*Quiet Rebels*

# *Quiet Rebels*

A History of Ontario Women Lawyers

**Mary Jane Mossman**

WILFRID LAURIER UNIVERSITY PRESS

LAURIER
*Inspiring Lives.*

This book has been published with the help of a grant from the Canadian Federation for the Humanities and Social Sciences, through the Awards to Scholarly Publications Program, using funds provided by the Social Sciences and Humanities Research Council of Canada. Wilfrid Laurier University Press acknowledges the support of the Canada Council for the Arts for our publishing program. We acknowledge the financial support of the Government of Canada through the Canada Book Fund for our publishing activities. Funding provided by the Government of Ontario and the Ontario Arts Council. This work was supported by the Research Support Fund.

Canada | Canada Council for the Arts | Conseil des Arts du Canada | ONTARIO ARTS COUNCIL CONSEIL DES ARTS DE L'ONTARIO an Ontario government agency un organisme du gouvernement de l'Ontario | Ontario

Library and Archives Canada Cataloguing in Publication

Title: Quiet rebels : a history of Ontario women lawyers / Mary Jane Mossman.
Names: Mossman, Mary Jane, author.
Description: Includes bibliographical references and index.
Identifiers: Canadiana (print) 20230163556 | Canadiana (ebook) 20230184464 | ISBN 9781771125925 (hardcover) | ISBN 9781771125932 (EPUB) | ISBN 9781771125949 (PDF).
Subjects: LCSH: Women lawyers—Ontario—History—20th century.
Classification: LCC KE332.W6 M68 2024 | DDC 340.09713—dc23--

Interior design by Sandra Friesen. The front cover image shows a drawing of a woman lawyer from a 1927 Women's Law Association of Ontario dinner invitation. The publisher and author gratefully acknowledge permissions granted by the Law Society of Ontario Archives and the Women's Law Association of Ontario for this image.


Waterloo, Ontario, Canada
www.wlupress.wlu.ca

FSC www.fsc.org MIX Paper | Supporting responsible forestry FSC® C016245

This book is printed on FSC® certified paper. It contains recycled materials and other controlled sources, is processed chlorine-free, and is manufactured using biogas energy.

Printed in Canada

Wilfrid Laurier University Press is located on the Haldimand Tract, part of the traditional territories of the Haudenosaunee, Anishnaabe, and Neutral Peoples. This land is part of the Dish with One Spoon Treaty between the Haudenosaunee and Anishnaabe Peoples and symbolizes the agreement to share, to protect our resources, and not to engage in conflict. We are grateful to the Indigenous Peoples who continue to care for and remain interconnected with this land. Through the work we publish in partnership with our authors, we seek to honour our local and larger community relationships, and to engage with the diversity of collective knowledge integral to responsible scholarly and cultural exchange.

For B.D.B.

# *Contents*

# *Preface*

> *The most important thing about research is to know when to stop ... Research is endlessly seductive; writing is hard work.*[1]

Barbara Tuchman's advice about knowing "when to stop" was especially apt during the many years I spent researching and writing this book. My interest began when I was asked to teach a seminar on Women and the Law as a Visiting Professor at Osgoode Hall Law School in 1975. A decade later, as a faculty member at the law school, I helped organize a special program about women lawyers' experiences for the Law Society of Upper Canada, an early effort to connect the histories of women in law with challenges then facing some Ontario women lawyers. In the years that followed, my research and teaching projects continued to include historical research about gender and legal professions in Canada and in other jurisdictions.[2] As important connections appeared between historical gendered patterns and contemporary challenges for some women lawyers in Ontario, this book evolved as a group biography of early women lawyers.[3] Although some early women lawyers became prominent members of the Ontario

1 B. Tuchman, *Practicing History* (New York: Alfred Knopf, 1981) 20–21.

2 M.J. Mossman, *The First Women Lawyers: A Comparative Study of Gender, Law and the Legal Professions* (Oxford: Hart Publishing, 2006).

3 R. Franklin, "Splinters and Mosaics: On Women's History and Group Biography," *Harper's Magazine* (June 2020) 76, a review of F. Wade, *Square Haunting: Five Writers in London Between the Wars* (London: Faber & Faber, 2020).

legal profession during their lifetimes, few remain household names in the twenty-first century. Moreover, unlike a number of biographical studies of male lawyers and judges in Ontario, stories of early women lawyers have been marginalized and hidden from history.[4]

This book's group biography focuses on the 187 women who were called to the bar of Ontario between 1897 and 1957, a period of almost six decades. During these years, all aspiring lawyers were required to attend lectures at the Law School at Osgoode Hall in downtown Toronto in the early mornings and late afternoons while articling in law firms for the rest of the day. Graduates of the law school were then eligible for admission to the Ontario bar.[5] Both as students and practitioners, these women were always a tiny minority, often the only woman in their law school classes—and the only woman in legal practice in many Ontario communities for decades. While there is considerable information about some women lawyers and their experiences, details for others often remain more elusive. Yet telling their stories as a group biography reveals how gendered patterns were embedded in a culture of male exclusivity, which defined the "gentleman's profession" of law for decades in the twentieth century. In addition to these 187 early women lawyers, this book explores significant changes in legal education and legal work, beginning in the 1960s and '70s, when the number of women lawyers began to increase—along with other changes, including greater diversity in the legal profession. Yet, as the book explores, exclusionary practices experienced by early women lawyers continue to create challenges for some contemporary members of the Ontario legal profession.

Many people have supported this project over the decades. Susan Lewthwaite and Paul Leatherdale patiently answered questions and arranged for me to review records at the Archives of the Law Society of

4 S. Rowbotham, *Hidden from History* (New York: Pantheon, 1974). See also L. Mulcahy and D. Sugarman, "Introduction: Legal Life Writing and Marginalized Subjects and Sources" (2015) 42:1 *Journal of Law and Society* 1. Until recently, only one Ontario woman judge merited a full-length biography: E. Anderson, *Judging Bertha Wilson: Law as Large as Life* (Toronto: University of Toronto Press/Osgoode Society for Canadian Legal History, 2001). For some recent studies, see C. Backhouse, *Claire L'Heureux-Dubé: A Life* (Vancouver: UBC Press/Osgoode Society for Canadian Legal History, 2017); and B. McLachlin, *Truth Be Told: My Journey Through Life and the Law* (New York: Simon and Schuster, 2019).

5 At least two women who graduated from Osgoode Hall in this period did not seek admission to the Ontario bar.

Ontario, including the fonds of the Women's Law Association of Ontario (WLAO). These WLAO archival records, and materials created for its important celebrations by WLAO historian, Abby Bushby, provided important information about individual women lawyers—as well as documenting the association's role in supporting early women in law. Canadian legal historians David Bell, Joan Brockman, Barry Cahill, Lori Chambers, Kathy Fisher, Philip Girard, Cameron Harvey, Lois Kernaghan, Mary Kinnear, Laurel Sefton MacDowell, Patricia McMahon, Jim Phillips, Wes Pue, and Lois Yorke all generously shared information about women lawyers and the legal profession. In addition, Minnie Niego at the Legislative Library in Iqaluit, and Beverley Speight, Court Librarian in Yellowknife, provided helpful advice about early women lawyers in these Territories. Friends, family, and colleagues, as well as staff in many archives, also offered information and help about the lives of individual women lawyers over the many years of this project: Adam Allentuck, Beverley Baines, Leo Barry, Naomi Black, Elizabeth Bruton, Dennis Cheng, Carol Creighton, Jon Creighton, Annette Demers, Richard Devlin, Meghan Dunn, Ruth Ellis, Ursula Franklin, Linda Gehrke, Jennifer Gold, John Gregory, Lynne Halley, Jane Banfield Haynes, Anita Herrmann, Bruce Karten, Charles Kaufmann, Fiona Kay, Caroline King, Mary Angela MacDonald, Marilyn Macfarlane, Wade MacLauchlan, Denis Magnusson, Alexander Malcolm, Alma Malcolm, Donna Mossman, David O'Connor, Shelley Quinn, Karen Schucher, Gemma Smyth, Lynda Tanaka, Margaret Thornton, Tory Tronrud, Lorna Turnbull, Lori Vaughan, Jo Veldman, Margot Warren, Elizabeth Wilson, Carol Wilton, and Heather Zordel. In addition, Laura Legge, QC, and Miriam Kelly, QC, kindly met with me to discuss the list of women called to the bar in Ontario, a list carefully created by Eileen Huckle at the Law Society for the years 1897 to 1975.

Many student research assistants provided excellent help with this project over the years, including Ami Atal, Cindy Baldassi, Tamara Barclay, Leanna Bayliss, Dena Bonnet, Gretta Fung, Wendy Greyling, Courtney Harris, Gail Henderson, Paisley Hillock, Thomas Hughes, Julie Jai, Christine Jenkins, Linda Knol, Craig Mazerolle, Victoria Mainprize, Eleanor Meslin, Erica Morassutti, Sheilagh O'Connell, Sahra Panjwanji, Alicia Puchta, Emma Rhodes, Nancy Riley, Jonathan Robinson, Claudia Schmeing, Amna Shakil, Anila Srivastava, and Christine Vanderschoot. My friend and former doctoral student, Elizabeth Archampong, created a draft bibliography, and Angus Lee tackled issues with the digital manuscript with expertise and efficiency. Two confidential readers of the draft manuscript offered helpful suggestions for revision, and library staff at Osgoode Hall Law School, including Yemisi Dina, Balfour Halévy, Tim Knight, Wayne Mah, Marianne Rogers and others, provided professional research advice for this project over many years.

Siobhan McMenemy, Clare Hitchens and Murray Tong at Wilfrid Laurier University Press provided continuing help and encouragement in the publication process. I especially thank historian Leslie Howsam, who read several chapters and offered encouragement; Janet Friskney, who provided expert help with the indexing for the book; Cheryl Hercules, whose kind assistance permitted me to complete this project; and Donna Mossman and Brian Bucknall for many years of patient listening.

PROLOGUE

# *Telling the Stories of Women Becoming Lawyers in Ontario*

## Toronto 1927: "A Toast to the Future of Women in Law"

> *How are those who cross the threshold received? If they belong to a group different from the group already "inside," what are the terms of their incorporation? How do the new arrivals understand their relationship to the place they have entered? What are the terms of identity they establish?*[1]

Joan Wallach Scott's questions about terms of identity among new arrivals are reflected in an historical puzzle about early women lawyers in Ontario, women who had recently "crossed the threshold" to enter the legal profession. Many of these women lawyers asserted ungendered terms of identity: they were lawyers, not women lawyers. In this context, an occasion in the spring of 1927 presents an interesting puzzle. One April evening, thirty-seven women lawyers gathered in the Yellow Room of the King Edward Hotel in Toronto for the annual dinner meeting of the Women's Law Association of Ontario (WLAO). The occasion was a celebration of two important milestones: the sixtieth anniversary of Canadian confederation in 1867, and the thirtieth anniversary of women's success in gaining

1 J. Wallach Scott, "American Women Historians, 1884–1984" in Wallach Scott, *Gender and the Politics of History* (New York: Columbia University Press, 1999) 178.

admission to the bar of Ontario.[2] In the thirty years since Clara Brett Martin had been called to the bar in 1897, becoming Canada's first woman lawyer,[3] fifty-six women had gained admission to the legal profession in Ontario—although not all of them were in active legal practice.[4] Thus, with thirty-seven women lawyers and law students present for this dinner meeting in 1927, about two-thirds of all women in law in Ontario participated in this celebratory event. Moreover, since other Canadian provinces, except Québec, had permitted women to become lawyers by 1918,[5] this WLAO dinner could also celebrate a "sprinkling" of women legal practitioners in most Canadian provinces by the late 1920s.[6]

Perhaps because of their small numbers, as well as their exclusion from most all-male professional organizations and collegial events, women lawyers in Ontario had established their own association almost a decade earlier in 1919. The WLAO automatically welcomed all women students at Osgoode Hall, as well as its women graduates, to join in activities such as these annual dinner meetings.[7] And since graduation from the profession's law school at Osgoode Hall was required for all those admitted to the Ontario bar until 1957, the WLAO provided collegial activities for women law students, as well as continuing support for women lawyers in Toronto and in other Ontario communities.[8]

These WLAO celebratory dinner meetings traditionally included a series of toasts. At this 1927 dinner, the evening began with a formal toast to the King. It was followed by a toast to the sixtieth anniversary of the Canadian

2 Law Society of Ontario (LSO) Archives, Women's Law Association of Ontario (WLAO) fonds, Scrapbook (SB), vol. 2, "Survey of Women Lawyers in Canada."

3 C. Backhouse, "'To Open the Way for Others of My Sex': Clara Brett Martin's Career as Canada's First Woman Lawyer" (1985) 1 *Canadian Journal of Women and the Law* 1; T. Roth, "Clara Brett Martin—Woman Lawyer" (1984) 18 *Law Society Gazette* 323; and S. Ryan, "A Pilgrim's Progress: Clara Brett Martin's Campaign for Admission to the Bar of Ontario" (1999) [unpublished, on file with M.J. Mossman].

4 E. Huckle, "List of Women Barristers and Solicitors in Ontario, 1897–1975" [unpublished, archived at Law Society of Ontario Archives].

5 See Chapter One and Appendix.

6 LSO Archives, WLAO fonds, SB, vol. 2: "Survey of Women Lawyers in Canada."

7 For the creation of the WLAO in 1919, see Part Two.

8 A. Bushby, "Creating Culture: The Early Years of Ontario Women in the Legal Profession" (Presentation to International Women's Day Celebration, Law Society of Upper Canada, Toronto, nd 2000).

federation, proposed by Grace Gordon (called to the bar in 1924)[9] and responded to by Apha Hodgins (1919). A toast to "our profession" was proposed by a student, Beatrice VanWart (1929), and responded to by Margaret Hyndman (1926). There was also a toast welcoming the women graduates of 1927, proposed by Lida Pearson Sturdy (1921) and responded to by Margaret Perney (1927).[10]

All these toasts were unremarkable at this celebratory dinner, but a final toast, proposed by Aileen Silk Bicknell (1919) and responded to by Florence Daley Harkins (1922), presents an intriguing puzzle. This toast was specifically directed to "the graduates of Osgoode Hall Law School of 1987," and it expressed hope that by 1987 "only a few stray men would be called to the Bar and ... all the judges would be women."[11] What was the meaning of this toast for women lawyers who were present at this 1927 WLAO dinner meeting? Was it just a light-hearted moment—looking back on women's presence in the legal profession for thirty years and, at the same time, looking ahead sixty years to the future for women in law? Or did this toast, masked in light-hearted humour, reveal an invisible—and complicated—relationship between gender and the legal profession in Ontario in 1927?

There appear to be no records of such a toast at other annual dinner meetings of the WLAO. In addition, information about the two women lawyers who proposed and responded to this final toast is sparse. Both Silk Bicknell and Daley Harkins had entered the law school as university graduates, and they had both been called to the bar, but by 1927, both had married and ceased to practise law, perhaps confirming the societal convention in the early twentieth century that marriage precluded careers for middle-class women.[12] Although Daley Harkins was the WLAO's representative to the Local Council of Women in Toronto, an umbrella

9 Huckle, "List of Women Barristers and Solicitors."

10 LSO Archives, WLAO fonds, SB, vol. 2.

11 LSO Archives, WLAO fonds, SB, vol. 2. A later report about this 1927 dinner meeting indicated (perhaps incorrectly) that this toast was proposed by Lida Pearson Sturdy (1921): LSO Archives, WLAO fonds, box 106, file 2006006-074. See also C. Morgan, "'An Embarrassingly and Severely Masculine Atmosphere': Women, Gender and the Legal Profession at Osgoode Hall, 1920s to 1960s" (1996) 11:2 *Canadian Journal of Law and Society* 19 at 56.

12 LSO Archives, WLAO fonds, SB, vol. 2.

organization that promoted a variety of women's interests,[13] there are no clues to explain the genesis of this toast in 1927—or its meaning for the graduates of Osgoode Hall Law School sixty years later in 1987.

Yet, this toast is significant because so many women who became lawyers in earlier decades of the twentieth century espoused identities, particularly in public, as lawyers rather than women lawyers. They never acknowledged their gender in public. As one prominent woman lawyer, Margaret Hyndman (1926), proclaimed in 1949, "Only the fact that I am a lawyer matters. That I am a woman is of no consequence."[14] Her comment about women lawyers' professional identity as lawyers—ungendered—confirms Nancy Cott's assertion that "professional ideology ... was increasingly magnetic ... The professional ethos, with its own promise of freedom from sex-defined constraints, was released to flourish in aspiring women's minds."[15] In the context of efforts by early women lawyers to adopt professional—and ungendered—identities as lawyers, the unusual emphasis on their female gender in this final toast at a formal public dinner of the WLAO may reveal, even fleetingly, some hidden tensions for women lawyers. As new arrivals, did their "terms of identity" require erasure of their gender as they crossed the threshold into the legal profession? And did this toast, imagining a future characterized by an extraordinary gender transformation in both the legal profession and the judiciary, suggest a need, especially at a major anniversary celebration, for these women lawyers to acknowledge their profound achievements, as women, in becoming lawyers?

13 Provincial and local chapters of the National Council of Women existed in Canada from the mid-1890s: V. Strong-Boag, "'Setting the Stage': National Organization and the Women's Movement in the Late 19th Century" in S. Mann Trofimenkoff and A. Prentice, eds., *The Neglected Majority: Essays in Canadian Women's History* (Toronto: McClelland and Stewart, 1977) 87.

14 M. Porter, "The Legal Lady," *Maclean's Magazine* (15 July 1949) 23.

15 N.F. Cott, *The Grounding of Modern Feminism* (New Haven, CT: Yale University Press, 1987) 232–33. Cott suggested that after suffrage was achieved, women professionals in the 1920s did not deny the instrumentality of feminism in breaking down barriers to women's first entry to the professions, but they assumed that no formal bar remained, and that the professions' supposedly neutral and meritocratic ideology was "not only their best armor but their only hope."

## Gender and History: Women and the "Gentleman's Profession" of Law

> *The ideal of the professional gentleman incorporated, among its other elements, images about a particular form of masculine identity, about the gendered distribution of knowledge and authority in both the "public" and the "domestic" sphere, which the entry of women on equal terms necessarily challenged. And the consequences of that challenge could not be foreseen ... [The] entry of young women might change the nature of an occupation fundamentally and forever ... [thus raising] anxiety among professional men themselves about their own future and their place in the social order ... [Women's admission to the professions] challenged the power relations, economic and otherwise, embedded in the ideology of separate spheres.*[16]

Women's admission to the professions, including law, posed a major threat to masculine identity, a female rebellion against the tradition of law as a "gentleman's profession." Male gender was fundamental to the concept of professionalism: an occupation could not be called a profession "if it was filled with women."[17] Although the transformation of the Ontario legal profession between 1870 and 1920 revealed an evolution from Georgian professionalism (based on worthy status) to modern professionalism (based on demonstrated and specialized expertise), the Law Society in Ontario apparently acquired the benefits of modern professionalism without abandoning "the patina of dignified and gentlemanly tradition."[18] Barriers to women's entry to the legal profession were based on longstanding traditions shared by the group who were "already inside": traditions of "gentlemanlyness, respectability and masculinity."[19] In this context, the

16 R.D. Gidney and W.P.J. Millar, *Professional Gentlemen: The Professions in Nineteenth-Century Ontario* (Toronto: University of Toronto Press, 1994) 329, 332.

17 Gidney and Millar, *Professional* Gentlemen 205–7, 239. The concept of the "professional woman" was a contradiction in terms at the end of the nineteenth century.

18 C. Moore, *The Law Society of Upper Canada and Ontario's Lawyers, 1797–1997* (Toronto: University of Toronto Press, 1997) 147, 152.

19 D. Sugarman and W.W. Pue, "Introduction: Towards a Cultural History of Lawyers" in W.W. Pue and D. Sugarman, eds., *Lawyers and Vampires: Cultural Histories of the Legal Professions* (Oxford: Hart Publishing, 2003) 14.

unusual toast at the WLAO dinner in 1927 might have acknowledged, albeit obliquely, the formidable challenges facing these pioneer women in law.

In her examination of women lawyers and professionalism in Manitoba prior to 1970, Mary Kinnear suggested that ideas of professionalism excluded women because concepts of competence and merit exist and flourish only within a social context—thus, early women lawyers were sometimes seen as "honorary men." Indeed, "women knocking at the door" may have promoted an obsession with ideas of professionalism, and particularly professional exclusivity, at the turn of the twentieth century.[20] Even after the first women succeeded in gaining admission to professions, new arrivals often encountered subtly revised forms of male power and exclusion strategies, masked within organizational struggles and institutional structures, which continued to create gendered segregation *within* the professions.[21] Thus, this final toast's audacious aspirations at the WLAO dinner in 1927, which prophesied an unprecedented gender transformation in the legal profession sixty years in the future, appear puzzling—but arguably significant.

---

20 M. Kinnear, *In Subordination: Professional Women, 1870–1970* (Montreal/Kingston: McGill-Queen's University Press, 1995) 97, 165. Kinnear assessed four strategies adopted by women professionals: separatism, superperformance, innovation, and subordination and concluded that the women professionals in her study tended to "subordination": 163–65. These strategies were identified in P.M. Glazer and M. Slater, *Unequal Colleagues: The Entrance of Women into the Professions, 1891–1940* (New Brunswick, NJ: Rutgers University Press, 1987). See also E. Smyth et al, "Introduction" in E. Smyth et al., eds., *Challenging Professions: Historical and Contemporary Perspectives on Women's Professional Work* (Toronto: University of Toronto Press, 1999) 3 at 4–6. In addition, ideals of professionalism may represent "something between a mystique and a conspiracy" rather than a series of admirable traits: M. Saks, "Removing the Blinkers? A Critique of Recent Contributions to the Sociology of Professions" (1983) 31 *Sociological Review* 1.

21 A. Witz, *Professions and Patriarchy* (London: Routledge, 1992) 102. See also C. Backhouse, "Gender and Race in the Construction of 'Legal Professionalism': Historical Perspectives" (Paper presented at Colloquium of the Chief Justice of Ontario's Advisory Committee on Professionalism, Toronto, 20 October 2003); U. Schultz and G. Shaw, eds., *Women in the World's Legal Professions* (Oxford: Hart Publishing, 2003); M. Thornton, *Dissonance and Distrust: Women in the Legal Profession* (Melbourne: Oxford University Press, 1996); and J. Brockman, *Gender in the Legal Profession: Fitting or Breaking the Mould* (Vancouver: UBC Press, 2001. In 1969, Williams suggested that women lawyers faced a "double prejudice to conquer"—the prejudice of the solicitor and the prejudice of the client: G. Williams, *Learning the Law* (London: Stevens and Sons, 1969) 195.

A second reason why this final toast at the WLAO dinner meeting remains interesting is its focus on connections between the aspirations of these early women lawyers and issues for more recent women in law. Although it could not have been foreseen in 1927, it happened that Osgoode Hall Law School, in its new location at York University, became embroiled exactly sixty years later, in 1987, in a human rights complaint about systemic sex discrimination, the result of controversy about the appointment of a new dean.[22] By 1987, the proportion of men and women law students was approaching parity at most Canadian law schools, and some women were being appointed judges, partners at major law firms, and professors and deans in Canadian law schools.[23] In addition, both the Law Society in Ontario and the Canadian Bar Association initiated studies about gender and the legal profession that were published in the early 1990s. These reports identified substantial differences in the experiences of men and women in the legal profession, and recommended changes to accommodate women and others—who were experiencing discriminatory practices as members of the profession.[24] Thus, by the later 1980s, women lawyers were increasingly asking, "What is the significance of a profession, which

22 The complaint alleging systemic sex discrimination, signed by 121 female lawyers, law professors, and law students in Ontario, was filed at the Ontario Human Rights Commission. See also the Epilogue.

23 D. Stager with H. Arthurs, *Lawyers in Canada* (Toronto: University of Toronto Press, 1990) 95 and Table 4.3: women constituted 47.6 per cent of students in Canadian law schools in 1987. Among Osgoode's full-time faculty in 1987, only 20 per cent were women: Osgoode Hall Law School calendar, 1986–87. See also B. Mazer, "An Analysis of Gender in Admission to Canadian Common Law Schools from 1985–86 to 1994–95" (1997) 20 *Dalhousie Law Journal* 135; B. Baines, "Women and the Law" in S. Burt, L. Code, and L. Dorney, eds., *Changing Patterns: Women in Canada* (Toronto: McClelland and Stewart, 1988) 157; and Law Society of Upper Canada, Symposium: "Women in the Legal Profession," May 1986.

24 F. Kay, *Transitions in the Legal Profession: A Survey of Lawyers Called to the Bar between 1975 and 1990* (Toronto: Law Society of Upper Canada, 1991); and Canadian Bar Association, *Touchstones for Change: Equality, Diversity and Accountability—The Report on Gender Equality in the Legal Profession* (Ottawa: Canadian Bar Association, 1993).

has been historically male, being rapidly transformed into one composed equally of men and women?"[25]

Yet, even after a decade of academic and court-based documentation of gender unfairness in the legal profession in the United States, such inquiries often failed to undermine the "resiliency of legal culture." That is, while such task forces might authorize inquiry, ask forbidden questions, and obtain information, professional culture seemed to remain impenetrable to profound change.[26] Moreover, as recently as 2008, Ontario's Law Society established its Justicia Project, especially designed to promote greater equality for women members of the legal profession.[27] The continuing need for such a program suggests that, even in the twenty-first century, Virginia Woolf's claim that women could enter the professions and "use them to have a mind of [their] own and a will of [their] own" remains profoundly contested.[28]

These conclusions suggest a need to examine how some contemporary gender issues in Ontario's legal profession may reflect the legacy of women lawyers who crossed the threshold into the profession in earlier decades. As American historians suggested, "the professional and personal challenges that confront women lawyers today ... reach back ... to the pioneer generation of women lawyers who were the first to grapple with the challenges facing women in the legal profession." Moreover, while some women did succeed in becoming lawyers in the United States in the late nineteenth century, they may have done so without effectively challenging the gender

25 M.J. Mossman, "Portia's Progress: Women as Lawyers—Reflections on Past and Future" (1988) 8 *Windsor Yearbook of Access to Justice* 252 at 261; and Mossman, "'Invisible' Constraints on Lawyering and Leadership: The Case of Women Lawyers" (1988) 20:3 *Ottawa Law Review* 567. See also Archives of the Law Society of Upper Canada, *Crossing the Bar: A Century of Women's Experience "Upon the Rough and Troubled Seas of Legal Practice"* (Toronto: Archives of the Law Society of Upper Canada, 1993) 41.

26 J. Resnik, "Ambivalence: The Resiliency of Legal Culture in the United States" (1993) 45 *Stanford Law Review* 1525 at 1535. See also C. Menkel-Meadow, "The Comparative Sociology of Women Lawyers: the 'Feminization' of the Legal Profession" (1987) 24 *Osgoode Hall Law Journal* 897.

27 Law Society of Upper Canada, *Final Report—Retention of Women in Private Practice Working Group*, 22 May 2008, executive summary, para 4. See also M.J. Mossman, "'The Law as a Profession for Women': A Century of Progress?" (2009) 30 *Australian Feminist Law Journal* 131.

28 V. Woolf, *Three Guineas* (London: Hogarth Press, 1977) 151.

premises of law and the legal profession.[29] Thus, experiences of exclusion among earlier cohorts of women lawyers, a tiny minority who studied and practised law within the constraints of the gentleman's legal profession, may have continuing relevance for some contemporary women lawyers.

In addition, women lawyers' experiences in the early decades of the twentieth century can provide historical insights about both women and the profession. For example, women lawyers' histories present a mirror of professional legal culture (its *habitus*) in relation to gender. Their stories reveal how they adopted a range of different strategies to confront, circumvent, or ignore the gender barriers they faced, that is, how they found "loopholes through which they [could] wriggle or interstices in which they [could] survive."[30] Their stories also document well-defined patterns of exclusion, some of which arguably continue to create challenges for contemporary women and others in the legal profession. In this way, this group biography of pioneer women lawyers may provide historical insights about contemporary gendered patterns in Ontario's legal profession.

29 V. Drachman, *Women Lawyers and the Origins of Professional Identity in America: The Letters of the Equity Club, 1887 to 1890* (Ann Arbor: University of Michigan Press, 1993) vii; and M. Grossberg, "Institutionalizing Masculinity: The Law as a Masculine Profession" in M.C. Carnes and C. Griffen, eds., *Meanings for Manhood: Construction of Masculinity in Victorian America* (Chicago: University of Chicago Press, 1990) 133 at 148. Drawing on Antonio Gramsci's work, Grossberg concluded that women might have created a "contradictory consciousness" in the legal community, but they did not create a "counter-hegemony." See also V. Drachman, *Sisters in Law: Women Lawyers in Modern American History* (Cambridge, MA: Harvard University Press, 2013); B. Babcock, *Woman Lawyer: The Trials of Clara Foltz* (Stanford, CA: Stanford University Press, 2011); J. Norgren, *Rebels at the Bar* (New York : New York University Press, 2013) and Norgren, *Stories from Trailblazing Women Lawyers: Lives in the Law* (New York: New York University Press, 2020).

30 P. Bourdieu, *Outline of a Theory of Practice,* translated by R. Nice (Cambridge: Cambridge University Press, 1977). Bourdieu's concept of habitus suggested "a way of recognizing the extent of individual freedom within certain limits set by culture": P. Burke, "Overture—The New History: Its Past and Future" in P. Burke, ed., *New Perspectives on Historical Writing*, 2nd ed. (Philadelphia: Pennsylvania University Press, 2001) 1 at 15–17.

## Gender and Biography: The "Woman Question," Puzzles, and Silences

> *What is acceptable, what is possible, what is imagined and attempted often differ. Women may be seen as eccentric rather than exceptional, and the world she is perceived to live in ... may be markedly different, especially in earlier times ... Feminism ... here reveals not only issues about gender and culture but an area of men's and women's lives that is still treated in culturally determined ways ... [And there are always] the "puzzles" that remain unsolved about the life.*[31]

Paula Backscheider's comment reveals some challenges for women's biographers. In this context, Hermione Lee lamented how we want to know about the whole "swarm of possibilities" that hum around women's experiences, but their stories are all too often full of absences, gaps, missing evidence, knowledge, or information.[32] Such challenges mean that telling women's stories requires biographers to reinvent the lives their subjects led, "discovering from what evidence they [can] find the processes and decisions, the choices and unique pain, that lay beyond the life stories of these women."[33] As Rosemary Auchmuty suggested, a crucial question in legal history is "Where are the women?"—a question that acknowledges a need to address the experiences of both women and "Outsiders," that is, those who are defined by racialization, ethnicity, religion, language, class or marital status, dis/ability, and/or sexuality.[34] In doing so, life writing must aspire to "transcend an authorized collective memory" by creating

31 P. Backscheider, *Reflections on Biography* (Oxford: Oxford University Press, 1999) 59, 132. See also M.J. Mossman, "Precedents, Patterns and Puzzles: Reflections on the First Women Lawyers" (2016) 5:4 LAWS 39, MDPI online: <http://www.mdpi.com/journals/laws>.

32 H. Lee, *Virginia Woolf's Nose: Essays on Biography* (Princeton, NJ: Princeton University Press, 2005) 1, 5.

33 C. Heilbrun, *Writing a Woman's Life* (New York: Ballantine Books, 1988) 31. See also C. Steedman, *Landscape for a Good Woman: A Story of Two Lives* (London: Virago Press, 1986); Sugarman and Pue, "Introduction" in Pue and Sugarman, eds., *Lawyers and Vampires* 15–16; and M. Burrage, K. Karausch, and H. Siegrist, "An Actor-Based Framework for the Study of the Professions" in M. Burrage and R. Torstendahl, eds., *Professions in Theory and History: Rethinking the Study of the Professions* (London: Sage, 1990) 223.

34 R. Auchmuty, "Recovering Lost Lives: Researching Women in Legal History" (2015) 42:1 *Journal of Law and Society* 34 at 43–44. See also Part Four.

a greater site of pluralism and inclusion. Perhaps women's lives might be better understood in terms of a kaleidoscope of changing and interconnected patterns: "each time you look you see something different, composed certainly of the same elements, but in a new configuration."[35]

There may also be the problem of "silences" in women's life stories:

> Like the frontiers-women silent about their physical strength and courage, pioneer women professionals were silent about their ambitions and recounted their lives as though their successes just happened to them, rather like the soprano's chance meeting with the tenor in the first act of an opera ... [S]he seems to have chanced upon the causes which elicit a lifetime commitment from her. She never acknowledges strategizing about how to advance the cause; she is as surprised as anyone else when success is at hand ... What are we to make of such silences?[36]

Traditionally, men's biographies adopted a quest plot: "life is an odyssey," a journey through many trials and tests, which the hero must surmount alone through courage, endurance, cunning, and moral strength. In contrast, Jill Ker Conway identified how the problem for women's life stories is one of censorship for public self-presentation—because "women cannot depart too dramatically from popularly accepted stereotypes," leaving silences where explanations are needed.[37] For centuries, even justifying ambition as a given for girls has taken some explaining—recall

35 D. Sugarman, "From Legal Biography to Legal Life Writing: Broadening Conceptions of Legal History and Socio-legal Scholarship" (2015) 42:1 *Journal of Law and Society* 7 at 27; and J. Purvis, "Biography as Microscope or Kaleidoscope? The Case of 'Power' in Hannah Cullwick's Relationship with Arthur Munby" in L. Stanley, *The Auto/biographical I: The Theory and Practice of Feminist Auto-biography* (Manchester: Manchester University Press, 1992) 158.

36 J. Ker Conway, *When Memory Speaks: Exploring the Art of Autobiography* (New York: Vintage Books, 1999) 15–16. See also Mulcahy and Sugarman, "Introduction," (2015) 42:1 *Journal of Law and Society* 1 at 2; C. Heilbrun, "Women's Autobiographical Writings: New Forms" in M.W. Brownley and A.B. Kimmich, eds., *Women and Autobiography* (Wilmington, DE: Scholarly Resources, 1999) 15; M. Maynard and J. Purvis, "Doing Feminist Research" in Maynard and Purvis, eds., *Researching Women's Lives from a Feminist Perspective* (London: Taylor and Francis, 1994) 1 at 2; and H. Buss, *Canadian Women's Autobiography in English: An Introductory Guide for Researchers and Teachers*, CRIAW papers, no. 24 (Ottawa: Canadian Research Institute for the Advancement of Women, 1991).

37 Ker Conway, *When Memory Speaks*, 7–11, 16.

that "women were appropriate subjects for biography only if fame was bestowed upon them, not if they seized or relished it themselves."[38] And while silence can simply be omission, it can also be "a powerful unspoken presence in the text."[39]

Silences are often frustrating in written accounts of women's lives, but silences also occur in oral histories because women may remember the past in different ways than men. Joan Sangster noted how women's narratives are more liable to be characterized by "understatements, avoidance of the first-person point of view, rare mention of personal accomplishments and disguised statements of personal power." Asking why and how women explain, rationalize, and make sense of their past offers "insight into the social and material framework within which they operated, the perceived choices and cultural patterns they faced, and the complex relationship between individual consciousness and culture." In addition, women's responses to interviewers' questions often depend on a host of variables: "the persistence of the researcher, the wording of the question, the tone in which it is asked in an oral interview, and the space for a reply in a written questionnaire."[40]

These insights help to identify the contrast between the subversively celebratory toast at the 1927 WLAO dinner meeting and the "silences" of many early women lawyers about their experiences of exclusion and

38 C. Sanger, "Curriculum Vitae (Feminae): Biography and Early American Women Lawyers" (1994) 46 *Stanford Law Review* 1245 at 1256. Sanger suggested that gender is always central to understanding a woman's life: 1254, citing S. Alpern et al., "Introduction" in Alpern et al., eds., *The Challenge of Feminist Biography: Writing the Lives of Modern American Women* (Urbana: University of Illinois Press, 1992) 1.

39 J. Woolf, "Silent Witness: Memory and Omission in Natalia Ginzburg's *Family Sayings*" in T.L. Broughton and L. Anderson, eds., *Women's Lives/Women's Times: New Essays on Auto/biography* (New York: State University of New York Press, 1997) 203 at 212. See also S. Groag Bell and M. Yalom, eds., *Revealing Lives: Autobiography, Biography and Gender* (New York: State University of New York Press, 1990).

40 J. Sangster, "Telling Our Stories: Feminist Debates and the Use of Oral History" (1994) 3:1 *Women's History Review* 5 at 6–7, citing C. Etter-Lewis, "Black Women's Life Stories: Reclaiming Self in Narrative Texts" in S. Berger Gluck and D. Patai, eds., *Women's Words: The Feminist Practice of Oral History* (New York: Routledge, 1991) 48. As Kinnear suggested, some interviewees may "deliberately reconstrue" to satisfy a personal agenda: Kinnear, *In Subordination*, 23. See also L. Stanley, "Moments of Writing: Is There Feminist Auto/biography?" (1990) 2:1 *Gender and History* 58; and M. Glucksmann, "The Work of Knowledge and the Knowledge of Women's Work" in Maynard and Purvis, eds., *Researching Women's Lives from a Feminist Perspective*, 149 at 154, 159.

discrimination. In her response to a survey of women lawyers in Canada in the late 1960s, Marguerite Ritchie, a prominent federal government lawyer, bluntly explained that women lawyers often fail to acknowledge discrimination:

> You may discover that some replies indicate an apparent lack of discrimination; in many cases, I have found that women are unwilling to admit discrimination, either because they are trying to conceal the fact from themselves or because they must play the role of "Uncle Tom" and their chances of promotion depend absolutely upon their conformity to and acceptance of the existing patterns. In other cases, I found that women who have been subject to great discrimination [have coped with it] by escapism ... These women very often do not want to remind themselves of the events and the years which were painful episodes in their career.[41]

In addition, the survey's author, Cameron Harvey, described how it focused on the "prickly question" of the treatment of women lawyers in the legal profession and that he had received some negative reactions to his questionnaire: some women respondents had asserted that "a lawyer is a lawyer and ... an article concerning women lawyers 'as a separate breed' [would] have about as much social value as an article on blue-eyed or left-handed lawyers."[42] In contrast, Carol Sanger concluded that modern women lawyers know that the biographies of women who chose to locate their professional lives in the law are likely to be "stories of piecemeal progress and circumscribed success."[43] Similarly, others have concluded that "it is far too facile to say that there were prejudices against women that they had to overcome. The ways in which the prejudice manifested itself were extremely complex and insidious.... As determined, aspiring

41 C. Harvey, "Women in Law in Canada" (1970–71) 4 *Manitoba Law Journal* 9 at 13; and *Toronto Daily Star* (1 February 1971). Marguerite Ritchie was called to the Alberta bar in 1944 and was later employed in the federal Department of Justice, where she was involved in initiatives to promote sex equality. She also recalled experiencing sexual harassment and discrimination. Ritchie was the first woman appointed a federal QC, in 1963, and in 1997 she received the Governor General's Award for *The Persons Case*. She died in 2016 at the age of 96. See *Ottawa Citizen* (17 October 1997): M. Bohuslawsky, "A Half-Century Battle for Women;" and *Globe and Mail* (28 May 2016), L. Fitterman, "Marguerite Ritchie: A Brilliant Champion of Women's Rights."

42 Harvey, "Women in Law in Canada," 9.

43 Sanger, "Curriculum Vitae (Feminae)," 1257–58.

professionals, women were not easily deterred [and] they found a variety of ways to respond to the discrimination they faced."[44]

Thus, telling the stories of early women lawyers means exploring puzzles and listening for silences in relation to their assertions that they were lawyers—ungendered—in a context of formidable exclusionary gender practices in the profession. Their experiences also point to an enigma: what prompted the subversive toast at the 1927 WLAO dinner meeting and its outspoken aspiration for a remarkable gender transformation in the legal profession by 1987? Was there a "powerful unspoken presence in the text"?

### Women Lawyers: Connecting the Past and Present

> *By definition, those who have been barred from entry into, or effective participation in, the legal world rarely occupy a prominent position in the official reports of cases or commentaries which form the basis of much legal scholarship ... Claims that these lives cannot be adequately charted because of insufficient information about them inevitably leads to a double marginalization: that which occurs during the lifetime of the subject and that which occurs when revisionist accounts of [only "important"] lives [are written].*[45]

In contrast to the many biographies and autobiographies of male lawyers and judges, stories about women lawyers and other Outsiders in the legal profession have often been marginalized, hidden from history.[46] Thus, telling the stories of early women lawyers in Ontario rescues them from marginalization. Significantly, their stories reveal how many of them were "quiet rebels," facing institutional obstacles and exclusionary practices, but without challenging them publicly. At the same time, a few early women lawyers rebelled against experiences of gender discrimination less quietly, and sometimes with individual success. Moreover, even after the "surge in numbers" of women lawyers, beginning in the 1960s, stories about how professional and societal norms discouraged women lawyers'

44 Glazer and Slater, *Unequal Colleagues*, 12–13. The authors suggested that "as professional success was increasingly predicated on character, on the presentation of self as the model of the gentleman as much as expert knowledge," it became increasingly difficult for women to carry out this role.

45 Mulcahy and Sugarman, "Introduction," 4. The authors suggested that biography is an "epistemological minefield" in relation to marginalized subjects.

46 S. Rowbotham, *Hidden from History* (New York: Pantheon, 1974).

aspirations provide insights about changing gender patterns in these different historical periods. Like a quilt that is created out of many individual patches, both the individual patches and the overall patterns are revealing.

This book's initial focus is the 187 women who were called to the Ontario bar between 1897 and 1957. As a group biography, it tells the stories of women with something in common, that is, the necessity of negotiating barriers created by societal mores and legal traditions to pursue their goals of becoming lawyers and practising law.[47] Most of these women were middle-class, white, and Protestant, although a few reflected some diversity in relation to religion, class, immigration status, and geographical location. Yet, in contrast to the admission of Black and Indigenous male lawyers in Ontario in earlier decades, Black and Indigenous women did not become lawyers in Ontario until the 1960s and '70s.[48] In addition, these early women lawyers constituted just a tiny minority, both at the law school and in legal practice, especially in contrast to the much larger number of women who began to enter the Ontario legal profession in the 1960s and later decades. In contrast to the 187 women admitted to the Ontario bar in six decades between 1897 and 1957, a total of 205 women were called to the bar in just six years between 1968 and 1974, a revolutionary transformation. Moreover, although more women than men have been called to the Ontario bar annually in recent years of the twenty-first century, women leave the legal profession more often than men, suggesting that exclusionary practices may continue to challenge some women lawyers.[49]

Exploring how and why 187 women began to enter the legal profession in the six decades up to 1957 necessitates an examination of their

47 Sugarman suggested that a group biography can reveal "a past we might otherwise overlook," especially in relation to women: Sugarman, "From Legal Biography to Legal Life-Writing," 23–24. See also Mulcahy and Sugarman, "Introduction."

48 See Part Four.

49 Huckle, "List of Women Barristers and Solicitors." By 1976, there were 557 women lawyers out of a total of 10,606 (5.3 per cent) in Ontario: D. Burnett, "The Society's Computer" (1977) 11 *Law Society Gazette* 70 at 73. See also Law Society of Upper Canada, General Membership Records, Spring 1989; R.L. Abel, "United States: The Contradictions of Professionalism" in R. Abel and P. Lewis, eds., *Lawyers in Society: The Common Law World*, vol. 1 (Berkeley: University of California Press, 1988) 186 at 202; and M. Choroszewicz and F. Kay, "Understanding Gender Equality in the Legal Profession" in R. Abel et al., eds., *Lawyers in 21st Century Societies, vol 2: Comparisons and Theories* (Oxford: Hart Publishing, 2022) 127. In 2018, 1,306 women and 1,083 men were called to the Ontario bar: Law Society of Ontario, *Annual Report, 2018*, at 34.

individual circumstances as well as gendered patterns in the profession. How did family backgrounds, geographical locations and individual personalities affect women lawyers' opportunities and choices, and how did women from Ontario communities far from Toronto (and a few from outside the province) arrange to attend compulsory lectures at Osgoode Hall in the early decades of the twentieth century? What strategies did these women lawyers adopt to find legal work in the gentleman's profession, and did they receive support from male lawyers and judges? How did some women lawyers succeed when they practised law as "lone voyagers," the only woman lawyer in their communities for decades, and did some women lawyers' careers reflect "winding tracks" rather than straight roads?[50] How did new opportunities for legal work, including in government, create spaces for women lawyers? Did these early women lawyers aspire to political or judicial roles, and did any women lawyers actively promote women's rights? To what extent did societal norms about appropriate roles for married women limit, or foreclose, the careers of early women lawyers, and how did some married women lawyers circumvent these societal constraints? And did the WLAO offer concrete support for its members, in addition to its social occasions, particularly in a context in which many legal organizations and established business and social clubs prohibited women members well into the second half of the twentieth century?[51]

Some women lawyers who enjoyed success as members of the legal profession in the first half of the twentieth century were "quiet rebels." While they clearly recognized their pioneering role in the legal profession, they also focused on fitting in rather than challenging its exclusionary practices. As their numbers increased in the later decades of the twentieth century, some women lawyers abandoned the "quiet rebel" strategy, while others have continued to focus on fitting in. In telling the stories of Ontario women lawyers in this book, historian Judith Bennett's studies of changes in women's work in different historical periods in England provides

50 G.J. Clifford, *Lone Voyagers: Academic Women in Co-educational Universities, 1870–1937* (New York: Feminist Press, 1989); and I. Elgqvist-Saltzman, "Straight Roads and Winding Tracks: Swedish Educational Policy from a Gender Perspective" (1992) 4:1–2 *Gender and Education* 41. See also M.C. Bateson, *Composing a Life* (New York: Penguin, 1989).

51 For example, the Lawyers Club, established in 1922 as an organization for continuing legal education, did not permit women members until 1974: Archives of the Law Society of Upper Canada, *Crossing the Bar*, 36. See also Part Three.

an important theoretical context. According to Bennett, changes in the patterns of women's work over time more often reflect continuity, rather than transformation. More specifically, Bennett identified a distinction between changes in women's experiences on one hand and transformation in their status, relative to men, on the other. As she argued, although women's work experiences may change, there is more often continuity rather than transformation in their work status in relation to men. Accordingly, Bennett suggested that women's history must move beyond "stirring tales of strong women who accomplished marvellous deeds against great odds" and be more attentive to continuities in exploring strategic lessons about the history of women's work.[52] Although Bennett's analysis did not focus on professional women, her theory is useful in identifying changes that occurred for women lawyers after 1957, and in assessing whether such changes more often constitute continuity, rather than transformation in status. For some contemporary women lawyers, gendered patterns may continue to create barriers.

### Researching the Stories of Women Lawyers

This project presented significant research challenges over several decades, especially because there is often considerable information about women who did "first things," but a dearth of similar details about those who followed—they left few written records "of the sense they made of their lives," they did not preserve their letters, and few of them wrote memorable autobiographies.[53] Thus the early discovery of a list of women called to the bar of Ontario from 1897 to 1975, compiled by Eileen Huckle, secretary to the Treasurer of the Law Society for many decades, was critical. In addition to identifying the exact date of each woman's call to the Ontario bar, Huckle's annotated list included brief notes about practice

52 J. Bennett, "Theoretical Issues: Confronting Continuity" (1997) 9:3 *Journal of Women's History* 73 at 74. See also reviews of this article in the same volume and J. Bennett, *History Matters: Patriarchy and the Challenge of Feminism* (Philadelphia: University of Pennsylvania Press, 2006) 5.

53 Kinnear, *In Subordination*, 22–23.

locations, as well as women's married names, essential finding aids for searches about them in other records.[54]

This project involved research in the Archives of the Law Society of Ontario, which also includes archival records of the Women's Law Association of Ontario; the Archives of Ontario; Library and Archives Canada; and numerous local archives in Ontario, in other Canadian provinces, and in other jurisdictions.[55] In addition, information about some early women lawyers was located in community and county bar association histories in Ontario, published studies of law firms, books published by the Osgoode Society for Canadian Legal History, university newspapers and publications, family biographical records online, and many law journals, especially the *Law Society Gazette*. In addition, women lawyers' practice locations were identified in the *Canadian Law Lists*, although its protocols did not always include lawyers working for government or corporations—and the names of women working in private law firms, often for many years, were sometimes missing or included in parentheses. Transcripts of oral histories of the Osgoode Society for Canadian Legal History, accessed in the Archives of Ontario before they became available online, also provided "real voices" for some early women lawyers. In spite of concerns about omissions and silences, and even though their voices can sometimes be awkward to handle and their memories complicated to interpret, oral histories can sometimes provide authentic testimony about "what women now think their life and work were really like."[56] Nonetheless, while stories of

54 Eileen Major, later Huckle, began employment in 1912 as a stenographer at the Law Society of Upper Canada. After her marriage, she was appointed assistant secretary in 1925 and worked with Earl Smith, QC, secretary of the Society, until her retirement in 1962: Moore, *The Law Society of Upper Canada*, 205, 211. Huckle's list was also identified in E. Mitchell Thomas, "The History of Women Lawyers in the County of Carleton Law Association" in W. Johnson, ed., *The First Century: Essays on the History of the County of Carleton Law Association by Various Hands on the Occasion of the Association's Centenary, 1888–1988* (Ottawa: Bonanza Press, 1988) 107 at 112. See also E. Mitchell Thomas, "The History of Woman Lawyers in the County of Carleton Law Association" (1988) 22:4 *Law Society Gazette* 397. Notably, two early women lawyers in the United Kingdom were referred to professionally as "Miss," even though both had married: "From an English Office Window" (1949) 27:5 *Canadian Bar Review* 583.

55 As Marlene Kadar suggested, archives are always "a complex site of influences and representations": M. Kadar, "Afterword" in H.M. Buss and M. Kadar, eds., *Working in Women's Archives: Researching Women's Private Literature and Archival Documents* (Waterloo, ON: Wilfrid Laurier University Press, 2001) 115.

56 Kinnear, *In Subordination*, 22–23.

many pioneer women lawyers in this book appear in the spotlight, others are glimpsed only in shadows—because records for many early women in law remain hidden, or at least undiscovered, at present. Yet, as a group biography, the book reveals details of gendered patterns in the legal profession, and how its professional culture created barriers, both direct and more subtle, for women lawyers. In addition, changes in social, political and economic contexts for legal work between 1897 and 1957 and in subsequent decades help to identify what choices were realistically available to women who wished to practise law in Ontario.

In telling their stories, this book also reveals how changing contexts for legal education at Osgoode Hall during these early decades sometimes encouraged or thwarted women's ambitions. It also demonstrates how the Law Society's school in Ontario reflected the "law practice" orientation of British legal education. That is, unlike university legal education programs in other Canadian provinces, Ontario law students in the decades before the 1950s spent most of their days articling at law firms: three years for university graduates and five years for those who were high school "matriculants." In addition, these articling students attended lectures in the early mornings and late afternoons at Osgoode Hall, usually presented by practitioners in accordance with the directions of the Law Society's Legal Education Committee.[57] After passing examinations and completing their articling requirements, students were eligible to be called to the bar, and a series of these ceremonies occurred before judges in Toronto courtrooms throughout the year. Notably, some judges were less than welcoming to new women lawyers.[58]

Parts One to Three identify all the women who were admitted to the bar in Ontario in order of their year of admission up to 1957. Each part begins with details about legal education and developments in legal practice within differing political, economic, and social contexts in which women were entering the Ontario legal profession. Recognizing that some readers may wish to focus on women lawyers in different periods, their stories appear chronologically according to their dates of admission to the Ontario in discrete sections or chapters in each part, separate from the contextual

57 There were changes in the arrangements for students at Osgoode Hall in different historical periods: see Chapters Two to Six.

58 See Chapters Three and Four re Margaret Hyndman and Ruby Wigle (1926) and Margaret Baird (1937).

information about different historical periods. The name index may also assist readers to locate stories of individual women lawyers quite easily. Each part also provides some tentative assessments of the accomplishments of women lawyers at different periods in Ontario history. Finally, Part Four focuses on some significant changes that occurred after 1957, the decades when the number of women lawyers were dramatically increasing.

Part One briefly examines the international contexts in which women began to enter the legal professions in the late nineteenth century in the United States, the British Commonwealth, and Europe. Chapter One explores the Canadian context with stories of the first women to succeed in opening the bar to women in Canada. Following Clara Brett Martin's success in gaining access to the Ontario bar in 1897, women in all the common law provinces became entitled to become lawyers by the end of the First World War in 1918 (prior to the enactment of similar legislation in Britain). In contrast, women's efforts to become *avocats* in Québec did not succeed until 1941. Chapter Two focuses on the ten women who graduated from Osgoode Hall and joined Clara Brett Martin as members of the Ontario bar up to 1918, becoming the earliest cohort of women lawyers in the province.

Part Two focuses on the interwar years between 1919 and 1939, exploring the changing contexts of both the 1920s and 1930s for the legal profession in Ontario, particularly for women lawyers. Chapter Three explores the experiences of women who were called to the Ontario bar up to 1929, including the first Jewish women lawyers and some women lawyers whose families were immigrants. Chapter Four focuses on the Depression years between 1929 and the outbreak of the Second World War in 1939, and it describes challenges faced by members of the legal profession, men as well as women, who were law students and practitioners during these years.

Part Three explores the stories of women who were called to the bar between 1940 and 1957, decades in which the legal profession was involved in debates about legal education, as well as significant expansion in legal work after 1945. Chapter Five explains how the Second World War offered new opportunities for some women in the legal profession, as male lawyers departed for the war. At the same time, these opportunities frequently disappeared at war's end, when male lawyers returned as veterans and received priority for articling experiences and employment. Chapter Six focuses on the period from 1950 to 1957, especially changes in legal education, including the Law Society's decision to introduce full-time lectures within a four-year course, while also providing limited recognition for the academic law program at the University of Toronto. This chapter also documents how societal views in the 1950s often tended to (re)emphasize women's roles as homemakers, creating new barriers for some women legal practitioners.

Part Four explores important changes for the Ontario legal profession after 1957: the accreditation of universities to provide academic legal education; the surge in the number of law students, especially women law students, in the 1960s and '70s in the context of second-wave feminism; new developments in legal work and its expansion, diversification, and globalization in the decades after 1957; and the impact of greater diversity among members of Ontario's legal profession, especially for Outsiders, both women and men.

In conclusion, the Epilogue assesses the legacy of early women lawyers as "quiet rebels," and explores whether changes in the legal profession represent "continuity" or "transformation" in the status of women lawyers. The Epilogue also briefly examines the human rights complaint at Osgoode Hall Law School in 1987 and its connections to the unusual toast at the WLAO dinner meeting in 1927.

# PART ONE

## *The First Women Lawyers: Making History*

# *Women in Law: An International Movement*

> *Canada can now boast of a very successful lady barrister. Miss Clara Brett Martin won over the Ontario Parliament to her side, and a special law was passed in her favour authorizing the Canadian bar to admit women to its privileges. So far, this young lady seems to be alone in the exercise of her profession, but the moment we pass over to the United States, the lady lawyer meets us here, there, and everywhere.*[1]

This press comment in November 1897, about eight months after Clara Brett Martin became Canada's first woman lawyer, noted how women in many parts of the world were challenging male exclusivity in the legal professions in the late nineteenth century. Indeed, the comment appeared just before Jeanne Chauvin presented her application for admission to the Paris bar on 24 November 1897, probably an effort by her enthusiastic

1 "Portias of Today," *Illustrated London News* (13 November 1897) 696. See also B. Harris, *Beyond Her Sphere: Women and the Legal Professions in American History* (Westport, CT: Greenwood Press, 1978) 110.

*avocat*, Louis Frank, to encourage a positive result for Chauvin's claim.[2] Frank, a Belgian barrister who had championed the admission of women as lawyers in Italy and Belgium prior to supporting Chauvin's challenge in Paris, had also published a major treatise supporting her admission to the bar.[3] Aspiring women lawyers in Canada were often encouraged by such reports of women gaining access to legal professions elsewhere. This Part provides a brief overview of this international movement, and then tells the stories of the first women who challenged male exclusivity in the legal professions in Canadian provinces and territories between 1897 and 1918. It also examines the experiences of ten women who entered Ontario's legal profession following Clara Brett Martin up to the end of the First World War.

Many women who aspired to enter professions in the late nineteenth century were attracted by contemporary ideas about professionalism, including its claims to objectivity, empiricism, rationality, impersonality, and collegially determined standards that offered freedom from sex-defined constraints.[4] In addition, new ideas about women's equality, which had been adopted in the United States at the Seneca Falls Convention in 1848,

2 E. Charrier, *L'évolution intellectuelle féminine* (Paris: Éditions Albert Mechelinck, 1931) 336–37; and Bibliothèque Royale, Brussels, Section des Manuscrits, Papiers Frank: photos and letters from women lawyers published in "Portias of Today." See also *New York Times* (1 December 1897) 7; S. Kimble, "Justice Redressed: Women, Citizenship and the Social Uses of the Law in Modern France, 1890–1939" (PhD diss., University of Iowa, 2002) [unpublished]; and M.J. Mossman, *The First Women Lawyers: A Comparative Study of Gender, Law and the Legal Professions* (Oxford: Hart Publishing, 2006).

3 L. Frank, *La femme-avocat: Exposé historique et critique de la question* (Paris: V. Giard et E. Brière, 1898) ii. *La femme-avocat* provided detailed historical information about women lawyers worldwide, along with Frank's enthusiastic endorsement of "l'affranchissement du sexe feminin." See also F. De Bueger-Van Lierde, "Louis Frank, Pionnier du Mouvement Féministe Belge" (1973) vol. 4: issue 3–4 *Revue Belge d'Histoire Contemporaine* 377.

4 N.F. Cott, *The Grounding of Modern Feminism* (New Haven, CT: Yale University Press, 1987) 233–34. See also B.J. Bledstein, *The Culture of Professionalism: The Middle Class and the Development of Higher Education in America* (New York: W.W. Norton, 1976); G.L. Geison, ed., *Professions and Professional Ideologies in America* (Chapel Hill: University of North Carolina Press, 1983); M. Sarfatti Larson, *The Rise of Professionalism: A Sociological Analysis* (Berkeley: University of California Press, 1979); M. Burrage and R. Torstendahl, eds., *Professions in Theory and History: Rethinking the Study of the Professions* (London: Sage Publications, 1990); A. Abbott, *The System of Professions: An Essay on the Division of Expert Labor* (Chicago: University of Chicago Press, 1988); and R. Stevens, *Law School: Legal Education in America from the 1850s to the 1980s* (Chapel Hill: University of North Carolina Press, 1983).

became widespread after women's support during the American Civil War: women looked forward to "the postwar Reconstruction as the dawn of a new era of equal rights for all Americans—Blacks and whites, women and men."[5] This sentiment was reflected in women's increasing access to higher education in the United States in the 1860s and '70s. In addition, high rates of mortality during the Civil War fundamentally changed demographic circumstances: "the assumption that every woman would become a wife became questionable, perhaps untenable." Thus, women increasingly sought financial independence, including in the legal profession.[6]

In 1869, Arabella Babb Mansfield became the first woman admitted to a state bar when Justice Springer in Iowa interpreted "male" statutory language to include females. And, in 1870, Ada Kepley became the first woman to obtain the LLB degree when she graduated from the one-year program at Union College of Law, now Northwestern.[7] Yet there were setbacks for some aspiring women lawyers in the United States, especially the decision of the United States Supreme Court, which denied Myra Bradwell's

5 C. Bolt, *The Women's Movement in the United States and Britain from the 1790s to the 1920s* (Amherst: University of Massachusetts Press, 1993); and I. Kugler, *From Ladies to Women: The Organized Struggle for Women's Rights in the Reconstruction Era* (Westport, CT: Greenwood Press, 1987). The "Declaration of Sentiments" espoused equal rights for women in higher education and the professions as well as the right to vote, hold property, and have full status in contracts and courts. See also E. Flexner, *Century of Struggle: The Women's Rights Movement in the United States* (Cambridge, MA: Belknap Press/Harvard University Press, 1959); and J. Hoff, *Law, Gender, and Injustice: A Legal History of US Women* (New York: New York University Press, 1991).

6 N.F. Cott, *Public Vows: A History of Marriage and the Nation* (Cambridge, MA: Harvard University Press, 2000) 78–79. See also Harris, *Beyond Her Sphere*, 98; and P.M. Glazer, and M. Slater, *Unequal Colleagues: The Entrance of Women into the Professions, 1891–1940* (New Brunswick, NJ: Rutgers University Press, 1987).

7 K.B. Morello, *The Invisible Bar: The Woman Lawyer in America, 1638 to the Present* (New York: Random House, 1986) 12; Hoff, *Law, Gender, and Injustice*, 162–63; V.G. Drachman, *Women Lawyers and the Origins of Professional Identity: The Letters of the Equity Club, 1887 to 1890* (Ann Arbor: University of Michigan Press, 1993) 235; and A.M. Bittenbender, "Women in Law" in A.N. Meyer, ed., *Women's Work in America* (New York: H. Holt and Company, 1891) 222. See also Stanford Women's Legal History project, online: <https://wlh.law.stanford.edu.>

eligibility for the legal profession.[8] Nonetheless, a press report in 1896 cheerfully concluded that "the prejudice and opposition which so long obstructed their progress are rapidly disappearing [and women] are now being received and recognized by their brother members of the legal profession."[9]

In contrast to these American decisions, Canadian judges followed British legal precedents with respect to women's access to the legal profession, and British courts had firmly rejected women at the bar and in the solicitors' profession. Bertha Cave's challenge to male exclusivity at Gray's Inn in 1903 was "politely declined" by the Benchers of the Inn, and her subsequent appeal to the House of Lords was rejected.[10] A decade later in 1913, when Gwyneth Bebb and three other women, all with outstanding university qualifications in law from Oxford, applied to take the solicitors' preliminary examinations, the Law Society refused their applications. Appeals to the courts failed as well because the judges concluded that statutory language using male pronouns should be interpreted in accordance with "long usage" in the common law.[11] Thus, legislative action was needed, and since Canadian courts generally deferred to British precedents, legislative action recognizing women lawyers became necessary in Canada as well.

8 *Bradwell v Illinois* 83 US (16 Wallace's Supreme Court Reports) 130 (1873); *In re Bradwell*, 55 Ill 535 (1869). Illinois and other states later amended their statutes to permit women lawyers: N. Gilliam, "A Professional Pioneer: Myra Bradwell's Fight to Practice Law" (1987) 5 *Law and History Review* 105; J. Friedman, *America's First Woman Lawyer: The Biography of Myra Bradwell* (Buffalo, NY: Prometheus Books, 1993); and "Myra Bradwell," Stanford Women's Legal History project, online. American precedents, especially *Bradwell*, were cited in cases in New Brunswick and Québec.

9 "Women Lawyers" (1896) 83 *Leslie's Illustrated Weekly* 363. See also L. Robinson, "Women Lawyers in the United States" (1890) 2 *Green Bag* 10.

10 "Lady Law Students," *Englishwoman's Review* (January 1904) 49; *The Times* (3 December 1903), cited in A. Sachs and J. Hoff Wilson, *Sexism and the Law: A Study of Male Beliefs and Legal Bias in Britain and the United States* (New York: Free Press, 1978) 28; and "Women and the Bar," *Law Journal* (12 December 1903) 620. See also E.M. Lang, *British Women in the Twentieth Century* (London: T. Werner Laurie, 1929) 146.

11 *Bebb v The Law Society* (1913) 29 TLR 634, aff'd [1914] 1 Chancery 286 (CA). The four women were Gwyneth Bebb, Karin Costelloe, Maud Ingram, and Lucy (Nancy) Nettleford: R. Auchmuty, "Whatever Happened to Miss Bebb? *Bebb v The Law Society* and Women's Legal History" (2011) 31:2 *Legal Studies* 199 at 213–14. See also (1914) 26 *Canadian Law Times* 629–30.

Legislative action was also required in the former British colonies of New Zealand and Australia. In New Zealand, a statute enabling women to become lawyers in 1896 preceded any woman's claim for admission to the bar, perhaps reflecting the government's wish to respond to newly enfranchised women voters—after female suffrage had been enacted in 1893.[12] Thus, when Ethel Benjamin graduated in law in 1897 from the University of Otago in Dunedin, she was admitted to the New Zealand bar in 1897, a few months after Clara Brett Martin's admission in Ontario—and Benjamin became the first Jewish woman lawyer in the British Empire.[13] Although Benjamin later married and moved to Britain, she never sought admission to legal professions there after the enactment of the *Sex Disqualification (Removal) Act, 1919*.[14]

Australia's first woman lawyer, Grata Flos Greig, was admitted to the bar of Victoria in 1905 after the enactment of a statute, sometimes referred to as the *Flos Greig Enabling Bill*, which permitted women lawyers.[15] In contrast, Ada Evans in the neighbouring state of New South Wales, who had obtained a university law degree even earlier in 1902, was unsuccessful in her efforts to obtain legislation permitting women to join the New South Wales bar until 1918. And although Evans then completed articles and was admitted to the legal profession in New South Wales in 1921, she never

12 S. Coney, *Standing in the Sunshine: A History of New Zealand Women since They Won the Vote* (Auckland: Viking, 1993) 28–31; and G. Gatfield, *Without Prejudice: Women in the Law* (Wellington: Brooker's, 1996) 25–40.

13 C. Brown, *Ethel Benjamin: New Zealand's First Woman Lawyer* (BA honour's thesis, University of Otago, 1985) [unpublished]; and J. November, *In the Footsteps of Ethel Benjamin* (Wellington: Victoria University Press, 2009) 54–ff.

14 *Sex Disqualification (Removal) Act, 1919*, 9 & 10 Geo 5 c 71; See also M. Takayanagi, *Parliament and Women, c 1900–1919* (PhD diss., King's College London, 2012) [unpublished], chapter 2; and J. Bourne, "Great Expectations and Hard Times: The Advent of the Sex Disqualification (Removal) Act 1919 and Women's Entry to the Legal Profession (2023) 32:6 *Women's History Review* 793.

15 M. Thornton, *Dissonance and Distrust: Women in the Legal Profession* (Melbourne: Oxford University Press, 1996) 50-51; R. Campbell, "That Girl with the Terrible Name" (1975) 49 *Law Institute Journal* 502; L. Kirk, "Portia's Place: Australia's First Women Lawyers" (1995) 1 *Australian Journal of Law and History* 75; and "Women and the Bar" (1905) 4 *Canadian Law Review* 464. See also G. Flos Greig, "The Law as a Profession for Women" (1909) 6 *Commonwealth Law Review* 145; and M.J. Mossman, "'The Law as a Profession for Women': A Century of Progress?" (2009) 30 *Australian Feminist Law Journal* 131.

practised law.[16] Nonetheless, it is significant that legislation permitting women's admission to legal professions was enacted in several British colonies, including New Zealand and Australia as well as Canada, before the 1919 statute in Britain—a pattern that suggests declining legal deference by former colonial legislatures.[17]

Moreover, in Britain, Eliza Orme became a pupil at Lincoln's Inn in the 1870s and then opened a law office in Chancery Lane, although she was not a member of the bar or enrolled as a solicitor. Orme later passed the final examination for the BCL degree at London University, becoming the first woman in the British Empire to acquire a university degree in law in 1888.[18] Orme had a successful legal business, working for barristers and solicitors in matters of conveyancing and patents for "half fees," and she also did work for private clients relating to wills and estates. In 1893, when she was one of only four women invited to participate at the Congress on Jurisprudence and Law Reform, part of the World's Columbian Exhibition in Chicago, the *Law Times* announced that "Miss Orme is regarded as one of the ablest women in England."[19] By 1919, when the statute was finally enacted by the British Parliament to permit women barristers and solicitors, Orme had been retired for almost two decades.[20] In contrast, Cornelia Sorabji, who had travelled from India to Britain to become the first woman to complete the BCL examinations at Oxford in 1892, eventually received her university degree and was admitted as a barrister in England after the First World War. In the intervening years, Sorabji had returned to India, becoming the first woman in the Empire to plead in a British court when she appeared for the defence on a murder charge in 1896. In the early decades of the twentieth century, Sorabji held a post in the British

16 J. Scutt, *Women and the Law: Commentary and Materials* (Sydney: The Law Book, 1990) 17–18; and B. McPaul, "A Woman Pioneer" (1948) 22 *Australian Law Journal* 1.

17 B. Kercher, "A Convict Conservative: George Crossley and the English Legal Tradition" (1999) 16:1 *Law in Context* 24. Kercher argued that the principle that British law was automatically applicable in its colonial settlements did not always prevail.

18 L. Howsam, "'Sound-Minded Women': Eliza Orme and the Study and Practice of Law in Late-Victorian England" (1989) 15 *Atlantis* 44. See also J.S. Anderson, *Lawyers and the Making of English Land Law, 1832–1940* (Oxford: Clarendon Press, 1992) 4; and H. Kirk, *Portrait of a Profession: A History of the Solicitor's Profession, 1100 to the Present Day* (London: Oyez, 1976) 173.

19 "Women in the Law Reform Congress," *Law Times* (2 September 1893) 402. See also E. Orme, "The Legal Status of Women in England" (1893) 25 *Chicago Legal News* 431.

20 "Women and the Bar," *Law Journal* (12 December 1903) 620.

administration in India, providing legal advice to *purdahnashins*, women living in *purdah* (seclusion), who were prohibited from interacting with men, including male lawyers. In addition to publishing several books and many journal articles, Sorabji later worked as a barrister in India and in Britain.[21]

In the late nineteenth century, European women were also challenging male exclusivity in the legal professions.[22] Early litigation challenges in the 1880s, presented by Lidia Poët in Italy and by Marie Popelin in Belgium, were unsuccessful, although both women used their university law degrees in later work. Poët became involved in penal reform while Popelin cofounded, with Louis Frank, La Ligue Belge du Droit des Femmes in 1892. Poët retired and Popelin died before legislation in Italy and Belgium permitted women to become lawyers after the First World War.[23] In contrast, women became eligible to become *femme-avocats* in France in 1900. Even though Jeanne Chauvin's application for admission to the Paris bar in 1897 had been initially rejected, she and others lobbied the French Chamber of Deputies and the Senate for amending legislation. After the new legislation came into force in December 1900, Chauvin was admitted as a *femme-avocat*.[24]

21 V. Brittain, *The Women at Oxford: A Fragment of History* (London: G. Harrap, 1960) 152–56; S. Gooptu, *Cornelia Sorabji: India's Pioneer Woman Lawyer* (New Delhi: Oxford University Press, 2006); R. Sorabji, *Opening Doors: The Untold Story of Cornelia Sorabji* (New Delhi: Penguin Books, 2010); and A. Burton, "The *Purdahnashin* in Her Setting: Colonial Modernity and the *Zenana* in Cornelia Sorabji's Memoirs" (2000) 65 *Feminist Review* 145. See also "Women Barristers" (1896) 32 *Canada Law Journal* 423; and "A Pioneer in Law," *Englishwoman's Review* (n.s.) (15 October 1896) 217–18.

22 J.C. Albisetti, "Portia Ante Portas: Women and the Legal Profession in Europe, ca. 1870–1925" (2000) 33 *Journal of Social History* 825. See also S. Kimble and M. Röwekamp, eds., *New Perspectives on European Women's Legal History* (New York: Routledge, 2017).

23 V. Olgiati, "Professional Body and Gender Difference in Court: The Case of the First (Failed) Woman Lawyer in Modern Italy" in U. Schultz and G. Shaw, eds., *Women in the World's Legal Professions* (Oxford: Hart Publishing, 2003) 419; and F. De Bueger-Van Lierde, "A l'origine du mouvement féministe en Belgique: 'L'Affaire Popelin'" (1972) 50 *Revue Belge de Philologie et d'Histoire* 1128. See also M. Popelin, "Laws of Marriage and Divorce in Belgium" in *Report of the International Congress of Women, June 24th–30th 1909* (Toronto: Geo Parker and Sons, 1910) 248; and Albisetti, "Portia Ante Portas," 830–38.

24 Charrier, *L'évolution intellectuelle féminine*, 337–45; A. Boigeol, "French Women Lawyers (*Avocates*) and the 'Women's Cause' in the First Half of the Twentieth Century" (2003) 10:2 *International Journal of the Legal Profession* 193; J. Savage, "The Problems of Wealth and Virtue: The Paris Bar and the Generation of the *Fin-de-Siècle*" in W.W. Pue and D. Sugarman, eds., *Lawyers and Vampires: Cultural Histories of the Legal Professions* (Oxford: Hart Publishing, 2003) 171.

The stories of these early women lawyers in other jurisdictions reveal different patterns, shaped by geography and political contexts, by different legal cultures in civil law and common law jurisdictions, and by evolving societal norms about gender roles—especially for women. Some women, particularly in the United States, gained admission to the bar and succeeded in legal practice in the last decades of the nineteenth century. Other women who obtained professional credentials encountered barriers in legal practice, and a few chose to engage in legal work "at the margins," without formal admission to the bar. In addition, some women who were excluded from legal practice used their legal knowledge in a variety of reform activities, including those relating to women's legal status. This international movement, which increasingly challenged male exclusivity in the legal professions, fostered new ambitions among women in Canada in the early twentieth century.

## CHAPTER ONE

# *Challenging Male Exclusivity in the Canadian Legal Professions, 1897–1918*

### The Canadian Context at the Turn of the Century

> *By the turn of the century, there were a few Canadian women who challenged quite vehemently both their domestic roles and their limited place in the workforce. Choosing to pursue a career ... some daughters of middle- and upper-class families, like their counterparts in Europe and the United States, began to demand entry into universities and into the new professions. Augusta Stowe-Gullen, Emily Stowe, and Amelia Yeomans, for example, breached the walls of male exclusivity in the medical profession. A few others pursued legal careers.*[1]

At the turn of the twentieth century and in the decades that followed, ideas about the "Woman Question" intersected with the new norms of legal professionalism and emerging opportunities for legal work in Canada's changing political economy. Although Canadian judges were unreceptive to women's claims to join provincial legal professions, some male lawyers

1 J. Errington, "Pioneers and Suffragists" in S. Burt, L. Code, and L. Dorney, eds., *Changing Patterns: Women in Canada* (Toronto: McClelland and Stewart, 1988) 64–65, describing a "progressive reform impulse" in North America between 1880 and 1920. See also N. Griffiths, *Penelope's Web: Some Perceptions of Women in European and Canadian Society* (Toronto: Oxford University Press, 1976); and R. Cook and W. Mitchinson, eds., *The Proper Sphere: Woman's Place in Canadian Society* (Toronto: Oxford University Press, 1976).

and legislators supported women's aspirations. In addition, political lobbying by women's reform organizations, particularly in the West, encouraged provincial legislators to enact female suffrage reforms as well as legislation to permit women lawyers—before women's suffrage was achieved federally in Canada in 1918.[2] In this context, women's efforts to become lawyers reveal individual qualities of ambition and perseverance, but their stories require attention to broader legal and political contexts—beyond claims of male oppression and female resistance.[3]

Although legal historian Wes Pue suggested that the "dominant cultural influence on Canadian lawyers" came from the United States, where a ready-made template of professionalization existed at the turn of the twentieth century, this template failed to recognize that American women had been entering the legal profession for three decades by 1900. Indeed, by 1910, there were 1,500 women lawyers in the United States.[4] At the same time, economic developments at the turn of the century in Canada—the construction of the new railway across Canada, the rapid spread of utilities, the need for more complex contracts and securities instruments, and an increasing number of new corporations—were creating a need for more sophisticated legal expertise. In addition, small law firms in major cities were increasing in size, lawyers were starting to specialize, and there was more mobility for lawyers who wanted to take advantage of new opportunities, particularly in the West. Canadian lawyers were also becoming concerned about standards for legal education and legal practice, and after

2 C. Cleverdon, *The Woman Suffrage Movement in Canada* (Toronto: University of Toronto Press, 1950); C. Bacchi, *Liberation Deferred? The Ideas of the English-Canadian Suffragists, 1877–1918* (Toronto: University of Toronto Press, 1983); and *An Act to confer the Electoral Franchise upon Women* SC 1918, c 20.

3 F. Iacovetta and M. Valverde, eds., *Gender Conflicts: New Essays in Women's History* (Toronto: University of Toronto Press, 1992) xvii. See also J. Sangster, *Through Feminist Eyes: Essays on Canadian Women's History* (Edmonton: Athabasca University Press, 2011).

4 W.W. Pue, "Cultural Projects and Structural Transformation in the Canadian Legal Profession" in W.W. Pue and D. Sugarman, eds., *Lawyers and Vampires: Cultural Histories of the Legal Professions* (Oxford: Hart Publishing, 2003) 367 at 387; and B. Harris, *Beyond Her Sphere: Women and the Professions in American History* (Westport, CT: Greenwood Press, 1978) 110.

the Canadian Bar Association was established in 1914, one of its earliest tasks was the creation of a model legal education curriculum in Canada.[5]

Male gender remained deeply ingrained in Canadian ideas of professionalism. An early leader of the CBA, James Aikins, envisaged legal education as aspiring to create "gentlemanly" instincts among law students: "law school was intended to make better men":

> What conferred privilege upon barristers ... was not simply the nature of the work ... but the fact that [this occupation was] taken up by gentlemen, by those who had acquired a liberal education, by those who had claims to belong to the respectable classes. To study the professions ... is to study not just the world of work and occupations but also Weber's triad of status, class and power—and one might add, gender as well.[6]

At the same time, male exclusivity in Ontario's legal profession did not preclude some limited diversity in the nineteenth and early twentieth centuries. Robert Sutherland, a Black lawyer and graduate of Queen's University, was called to the Ontario bar in 1855, and another Black

5 C. Wilton, "Introduction" in C. Wilton, ed., *Inside the Law: Canadian Law Firms in Historical Perspective* (Toronto: Osgoode Society for Canadian Legal History/ University of Toronto Press, 1996) 1 at 13; and "Women Barristers" (1896) 32 *Canada Law Journal* 423. See also Pue, "Cultural Projects" 367; and C. Moore, *The Law Society of Upper Canada and Ontario's Lawyers, 1797–1997* (Toronto: University of Toronto Press, 1997).

6 R.D. Gidney and W.P.D. Millar, *Professional Gentlemen: The Professions in Nineteenth-Century Ontario* (Toronto: University of Toronto Press, 1994) 12; and W.W. Pue, "Common Law Legal Education in Canada's Age of Light, Soap and Water" (1996) 23 *Manitoba Law Journal* 654 at 682–83. See also B. Baines, "Women and the Law" in S. Burt, L. Code, and L. Dorney, eds., *Changing Patterns: Women in Canada* (Toronto: McClelland and Stewart, 1988) 157.

lawyer, Delos Rogest Davis, was admitted in 1884.[7] Two men with partial Indigenous heritage were also admitted to the bar in the nineteenth century: William Kerr in 1862 and Solomon White in 1865. In addition, John O'Connor, a disabled lawyer who became Ontario's first Irish Catholic judge in 1884, and Archibald MacLellan and his brother, Duncan, who were both blind, were called to the Ontario bar, as well as Catholic lawyers, with both Irish and Francophone heritage.[8] Moreover, among lawyers with German heritage, Michael Ludwig won the Gold Medal at Osgoode Hall and was called to the Ontario bar in 1889, and he later became President of the Ontario Bar Association and the first Treasurer of German heritage at the Law Society of Upper Canada. Samuel King, who was called to the bar in 1891, was among the earliest Jewish lawyers in Ontario. As an assimilated, educated, and well-to-do Jew, King's presence in the profession did not provoke concerns—in contrast to children of Yiddish-speaking Eastern European poor immigrants. Nonetheless, in spite of this diversity,

7 Law Society of Ontario (LSO), "Diversifying the Bar": Robert Sutherland and Delos Rogest Davis. In 1910, Davis became the first Black KC in the British Empire: L. Talbot, "History of Blacks in the Law Society of Upper Canada" (1990) 24:1 *Gazette* 65; and J. Isaac, "Delos Rogest Davis, KC" (1990) 24: 4 *Gazette* 293. Sutherland was born in Jamaica whereas Davis was born in Maryland in the United States. Thus, Abraham Beverley Walker, who was born in New Brunswick, is regarded as the first Canadian-born Black lawyer. Walker studied law at the National Law School in Washington and was called to the New Brunswick bar in 1882. He later attended King's College of Law in Saint John in the early 1890s: D.G. Bell, *Legal Education in New Brunswick: A History* (Fredericton: University of New Brunswick, 1992) 83, 92–94. Walker experienced racism in his efforts to practise law in his lifetime, but in 2019 he was awarded the Order of New Brunswick posthumously: K. Bissett, "Canadian-Born Black Lawyer Honoured a Century after Death," *Toronto Star* (28 October 2019) A7. See also *Dictionary of Canadian Biography* online (University of Toronto Press and Les Presses de l'Université Laval).

8 LSO, "Diversifying the Bar," William Simcoe Kerr and Solomon White. Kerr's ancestry included Chief Joseph Brant of the Mohawk and Sir William Johnson, superintendent of "Indians" in the eighteenth century. White's father was a Wyandot Chief, and his mother was francophone. White was elected to the provincial legislature and named KC in 1908. See also "Diversifying the Bar," John O'Connor, Archibald MacLellan, Duncan MacLellan, Angus Macdonelle, and Charles Baby.

male exclusivity remained: "It was women ... who posed the challenge most acutely."[9]

By the 1890s, ideas about women's "proper roles" were in flux, and some women's reformist organizations, including the Dominion Women's Enfranchisement Association, actively supported Clara Brett Martin's application for admission to the Ontario bar.[10] The National Council of Women had been established in Canada in 1893, with Lady Aberdeen, wife of the Governor General, as its President, and the first Women's Institute was established at Stoney Creek, Ontario, in 1897. In the early 1890s, the Woman's Christian Temperance Union (WCTU) in Manitoba had adopted women's suffrage as a strategy to achieve prohibition, and the WCTU staged its first Mock Parliament on the suffrage issue. Although the WCTU relied on arguments about the need for women's "purifying influence" in the public sphere, other suffragists adopted arguments about women's rights to "equality and justice," a more radical approach that might have inspired women lawyers.[11] By the turn of the twentieth century, women in some provinces had become eligible for election to school boards and to vote in municipal elections, married women's property reforms ensured that most

9 LSO, "Diversifying the Bar," Michael Ludwig. See also E. Bloomfield, "Lawyers as Members of the Urban Business Elites in Southern Ontario, 1860 to 1920" in C. Wilton, ed., *Beyond the Law: Lawyers and Business in Canada 1830 to 1930* (Toronto: Osgoode Society for Canadian Legal History, 1990) 112 at 134–35; and Moore, *The Law Society of Upper Canada*, 180.

10 T. Roth, "Clara Brett Martin—Canada's Pioneer Woman Lawyer" (1984) 18 *Law Society Gazette* 323 at 328.

11 V. Strong-Boag, "Setting the Stage" in S. Mann Trofimenkoff and A. Prentice, eds., *The Neglected Majority: Essays in Canadian Women's History* (Toronto: McClelland and Stewart, 1977) 87; N. Griffiths, *The Splendid Vision: Centennial History of the National Council of Women of Canada, 1893–1993* (Ottawa: Carleton University Press, 1993); C. MacDonald, *Adelaide Hoodless: Domestic Crusader* (Toronto: Dundurn Press, 1986); L. Kealey and J. Sangster, eds., *Beyond the Vote: Canadian Women and Politics* (Toronto: University of Toronto Press, 1989); G. Cuthbert. Brandt et al., *Canadian Women: A History*, 3rd ed. (Toronto: Nelson Education, 2011); and S. Bashevkin, "Independence versus Partisanship: Dilemmas in the Political History of Women in English Canada" in V. Strong Boag and A.C. Feldman, eds., *Rethinking Canada: The Promise of Women's History* (Toronto: Copp Clark Pitman, 1986) 246.

Canadian women could retain their own earnings, and some provinces had begun to enact laws to provide financial assistance to deserted wives.[12]

Ontario enacted female suffrage in 1917, and Prime Minister Borden's Union Government enacted the *Military Voters' Act* in the same year.[13] The federal statute enfranchised women with close relatives in the armed forces, apparently a "blatant attempt" to ensure success in the election that year. The movement for the vote had begun earlier at local and provincial levels, where municipalities had granted the franchise to all property owners, including married women, between 1880 and 1900. By 1910, female suffrage organizations existed in each province, and in addition to support from labour groups and the press, the National Council of Women endorsed women's suffrage that year. In March 1918, the *Women's Franchise Act* was introduced in the federal Parliament, providing suffrage for many, but not all, Canadian women in federal elections.[14] In addition, although the suffrage cause involved many Canadian women, it seems that only

12 Most early women's organizations did not include Indigenous or Black women, and many were organized along class lines, with married women who did not work outside the home as leaders. Nonetheless, these organizations succeeded in politicizing "long-standing concerns involving women, children, the family, the church and the community": Brandt et al., *Canadian Women*, 230–40. See also M. Dumont et al., *Québec Women: A History*, trans. by R. Gannon and R. Gill (Toronto: Women's Press, 1987).

13 Errington, "Pioneers and Suffragists," 70–73. See also *Ontario Franchise Act, 1917*, 7 Geo V, c 5. Prime Minister Borden created a Union Government in 1917, and Newton Rowell, leader of the Liberal Party in Ontario, was appointed chair of the Cabinet's war committee. Borden also established Canada as an autonomous Dominion at the Paris Peace Conference in 1919: T. Cook: "Canada's Warlord: Prime Minister Sir Robert Borden's Leadership during the Great War" (2011) 13:3 *Journal of Military and Strategic Studies* 1; and M. Prang, *N.W. Rowell, Ontario Nationalist* (Toronto: University of Toronto Press, 1975).

14 *An Act to confer the Electoral Franchise upon Women*, SC 1918, c 20. See also Bacchi, *Liberation Deferred?*, 142-43; Cleverdon, *The Woman-Suffrage Movement in Canada*; and Brandt et al., *Canadian Women*, 289–ff. The statute did not extend the vote to Canadians of Chinese, Japanese, or East Indian parentage until after the Second World War, and registered Indians in Canada were not permitted to vote until 1 July 1960: Royal Commission on the Status of Women, *Report of the Royal Commission on the Status of Women* (Ottawa: Information Canada, 1970) 164, 336–38; and L. Marsden, *Canadian Women and the Struggle for Equality* (Don Mills, ON: Oxford University Press, 2012) 70, 198. Most Canadian provinces had enacted female suffrage by 1918, but New Brunswick did so in 1919, Prince Edward Island in 1922 and Newfoundland in 1925. Québec did not permit women to vote until 1940: Dumont et al., *Québec Women*, 262–65.

a few women lawyers in this early cohort up to 1918 were involved in this reform movement.

Canadian women also attained access to higher education in the late nineteenth century. In May 1875, Grace Annie Lockhart received the first Bachelor of Science degree in the British Empire at Mount Allison University. Both Dalhousie and McGill Universities opened their Arts faculties to women in the 1880s, as did Manitoba College and both Trinity and University Colleges in Toronto. Although there was greater resistance to women's entry to medicine and law, a few women began to study medicine in the 1880s. In contrast to women doctors who could argue that they were responding to privacy needs for women patients, opponents of women lawyers resisted their claims because they might have to enter boisterous courtrooms where criminals and individuals of ill repute were brought to justice.[15]

In addition, male culture in traditional apprenticeship arrangements for law students posed challenges for some women, and the creation of formal law lectures in Ontario and New Brunswick, in which women could demonstrate their expertise in competitive examinations, may have encouraged women to become law students. It is significant that Clara Brett Martin applied to the Law Society in Ontario just two years after the establishment of Osgoode Hall's permanent lecture program in 1889, while Mabel Penery French began to study at King's College of Law in Saint

15 V.G. Drachman, *Sisters in Law: Women Lawyers in Modern American History* (Cambridge, MA: Harvard University Press, 1998) 5, 149; and M.R. Walsh, *"Doctors Wanted: No Woman Need Apply": Sexual Barriers in the Medical Profession, 1835–1975* (New Haven, CT: Yale University Press, 1977). See also Royal Commission on the Status of Women in Canada, *Report,* 164; Mount Allison University history, online: <https://www.mta.ca>; and V. Strong-Boag, "Canada's Women Doctors: Feminism Constrained" in L. Kealey, ed., *A Not Unreasonable Claim: Women and Reform in Canada 1880s–1920s* (Toronto: Women's Press, 1979) 109 at 117–18. Strong-Boag identified two women's medical colleges, founded in 1883 in Toronto and Kingston, that had admitted 146 students before closing, after universities began to admit women medical students. Canadian women also studied medicine in the United States. Among them, Jennie Trout graduated from the Woman's Medical College of Pennsylvania in 1875, becoming Canada's first licensed female doctor: C. Hacker, *The Indomitable Lady Doctors* (Toronto: Clarke, Irwin and Company, 1974).

John about a decade after it was established in the 1890s.[16] In contrast, Ada M. Read, the daughter of a Toronto lawyer, who served as Librarian at the County of York Law Association from 1886 to 1919, "may very well have been attracted to the law," even though the profession was then closed to women. Read was highly regarded by the legal profession, especially because she noted up decisions in the library's law reports as precedents were applied, distinguished, or overruled."[17] In addition to other challenges, comments in Canadian legal journals in the late nineteenth century were quite dismissive of women lawyers: "As conveyancers, or as compilers of text-books, there may be no reason why some women should not succeed as well as some men: but to refuse to allow them to embark on the rough and troubled sea of actual legal practice, is, as it appears to us, being cruel only to be kind."[18]

Although such views remained prevalent in the 1890s, the legal profession faced new challenges as Ontario experienced rapid industrialization, urbanization, and immigration. In addition, the number of lawyers was

16 Two women, Isabel Mowatt and Edith Hanington, began to study law in 1892 at King's College of Law in Saint John, but neither completed their legal studies: Bell, *Legal Education in New Brunswick*, 83. In the West, Erella Laurena Leona Alexander of Calgary enrolled as an articling student with the Law Society of the Northwest Territories in 1896. Although she passed the intermediate examination in 1900, there is no evidence that she was called to the bar: S. Petersson, "Ruby Clements and Early Women of the Alberta Bar" (1997) 9 *Canadian Journal of Women and the Law* 365 at 366–67.

17 J. Honsberger, *The County of York Law Association: A History of the First Hundred Years 1885–1985* (Toronto: The County of York Law Association, 1989) 18; and (1891) *Canadian Law Times* 42 at 46. In later decades, women lawyers were often employed in law libraries. For example, Diana Priestley, who had obtained a law degree after service in the Second World War, pursued a law library degree at the University of Washington and became a law librarian at the University of British Columbia in 1953. Ten years later, Priestly moved to the University of Toronto Law Library and then to the Law Library at Osgoode Hall Law School at York University (1967–70). Eventually, Priestly returned to British Columbia to establish the law library at the University of Victoria's new law school: Provincial Archives, Victoria BC, "Aural History Interview": Diana Priestly, 1990.

18 See (1880) 16 *Canada Law Journal* 160–61. See also (1869) 5 *Canada Law Journal* 307; and (1879) 15 *Canada Law Journal* 146. Myra Bradwell responded to these views in the *Chicago Legal News* (19 June 1880): "According to our Canadian and English brothers it would be cruel to allow a woman to 'embark upon the rough and troubled sea of actual legal practice,' but not to allow her to govern all England with Canada and other dependencies thrown in. Our brothers will get used to it and then it will not seem any worse to them to have women practicing in the courts than it does now to have a queen rule over them."

growing, and the volume of litigation was increasing, and "many lawyers felt that the bar's traditional position of status and power was threatened by a levelling spirit of the age." Thus, the Law Society's decision to establish a law school with mandatory lectures in 1889 was welcomed as a means of ensuring the bar's control of the profession and legal education. Yet lectures at the Society's law school were designed to augment, not replace, the traditional apprenticeship arrangement for legal training in law offices, even though, by the turn of the twentieth century, "the telephone, typewriter and stenographer [were altering] the role of the legal clerk and [making] his duties ever more menial."[19] Rejecting the pleas of lawyers outside Toronto, who had expressed grave concern about the loss of their articling students for several months each year, the Law Society's Benchers also rejected a proposal from the University of Toronto to collaborate in the creation of a law faculty. Thus, after 1889, all law students in Ontario were required to article in law firms and to attend lectures at the law school. University graduates were required to article and attend lectures for three years, while matriculants (high school graduates) needed to complete five years of articles and attend the Law School's compulsory lectures during the final three years of articling.[20]

To accommodate law lectures, the Law Society's Benchers authorized the creation of a school building on the grounds of Osgoode Hall, and a new student library, the Phillips Stewart Student Library, was established following a generous bequest. Although the school's new principal, William Reeve, arranged the lectures, the Law Society's Legal Education Committee retained full authority for appointing lecture staff, regulating the lectures, and defining both the subjects to be taught and the books to

19 C. Cole, A History of Osgoode Hall Law School, 1889–1989 [unpublished, 1995, archived at Osgoode Hall Law School library] 41, 50–51; and E. Brunet, "The Law Office at the Turn of the Century" *Ontario Lawyers Gazette* (May/June 1999) 32. See also Gidney and Millar, *Professional Gentlemen*, 299, 313–14.

20 C. Cole, *"A Learned and Professional Body": The Professionalization of the Ontario Bar, 1867–1929* (PhD diss, University of Western Ontario, 1987) [unpublished], citing *Canada Law Journal* (1 February 1889) 52. In 1889, 37 per cent of articling students lived in Toronto: Cole, *"A Learned and Professional Body,"* 210. See also B. Baker, "Legal Education in Upper Canada, 1785–1889: The Law Society as Educator" in D. Flaherty, eds., *Essays in the History of Canadian Law*, vol. 2 (Toronto: Osgoode Society for Canadian Legal History/University of Toronto Press, 1983) 49.

be studied.[21] In contrast to university law programs in New Brunswick, Nova Scotia, and Québec and similar arrangements adopted in some western provinces in the early twentieth century, and in spite of demands for more specialized and sophisticated legal expertise, law office work remained the major focus of Ontario legal education for decades. Formal lectures at Osgoode Hall were arranged for early morning and late afternoon, leaving most of a student's day free for office work.[22]

Notwithstanding these different arrangements for legal education, Canadian women gained access to all the common law legal professions in Canada, including pre-Confederation Newfoundland, by 1918, a year before women became entitled to become barristers and solicitors in Britain. In contrast, even though women in France had become *femme-avocats* in 1900, both the courts and the legislature in Québec denied women's claims until 1941.[23] The stories of the first women lawyers in Canadian provinces reveal how women challenged male exclusivity in the gentleman's profession of law.

21 B. Bucknall, T. Baldwin and J.D. Lakin, "Pedants, Practitioners and Prophets: Legal Education at Osgoode Hall to 1957" (1968) 6 *Osgoode Hall Law Journal* 141 at 165–68; and Moore, *Law Society of Upper Canada*, 170. In 1893–94, there were 785 lectures, prompting the *Canadian Law Times* to complain that the process was more like "stuffing sausages" than education: (1893) 13 *Canadian Law Times* 153.

22 Bucknall, Baldwin, and Lakin, "Pedants, Practitioners and Prophets," 161, 169, 173–74. See also P. Girard, "The Making of the Canadian Legal Profession: A Hybrid Heritage" (2014) 21 *International Journal of the Legal Profession* 145; and Gidney and Millar, *Professional Gentlemen*, 370–75. Although the law school's first principal (Reeves) had demonstrated support for university legal education, he died in 1894 and was succeeded by Principal Hoyles, who had less interest in the American system of university legal education.

23 Women also practised law in the territories in northern Canada. In the Northwest Territories, women lawyers were permitted to practise law without statutory changes: Beverley Speight, Court Librarian, Yellowknife, email communication to author (22 June 2005). In Yukon, an Ordinance respecting the Legal Profession was enacted in 1914, after Yukon's separation from NWT; section 4 referred to "persons," but without details about gender. Although the register may be incomplete, Mildred Gordon, later Cross, practised in Yukon between 1925 and 1930, and two women were later called to the bar: R. MacDonald in 1949 and E.D. Walters in 1973. By the early 1990s, one-third of Yukon lawyers were women: Canadian Bar Association, Task Force on Gender Equality, Yukon Report, 1993, at 18. See also D. Chunn and J. Brockman, "'She Never Did Anything by Halves': Mildred Elizabeth Louise Gordon" (2003) 61:5 *The Advocate* 725. When Nunavut was created in 1999, laws in force in the NWT were duplicated for Nunavut: *Nunavut Act*, SC 1993, c 28: Minnie Niego, Legislative Library, Iqaluit, email communication to author (14 June 2005).

### The "First" Women Lawyers in Canada

> *I imagine that very few of the students are aware that this neat little announcement ["women may be admitted as students-at-law on the same terms as men"] appears in the Calendar of the Law School. Doubtless its original purpose was to inform ambitious young women who were so bold as to attempt to invade a field, formerly regarded as belonging exclusively to men, that the way was now thrown open to them ... [These words also] form a rather fitting memorial to the woman who, only after a long struggle, was successful in having them inserted.*[24]

In 1891, Clara Brett Martin wrote to the Law Society of Upper Canada, requesting permission to become a student at the new law school at Osgoode Hall, noting that, even though she was a woman, she was relying on the "broad spirit of liberality and fairness that characterizes members of the legal profession."[25] Six months later, the Law Society rejected her request, stating that neither the statutes nor the rules of the society authorized the admission of women members. As the press reported, "the applicant [then] hied her to the Legislature, and this august body freed itself from its embarrassment by granting power to the Law Society to admit women as solicitors." Premier and Attorney General Oliver Mowat, who had introduced the necessary amendment in the legislature, then participated as an *ex officio* Bencher to achieve a positive outcome for Martin at the Law Society.[26] Press reports were critical of Mowat's support for Martin, suggesting that discussion of sex crimes in classes would create embarrassment for both lecturers and women students and that the vote

24 M. Appleby, "The Entry of Women into the Profession of Law and their Hopes," *Obiter Dicta* (17 January 1934) n.p. See also P. Axford, "Portias of the Province" *Saturday Night* (18 February 1948).

25 C. Backhouse "'To Open the Way for Others of My Sex': Clara Brett Martin's Career as Canada's First Woman Lawyer" (1985) 1 *Canadian Journal of Women and the Law* 1. See also Roth, "Clara Brett Martin;" and S. Sperdakos, "A Woman's Proper Place: The Entry of Women into the Legal Profession" (Presentation to Law Society of Upper Canada, Toronto, June 1997).

26 See 12 *Canadian Law Times* (May 1892) 111. Backhouse suggested that Mowat may have supported women's access to the legal profession rather than responding to more "radical" requests for women's enfranchisement: Backhouse, "To Open the Way for Others of My Sex," 26.

did not "represent the opinion of the profession, nor for that matter, the real opinion of the Benchers."[27] Clearly, Martin's claim challenged not only the idea of law as a gentleman's profession but also some male lawyers.

Martin eventually obtained an articling position in 1893 with William Mulock, apparently after his daughter Ethel had explained that Martin wanted to become a lawyer.[28] Mulock thus became the earliest male lawyer to offer concrete support to an aspiring Ontario woman lawyer. Martin began her legal studies and was admitted as a solicitor, and she then requested a legislative amendment in 1895, permitting women to be called to the bar. The legal press was not supportive:

> Admission to the Bar means a qualification for the Bench. To allow women to be called to the Bar, and to deny them the legitimate aspiration of attaining a seat on the Bench, would seem unreasonable. The question, then, is, Is the public prepared to see, and is it in the public interest that it should see, female judges on the Bench? We are firmly persuaded that neither the one nor the other is the case, and the only legitimate way of keeping women off the Bench is by excluding them from the Bar.[29]

Nonetheless, the Benchers eventually adopted rules for the admission of women to the bar in November 1896, and Martin was duly called to the bar of Ontario on 2 February 1897, the first woman lawyer in Ontario and

27 See 12 *Canadian Law Times* (December 1892) 296–97. See also (1893) 4:1 *Western Law Times* 1.

28 Obituary, "Mrs. Ethel Kirkpatrick" (formerly "Mulock"), *Stratford Beacon Herald* (14 February 1957). Although Backhouse described Ethel Mulock as a girlhood friend of Martin, Mulock may have been one of Martin's students while Martin worked as a teacher after completing her first degree at the University of Toronto. Martin was about six years older than Mulock: Backhouse, "To Open the Way for Others of My Sex," 22; Roth, "Clara Brett Martin," 325 n9; and LSO Archives, "Clara Brett Martin" name file. See also Moore, *The Law Society of Upper Canada*, 183; and S. Gibson, "Fairly Determined" (2002) 29:3 *University of Toronto Magazine*, souvenir ed. 46 at 49. William Mulock had been called to the bar in 1866 and served as a Liberal MP from 1882 to 1905: J. Sedgwick, "Sir William Mulock, PC, KCMG, A Recollection" (1991) 25 *Law Society of Upper Canada Gazette* 287.

29 See (1895) 31:8 *Canada Law Journal* 253 at 254. See also (1896) 32:10 *Canada Law Journal* 747.

in Canada.[30] The *Canada Law Journal* graciously congratulated her on her achievement, but added that "it will not be disloyal to her as now one of the brethren of the gown, also to express the hope that she may be the one brilliant exception to the time-honoured rule which has hitherto closed our ranks to those who are not of the male persuasion.[31]

For several years, Martin was the "one brilliant exception." She eventually established her own sole practice, which she carried on in the Temple Building at Bay and Richmond Streets. She was well regarded in the profession and handled cases of domestic relations, drawing settlements and agreements, as well as conveyancing, mortgages, and wills.[32] Martin was later elected a trustee of the Toronto Board of Education, and she responded to a request from the National Council of Women to submit an article on the legal status of women in Canada (outside Québec) for its publication *Women of Canada,* in 1900.[33] At that date, even though there were nearly one hundred women doctors in Canada, Martin was still

30 *Toronto Star* (2 February 1897), identifying Martin as "the pioneer lady lawyer of Canada." Apparently, Oliver Mowat cast the deciding vote for her admission: Axford, "Portias of the Province."

31 See (1897) 33:4 *Canada Law Journal* 1: Martin was entitled to be called to the bar after graduating from the Law School in 1896. She later obtained the BCL degree at the University of Toronto in 1897, and the LLB degree in 1899: H.J. Morgan, ed., *The Canadian Men and Women of the Time: A Handbook of Canadian Biography* (Toronto: W. Briggs, 1898). These degrees probably resulted from law courses in the Faculty of Arts, since the university's law faculty was not formed until 1949: LSO Archives, letter from P. Dawson, Administrative Secretary, Dean's Office, Faculty of Law, University of Toronto (2 April 1984).

32 LSO Archives, Women's Law Association of Ontario (WLAO) fonds, Scrapbook (SB), vol. 1. Martin defended John (James) Doughty, who was charged with the murder of Ambrose Small. Apparently, she "took a severe cold" while returning from a trip to Ottawa on Doughty's behalf in 1921, which contributed to her death in 1923.

33 "Clara Brett Martin," *Canadian Who's Who* (1916); and "Book Nearly Ready," *Toronto Star* (13 January 1900). Prepared for the Paris International Exhibition in 1900, the book included Martin's contribution, "Legal Status of Women in the Dominion of Canada (Except in the Province of Québec)" in National Council of Women of Canada, *Women of Canada: Their Life and Work* (Paris: Paris International Exhibition, 1900) 34. A contribution by H. Gérin-Lajoie, "Legal Status of Women in the Province of Québec," was also included. In the 1920s, Martin forwarded correspondence to Ontario's Attorney General that criticized Jewish lawyers; discovery of the letter in the 1990s resulted in controversy and revisions to Martin's history: L.R. Betcherman, "Clara Brett Martin's Anti-semitism" (1992) 5:2 *Canadian Journal of Women and the Law* 280, and related articles in this volume.

Canada's only woman lawyer. Martin later created several articling opportunities in her office for women law students at Osgoode Hall, and her pioneering efforts to "open the way for others of my sex" probably created encouragement for other women to become lawyers in Canada.[34]

Although women had begun to study law at King's College of Law in Saint John in the early 1890s, the first challenge to the profession's male exclusivity in New Brunswick occurred when Mabel Penery French graduated in 1905 after three years of study. She began work as an articling student in the firm where she had previously been a secretary, and also submitted her application to the court for admission as a barrister.[35] Stephen Bustin, a partner at the firm, presented arguments supporting her application, along with two other male lawyers, including Charles Skinner KC, who argued:

> The trend of recent legislation, both political and judicial, is to remove the disabilities of women and open to them every avenue leading to avocations which may enable them to earn a livelihood. Why delve into the dark ages for a precedent to justify holding them incompetent or by law disqualified from exercising a calling to which we have every reason to believe, from their successes in our universities and in the professions (which have been opened to them), they will bring to bear equal intelligence, greater diligence and devotion to duty than men?[36]

Rejecting these arguments, the judges focused on the tradition of law as a gentleman's profession. Justice Frederic Barker reviewed and rejected American precedents permitting women to become attorneys, instead

34 Gidney and Millar, *Professional Gentlemen*, 349. A decade earlier, in 1891, the census had recorded seventy-six women doctors in Canada, with thirty-seven in Ontario: Strong-Boag, "Canada's Women Doctors," 127–29. See also *Buffalo Express*, ca. 1896, cited in Backhouse, "To Open the Way for Others of My Sex," 22; and *Toronto Star* (9 January 1901 and 26 February 1904). Martin was a scheduled speaker at the International Congress of Women in Toronto in 1909 but sent her regrets: National Council of Women of Canada, *Report*, vol. 2, at 173–74. Martin died suddenly of a heart attack at the age of forty-nine in October 1923: Backhouse, "To Open the Way for Others of My Sex," 35.

35 Bell, *Legal Education in New Brunswick*, 95. See also L. Yorke, "Mabel Penery French (1881–1955): A Life Re-created" (1993) 42 *University of New Brunswick Law Journal* 3.

36 *In re French* (1905) 37 *New Brunswick Reports* 359 at 360. Skinner also argued the absence of direct British authority and the evenly balanced decisions in US states, and noted that male pronouns in other statutes, such as the *Medical Act*, did not preclude women doctors.

quoting the U.S. Supreme Court's decision denying Myra Bradwell's application for admission to the bar in 1873: "The natural and proper timidity and delicacy which belongs to the female sex evidently unfits it for many of the occupations of civil life." Chief Justice William Tuck curtly stated his disavowal of ideas based on "the advanced thought of the age and the right of women to share with men in all paying public activities": rather than competing with men, women should attend to their own legitimate business.[37] Notwithstanding this outcome, French and her supporters sought legislative help from New Brunswick's sympathetic Attorney General William Pugsley, who was known to support reforms to encourage women's independence. The provincial statute was revised in 1906. Following enactment of the legislation, French was admitted to the bar of New Brunswick on 22 November 1907, the first Canadian woman lawyer beyond Ontario.[38]

French and Bustin initially established a new partnership, and French also became involved in suffrage activities in New Brunswick.[39] Like other lawyers from the Maritimes who moved west, French subsequently decided to seek new opportunities in British Columbia, and in 1911 she became a legal assistant in the Vancouver firm of Russell, Russell and Hannington, whose partners were originally from New Brunswick. Joseph Russell argued French's application for admission by transfer to the bar of British Columbia, but both the lower court and the British Columbia Court of Appeal denied the application.[40] French sought legislative support once again, but British Columbia's Attorney General, William Bowser, declined to amend

37 *In re French*, 360–62, 365, citing *Bradwell v Illinois* (1873).

38 Yorke, "Mabel Penery French," 17–18.

39 French presented a paper at the meeting of the International Congress of Women in Toronto in 1909: "The Legal Parental Rights of Women in New Brunswick" in International Congress of Women, *Report of the International Congress of Women, June 24th–30th, 1909* (Toronto: Geo Parker and Sons, Printers, 1910) 203. Only a few women sought admission to the New Brunswick bar in subsequent years: Muriel Corkery was admitted in 1921; and Muriel McQueen Fergusson, the first woman Speaker of the Senate in Canada in 1972, was admitted in 1925: M.L. Lynch, "Women in the Law" (1950) 3 *University of New Brunswick Law Journal* 12 at 13–14.

40 Hannington's father was Daniel Hanington, one of the judges in French's case in New Brunswick: Yorke, "Mabel Penery French," 29. See also C. Mullins and A. Harvey, *Russell & Dumoulin: The First Century, 1889–1989* (Vancouver; Russell and Dumoulin, 1989), private memoir archived at the firm. See also *Re French* (1910–12) 17 *British Columbia Reports* 359; and M.J. Mossman, "'Invisible' Constraints on Lawyering and Leadership" (1988) 20:3 *Ottawa Law Review* 567.

the statute. Statutory change was eventually achieved, apparently as a result of the efforts of Evlyn Farris, a tireless supporter of women's rights and leading member of the University Women's Club in Vancouver. After discussion at a game of bridge between Farris and Robert Hannington, a partner at Russell, Russell & Hannington, Farris attended on the Attorney General to seek support for amending legislation. When the Attorney General suggested that he planned to postpone any action, "family lore has it that [Evlyn Farris] refused to move from his office until he promised to bring the bill to the legislature" during the current session.[41] After the statute was enacted, French completed the required examinations and was called to the bar of British Columbia on 1 April 1912. The minutes recorded the admission of "twenty gentlemen, including Mabel Penery French," confirming French's admission to the gentleman's profession.[42]

By 1912, there were only five women lawyers in Canada, and French was the only one outside Ontario and the only one qualified to practise law in two Canadian provinces. French worked as a legal practitioner for just a few years, initially in Saint John and later in Vancouver, but she eventually left Canada to live in England, where she married and never practised law again. Lois Yorke suggested that French may not have been committed to either the legal profession or the women's movement, instead using her career in law to achieve social advancement. Yet, her story also suggests that aspiring women lawyers, who succeeded in gaining admission to the bar, faced daunting challenges in legal practice. French's success in

41 Yorke, "Mabel Penery French," 36–41; and S. McClean, *A Woman of Influence: Evlyn Fenwick Farris* (Victoria: Sono Nis Press, 1997) 81–82. Farris was the wife of prominent lawyer and later senator John W. Farris. See also Antoinette, "Another Victory Scored by Woman," *My Lady's Realm* (28 February 1912); R. Pazdro, "Of British Columbia Suffragists and Barristers" (1980) 2:4 *Canadian Women's Studies* 15; and J. Brockman and D. Chunn, "'A New Order of Things': Women's Entry into the Legal Profession in British Columbia" (2002) 60:3 *The Advocate* 185.

42 A. Watts, *History of the Legal Profession in British Columbia, 1869–1984* (Vancouver: Law Society of British Columbia, 1984) 134. A second woman lawyer, Edith Paterson (a graduate of Osgoode Hall) was called to the British Columbia bar in 1916: see Chapter Two. See also J. Brockman, "Exclusionary Tactics: The History of Women and Minorities in the Legal Profession in British Columbia" in H. Foster and J. McLaren, eds., *Essays in the History of Canadian Law*, vol. 6, *British Columbia and Yukon* (Toronto: Osgoode Society for Canadian Legal History, 1995) 508, 517; and W.W. Pue, *Law School: The Story of Legal Education in British Columbia* (Vancouver: University of British Columbia Faculty of Law, 1995) 223–32.

becoming a lawyer in two provinces reveals her ambition as well as strategic alliances with sympathetic male supporters, but her experience in legal practice may not have met her stated goals of establishing a "useful and independent career."[43]

While French was practising law in New Brunswick, a woman in St. John's, Newfoundland, was beginning to read law in the office of her uncle, Donald Morison. Janet Miller was seeking admission to the bar according to the British tradition of serving articles in a firm and completing examinations. In 1910, she petitioned the Law Society to do the initial examination, but the Society rejected her request because she was a woman. Thus, at the next general meeting, Donald Morison proposed a motion to change the Society's rules to permit women to become lawyers, but a majority of members did not see "the necessity for or the expediency of any such radical change" in the Society's constitution, and the motion was defeated. Since Morison was also serving as Attorney General, he prevailed on his Cabinet colleagues to revise the statute in 1910, thus permitting women to join the profession. Miller began to article in Morison's office, and she was duly admitted as a student member of the Society on 12 April 1913 as "Miss Janet M. Miller of St John's, Gentleman."[44]

Although Miller successfully opened the bar to women in Newfoundland, she did not complete her studies and was never called to the bar. The First World War intervened, and in 1915 she moved to Glasgow to marry Eric Ayre, a fellow Newfoundlander who was in training there for combat,

43 Yorke, "Mabel Penery French," 44–49. When the Vancouver law firm was reorganized in 1912, French accompanied Russell to England, and he returned to Vancouver in 1914. French may have been in Saint John in 1914, with plans to return to Vancouver, but there is little information until her marriage in England in 1923: M.J. Mossman, *The First Women Lawyers: A Comparative Study of Gender, Law and the Legal Professions* (Oxford: Hart Publishing, 2006) 109–10; and "Vancouver's Lady Barrister in Town," *Saint John Globe* (4 May 1914). See also J.S. Cowper, "Confidences of a Woman Lawyer" (1912) 39 *Canadian Magazine* 142, cited in Yorke, "Mabel Penery French," 44.

44 B. Riggs, "Janet Miller Helped Pave the Way," *Archival Treasures*, Centre for Newfoundland Studies Archives, Memorial University: undated news report. See also Heritage Newfoundland and Labrador, "The First World War: Newfoundlanders and Labradorians Served on Land, at Sea, and in the Air during the first World War," online: <https://www.heritage.nf.ca. Donald Morison, a prominent lawyer and politician, represented Bonavista in the House of Assembly in 1888–97 and in 1906–13, and he was a judge of the Supreme Court of Newfoundland in 1898–1904: *Encyclopedia of Newfoundland and Labrador*, Centre for Newfoundland Studies, Memorial University, 397–98.

and Miller spent the next year in Glasgow. Tragically, on 1 July 1916, Ayre became one of the many casualties of the Newfoundland Regiment at Beaumont-Hamel and the Battle of the Somme. Miller Ayre then moved south to London and joined the Volunteer Aid Detachment, training as an ambulance driver. In 1917, her only brother died of pneumonia in London, after serving sixteen months in the war. Returning to St. John's after the war, Miller Ayre decided that too much time had passed to resume her law studies. She became actively involved in suffrage activities and married a St. John's businessman, Andrew Murray, in 1924. Miller Ayre Murray died at age fifty-four in 1946.[45]

Although she was never admitted to the Newfoundland bar, Miller's story is important for two reasons. The first is that "Miller would probably have been Newfoundland's first practising female lawyer had not World War I intervened." Indeed, after Newfoundland became Canada's tenth province after the Second World War, Miller would have been recognized among the earliest cohort of women lawyers in Canada. It was not until 1933 that Louisa Saunders was called to the bar in Newfoundland, pursuant to the statute enacted for Miller in 1910, thus becoming the first woman member of the Newfoundland Law Society.[46] The second reason for the significance of Miller's experience is the relative autonomy exercised by the government in Newfoundland in 1910—at a time when women in Britain continued to be excluded from the professions of solicitor and barrister.[47]

45 Riggs, "Janet Miller Helped Pave the Way." Miller's certificate of admission to the legal profession as a student was presented by her daughter to the Memorial University Archives: M. Porter, "Memorial: Gert Crosbie," *St. John's Status of Women Council Magazine* (Spring 2004). Eric Ayre was a captain in command of "D" Company and led "his men over the top at Beaumont-Hamel." His brother Bernard and cousins Gerald and Wilfrid were killed in the same action: "Brothers in Arms," *Telegram* (14 August 2015): see also Petersson, "Ruby Clements," 384.

46 Riggs, "Janet Miller Helped Pave the Way." See also C. Harvey, "Women in Law in Canada" (1970–71) 4 *Manitoba Law Journal* 9 at 17. Saunders practised law continuously until the late 1960s in a firm that initially included Richard Squires: *Canadian Law Lists.*

47 Although it is somewhat unclear, Newfoundland was an independent Dominion in 1910. For example, at the Imperial Conference in 1911, Newfoundland was present along with other Dominions of the British Empire, and its Dominion status may have been established in 1907: D. Coffey, "Newfoundland and Dominion Status" (Presentation to Legal History Workshop, University of Toronto, faculty of law, nd). See also W.C. Gilmore, *Newfoundland and Dominion Status: The External Affairs Competence and International Law Status of Newfoundland, 1855–1934* (Toronto: Carswell, 1988); and "Women Legal Practitioners in the Dominions" (1923) 156 *Law Times* 426–27.

In addition, the positive involvement of a sympathetic male relative, who was also a lawyer and Attorney General, was clearly significant to Miller's success in gaining admission as a student-at-law in Newfoundland.

While Miller was seeking admission as a law student in Newfoundland, women in the western provinces were also applying for admission to the bar, and the introduction of systematic lectures for law students may have encouraged their interest. Law lectures were introduced in Manitoba about 1911, in Saskatchewan in 1913, and in Alberta in 1912.[48] In addition, women's opportunities for legal careers may have been enhanced when the legislatures of Manitoba, Saskatchewan, and Alberta enacted provincial suffrage legislation for women in 1916.[49]

In 1915, the Law Society of Alberta, without any legislative intervention at all, admitted Lillian Ruby Clements as its first woman lawyer. A retrospective statute was enacted in 1930.[50] Clements's family originated in Ontario, but they had moved west to Edmonton and later Vegreville at the turn of the century. Clements graduated from high school in 1905 and then worked as a teacher for a few years before attending McMaster University, then located in Toronto. When she applied to the Law Society in Alberta for admission as a student, the society granted conditional approval because of uncertainty about the eligibility of women to become lawyers. Clements attended the requisite Law Society lectures and articled in Vegreville, and obtained the LLB degree from the University of Alberta,

48 D. Gibson and L. Gibson, *Substantial Justice: Law and Lawyers in Manitoba, 1670–1970* (Winnipeg: Peguis, 1972) 215–16; B. Bilson, "'Prudence Rather than Valor': Legal Education in Saskatchewan 1908–23" (1998) 61 *Saskatchewan Law Review* 341; (1913) 33 *Canadian Law Times* 923–94; and W.G. Morrow, "An Historical Examination of Alberta's Legal System: The First Seventy-Five Years" (1981) 29 *Alberta Law Review* 148.

49 *Act to amend "The Manitoba Election Act,"* SM 1916, c 36; *Act to amend The Statute Law*, SS 1916, c 37, s 1; and *Act to provide Equal Suffrage*, SA 1916, c 5. Female suffrage was enacted federally in 1918, although this legislation excluded Indigenous and Asian women: Brandt et al., *Canadian Women*, 253-273. See also *Dominion Elections Act*, SC 1920, c 46.

50 The *Sex Disqualification (Removal) Act, 1930*, SA 1930, c 62, was enacted in response to the *Persons Case* in the Privy Council and was retroactive to 1 September 1905, the date when Alberta became a Canadian province. See *Edwards v Attorney General of Canada* [1930] AC 124; and R. Sharpe and P. McMahon, *The Persons Case: The Origins and Legacy of the Fight for Legal Personhood* (Toronto: University of Toronto Press, 2007).

one of ten graduates in 1915.[51] When she was admitted to the bar in Alberta on 20 September 1915 the press reported comments by Oliver Mowat Biggar at the ceremony:

> "I have the pleasure in presenting to the bar Miss Lillian Ruby Clements" and he said it as though it were a real "pleasure" not a mere society formula; and added: "This event is worthy of note as Miss Clements is the first woman in Alberta to be admitted to the bar, and it is timely, for according to the newspapers, she will soon be able to exercise her franchise as well."
>
> The whole proceeding occupied just seven minutes by the court clock, and yet those few minutes preceded by many years of hard and faithful work on the part of Miss Clements, will serve to make the future path of the young women of Alberta, legally inclined, much less difficult to follow.[52]

Mowat Biggar, the grandson of Oliver Mowat in Ontario, may have provided support for Clements and other women lawyers. In addition, "frontier feminism" in western Canada and the United States may have resulted in fewer barriers for women professionals. In spite of Clements's success, she never practised law because she married soon after her call to the bar, and "while the educational merit made law a suitable field for

51 Petersson, "Ruby Clements." The University of Alberta established its faculty of law in 1921, and Petersson identified the first women to attain the LLB degree from the faculty between 1922 and 1924. Thus, Clements' degree may have been granted by the university rather than the law faculty. Harvey incorrectly identified E. Fagan as the first woman to attain the LLB degree in 1921: Harvey, "Women in Law in Canada," 17. For Fagan, see Chapter Five.

52 "An Event in the Supreme Court: First Woman Admitted to the Bar," *Edmonton Journal* (20 September 1915) 10, quoted in Petersson, "Ruby Clements," 377–78. A hundredth anniversary celebration of Clements' admission to the bar was organized by the Women's Legal Forum at the University of Alberta on 10 September 2016, in the presence of Alberta's Chief Justice Catherine Fraser. Justice Suzanne Coté of the Supreme Court of Canada gave a keynote address: Legal Education Society of Alberta (blog), online: <https://www.lesaonline.org.>

women to study, women could only practise law within the confines of societal norms."[53]

In Manitoba, two women lawyers—Melrose Sissons and Winnifred Wilton—were called to the bar in 1915. Although Sissons, a farmer's daughter and silver medallist in political economy and history at the University of Manitoba's College, is regarded as the first to apply for admission to the Law Society of Manitoba in 1911, there was an earlier inquiry. In February 1910, M.J. Finkelstein inquired on behalf of Gladys McHugh, who was employed in the office of Finkelstein & Morrisey, as to "whether the rules of our Law Society permit ladies to engage in the practice of law," adding that "personally I cannot see why any distinction should be made between the sexes in this regard." Ten days later, the Law Society responded, "The question of the admission of women as law students in this province was considered by the Benchers several years ago and it was then decided that Convocation had no jurisdiction in the then present state of the law to admit women to practise as Barristers or Attorneys. No change has been made since that resolution was passed, and there seems no reason for not affirming it."[54]

Although no further record exists with respect to Finkelstein's inquiry, the Law Society requested a legal opinion from E.A. Anderson in 1911, perhaps prompted by Sissons' application as to whether women were eligible for admission to the Law Society, and whether the Benchers had power to admit them. Anderson's opinion in October 1911 concluded that "a woman cannot, as a matter of right, compel the Benchers to admit her as a student at law," and he expressed uncertainty about the Benchers' power to admit a woman, citing the *French* case in New Brunswick, and pointing to the statutes enacted in Ontario. Anderson recommended that the Benchers seek

53 Petersson, "Ruby Clements," 379–80, 391; M. Matsuda, "The West and the Legal Status of Women: Explanations of Frontier Feminism" (1985) 24 *Journal of the West* 47; and A. Acorn, "Snapshots Then and Now: Feminism and the Law in Alberta" (1996) 35:1 *Alberta Law Review* 140. Oliver Mowat Biggar's mother was the daughter of Premier Oliver Mowat in Ontario. Two Alberta women (Emily Murphy and Alice Jamieson) were the first to be appointed police magistrates in Canada in 1916, and Louise McKinney and Roberta MacAdams became the first Canadian women to be elected to a provincial government in 1917. Five Alberta women had launched the *Persons Case*: see L. Dranoff, *Women in Canadian Law* (Toronto: Fitzhenry and Whiteside, 1977) 91–94; and Sharpe and McMahon, *The Persons Case.*

54 Wilton Wilson Family Archive (on file, M.J. Mossman), letter from M.J. Finkelstein to Campbell (5 February 1910). The Law Society's reply (16 February 1910) is unsigned.

a statutory amendment, or perhaps arrange a friendly suit "so that the applicant referred to in your letter could take some proceedings to have it declared that she was entitled to be admitted."[55] After the Law Society refused Sissons's application, on the basis that the word "person" in the statute included only males, the Manitoba legislature amended the statute in 1912, and Sissons began her articling position immediately. In addition, Winnifred Wilton commenced articles with Frederick James Sharpe in November 1912. Both Sissons and Wilton passed their final examinations in 1915, with Wilton gaining the highest marks of all students in the examinations.[56]

Sissons practised law for two years, but then married and relinquished legal practice.[57] Wilton also married, but only after some years of legal work. Initially, she had joined her brother, Jack Wilton, in his law practice in Winnipeg, but after just a few months she was appointed a legal representative with the Estates Department of the Canadian Expeditionary Force at their London headquarters. She was responsible for organizing the belongings of Canadian soldiers who were killed in action in the First World War. A press report in England in 1917 quoted her wry comment, in an interview with the *London Daily Mail*, on Londoners' shock at learning she was a lawyer. As she quipped, "I am trying to discover why people think that a woman lawyer must be a freak of some sort."[58] When the United States joined the war effort, Wilton requested a transfer to the American

55 Wilton Wilson Family Archive (on file, M.J. Mossman),"Re Melrose Sissons," letter from E.A. Anderson, KC, (Moran, Anderson & Guy) to W.A. Taylor, Assistant Secretary, Law Society (26 October 1911); and "Law Society Refuses Woman's Application," *Manitoba Free Press* (1 December 1911).

56 M. Kinnear, *In Subordination: Professional Women, 1870–1970* (Montreal/Kingston: McGill-Queen's University Press, 1995) 78–79, citing *Manitoba Free Press* (26 November 1915). See also C. Harvey, ed., *The Law Society of Manitoba, 1877–1977* (Winnipeg: Peguis, 1977) 36–37.

57 Kinnear, *In Subordination*, 205. Sissons had three children and was active in women's organizations in McCreary, Manitoba.

58 "Winnipeg Girl Lawyer Surprises Londoners," *London Daily Mail*, ca. 1917. See also P. Wilton, "Inappropriate for Women ..." *Law Now* (November 1992) 23–24; and J. Wilton, "Any Man" [unpublished memoir of Winnifred's brother, on file, M.J. Mossman]. Jack described meeting Winnifred in London "in all the glory of her womanhood," when she was twenty-six. Wilton's older sister Jean was working as a nurse in London, where she had married a soldier in the Welsh battalion who was killed in action shortly after their marriage: Wilton, "Any Man," 246–47.

Red Cross in Paris, where she met and married an American officer, Archibald Wilson from New York City, in 1919.

Wilton's letter to her parents in Winnipeg in May 1919 reveals that she had married Wilson only a few weeks after their first meeting: "Before you will have received this I will have been married." Although the couple intended to return to New York, Wilton promised that they would visit Winnipeg to introduce Wilson, who was from a very good family and of English descent. But she also noted that her career plans might change:

> The only trouble is that my legal career for which I had wonderful ambitions is cut short. I have always thought that when I got home this time I would be finished wandering and get to work and make you and Dad very proud of my accomplishments at the Bar. But somehow, I feel that you will be almost glad that I shall be with such a man for the rest of my life even at the sacrifice of all my study and your hard work to help make it possible.[59]

There is some evidence that Wilton Wilson may have wished to practise law after the couple settled in New York, since she wrote and passed the New York bar exams in 1922, becoming "the first English-born woman to be admitted to the American bar."[60] Perhaps the arrival of three sons in the 1920s prevented her from engaging in much legal practice, although she worked part-time in the 1930s as a legal referee, including in a dispute

59 Wilton Wilson Family Archive (on file, M.J. Mossman), letter from Wilton to her parents on American Red Cross letterhead (28 May 1919), explaining that they would marry in the Church of England. Archibald Wilson's letter to his mother on American Expeditionary Forces letterhead described Winnifred as "an entirely different kind of girl" and explained that three of her brothers were in the war, although one had been killed and another injured. Wilson said that they would marry at the Mairie of the 16th arrondissement. Wilson was an engineer at the US Embassy in Paris: Kinnear, *In Subordination,* 79; the couple may have had a courtship of just six days: P. Wilson, "Inappropriate for Women," 24.

60 *New York Times* (7 January 1923); and Wilton Wilson Family Archive (on file, M.J. Mossman), letter from State of New York, Office of Court Administration, to Elizabeth Wilson, Winnifred Wilson's granddaughter (17 October 1994), confirming Wilton Wilson's admission to the New York bar. Wilton's business card identifies "Winifred Wilton Wilson, Counselor at Law, 65 Edgar Lane, Hastings-on-Hudson and 342 Madison Avenue, New York."

about electrical rates at the local utility. Wilton Wilson died in New York in 1962 and was buried there. She never returned to live in Winnipeg.[61]

In 1917, Isabel MacLean also joined the Manitoba bar, the first woman to obtain the LLB degree at the University of Manitoba in 1916, and also the first to practise law in Grandview in rural Manitoba. In 1920, she married Albert Hunt and the couple moved to Cornwall, Ontario, where they had two children. When her husband died after just four years of marriage, MacLean Hunt moved back to Manitoba, and became the first woman lawyer in the legal department of the City of Winnipeg. She supported her family as a Solicitor, and later Assistant Solicitor, for the City of Winnipeg for thirty years, and she became the first woman lawyer in Manitoba to be appointed QC in 1953.[62]

The Law Society of Saskatchewan had established lectures on law at its part-time law school in Regina in 1913,[63] even though plans were underway as early as 1907 to establish the University of Saskatchewan. Significantly, the university's first President, Walter Murray, a former professor of philosophy at Dalhousie, supported university legal education based on the Harvard model of full-time study. Although the Regina school continued

61 P. Wilton, "Inappropriate for Women," 24; and Wilton Wilson Family Archive (on file, M.J. Mossman), "Foreclosure Notice," unidentified news report (June 1935). Wilson's family suffered financial losses in 1929, which may have prompted Wilton Wilson to work part-time. She was buried in the Wilson plot in Greenwood Cemetery in Brooklyn, New York: E. Wilson, "Winnifred Wilton Wilson" Wilton Wilson Family Archive (on file, M.J. Mossman), [unpublished biography, 1994] 7; and obituaries, *New York Press* and *Winnipeg Free Press*.

62 Kinnear, *In Subordination*, 79; Gibson and Gibson, *Substantial Justice*, 215; obituary, *Toronto Star* (6 January 1990) A6; and MacLean Hunt Family Archive (on file, M.J. Mossman): biography of Isabel Ross MacLean Hunt. MacLean Hunt was a founding member of the Portia Club in 1907 and president of its successor organization, the Women Lawyers' Association: MacLean Hunt Family Archive (on file M.J. Mossman), biography of Isabel Hunt for the Governor General's Award commemorating the *Persons Case* in 1983. In 1960, MacLean Hunt and her son John established a practice together, and she also donated her legal services to the Age and Opportunities Bureau of Greater Winnipeg to assist elderly women with limited means of support. She retired in 1978. In 1917, Genevieve Lipsett Skinner also graduated with an LLB degree at the University of Manitoba. She became parliamentary correspondent for the *Vancouver Sun*, the only woman member of the press gallery for many years: LSO Archives, WLAO fonds, SB vol. 3.

63 Between forty and fifty students were enrolled in 1913: (1913) 33 *Canadian Law Times*, 924–95. The initial term was six months, and there were to be few holidays "in order to cover all the required work."

to provide lectures to supplement daily office work by students, it closed in 1922 because of financial pressures. Moreover, the Canadian Bar Association's preference for university-based legal education encouraged recognition of the law program at the University of Saskatchewan, and it became the sole provider of legal education in Saskatchewan in the early 1920s.

Mary Cathcart was the first woman admitted to the bar of Saskatchewan on 18 April 1917, probably after articling and attending lectures at the Regina law school. The press reported positively on Cathcart's admission to the bar, noting that women lawyers were offering little competition in legal practice, and concluding that "opening the door of the profession to women may not prove to be a matter of much practical importance." Cathcart practised briefly with Chisholm & Company before leaving the province a year after her call to the bar.[64]

In 1918, Margaret Burgess was admitted to the bar in Saskatchewan, even though her initial application had been rejected in 1912. She had reapplied in 1913 after an amendment to the *Legal Profession Act*, and practised law initially with M.A. Miller in Weyburn, winning the first case in which she appeared in court. In the 1920s, Burgess moved to Regina, becoming the first Saskatchewan woman lawyer to open her own law office in the city, and in 1935, she was appointed a judge of the Juvenile Court in Saskatchewan.[65] The first woman to obtain the LLB degree at the University of Saskatchewan was Elsie Hall in 1920. As E.M. Hall, she practised law in Wadena in the Judicial District of Humboldt in the 1920s, and later in a number of small firms in Saskatoon. By 1956, she was practising law in Nanaimo, British Columbia after being called to the bar there in 1948.[66]

In contrast to the success of women in the three Prairie provinces, Annie Macdonald Langstaff's efforts to gain admission to Le Barreau du Québec ended unsuccessfully. Langstaff had moved from eastern Ontario to Montreal, after her husband deserted her and her young daughter. She

64 "Woman Suffrage and Women Solicitors" (1917) 53 *Canada Law Journal* 130 at 131. No record of "Mary Cathcart" appears in the *Canadian Law Lists*. See also Bilson, "Prudence Rather than Valor" 345–ff, 374; and Pue, "Common Law Legal Education," 654.

65 *Regina Morning Leader* (29 November 1924); and *Canadian Law Lists*.

66 Harvey, "Women in Law in Canada," 17; and Law Society of Saskatchewan blog, online. In Saskatchewan, Hall practised law at Hall & Fyfe in 1931 and at Hall & Maguire in 1939. After she relocated to British Columbia, she was listed in 1956 in Nanaimo as "E.M. Hall, 22 (Sask), 48 (BC)": *Canadian Law Lists*.

found work in the law firm of Sam Jacobs, and it was Jacobs who contacted Dean Walton at McGill's Faculty of Law to request permission for Langstaff to study law. The Dean replied that although no woman had previously done so, there was no objection to her following lectures in law at the university.[67] Langstaff entered McGill's academic law program in 1911 and graduated in 1914 with first-rank honours, an overall standing of fourth place, and a prize. In spite of this success, her application for permission to take the preliminary bar examinations was summarily refused by the Barreau. Jacobs applied for a writ of mandamus, but the suit was denied in the Superior Court in 1915, based on the use of male pronouns in the Civil Code. In the context of graphic descriptions in the press about women's non-traditional work during the First World War, moreover, Justice Henri Saint-Pierre concluded that such work constituted major exceptions to women's "proper role":

> A woman may be as brave as any man, and scenes which are in the present time, daily depicted to us, show that many of them are proving their usefulness as nurses on the field of battle; but the physical constitution of woman makes it plain that nature never intended her to take part along with the stronger sex in the bloody affrays of the battlefield ... I would put within the range of possibility though by no means a commendable one, the admission of a woman to the profession of solicitor or to that of *avoué*, but I hold that to admit a woman and more particularly a married woman as a *barrister*, that is to say, as a *person who pleads cases at the bar before judges or juries in open court and in the presence of the public*, would be nothing short of a direct infringement upon public order and a manifest violation of the law of good morals and public decency.[68]

Saint-Pierre's decision provoked negative commentary in both English and French newspapers, and Montreal's Local Council of Women sponsored a mass protest meeting at the YMCA, attended by six hundred people, including one hundred men. The meeting was chaired by the mayor of Montreal, and a number of prominent speakers supported women's

67 M. Gillett, *We Walked Very Warily: A History of Women at McGill* (Montreal: Eden Press Women's Publications, 1981) 304.

68 *Langstaff v Bar of Québec* (1915) 47 *Rapports Judiciares du Québec* (CS) 131 at 139 (emphasis in original); and Gillett, *We Walked Very Warily*, 304.

admission to the bar.[69] Moreover, as Langstaff, a single parent who needed to work, had argued in a speech in 1915: "It is all very well to say that women's sole sphere should be the home, but it shows most lamentable blindness to the economic conditions which one would think were potent. The plain fact ... is that many women have to earn their living outside the home, if they are to have homes at all ... [All] that is asked for women who desire to practise [law] is that they shall prove [their abilities] as men have to prove them."[70]

In spite of support from women's organizations, the legal profession, and politicians in Québec, Macdonald Langstaff's appeal to the Court of King's Bench in November 1915 was similarly rejected by four of the five presiding appellate judges. Yet, the opinion of Justice Joseph Lavergne, the only dissenting judge, was important as it was the first time that a person in a position of power had recognized women's eligibility for admission to the Barreau du Québec. Jacobs adopted Lavergne's views in his subsequent arguments to a legislative committee, but the committee's proposed reform bill was narrowly defeated in the legislature—by a vote of twenty-one in favour and twenty-two opposed. Another bill, presented after the election in 1916, also failed to win sufficient support.[71] Other bills were regularly presented to the legislature, but it was not until 1941, in the midst of the Second World War, that legislation in Québec permitted women to join the Barreau: "History was made in Québec on Thursday, when two women [Elizabeth Monk and Suzanne Raymond-Filion] were admitted to the practice of law,

69 The meeting was well reported: see *La Presse* (13 February 1915); *Gazette* (19 February 1915); and *Toronto Saturday Night* (27 February 1915). Senator Dandurand and the Syndic of the Montreal bar supported a motion to permit women to enter the bar on the same terms as men; and Carrie Derick, the first woman university professor in Canada, at McGill, also spoke in support of opening the professions to both women and men. See also Gillett, *We Walked Very Warily*, 306; and Dumont et al., *Québec Women*, 244.

70 Langstaff, speech to the Insurance Underwriters' Dinner, 1915, reproduced in Gillett, *We Walked Very Warily*, 306.

71 *Langstaff v Bar of Québec* (1916) 25 *Rapports Judiciares de Québec* (CBR) 11; and G. Gallichan, *Les Québécoises et le barreau: L'histoire d'une difficile conquête, 1914–1941* (Québec City: Septentrion, 1999) 35–36, 40–42. Grace Ritchie England and activist Marie Gérin-Lajoie, the women who accompanied Jacobs in the presentation to the legislature, were involved in women's reform organizations, including Montreal's Local Council of Women, established in 1893. Gérin-Lajoie later founded the Féderation nationale Saint-Jean-Baptiste in 1907: Dumont et al., *Québec Women*, 251.

[marking] the culmination of a long struggle for recognition of women's right to an equal place in the professions alongside men."[72]

Elizabeth Monk had graduated from McGill with a BA in 1919 and then obtained an MA at Radcliffe in French and German in 1920. She studied for a year at Oxford and then enrolled in law at McGill, graduating in 1923 with the highest standing in the civil law program. After being called to the bar of Nova Scotia in 1934, Monk worked for many years as a legal researcher in Québec law firms, and she also worked tirelessly behind the scenes drafting the legal arguments for women who were fighting other "monumental struggles of the time" (the right to vote, the right to equal salary for equal work, and the right to enter the professions). By 1942, when Monk was called to the bar, all the judges in the *Langstaff* case, as well as Sam Jacobs, had died.[73]

In 1942, Annie Macdonald Langstaff was not eligible to join the bar because the new statute required both an undergraduate degree as well as a degree in law, and Langstaff had only a law degree. Thus, "Mrs. Langstaff" continued to support legal work at the law firm, having remained there as the firm's formidable manager after Jacobs was elected to the House of Commons in 1917.[74] In addition, Langstaff authored the *French-English/English-French Law Dictionary* in 1937,[75] and she took up flying as a hobby

72 *Montreal Star* (17 January 1942); and Harvey, "Women in Law in Canada," 18.

73 M. Ryval, "Women in Law: Ladies No Longer in Waiting," *Canadian Lawyer* (December 1977): "Elizabeth Monk." Prior to 1941, Monk was an employee at Perron, Vallee & Perron, but from 1941–43, she was listed as a member of the firm. In 1966, she joined Tansey firm, now Lavery Lawyers, practising corporate law. Monk died at the age of eighty-two in 1980, five months after she had ceased to practise law: K. Leger, "Pioneering Female Lawyer Honoured," *Montreal Gazette* (28 October 2011).

74 Langstaff was employed at the law firm for sixty-seven years: McGill University, Faculty of Law Archives, letter from Michael Vineberg of Phillips Vineberg to Dean Brierley (16 December 1981). See also I. Pilarczyk, *"A Noble Roster": One Hundred and Fifty Years of Law at McGill* (Montreal: McGill University Faculty of Law, 1999) 58–59; and G. Morgentaler, "McGill Alumnae through the Decades: Part II" *McGill News* (Fall 1984) 20–21. Jacobs was a federal MP for Montreal-Cartier for the Liberals from 1917 until his death in 1938: Gallichan, *Les Québécoises*, 26; B. Figler, *Sam Jacobs, Member of Parliament* (Gardenvale Québec: Harpell, 1959); and L. Crawford, "Current Events," *Canadian Magazine* (November 1914) 10.

75 A.M. Langstaff, *French-English, English-French Law Dictionary* (Montreal: Wilson and Lafleur, 1937). After a signed copy of this book was discarded by the McGill library, it turned up in a second-hand bookstore and was purchased and gifted to the Faculty of Law by Kathy Fisher: email communication to M.J. Mossman.

after the First World War. She retired at the firm in 1965 at the age of seventy-eight and died ten years later in June 1975. In 1981, McGill's Board of Governors voted to name a seminar room at the law faculty in her honour, but the plaque outside the room makes no mention of her persistent but unsuccessful efforts to gain admission to the bar. Langstaff's accomplishment was finally recognized in September 2006, on the sixty-fifth anniversary of Québec's legislation permitting women to become lawyers. In a special ceremony, the Bar of Montreal formally admitted Annie Macdonald Langstaff to the legal profession in Québec and posthumously named her recipient of the profession's rarely awarded Medal of Honour.[76]

In contrast to the longstanding controversy in Québec, discussion was relatively muted when the Nova Scotia legislature enacted its reform in 1917—in anticipation of women's applications for admission to the bar. At the time, some Nova Scotia lawyers had circulated a petition calling on the legislature not to pass the proposed bill because it was "not in the interests of the female sex nor of the Public." Thirty barristers had signed the petition, but others refused to do so, and as John Hood, a Shelburne barrister, commented, "I have always thought that the woman's place was in the Home, but if an occasional one wants to put on pants, I have no objection under Heaven to her doing so." Although the dissenting petition was presented to the Legislative Council, the bill received Royal Assent on 9 May 1917.[77]

In 1917, three women were enrolled in the law program at Dalhousie University, and all were subsequently called to the bar. One was Frances Fish, a lawyer's daughter from Newcastle, New Brunswick. Fish had obtained a BA from the University of New Brunswick in 1910 at the head of her class and an MA in classics at the University of Chicago. Although she began a PhD in Chicago, she did not complete it. Instead, she worked

76 See McGill University, Faculty of Law Archives, memo from Dean Brierley to Librarian Michael Renshawe, ca. 1981. See also K. Leger, "Woman's Struggle Recognized," *Gazette* (15 September 2006); and "Enfin Avocate!," *Le Journal (Barreau du Québec)* (October 2006). Julie Latour, Bâtonnier du Québec, presented the medal to Lucien Bouchard, representative of Davies Ward Phillips Vineberg, successor to Jacobs's firm, and it is permanently displayed in McGill's faculty of law: *McGill News* (Winter 2007) 13.

77 L. Kernaghan, "The Madonna of the Law," *Hearsay* (Dalhousie Law School) (Fall 1991) 26–27. See also J. Willis, *A History of Dalhousie Law School* (Toronto: University of Toronto Press, 1979) 76–77. Willis identified Emelyn MacKenzie as the woman law student who appeared before the legislative committee that recommended women's eligibility for admission to the bar in Nova Scotia.

as a teacher, including one year in Winnipeg in 1911–12, at a time when press reports were circulating about Melrose Sissons and Winnifred Wilton becoming law students at the University of Manitoba. Fish returned to New Brunswick in 1913 and continued to teach, but she also enrolled as a student at law. Two years later, Fish entered Dalhousie Law School, just a few months after two other women had been accepted as articling clerks by the Nova Scotia Barristers Society: Emelyn Laura MacKenzie and Caroline Isabel McInnes.[78]

Fish commenced articles in 1913 in New Brunswick with W.A. Trueman, a Campbellton barrister, and after his death in 1917, she transferred to the office of E.P. Williston in Newcastle. She received the LLB degree at Dalhousie in May 1918 and completed a further three months of articles with Robert Yeoman, a sole practitioner in Halifax.[79] She became Nova Scotia's first woman lawyer when she was called to the bar in September 1918; and both MacKenzie and McInnes were called to the bar in May 1919. Fish's legal career began with the Halifax Relief Commission, assisting in the reconstruction of Halifax's North End after the devastating explosion of

78 B. Cahill, "'Everybody Called Her Frank': The Odyssey of an Early Woman Lawyer in New Brunswick" (2001) 2 *Journal of New Brunswick Legal Studies* 55 at 56–58. Fish had been appointed principal of the Campbellton High School on her return to New Brunswick: Kernaghan, "The Madonna of the Law," 26. The entry of these first women law students was announced in the *Dalhousie Gazette* (1 December 1916) 10, and both Fish and MacKenzie participated in the Mock Parliament late in 1916: *Dalhousie Gazette* (20 December 1916) 10. McInnes and MacKenzie articled with Hector McInnes, Caroline's father, who was a partner at McInnes, Jenks & Lovett, and Caroline McInnes worked for twenty years as a general practitioner in the firm. According to MacKenzie, the dearth of places for students in Halifax law firms resulted in her moving to New York, where she practised as a corporate solicitor: "Emelyn MacKenzie" (1976) *Ansul* (Dalhousie Law School) 5–6: MacKenzie recalled that the war meant fewer law students, and she described her experience of the Halifax Explosion in 1917. Although MacKenzie arrived in New York around the same time as Wilton Wilson from Manitoba, there is no evidence that the two women met. See also Kernaghan, "The Madonna of the Law," 27; and Willis, *A History of Dalhousie Law School*, 76–78.

79 Kernaghan, "The Madonna of the Law," 27. Yeoman had been called to the Nova Scotia bar in 1915. He later provided an articling position to Grace Wambolt, who was called to the bar in Nova Scotia in 1925, and they formed a partnership in 1929. Wambolt practised law for many years and was the first woman lawyer elected to the council of the Nova Scotia Barristers' Society and the first woman lawyer in Nova Scotia appointed KC: "M. Grace Wambolt" (1977) *Ansul* (Dalhousie University); and J. Servinis, "The Exclusiveness of the Legal Profession in Canada and How One Nova Scotian Woman Rose to the Challenge: M. Grace Wambolt" [unpublished paper, 1998: Dalhousie Law School].

1917, and she was later employed in 1921 at Maclean, Burchell & Ralston, a Halifax law firm. A few years later, through her family's political connections, she worked in Ottawa at the Department of Finance, and then in the legal department of Metropolitan Life. In the 1920s, she was hired as a legal assistant in the Montreal office of C.H. Cahan, KC, a federal politician whose law office handled the legal affairs of another Campbellton native, Lord Beaverbrook. In 1927, Fish attended a Canadian Bar Association meeting in Toronto, where she may have met some members of the Women's Law Association of Ontario.[80]

When her father died suddenly in 1933, Fish returned to New Brunswick to practise law in Newcastle, and she was admitted to the bar there in 1934. Her decision to work as a sole practitioner at age forty-five created a "hard row to hoe" because of an oversupply of lawyers and her lack of familiarity with practice in New Brunswick: "not only had she not practised for fifteen years, [but] she had not practised in New Brunswick at all." Nonetheless, Fish had some success, and she became the first woman lawyer to argue before the appeal division of New Brunswick's Supreme Court in 1935. She also became an expert in divorce law, but she may have struggled for acceptance in the legal profession. When she was appointed deputy county magistrate for Northumberland, both of Newcastle's newspapers greeted her appointment with "deafening silence." In 1972, Fish was appointed QC, and she continued as a sole practitioner until a few months before her death in 1975.[81]

Fish's accomplishments as a woman lawyer were significant. Only thirty-eight women joined the bar in New Brunswick in the six decades after Mabel French's admission in 1907, and not all these women practised law. Moreover, Fish practised law in Newcastle, the only woman lawyer north of Fredericton, and she seems to be the first woman lawyer in New Brunswick to engage in a conventional legal practice for many years. Just as French had overcome the barriers to admission, "Fish courageously

80 Cahill, "Everybody Called Her Frank," citing "Social and Personal News," *Ottawa Journal* (31 August 1927) 59–60; and Kernaghan, "The Madonna of the Law," 27. See also J. Kitz, *Shattered City: The Halifax Explosion and the Road to Recovery* (Halifax: Nimbus, 2004); and Willis, *A History of Dalhousie Law School*, 76–78. Willis reported that Fish was not eligible to practise law in either Québec or New Brunswick in 1917, perhaps unaware of the New Brunswick statute of 1906 and its first woman lawyer, Mabel French.

81 Cahill, "Everybody Called Her Frank," 60–62. In 1934, Fish was only the ninth woman called to the New Brunswick bar: Lynch, "Women in the Law."

faced and overcame the obstacles confronting her as a female practitioner in New Brunswick." Yet, Fish "was not only a 'woman lawyer' but a lawyer who incidentally was a woman and none the worse a lawyer for it. Nor was she a feminist in any meaningful sense of the word; in her view, that would have damaged her credibility as a lawyer and jeopardized her career prospects ... Though not a feminist, much less a feminist lawyer, she was an emancipated professional woman who opened up for women lawyers the realistic prospect of making a living practising mainstream law."[82] Although Fish is among the "first" Canadian women lawyers because of her admission to the Nova Scotia bar in 1918, her experience in practice in New Brunswick from the 1930s to the 1970s corresponds more closely to the lives of women who engaged in legal practice in Canada several decades after the "first" women lawyers.

Finally, a year after Nova Scotia enacted its reform statute for women lawyers, similar legislation was enacted in Prince Edward Island, without controversy, on 26 April 1918, when the bill was read a third time in the Legislative Assembly and "resolved in the affirmative." There is no record of any dissent.[83] Although no woman was seeking admission to the bar in Prince Edward Island in 1918, Attorney General Johnston presented a petition at the Summerside sittings of the Supreme Court in November 1919 for the admission of Wanda Wyatt, who had a BA from McGill, as a law student. Wyatt's principal was her father, J.E. Wyatt, KC, of Summerside. The press reported this event positively, noting that Wyatt was the first admission of a lady to the study of law in the province, and suggesting that "the appearance of women in the various professions and administrative capacities of life is accepted as a development of the times." Although Wyatt apparently assisted in her father's office on occasion, she never applied for admission to the bar. Since her family's social prominence and financial security allowed her to attend ceremonial occasions involving royal

82 Cahill, "Everybody Called Her Frank," 62–63, 69; and Lynch, "Women in the Law." Lynch and Fish were called to the bar in New Brunswick on the same date in 1934, and Lynch practised law briefly in Saint John before being appointed registrar at the University of New Brunswick. She later worked with Lord Beaverbrook. Lynch described Fish as "a prominent lawyer in Newcastle." Cahill concluded that Fish might not have approved of the "Frances Fish Women Lawyers Achievement Awards," created by the Nova Scotia Association of Women and the Law, but that "though not a feminist, Fish was a pioneer within the age of feminism—in spite of herself."

83 Minutes of the Legislative Assembly, Prince Edward Island (19 April 1918) at 51–ff.

visitors and Canadian political figures, she may not have aspired to be admitted to the bar.[84]

In February 1926, the first woman was admitted to the bar of Prince Edward Island: Roma Stewart, daughter of the island's Premier. Stewart articled in her father's office in Charlottetown, then attended Dalhousie law school for one year. Although she excelled in her law school examinations, she returned to complete her articles in Charlottetown, perhaps because her father's role as Premier necessitated her help at the firm.[85] After her call to the bar, she practised law briefly and then moved to Montreal. Since women could not practise law in Québec, Stewart worked in a trust company for a few years and then married George Goodwin, a businessman, and ceased her employment. The Goodwins were active in liberal/social democratic circles and Stewart Goodwin was involved in suffrage-related activities in Québec in the 1940s. After Goodwin's death in 1963, Stewart married William Blackburn, a professor of creative writing at Duke University. Her memoir reveals her satisfaction with a happy and interesting life, but it also confirms that Roma Stewart Goodwin Blackburn never practised law after she left Prince Edward Island in 1926.[86]

84 D. Kessler, *A Century on Spring Street: Wanda Lefurgey Wyatt of Summerside, Prince Edward Island 1895–1998* (Charlottetown: Indigo Press, 1999) 196–99, 225–26, 347, and Chapter 8. Wyatt's petition was received in court on 25 November 1919, and her articles and fees were submitted on 15 December 1919. In 1929, she enjoyed a cruise around the world, and she was presented to Princess Elizabeth during her visit to the island in 1951. At Wyatt's death, her steadfast commitment to the island and its communities was manifested in her generous bequests to the province.

85 Stewart's call to the bar was noted in Toronto: *Daily Star* (13 February 1926). This report identified her as "Roma Steward." Apparently, the depression in the early 1920s affected Stewart's father's financial circumstances, perhaps explaining her decision to complete articles in Charlottetown rather than return to Dalhousie's law program. Even though Professor John Read had awarded his highest grade ever to Stewart, her Dalhousie classmate Mary McIntyre became the first PEI woman to obtain a Dalhousie law degree: Roma Goodwin Blackburn, "Heart and Home: A Memoir" (2008) 32 *Legal Studies Forum* 683 at 714–15. Dalhousie University law school records identified Stewart as a graduate with "Sp Law" in 1923–24: communication from Dalhousie University to M.J. Mossman (30 November 2017).

86 Stewart reported being called to the bar in PEI on 26 January 1926, that is, two years after her study at Dalhousie's law school. See also K. Fisher, "Sounding Down the Years: Roma Stewart Goodwin Blackburn's Journey in Law" (1994) [unpublished paper, on file, M.J. Mossman], cited in Petersson, "Ruby Clements," 384; Blackburn, *Heart and Home*, Chapters 8 and 9; and Roma Stewart archival papers, Duke University, online: <http://library.duke.edu/rubenstein/findingaids/blackburnroma/>.

### A Legacy of Gendered Precedents and Patterns

> *Any account of a woman's life is always constructed within a gendered historical context, so that both individual experiences and the overall social context are important. Thus, "a conception of experience lies at the intersection of theory and practice in women's history writing."*[87]

In challenging the gendered culture of Canada's legal professions in the first decades of the twentieth century, did these pioneer women lawyers establish useful precedents or patterns of legal practice for later cohorts of women in law? At the outset, it seems significant that in just two decades between Clara Brett Martin's controversial admission to the Ontario bar in 1897 and the more prosaic enactment of legislation in Prince Edward Island in 1918, women in all of Canada's common law provinces became eligible to enter provincial legal professions. In contrast, Québec's legislature remained unpersuaded until 1941, notwithstanding recognition of *femme-avocats* in France in 1900. Stories about Canada's first women lawyers suggest the impact of the women's movement, especially its support for women's access to higher education and female suffrage, and the attraction of ideas of professionalism in the early twentieth century. The carnage of the First World War also meant that some women, including widows and young women with few marriage prospects, needed paid work. For some women, there was also crucial support on the part of individual men, including family members, lawyers, judges, and provincial politicians.

Most of these first women lawyers shared similar social characteristics, and several grew up in middle-class families that encouraged women's higher education. At a time when few women obtained university degrees, Martin (Ontario), Clements (Alberta), Sissons (Manitoba), and Fish (Nova Scotia and New Brunswick) all completed university degrees before studying law. Langstaff in Québec and French in New Brunswick had worked in administrative roles in law firms before embarking on legal studies, and both women received considerable support from their lawyer employers.

87 R. Roach Pierson, "Experience, Difference, Dominance and Voice in the Writing of Canadian Women's History" in K. Offen et al., *Writing Women's History: International Perspectives* (Bloomington: Indiana University Press, 1991) 79 at 91.

Most of these pioneer women lawyers were resident in cities, although Martin, Sissons, and Langstaff grew up in farming communities. Moreover, all of these women were white, and most were of British descent—even in Québec, Langstaff was an anglophone from eastern Ontario.

Several women who gained admission to the bar had male relatives who were lawyers: Miller in Newfoundland, Wilton in Manitoba, Fish in New Brunswick, both Wyatt and Stewart in Prince Edward Island, and McInnes in Nova Scotia. Some also had useful legal and political connections, including Martin in Ontario, French in New Brunswick and British Columbia, Miller in Newfoundland, and Fish in Nova Scotia and New Brunswick. Langstaff also had significant support from Jacobs, a lawyer and later politician in Québec, but even though she was a single parent and needed paid work, her application to become a *femme-avocat* was repeatedly rejected for decades. MacLean Hunt, who became a single parent after just a few years of marriage, was more fortunate and established a successful legal career in Winnipeg's legal department in the 1920s.

Nonetheless, although women gained admission to the legal professions in nine Canadian provinces by 1918, success in private practice was more elusive. Some women did not practise for long, and sometimes not at all: French in New Brunswick and British Columbia, Sissons and Wilton in Manitoba, Clements in Alberta and Stewart in Prince Edward Island. For some of these women, societal norms that precluded married women from engaging in paid work tended to block careers in legal practice. In addition, potential clients were probably unfamiliar with women lawyers in the years before 1918—as Wilton's comment in London revealed, people continued to be surprised to meet a woman lawyer in the early twentieth century. In Québec, women lawyers were employed in law firms, but without being called to the bar for decades: Langstaff managed Jacobs' law firm for most of her life, and Elizabeth Monk and others worked as legal researchers until 1941. A few women were active in promoting women's legal rights in Québec, including Monk and Stewart Goodwin, while Martin in Ontario and French in New Brunswick had some connections to the women's movement in their provinces.

Among these first women lawyers in Canada, only Martin succeeded in winning political office in the early twentieth century. In addition, Martin was engaged in private practice in Ontario for more than two decades until her early death in 1923. In contrast, although French engaged in practice briefly in New Brunswick and British Columbia before 1920, as did Wilton and Sissons in Manitoba, most of these early women lawyers began to practise law in the 1920s: Hall and Burgess in Saskatchewan, McInnes and Wambolt in Nova Scotia, MacKenzie in New York, Stewart very briefly in Prince Edward Island, and MacLean Hunt in Winnipeg. Others, including Fish in New Brunswick and Saunders in Newfoundland, did not begin their lengthy practices until the mid-1930s, a full decade after Martin's death. At the same time, many "first" women lawyers experienced being the only women lawyer in their communities for years.

In addition, even after being admitted to the bar, early women lawyers frequently faced exclusionary practices in the legal profession, including prohibitions on participation in professional and social activities—which often created barriers to success as private practitioners. For others, the absence of robing facilities in courts required considerable creativity well into the middle of the century. As Grace Wambolt (1925) in Halifax later explained:

> I had the choice of a public washroom on the ground floor, open to the general public of both sexes, or of getting a key from the registry of deeds to a room on the ground floor used by the female clerical staff of the courthouse. [Instead, Wambolt often resorted to robing in the law library behind the more remote bookshelves, where] it was a bit embarrassing when people would come around to find a book while I was dressing or undressing.[88]

It also seems significant that Martin, who was employed at several law firms early on, established her own law firm around 1901.[89] Moreover, although she enjoyed some success in legal practice, and employed women lawyers and articling students in her firm, professional recognition may have been elusive. When she addressed women law students at Osgoode Hall in 1919, one member of the audience recorded her impression:

88 "G. Wambolt," *Ansul* (Dalhousie University) (December 1977), vol. 2. See also G. Wambolt, "MGW 'Reminiscences, Reflections of a Woman Lawyer—A Sacred Oath,'" Nova Scotia Archives & Record Management (Private Sector Archives Section, MG 1, vol. 1596, no. 53, cited in Servinis, "The Exclusiveness of the Legal Profession in Canada," 14.

89 Martin had articled initially with Mulock, Miller, Crowther and Montgomery but then transferred her articles to Blake, Lash, Cassels: Backhouse, "To Open the Way for Others of My Sex," 22. In 1901, when she was first elected a public school trustee, Martin was working at the firm of Shelton, Wallbridge and Martin, but she established her own firm soon thereafter: *Toronto Star* (9 January 1901).

"Victories are seldom enjoyed by those who win the battles. It is later generations who may benefit. I would say that my impression of Clara Brett Martin was that it had not brought her the satisfaction she had expected, and that the younger women lawyers who appeared to be heading for greater success than she had, were not particularly aware of what she had had to take."[90]

At the same time, it seems clear that Martin was not just the first woman lawyer in Canada, but perhaps one of the only women in this initial cohort who achieved modest success in private practice before 1918. Prior to the First World War, societal norms powerfully shaped women lawyers' opportunities—and their choices. In this context, although women established important precedents in "gendering" the legal professions in the common law provinces, they still remained subject to gender patterns in society and in the legal profession. And although some women who followed the "first" women lawyers in Canadian provinces had greater opportunities, some early patterns proved remarkably persistent. Thus, the legacy of these "first" women lawyers includes both their important precedents and the challenges of gendered patterns within the legal profession.

90 A. Anderson, "The First Woman Lawyer in Canada: Clara Brett Martin" (1980) 2:4 *Canadian Women's Studies* 9 at 11. Anderson identified Apha Hodgins (1919) as the source of this quote and that it occurred at a meeting of the Women's Law Association of Ontario in 1919. See also Roth, "Clara Brett Martin," 339 n79: letter from Apha Hodgins to Helen Woodridge (22 November 1973). For Hodgins, see Chapter Three.

CHAPTER TWO

# *After Clara Brett Martin: Ontario's Early Women Lawyers*

## New Challenges in the Legal Profession

> *I do not think that the most fervent advocate of women's rights could claim that the admission of women to the practice of law has had any appreciable effect on the Bar, the practice of law, the Bench or the people. It is claimed that it was a measure of justice and fair play, that it removed a grievance and has had no countervailing disadvantage. That claim may be fairly allowed: in other respects, the admission of women is regarded with complete indifference by all but those immediately concerned.*[1]

As Justice William Riddell noted in 1918, the number of women lawyers "is increasing slowly if at all." Indeed, after Clara Brett Martin's admission to the Ontario bar in 1897, only ten more women entered the legal profession by 1918—and not all of them practised law. Riddell also assured readers that "the women who practise law are not 'wild women'; they are earnest, well-educated women who ask no favours but are quite willing to do their share of the world's work on the same conditions as men." Moreover, he

1 Justice W. Riddell, "Women as Practitioners of Law" (1918) *Journal of Comparative Legislation* 200 at 206. Riddell had been a litigator in the firm of Beatty Blackstock: C. Moore, *The Law Society of Upper Canada and Ontario's Lawyers, 1797–1997* (Toronto: University of Toronto Press, 1997) 155; and C. Moore, "The Ontario Lawyers' Alphabet: R is for Riddell," *Law Times* (15 November 2002) 7.

confirmed that the Bench "can discover no difference in the ability and acumen in man and woman. It is the individual talent and industry which tell, not the sex."[2] Apparently, Riddell had concluded that these few women lawyers represented just a "few brilliant exceptions"—who would not challenge the status quo in the gentleman's profession.[3]

Societal changes in the early twentieth century may have prompted women's aspirations to become lawyers. As a report in the 1890s had suggested, "circumstances [often] make it a matter of necessity for [women] to earn their living," either to increase their standard of living or to prepare for emergencies and future risks.[4] After 1900, moreover, women's organizations were becoming more active in reform efforts, and women were increasingly seeking higher education.[5] In addition, the enactment of female suffrage in Ontario in 1917 and by the federal Parliament in 1918 may have encouraged women's interest in law and legal careers.[6] Although

2 Riddell, "Women as Practitioners of Law," 209. As he noted, "There seems to be no more fear of man losing his lead in law than in the sister profession of medicine." Riddell described himself as a reformer: H. Bates Neary, *William Renwick Riddell: A Biographical Study* (MA thesis, University of Western Ontario, 1977) [unpublished] 9, even though he had opposed the admission of Clara Brett Martin to the Ontario bar in 1892: C. Backhouse, "'To Open the Way for Others of My Sex': Clara Brett Martin's Career as Canada's First Woman Lawyer" (1985) 1 *Canadian Journal of Women and the Law* 1 at 19, citing Law Society of Upper Canada, Minutes of Convocation (9 December 1892).

3 The *Canada Law Journal* had expressed this hope in relation to Martin's admission to the bar: (1896) 32:10 *Canada Law Journal* 747.

4 J. Thomson Scott, "Introduction" in *The Conditions of Female Labour in Ontario* (Toronto: Warwick and Sons, 1892). The author noted that married women were not usually employed "as long as their husbands are at all able to support them" (25). In contrast to middle-class women, many immigrant women were employed as domestic servants in Ontario: M. Barber, "The Women Ontario Welcomed: Immigrant Domestics for Ontario Homes, 1870–1930" in A. Prentice and S. Mann Trofimenkoff, eds., *The Neglected Majority: Essays in Canadian Women's History, Volume Two* (Toronto: McClelland and Stewart, 1985) 102.

5 Strong-Boag, "'Setting the Stage': National Organization and the Women's Movement in the Late 19th Century" in S. Mann Trofimenkoff and A. Prentice, eds., *The Neglected Majority: Essays in Canadian Women's History* (Toronto: McClelland and Stewart, 1977) 87, and Chapter 1. See also W. Roberts, "'Rocking the Cradle for the World': The New Woman and Maternal Feminism, Toronto, 1877–1914" in L. Kealey, ed., *A Not Unreasonable Claim: Women and Reform in Canada, 1880s–1920s* (Toronto: Women's Press, 1979) 15; and G. Cuthbert Brandt et al., *Canadian Women: A History*, 3rd ed. (Toronto: Nelson Education, 2011) 289–ff.

6 *Ontario Franchise Act, 1917*, 7 Geo V, c 5; and *An Act to confer the Electoral Franchise upon Women*, SC 1918, c 20. See also Chapter One.

only ten more women had been called to the Ontario bar by 1918, the number of women law students at Osgoode Hall increased during the First World War, when male students were absent overseas. Thus, twenty women were called to the bar in just three years between 1919 and 1921, and these increasing numbers may have prompted creation of their own legal organization in 1919, the Women's Law Association of Ontario.[7]

Women who were admitted to the bar up to 1918 joined a relatively small legal profession in Ontario. Although a comparison of the number of lawyers to the Ontario population over six decades in the late nineteenth and early twentieth centuries revealed considerable fluctuation in the profession's growth rates, the rate between 1901 and 1911 was a negative—0.07 per cent—even though Ontario's population was increasing at a modest rate. The profession's growth rate between 1911 and 1921 was substantially higher at 7.9 per cent, although much of this increase reflected the return of soldiers after the war: many enrolled as law students in the 1918–19 academic year and were called to the bar by 1921.[8] The geographic distribution of lawyers in Ontario also changed between 1900 and 1920 as new forces of industrialization concentrated business growth and provided opportunities for specialized corporate practices. More lawyers became concentrated in Toronto and some county towns, changes which probably benefitted male lawyers more often than women. Moreover, after 1900, women were increasingly employed in offices in clerical positions, perhaps

7 E. Huckle, "List of Women Barristers and Solicitors in Ontario, 1897–1975" [unpublished, archived at Law Society of Ontario Archives] ; and A. Bushby, "The Early Years: Sources of an Enduring Tradition—The Women's Law Association of Ontario, 1919–1950" (80th Anniversary Celebration, 14 January 2000) 1. See also Chapter Three.

8 C. Cole, "A Developmental Market: Growth Rates, Competition and Professional Standards in the Ontario Legal Profession, 1881–1936" (1984) 7 *Canada-United States Law Journal* 231 at 232–33, citing Principal Hoyles's report to convocation, May 1919. Cole also noted an increased growth rate for the legal profession in the 1920s and a decline during the Depression: Cole, "A Developmental Market," Figures 1–4.

contributing to subordinate patterns experienced by early women lawyers in many law firms.[9]

During the first decade of the twentieth century, corporate legal practice became a leading source of wealth and prestige for lawyers, and Canada's largest law firm between 1901 and 1911, Beatty Blackstock (a forerunner of the Fasken firm) had grown to fifteen lawyers. In other Ontario cities and towns, lawyers provided services to industries such as mining, pulp and paper, and manufacturing, but their work also focused on minor court cases and real estate conveyancing. After the enactment of Ontario's workmen's compensation legislation in 1914 eliminated the lucrative business of employment liability cases, some lawyers developed new specializations in negligence and motor-vehicle law.[10] In addition, while some lawyers faced external competition in relation to conveyancing and the drawing of wills, there was little internal competition before the 1920s. Thus, for the ten women lawyers who were called to the Ontario bar between 1902 and 1918, their experiences of exclusion often resulted from gendered patterns in the practice of law.

Several early women lawyers established their own law firms, often outside Toronto, perhaps confirming women's exclusion from Toronto's elite corporate firms. A similar pattern occurred in the United States, where changes in legal education and practice in the early twentieth century encouraged the creation of elite law firms, which generally excluded

9 E. Bloomfield, "Lawyers as Members of Urban Business Elites in Southern Ontario, 1860 to 1920" in C. Wilton, ed., *Beyond the Law: Lawyers and Business in Canada 1830 to 1930* (Toronto: Osgoode Society for Canadian Legal History, 1990) 121. See also C. Moore, "1902 Not So Different from 2002 for Lawyers," *Law Times* (14 January 2002) 8; G. Lowe, "Women, Work and the Office: The Feminization of Clerical Occupations in Canada, 1901–1931" in V. Strong-Boag and A. Claire Fellman, eds., *Rethinking Canada: The Promise of Women's History* (Toronto: Copp Clark Pitman, 1986) 107; and J. Sangster, "The 1907 Bell Telephone Strike: Organizing Women Workers" in Strong-Boag and Fellman, *Rethinking Canada*, 137.

10 Moore, *The Law Society of Upper Canada*, 154–57, 195. See also C.I. Kyer, *Lawyers, Families, and Businesses: The Shaping of a Bay Street Law Firm, Faskens, 1863–1963* (Toronto: Osgoode Society for Canadian Legal History/Irwin Law, 2013); E. Tucker, *Administering Danger in the Workplace: The Law and Politics of Occupational Health and Safety Regulation in Ontario, 1850–1914* (Toronto: University of Toronto Press, 1990); and R. Risk, "The Nuisance of Litigation: The Origins of Workers' Compensation in Ontario" in D. Flaherty, ed., *Essays in the History of Canadian Law*, vol. 2 (Toronto: Osgoode Society for Canadian Legal History, 1983) 418.

women lawyers.[11] Moreover, while male lawyers who were Black, Jewish, French Canadian, or German might hope that their own communities could become a source of clients, few women were in business or had responsibility for household decisions about legal work. Thus, women lawyers competed for clients directly with men. The necessity to attend compulsory lectures in Toronto for several months each year may have created financial barriers for some aspiring students who lived in other parts of the province, and it is unclear whether such issues concerned the Law Society.[12] For women students, attendance at lectures in Toronto involved specific gender challenges in these years, including travel arrangements and appropriate accommodation. Such challenges may explain why only four women were called to the Ontario bar after Martin and before the outbreak of the First World War in 1914.[13]

When Principal Reeve died suddenly in 1894, he was replaced by Newman Hoyles, who remained Principal until 1923. It was not until 1919 that the law school hired a second full-time faculty member, John Falconbridge. Thus, for students at Osgoode Hall up to 1918, most lecturers were part-time appointees, mainly practitioners, selected by the Legal Education Committee. Tuition fees that started at $10 in 1891 were regularly increased, and, by 1907, the fees were $100 per session. Commendation for the new law school appeared in the press in 1893, where an anonymous author expressed enthusiasm for the altered conditions of Osgoode's advanced and practical curriculum, making the new Law School "fully equal, if not

11 M. Grossberg, "Institutionalizing Masculinity," in M.C. Carnes and C. Griffen, eds., *Meanings for Manhood: Construction of Masculinity in Victorian America* (Chicago: University of Chicago Press, 1990) 143–44; and J.S. Auerbach, *Unequal Justice: Lawyers and Social Change in Modern America* (New York: Oxford University Press, 1976) 22–32.

12 Moore, *The Law Society of Upper Canada*, 171–72, 184. As Moore suggested, the decline in male lawyers between 1895 and 1910 may have resulted from the requirement to attend lectures in Toronto. See Chapter One.

13 Toronto was not always attractive for law students in these years. The use of coal by industry and homeowners created significant air pollution. There was also a crowded immigrant-receiving area in the Ward, an area bounded on the southwest by Queen Street and University Avenue, the exact location of Osgoode Hall: M. Potter, "When Fresh Air Was Rare in the City," *Toronto Star* (9 July 2016) A3; and J. Lorinc et al., eds., *The Ward: The Life and Loss of Toronto's First Immigrant Neighbourhood* (Toronto: Coach House, 2015).

superior, to any institution of the kind on the continent."[14] In contrast, a contemporary student's account suggested more prosaic arrangements:

> Daily records of attendance were kept, and students were required to attend five-sixths of all lectures and four-fifths of each series. Failure to pass any exams required re-attendance at the same series of lectures ... Exams for the year had to be passed with an aggregate of 55% of total marks or better, and not less than 29% on any one paper. In order to gain honours, a student had to make an aggregate of over 75% of all marks and the same percentage on the honours exam.[15]

As Cecilia Morgan suggested, some arrangements at the law school may have been experienced as particularly challenging by women students: "[There were recorded] incidents of clear-cut harassment at the hands of both instructors and students, designed to humiliate them and make them feel unwelcome. Clara Brett Martin complained of instructors whose lectures emphasized sexual matters in order to embarrass her and of male students who hissed whenever she walked in the room."[16] Since Martin may not have spent much time at lectures, attendance may not have been strictly enforced for women. Moreover, even for male students, there were few Law School activities, although the Legal and Literary Society had been established as early as 1876.[17]

---

14 B. Bucknall, T. Baldwin, and J. Lakin, "Pedants, Practioners and Prophets: Legal Education at Osgoode Hall to 1957" (1968) 6:2 *Osgoode Hall Law Journal* 139 at 176–79; and Historicus, "The Ontario Law School" (1893) 1 *Canadian Magazine* 699–700. Lectures at Osgoode Hall, in conjunction with full-time articling, reflected the "practical" arrangements for legal education in Britain. Significantly, the *Historicus* article did not mention university law schools at McGill or Dalhousie, and in the United States.

15 Bucknall, Baldwin, and Lakin, "Pedants, Practitioners and Prophets," 177, citing Gillis, "Legal Education in Ontario: An Historical Sketch" (1904) 4 *Canada Law Review* 197. Students were assigned numbered seats in lecture rooms so that absentees could be noted easily and so that lecturers could call on students by number (for example, "Seat 38") to respond to questions.

16 C. Morgan, "'An Embarrassingly and Severely Masculine Atmosphere': Women, Gender and the Legal Profession at Osgoode Hall, 1920s to 1960s" (1996) 11:2 *Canadian Journal of Law and Society* 19 at 31; and Bucknall, Baldwin, and Lakin, "Pedants, Practitioners and Prophets," 178. See also V.G. Drachman, *Sisters in Law: Women Lawyers in Modern American History* (Cambridge, MA: Harvard University Press, 1998) 52–53.

17 Bucknall, Baldwin, and Lakin, "Pedants, Practitioners and Prophets," 155–56.

The number of women called to the bar between 1914 and 1918 rose to six, and the number of women students at the Law School increased as male students joined the war effort. By the end of 1915, out of about 1,600 lawyers in practice in Ontario, 116 lawyers and 97 law students were already on active service in Europe; by the end of the war, 300 lawyers and a larger number of students had served in the forces.[18] Although the war may have encouraged women to become law students, the Law Society may have been more accepting of women students, and their fees, while male students were absent.[19]

At the end of the war, male lawyers and law students were treated generously by the law society. "With more gallantry than caution," Convocation had passed a motion in 1915

> that all students of the Law Society who volunteer and enlist for the present War, qualify and go to the front, and who return in good standing and have borne themselves as members of the Law Society and soldiers ought to do, shall be advanced as follows:
>
> First year students to the second year without examination. Second year students to third year without examination. Third year students to Call to the Bar and Certificate of Fitness without examination.[20]

More than 60,000 members of the Canadian Expeditionary Force died in the war, and many others returned with physical and mental challenges. Wartime grievances related to the Borden government's actions, especially conscription, continued to fester for some years after 1918, and the

18 Moore, *The Law Society of Upper Canada*, 191–93. In 2014, the centennial of the outbreak of the First World War, the Law Society arranged posthumous calls to the bar for sixty law students who had died in the war. This centennial honour resulted from biographies created for these former students by Patrick Shea: *Law Times* (21 July 2014) at 1, 4.

19 In 1917, Convocation discussed refunds of fees for (male) law students if they were drafted for active service pursuant to conscription: "Local and Personal" (1917) 37:19 *Canadian Law Times* 746.

20 Bucknall, Baldwin, and Lakin, "Pedants, Practitioners and Prophets," 180. Only one unidentified woman student, with military nursing service, received this benefit: Moore, *The Law Society of Upper Canada*, 194. The Prince of Wales (later Edward VIII) commended the Law Society for the war efforts of its members: S. Denison, "Legal Education in Ontario" (1924) 2 *Canadian Bar Review* 85 at 88. A First World War Memorial by the sculptor Frances Norma Loring was unveiled in 1928: J. Honsberger, *Osgoode Hall: An Illustrated History* (Toronto: Osgoode Society for Legal History, 2004) 221–23.

influenza epidemic (Spanish flu) spread in Canada. Although 2 million Canadians became sick and 50,000 died, with 1,300 deaths in Toronto in October 1918 alone, there are few reports about its impact on the law school and the legal profession.[21] Although the law school remained open during the summer for two years after 1918 to provide lectures for returning soldiers, standards may not have been high. As Principal Hoyles stated, "That is the veterans' class, we're not going to plow anyone." While such measures demonstrated patriotism, a consensus later emerged that these Law Society concessions had produced too many "inadequately trained, incompetent lawyers" in Ontario.[22]

Thus, the decades between Clara Brett Martin's admission in 1897 and the end of the First World War in 1918 included political and economic changes in Ontario, and some modest developments for the legal profession and the law school at Osgoode Hall. In addition, stories of the ten women who were called to the bar in these decades reveal how gendered patterns were becoming embedded in Ontario's legal profession.

21 D. Morton, *Canada and War: A Military and Political History* (Toronto: Butterworths, 1981); T. Cook, *At the Sharp End: Canadians Fighting the Great War, 1914–1916* (Toronto: Viking, 2007); and T. Cook, *Shock Troops: Canadians Fighting the Great War, 1917–1918* (Toronto: Penguin Canada, 2009). See also J.W. Walker, "Race and Recruitment in World War I: Enlistment of Visible Minorities in the Canadian Expeditionary Force" (1989) 70:1 *Canadian Historical Review* 1; and I.H.M. Miller, *Our Glory and Our Grief: Torontonians and the Great War* (Toronto: University of Toronto Press, 2002) 187–88. Helen Palen and Theresa Cherrier were called to the Ontario bar in September 1918, a month before the influenza epidemic reached Ontario.

22 Bucknall, Baldwin, and Lakin, "Pedants, Practitioners and Prophets," 181. The special arrangements for students, adopted by the Law Society in 1915, were modelled on those provided after the War of 1812.

### Challenging Ontario's "Gentleman's Profession"

> *In the case of Osgoode Hall Law School, the admission of the first woman law student [Martin] did not result in a real "revolution" for women in this particular profession but neither did it result in a complete maintenance of the status quo ... Like Martin, the women students who followed her resembled their male brethren, but their gender meant that they were faced with the need to negotiate their way through a variety of structures, attitudes, and practices in which the overriding assumption was that lawyers and law students were gentlemen, a cultural and social definition that persisted throughout this period.*[23]

Masculine norms, which remained prevalent in Ontario's legal profession after Clara Brett Martin, were revealed in a variety of different behaviours: "gentlemanly, paternalistic, boyish teasing or clear-cut misogyny." In addition, societal ideas about gender roles influenced women in the legal profession—as in society more generally, and responses to women's presence as lawyers ranged from "outright hostility, thinly-veiled animosity, condescension, and indifference" to individual acts of kindness and generosity.[24] Moreover, strategies to overcome gender challenges reflected both professional possibilities and personal choices.

Five years after the admission of Martin to the Ontario legal profession, a second woman was called to the bar in 1902: Eva Maude Powley from Port Arthur, now Thunder Bay. Powley had contacted the society as early as 1893 to request information about the admission of women as solicitors, and it is possible that extensive publicity about Martin's admission pursuant to the 1892 statute may have inspired Powley's interest in a legal

23 Morgan, "An Embarrassingly and Severely Masculine Atmosphere," 22. While Morgan's focus was the 1920s to the 1960s, the context for the ten women admitted to the bar up to 1918 was similar and sometimes even more challenging because they were so few in number.

24 Morgan, "An Embarrassingly and Severely Masculine Atmosphere," 22. See also discussion about Grace Hewson (1905) in this chapter.

career.[25] Powley was advised that she needed full standing as a high school matriculant, including Latin, and after successfully meeting this requirement in 1894, she enrolled as a matriculant in 1895.[26] Yet, Powley decided to postpone her plans for legal education, and she later attended Trinity College in Toronto on scholarship, graduating in 1899. After articling for three years, she was admitted to the bar as a university graduate in 1902, with the press announcing that "Ontario has now its second lady lawyer."[27]

A possible motive for Powley's interest in law may have been her father's lawsuit in the 1880s, when he was represented by a Port Arthur lawyer, F.H. Keefer. William Powley was involved in the lumber business, and he had moved from Ottawa to Port Arthur to manage the woods operations owned by Colonel F.C. and Mme Josephine Farijana. After he was dismissed from this employment in 1887, he sued the owners for wrongful dismissal, claiming a balance of wages owing. At trial in District Court in June 1887, the jury accepted Powley's claim, and he was awarded $591.66 in damages and full costs. Powley continued to work in the lumber business, and he was later appointed a tax collector for Port Arthur and clerk-treasurer of the Municipality of Shuniah.[28] Both the Powley and Keefer families were prominent

25 Morgan, "An Embarrassingly and Severely Masculine Atmosphere," 24 n11. Powley may have delayed her law studies for administrative and financial reasons, but her difficulties with the Benchers may suggest that they did not wish to have two women law students at the same time. See also Law Society of Ontario (LSO) Archives, Minutes of Convocation (June 1895). There is a discrepancy about Powley's age: the 1901 Port Arthur census indicates her birth date as 28 December 1875, while the 1911 census reports it as 1878.

26 LSO Archives, Ontario Bar Biographical Research Project (OBBRP) Eva Maude Powley."

27 LSO Archives, Women's Law Association of Ontario (WLAO) fonds, Scrapbook (SB), vol. 1, "Eva Maude Powley," *Telegram* (25 June 1902). See also "Miss Eva Powley," *Winnipeg Tribune* (3 March 1923).

28 Thunder Bay Museum Archives, "William M. Powley (1838–1912)"; *Thunder Bay Sentinel* (14 June 1887 and 17 June 1887) 4. Powley's award represented two-months' salary and damages. See also *Fort William Daily Journal* (17 September 1896) 3, reporting on his work relating to a pulpwood camp.

in Port Arthur, and Keefer was later elected to the federal Parliament and the Ontario legislature.[29]

Eva Powley was an excellent student, becoming one of three candidates, out of nine, who succeeded in the examination for a teacher's certificate in 1892, and she may have worked as a teaching assistant in early 1892.[30] By June 1897, she had pursued university and law studies in Toronto for a year.

> Miss Eva Powley who left Port Arthur in April with her sister Mrs Hazelwood for Toronto has successfully passed the first intermediate law examination at Osgoode Hall which began on April 27th last. There were some 78 candidates, Miss Powley being the only woman. 63 were successful and Miss Powley was in the first half of these. Considering that the majority of the other candidates had the benefit of lectures at the law school in Toronto and are university students, Algoma can well feel proud of her success. She is the second woman to enter the legal profession, Miss Martin who is practising in Toronto being the first. Miss Powley is at present at St Hilda's College, the woman's residential college of Trinity University, and will present herself at the examinations commencing on the 10th inst for the first year's work of the BA degree for Trinity which studies she has along with her law course and office work prepared in Port Arthur during the last winter.[31]

29 "Obituary for Francis Henry Keefer, KC, MA, LLD," *Port Arthur News Chronicle* (5 December 1928). Called to the Ontario bar in 1883, Keefer served as town and city solicitor of Port Arthur from 1889 to 1892 and from 1905 to 1910. He served in Parliament (1917–23), and he was counsel and general advisor to the Canada Food Board in 1917 and Parliamentary Secretary of External Affairs in 1918–21. He served in the Ontario Legislature (1923–26) as legislative secretary for northern Ontario, and he was appointed a public trustee in 1928.

30 *Port Arthur Weekly Herald* (5 September 1891) 4; and *Fort William (Weekly) Journal* (24 February 1892). All five of Eva's sisters "married well": Edna married Gilbert Murray, Toronto; Margaret married Alfred Allen, London, England, and Calgary; Hilda married Richard Hazelwood; Flora married Captain Featherstonhaugh; and Maria Louise married C.W. Jarvis. Obituary, "William Powley," *Fort William Morning Herald* (8 June 1912); and email communications to M.J. Mossman from Thunder Bay Museum archivist, October/November 2015.

31 "A Clever Woman," *Fort William Daily Journal* (7 June 1897) 1: Powley wrote exams but did not attend lectures in Toronto in her first year, which may have prompted Principal Hoyles's recommendation in 1898 that lectures at the law school become compulsory for first-year students, as well as for those in second- and third-year: Bucknall, Baldwin, and Lakin, "Pedants, Practitioners and Prophets," 174.

In July, the press reported that Powley had taken first-class honours at Trinity College in literature and history and second-class honours in mathematics and physical science. Two years later, on 3 July 1899, there were reports that Eva Powley had passed the examinations for the BA, standing first in the first-class honour list and winning prizes.[32] Indeed, Powley graduated in 1899 as "the top student of a strong class of four firsts and one second."[33]

These reports suggest Powley prepared for her first-year examinations—both at Osgoode Hall and at the university—in Port Arthur, prior to April 1897. In the next two years, she combined her studies for the BA at the university with the lectures and exams at Osgoode Hall, and then returned to Port Arthur to article. Although there is no record of Powley's articling principal, she may have worked at Keefer's office prior to travelling to Toronto, and it is possible that she articled at Keefer's firm from 1899 to 1902. Eva Powley was called to the Ontario bar in 1902, the only woman among sixty-five new lawyers that year, and the second woman among 1,800 Ontario lawyers.[34] Curiously, there was also a suggestion that "Miss Powley, who was recently called to the bar at Toronto, will practise

32 *Fort William Daily Journal* (2 July 1897 and 3 July 1899). The 1899 report congratulated Miss Kittridge, who had studied for her BA exams at Trinity University while doing office work for her uncle F.H. Keefer in Port Arthur, confirming Keefer's support for women students.

33 J.G. Slater, *Minerva's Aviary: Philosophy at Toronto, 1843–2003* (Toronto: University of Toronto Press, 2005) 517.

34 LSO Archives, OBBRP, "Eva Maude Powley," and letter from Isabel Kelly MacKay to the Dean of Arts and Science, University of Toronto (19 November 1983). See also Moore, "1902 Not So Different from 2002." The University of Toronto confirmed "Miss E.M. Powley" as the university's first woman law graduate in Ontario, although the law program was then part of the Faculty of Arts: LSO Archives, "Re: 100 Years—Women in Toronto," letter from Patricia Dawson, Administrative Secretary, Dean's Office, Faculty of Law, University of Toronto, to Anne Rochon Ford, New College (7 April 1984). Dawson also referred to an Alumni Address Book for law graduates, created in 1901, which listed Powley as the first woman law graduate, although Clara Brett Martin had graduated with a BCL degree in 1897: H.J. Morgan, ed., *The Canadian Men and Women of the Time: A Handbook of Canadian Biography* (Toronto: W. Briggs, 1898): "Clara Brett Martin."

at Rat Portage," but there is no evidence of such a practice in Rat Portage, now Kenora.[35]

Records of Powley's law practice are unclear. Although she may have practised independently in Port Arthur until 1912,[36] newspaper advertisements in Port Arthur and Fort William identify Powley as the second lawyer in F.H. Keefer's firm as early as February 1906.[37] Keefer, who had been appointed KC in 1897 and was also town and city solicitor for Port Arthur, may have been contemplating a political career in 1906 and thus hired Powley to assist with his legal practice. Similar advertisements for the Keefer firm, including Powley as a firm member, appeared in the press in subsequent years.[38] At the same time, Powley may also have been seeking new opportunities. In March 1908, she wrote to the Law Society of British Columbia with an inquiry about women's eligibility for legal practice. Oscar Bass, the Law Society's secretary, responded in a letter addressed to "E.M. Pawley."

> Dear Sir:
> In reply to your enquiry of the 10th instant, I beg to say that the fair sex have not yet threatened to invade the legal profession in British Columbia. Their efforts so far have been confined to the trials of suffragettes in Municipal elections, or else they consider that their interests are fully protected by the male sex so far as forensic science is concerned. The Benchers not yet having had to consider the application of a modern Blackstone in petticoats to enter

35 Email communication from Lake of the Woods Museum archivist, Lynne Halley, in Kenora, 10 November 2015. Rat Portage (portage to the country of the muskrat) changed its name to Kenora in 1905. A thriving community in the early decades of the twentieth century, with gold mines, logging, and the Canadian Pacific Railway, it became part of Ontario in 1889 after a Privy Council decision in the boundary dispute between Ontario and Manitoba: D. and L. Gibson, *Substantial Justice: Law and Lawyers in Manitoba, 1670–1970* (Winnipeg: Peguis, 1972) 155–56.

36 L. Yorke, "Mabel Penery French (1881–1955): A Life Re-created" (1993) 42 *University of New Brunswick Law Journal* 18 n57. No records of Powley's practice exist in *Canadian Law Lists.*

37 Advertisement for the law firm F.H. Keefer, Barristers and Solicitors, *Port Arthur Daily News* (4 February 1906). The firm names included "F.H. Keefer, LLB" and "E.M. Powley, BA." See also obituary, "F.H. Keefer," *Port Arthur News Chronicle* (5 December 1928), describing Powley as "a graduate of Mr Keefer's office."

38 *Port Arthur Daily News* (25 June 1907) 4; advertisement for the Keefer firm, naming only Keefer and Powley, *Port Arthur Daily News* (27 August 1914).

> the profession it is difficult to say what their feelings would be or what decision they would reach when the moment of decision arises. I am sending you a copy of the Rules.[39]

While it is easy now to dismiss Bass's views as misogynistic, they were not atypical at the time. Moreover, Powley's inquiry occurred four years before Mabel Penery French's unsuccessful litigation led to the legislative amendment permitting her to gain admission to the British Columbia bar in 1912.[40]

Thus, Powley continued to work at the Keefer firm. In 1911, she became one of several provincial directors of a new corporation, the Rocmac Road Corporation of America Ltd. Then, after Keefer's son, Hugh, as well as N.E. Towers, joined the firm, its name changed to Keefer, Keefer and Towers in 1912. In advertisements in the press, Powley's name continued to be placed immediately after F.H. Keefer in the list of lawyers at the firm, but "Powley" never became part of the firm's name.[41] In 1912, Powley's father died, and in July 1913 the press announced that Eva Powley, a lawyer at Keefer, Keefer and Towers, was resigning from the firm: "Miss Powley is one of the few lady lawyers practicing in Canada, and during her association with this well-known legal firm has, through hard work and ability established a

39 A. Watts, *History of the Legal Profession in British Columbia, 1869–1984* (Vancouver: Law Society of British Columbia, 1984) 133. See also J. Brockman, "Exclusionary Tactics: The History of Women and Minorities in the Legal Profession in British Columbia" in H. Foster and J. McLaren, eds., *Essays in the History of Canadian Law*, vol. 6, *British Columbia and Yukon* (Toronto: Osgoode Society for Canadian Legal History, 1995) 508 at 510; and W.W. Pue, *Law School: The Story of Legal Education in British Columbia* (Vancouver: University of British Columbia Faculty of Law, 1995) 223–27. Powley's letter to Bass explained that she was writing an article about women in the legal profession in Canada, but no such article has been located.

40 Pue, *Law School*, 224. French was admitted to the bar of British Columbia in 1912: see Chapter One.

41 "Rocmac" was a waterproof binder for macadam road building; it was used to build Fort William Road between Port Arthur and Fort William: obituary, "F.H. Keefer," *Port Arthur News Chronicle* (5 December 1928). The other directors included F.H. Keefer and his sons, Hugh and Harold Keefer, as well as Alfred Paterson: *Fort William Morning Herald* (16 January 1911). Norman E. Towers graduated from the University of Toronto and enrolled at Osgoode Hall in 1908. He was called to the bar in 1911 and practised briefly in Toronto and then in Port Arthur before joining the war effort. He was fatally wounded at Courcelette in 1916 and died in hospital in Rouen: LSO Archives, OBBRP, "Norman Ewart Towers."

name and reputation as a lawyer that extends not only throughout the city, but the Dominion." Powley left Port Arthur for Toronto in October 1913, planning to board a ship in Québec to visit "the old country and Europe." By December 1914, her plans had changed, as she had become involved in war work, serving with the Red Cross Society in Europe. By July 1915, Powley was secretary of a field comforts department for the Canadian army, headquartered at Shorncliffe, England.[42]

In 1917, Powley returned to Port Arthur, and she and her widowed mother then moved to Winnipeg, where the 1921 census reported her as being the head of a household in the Chelsea Court apartments, built in 1914. Powley's occupation was identified as "manager" with an annual income of $3,600, and she was featured in a press report in 1923.

> As retiring as she is charming, few people know that Miss Eva Powley, secretary-treasurer of the Cadomin Coal Company, is a graduate of Trinity University in arts and law, and a graduate of Osgoode Hall. Miss Powley practised law in Port Arthur with Mr Frank Keefer, KC, until the war broke out. She then went to England, where she was engaged in war work throughout the war. Since her return to Canada, she has looked after the finances of the Cadomin Coal Mine, 160 miles northwest of Edmonton, of which she is also a shareholder and director.[43]

There is no evidence that Powley wished to practise law in Manitoba, or that she applied to the Law Society in Manitoba for admission to the bar.

Although her mother died in 1933, Powley remained in Winnipeg for the rest of her life, engaging in a variety of social and philanthropic activities. Among others, she was a member of the committee in charge of billeting visitors to the Dominion Drama Festival in 1938, and she chaired the purchasing department of the United Services Centre to support a

42 *Port Arthur Daily News* (3 July 1912 and 17 September 1913). It is unclear what role Powley held in the Keefer firm. See also *Port Arthur Daily News* (3 October 1913) 6, and obituary for Captain Featherstonhaugh, Powley's brother-in-law (4 December 1914); and "Zeppelin Raid a 'Fuss' Thought Miss J. Arnoldi" *Winnipeg Evening Tribune* (14 July 1915) 6. Arnoldi was involved in establishing the field comforts division, a new military department providing supplies for Canadian soldiers stationed in England.

43 Canada, Bureau of Statistics, Census 1921, Winnipeg; and *Winnipeg Evening Tribune* (3 March 1923).

recreational centre for military personnel during the Second World War.[44] Social pages in the Winnipeg press record occasions when she and her friends spent time at her shooting lodge on Lake Manitoba as well as her frequent travels, often with her niece Marjorie Hazelwood. Eva Powley died in Winnipeg in 1969 and was buried in Port Arthur. One obituary identified her as "the first woman lawyer" in Ontario.[45]

In 1907, five years after Powley was admitted to the Ontario bar, the *Telegram* announced the admission of the "second female lawyer" in Ontario while the *Globe* correctly noted that she was the third. Geraldine Robinson was the daughter of J.A. Robinson, a well-known lawyer in St. Thomas, who died before his daughter was called to the bar.[46] Robinson's call to the bar ceremony, along with seven new male barristers, was greeted enthusiastically. "The gloomy old corridors of Osgoode Hall were enlivened this morning by one of the rarest ceremonies ever seen in the temple of the goddess of justice—the swearing in of a girl student as a full-fledged barrister of His Majesty's High Courts." The report continued:

> The swearing in of Miss Robinson created a mild sensation [at Osgoode Hall]. She is a general favorite among the students, and during her course of five years, has become popular among acquaintances. Nevertheless, the older heads among the lawyers stood in the corridors and stared as the pretty young lawyer, robed in black, and with a rosy flush on her cheeks, walked out of the Courtroom and received the hearty congratulations of half

44 Obituary for Mrs. Powley, which identified both Eva and her sister Hilda as residents of Winnipeg, *Port Arthur News Chronicle* (25 September 1933). See also *Winnipeg Tribune* (11 May 1938) 5; and "Rush Work on Centre," *Winnipeg Evening Tribune* (8 February 1943) 11. These news reports identified Eva Powley as a graduate lawyer/barrister, although she had ceased to pay Law Society fees in Ontario in 1928: LSO Archives, OBBRP, "Eva Maude Powley."

45 *Winnipeg Tribune* (20 September 1941) 13, (10 October 1942) 9, and (5 October 1943). Powley travelled often with her sister Hilda and her niece Marjorie Hazelwood, including trips to the West Indies, Bermuda, England, and Europe. See also Thunder Bay Museum Archives, unidentified obituary, Port Arthur, "Became First Woman Lawyer in Ontario."

46 LSO Archives, OBBRP, "Geraldine Bertram Wright." This record identifies her birth surname as Robinson and also her surname when she was called to the bar. See also *Telegram* (20 September 1907); and *Globe* (21 September 1907). *The Globe* reported that the second woman lawyer was "E.M. Powley of Port Stanley," but there is no confirmation for Powley at this location.

> a dozen enthusiastic female friends. "See the bewitching vision," said one KC to his fellows. "We'll soon be crowded out of the profession if this keeps on," remarked another legal light. Miss Robinson told the Herald that she would return to St Thomas, and take up the legal duties [in her late father's firm]. She does not intend to begin work in the courts as yet.[47]

The report described Robinson as "a modern Portia," the third lady lawyer in Ontario following Martin and Powley.

Robinson had been admitted as a student-at-law in 1902, at the age of seventeen, the only woman student at the Law School that year. In contrast to Martin and Powley, Robinson was a matriculant, required to article for five years and to attend the Law School's lectures during the final three years. Although no formal record of her articling principal exists, she may have articled in her father's firm in St. Thomas, and it is unclear whether she practised law in her father's firm for two years after her call to the bar. In 1909, Robinson married Ward Wright, of the firm of Rowell, Reid, Wright, McMillan, and although she remained a dedicated member of the Women's Law Association of Ontario (WLAO) and other Toronto organizations, Robinson Wright never practised law after her marriage.[48] In 1920, Robinson Wright was elected WLAO President, and her many contributions to the organization were recognized in 1932, on the twenty-fifth anniversary of her admission to the bar, with a reception in her honour and presentation of a silver plate. The social mores of the 1930s were reflected in the guests at this reception—women lawyers and the wives of judges. Robinson Wright also devoted time to painting, and her work was exhibited at the Studio Guild in New York City in the 1930s. There was also an exhibition and sale of her watercolours in support of the Royal Regiment of

47 *Fort William Morning Herald* (23 September 1907). Robinson was admitted to the bar at Easter, 1907: Huckle, "List of Women Barristers and Solicitors."

48 LSO Archives, OBBRP, "Geraldine Bertram Wright"; and LSO Archives, "Diversifying the Bar," Geraldine Bertram Wright. Ward Wright was later elected a Bencher, and the couple's son Peter became a lawyer and a judge: LSO Archives, OBBRP, "Geraldine Bertram Wright." See also LSO Archives, WLAO fonds, SB, vol. 1; and *Canadian Law Lists*.

Canada and the Red Cross Prisoner of War Parcel Fund in Toronto during the Second World War.[49]

As a former president of the WLAO, Wright hosted an evening reception in the spacious drawing room of her home in October 1936, so that WLAO members could meet Lord Thankerton of the Privy Council during his visit to Toronto. Although arrangements had been made for him to speak at a call to the bar ceremony, and to attend both a lunch with the Benchers and a dinner meeting of the Lawyers Club, Wright suggested the evening reception for women lawyers because they were, of course, excluded from all other occasions. Thus, women lawyers met Lord Thankerton, along with Arthur Roebuck, Attorney General of Ontario, and Justice Henry Davis, of the Supreme Court of Canada, both of whom had attended the meeting of the Lawyers Club with Ward Wright. Lord Thankerton's informal talk at this WLAO evening focused on his recollections of a Scottish lady who had achieved success in the courts. Apparently, "his cordial manner was highly refreshing to the listeners [in their pretty evening clothes], weary as they are of being constantly told to tend to their knitting."[50]

Among the early cohort of Ontario women lawyers in Ontario, Robinson Wright was the first to enter the Law School as a matriculant. She was also the first of many women students whose father was a lawyer, and, like several others in this early cohort who married, she did not practise law. Yet, her continuing involvement in the WLAO suggests that she remained closely connected to other women lawyers, including those in legal practice. Although she was not "a fierce proponent" of women's rights, she appreciated from her own experience, "the difficulties for a woman in what so

49 The reception in honour of Robinson Wright was held at the home of Mrs. Victor Sinclair: LSO Archives, WLAO fonds, SB, vol. 1, and SB, vol. 3. Mrs. Sinclair's daughter was Gertrude Sinclair, later Haines (1927): Huckle, "List of Women Barristers and Solicitors." The silver tray was returned to the WLAO in 1959 and later presented to the Law Society in 1983: LSO Archives, WLAO fonds, box 106, no. 076. The painting exhibition lasted two weeks at Mellors' Fine Art Galleries at 759 Yonge Street: LSO Archives, WLAO fonds, SB, vol. 2. See also SB, vol. 1.

50 There is no information about the Scottish woman identified by Lord Thankerton, although there are reports of women practising in medieval Scottish courts: E. Ewan, "Scottish Portias: Women in the Courts of Mediaeval Scottish Towns" (1992) 3 *Journal of the Canadian Historical Association,* new series, 27. See also Grace Hunter, "Lady Lawyers and Lord Thankerton," *Saturday Night* (10 October 1936). Hunter (1926) was also a lawyer: Huckle, "List of Women Barristers and Solicitors." See also LSO Archives, WLAO fonds, SB, vol. 3.

many men regard[ed] as a man's profession." As her obituary noted in 1967, moreover, she also had "the unique distinction of being the daughter, wife, mother, niece, sister, aunt and cousin of members of the Ontario bar."[51]

In 1903, a year after Robinson's enrolment as a law student, another woman, Grace Hewson, registered as a matriculant at Osgoode Hall. The daughter of Judge Charles Hewson of the Barrie, Sudbury, and District of Manitoulin Court, Hewson began working in her father's law office in Barrie at the age of sixteen. She articled with her father's partner, who was her mother's brother, for two years and she then began attending lectures at Osgoode Hall.[52] As the only women students in their respective classes at Osgoode Hall, Hewson and Robinson were easily identified. A decade after Martin had suffered indignities from male students, Hewson was the object of a male prank in her first year at the Law School:

> In 1905, male students plotted to humiliate the lone woman in their class, Grace [Hewson], by letting a mouse loose in the lecture hall to scare her and "show her up" as a coward. The efficacy of their plan rested on notions of "ladylike" timidity, nervousness, and a lack of self-control, in contrast to their own manly dignity and courage. Unfortunately for them, it was thwarted when other male students warned [Hewson] of what was in store for her. The runaway mouse apparently did not have the desired effect and at least two of the students openly admired her calm and control.[53]

51 E. Mitchell Thomas, "Sisters-in-Law" (1991) 25:3 *Gazette* 298 at 301; obituary, Geraldine Wright (1967) 1:1 *Law Society Gazette* 66; and LSO Archives, "Diversifying the Bar," Geraldine Bertram Wright. The obituary described Mrs. Ward Wright as "the senior woman lawyer in the Province" for many years and stated that she was survived by her son, Peter Wright, a Bencher. The *Gazette*'s obituary incorrectly identified Robinson Wright as the third woman to be admitted to the bar in the British Empire in 1907. Ethel Benjamin was admitted to the bar in New Zealand in 1897, and Grata Flos Greig was admitted to the bar of Victoria, Australia, in 1905: See Part One, Women in Law: An International Movement. Robinson Wright was the third woman lawyer in Canada and the fifth woman lawyer in the Empire. See also P. McWilliams, "Leaders among the Women Lawyers of Ontario—Revisited" (1987) 21:2 *Gazette* 157 at 161.

52 "Grace Knight Dies," *Woodbridge and Vaughan News* (16 January 1974); LSO Archives, "Diversifying the Bar," Grace Ellen Hewson; and *Toronto Star* (2 January 1974) A14.

53 Morgan, "An Embarrassingly and Severely Masculine Atmosphere," 31, citing the Osgoode Society for Canadian Legal History, oral history interview, E. Mitchell Thomas, 1988–89, at 10. According to Mitchell Thomas, it was her father, called to the bar in 1906, who was one of the men who warned Hewson. She also reported that Hewson remained silent as the mouse scampered over her boots.

Clearly, there were male challengers, but also male supporters, of women law students at the Law School.

After Hewson's call to the bar in 1908, she was employed as a solicitor with the real estate firm of Robins Limited, which had sixty salesmen; she described this period as three years of strenuous work. In 1912, she resigned her position when she married Cyril Knight, an Ontario Associate Provincial Geologist, and the couple lived in mining districts in northern Ontario for many years.[54]

By 1944, Hewson Knight had returned to Toronto as one of many older women doing war work in a plant. She had two sons in the war, and she firmly believed that younger women also needed to be involved in war work because "their menfolk are going to suffer if they don't give an all-out effort."[55] Hewson's obituary, which identified her as the fourth woman to be called to the bar in Ontario, reported that she preferred to be known as the fourth woman lawyer in the British Empire "to demonstrate how slow all countries were in recognizing women's rights."[56]

When Hewson ceased her employment in 1912, Martin and Powley were the only women legal practitioners in Ontario—more than a decade after

54 LSO Archives, WLAO fonds, SB, vol. 1. Law Society records suggest that Hewson practised law in Port Arthur as well as in Toronto, but this information is unconfirmed: LSO Archives, OBBRP, "Grace Ellen Hewson." Hewson's obituary reported that she was president of the Women's Association of the Mining Industry from 1932 to 1934: *Toronto Star* (2 January 1974) A14. She died at the age of eighty-eight in December 1973 in Woodbridge, near her two sons and their families. Hewson's husband died in 1960: "Grace Knight Dies," *Woodbridge and Vaughan News* (16 January 1974).

55 LSO Archives, WLAO fonds, SB, vol. 2. Hewson Knight's war work involved high explosives at the General Engineering Company: LSO Archives, Clara Brett Martin fonds. Another news report included a photo of "Mrs. Cyril Knight at her Machine": LSO Archives, WLAO fonds, unidentified press report (13 May 1944). Her obituary recorded that she had three sons, but her eldest son, Captain Archie Knight, was with the Third Canadian Armoured Corps and was a casualty of the war: LSO Archives, WLAO fonds, SB, vol. 2, unidentified obituary and funeral announcement; and *Toronto Star* (2 January 1974) A14.

56 LSO Archives, "Diversifying the Bar," Grace Ellen Hewson, citing her obituary reprinted in the journal *Through the Years: Manitoulin District History and Geneology,* September 1986. Like others, Hewson Knight was unaware of other early women lawyers in common law jurisdictions: Mabel French, called to the bar in New Brunswick in 1907; Ethel Benjamin, called to the bar in New Zealand in 1897; and Grata Flos Greig, called to the bar in Victoria, Australia, in 1905. See Part One, Women in Law: An International Movement, and Chapter One.

Martin's admission to the bar in 1897. Moreover, when Powley abandoned legal practice in early 1913, Martin remained the only woman practitioner in the province.

In Trinity term in 1913, Jean Cairns was called to the Ontario bar and she began a law practice that continued for many decades. Cairns had grown up on farms just north of Toronto and later near Huntsville, and she had initially qualified as a teacher. After teaching for a few years, she persuaded her parents, who had supported her three brothers to attend the University of Toronto, to assist her as well, and she graduated with a BA in political science and economics from University College in 1910. She enrolled at the Law School as a university graduate at the age of twenty-four, probably the only woman in her class, and articled with Donald Grant in Huntsville. She was called to the bar along with twenty-seven men.[57]

Some reports indicated that Cairns intended to return to Huntsville to practise law, but she worked as a sole practitioner for several years in Toronto, where she claimed to have "nearly starved" because of a lack of clients—although she also received a glowing report after her appearance in Weekly Court in 1915.

> We deem well worthy of notice in this column almost if not quite, the first appearance in the history of the Bar of Upper Canada of a lady lawyer as counsel in Weekly Court. This honour fell to Miss Jean Cairns on the 21st ult., who moved before Mr Justice Hodgins in an opposed motion for an injunction, which was granted. We have it from those present in Court that Miss Cairns, whose name is a good omen of professional success, conducted her case in a very able manner. There can be no reason why in certain departments of legal practice women should not succeed, and every mere man, who is a man, will wish them every success in overcoming the handicap which their sex places them under in this and many other fields of work.[58]

57 LSO Archives, OBBRP, "Jean Cairns Morris"; Huckle, "List of Women Barristers and Solicitors"; *Globe* (13 September 1913) 18; "Another Woman to Practice in Ontario Courts," *Toronto Daily Star* (12 September 1913); and Alma Morris Tefft/Malcolm, daughter of Jean Cairns Morris, telephone interview with M.J. Mossman (18 November 2015).

58 "Locals and Personals" (1915) 35 *Canadian Law Times* 459; and "Miss Jean Cairns, BA to Practise in Huntsville," *Globe* (22 November 1913); Alma Morris Tefft/Malcolm, telephone interview with M.J. Mossman (18 November 2015); and letter from Malcolm to M.J. Mossman, 23 November 2015. See also (1913) 33 *Canadian Law Times* 863. No information about Cairns's Toronto practice appears in the *Canadian Law Lists*.

Cairns was actively involved with the Women Lawyers Association in the United States. In June 1914, a brief note appeared in the association's journal about "Californian and Canadian Pioneer Women Lawyers," identifying Clara Shortridge Foltz in California and Jean Cairns in Canada.[59] This report confirmed that, after her call to the bar, Cairns had "immediately opened an office in Toronto ... [and she] is doing well and finds the work interesting." The same report noted that Cairns was the fifth woman called to the Ontario bar, but that two other women lawyers had married and were not practising. It noted that Martin was in practice in Toronto, that Powley was in Port Arthur, and that French had been admitted to the bar in Vancouver. The article thanked Jean Cairns, "who takes a profound interest in the progress of women in the profession," for these details.[60]

Cairns remained active in this American association, contributing an article, "The Law Affecting Married Women's Property in Ontario," in 1915 and an article about wills in Ontario in 1916, when Cairns became Vice-President of the association for Canada. This appointment was announced in the Canadian legal press in 1917.[61] Cairns appears to be the only Ontario woman lawyer to become involved with this American women lawyers' association in these early years, suggesting her interest in connections to other women lawyers when their numbers were very small in Ontario and in other Canadian provinces.[62]

59 See B. Babcock, *Woman Lawyer: The Trials of Clara Foltz* (Stanford, CA: Stanford University Press, 2011).

60 "Californian and Canadian Pioneer Women Lawyers" (1914) 3:9 *Women Lawyers' Journal* 72. Cairns's information about Powley was outdated in 1914.

61 J. Cairns, "The Law Affecting Married Women's Property in Ontario" (1914) 5:3 *Women Lawyers' Journal* 19, identifying Cairns as vice-president, 23. Two other Canadians were listed as members: Alice Jamieson and Annie Langford, both of Calgary. See also J. Cairns, "Wills—Ontario" (1916) 5:7 *Women Lawyers' Journal* 52; and (1917) 31 *Canadian Law Lists* 746 at 747.

62 After Cairns's marriage to Philip Morris in 1917, she was listed twice in the *Journal* in 1918 as "Jean Cairns (VP)," at 121 Simcoe St., Toronto, and as "Jean Cairns Morris, at 49 Sun Life Building, Hamilton: (1917–18) 7:5 *Women Lawyers' Journal* 33 at 39. In June 1918, she was listed as "Jean Cairns Morris": (1918) 7:9 *Women's Lawyers' Journal* 71. By November 1922, Cairns Morris was listed as the vice-president for Ontario, while Alice Jamieson was vice-president for Alberta: (1922–23) 12:1 *Women's Lawyers' Journal* 1 at 6, 8. A few years later, all the non-American members were listed as "honorary" members: (1925–26) 14 *Women's Lawyers' Journal* 17. See also LSO Archives, "Diversifying the Bar," Jean Cairns.

In April 1917, Cairns married Philip Morris, one of her law school classmates, who had been called to the bar in the fall of 1913.[63] Cairns Morris joined her spouse in his general practice firm in Hamilton and she also joined the Hamilton Bar Association, becoming its first woman member. Cairns Morris was especially interested in laws for women and children, and as an active participant in the Local Council of Women in Hamilton, she later represented Hamilton at the Provincial Council of Women. She also assisted the National Council of Women and its local and provincial chapters in their efforts during the Great War, and in postwar arrangements for veterans and their families. In the 1930s, her contributions resulted in an invitation to be part of the Canadian delegation to a meeting of the International Council of Women in Vienna, but she declined this invitation because of her responsibilities in Hamilton.[64]

Indeed, by the mid-1930s, Cairns Morris had significant responsibilities. Her husband and law partner, Philip Morris, had participated actively as an investor during the 1920s, but the market crash in 1929 eroded many of his investments, and he filed for bankruptcy. In addition, the Law Society disbarred him on 21 June 1934, one of eighty lawyers disbarred in the 1930s—almost four times the number disbarred in the previous decade. The peak years were 1933 and 1934, and, although the overwhelming majority of disbarrings were for stealing from clients and related offences, the precise reason for Morris's disbarment is unknown. By 1936, the Benchers formally agreed to require lawyers to deposit clients' monies into separate trust accounts, and to keep records of these accounts to be audited by the

63 Philip Morris had graduated with a BA at the University of Toronto in 1911, but he was admitted as a law student in Michaelmas term 1910. He articled with T. Haslett in Hamilton and was called to the bar in Michaelmas term, 1913: LSO Archives, OBBRP, "Philip Morris"; and "Personal" (1913) 33 *Canadian Law Times* 1122 at 1125. The couple's marriage registration indicated that both Cairns and Morris were "about" twenty-nine years old when they married, but Cairns was actually thirty-one: *Ontario Marriages 1801–1928*, online: <http://www.archives.gov.on.ca>. Cairns may have misstated her age so that she was not older than her husband, but this marriage certificate information later delayed her entitlement to Old Age Security: Alma Morris Tefft/Malcolm, telephone interview with M.J. Mossman (18 November 2015). See also LSO Archives, OBBRP, "Jean Cairns Morris."

64 LSO Archives, "Diversifying the Bar," Jean Cairns; LSO Archives, WLAO fonds, SB, vol. 1; R. Shaw, *Proud Heritage: A History of the National Council of Women of Canada* (Toronto: Ryerson Press, 1957); and Alma Morris Tefft/Malcolm, telephone interview with M.J. Mossman (18 November 2015).

society.[65] For the Morris family, the disbarment was extremely difficult, but the Morris firm continued in Hamilton and "J.C. Morris" continued to practise law.

In spite of this major setback, Cairns Morris's story is remarkable. Only the fifth woman to be called to the bar in Ontario, she was the first to join her husband in the practice of law and the first to have two children, although she may have worked part-time for some years. After 1934, she was both a mother and head of the law firm, and her "feisty and spirited nature [and] a wry sense of humour" helped her through difficult days. Significantly, she also established a "women lawyers dynasty." The Morris firm became the first mother-daughter law practice in Ontario when Cairns Morris's married daughter, Alma Tefft, later Malcolm, graduated from the University of Toronto in law and was called to the bar in 1959. She joined her mother in the firm at its new location on John Street North and carried on the firm's practice after Cairns Morris's retirement in 1967, following fifty-three years in legal practice.[66] In addition, the twin daughters of Cairns Morris's son also became lawyers after attending Dalhousie Law School: Janet Morris graduated in 1979, and her twin, Jean Cairns Morris, in

65 Disbarment records are missing because minutes of Convocation were not published between 1928 and 1935, probably because of the Depression: communication from Paul Leatherdale, LSO archivist, 14 December 2015. Philip Morris's younger brother, William, who had been called to the bar in 1921, also practised at the Morris firm in Hamilton for some years, but he moved to a practice in Toronto. According to his daughter, Philip Morris was a "firebrand," which may have attracted the Society's attention: Alma Morris Tefft/Malcolm, telephone interview with M.J. Mossman (18 November 2015). See also Moore, *The Law Society of Upper Canada*, 209–10.

66 Alma Morris Tefft graduated in law from the University of Toronto in 1957 and was called to the Ontario bar in June 1959. Cairns Morris attended the call to the bar ceremony to congratulate her daughter: Huckle, "List of Women Barristers and Solicitors"; and *Telegram* (26 June 1959). Malcolm considered that women who were called to the bar in the 1950s faced greater difficulties in legal practice than women in her mother's generation because, after the Second World War, "everyone was staying home and having babies": Alma Malcolm "Women in Law through the Decades," University of Toronto. After her first husband's death, Tefft married William Malcolm, a Hamilton lawyer, and when she retired, the files at Morris and Morris were transferred to Malcolm: Alma Morris Tefft/Malcolm, telephone interview with M.J. Mossman, 18 November 2015.

1980.[67] The feisty and spirited lawyer matriarch, Jean Cairns Morris, admitted to the Ontario bar in 1913, died in 1982 at the age of ninety-six.[68]

In the fall of 1913, the press announced that the law school at Osgoode Hall was "the busiest Blackstonian mill in all its history," with 118 students in the first-year class and more than 300 students in all three years. In addition, the first-year register suggested "indications of an imminent militancy in the jurisprudence of this province" because there were four women's names on the first-year register, as well as two women students in second year.[69] The second-year students included Edith Paterson from Vancouver, who had won a scholarship in her first year in a class of one hundred, and Mrs. H.V. Laughton, formerly Miss Mary Buckley, whose husband was a barrister practising law in Toronto.[70] Both women were university graduates, and they were called to the bar together at Easter in 1915,

67 C. McLeod, "The Morris Dynasty," *Canadian Lawyer* (August/September 1992) 52; and C. Wiktor, ed., *Dalhousie Law School Register, 1883–1983* (Halifax: Dalhousie Law School, 1983). McLeod reported that Janet Morris was a sole practitioner in 1992 and that Jean worked for Legal Aid in Halifax. In 2015, Tefft/Malcolm explained that Janet had practised law for ten years after her call to the bar, and that Jean had recently retired: Alma Morris Tefft/Malcolm, telephone interview with M.J. Mossman (18 November 2015). See also LSO Archives, "Diversifying the Bar," Alma Malcolm. Her son, Alexander Malcolm, became a lawyer in Hamilton, and his website identified his grandmother Cairns Morris as a "fearless trailblazer," online: <http://www.malcolmlawyer.net/a-tradition-of-legal-practice/>.

68 LSO Archives, OBBRP, "Jean Cairns Morris." Inspired in the 1920s by Sir Henry Mill Pellatt, the Canadian financier whose legacy is Casa Loma in Toronto, Philip Morris began to construct a mansion in Fruitland, using materials, sometimes entire sections, of old buildings being torn down in Hamilton. After his disbarment, the mansion remained uncompleted. In the 1940s, his son, Alan Morris, an engineer, decided to complete the Fruitland mansion and convert it to apartments. His mother provided financial assistance and named the building Cairngorm. In 1952, the son's family moved into an apartment, and Cairns Morris might have lived in an apartment there as well. The building was sold in the 1970s and was purchased and renovated in the mid-1990s as Edgewater Manor, a fine-dining restaurant: Alma Morris Tefft/Malcolm, telephone interview with M.J. Mossman (18 November 2015).

69 "Personal" (1913) 33 *Canadian Law Times* 919 at 931. The names on the first-year register included Gertrude Alford from Belleville, who was called to the bar in 1916. The others in first-year were Charlotte Wegg, BA, from St. Thomas; Mary Maund, from Kingston; and Lena Richardson, from Toronto. There is no record that Wegg, Maund, and Richardson were called to the Ontario bar.

70 LSO Archives, OBBRP, "Edith Paterson" and "Mary Elizabeth Laughton." Mary Buckley married H.V. Laughton in June 1913, after completing the first year of lectures at the law school.

the first occasion when two women were admitted to the Ontario bar in the same year.

Paterson was born in 1891 and grew up in Shaughnessy Heights in Vancouver. She attended McGill University for an MA and then enrolled at Osgoode Hall in the spring of 1912. She was admitted to the Ontario bar in 1915 after articling with Frank Denton, KC, in Toronto, and attending the required lectures at the law school. Paterson returned to Vancouver in July 1915 and was admitted to the bar of British Columbia on 3 January 1916, the second woman to enter the legal profession there after Mabel Penery French in 1912.[71] Paterson initially worked at the firm of McNeil, Bird & MacDonald, and then with Tupper and Bull, the law firm of Sir Charles Tupper, KC, but she opened her own law office on 1 December 1919, the first woman lawyer to do so in Vancouver. A few years later, in 1923, she entered a long-standing law partnership with Hamilton Read.[72]

For several decades, Paterson's practice included significant counsel work, including many appearances in all the courts, and she was probably the first woman lawyer to appear in the British Columbia Court of Appeal. Her practice focused on both civil and criminal law in many different areas

71 LSO Archives, OBBRP, "Edith Paterson," identifying her university degree in 1911 as a BA. In contrast, the Legal Archives of British Columbia (LABC), which includes ten volumes of materials (1897 to 1970) identifies her university degree as an MA and claims she resided at Royal Victoria College in 1909–1911: LABC, Edith Louise Paterson fonds, "Biographical Sketch" and "Series Descriptions." The archive says she was born in 1891, although the 1921 census recorded her age as twenty-five. The LABC fonds include Paterson's notes from lectures at Osgoode Hall on contracts, criminal law, municipal law, equity, and practice, as well as a letter from her principal, Frank Denton, dated 15 July 1915. Denton's letter stated: "I hope that your every dream of success may be more than realized. May all your squares become cubes and the fourth dimension be discovered by and named after you. I regret you are not remaining in Toronto—However, Vancouver will gain by what the former loses": LABC, Edith Louise Paterson fonds, "Biographical Sketch"; *Vancouver Daily World* (23 July 1915); and Brockman, "Exclusionary Tactics," 529–34. See also P. Proudfoot and G. Pun, "Edith L. Paterson" (2010) 68:1 *The Advocate* 84 at 85; Huckle, "List of Women Barristers and Solicitors"; and LSO Archives, WLAO fonds, SB, vol. 1. For Mabel French, see Chapter One.

72 Percy Hamilton Read had been admitted to the bar in England in 1901, and he immigrated to British Columbia in 1910 to practise law: Proudfoot and Pun, "Edith L. Paterson, 84-85, 87 n12. Read's first wife died in 1943, and Paterson and Read married in 1944, although they had been romantically involved from the 1920s: Brockman, "Exclusionary Tactics," 559 n200. After Read died in Vancouver in 1961: (1962) 20 *The Advocate* 219, Paterson changed her surname to Read in the *Canadian Law Lists*.

of law: trusts, corporations, contracts, family law, collections, administrative law, personal injury, and insurance. Paterson was the first woman elected to the executive of the Vancouver Bar Association, and she was a member of the Association's Legal Aid Committee.[73] Moreover, Paterson believed that many clients preferred a woman lawyer:

> There are a large number of men who prefer to seek the advice of a woman lawyer. Many women too ... Both my women and men clients usually explain that their reasons for coming to me—a woman lawyer—they would rather talk to a woman—they can tell me "things." Law is after all quite a usual profession and I deserve no extra credit because I am a woman. I have found very little prejudice against women in the legal profession and the men have been particularly helpful to me in every instance—all of them from judges to gaolers.[74]

As Joan Brockman concluded, such a statement may not have been entirely true, but "it would have been suicidal to their career[s]" for early women lawyers to acknowledge any prejudice.[75]

Paterson was also an active member of the Conservative Party in British Columbia. As early as 1916, she was President of the Ward VI Women's Conservative Association and an invited speaker at Association meetings in other wards where she advocated for women's suffrage. In 1920, she became a candidate for the Conservative Party in the provincial election, and while her speeches were well received, she was not elected. Nonetheless, by 1918, she had been elected to the executive council of the University of British Columbia and, in the following year, she was an

73 Proudfoot and Pun, "Edith L. Paterson," 85. See also Pue, *Law School,* 225–36. One of Paterson's major cases was *Brown v Storoschuk,* [1947] 1 DLR 227 (BCCA): Proudfoot and Pun, "Edith L. Paterson" 88 n13, in which she was listed as "Edith Hamilton Read."

74 Brockman, "Exclusionary Tactics." 531–32; and A. Paige, "Base Charge Is Refuted: Professional Women Not Misfits, says Ann," *Vancouver Daily World* (30 May 1923). Brockman also reported the consternation of a client for whom Paterson had drafted a letter, signing it with just her initials, after he discovered that she was actually a woman: Brockman, "Exclusionary Tactics," 533.

75 Significantly, Brockman noted that women lawyers seventy years later would also refrain from public criticism of the male-dominated profession unless "their anonymity was assured": Brockman, "Exclusionary Tactics," 533 and 561 n223.

honoured guest of the Vancouver Bar Association at a luncheon for Jacqueline Bertillon of the Paris bar.[76]

Paterson's support for the provincial Conservatives was rewarded when they were elected in 1928, and Paterson was appointed a judge of the Juvenile Court of British Columbia, serving from 1929 to 1934. She thus became the first woman law graduate in Canada, and the first woman graduate of the law school at Osgoode Hall to be appointed a judge in Canada.[77] Established in 1917 with the support of the University Women's Club in Vancouver and the advocacy of Helen Gregory MacGill, the court was intended to respond to the inequities faced by women before the law. Although she did not have formal legal training, MacGill had been appointed as one of the first two magistrates, and the only woman, of the Juvenile Court in 1917. The political nature of such appointments was revealed in 1933, when the Liberals regained power in the province and MacGill was reappointed to the court. Paterson returned to practising law with Read.[78]

In the 1940s, Paterson presented a series of radio broadcasts on legal issues generally but not exclusively of interest to women, and she continued to encourage women to vote. In 1969, she was honoured with a fifty-year certificate from the British Columbia Law Society along with other male leaders of the bar. The report of the Treasurer identified the thirty-seven "gentlemen" receiving this honour, echoing a similar announcement of Mabel Penery French's admission to the bar as one of

76 *Vancouver Daily World* (21 July 1916) 5, (6 May 1916) 11, and (6 April 1916) 20. Paterson's activities were regularly reported in this press: see *Vancouver Daily World* (3 May 1918) 10, (12 November 1920) 12, and (18 November 1920) 15.

77 Executive Council report to the Lieutenant Governor, Victoria BC (20 February 1929), noting a salary of $1,500 per annum, payable monthly; and G. Paterson Lane, "She Is Canada's Youngest Woman Judge," *MacLean's Magazine* (1 May 1929) 81–82. Paterson Lane was Edith Paterson's younger sister: 1921 census, Dominion Bureau of Statistics, Point Grey Municipality, 11. See also LSO Archives, "Diversifying the Bar," Edith Louise Paterson; and Watts, *History of the Legal Profession in British Columbia*, 135.

78 E.G. MacGill, *My Mother, the Judge* (Toronto: Ryerson Press, 1955) 165–ff. This account suggested that Evlyn Farris, whose husband was Attorney General, was instrumental in the appointment of Helen Gregory MacGill as a judge of the Juvenile Court, 155–56. See also J. Bannerman, *Leading Ladies: Canada. 1639–1967* (Galt, ON: Highland Press, 1967); J. Bannerman, *Leading Ladies* (Mika, 1977); and C. Sissons, *Elsie Gregory MacGill: Engineering the Future and Building Bridges for Canadian Women, 1918–1980* (PhD diss., University of Ottawa, 2008) [unpublished] 32 n33.

twenty "gentlemen" nearly sixty years earlier. In 1970, Paterson suffered a stroke, and her practice was placed in custodianship. She died in 1980 after a long period in hospital. As a major tribute stated in January 2010, "Edith Paterson, so remarkable by the lights of her time in the early and mid 20th century, would scarcely be noticeable now. Her legacy is practically invisible by its very prominence."[79]

The second woman admitted to the Ontario bar at Easter in 1915 was Mary Buckley Laughton. Buckley had received a BA at the University of Toronto in 1912 and enrolled at the law school while articling with Gordon Shaver in Toronto. In June 1913, after completing first-year, she married a lawyer, Harry Laughton, becoming the first married woman student at the law school, and then the first married woman to be called to the bar.[80] Harry Laughton and Mary Buckley were both from Parkhill, now North Middlesex, northwest of London, and Mary had been a university friend of Harry's younger brother, George. The couple had a home on Glengrove Avenue in north Toronto and were "part of the upper social structure in Toronto." They had one son, a brilliant student and musician who died during the Second World War.[81] Mary Laughton may have worked for some months as a junior in Martin's law office, but in 1917, she enrolled in a social service course at the University of Toronto and became General Secretary of the Big Sisters Association. She resigned this position in 1921 because of ill health, although she remained a volunteer with the Big Sisters at least until the 1930s. She ceased paying Law Society fees in 1922, after discontinuing legal practice.[82]

In the history of the Women's Law Association of Ontario, Buckley Laughton is remembered fondly because it was at her summer home on Centre Island that an important organizational meeting in October 1923 led to the Association's first annual report. In 1920, she authored an article in *Maclean's Magazine* about "Women in Law," providing an encouraging description of the opportunities for women who aspired to join the legal

79 Proudfoot and Pun, "Edith L. Paterson," 85–86 and n27.

80 LSO Archives, OBBRP, "Mary Elizabeth Laughton."

81 Harry Laughton KC was employed at National Trust, and became vice-president and general manager there in the 1940s, and he was also elected a director of the Canada Life Assurance Company in 1947: *Canadian Law Lists*.

82 LSO Archives, "Diversifying the Bar," Mary Elizabeth Laughton. Buckley Laughton may also have obtained a degree from the Conservatory School of Expression: LSO Archives, WLAO fonds, SB, vol. 1.

profession. She noted increasing numbers of women lawyers and law students, including sixteen women who had been called to the bar by 1920, and another fifteen "prospective Portias" currently enrolled as students in the three years at the law school.[83] Laughton argued that no woman need feel she would be a lone female if she aspired "to tread the labyrinth of legal learning," a significant change from the experiences of several lone women law students before 1918. She also explained that the three-year law program involved ten one-hour lectures each week for six months, and that students would also be involved in "practical experience in a law office for a remuneration which amounts to a little more than carfare."[84]

Buckley Laughton's article firmly rejected the idea that the study of law was more difficult for women, arguing that women are often well-suited to detailed work: "a woman could have as much aptitude for [law studies] as she has for grasping the intricacies of a new crochet pattern." Her article asserted that women needed to earn their own living to avoid becoming parasites on society, as well as to engage in the reform of man-made laws to ensure justice and fairness for women: "None but a woman is aghast at the lightness of the penalty imposed for offences against her sex and the heaviness of the punishment for the crime of taking another man's property." In spite of these arguments, Buckley Laughton did not practise for long, probably because of her status as a married woman, but she remained active in the WLAO, serving as honorary president and toast mistress at the first annual dinner meeting in February 1920, and as the WLAO representative to the Local Council of Women in 1923. In addition, she was featured as a founding member of the WLAO in a commemorative article about the organization's eighty-fifth anniversary in 2004.[85]

In 1916, Gertrude Alford was the only woman called to the Ontario bar. The daughter of William Alford, a contractor in Belleville, she was the third

83 M.E. Laughton, "Women in Law," *Maclean's Magazine*, ca. 1920 at 74. See also C. Harvey, "Women in Law in Canada" (1970–71) 4 *Manitoba Law Journal* 9 at 27–28; and Chapter Three.

84 Laughton, "Women in Law."

85 Laughton, "Women in Law," 74–75; *Globe* (17 February 1920); and LSO Archives, WLAO fonds, Women's Law Association of Ontario, annual report, 1923–24, at 2. See also *Toronto Telegram* (7 February 1953), which identified Laughton's painting of her spouse in his KC silks and Robinson Wright's paintings of flowers at the WLAO Hobby Show; and "Women's Law Association of Ontario—Celebrating 85 Years," 2004, unidentified news report featuring Buckley Laughton's photo and biography.

woman called to the bar as a matriculant, following Robinson Wright and Hewson Knight. Alford had worked as a "typewriter" in the City Clerk's Office in Belleville prior to enrolling at the law school in 1911 at the age of nineteen, and she articled with W.C. Mikel, KC, in Belleville.[86] The press reported on her call to the bar: "Miss Gertrude Alford, of Belleville, is the only young woman to graduate this year in law at Osgoode Hall. She was born and educated in Belleville ... Miss Alford obtained high standing throughout her entire course, and [she] will be the first lady lawyer Belleville has produced."[87] Although some reports indicated that Alford had joined the legal department of the Canadian National Railway, she joined Mikel's firm immediately after her call to the bar, and she was soon in charge of the firm's second office in Trenton. By 1922, the firm of Mikel & Alford in Belleville included both Mikel and Alford as members, while Alford was the sole member of the Mikel & Alford firm in Trenton.[88]

Alford was appointed KC in December 1945, the only woman among forty male lawyers, including eleven war veterans. Although she was not the first woman lawyer in Ontario to be appointed KC, Alford is the earliest woman graduate of the law school at Osgoode Hall to receive this recognition.[89] She was also the first woman lawyer in eastern Ontario, and the only one for decades. Her small office in Trenton was located at 80 Division Street on the second floor above a store, and she had a general practice that included estates work, some commercial law, and real estate. After Alford's father died in 1929, her mother moved to Trenton to live with her in a home just east of the Trenton airbase overlooking the Bay of Quinte. Alford's married sister lived nearby in Consecon.[90]

86 LSO Archives, OBBRP, "Gertrude Alford"; and LSO Archives, "Diversifying the Bar," Gertrude Alford.

87 *Ottawa Journal* (16 May 1916) at 9.

88 WLAO, annual report, 1923–24. *Canadian Law List* entries identified Alford as a member of the firm of Mikel & Alford in Trenton from 1922 and then as a sole practitioner in Trenton from 1936 to 1970. In the 1930s, Mikel became a local Master in Belleville, and he was later appointed a special examiner. Alford may have worked for several years in the Department of the Attorney General in Ontario: LSO Archives, "Diversifying the Bar," Gertrude Alford.

89 *Globe and Mail* (21 December 1945) 11; and Huckle, "List of Women Barristers and Solicitors."

90 Bruce Karten, a lawyer who purchased Alford's practice in 1970–71, telephone communication with M.J. Mossman (November 2015). See also obituary, "Mrs. William Alford," *Globe* (9 August 1934) 11.

At least in the early years of practice, Alford attended some WLAO events in Toronto, including a luncheon in February 1917 hosted by Helen Palen, Marie McNulty, and Theresa Cherrier, all of whom were called to the bar in 1918. Their guests were women lawyers and law students, including Mary Buckley Laughton, Jean Cairns, and Clara Brett Martin. Alford also attended the first dinner of "the new and epoch-making society, the Women's Law Association of Ontario," in February 1920, along with a large number of women lawyers and women law students.[91] As a woman who practised law in Trenton until the early 1970s, during decades when few women were in practice in eastern Ontario, Alford probably found these WLAO connections important. She died in 1975 and, after a funeral in Trenton, she was buried in the Belleville cemetery.[92]

In 1918, three women gained admission to the legal profession in Ontario, a number described as "extraordinary" for one year.[93] In May 1918, Mary (Marie) McNulty from Ottawa, aged twenty-two, was called to the bar. McNulty and her law school colleague, Teresa Cherrier, were the first Catholic women to be called to the Ontario bar. McNulty and her family lived on Lisgar Street and after graduating from the Ottawa Collegiate, she had enrolled as a matriculant in 1913 at the age of eighteen. A press announcement confirmed that "Ottawa's first woman lawyer will be formally called to the bar on May 23rd next, and after a short vacation, Miss Mary McNulty will be a general practitioner here." The woman journalist who interviewed McNulty asked why she had chosen to become a lawyer.

> "It seemed to me," Miss McNulty replied, choosing her words with quiet care which should make them highly effective in her profession, "women in Ontario have been neglecting an opportunity for, although the legal profession has been open to women since 1892, few girls have taken advantage of

91 "Social Events," *Globe* (20 February 1917) 8, and (17 February 1920) 10.

92 For 1971–73, the firm name was "Alford and Karten": *Canadian Law Lists.* However, Alford was quite frail by then, and her long-time assistant, Florence Smith, was providing continuity for the practice. When Karten purchased the practice in 1970–71, he inherited the firm library, including several volumes from the early decades of Ontario legal practice: Karten telephone interview with M.J. Mossman (November 2015). See also minutes of Convocation (17 October 1975), noting the death of Alford on 7 August 1975; and Belleville Public Library, unidentified obituary and funeral notice.

93 Helen Palen obituary, *Globe and Mail* (29 December 1971). Palen was called to the bar in September 1918: Huckle, "List of Women Barristers and Solicitors."

> the fact." General practice appeals to Miss McNulty, and she has no vision of seeing the walls of prejudice fall at the first march ... [The report also noted that] throughout her course, she had been met with the utmost kindness, [stating] "In fact sometimes I was afraid that men gave way because I happened to be a girl, and while I appreciate the little courtesies extended, I want to take my turn just as a man would."[94]

McNulty articled with E.F. Burritt at the firm of Code & Burritt in Ottawa, and her principal stated warmly in May 1918 that "I know that the male portion of the Ottawa bar will welcome her as a practising member of the profession." McNulty was a confident young woman: she was an ardent supporter of suffrage for women, having joined the Women's Franchise Association at the age of sixteen, and she claimed to have been involved, during her time as a law student, in drafting legislation for women's suffrage. She was also the first woman student to participate on the law school's debating team.[95] After being called to the bar, moreover, McNulty "hastened to her brother's [law] office" to assist with his law practice while he, John Hugh McNulty, was in uniform in World War I.[96]

Notwithstanding her confidence about a legal career, McNulty left the law firm only a few years later to work as legal secretary for Henry T. Ross, head of the Canadian Bankers' Association. She was more interested in business than law, although it is possible that she had not been welcomed into legal practice in Ottawa. She soon changed occupations again, working for a small, exclusive Ottawa clothing store as its European buyer and

94 LSO Archives, WLAO fonds, SB, vol. 1, "First Woman Lawyer Here Is Charmingly Feminine," *The Journal*, ca. 1918. "Coming down from the pedestal of *The Journal* interviewing a lady lawyer, [and] talking as two girls," McNulty and the interviewer agreed that men in business were considerate to women.

95 LSO Archives, WLAO fonds, SB, vol. 1; and LSO Archives, OBBRP, "Mary McNulty." According to a later press report, McNulty's mother, Anna O'Riley McNulty, was the first general correspondent for a newspaper in Canada: LSO Archives, Mary (McNulty) Fix fonds, *Toronto Telegram* (18 February 1959) and *Globe and Mail* (10 January 1953). See also LSO Archives, "Diversifying the Bar," Mary McNulty; and WLAO fonds, SB, vol. 10, obituaries.

96 E. Mitchell Thomas, "The History of Woman Lawyers in the County of Carleton Law Association" in W. Johnson, ed., *The First Century: Essays on the History of the County of Carleton Law Association by Various Hands on the Occasion of the Association's Centenary, 1888–1988* (Ottawa: Bonanza Press, 1988) 107 at 107–8. Mitchell Thomas' report that McNulty left her brother's firm to practise law in central Ontario is unconfirmed.

business manager, and she was later hired as a department manager for the new Eaton's store in Montreal. She then worked for Eaton's as a foreign buyer, initially in New York and for two years in Paris. Although a press report in 1959 explained that "she didn't like [law] and quit," McNulty may have been searching for challenges missing in legal practice in Ottawa. But it may also be significant that "there is no trace of another woman venturing into practice in Ottawa until 1950."[97]

McNulty returned to Canada and married Albert Fix, a Vienna-born pianist, in 1931. They built a house in Port Credit and began to breed dachshunds. After her husband's death in 1945, McNulty Fix opened the Cloverleaf Dress Shop in her home, and she later became involved in local politics. At a rate payers' meeting in 1952, she spoke up about financial issues in the township, and in 1953, she was elected Deputy Reeve, the first woman to serve on a municipal council in Peel County. She received the largest majority of votes in Toronto Township history. Then, in 1955, she became Peel County's first woman Reeve, and although she was defeated the next year, she was again elected Reeve in 1957 and 1958. In 1959, she was appointed Warden of Peel County.[98]

McNulty Fix considered that she was "not the ball-of-fire type" like Charlotte Whitten, mayor of Ottawa, but "I hope I can do as much for my municipality." In 1959, she reported on her efforts to attract industry to the township, noting that six years earlier, when she had first been elected, industry comprised only 19.5 per cent of the total assessment for

97 LSO Archives, Mary (McNulty) Fix fonds, *Globe and Mail* (10 January 1953). McNulty discontinued practice in 1921, although she did not pay fees after 1919: LSO Archives, OBBRP, "Mary McNulty." The biography of Mary McNulty Fix notes her role as a buyer of women's clothing for Eaton's and that McNulty claimed responsibility for "introducing Canadian women to shorts": Dufferin-Peel Counties District School Board, biography of Mary Fix, online http://w3.dpcdsb.org/MAFIX/School+History/Naming+of+school.htm. See also *Toronto Telegram* (18 February 1959); and Mitchell Thomas, "The History of Women Lawyers," 108. Significantly, Mitchell Thomas (1942) documented difficulties that she had encountered in Ottawa after the Second World War, including being questioned by a judge about whether she was a "full fledged lawyer"—decades after McNulty's practice in the early 1920s. Moreover, there were still no proper robing rooms for women lawyers in the Ottawa courthouse in the 1950s: Mitchell Thomas, "The History of Women Lawyers," 111–12.

98 *Toronto Telegram* (18 February 1959); and Dufferin-Peel Counties District School Board, biography of Mary Fix. See also *Port Credit Weekly* (2 December 1954), which indicated that McNulty practised law for (only) two years.

the southern sector of the township but had grown to 37.88 per cent by 1959 (close to the 40 per cent recommended by planners for a healthy assessment base.)[99] In the 1960s, she was actively involved in heritage issues and a member of the Library Board and other municipal projects, and she published articles on a variety of topics. She served on the Mississauga Centennial Committee, contributing both the introductory chapter and a chapter about the history of industry for the *Peel County Centennial History* in 1967. McNulty Fix died in 1972, with a funeral mass held in Port Credit. She left her estate to the City of Mississauga, and the Dufferin-Peel Roman Catholic Separate School Board named a school in her memory.[100]

In September 1918, two women were admitted to the bar. One was Helen Palen, who had enrolled as a matriculant in Trinity term 1913 at the age of twenty-eight, and then graduated from Osgoode Hall with honours. Palen had worked as Deputy County Court Clerk in Belleville before moving to Toronto, where she articled in the offices of J. Webber Payne and then Holden & Murdoch. She also articled with Peter Anderson in Belleville, probably for two years before relocating to attend lectures in Toronto in 1915.[101] Palen and McNulty became friends, and Palen visited Ottawa in 1920. A report about Palen's appearance before Justice Logie, on appeal from a master's order, noted her "clever argument and presentation of the case," and suggested that "the appearance of a woman counsel in the Supreme Court of Ontario has been a very rare occurrence in the past, but it is anticipated that it will be more frequent in the days to come."[102]

99 LSO Archives, Mary (McNulty) Fix fonds, *Globe and Mail* (10 January 1953); and *Toronto Telegram* (18 February 1959).

100 McNulty Fix willed her property, at the corner of Highway 10 (Hurontario Street) and Queen Elizabeth Way, to the city for a public park, and her home was later used as a crisis centre: Mitchell Thomas, "The History of Women Lawyers," 108; LSO, "Diversifying the Bar," Mary McNulty; and Dufferin-Peel Counties District School Board, biography of Mary Fix. See also LSO Archives, Mary (McNulty) Fix fonds, unidentified report of her funeral in 1972, with six former Reeves as pall bearers.

101 LSO Archives, OBBRP, "Helen Beatrice Palen"; and LSO Archives, WLAO fonds, SB, vol.1. Law Society records indicate that Palen was a court reporter in Belleville before studying law: LSO Archives, "Diversifying the Bar," Helen Beatrice Palen.

102 *Ottawa Journal* (5 January 1920). The young McNulty may have discussed her legal prospects with Palen, who had more experience as a working woman. See also "Judge Compliments Lady," LSO Archives, WLAO fonds, SB, vol. 2, unidentified press report.

Records about Palen's legal work suggest that she was in private practice in Toronto during the 1920s, but the details are unclear.[103] In 1930, she was appointed Deputy Registrar under the *Security Frauds Prevention Act* in the Provincial Secretary's Department, working with W.W. Denison, Registrar of Companies and Brokers, a government department that later became the Ontario Securities Commission. Palen was one of three women lawyers employed by the Ontario government at that time. In 1933, she became the first woman appointed Assistant Registrar of the Supreme Court of Ontario, and she was appointed KC in November 1945.[104] Five years later, in 1950, she became the first woman Deputy Registrar of the Supreme Court of Ontario. Since Palen had long been an active member of the WLAO, the Association celebrated this new appointment with a tea in her honour at the University Women's Club in February 1951.[105]

John Honsberger described Palen presiding in Weekly Court in the 1940s:

---

103 Some records indicate that Palen practised law with Holden Murdoch and then with T.R.J. Wray and R.J. Russell, and that she had a sole practice in the late 1920s: LSO Archives, OBBRP, "Helen Beatrice Palen." In contrast, WLAO records suggest that she worked with Corley, Gordon for about five years and then established her own practice at 2531 Yonge Street: WLAO, annual report, 1923–24. Palen's obituary reported that she worked for T.R.J. Wray for five years and then established her own practice: "First Women in Court Role," *Globe and Mail* (29 December 1971). Another record (probably inaccurate) suggested that she worked for some time as an assistant to Toronto police magistrate, George Denison, and that she was appointed Deputy Registrar of the Ontario Securities Commission in 1923: LSO Archives, "Diversifying the Bar," Helen Beatrice Palen.

104 LSO Archives, "Diversifying the Bar," Helen Beatrice Palen, quoting unidentified report, "Government Employs Three Women Lawyers." See also *Globe* (27 February 1931) 12. Public accounts reveal that Palen worked in 1930–31 for eight and a half months as Deputy Registrar under the *Security Frauds Prevention Act* and was later employed for nearly five months as Assistant Registrar of the Supreme Court: Ontario, *Public Accounts of the Province of Ontario, 1930–31* (Toronto: Herbert H. Ball, 1932); and Ontario, Public Accounts of the Province of Ontario, 1932–33 (Toronto: Herbert H. Ball, 1934). See also *Globe and Mail* (5 November 1945) 8: among the new KC appointments, including Palen, were seven men who had served in the Armed Forces. Law Society records incorrectly identify the year of Palen's KC appointment as 1935: LSO Archives, "Diversifying the Bar," Helen Palen.

105 LSO Archives, WLAO fonds, SB, vol. 3, *Globe and Mail*, unidentified news report; and *Toronto Telegram* (22 June 1950). See also LSO Archives, WLAO fonds, SB, vol. 3, *Globe and Mail* (21 February 1951).

> She was an imposing woman. She wore her hair in a braid wound into a bun and pinned to the back of her head. She wore dresses, usually with a belt, but never suits. She was competent, ran a good office and was not difficult to approach. She was, however, a stickler in respect to grammar, punctuation and spelling. She preferred the Oxford dictionary over the Old Testament for the spelling of "judgment." She also had strong views on commas; behind her back, lawyers would refer to "Palen on Commas." It was often a lengthy procedure to have her settle an order: she would go through it word by word, line by line, and, if there were any changes, she would not sign it until it had been retyped.
>
> She used to tell a story about herself when she sat in weekly court as registrar. It was a few moments before eleven, when court was to open. She was frantically matching counsel slips, which gave the name of counsel appearing on a matter, with the papers for each. She found that she was missing one slip. A quick look around the courtroom suggested to her that it was the very junior barrister a few rows back who had not handed in a slip. She beckoned him to her desk. "Quick, I haven't a slip." The blushing young man replied, "I'm sorry; what do you want me to do?"[106]

A woman lawyer also recalled Palen's "lesson in drafting and the precise use of language, as her spidery writing went around the paper, changing every paragraph of a draft order in Weekly Court, and providing a glimpse of the clear and precise legal mind that was hers."[107]

Palen was one of four women lawyers who presided over a tea in honour of the justices of the Supreme Court of Ontario and their wives in 1946, and she was present, with other women lawyers, at a meeting of the Ontario section of the Canadian Bar Association in Ottawa in 1951. When Palen

106 Honsberger, *Osgoode Hall*, 231–32. Some years later, when Palen was asked to write an article about "Drafting a Judgment or Order" for *Obiter Dicta*, she lamented the problem of punctuation: "Proper punctuation is an almost lost art, and one mentions it rather hopelessly. The trouble seems to be that draftsmen leave the punctuation to their typists, many of whom use commas as some cooks use sprigs of parsley—just to make things look prettier": H.B. Palen, "Drafting a Judgment or Order" (January 1950) 24:2 *Obiter Dicta* 15. She also instructed students that since courts decide issues between litigants, not counsel, "it follows that a written emanation of the Court should be couched in language which can be understood by a layman of ordinary intelligence and education without legal training. The use of Latin should be avoided."

107 E. Mitchell Thomas, "Sisters-in-Law," (December 1972) *Gazette* 301, reprinted in (1991) 25:3 *Gazette* 298.

retired in 1956, she was honoured for her work by the WLAO with the presentation of a silver tray.[108] Palen died in Toronto on 26 December 1971, a life member of the Law Society of Upper Canada. Her funeral and burial took place in Belleville.[109]

The third woman called to the bar in 1918, along with Palen, was Theresa Cherrier. Cherrier had worked as a stenographer in a law office in Hamilton prior to enrolling as a matriculant at the Law School in Trinity term 1913. There is no information about her articling principal, either in Hamilton or Toronto, but given that she later practised with W.T. Evans and then carried on the firm's practice after Evans was appointed to the Bench, Cherrier may have articled with Evans.[110] Among the cohort of women called to the bar up to 1918, Cherrier was the third, after both Palen and Alford in 1945, to be appointed a QC. Cherrier's appointment occurred in March 1953.[111]

Cherrier practised law in Hamilton for over forty years, mainly in real estate and probate, and she was also widely known for giving help to women with family court problems. Indeed, she "had a reputation as a kind and generous woman ready to assist anybody, including many who had no

108 "Personal Notes," *Globe and Mail* (1 January 1946). The other women lawyers involved at the tea event were Mrs. Ward Wright (1907), Miss Vera Parsons (1924), and Miss Sybil Bennett (1930). See also "Social and Personal," *Ottawa Journal* (2 April 1951). Palen also assisted in organizing a garden party in 1948 in honour of J.D. Falconbridge, dean emeritus: "Personal Notes," *Globe and Mail* (25 June 1948). See also LSO Archives, WLAO fonds, SB, vol. 3; and *Toronto Daily Star* (2 June 1956). Law Society records indicate that Palen was born in 1885, confirming that she retired at the age of seventy-one: LSO Archives, "Diversifying the Bar," Helen Beatrice Palen; and *Toronto Telegram* (22 June 1950).

109 Obituary, "Helen Palen First Woman in Court Role" *Globe and Mail* (29 December 1971); *Chatham News* (29 December 1971); Minutes of Convocation, 1971–73, *Ontario Reports*, ca. 1973, viii; and LSO Archives, OBBRP, "Helen Beatrice Palen." Palen was eighty-six at the time of her death.

110 Law Society records identify Cherrier's age in 1913 as twenty-two, based on her birth in 1890. However, press reports at her death in 1961 identified her as seventy-three, suggesting she may have been twenty-five in 1913: obituary, *Hamilton Spectator* (23 May 1961). See also LSO Archives, "Diversifying the Bar," Theresa Cherrier; and LSO Archives, OBBRP, "Theresa Cherrier."

111 LSO Archives, WLAO fonds, SB, vol. 6, unidentified press report, "Announce Appointment of 67 Men, Two Women as Queen's Counsel," 1953. The other woman appointed QC was Lily Sherizen (1930). See also obituary, *Hamilton Spectator* (23 May 1961); and LSO Archives, "Diversifying the Bar," Theresa Cherrier. A Law Society record indicated the QC appointment occurred in 1952 (LSO Archives, OBBRP, "Theresa Cherrier") while the *Hamilton Spectator* identified the appointment as in March 1953.

hope of ever paying lawyers' fees." In addition, Magistrate Albert Marck, who handled her practice for four years prior to her death, suggested that Cherrier was very much a personal forerunner of social agencies dealing with women and families.[112]

Cherrier was a devout Catholic who attended mass at St. Patrick's Church in Hamilton every day. She was also active in Catholic organizations, including the Catholic Women's League and the Children of Mary, and she was a member of the Hamilton Bar Association and the Ontario Bar Association. She attended a WLAO tea in Hamilton in 1938, along with "Mrs. Philip Morris" and other women lawyers, hosted by Mrs. W.S. McLay (Florence Thompson, 1922), but Cherrier was not listed among active WLAO members in the early 1950s.[113] Based on her surname, Theresa Cherrier may be "la première avocate franco-ontarienne," although her obituary did not identify a francophone heritage.[114] The obituary stated that Cherrier was the first woman from Hamilton to be admitted to the Ontario bar," although Cairns Morris, who had married and relocated to practise law

112 Obituary, *Hamilton Spectator* (23 May 1961). There is information that Anita Dateman Lawson was a graduate of the Law School in 1918. But she married her spouse, James Lawson MP, while she was a student and identified herself "with her husband's career: social, legal and political" and was not called to the bar: LSO Archives, WLAO fonds, SB, vol. 1. James Lawson was elected to Parliament in 1928–1940 for York West and York South. Anita Lawson is not included in Huckle, "List of Women Barristers and Solicitors."

113 Obituary *Hamilton Spectator* (23 May 1961); and LSO Archives, WLAO fonds, SB, vol. 3, "Active Members of WLAO, 1950–51"; and SB, vol. 2, "Women Barristers at Hamilton Tea," ca. 1938. The other Hamilton women lawyers present for this occasion included Phyllis Eileen Harron (1921), Mrs. M. McLean (Mary Constance Hunt, 1934), Margaret Sullivan (1929), Constance Nelson (1937), and Frances Milne (1929). Women lawyers from other Ontario communities, and a large number from Toronto, were also in attendance, including both women practitioners and others who were married and not practising law.

114 LSO Archives, letter from E. Brunet to G. Lévesque, 28 October 1993, in response to his inquiry about the first Franco-Ontario woman lawyer. The letter, written in French, expressed concern that a francophone name might not necessarily correspond to an individual's language or identity. The letter suggested Cherrier as possibly the first francophone avocate. Cherrier's parents were Flavian and Theresa Cherrier, but there is no confirmation of francophone heritage: obituary, *Hamilton Spectator* (23 May 1961). The letter from Brunet also identified another possible francophone woman, Lovedy Campeau (1919), who practised law in Essex County: see Chapter Three.

in Hamilton in 1917, a year prior to Cherrier's call to the bar, was the first woman practitioner in Hamilton. Cherrier died in 1961.[115]

### A Kaleidoscope of Patterns and Puzzles

> *For some critics, biography is a fiction, a creation of the biographer who weaves a seamless narrative, creating coherence and causal connections that bear little relation to the lived experience of the person being studied. The self, it is sometime argued, is not unitary and coherent but shifting and fragmented ... [It may be more appropriate] to see biography as a "kaleidoscope": each time you look you see something rather different, composed certainly of the same elements, but in a new configuration.*[116]

Stories of early women lawyers provide historical insights into the gendered culture of Ontario's legal profession in the first two decades of the twentieth century, and the kaleidoscope metaphor is useful in exploring shifting patterns in their lives. One pattern is the extent to which connections to the legal profession may have influenced women's decisions to pursue admission to the bar, and which may have assisted some women in practice.[117] Although American scholars identified family connections to the profession as being quite significant, only four of these ten women called to the Ontario bar up to 1918 had family members in the legal profession: Robinson Wright was the daughter of a lawyer, Hewson Knight's father was a judge, McNulty Fix was the sister of a lawyer, and Buckley Laughton married a lawyer after completing her first year at the law school. In addition to family connections, three women had worked in supportive roles in the courts or law offices: Alford and Palen in Belleville and Cherrier in Hamilton. All of these early women lawyers articled with male lawyers, but only

115 Obituary, *Hamilton Spectator* (23 May 1961). Law Society records incorrectly identify Cherrier as the "first woman to be admitted to the bar in Hamilton": LSO Archives, OBBRP, "Theresa Cherrier."

116 J. Purvis, *Emmeline Pankhurst: A Biography* (London: Routledge, 2002) 6; and L. Stanley, "Biography as Microscope or Kaleidoscope? The Case of 'Power' in Hannah Cullwick's Relationship with Arthur Munby" in L. Stanley, *The Auto/biographical I: The Theory and Practice of Feminist Auto-biography* (Manchester: Manchester University Press, 1992) 158; see also P. Backsheider, *Reflections on Biography* (Oxford: Oxford University Press, 1999).

117 Drachman, *Sisters in Law*, 40-ff. Both Arabella Mansfield and Ada Kepley, two pioneer women lawyers in the United States, articled with male relatives. See Chapter One.

Robinson Wright and Hewson Knight articled with family members. Significantly, the four women with family connections to the legal profession did not practise law for long. Robinson Wright, Hewson Knight, and Buckley Laughton married during or soon after law school and then ceased to practise law, and McNulty Fix married somewhat later, after leaving law practice for a business career.[118] In contrast, the three women who worked in law settings and then entered the law school as matriculants never married and practised law for many years in Ontario: Alford in Trenton and Cherrier in Hamilton had their own private practices, and Palen had a successful career in the public service after a decade in private practice.

In addition to family connections to the legal profession, several early women lawyers obtained articling experiences through family business connections to the legal profession.[119] Thus, William Powley's business in Port Arthur, including his suit for wrongful dismissal, may have established a connection to F.H. Keefer for Eva Powley.[120] Similarly, William Alford's business in Belleville may have opened up an opportunity for his daughter at the firm of M.C. Mikel. In addition, several early women lawyers were from middle-class families: Paterson's family supported her studies at McGill and at the law school in Toronto, and Cairns Morris's parents were farmers who supported her and her three brothers at university. In contrast to these family and business connections, there is less information about the economic circumstances of Cherrier in Hamilton and Palen in Belleville, both of whom were matriculants and older than most women in this cohort. They may have financed law studies after working for several years, as did Cairns Morris. Thus, although some pioneering professionals came from modest origins, a majority entered the legal profession from middle-class backgrounds."[121]

118 These early women lawyers conformed to the societal convention of the marriage-career dichotomy identified by Petersson: S. Petersson, "Ruby Clements and Early Women of the Alberta Bar" (1997) 9 *Canadian Journal of Women and the Law* 365 at 388–89. See also Chapter One.

119 E. Smyth et al., *Challenging Professions: Historical and Contemporary Perspectives on Women's Professional Work* (Toronto: University of Toronto Press, 1999) 5.

120 Powley's communication to the Law Society in the mid-1890s, explaining that she was postponing law school because she did not have sufficient funds, is somewhat puzzling. Her later attendance at Trinity College on scholarship while also attending law school lectures may suggest she did not have her parents' support, or perhaps their approval.

121 Smyth et al., *Challenging Professions*, 7.

In addition, all the women lawyers in this earliest cohort were white. Although some had parents who had immigrated to Canada, they had generally originated in the British Isles. With the possible exception of Cherrier in Hamilton, they were all anglophones, and all except McNulty and Cherrier were Protestant. Significantly, both these Catholic women came from Ottawa and Hamilton at a time when 75 per cent of Toronto's population was Protestant, especially Anglican, Presbyterian, and Methodist.[122] Moreover, although the Jewish population in Toronto was increasing, especially after the First World War, the first Jewish women were not called to the bar until the late 1920s, and the first Black and Indigenous women did not become lawyers until the 1960s and '70s. In contrast to male members of the legal profession, issues about diversity did not challenge the culture of women lawyers until later decades.[123]

Only four of these women were university graduates like Martin: Powley, Cairns Morris, Paterson Read and Buckley Laughton. All the others, including three of the women with family members in the legal profession (Robinson Wright, Hewson Knight, and McNulty Fix), were admitted to the bar as matriculants after five years of articles. This pattern may suggest that, among members of the legal profession, articling was regarded as the preferred path to the profession, a "culture of legal practice" that was preferable to university education. There is also evidence that some male lawyers were supportive of women's aspirations to be admitted to the legal profession—although they may have been less enthused about women in private practice. Indeed, only Powley, Alford, Cherrier, and Palen worked in private practice, and both Powley and Palen did so for only a decade. Significantly, none of these four women married. Were they primarily seeking financial independence, or simply recognizing that marriage was not an option in the context of the carnage of the First World War? Or did they

122 Miller, *Our Glory and Our Grief*, Appendix B.

123 Some Jewish women lawyers experienced exclusion from both the WLAO and the women lawyers' sorority, Kappa Beta Pi: see Part Two. In addition, the discovery in the 1990s of antisemitic sentiments in Martin's letter to the Attorney General suggests that some women challenged male exclusivity in the legal profession but without recognizing its other exclusionary practices: see Chapter One. Christopher Moore concluded that although the Law Society did not practise formal discrimination itself, law firms often precluded articling or employment for Jewish students, both male and female: Moore, *The Law Society of Upper Canada*, 199–202. See also Parts Two and Three.

intentionally eschew marriage so as to "adopt professional lives parallel to men's"?[124]

Interestingly, the two women who married and continued to practice law constitute a significant pattern because both practised law with their spouses. Paterson Read was a sole practitioner for a few years and then became the law partner of Hamilton Read in Vancouver. The partners married after the death of Read's first wife, and Paterson Read engaged in a successful legal practice in Vancouver for more than fifty years. More significantly, Cairns Morris in Hamilton was not only the first Ontario woman lawyer to marry a classmate and practise law alongside her spouse, but she also seems to be the first woman to practise law as a mother. Then, after her husband declared bankruptcy and was disbarred in the 1930s, she took over the firm. Later, she practised law with her daughter, who was called to the bar in 1959. Although Cairns Morris's practice was partly a response to her husband's misfortune, her success confirms her legal ability and a strong determination to persevere.

There is evidence that some early women lawyers were interested in women's organizations and politics. Mary Buckley Laughton's work at the Big Sisters Associations and Jean Cairns Morris's participation in the Provincial Council of Women suggest that they used their legal education to support women's interests. Moreover, like Clara Brett Martin, who was elected a school trustee, Mary McNulty Fix was highly successful in the 1950s as a local politician in Mississauga, and Edith Paterson became a Conservative candidate just a few years after her call to the bar in British Columbia. Most women lawyers in this cohort also joined the WLAO, although not all remained active, especially if they were practising law in communities outside Toronto. Moreover, some women lawyers who married remained welcome members of the WLAO, even though they were not in legal practice, an arrangement that resulted in the creation of a second organization, Kappa Beta Pi, for women lawyers in active legal practice.[125]

Another similarity among these women is quite striking: only Clara Brett Martin and Mary Buckley Laughton developed connections to

124 A. Harris, *Broken Patterns: Professional Women and the Quest for a New Feminine Identity* (Detroit: Wayne State University Press, 1995). See also N.F. Cott, *The Grounding of Modern Feminism* (New Haven, CT: Yale University Press, 1987), which presents the argument that the loss of men's lives in war necessitates women's financial independence; and Moore, *The Law Society of Upper Canada*, 191–94.

125 See Part Two.

Toronto after arriving from nearby communities. All the others came to the law school at Osgoode Hall from relatively distant parts of Ontario: Ottawa and Belleville in the east; Port Arthur, Huntsville, and Barrie in the north; and Hamilton and St. Thomas southwest of Toronto. And, of course, Paterson Read came from Vancouver. Clearly, travel and accommodation arrangements for women in the early decades of the twentieth century often created special challenges. Significantly, Powley was accompanied by her married sister, Hilda Hazelwood, when she travelled to Toronto for exams in April 1897.

While it is puzzling that few women in Toronto responded to Martin's success in opening the bar to women, this pattern may confirm the highly exclusive professional culture in Toronto in these decades, when the gentleman's legal profession was clearly defined in terms of class and family connections—as well as gender. In this context, all but Palen returned to their home locations to practise law, and Palen eventually abandoned private practice to work in government. These early patterns suggest a dominant elite male culture in private practice in the early twentieth century, and especially in Toronto.

Overall, these stories of women who became lawyers in Ontario in this cohort between 1897 and 1918 reveal early gendered patterns in the legal profession in relation to women's aspirations to become lawyers. In documenting how early women lawyers confronted the constraints of both legal traditions and societal norms, stories of their experiences reveal a kaleidoscope of puzzles and patterns, some of which continued to challenge later generations of women lawyers. Thus, as Backscheider suggested, "the great questions of biography are the essential questions about human experience in the world."[126]

126 Backsheider, *Reflections on Biography*, 59.

# PART TWO

## *Opportunities and Barriers: The Interwar Years, 1919–39*

# *After the First World War: A "Turning Point" for Women?*

> *World War I ... was a turning point for Canada as a nation. The Canada of 1919 was profoundly different from the Canada of 1914 in several fundamental aspects—demographic, economic, political, and social. Wracked internally by divisions between French and English, east and west, labour and capital, and plunged into a serious recession, the emerging nation stood poised on the brink of an uncertain future ... The Canadian inter-war experience can best be described as turbulent. The transition from a wartime to a peacetime economy was a painful one, particularly for women workers.*[1]

When the First World War ended in November 1918, "it was expected that women would cheerfully surrender their newly acquired positions in the workforce." The social and economic dislocation at war's end reinforced the belief, prevalent before 1914, that working women should not compete for men's jobs but rather work in traditional female jobs, often with inadequate wages. Moreover, although "the 1920s were difficult years for women workers, the 1930s were disastrous." As the Depression spread, the "deep-seated prejudice against married women working outside the home intensified, and the appropriateness even of single women working for

1 A. Prentice et al., *Canadian Women: A History*, 2nd ed. (Toronto: Harcourt Brace Canada, 1996) 244. Although the Canadian economy was relatively buoyant in the mid- to late 1920s, the Depression after 1929 created hardships for many Canadian families.

wages, widely conceded during the 1920s, was now called into question." Women professionals also faced criticism for taking away men's jobs, and traditional views about women's frailty as well as exclusion from articling positions created major barriers for women as law students and lawyers.[2]

Canada's contributions to the war effort resulted in a modest presence, along with other Dominions and India, at the Peace Conference that led to the Treaty of Versailles in 1919. Canada also became a member of the League of Nations and the International Labour Organization, providing additional opportunities to participate as an independent nation in the international sphere.[3] Changes also occurred in Canadian politics when Mackenzie King succeeded Laurier as leader of the Liberal Party in 1919 and became Prime Minister in 1921. In addition, Agnes Macphail became the first woman elected to the House of Commons in 1921, as a member of the National Progressive Party (later CCF). Her success may have inspired women to seek roles in public life.[4] Except for a brief period in 1926 and then during the Conservative government of R.B. Bennett (1930–35), King's Liberals formed the federal government throughout the interwar period and the Second World War.[5]

In Ontario, Premier William Hearst's Conservatives were defeated in the provincial election in 1919 by a coalition of the United Farmers of Ontario and the Independent Labour Party, under the leadership of E.C. Drury, the "Farmer Premier." In 1921, the Drury government enacted legislation to finance and support agricultural development, including

2 G. Cuthbert Brandt et al., *Canadian Women: A History*, 3rd ed. (Toronto: Nelson Education, 2011) 289, 301–8. Many women lawyers found employment in government rather than private practice.

3 D. Creighton, *Canada's First Century, 1867–1967* (Toronto: MacMillan, 1970) 151–57.

4 R. Wyatt, *Agnes Macphail: Champion of the Underdog* (Lantzville, BC: XYZ Publishing, 2000). Macphail joined the National Progressive Party and participated in founding the CCF in the 1930s. She was re-elected federally until 1940, and in 1943, Macphail and Rae Luckock became the first women elected to the Ontario legislature: D. French, "Agnes Macphail" in M.Q. Innis, ed., *The Clear Spirit: Twenty Canadian Women and Their Times* (Toronto: University of Toronto Press, 1966) 179; T. Crowley, *Agnes Macphail and the Politics of Equality* (Toronto: Lorimer, 1990); and *Globe and Mail* (4 December 2021) O4.

5 The Liberals had requested a dissolution of Parliament in 1926, which Governor General Viscount Byng refused to grant. The incident is known as the King-Byng Affair. See Creighton, *Canada's First Century*, 198–99, 252; H. Blair Neatby and R. MacGregor Dawson, *William Lyon Mackenzie King: The Lonely Heights, 1924–1932* (Toronto: University of Toronto Press, 1963); and P.B. Waite, *In Search of R.B. Bennett* (Montreal and Kingston: McGill-Queen's University Press, 2012).

the Agricultural Development Board and the *Ontario Farm Loans Act*, and a number of women lawyers obtained employment in these public-sector positions from the late 1920s to the 1940s.[6] Prohibition, initially enacted by the Hearst government in 1916, was enforced more vigorously by Premier Drury's coalition government, but alcohol remained widely available at social occasions, including at Osgoode Hall. The Conservatives remained in power in Ontario until 1934, when Premier Mitch Hepburn's Liberals formed a government with promises to introduce austerity programs, some of which affected employment for women lawyers in government, creating a "cause célèbre" for the Women's Law Association of Ontario (WLAO) in the 1930s.[7]

Some women lawyers in the interwar years became involved in the social causes of these decades, including support for strikes and labour unrest after the war. One report identified 428 strikes in Canada involving 150,000 workers, including the Winnipeg General Strike in May and

6 P. Oliver, *Public and Private Persons: The Ontario Political Culture, 1914–1934* (Toronto: Clarke, Irwin, 1975) 20–21, 30; J.D. Hoffman, *Farmer-Labour Government in Ontario* (MA thesis, University of Toronto, 1959) [unpublished]; and J. MacLeod, *The United Farmer Movement in Ontario* (MA thesis, Queens University, 1958) [unpublished]. See also *Agricultural Development Finance Act* (1921); *Agricultural Development Act* (1921); and *Ontario Farm Loans Act* (1921). The Agricultural Development Board issued bonds and debentures, secured by mortgages held by the board, and the funds provided loans to recipients to acquire land for agricultural purposes and erect farm buildings: E. Lang, *Handy Guide to the Laws of Ontario* (Toronto: Copp Clark, 1918, 1923, 1929).

7 *Ontario Temperance Act*, SO 1916, c 217. Doctors, who could write prescriptions for alcohol, wrote 650,000 prescriptions in 1920. See also G. Hallowell, *Prohibition in Ontario, 1919–1923* (Ottawa: Lowe, 1972); C. Heron, *Booze: A Distilled History* (Toronto: Between the Lines, 2003); Oliver, *Public and Private Persons*, 22–25, 76–77; P. Oliver, *G. Howard Ferguson: Ontario Tory* (Toronto: University of Toronto Press/Ontario Historical Studies Series, 1977); C.I. Kyer, "Parading Their Ignorance of Financial Transactions: The Smith/Jarvis Fraud Trial of 1924" (2021) 36 *Banking and Finance Law Review* 339; Creighton, *Canada's First Century*, 198–99, 211–12, 238–39, 252; J. Saywell, *"Just Call Me Mitch": The Life of Mitchell F. Hepburn* (Toronto: University of Toronto Press, 1991); and Chapter Four.

June 1919, which included workers in both private and public sectors.[8] Although women workers and returning soldiers both faced difficulty finding employment as the immediate economic boom after the war deteriorated briefly into a depression in 1921, an "upward swing" in the economy occurred in 1923 and remained throughout the 1920s. Export prices moved upwards, Canada's share of the world wheat market was three times more than it had been during the early twentieth-century boom, immigration rose, and capital returned to support construction projects. In addition, there was expansion of the railways and new utilities, growth in cities and an emerging financial services sector, all of which created significant legal work. Thus, in the first decade after the First World War, there were rising economic prospects in Canada, including for lawyers: "Business [was] good throughout the 1920s, as the profession put the war behind it . . . with industrial development, resource exploitation, a booming securities trade, and the rise of new fields of litigation."[9] At the same time, male lawyers—more often than women lawyers—benefitted from many of these changes.

After some stagnation at the beginning of the twentieth century, the number of lawyers began to increase significantly. A report in 1922 noted that while Ontario's population had increased 16 per cent since 1911, the number of lawyers had increased by 40 per cent. Moreover, between 1921 and 1931, there was a one-third increase in the number of lawyers in Ontario, a situation that resulted in protests about overcrowding—as well

8 R. Kramer and T. Mitchell, *When the State Trembled: How A.J. Andrews and The Citizens' Committee Broke the Winnipeg General Strike* (Toronto: University of Toronto Press, 2010); and *Globe and Mail* (11 May 2019) 1, 6–7. These strikes arguably frightened some of the Canadian middle class, who regarded them as "a prelude to the establishment of a Soviet form of government in Canada": L.-R. Betcherman, *The Little Band: The Clashes between the Communists and the Canadian Establishment 1928–1932* (Ottawa: Deneau Publishers, 1982), "Introduction" and "Epilogue," 215. Betcherman reveals how law-and-order forces were used to overcome democratic freedoms, including the enactment of section 98 of the *Criminal Code*, which criminalized attendance at meetings deemed revolutionary. Some lawyers, including women lawyers, were members of the Communist Party in Ontario.

9 Creighton, *Canada's First Century*, 177–78; C. Wilton, "Introduction" in C. Wilton, ed., *Inside the Law: Canadian Law Firms in Historical Perspective* (Toronto: Osgoode Society for Canadian Legal History/University of Toronto Press, 1996) 13 at 16; and C. Moore, *The Law Society of Upper Canada and Ontario's Lawyers, 1797–1997* (Toronto: University of Toronto Press, 1997) 195.

as increasing concerns about lax admission standards at Osgoode Hall.[10] In addition, the prosperity enjoyed by the legal profession in the 1920s was sharply curtailed for many, including women lawyers, following the Stock Market crash in October 1929. Mass unemployment and poverty spread across much of Canada, and the situation was exacerbated by the collapse of the international wheat market in 1929 and drought on the Prairies during the 1930s:

> At the nadir of the Depression, half the wage earners in Canada were on some form of relief. One Canadian in five was a public dependant. Forty per cent of those in the workforce had no skills; the average yearly income was less than five hundred dollars at a time when the poverty line for a family of four was estimated at more than twice that amount. [Moreover,] the army of the deprived was treated shabbily by ... government.[11]

Although Ontario lawyers were not immune to these challenges in the 1930s, some continued to enjoy the prosperity they had experienced in the

10 *Globe* (16 March 1922), reporting a comment by the president of the Ontario Bar Association. See also Moore, *The Law Society of Upper Canada,* 195–96, who noted that lawyers' numbers decreased in the 1930s. Significantly, the Ontario Bar Association passed forty resolutions relating to "unqualified practitioners" in 1919 and 1920: P.J. Giffen, "Social Control and Professional Self-Government: A Study of the Legal Profession in Canada" in S.D. Clark, *Urbanism and the Changing Canadian Society* (Toronto: University of Toronto Press, 1961) 127. For the Law Society's "relaxed" academic standards after the First World War, see Chapter Two.

11 P. Berton, *The Great Depression, 1929–1939* (Toronto: McClelland and Stewart, 1990) 9–10. Regarding the federal government's decision to service the railroad debt rather than provide help to Canadians, Berton argued, "Without that burden of debt the government could have doubled its relief payments to every family in Canada." See also M. Horn, ed., *The Dirty Thirties: Canadians in the Great Depression* (Toronto: Copp Clark, 1972); and J. Struthers, *No Fault of Their Own: Unemployment and the Canadian Welfare State, 1914–1941* (Toronto: University of Toronto Press, 1983). The Communist Party of Canada, established in the 1920s, began to organize nationwide protests of the unemployed: Betcherman, *The Little Band,* 86–88. Relief programs, which often focused on temporary and seasonal assistance, were unable to cope with the number of needy families. In Toronto, 35,000 people had registered with the city's Unemployment Bureau by the mid-1930s, but neither the city's Welfare Commissioner nor Ontario Premier Hepburn wanted to create an accommodation that was "too comfortable." The premier remained convinced that "any single boy with initiative and backbone" could find a job: G. Heroux and B. Palmer, "Housing the Poor during the Great Depression," *Toronto Star* (30 July 2017) A15.

1920s, while others, including some women lawyers, faced grave economic challenges.

By 1919, the Legal Education Committee of the Canadian Bar Association (CBA) was earnestly developing recommendations to promote uniformity in legal education in Canada, including higher admission requirements, such as completion of at least one year of a university BA program. The CBA committee also recommended that office attendance be suspended during months when students were attending law school lectures, enabling students to better focus on their studies. In September 1920, a proposed standard curriculum for legal education was adopted at the Association's annual meeting: it included eight courses in year one: Contracts, Torts, Property I, Constitutional History, Criminal Law, Practice and Procedure (Elementary), History of English Law, and Jurisprudence. There were also eleven mandatory courses in year two and fourteen in year three. Although some Ontario lawyers expressed support for these proposed reforms, the Law Society in Ontario expressed no interest in substantive changes to its admission requirements, the curriculum of its law school or its primary focus on office work for Ontario law students.[12]

In 1923, Principal Hoyles resigned at the age of seventy-nine, after twenty-eight years as Principal of the Law School. He was remembered fondly by students, including women law students, for his gentlemanly qualities and graciousness, but students also recalled his difficulty teaching divorce cases in Conflicts of Laws: "Only by endless circumlocutions

12 B. Bucknall, T. Baldwin, and J. Lakin, "Pedants, Practitioners and Prophets: Legal Education at Osgoode Hall to 1957" (1968) 6:2 *Osgoode Hall Law Journal* 139 at 182–84, citing (1920) 5 *Proceedings of the Canadian Bar Association* 250. The CBA model was based on the Dalhousie Law School curriculum, and it also reflected "prairie social thought, political vision and legal culture" and the views of practising lawyers such as James Aikins and H.A. Robson of Manitoba: Moore, *The Law Society of Upper Canada,* 215; and W.W. Pue, "Common Law Legal Education in Canada's Age of Light, Soap and Water" (1996) 23 *Manitoba Law Journal* 654 at 674–85. The Law Society in Ontario made no effort to adopt the standard curriculum: (1921) *Proceedings of the Canadian Bar Association* 242. See also W.W. Pue, "Canadian Legal Education, 1900–1930" in R. McQueen and W.W. Pue, eds., *Misplaced Traditions: British Lawyers, Colonial Peoples,* symposium issue (1998–1999) 16:1 *Law in Context* 80; W.W. Pue, "Cultural Projects and Structural Transformation in the Canadian Legal Profession" in W.W. Pue and D. Sugarman, eds., *Lawyers and Vampires: Cultural Histories of the Legal Professions* (Oxford: Hart Publishing, 2003) 367; and R.V. Maclennan, "Legal Education in Canada" (1922) *Canadian Law Times* 319. Maclennan's daughter Elizabeth was called to the Ontario bar in 1927: see Chapter Three.

could he reconstruct an adultery in words discreet enough for ladies' ears." The new Dean, John Falconbridge, had been associated with the law school for two decades as an examiner and lecturer, and he was much more enthusiastic about research and scholarship than his predecessor. In 1923, Falconbridge was the only full-time staff member at the law school, along with four part-time lecturers, and the law school consisted of three overcrowded classrooms and a library of only 2,500 books. In addition, the school had "no name, no yearbook, no separate budget and no public functions." The Lawyers Club, established in 1922, made a series of recommendations to the new Dean, suggesting a full-time program of study for three years followed by one year of full-time articling, as well as recommending that the law school's Dean should have control over courses of study and law school staff, replacing the role of the Law Society's Legal Education Committee. These suggestions were studiously ignored, with the result that "the Ontario law student [in 1923] found himself in a position essentially unchanged from that occupied by his predecessors of twenty or thirty years earlier."[13]

At the same time, Dean Falconbridge obtained the Law Society's approval for a library budget four times larger than in the previous year, and the Legal Education Committee approved the appointment of a second full-time staff member, the introduction of new teaching methods, and the elimination of examiners appointed by the Law Society. In 1923, the law school also finally acquired its own name: "Osgoode Hall Law School." Dean Falconbridge attracted Donald MacRae from Dalhousie Law School, whose credentials included a PhD and experience as past Chair of the Legal Education Committee of the CBA. He was a "kindred spirit" to Dean Falconbridge when it came to reform of legal education. In 1925, Sidney Smith became the third full-time member of staff, and in 1927, a recent graduate, Cecil (Caesar) Wright, was appointed after completing graduate

13 Bucknall, Baldwin, and Lakin, "Pedants, Practitioners and Prophets," 184–89. As the authors noted, students contributed about 60 per cent of the Law Society's total budget, although law school costs amounted to only 20 per cent. See also S. Denison, "Legal Education in Ontario" (1924) *Canadian Bar Review* 85 at 87, 90.

work at Harvard.[14] As early as 1931, some women lawyers forwarded a suggestion to the Law Society that a woman lecturer should be appointed, but the recommendation was not seriously considered—if at all.[15]

In May 1926, with strong support from the CBA, Dean Falconbridge raised the admission requirements for new entrants to at least two years of university studies, thereby eliminating the admission of matriculants after 1926. He also expanded the number and scope of lectures; by 1928, nine hundred lectures were being presented annually from September to May. The case method of teaching, introduced at Harvard in the late nineteenth century, was reportedly being used in nine courses, and English and American texts were being replaced by in-house Canadian legal course materials. By 1931, seventeen out of twenty-two subjects being taught at the law school were using materials prepared by Osgoode faculty. Despite these reforms, the Law Society continued to suggest that the "tendency to emphasize unduly the academic training at the expense of efficient office

14 Bucknall, Baldwin, and Lakin, "Pedants, Practitioners and Prophets," 192–ff. The Legal Education Committee suggested that teaching staff adopt different methods to replace formal lectures, noting that some students were passing examinations by "reading typewritten notes purchased from their predecessors." Sidney Smith was later appointed president of the University of Toronto. MacRae had initiated significant reform at Dalhousie Law School during the First World War, and his work with the CBA resulted in the Dalhousie curriculum becoming the template for the CBA recommendations and common law schools in Canada. Like Dean Falconbridge, MacRae published articles on legal topics, particularly after the establishment of the *Canadian Bar Review* in 1923: Willis, *A History of Dalhousie Law School* (London: Stevens and Sons, 1969) 74–75, 78–80, 87.

15 Law Society of Ontario (LSO) Archives, Women's Law Association of Ontario (WLAO) fonds, Scrapbook (SB), vol. 2, *Mail* (24 January 1931). At a WLAO meeting concerning the appointment of a woman judge in the Juvenile Court in Hamilton, members adopted a motion based on a report by WLAO President Grace Hunter (1926): "That the time has also arrived when there should be a woman lecturer on the staff of Osgoode Hall Law School."

training" was inappropriate, and that the study of authoritative textbooks was preferable to the case method.[16]

During the First World War, there had been a modest increase in the number of women law students, so larger numbers of women were called to the bar in the early 1920s. Like Mary McNulty (1918) in Ottawa, some women may have decided to study law to replace brothers, cousins, and friends who were lawyers and serving in the war.[17] Prior to 1926, both men and women students had been admitted to the bar as matriculants, after serving five years in articles. Admission requirements were again relaxed during the Depression in 1932 to ensure that "the student who was less favoured with worldly goods" might still enter the legal profession.[18] In this way, some women, as well as men, were called to the bar without attending university in both decades of the interwar years.

The number of women lawyers increased in the interwar years, especially in the 1920s. Even though organizers of women's war work regularly emphasized that women were needed to replace enlisted men *only* for the duration of the war, women employed in war industries acquired new skills, as well as greater confidence, in the paid workforce. At the Canadian

16 Bucknall, Baldwin, and Lakin, "Pedants, Practitioners and Prophets," 193–95, 199–201. Dean Falconbridge was publicly congratulated on his achievement in raising admission standards by the editor in (1926) 4 *Canadian Bar Review* 329. Significantly, matriculants became eligible for admission again during the Depression in the 1930s. To support the emphasis on office training, the law school's calendars after 1937 included an essay on "Office Training." In addition, oral examinations by eminent practitioners were reintroduced. At the same time, the Law Society's regulation of articling arrangements for students often revealed important lapses.

17 E. Huckle, "List of Women Barristers and Solicitors in Ontario" (1897–1975) [unpublished, archived at Law Society of Ontario Archives]. See also J. Hagan and F. Kay, "Hierarchy in Practice: The Significance of Gender in Ontario Law Firms" in Wilton, ed., *Inside the Law*, 530 at 535; and Moore, *The Law Society of Upper Canada*, 205. For McNulty (1918), see Chapter Two. Elizabeth Maclennan (1927) also entered the legal profession after her brother died in the First World War: "The Way Things Were: The Alumni Voices Project" (Winter 2014) *Continuum* (Osgoode Hall Law School) 32.

18 Bucknall, Baldwin, and Lakin, "Pedants, Practitioners and Prophets," 196–97; and "Low Standards Deplored," *Obiter Dicta* (December 1932), reprinted in Law Society of Upper Canada (2002) *Gazette*, 40–41. Incongruously, the Law Society raised the articling fee in the 1930s from $50 to $100 and tuition fees from $100 to $150. The revival of matriculant admission may have had little impact. By 1937, there were ninety-two university graduates and only nine matriculants in the first-year class: Bucknall, Baldwin, and Lakin, "Pedants, Practitioners and Prophets," 200, citing F.C. Cronkite, "Legal Education—Which Trend" (1935) 13 *Canadian Bar Review* 359 at 366.

National Exhibition (CNE) in 1918, for example, women participated in demonstrations of wartime nursing but also in using lathes, handling tractors, and working industrial machinery: "They did not seem like the same women of a year ago." Historian Naomi Griffiths also identified how, after the war, "women . . . were entering work that had previously been the preserve of the male," including not only the professions (lawyers and doctors) but also construction work, and fishing and trapping.[19] Women's work experiences during the war—as well as a need for financial independence following it, when the carnage of war made the prospect of marriage less likely and when some women had no interest in marriage at all—enhanced their aspirations for legal work.[20]

Nonetheless, women who engaged in paid work represented just a small minority of adult women. For example, the 1931 census reported that 82.7 per cent of Canadian women had married by the age of forty-four, and many of them were not employed in the workforce after marriage.[21] At the same time, an article in a woman's magazine in 1919 encouraged some

19 I.H.M. Miller, *Our Glory and Our Grief: Torontonians and the Great War* (Toronto: University of Toronto Press, 2002) 128, 183, citing *News* (29 August 1918) 7; and N. Griffiths, *Penelope's Web: Some Perceptions of Women in European and Canadian Society* (Toronto: Oxford University Press, 1976) 184–85. By 1931, 46 per cent of Canadian women aged twenty to twenty-four were involved in paid work. In addition, more women were entering higher education: the percentage of women university students rose from 11 per cent in 1900 to 14 per cent in 1919–20, and the creation of women's organizations in earlier decades provided many women with experiences of organizing for change: Prentice et al., *Canadian Women,* 2nd ed., 175, Tables A.8, A.9, and 214–20. The goals of "maternal" suffragists, often married women who were not engaged in paid work, tended to differ from those of women seeking financial independence by working alongside men: S. Bashevkin, "Independence versus Partisanship: Dilemmas in the Political History of Women in English Canada" in V. Strong-Boag and A. Claire Fellman, eds., *Rethinking Canada: The Promise of Women's History* (Toronto: Copp Clark Pitman, 1986) 246 at 250, 253–54; and D. Gorham, "Flora MacDonald Denison: Canadian Feminist" in L. Kealey, ed., *A Not Unreasonable Claim: Women and Reform in Canada, 1880s–1920s* (Toronto: Women's Press, 1979) 47.

20 L. Marsden, *Canadian Women and the Struggle for Equality* (Don Mills, ON: Oxford University Press, 2012) 65–72, 108–116. As Marsden noted, the ratio of men to women at different times in Canada encouraged or curtailed women's marriage prospects.

21 N.E.S. Griffiths, *The Splendid Vision: Centennial History of the National Council of Women, 1893–1993* (Ottawa: Carleton University Press, 1993) 177, citing Dominion Bureau of Statistics. Although Griffiths acknowledged the NCW's "bourgeois" membership, similar issues affected women in working-class families: J. Sangster, *Dreams of Equality: Women on the Canadian Left, 1920–1950* (Toronto: McClelland and Stewart, 1989) 236–37.

women to study law. It explained, in copious detail, the unpleasant—and unjust—proceedings of a typical theft case in a Toronto court "through the eyes of a woman," suggesting that men had long seen the court as a "dirty, dingy room filled with dirty, dingy, restless people" but had done nothing to improve it. The author argued that the obvious solution to this problem was to have women lawyers and judges.[22]

As early as 1919, women lawyers created their own legal organization. In that year, two women students at the law school, Laura Denton (1920) and Helen Currie (1921) called an initial meeting, which attracted four others: Mary Buckley Laughton (1915), Helen Palen (1918), Apha Hodgins (1919), and Evelyn Harrison (1921). The meeting took place in the law offices of Frank Denton, KC, Laura's father. Although few details of the meeting exist, the group planned an annual meeting for their new organization, the Women's Law Association of Ontario (WLAO). From the beginning, the WLAO welcomed all women admitted to the Ontario bar, including many who were not in active legal practice, as well as all current women students at the law school. The first WLAO meeting took place in 1919 at the Inglewood Tea Rooms on the southwest corner of Spadina Avenue at Bloor Street. Clara Brett Martin was the keynote speaker.[23]

WLAO records indicate that the organization was continuous from 1919, with Mrs. Ward Wright (Geraldine Robinson, 1907) elected president in 1920–21. The first record of the Association, its annual report for 1923–24, provided brief details about each woman called to the bar by that date and noted that eighteen women were then enrolled as student members

22 D.C. Mills, "My Day in Court," *Ladies Home Journal* (February 1919) 15. The *Journal* appeared to anticipate women's admission to the bar: "In this New Day for Women, when her counsel and advice are being sought on every hand but one, why the delay there? Probably because Woman herself hasn't quite 'got around to it yet.' But the day of her getting 'around to it' is so close at hand ... [and] this article is offered for the perusal of our honoured judges, bailiffs, tipstaves and other assistants in our courts."

23 A. Bushby, "The Early Years: Sources of an Enduring Tradition—The Women's Law Association of Ontario, 1919–1950" (80th Anniversary Celebration, 14 January 2000) 2–3. The WLAO's two cofounders addressed the tenth anniversary celebrations of the WLAO on 13 April 1929. In addition, Joy Kennedy Clarry (1951), WLAO President, recounted stories told by her aunt Laura Denton Duff (1920) at a WLAO meeting in 1956. A report of this meeting noted that "five original members" of the 1919 meeting were present for Kennedy Clarry's presentation: Buckley Laughton, Palen, Harrison, Hodgins, and Maw, but it is unclear whether Irene Maw (1925) was a law student in 1919: LSO archives, WLAO fonds, SB, vol. 6, box 98.

of the Association. The report's details of meetings in 1923–24 included a welcome meeting in October, at the summer home of Mary Buckley Laughton (1915) on Centre Island: "Ideal weather and the opportunity of meeting our new members and renewing past acquaintances combined to make a very successful meeting." Another meeting in 1923 recorded the death of Clara Brett Martin and the Association's decision to establish a scholarship in her honour at the law school.[24] The WLAO offered educational lectures as well as social events, fostering a support network for women lawyers in Ontario communities. Since all aspiring lawyers in Ontario were required to attend the "law school" (after 1923, "Osgoode Hall Law School"), the Association easily communicated with the school's women students and graduates, organizing regular events in Toronto and elsewhere in the province. As Cameron Harvey concluded, the WLAO became "the grandmother of the many women lawyers' organizations which exist across Canada in virtually every province."[25]

One special WLAO event occurred in April 1925, when forty-five women lawyers and law students gathered for a celebratory lunch at the King Edward Hotel in honour of Principal Hoyles after his retirement:

> The luncheon was really a corporate declaration of love for one who had during their memorable years, in an embarrassingly and severely masculine atmosphere, been a real father to them all, a model of kindness, a fountain of unfailing sympathy. The luncheon was therefore not a formal affair,

24 For a list of WLAO presidents, see Bushby, "The Early Years." Other WLAO meetings in 1923–24 included presentations about immigration conditions in Canada and about the Juvenile Court. The association held a dance on 14 February 1924 and its annual dinner on 29 March, at which a new executive was appointed. Mrs. Ward Wright rejoined the executive as honorary president. The new executive included both practitioners and non-practitioners, as well as women law students: President Verona Taylor (1920); Vice-President Florence Daley, later Harkins (1922); Secretary Treasurer Edith Sheppard, later Revel (1925); Corresponding Secretary Irene Maw (1925); Archivist Grace Hunter (1926); and the representative to the Local Council of Women, Mary Buckley Laughton (1915): LSO Archives, WLAO fonds, WLAO, annual report, 1923–24. The same report noted that the Ontario Bar Association had extended an invitation to WLAO members to attend the Ontario Bar Association (OBA) meetings in May, even if they were not OBA members.

25 C. Harvey, "Women in Law in Canada" (1970–71) 4 *Manitoba Law Journal* 9 at 27–28. Cameron reported that the first WLAO meeting occurred in October 1923 on Centre Island, but WLAO records are clear that earlier meetings occurred in 1919 and perhaps in 1920–22, even though the first WLAO annual report was not published until 1923–24.

> but an affair of the heart ... Until later years there were seldom more than one or two women in a class. It was Dr. Hoyles who gave them courage to persevere.[26]

In Principal Hoyles' speech, he identified "a special place" for women in law: "He urged them to strengthen the WLAO, keep studying, and attempt to improve laws that concerned women and children." Many women students expressed particular gratitude for Hoyles' support, perhaps hinting at some hidden "silences" about continuing challenges for women law students.[27]

Newspaper social pages in the interwar years recorded regular WLAO lunch and dinner meetings as well as special afternoon tea and garden party events to honour achievements of individual women members. Judges and lawyers were often invited speakers. For example, as President of the CBA, James Aikens addressed a WLAO meeting to report on its

26 *Toronto Daily Star* (25 April 1925). This report stated that forty-five women had graduated from Osgoode by 1925; twenty of them practised law—ten in Toronto, and the others in Trentón, Hamilton, Guelph, Port Colborne, Windsor, Preston, London, and Fort William. This information is confirmed in Huckle, "List of Women Barristers and Solicitors." The report also noted that there were fourteen women students at Osgoode Hall in 1925. See also C. Morgan, "'An Embarrassingly and Severely Masculine Atmosphere': Women, Gender and the Legal Profession at Osgoode Hall, 1920s to 1960s" (1996) 11:2 *Canadian Journal of Law and Society* 19 at 38–39. Morgan suggested that although Hoyles' courtesy and generosity toward women students may have made matters easier for them as individuals, he did little to change the general "atmosphere" at the law school.

27 Morgan, "An Embarrassingly and Severely Masculine Atmosphere" 28. Hoyles also emphasized the need for women judges, perhaps a "swipe at existing juvenile courts" presided over by Margaret Patterson, a woman magistrate who was not a lawyer. See also A. Glasbeek, *Feminized Justice: The Toronto Women's Court, 1913–1934* (Vancouver: UBC Press, 2009); and D. Chunn, *From Punishment to Doing Good: Family Courts and Socialized Justice in Ontario, 1880–1940* (Toronto: University of Toronto Press, 1992). Dean Falconbridge and his wife were also lunch guests; curiously for this occasion, Falconbridge noted Hoyles had "endeared himself" to male law students by his scholarship, industry, and strong sympathy for young men.

activities; he also noted his admiration for women lawyers' "pluck."[28] In this way, the WLAO created an important network for women lawyers, perhaps fostering Clara Brett Martin's hiring of Buckley Laughton (1915) and Dorcas Kelly, later Landriau (1920), as junior lawyers in her firm, as well as Lorna Wilson, later Brigden (1923) as an articling student.[29]

In the mid-1920s, the WLAO's willingness to include members who were non-practising lawyers, frequently because they had married and ceased practice, prompted the creation of a separate women lawyers' organization in 1926: the Alpha Mu chapter of the American woman lawyers' sorority, Kappa Beta Pi. The first legal sorority in the United States, Kappa Beta Pi had been founded by ten women law students at the Chicago Kent College of Law in 1908 to promote high professional standards among women lawyers and students.[30] There were many Kappa Beta Pi chapters in the United States, but the Alpha Mu chapter at Osgoode Hall appears to be the first and only chapter established in Canada.[31] Its membership was restricted to

28 For example, in 1920, three of the women called to the bar in 1918 (Helen Palen, Marie McNulty, and Theresa Cherrier) hosted a lunch for women lawyers and law students, including women in practice outside Toronto: *Globe* (17 February 1920) 10; and LSO Archives, WLAO fonds, SB, vol. 2, unidentified press reports, ca. early 1920s. Aikens spoke to the WLAO at a lunch at the King Edward Hotel about legal and legislative points of national interest and the role of the Canadian Bar Association, "especially in effecting the uniformity of legislation throughout Canada." Dorothy Hennigar, a law graduate of McGill University who was not entitled to practise law in Québec, also attended this meeting: LSO Archives, WLAO fonds, SB, vol. 2. For Sir James Aikens, see Pue, "Common Law Legal Education," 679–83.

29 LSO Archives, WLAO fonds, SB, vol. 1.

30 University of Texas at Austin, Tarlton Law Library, Rare Books and Special Collections, Records of the Kappa Beta Pi legal sorority. See also "History of Kappa Beta Pi Legal Sorority (International)" in *Handbook of Kappa Beta Pi Legal Sorority (International)*, revised 1972, at 9. Since there were no organizations for women lawyers when the sorority was established, it helped "to bind these women lawyers together, to inspire them, or to encourage other women to enter the profession."

31 The Alpha Mu chapter was established at Osgoode Hall Law School on 12 November 1925. Its student members who were later called to the bar included Emily Lynch (1925), Ruby Wigle (1926), Elizabeth Davies (1926), Margaret Hyndman (1926), Laura Lees (1926), Grace Hunter (1926), Ethel Mary Renwick (1926), Bertha Hawkins (1926), Elizabeth Maclennan (1927), Margaret Perney (1927), Elva Dunn (1927), and Gertrude Sinclair (1927). Other student members, including Constance Godfrey, Kathleen Lee, and Elizabeth Mustard, were not admitted to the bar: Huckle, "List of Women Barristers and Solicitors." See also E. Mitchell Thomas, "Sisters-in-Law" (1991) 25:3 *Gazette* 298 at 301.

women students who had achieved good academic records and who later engaged in legal practice, and most members of the sorority in Ontario, at least in early decades, were unmarried. Some Canadian members achieved prominence in the international sorority,[32] and the sorority held two national conventions in Canada. The first took place at the Seigniory Club near Montréal in Québec in 1937, described as "a province which at that time did not permit women to study or practice law!" The second meeting occurred at Niagara Falls in 1947, when Margaret Hyndman (1926) was elected Grand Dean.[33] Some Ontario women lawyers were members of both the WLAO and Kappa Beta Pi. They participated in these two organizations at a time when women lawyers were excluded from male-only clubs and from membership in most professional legal organizations. Thus, these organizations offered women important professional and social support.[34]

32 In 1947, Margaret Hyndman (1926) became the first woman lawyer outside the United States to be elected Grand Dean of Kappa Beta Pi (1947–49). In that year, Margaret Perney (1927) was Grand Registrar and an officer of the sorority, and Judge Helen Kinnear (1920) was an honorary member, along with women judges in the United States: L.Miller Derry, *Digest of Women Lawyers and Judges* (Louisville, KY: Dune Press, 1949) 430–31.

33 "The Golden Anniversary History of Kappa Beta Pi, 1908–1958" (1958) 42:4 *Kappa Beta Pi Quarterly* 1 at 14, 22. See also (1937) 21:2: *Kappa Beta Pi Quarterly*; and LSO Archives, WLAO fonds, SB, vol. 2, "Law Ladies Sorority at Seigneury Club" (1937) 7:7 *Bench and Bar*, identifying Margaret Hyndman (1926), Margaret Perney (1927), and Jean O'Rourke (1931) as attendees. Of course, women could study law in Québec as early as 1911, but they were not eligible to be admitted to the legal profession until 1941: see Chapter One. In 1963, another meeting of Kappa Beta Pi was held at the Royal York Hotel in Toronto, and it included a buffet supper party, a visit to the O'Keefe Centre, and a tour of Osgoode Hall. Justice Gale was the banquet speaker, and the convention chair was Mrs. Helen (Burden) Murray (1954): *Telegram* (22 June 1963). There are no records of Kappa Beta Pi chapters elsewhere in Canada, although an Ontario woman lawyer was instrumental in creating a chapter in Paris: E. Mitchell Thomas, "Sisters-in-Law," 301; and see Gertrude Sinclair (1927), Chapter Three.

34 The sorority's Alpha Mu chapter was disbanded in the 1980s. At a celebratory dinner in 1983, after the election of Laura Legge (1948) as the first woman Treasurer of the Law Society, Margaret Hyndman (1926) presented the Alpha Mu charter to Legge: *Globe and Mail* (27 October 1983). The charter is now lodged in the Law Society Archives, but few other records of the Alpha Mu chapter have been located. In contrast, the WLAO celebrated its centenary in a gala event in 2019, and it continues as a networking organization for Ontario women lawyers. WLAO records are in the Law Society of Ontario Archives.

CHAPTER THREE

# *Pioneers and Prejudice: After the War, 1919-29*

> *During the past year in Ontario women barristers could be heard in the Courts from Police to Appellate and a Toronto paper quotes its Ottawa correspondent as follows: "And it is no longer a frontpage news item if a Portia appears in a Canadian Law Court." In spite of this encouraging newspaper note, Law is a pioneer field for women although prejudice is fast disappearing and people are acknowledging that women practise Law for the same reasons as do their fathers, brothers or cousins and with as much earnestness and ambition. Possibly there are a few gentlemen—even in the profession who speak disparagingly of women lawyers and in the next breath quote the Statutes of Ann, Elizabeth and Victoria.*[1]

Ruby Wigle's article about women in law appeared not long after she was called to the Ontario bar in January 1926. Among other issues, she explained that a large number of women lawyers left practice for marriage, describing the "marriage or career dichotomy" as "regrettable, but too complicated to discuss here."[2] An American study of women's lives between 1920 and 1940 explained in more detail that marriage often precluded paid work for most white women in the interwar years: "Most

1 R. Wigle, "Sisters in Law" (1927) 6 *Canadian Bar Review* 419 at 420.

2 Wigle, 422. Wigle (1926), discussed later in this chapter, eventually married and continued to practise law for some years.

married white women resisted gainful employment because, in spite of economic pressures, societal and domestic demands exerted an even greater influence. Housework and childcare took up much of their time, and society did not provide the necessary services to lighten that load. Public opinion was also resistant to the employment of married women and jobs were rarely available."[3] This context is reflected in the stories of some women law graduates in the 1920s, although others who married sometimes practised law in the 1930s because of financial necessity. Other women lawyers—who did not marry—engaged in the practice of law for many years, and often into old age.

In 1919, five women were called to the bar. Prior to their graduation, they were honoured guests at a celebratory dinner hosted by women students in the first and second years at the law school.[4] Among these five women, two engaged in private practice for many years. One practitioner was Apha Hodgins, who was present at the WLAO's founding meeting. She graduated with honours, and she was the first woman to earn the highest mark in a law school course when she won the Bicknell Prize for highest standing in Commercial Law. Hodgins was born in Lucan (now Lucan Biddulph) in southwestern Ontario, and although she attended the University of Toronto and enrolled as a student at the law school for one year in 1913, she was called to the bar as a matriculant. Hodgins articled with A.J.R. Snow, KC, and George Kappelle, office referee, and later with F.C. Jarvis of McPherson, Campbell & Jarvis in Toronto.

After her call to the bar in June 1919, she worked for two years as secretary to Ralph Hodder-Williams who was writing a regimental history. She later did legal work related to wills and trust agreements in insurance agency offices. In the early 1930s, she may have established a sole practice, and she was briefly associated later in that decade with G.M. Wilton's mining-law practice in Toronto. In the 1940s, Hodgins relocated to

3 W. Wandersee, *Women's Work and Family Values, 1920–1940* (Cambridge, MA: Harvard University Press, 1981) 2. A report in 1929 about women doctors, dentists, and lawyers quoted WLAO President Marion James (1922), who identified sixty-eight women lawyers. Nineteen were married, and some married women lawyers were practising law: Law Society of Ontario (LSO) Archives, Women's Law Association of Ontario (WLAO) fonds, Scrapbook (SB), vol. 1, unidentified news report, ca. 1929–30. See also N. Griffiths, *The Splendid Vision: Centennial History of the National Council of Women of Canada, 1893–1993* (Ottawa: Carleton University Press, 1993) 177; and the Epilogue.

4 *Globe* (3 April 1919) 8.

Bowmanville and set up a sole practice. Her obituary stated that she had been self-employed in Bowmanville for forty years and was a well-known and respected citizen. Hodgins was Bowmanville's only woman legal practitioner for many decades, and she became the first woman President of the Northumberland Law Association in the 1950s. She was a regular participant in WLAO activities, serving as President between 1933–34 and 1935–36, and she became a life member of the Law Society in 1969. Hodgins died in 1983 at the age of ninety-one, having retired from her legal practice just five years earlier.[5]

Norma Lown, who was also admitted to the bar in June 1919, may have engaged in a sole practice in the mid-1920s on Richmond Street West. She had entered the law school as a matriculant and was called to the bar at the age of thirty. For a few years in the early 1930s, she was employed at Starr, Spence & Company, doing stock certificate transfers and company law, but she discontinued practice in 1936 because of illness.[6]

In September 1919, two women were called to the bar, both having passed the final exams with honours. Aileen Silk, later Bicknell (the woman who had proposed the toast at the WLAO's celebratory dinner in 1927 "to the Osgoode Hall graduates of 1987") had graduated from the University of Toronto in 1916 and articled with Judge Gauld in Hamilton and at Johnston, McKay, Dodds & Grant. She worked briefly as a junior solicitor with the latter until her marriage to James Bicknell in 1923, but she did not practise law thereafter. Silk Bicknell died in 1943.[7]

Muriel Lee, also a graduate of the University of Toronto in 1916, articled and was called to the bar in September 1919. She worked in the law firm of her father, Lyman Lee, KC, in Hamilton. Lee was the fifteenth woman to be

5 LSO Archives, Ontario Bar Biographical Research Project (OBBRP), "Apha Hodgins"; and LSO Archives, "Diversifying the Bar," Apha Hodgins. Hodgins was listed in Toronto at 48 King Street West in 1931 and at 30 University Avenue the following year. In 1938, her name was listed in parentheses at the firm of G.M. Wilton in the Victory Building in Toronto. By 1946, Hodgins was practising in Bowmanville at 10 Duke Street, and she continued to practise law there until her retirement: *Canadian Law Lists*. See also LSO Archives, WLAO fonds, SB, vol. 1, obituary; and LSO Archives, WLAO, annual report, 1923–24.

6 LSO Archives, "Diversifying the Bar," Norma Lown; LSO Archives, OBBRP, "Norma Lown"; and *Canadian Law Lists*.

7 Silk Bicknell had served with Lovedy Campeau on the Fourth-Year Executive at University College: (1916) *Torontogenesis* 39; and *Globe* (6 May 1919). See also LSO Archives, WLAO annual report, 1923–1924, and SB, vol. 1; LSO Archives, OBBRP, "Aileen Silk"; LSO Archives, "Diversifying the Bar," Aileen Silk; and *Canadian Law Lists*.

called to the Ontario bar, but she discontinued practice after she married Bruce Monroe in about 1921. She later lived in Port Credit.[8]

Lovedy Campeau, later Scott, became the second long-time woman practitioner in the class of 1919. The daughter of a doctor in Amherstburg, Campeau graduated from the University of Toronto in 1916, and then articled in Toronto with Daniel Coffey while attending lectures at Osgoode Hall. After she was called to the bar in October 1919, she moved to Windsor to practise law, becoming the first woman lawyer in Essex County. In the 1930s, she had an extensive real estate and estates practice, and she also engaged in court work and acted as a legal agent for the Agricultural Development Board, County of Essex. After she married Grover Scott in 1941, she continued to be listed as "Miss L.J. Campeau." She was often present at WLAO events, and in 1927 she attended a meeting of the Canadian Bar Association in Toronto. Campeau Scott was appointed KC in 1950 and a life member of the Law Society in 1969. She died on 1 May 1980.[9]

The number of women lawyers continued to increase. Six women were called to the bar in the fall of 1920, and most engaged in legal practice for at least a few years. Marjorie Rowland, later Blatz, articled with Fasken, Robertson & Company, but she was not invited to join the firm as it excluded women as employed lawyers until the 1950s.[10] Rowland married and moved

---

8 LSO Archives, "Diversifying the Bar," Muriel Lee; LSO Archives, WLAO fonds, SB, vol. 1; and *Globe* (6 May 1919).

9 Dr. Campeau practised medicine in Amherstburg for twenty-four years before his death in 1924. Although he was of French ancestry, there is no confirmation that he or his daughter spoke French. See also Amherstburg Bicentennial Book Committee, *Amherstburg: 1796-1996* (http://marshcollection.org/online-publications/amherstburg-1796-1996-the-new-town-on-the-garrison-grounds-book-ii/) 182–83. As a member of the University College Fourth-Year Executive, Campeau was designated the "Poetess": (1916) 18 *Torontogenesis* 39. Campeau passed her final exams at the law school with honours, standing twelfth in her class: *Globe* (6 May 1919). She often attended WLAO and other legal events in Toronto: *Globe* (7 April 1925), (25 August 1927), and (16 April 1928). She was photographed at the Canadian Bar Association meeting in Windsor in 1953, along with Helen McTague (1924) of Windsor and Harriet Clark (1947) of Toronto: LSO Archives, WLAO fonds, SB, vol. 6, *Windsor Daily Star* (2 February 1953). See also marriage notice, *St. Thomas Times-Journal* (24 June 1941); LSO Archives, OBBRP, "Lovedy Campeau"; LSO Archives, "Diversifying the Bar," Lovedy Campeau; LSO Archives, WLAO fonds, SB, vol. 1; *Canadian Law Lists*; and obituary, *Amherstburg Echo* (May 1980).

10 C.I. Kyer, *Lawyers, Families, and Businesses Lawyers, Families, and Businesses: The Shaping of a Bay Street Law Firm, Faskens, 1863–1963* (Toronto: Osgoode Society for Canadian Legal History/Irwin Law, 2013) 224.

to Chicago, where her husband did graduate work in psychology, and Rowland Blatz worked in administration in the dean's office. After returning to Toronto, Rowland Blatz completed an MA degree at the University of Toronto and began a PhD focused on issues relating to mental illness, particularly its relationship to crime. She also visited western provinces on behalf of the Board of Social Hygiene. In addition, she became an early expert on adoption law in Ontario. In 1933, her paper on adoption was read at a meeting of the Local Council of Women in Toronto by another woman lawyer, Elizabeth Newton (1921). The paper argued that adoption should occur only if a "really good home" could be identified. Rowland Blatz also became engaged in lobbying for law reform to permit more than one man to be held liable for child support for "illegitimate" children when a father's identity could not be established. As these activities confirm, Rowland Blatz used her legal education to promote law reform.[11]

Another graduate of 1920, Dorcas Kelly, later Landriau, obtained a BA at Queen's University in 1916 and then attended Osgoode Hall. She may have worked briefly as a junior solicitor in the office of Clara Brett Martin prior to Martin's death in 1923. Kelly, who was from Sudbury, may have returned there briefly after her call to the bar, and she later worked as a solicitor with the Detroit Trust Company. She ceased legal practice after her marriage to Frank Landriau, a practising solicitor in Windsor. The couple had three children, and Kelly Landriau remained in Windsor until she died in 1992 in her ninety-seventh year.[12]

Laura Denton, later Duff, who had initiated the founding meeting of the WLAO in the office of her father, Frank Denton, during her second year at the law school, was also called to the bar in 1920. She had graduated from

11 LSO Archives, WLAO fonds, SB, vol. 1; and LSO Archives, WLAO, annual report, 1923–1924. A later report, ca. 1933, indicated that Rowland Blatz had worked as a junior at the Fasken firm for two years. See also LSO Archives, WLAO fonds, SB, vol. 2, "Adoption Shown No Panacea for Welfare of Children," *Mail and Empire* (10 March 1933) 8. According to Eileen Huckle, Rowland Blatz later became Mrs. Spaulding: Huckle, "List of Women Barristers and Solicitors in Ontario" (1897–1975) [archived at Law Society of Ontario Archives].

12 LSO Archives, WLAO fonds, SB, vol. 1 and box 106:2006006-079, obituary; and Huckle, "List of Women Barristers and Solicitors." *Canadian Law Lists* do not record Kelly's practice in Martin's firm or elsewhere prior to her marriage, although WLAO records suggest that she may have practised law in Sudbury after her call to the bar. See also LSO Archives, WLAO fonds, SB, vol. 3, J.D. Pearlstein, "Fourteen Graduate, Four Practising Law," unidentified press report about early women lawyers (August 1933).

the University of Toronto in 1911, and entered the law school in 1917 at the age of twenty-six. She articled with A.A. Macdonald. After her call to the bar, she worked with her brother at their father's firm, thus establishing the first father/son/daughter law firm in Ontario. In 1923, she married George Duff and accompanied him to England for his graduate studies. On her return to Toronto, after their father's death, she and her brother carried on the firm's practice as Denton and Denton. Denton Duff was later associated for two years with the Provincial Law Clerk at the Parliament Buildings, but she then ceased legal practice. In 1919–20, she had served as President of the WLAO with Helen Currie, and she remained active in the organization thereafter. She was also an elected member of the Senate of Victoria University for many years.[13]

Verona Taylor, later Whatmough, graduated from the University of Toronto in 1917, and obtained a degree from the Toronto Conservatory of Music the following year. After her call to the bar, she practised briefly with Irwin, Hales & Irwin, but she was appointed Librarian of the County of York Law Association in 1920, following the illness and resignation of Ada Read. Taylor was the Association's librarian for ten years and she coauthored *Annotations to the Revised Statutes of Ontario, 1927*. She was active in the WLAO and served as President in 1923–24, but she resigned her library position in 1930 to marry Joshua Whatmough, a professor of philology, and moved to Cambridge, Massachusetts. She ceased legal practice after her marriage.[14]

In contrast to these four women, two others who joined the Ontario legal profession in 1920 engaged in legal work for many years. Vera Robinson, later Cartwright, from London, Ontario, attended secondary school in Toronto and then obtained an honours BA in modern languages from the

13 LSO Archives, WLAO, annual report, 1923–24; WLAO fonds, SB, vol. 1. See also LSO Archives, "Diversifying the Bar," Laura Denton; A. Bushby, "The Early Years: Sources of an Enduring Tradition—The Women's Law Association of Ontario, 1919–1950" (80th Anniversary Celebration, 14 January 2000); and *Canadian Law Lists.*

14 G.V. Taylor and F.C. Snider, *Annotations to the Revised Statutes of Ontario, 1927* (Toronto: Carswell, 1927). The trustees of the library congratulated her on producing a "book which will be of great benefit to all members of the profession." Significantly, a succession of three librarians had replaced Read, prior to Taylor's appointment: J. Honsberger, *The County of York Law Association: A History of the First Hundred Years, 1885–1985* (Toronto: County of York Law Association, 1989) 66–67. See also LSO Archives, WLAO fonds, SB, vols. 1, 3; LSO Archives, WLAO, annual report, 1923–1924; and *Canadian Law Lists.* For Ada Read, see Chapter One.

University of Toronto in 1917. She articled with Aylesworth & Company, attended lectures at the law school, and then opened her own office at 33 Richmond Street West after her call to the bar in September 1920. After Helen Currie (1921) was called to the bar, she joined Robinson in a partnership, thus establishing Robinson & Currie as the first women lawyers' partnership in Ontario in 1921. Among other legal work, Robinson handled court appearances for N.L. Martin, trustee in bankruptcy. After Currie left the partnership to work with her father a few years later, Robinson joined the Provincial Land Tax Office as a solicitor. In 1927, Robinson was appointed Assistant Librarian at the Phillips Stewart Library at Osgoode Hall Law School, and three years later, after Verona Taylor's resignation, Robinson was appointed Librarian at the County of York Law Association. Robinson was actively involved in the WLAO, and she was elected Vice-President at the special annual meeting in the Yellow Room at the King Edward Hotel in 1927. She served as President in 1928–29, and later as Vice-President when Apha Hodgins (1919) became President in the mid-1930s.[15]

In 1935, Robinson married Henry Cartwright, a Kingston lawyer. In that year, Robinson had published *The Canada Statute Citator, 1935*, while Cartwright had published *The Ontario Statute Citator, 1935*. Both publications were described as highly efficient in providing updates for ever-increasing numbers of statutory amendments, a relatively new but mounting challenge for practitioners.

> As the years roll on and legislatures come and sprawl over the statute books and pass along, the amendments to the statutes since the last revision become so numerous and ubiquitous that it is not only unsafe but impossible to refer intelligibly to any statute without some handy means of obtaining a reference to those amendments. That is the function of these Citators and they discharge that function with complete efficiency. Not only that but they give you a reference to every relevant case on any statute

15 LSO Archives, WLAO fonds, SB, vol. 1; LSO Archives, OBBRP, "Vera Robinson Cartwright"; LSO Archives, "Diversifying the Bar," Vera Robinson; *Globe* (11 April 1927) 16. The OBBRP report identified Robinson's articling principal as Valentine McNamara in Sault Ste. Marie. As WLAO President, Robinson received guests for a dance in February 1929 at the "lovely home on Roxborough Drive" of Janet Gibson, later VanEvery (1929): *Globe* (25 February 1929) 18.

you are interested in. These two functions are indispensable ... You will find these books the biggest value in law books that you ever bought.[16]

Both *Citators* were republished in 1937 by the Cartwrights and praised for being indispensable with "the annual incessant grinding of the legislative mills."[17]

After her marriage, Robinson moved to Kingston, where she joined her husband's firm, and they practised law as Cartwright and Cartwright. In 1937, Robinson Cartwright gave birth to a son and a few years later, a daughter.[18] In 1951, Robinson Cartwright was the unsuccessful candidate for the CCF in the Kingston riding, and her candidacy was celebrated at a meeting in Toronto at Woodsworth House, at which Thérèse Casgrain was the featured speaker.[19] In the 1950s, as the only woman lawyer in Frontenac County, Robinson Cartwright was asked to provide legal aid to an inmate

16 LSO Archives, WLAO fonds, SB, vol. 1; and LSO Archives, WLAO, annual report, 1923–1924. By 1923–24, Robinson's office was still at 33 Richmond St. West, but Currie was employed with the Continental Bond Company at 302 Bay Street. In 1931, Robinson was listed at 481 Dovercourt Road, and she may have conducted a limited practice alongside her position at the County of York Law Library: *Canadian Law Lists*. See also Honsberger, *The County of York Law Association*, 67; and *Globe* (7 February 1935).

17 *Fortnightly Law Journal* (1 October 1937) 75. The reviewer suggested that the *Citators* "are veritable life preservers among the turbulent paper waves of legislative hash." See also H. Cartwright, *The Ontario Statute Citator, 1935* (Toronto: Canadian Law List, 1937); and V. Robinson Cartwright, *The Canada Statute Citator, 1935* (Toronto: Canadian Law List, 1937).

18 *Globe and Mail* (17 August 1937). Robinson was about forty years old in 1937: LSO Archives, "Diversifying the Bar," Vera Robinson. She may have practised law only part-time for some years: LSO Archives, OBBRP, "Vera Robinson Cartwright." In the late 1930s, the Cartwright spouses were named as "solicitors for the respondents" in litigation about a land dispute at the Supreme Court of Canada: *Cartwright v Cartwright* [1940] SCR 659 at 670. The *Canadian Law Lists* identified the firm of Cartwright and Cartwright in the 1950s, although it named the partners as Henry Cartwright and Vera Robinson. From 1954, Robinson Cartwright was no longer named as a member of the firm; and at some point, the Cartwrights divorced.

19 Casgrain was national vice-chair of the CCF and leader of the CCF in Québec: S. Mann Trofimenkoff, "Thérèse Casgrain and the CCF in Québec" in L. Kealey and J. Sangster, eds., *Beyond the Vote: Canadian Women and Politics* (Toronto: University of Toronto Press, 1989) 139. Sangster suggested that all parties tended to place women in unwinnable ridings: J. Sangster, "The Role of Women in the Early CCF" in Kealey and Sangster, *Beyond the Vote*, 118 at 127. Henry Cartwright's obituary noted that he had also been an unsuccessful candidate for the CCF in Kingston: obituary, *Kingston Whig-Standard* (30 October 1989).

at the Women's Penitentiary, work that resulted in her long-standing involvement with the Elizabeth Fry Society. For many years, she provided voluntary representation for women prisoners and participated in public discussions about their needs.[20] Robinson Cartwright became a life member of the Law Society in 1970 and died in 1979.[21] Her story not only reveals a wide variety of legal and voluntary activities, but also how she challenged the "marriage or career" pattern. Her daughter, Katherine Cartwright (1967), became the second Ontario woman lawyer whose mother was a lawyer.[22]

The other woman in the class of 1920 with a long legal practice was Helen Kinnear from Port Colborne. Her father was a lawyer and an ardent member of the Liberal Party, and Kinnear followed closely in his footsteps. She graduated from the University of Toronto in 1917 and with her father's support entered the law school. After graduating with honours at the age of twenty-six, she immediately joined her father's practice in Port Colborne, which became Kinnear and Kinnear. She was the first woman lawyer in the Niagara Peninsula.[23] She also became involved in Liberal politics: in 1923, she was elected Recording Secretary for the Ontario Women's Liberal

20 *Globe and Mail* (14 May 1964) and *Ottawa Journal* (22 and 24 November 1966). See also "Elizabeth Fry Societies Study Sentence Injustices," *Ottawa Journal* (10 April 1968), reporting Robinson Cartwright's view that Indigenous girls were given "stiff sentences for minor offences." See also V.A. Cartwright, "Friend to Forgotten Women: The Elizabeth Fry Society at Kingston," (1958) 32:1 unidentified law journal 31 (Law Society of Ontario Archives).

21 LSO Archives, OBBRP, "Vera Cartwright"; and obituaries: Law Society of Upper Canada, "Minutes of Convocation," vol. 4, at 253; and *Globe and Mail* (27 February 1979) 41. News reports about Robinson Cartwright include a curious one, in which a caption for a photo of a typhoon fighter plane identified Vera Cartwright in the cockpit as one of several girls attending the Canadian Army Show at an RCAF station in Holland: *Globe and Mail* (23 October 1944).

22 Katherine Cartwright later practised law in her father's firm in Kingston after her call to the bar in 1967: Huckle, "List of Women Barristers and Solicitors"; and *Canadian Law Lists*. See also discussion of Jean Cairns Morris and her daughter, Alma Morris Tefft, later Malcolm (1959), Chapter Two.

23 M. Corbett and D. Corbett, "Helen Kinnear (1894–1970)" in R.M. Salokar and M.L. Volcansek, eds., *Women in Law: A Bio-biographical Sourcebook* (Westport, CT: Greenwood Press, 1996) 129–30. The Kinnear family were long-time Liberals: Helen Kinnear's grandfather James had nominated William Lyon Mackenzie as Liberal candidate for the Parliament of Upper Canada in 1851, and her father, Louis Kinnear, was an unsuccessful candidate for the Liberals in Welland in 1911. See also *Canadian Law Lists*.

Association, and during the 1920s, she "travelled around the Niagara Peninsula organizing campaigns, chairing committees, and holding offices in local and regional branches of the Liberal Party." She argued that women, as 52 per cent of the voting public, should have a "definite place" in Canada's political system.[24]

When her father died suddenly in 1924, Kinnear took over the practice, and she later formed a partnership, Kinnear and Hazelwood, which was dissolved in 1930. Kinnear then travelled with her mother and sister in the United States, where she investigated legal issues about juvenile defenders and the role of the insanity defence. She returned to Ontario in 1932–33, and opened a sole practice in Port Colborne, with her sister Jennie as her office manager. Well regarded as a lawyer, Kinnear appeared frequently in the courts and gained the respect of clients such as the International Nickel Company and the Canada Cement Company.[25] Kinnear became the first woman to plead a case before the Supreme Court of Ontario, where Justice Logie suspended proceedings to welcome her as "the first modern Portia" in his court.[26]

In 1934, Kinnear became Ontario's first woman KC, appointed by Premier Hepburn's newly elected Liberal government. By then, Kinnear had been practising law since 1920, and she was president of the Ontario Women's Liberal Association and a former president of the Liberal Association in Welland. The press proudly announced that her appointment as

24 *Globe* (4 May 1923). At a meeting in 1923, Kinnear moved to allow women to retain their nationality after marriage to an alien. She was also present for an executive meeting in 1924 when Grace Ritchie England, president of the Montreal Women's Liberal Club, was among the speakers: *Globe* (28 February 1924). See also Corbett and Corbett, "Helen Kinnear," 130.

25 Corbett and Corbett, "Helen Kinnear," 130–31; LSO Archives, WLAO fonds, SB, vol. 1; and *Canadian Law Lists*.

26 K.B. Munro, "The Hon. Helen Kinnear, a Personal Memoir," *Canadian Lawyer* (June/July 1993) 15 at 18. Kinnear acted for the defendant and succeeded to the extent of reducing the plaintiff's claim from $5,000 to $500, and the costs were also reduced. The date of this appearance is unconfirmed, but it was probably in the late 1920s or early 1930s, since Justice W.A. Logie served on the High Court of Justice from 1918 to 1933: list of former Supreme Court judges, online: <https://ontariocourts.ca/en/formerjudges>.

KC "is the first [for a woman lawyer] in the annals of the British Empire."[27] Although Kinnear's appointment probably reflected her loyal support for the Liberal Party,[28] her legal competence was never in doubt. Indeed, in 1935, she became the first woman lawyer to appear as counsel in the Supreme Court of Canada.[29]

Kinnear was also active in the WLAO. She was present at a tea hosted by Florence Thompson McLay (1922) in Hamilton in May 1938, along with a large number of WLAO members, and she regularly attended annual dinner meetings and other WLAO activities. She was also an invited speaker at other women's organizations. In early 1940, she addressed the Ontario Women's Liberal Association, stressing the need to re-elect the government of Mackenzie King.[30] In 1941, she announced her intention to seek the Liberal nomination in a by-election in Welland, necessitated by the death of the incumbent, A.B. Damude. Prior to the voting, Kinnear had "pleaded

27 *Globe* (22 December 1934) 4. The report quoted Kinnear as being "pleasantly surprised." Fifteen years later, in 1949, the first two women lawyers in England were appointed KCS in a ceremony on the thirtieth anniversary of women becoming eligible to join the legal professions in the United Kingdom in 1919. They were Helena Normanton and Rose Heilbron. See J. Bourne, *Helena Normanton and the Opening of the Bar to Women* (Hook, Hampshire: Waterside Press, 2016); and H. Heilbron, *Rose Heilbron: The Story of England's First Woman Queen's Counsel and Judge* (Oxford: Hart Publishing, 2012).

28 *Globe* (22 December 1934) 6. This press report noted the appointment of eighty-two KCS in 1934 as a "relatively modest" number, and stating, "Congratulations especially will go out to Miss Helen Kinnear of Port Colborne, who is said to be the first woman in the Empire to achieve the honor." In 1933, Kinnear was vice-president of the Welland Liberal Riding Association, president of the Hamilton District Women's Liberal Association, and legal adviser to the National Federation of Liberal Women. She was also past president of the Port Colborne Women's Liberal Association, and she had been secretary of the Ontario Women's Liberal Association for two years: LSO Archives, WLAO fonds, SB, vol. 1.

29 Munro, "The Hon. Helen Kinnear," 18. Kinnear won the appeal. In 1937, the Welland County Women's Liberal Association held a luncheon in honour of Kinnear: *Globe and Mail* (26 June 1937) 12, and she was seated at the head table at the conference of the Ontario Women's Liberal Association in Toronto in 1937: *Globe and Mail* (4 May 1937) 11. See also the Helen Kinnear Women's Liberal Association of Galt: *Globe and Mail* (29 April 1939) 10.

30 *Globe and Mail* (16 May 1938) 12; *Globe and Mail* (24 April 1939) 13; and *Globe and Mail* (26 February 1940). In an address at the outbreak of the Second World War in September 1939, Kinnear asserted that "if we have any hope at all for freedom, we must fight on until we have completely vanquished Hitlerism and all it stands for, and that will involve the concerted effort of all individuals in the British Commonwealth": *Globe and Mail* (26 September 1939) 8.

with the delegates not to allow the fact that she was a woman to influence their vote." As it was her third attempt to gain political office, she was thrilled to win the nomination on the second ballot with slightly more than 50 per cent of the vote.[31]

Surprisingly, shortly after her victory, Kinnear formally requested the Welland County Liberal Association to permit her to withdraw her candidacy in favour of Humphrey Mitchell, the newly appointed Minister of Labour in the federal Cabinet who did not have a seat in Parliament.[32] Kinnear had visited Ottawa in December 1941 to meet with the Prime Minister, and she had confirmed her willingness to step down as the Liberal candidate, but only after a formal vote of the Welland Liberal Association.[33] At an urgent meeting of the Association's executive on 22 December 1941, Kinnear emphasized how thrilled she had been to receive the nomination for the Welland riding, but she also stressed the Prime Minister's urgent need for Mitchell in the Cabinet "to handle the tense labour situation in Canada today to the satisfaction of Labour and yet in the best national interests."

> I am well aware of the sacrifice I am asked to make in giving up the nomination which has come to me as the culmination of twenty years' work for the

31 Damude had held the seat for nine years prior to his death: *Globe and Mail* (15 October 1941) 9 and (27 October 1941) 13. Kinnear advised Prime Minister Mackenzie King that the Liberals might win the riding by acclamation if the Conservatives failed to contest it, thus ensuring her election as a federal MP. See also Library and Archives Canada (LAC), microfilm reel C 4864 at 259532, letter from Kinnear to Mackenzie King (6 November 1941), requesting time to organize her practice prior to the by-election.

32 Humphrey Mitchell, a trade unionist, was first elected to the House of Commons as a Labour candidate in the Hamilton East by-election in 1931, but he was defeated in 1935 and declined to run in 1940. However, he was appointed to Cabinet as Labour Minister in 1941, a year after the introduction of unemployment insurance, and he "was elected shortly thereafter as the new Liberal MP for Welland." He oversaw mobilization of the labour force (including women) during the Second World War, but his role in implementing the detention of Japanese Canadians was controversial. He remained labour minister until his death in 1950: The Canadian Encyclopedia "Humphrey Mitchell" online: <https://www.thecanadianencyclopedia.ca>.

33 LAC, microfilm reel C 4864 at 259533, telegram from Prime Minister Mackenzie King to Kinnear (24 December 1941), confirming that the he was "greatly relieved" to learn from Colonel Gibson that Kinnear had agreed to ask the Welland Liberal Association's executive to accept her resignation as the candidate in the by-election. The telegram expressed "very sincere appreciation of this patriotic action." Gibson was a member of Cabinet and represented the Hamilton West riding.

> Liberal Party in Welland County and beyond. I know that not only Welland County was interested in this contest, but also the women of Canada who for twenty years have worked with little success for adequate representation and who felt at last that they would be represented in Ottawa by a woman who had come up the hard way... We are Canadians first and Liberals afterwards ... *I ask you not to consider me personally at all.* I ask you to consider Mr King's request to open this seat for Mr Mitchell in the light of the fact that I am ready and willing to accede to Mr King's request if you will let me.[34]

Kinnear's request was unanimously refused by the Association's executive after a "very comprehensive" discussion, and the Association's letter to the Prime Minister noted that it was a "matter of considerable concern to the members of the Executive that they did not feel they could accede to your request." At the same time, the Association confirmed its formal motion that "the best interests of all concerned would not be served'" by releasing Kinnear as the riding's candidate, while also recognizing this wartime "very grave situation."[35]

A week later, Kinnear called another meeting of the Association executive, at which a motion was passed, with Kinnear's endorsement, acceding to the prime minister's request.[36] Although the paper trail is incomplete, the press began to report rumours in April 1942 of a potential judicial appointment for Kinnear, and in June 1943 Kinnear was sworn in as County Court judge for Haldimand County. Clearly, Kinnear's legal expertise made her a fine candidate for judicial appointment, but her long-standing support for the Liberal Party was probably significant. Moreover, as Justice Marie Corbett later suggested, "Kinnear wouldn't have let go of the victory [in the Welland riding]—her third attempt at public

34 LAC, microfilm reel C 4864 at 262406–409, text of Kinnear's address to the Welland Liberal Association's executive, enclosed in a letter from the association's secretary to the Prime Minister (23 December 1941) (emphasis added). Kinnear's address to the executive acknowledged that Mitchell was likely to be an "absentee Minister of the Crown," as his role in Cabinet would not permit significant attention to the riding's local needs.

35 LAC, microfilm reel C 4864 at 262404–405, letter from Association Secretary E.M. Murray to the Prime Minister (23 December 1941). See also *Globe and Mail* (24 December 1941) 9.

36 LAC, microfilm reel C 4864 at 262410–411, (1 January 1942).

office—without getting something in return."[37] Kinnear's inauguration at the Cayuga courthouse on 23 June 1943 was a joyful occasion. The presiding judge declared that Kinnear had "the logic of a man and the intuition of a woman," adding that "this event makes a milestone in a long and sometimes furious struggle to achieve the utmost in female endeavour." More than one hundred people attended this ceremony, including seventeen women lawyers.[38]

Kinnear described the jurisdiction of a county court judge as "the Jack of all trades in the administration of justice in Ontario," and she thrived in this environment. "Diminutive in stature—5 feet, 4 inches—her quiet demeanour and infectious smile belied a keen legal mind." Kinnear also had jurisdiction as a surrogate court judge, hearing issues about estates and custody and guardianship of children, and she was a local judge of the High Court of Justice. Her judgments were praised as models of clarity.[39] Respect for Kinnear's expertise was evident when the Local Council of Women in Toronto invited her to be the first speaker in a lecture series about law in 1945, all presented by women lawyers. Kinnear's lecture, "The Machinery of the Law," attracted more than five hundred people

37 Comment of M. Corbett, quoted in D.-L. Carlson, "Portrait of the Judge as a Trail-Blazing Woman," *Law Times* (10–16 May 1993) 4. See also *Globe and Mail* (23 April 1942) 8. Kinnear's statement to the association's executive, "I ask you not to consider me personally at all," may be innocuously patriotic, but it might also reflect her satisfaction after a successful negotiation with the Prime Minister.

38 Munro, "The Hon. Helen Kinnear," 15. The WLAO held a dinner in Kinnear's honour: LSO Archives, WLAO fonds, SB, vol. 3, unidentified news report, "Judge H. Kinnear Honored by WLAO." See also E. Jenkins, "Hi, Judge!" *Chatelaine* (May 1949) 15. Significantly, Kinnear's appointment predated the appointment of Sybil Campbell as the first woman Stipendiary Magistrate in England in 1945, and the Supreme Court appointments of both Elizabeth Lane in Great Britain and Roma Mitchell in Australia, in 1965: U. Schultz and G. Shaw, eds., *Gender and Judging* (Oxford: Hart Publishing, 2013) 12–13. See also S. Magarey and K. Round, *Roma the First: A Biography of Dame Roma Mitchell* (Adelaide: Wakefield Press, 2007).

39 Corbett and Corbett, "Helen Kinnear," 132–34. As the authors noted, moreover, there were additional responsibilities assigned by statute, including summary-conviction matters in criminal law. In addition, Kinnear travelled to the Welland County Court once a week for two years, and she assumed responsibility for the County of Lincoln in 1948–49. Kinnear also published two articles about the jurisdiction of the County Court: "The County Judge in Ontario" (1954) 32:1 *Canadian Bar Review* 21; and "The County Judge in Ontario" (1954) 32:2 *Canadian Bar Review* 127. Kinnear's judicial decisions are archived in the Cayuga Court House Library. See also Munro, "The Hon. Helen Kinnear," 15; Jenkins, "Hi Judge!"; and *Toronto Star* (9 January 1943) 16.

who "jammed every available foot of ... space" to hear her speak.[40] In 1955, Kinnear joined one thousand Canadian lawyers and judges at the first Commonwealth and Empire Law Conference in London, where her prominence was confirmed by the press: "There are 32 judges in the Canadian delegation, including the Chief Justices of Québec, Ontario, and Alberta, and Helen A. Kinnear of Cayuga, the only woman in the Commonwealth to have been made a county court judge."[41]

Kinnear continued to be involved with the WLAO as its honorary president, attending many events and dinners. In August 1958, she was present at the WLAO luncheon for Canadian women lawyers, held in conjunction with the Canadian Bar Association's meeting in Toronto. As WLAO President, Mabel Van Camp (1948) presided, and a new woman lawyer from Nova Scotia, Mrs. B. Wilson, was among the guests. As a result, the first woman appointed a judge in Ontario (Kinnear, in 1943), the first woman appointed to the Ontario High Court (Van Camp, in 1971), and the first woman appointed to the Ontario Court of Appeal (Wilson, in 1975) and then to the Supreme Court of Canada (Wilson, in 1982) were all in attendance at this WLAO event in 1958.[42]

Kinnear also served as a Juvenile Court Judge, and she became the founding president of the Juvenile and Family Court Judges Association (1952–54). In addition, she was active in the John Howard Society and received the Society's medal for her contributions. In the 1950s, she was appointed to the Royal Commission on the Defence of Insanity, chaired by Chief Justice McRuer, and then to the Royal Commission on Criminal Sexual Psychopaths. Both inquiries resulted in significant background studies for the federal *Criminal Code* reform process.[43] Judge Kinnear retired in 1962 and died in 1970. In 1993, on the fiftieth anniversary of her judicial appointment, her exemplary achievements were recognized on

40 *Globe and Mail* (4 October 1945) 12. See also her complaint about the judicial collar button in an address to the WLAO in 1948: *Globe and Mail* (19 April 1948) 14.

41 *Globe and Mail* (27 July 1955) 2. In 1953, Kinnear received an honorary doctorate in law from the University of Toronto: Munro, "The Hon. Helen Kinnear," 16.

42 *Globe and Mail* (12 September 1958).

43 Corbett and Corbett, "Helen Kinnear" 133–34; *Globe and Mail* (15 November 1956) 19; and LSO Archives, "Diversifying the Bar," Helen Kinnear. See also Canada, J.C. McRuer, *Report of the Royal Commission on the Law of Insanity as a Defence in Criminal Cases* (Hull: Queen's Printer, 1956); and *Report of the Royal Commission on the Criminal Law Relating to the Criminal Sexual Psychopaths* (Ottawa: Queen's Printer, 1958).

International Women's Day, when the Canadian postal service issued a commemorative stamp with the words "Helen Alice Kinnear 1894–1970—Legal Pioneer."[44]

In the fall of 1921, the number of women lawyers in Ontario increased significantly when nine women graduates were called to the bar, part of the female contingent who entered Osgoode Hall at the end of the First World War—and the largest number of women called to the Ontario bar in the same year until after the Second World War. Graduation photographs of these nine women were placed together at the bottom of the 1921 Osgoode Hall class photograph.

Two of these women lawyers became employed outside legal practice: Mary MacDonald became Librarian at the Agricultural College in Guelph, and Eileen Harron worked (perhaps briefly) for the Society for the Prevention of Cruelty to Children in Boston, Massachusetts.[45]

Two women called to the bar in 1921 combined marriage and legal practice, at least to some extent. Vida Harris, later Grover, had graduated from the University of Toronto in 1917 and then worked at the Standard Bank in Campbellford. She articled at Grover & Grover, and may have continued to work there for two years after her call to the bar. Harris was elected WLAO President in 1921–22. She was also employed at the T. Eaton Company for five years until her marriage to George Grover, and she may have worked at the Grover firm with her spouse. After her husband's death, Harris Grover was associated with Holden, Murdoch, Walton, Finlay & Robinson in Toronto. She died in 1951.[46]

Marjorie Brigden, later Henry, also a graduate of the University of Toronto, married shortly after she was called to the bar, and she may have

44 Corbett and Corbett, "Helen Kinnear" 129. See also M.J. Mossman, "Becoming the First Women Judges in Ontario: Women Lawyers, Gender and the Politics of Judicial Appointment" in Schultz and Shaw, eds., *Gender and Judging*, 51.

45 LSO, WLAO, annual report, 1923–1924. According to Huckle, "List of Women Barristers and Solicitors," Harron was located in Hamilton, and she was present at the event hosted by Thompson McLay in Hamilton in 1938: "Women Barristers at Hamilton Tea," *Globe and Mail* (16 May 1938). Harron may not have practised law.

46 LSO Archives, WLAO fonds, SB, vols. 1, 3, including an unidentified report in the *Star Weekly*, which identified "Mrs. George Grover" practising with her husband in 1938. See also obituary "Mrs. V.I. Grover," *Lex* (June/July 1951); and WLAO, annual report, 1923–24. George Grover, KC, is listed at 371 Bay Street, but there are no references to Harris Grover in the 1930s in *Canadian Law Lists*, and she may have resigned as a member of the Law Society in 1925: Pearlstein, "Fourteen Graduated, Four Practising Law."

practised law in Flesherton for two years before moving back to Toronto. In the 1980s, P.K. McWilliams, the son of Lorna Ireland McWilliams (1922), published memories of early women lawyers, his mother's colleagues. He recalled a garden party for women lawyers at which "the most colourful in every sense was Marge Henry," and he identified her as the daughter of the artist, Fred Brigden. There is little information about her in the 1920s, but she worked at the Agriculture Development Board at the Parliament Buildings in the 1930s, and she may have worked with the Office of the Official Guardian in 1939. In the 1940s and early 1950s, Brigden Henry had an office in the Kent Building, and she represented wives who had been deserted or were unhappy in their marriages in divorce proceedings. She was still practising in the 1950s.[47]

Two women, Edyth Dyke and Helen Currie, who were called to the bar in 1921, also practised law for several years. Dyke, who had graduated from the University of Toronto, became the first woman lawyer to practise in Fort William, a city full of immigrant families "from more countries than are in the United Nations."[48] Since Eva Powley (1902) had ceased practice in Port Arthur a decade earlier, Dyke was the only woman practising law in northwestern Ontario in the 1920s, and she described her work as a general real estate business. Dyke may have ceased practice at some point in the 1930s, but she was again listed as a Fort William practitioner in the late 1940s and 1950s.[49]

Dyke's law school colleague, Helen Currie, had also graduated from the University of Toronto, and then attended the College of Education for a year. She articled in Toronto with E.T. Malone and later with J.B. Clarke, and she practised briefly with Clarke, Swabey & McLean. In 1921, Currie joined Vera Robinson (1920) in the first women's law partnership in Ontario. Currie left the partnership to work as solicitor for the Continental Bond Company on Bay Street until her father's health forced him to give up business. Her father, John A. Currie, had been an MPP, and it is possible that Helen Currie was inspired by him to run (unsuccessfully) for election

47 P.K. McWilliams, "Leaders among the Women Lawyers of Ontario—Revisited" (1987) 21:2 *Gazette* 157 at 159; LSO Archives, WLAO fonds, SB, vol. 1; and *Canadian Law Lists*.

48 I. Abella, "The Making of a Chief Justice: Bora Laskin, the Early Years" (1991) 25:3 *Gazette* 422 at 427.

49 LSO Archives, WLAO fonds, SB, vol. 1. "E. Dyke" appears in Fort William in the *Canadian Law Lists* until the early 1930s and then is absent from these records until the late 1940s and early 1950s. For Powley, see Chapter Two.

in Ontario in 1928. She may have established a sole practice in 1929, but by 1930–31, she was not employed, and she resigned as a member of the Law Society in 1931. By that date, she had obtained employment with the Office of the Superintendent of Schools in Toronto, where she worked in a non-legal capacity in the Statistical Department.[50]

A decade later, during the Second World War, Currie was employed in the Department of National Revenue in Ottawa, and in a legal capacity from 1944, and she may have been a member of the Tax Appeal Board.[51] Currie's experiences reveal that legal work available to women lawyers in the 1920s diminished during the Depression but rose again during the Second World War. Currie was present at the thirtieth anniversary celebration of her class in 1951, when she and other women classmates were photographed by the press at the King Edward Hotel with Premier Leslie Frost, who had also been called to the Ontario bar in 1921. This press report identified Currie as an employee in the income tax department at that time.[52]

Three women who were admitted to the bar in 1921 were later appointed KC or QC. Elizabeth Newton was appointed KC in 1947. Originally from Hamilton, she had graduated from the University of Toronto in 1911 with the MA degree, specializing in Italian, Spanish, and philology, and she then

50 In 1922, the firm of Robinson & Currie was located at 33 Richmond Street West. In 1925, Robinson was still listed at this address, but Currie was listed at 302 Bay Street, and in 1929 at 217 Bay Street: *Canadian Law Lists.* See also LSO Archives, WLAO fonds, SB, vol. 1; LSO Archives, WLAO, annual report, 1923–24; LSO Archives, OBBRP, "Helen Currie"; McWilliams, "Leaders among the Women Lawyers of Ontario," 160; and Pearlstein, "Fourteen Graduate, Four Practising Law."

51 LSO Archives, OBBRP, "Helen Currie." Mitchell Thomas reported that Currie practised "as a member of the Department of Revenue prior to and during World War II and for some years thereafter": E. Mitchell Thomas, "The History of Women Lawyers in the County of Carleton Law Association" in W. Johnson, ed., *The First Century: Essays on the History of the County of Carleton Law Association by Various Hands on the Occasion of the Association's Centenary, 1888–1988* (Ottawa: Bonanza Press, 1988) 107–13.

52 LSO Archives, WLAO fonds, "Premier Frost, 1921 Classmates, at Reunion," unidentified news report, 1951: The other women graduates of 1921 with the Premier were Mrs. G.S. Sturdy of Preston; Mrs. L. McWilliams, "formerly of the wartime legal services"; Evelyn Harrison, KC, of London; and Elizabeth Newton, KC, librarian of the York County Law Society. According to Huckle, "List of Women Barristers and Solicitors," McWilliams was called to the bar in May 1922, but she may have been a member of the class of 1921. Currie resigned voluntarily (for a second time) in 1965, but no record of her date of reinstatement after 1931 exists. Her government work in Ottawa may not have required membership in the Law Society.

taught school in Vancouver for several years. She was thirty-four years old when she was called to the bar in Ontario. Newton initially practised law in Toronto, working at Jones & Leonard in the early 1920s, where she did corporate, mortgage, and real estate work, along with wills and estates. When Vera Robinson Cartwright resigned her post at the York County Law Association Library in 1935, Newton was appointed the new Librarian. Newton's salary was twenty-five dollars per month less than Robinson's, "evidence of how the continuing Depression eroded salaries," even though her salary may have been higher than many of the association's members.[53]

The York County Law Association library was located in Old City Hall, along with the Supreme Court trial courtrooms, and "Miss Newton" had the key to the robing rooms. In addition, she was helpful to counsel.

> All the lawyers who were on trials, including the late Chief Justice McRuer, would come dashing in to [consult] Miss Newton if they needed something in a hurry and she had all the reports ... She kept right up to date on law. And she was a tremendous help. And I think a lot of cases were certainly helped by a five-minute little chat at Miss Newton's desk, or Miss Newton going to get the right case and the right annotation ... She was highly respected by the bar.[54]

Newton was also active as a member of the Board of Directors and executive of the Alumnae Federation of the University of Toronto, and she served in similar roles at Trinity College and St. Hilda's College. She also served in the WLAO for many years, including as President in 1926–27. Newton was also co-convenor, with Lily Sherizen (1930), of a popular WLAO Hobby Show for lawyers in the early 1950s. She retired from her post as Librarian in her early seventies in 1958 and perhaps continued a limited private practice after retirement. Newton died in 1971. She was highly

53 LSO Archives, OBBRP, "Elizabeth Newton"; LSO Archives, WLAO fonds, SB, vol. 1; and obituary, *Toronto Telegram* (10 March 1971). Newton's name was not included at Jones & Leonard in the *Canadian Law Lists* in the late 1920s, so she may have worked as a legal assistant. See also Honsberger, *The County of York Law Association*, 67.

54 A recollection of Elizabeth Newton by Margaret Smith (1944): Osgoode Society for Canadian Legal History (OSCLH), oral history, "Margaret Smith," 84.

respected in the legal community—indeed, she was frequently described as "a saint."[55]

The second woman in the class of 1921 to be appointed a KC was Evelyn Harrison from London. Harrison had graduated from the University of Toronto in 1917 and articled with U.A. Buchner in London. She became the first woman to practise law in London and the first woman lawyer to join the Middlesex Law Association. Harrison's decision to enter the legal profession was partly inspired by her lawyer uncle, but she also wished to obtain legal expertise to avoid the challenges her mother had faced after the death of her father. After her call to the bar, she was associated for a few years with Brickenden & Company in London, perhaps in its part-time office in Port Stanley. In 1928, Harrison established her own firm in London, specializing in real estate law, and until the early 1940s she practised law as London's only woman lawyer. She was appointed KC in 1949.[56]

Harrison was also active in public service in London: she served for nineteen years as a trustee of London's Board of Education, three terms as Chairman, and she was active in the Red Cross and a past president of both the London Council of Women and the University Women's Club. She was a charter member of the Professional Women's Club and the WLAO, and she frequently attended WLAO events in Toronto. In addition to her appointment as KC, she became a life member of the Law Society in 1971. In that year, Harrison was one of nine lawyers—and the only woman—to be

55 Obituary, *Toronto Telegram* (30 March 1971). Newton was buried in Hamilton Cemetery. See also LSO Archives, WLAO fonds, SB vol. 1; and LSO Archives, OBBRP: "Elizabeth Newton." Newton may have been supporting her brother who had been invalided during World War I: McWilliams, "Leaders Among the Women Lawyers of Ontario" 160.

56 LSO Archives, OBBRP: "Evelyn Harrison"; LSO Archives, WLAO Annual Report, 1923–24; and Morgan, "An Embarrassingly and Severely Masculine Atmosphere" 28. Harrison remained a sole practitioner, although her office location changed over the years: *Canadian Law Lists*. It was not until 1941 that Beth Underhill became the second woman lawyer in London, practising in a firm with her spouse. Eileen Mitchell Thomas (1942) reported that she had received support from Harrison when she practised briefly in London: see Chapter Five. A list of women members of the Middlesex Law Association includes Harrison: F. Carter, *The Middlesex Bench and Bar* (London: Middlesex Law Association, 1969) 118. In addition to the names of other women practitioners, this list includes Efleda Louise Clarke (1918), but no records of Clarke as an Ontario lawyer exist in LSO Archives.

honoured by the Middlesex Bar Association for being called to the Ontario bar for fifty years or more. Harrison died in 1982 at the age of eighty-six.[57]

The third member of the 1921 class who became a QC was Lida Pearson, later Sturdy. She was appointed QC in 1962, forty-one years after her call to the bar. In the early twentieth century, Pearson's father had been Mayor of Newmarket, then Warden and Reeve of York County, and MPP for North York. Her father encouraged Pearson to study law after she graduated from the University of Toronto in 1918. Pearson recalled that her class "was full of returning veterans from the First World War" and that "all the women sat in a row at the front, and ... were studiously ignored by both male classmates and lecturers." Pearson decided to practise law west of Toronto and chose Preston, now part of Cambridge, which had only one (male) lawyer in 1921. At the time, a physician friend advised Pearson that "there's room for another lawyer here but whether or not there's room for a woman lawyer, I don't know."[58]

Pearson opened a one-room office, above a meat store and next to a dentist's office. Her first client arrived three weeks later, needing help from the town council regarding a flooded cellar. Pearson's assistance proved successful. Her fee was fifty cents, and her reputation and clientele gradually increased. Nonetheless, as her lawyer son later explained, her early experiences were sometimes challenging:

> I know her early practice was difficult in that the male lawyers in Galt, Preston and Kitchener were very reluctant to accept a woman lawyer on an equal basis. I recall that my mother told me [that] when she first went to the registry office, the male solicitors would immediately gather around her to tell each other obscene jokes, and she would leave the registry office in tears and sit in a small park until noon hour [when] the men went for lunch. Mother would then hurry back to the registry office in the hopes of completing her work before they returned.[59]

57 LSO Archives, WLAO fonds, SB vol. 10: (11 January 1971) *London Free* Press 9: "Association Honors Veteran Lawyers"; and obituary, *London Free Press* (7 april 1982).

58 L. Foster, "Lida B. Pearson Sturdy, 1895–1987" (1991) 79 *Waterloo Historical Society (Journal)* 40; and "She Founded a Cambridge Law Firm," *Kitchener-Waterloo Record* (19 February 1975).

59 LSO Archives, P.R. Sturdy, "Memo re Lida B. Pearson Sturdy, 3 November 1992." P.R. Sturdy was the son of Pearson Sturdy and a lawyer. See also Foster, "Lida B. Pearson Sturdy, 45–46; *Kitchener-Waterloo Record* (19 February 1975).

Pearson practised law for several years, but after she married Gerald Sturdy, a cabinet maker, in 1927, she sold her practice to Ruby Wigle (1926) and moved to Chicago for her husband's work. The couple moved back to Ontario in 1928, where their son, Peter, was born, and then a daughter, Marilyn, in the following year. By 1930, they were back in Preston, and as the Depression deepened, Pearson Sturdy's husband became unemployed. Meanwhile, Wigle had succeeded in the Preston practice, including being appointed town solicitor in 1931, and another lawyer, Patrick Flynn, had also opened an office in Preston. In 1933, when Wigle married and planned to move with her spouse to Sault Ste. Marie, she sold the practice back to Pearson Sturdy. Pearson Sturdy resumed her practice, focusing on wills, conveyancing, litigation, and family law, and she became town solicitor in 1934, replacing Wigle.[60]

Pearson Sturdy's son recalled that his mother provided legal services for Ukrainian and Polish immigrants who had arrived after the First World War. Moreover, in the absence of shelters for abused women, she sometimes housed a mother and her children in her own home until she could make other arrangements for them. In the mid-1930s, Pearson Sturdy ran for School Trustee in 1935 and was defeated, but she was "the runaway first" in the election the following year. She was Vice-Chairman in 1937 and Chairman the following year, and she remained a school trustee until 1945. During the Second World War, Pearson Sturdy opened her home to members of the Women's Royal Navy Service (WRENS) who were training in Galt and to hitchhiking soldiers on leave. Overworked, she suffered a breakdown, but in 1946 she formed a partnership with Flynn after he returned from war service. When Pearson Sturdy's son was called to the bar in 1955, he joined the firm of Pearson, Flynn & Sturdy in 1961, thus establishing the first mother-son legal partnership in Ontario.[61]

Pearson Sturdy was active in community activities, including her church, and she continued her legal practice until 1967. She died twenty years later at the age of ninety-one, and was afflicted with Alzheimer's in her last years. Pearson Sturdy was a strong woman and an excellent lawyer.

60 Foster, "Lida B. Pearson Sturdy," 47-48.

61 LSO Archives, P. Sturdy, "Memo re Lida B. Pearson Sturdy"; McWilliams, "Leaders among the Women Lawyers of Ontario," 158; and *Canadian Law Lists*. See also LSO Archives, "Mrs. Gerald Sturdy Marks 40 Years in Law Field," unidentified press report (November 1961).

> Although she contributed to many organizations, Lida B. Sturdy was first and foremost her own woman, an individual. She never saw herself in the vanguard of any kind of women's movement, nor did she ever join any women's rights groups. She was undoubtedly aided in her career by the sweeping changes in Canada regarding the status of women. Her example must have made many local people re-think their own ideas about the capabilities and the position of women around them. Lida's most significant contribution to local history is as the first woman lawyer, a professional job with a high profile that she performed well and with love. Her sense of duty and interest in people made her a leader in her church, her profession and her community.[62]

In contrast to the large cohort who studied during the war and were called to the bar between 1919 and 1921, only four women were called in 1922 and three in 1923, perhaps suggesting the Law Society's renewed preference for male applicants at war's end. Among the women graduates of 1922 was Lorna Ireland, later McWilliams, from St. Catharines, who had begun her studies at Osgoode Hall in 1917 as a matriculant. During her five years of articles, she worked with Judge Kingstone in St. Catharines before his judicial appointment and then with Crown Attorney Lancaster and Burson & Johnston, also in St. Catharines. Then, while attending lectures at the law school during her final three years, she articled with Kayne & Bissett.[63] Ireland vividly recalled her arrival at Osgoode Hall for lectures in 1919, when "she found herself amongst a large class of mature veterans of World War I [who] regarded her as a child and did not take her seriously until she passed her first set of exams." Prior to her call to the bar, Ireland married David McWilliams, and although she was not in active legal practice, she asserted that "her interest [was] still keen." According to her son, P.K. McWilliams, Ireland also faced challenges as a woman lawyer: "it was difficult for women lawyers to make their way in the profession. Indeed, it was difficult for male lawyers as well. The social conditions were more settled, and it was a slow business to become established. Then the

62 Foster, "Lida B. Pearson Sturdy," 52-53. Of the thirty-one women called to the bar up to 1921, eight were later appointed KC: Alford (1916), Palen and Cherrier (1918), Campeau Scott (1919), Kinnear (1920) and Newton, Harrison, and Pearson Sturdy (1921). Most practised law for lengthy periods, mainly in communities outside Toronto. In Toronto, Palen later became deputy registrar of the Supreme Court of Ontario, and Newton was appointed librarian of the County of York Law Library.

63 LSO Archives, WLAO fonds, SB, vol. 1.

depression blighted the lives of most in the thirties."[64] In the 1950s, she worked at the Parliament Buildings and later for the Department of Agriculture. She was appointed QC in 1966, along with her son, Peter, "the first time a mother and son ... received this honour together."[65]

Two women graduates in 1922—Florence Daley, later Harkins, and Florence Thompson, later McLay—established the second women's law partnership in Ontario at 57 Queen Street West in Toronto, probably early in 1923. Daley's father was J.J. Daley, Chief Librarian at Osgoode Hall's Great Library. She had graduated from the University of Toronto in 1919, and then articled with George Keogh while attending lectures at Osgoode Hall. Daley practised with Thompson at their firm for several years, but she resigned her practice prior to her marriage to J.M. Harkins in 1926. Daley Harkins remained active in the WLAO and served on the executive as its representative to the Local Council of Women in Toronto. It was Daley Harkins who responded to Aileen Silk Bicknell's toast to graduates of 1987 at the WLAO's celebratory dinner in 1927. She died in 1948.[66]

Florence Thompson obtained a BA and MA from McMaster University and possibly combined her courses in arts and law; as the press noted, she was "the first girl in Toronto to have achieved such phenomenal success in the university world."[67] After her call to the bar in 1922, she worked briefly with Freeman, Moss & Latimer before establishing a partnership with Daley. After Daley married and left the partnership, Thompson continued as a sole practitioner at the same location until her marriage to W.S. McLay several years later. She remained involved in the WLAO, but she was no longer in practice at the time of her WLAO garden party at her Hamilton home in 1938.[68]

64 LSO Archives, WLAO fonds, SB vol. 1.; and McWilliams, "Leaders among the Women Lawyers of Ontario—Revisited," 158–59. After raising her two sons, Ireland McWilliams served in the Canadian Women's Army Corps during the Second World War, and afterward enjoyed a modest career with the Ontario government.

65 *Globe and Mail* (1 January 1966). This report identified Lorna McWilliams as Acting Senior Solicitor of the Junior Farmers Loan Branch in the Department of Agriculture. See also *Canadian Law Lists.*

66 LSO Archives, OBBRP, "Florence Daley"; and LSO Archives, WLAO fonds, SB, vol. 1.

67 LSO Archives, WLAO fonds, SB, vol. 1, unidentified press clipping. By 1922, no memory of Eva Powley's attendance at both arts and law programs in the late 1890s had survived: see Chapter Two.

68 *Globe and Mail* (16 May 1938) 12; LSO Archives, WLAO fonds, SB vol. 1; and *Canadian Law Lists.*

Marian James, later Lamey, who graduated with an MA from the University of Toronto, was also called to the bar in 1922, after articling in Hamilton with L.F. Lambier. James was one of seven students who won scholarships in her second year at Osgoode Hall. In 1923–24, James was practising law on John Street in Hamilton, but she later worked in Toronto as Assistant Supervisor of sessional stenographers at the Agriculture Development Board. She was eventually appointed to the board permanently—perhaps the board's first woman lawyer employee. James was an active member of the WLAO, serving as President in 1929–30. In 1936, she married Dr. M.P. Lamey, but it appears that she continued in legal practice. She was appointed QC in 1958 and a life member of the Law Society in 1972. Marian James Lamey died in 1987.[69]

Among the three graduates of 1923 was Donella McRae. In 1923–24, she was practising with W.H. Kirkpatrick at 2836 Dundas Street West, but there is no record of her at this firm in 1925 or thereafter. McRae attended some WLAO events after her call to the bar—there is a brief report of her winning a prize at a WLAO bridge tournament in December 1927—but there are no further records of her in legal practice.[70] Similarly, although Mary Taylor, later Odell (1923),worked as Secretary to Thomas Low in the Parliament Buildings in Ottawa in 1923, she later married J.H. Odell and was living in Boston in the 1930s. There are no records of her in legal practice.[71]

Lorna Wilson, later Brigden, who obtained a BA from the University of Toronto in 1919, attended the Faculty of Education the following year before entering the law school. She initially articled with the women lawyers' firm Robinson & Currie, and she became a student in the office of Clara Brett Martin in 1922–23. In the mid-1920s, after her call to the bar, she was employed at Gregory & Gregory at 371 Bay Street in mortgage and

69 LSO Archives, OBBRP, "Marion James Lamey"; Huckle, "List of Women Barristers and Solicitors"; and LSO Archives, WLAO fonds, SB, vols. 1, 2, and "Queens of the Bar Gather at Banquet," unidentified press report. The *Canadian Law List* in the 1920s has no entries for James, perhaps suggesting that she worked as a legal assistant in Hamilton. Margaret Smith (1944) recalled that Lamey later practised law at the firm of Matthews Stivers in Newmarket: OSCLH, oral history, "Margaret Smith," 87.

70 *Canadian Law Lists*; Huckle, "List of Women Barristers and Solicitors"; and LSO Archives, WLAO fonds, SB, vol. 2, unidentified press report of the WLAO meeting ca. December 1927. There is no record of McRae in a list of women lawyers in LSO Archives, WLAO fonds, SB, vol. 1.

71 LSO Archives, WLAO fonds, SB, vol. 1; LSO Archives, WLAO, annual report, 1923–24; and *Canadian Law Lists*.

conveyancing work. She later spent nine months in the statistics branch of the Board of Education and then two years in the personnel department of the Robert Simpson Company. Wilson married G.G. Brigden in 1928 and ceased to practise law, although she remained actively involved in WLAO activities.[72]

In 1924, four women were called to the bar and all practised law for many years. All four were later appointed KC or QC, and none of them ever married. Grace Gordon, the daughter and granddaughter of lawyers, attended the University of Toronto prior to entering the law school. She articled in Peterborough with her brother, G.N. Gordon, a city solicitor and member of City Council. After her call to the bar in May 1924, she practised law for some years, perhaps as a sole practitioner as well as in the firm of Gordon, Elliott & Gordon at 73 Richmond Street West.[73] In 1934, she was appointed to the Office of the Official Guardian in the provincial government, handling children's estates, a position she held for twenty-five years. Gordon was also an executive member of the Local Council of Women for thirty years and its president in 1962–64, and she was the organizer of the council's lecture series on law in Toronto after the Second World War, at which Helen Kinnear (1920) was the first speaker. Gordon was an active member of the WLAO and the National Council of Women, and she was appointed QC in 1959. She died in 1967.[74]

Helen McTague was born in Guelph and attended the University of Toronto, but she was admitted to Osgoode Hall as a matriculant in 1919. She articled in Guelph with C.L. Dunbar. After being called to the bar in November 1924, she practised law in Windsor, doing corporate and real

72 LSO Archives, WLAO fonds, SB, vol. 1; and LSO Archives, WLAO, annual report, 1923–24. See also *Canadian Law Lists*: Wilson was listed as "L.G. Wilson" at the Gregory firm in 1925.

73 OSCLH, oral history, "W.B. Gordon" (Grace Gordon's nephew); and obituary, Grace Gordon, *Peterborough Examiner* (2 June 1967). Grace Gordon's brother was later elected to the House of Commons, serving as deputy speaker and Minister of Immigration. See also *Canadian Law Lists* in the 1920s and early 1930s; and Pearlstein, "Fourteen Graduate, Four Practising Law," confirming Gordon's employment in her father's firm in 1933.

74 LSO Archives, WLAO fonds, SB, vol. 1; LSO Archives, OBBRP, "Grace Gordon"; obituary, *Peterborough Examiner* (3 June 1967); and obituary, *Globe and Mail* (3 June 1967). Gordon supported several contemporary political causes, including nationalization of the liquor industry and abolition of capital punishment, and she promoted divorce reform and housing for the elderly. Gordon was the first woman chair of the Committee of Stewards of Trinity United Church, Toronto.

estate work. Initially, she joined her brother's firm, and after her brother, C.P. McTague, was elected a member of the Ontario legislature and then appointed Securities Commissioner, she continued practice at this Windsor firm. In later decades, the McTague firm grew substantially; by 1970, McTague, Clark, Holland, Whiteside, Coughlin, Ouellette & Mailloux also included several junior lawyers. Along with Lovedy Campeau Scott (1919), McTague was appointed KC in 1950, the only women lawyers included in the KC list that year. At a meeting of the Canadian Bar Association in Windsor in 1953, McTague was photographed with Campeau Scott and a Toronto woman lawyer. She served as President of the Essex Law Society, and she became a life member of the Law Society in 1974. McTague retired in 1972 and died in 1986 at the age of ninety-three.[75]

In October 1924, Mary Waddell, a 1903 graduate of the University of Toronto with a BA in mathematics, was called to the bar. Waddell also completed graduate work at Bryn Mawr in the United States, and she was appointed a Maths lecturer at the University of Toronto. After she began to practise law, she explained that she had "discovered it was easier to be a lady lawyer than a lady mathematician. All that was necessary was to get along with your clients." Waddell was admitted to the law school in 1921 at the age of thirty-seven. She articled with her brother, R.R. Waddell, in his office at 302 Bay Street but "while taking her studies leading to her call to the bar, she was never off the University staff." She continued to teach at the university, perhaps practising law part-time, until 1947, when she began to practise law full-time—and she was still practising at the age of eighty-two in 1960.[76] In September 1960, Waddell spoke to the press on her return from the second Commonwealth and Empire Law Conference in Ottawa.

75 LSO Archives, OBBRP, "Helen McTague"; and LSO Archives, WLAO fonds, SB, vol. 1, *Toronto Telegram* (27 December 1950), *Windsor Daily Star* (2 February 1953), and *Canadian Law Lists.*

76 LSO Archives, OBBRP, "Mary Waddell"; LSO Archives, WLAO fonds, SB, vol. 1; and *Toronto Telegram* (4 October 1960). Waddell began tutoring in mathematics "with the returned men in 1917–18," and one of her students at the university was Dalton Wells (later a judge of the Court of Appeal of Ontario, 1964–67): *Bowmanville-Canadian Statesman* (13 October 1960), and *Telegram* (4 October 1960). Waddell also explained that she "couldn't go far at the university as a woman": *Orono Weekly Times* (6 October 1960). Waddell had also attended the first Commonwealth Law Conference in London in 1955 and hoped to attend the next one in Australia in 1965. In addition to his Bay Street office, Waddell's brother had a branch office in Orono, which later became his main office: *Canadian Law Lists.*

She was described as probably "the oldest practicing woman lawyer at the conference, and possibly in Canada." Waddell practised from her home on Madison Avenue and was appointed a QC in 1961. She died in 1967.[77]

Vera Parsons, who was called to the bar in September 1924, became one of the few women before the 1960s to challenge the prevailing view that female lawyers were not suited for court work. The daughter of an executive at the Robert Simpson Company, Parsons became Ontario's first woman criminal defence lawyer and "stood out as an excellent counsel in court."[78] After Parsons obtained a BA at the University of Toronto in 1911 and then an MA at Bryn Mawr, in Pennsylvania, she began doctoral studies in Rome but returned home to Toronto without completing a PhD.[79] "Back in Toronto, she found her most useful immediate asset was the ability to speak Italian," assisting residents of "the Ward." Bounded by Yonge Street, Queen Street, University Avenue, and College Street, the Ward was home to thousands of poor immigrants who had arrived in Toronto between the 1890s and the 1920s.[80] In 1919, a report about the new quarters of the Central Neighbourhood House at 27 Elm Street identified Parsons as the "Italian and Slavic worker," and she was elected to the organization's executive in

77 See also press report, *Orono Weekly Times* (6 October 1960); LSO Archives, WLAO fonds, SB, vol. 1; Huckle, "List of Women Barristers and Solicitors"; and *Toronto Telegram* (4 October 1960).

78 M. Brunet, "'One of the Most Capable and Astute Barristers Practicing in Our Criminal Courts': Vera Parsons (1889–1973)" (2011) 32:4 *For the Defence* 31, quoting E.P. Hartt, "The Bench and the Bar," *Obiter Dicta* (Spring 1952) 23. See also OSCLH, oral history, "Margaret Smith," 90–91; and P. Platt, "Vera Parsons: Some Pieces of a Life" (1975) 11:5 *The Advocate* (University of Toronto Faculty of Law) 11.

79 LSO Archives, OBBRP, "Vera L. Parsons"; and LSO Archives, "Diversifying the Bar," Vera L. Parsons. Parsons may have remained in Pittsburgh after her MA: "Tea for Visitors," unidentified press report (31 December 1913), identifying two guests from Toronto, including Parsons. Her portrait was painted in Pittsburgh in 1915-16 by the American artist, Fred Demmler, and the portrait is now in the Carnegie Art Museum: email communication from Charles Kaufmann to M.J. Mossman (25 June 2020).

80 M. Rosenfeld, "The Lady ... and the Crooks," *Maclean's Magazine* (3 March 1956) 48; and J. Lorinc, "Bringing Back the Ward," *Toronto Star* (19 May 2013) IN1. Immigrants from China, Russia, and Italy joined earlier Irish immigrants and a Black community of former slaves who had arrived in Ontario on the underground railway: J. Lorinc, "The Slum We Buried in the Heart of Toronto," *Toronto Star* (23 May 2015) M1. See also J. Lorinc et al., *The Ward: The Life and Loss of Toronto's First Immigrant Neighbourhood* (Toronto: Coach House, 2015); and Bureau of Municipal Research, *What Is "The Ward" Going to Do with Toronto? A Report* (Toronto: The Bureau, 1918).

May 1919. Apparently, Parsons decided to become a lawyer when an Italian girl was jailed for vagrancy and Parsons "could do nothing about it."[81]

Parsons graduated from Osgoode Hall Law School in September 1924. She was the first woman to win the silver medal. Prior to her call to the bar, she successfully appeared for a complainant in police court after a motor car collided with the complainant's horse-drawn buggy. As frequently occurred at this time, a report of the case described how the "usual drab grey of court proceedings was considerably enlivened" by Parsons's appearance: she was "attired in a chic black hat, a fox stole neck piece, brown suit, brown walking boots, and carried a mannish cane."[82] Even more enthusiasm greeted Parsons's appearance in March 1925 on behalf of a plaintiff in a civil case involving a jury, when Judge Coatsworth remarked that he could not recall an occasion when "a lady barrister had appeared to plead a case before a jury in Toronto." The press described Parsons's expertise: "Miss Parsons stands quietly behind her table and quietly puts her questions. There is no hesitation about them. She apparently knows what answer she wants and ... she knows how to go about getting it. Her voice is not loud, nor does she appear to exert herself to make it heard by judge, jury, witness and opposing counsel."[83]

Parsons articled and then practised law at Horkins & Graham in Toronto, eventually becoming a partner; since Horkins preferred trial work, "Parsons, the cerebral scholar, became her firm's appellate specialist."[84] Parsons also did trial work, especially on behalf of young persons, and she was described as "a Portia who has [often] appeared ... to plead for erring mankind." Parsons appeared in the Women's Court before Magistrate

81 *Globe* (20 May 1919) 10. Parsons's volunteer work was commended at a meeting the next year. The Central Neighbourhood House provided medical, health, and educational activities, along with a summer camp at Allendale for 396 children in the Ward: *Globe and Mail* (27 February 1960) 9. See also obituary, "Vera Parsons, 83, Criminal Lawyer," *Toronto Star* (20 February 1973).

82 "Fair Portia in Court Wins Case for Client," *Toronto Star* (14 August 1924) 3. Press reports often commented on Parsons's use of a cane, necessitated by her childhood polio.

83 LSO Archives, WLAO fonds, SB, vol. 2, "Miss Vera L. Parsons' Appearance Before Jury is Event in Legal History: Bench is Impressed," *Toronto Star* (11 March 1925).

84 C. Moore, "Breaking Ground for Women Lawyers" *Law Times* (26 August 2002) 8. William Horkins was called to the bar in 1917 and was appointed KC in 1933. He had worked with T.C. Robinette before establishing his own firm. He retired in 1942 because of ill health and died in 1952: LSO Archives, OBBRP, "William B. Horkins"; and obituary, unidentified press report.

Margaret Patterson to assist a young woman who had placed her two-week-old baby in a car, which happened to be parked beside the University of Toronto's Anatomy building. The young mother later explained that the baby's father had died and that she had only one cent in her purse, but since she expected the story of her baby to be in the papers, she knew she would find her child. In this case, Parsons pleaded the precise wording of the *Criminal Code* offence—that the life of the child "*is* endangered" rather than "*is likely* to be endangered." In addition, she provided a practical solution: she had identified three families willing to take in the young mother and her baby. Thus, Magistrate Patterson remanded the case to the Catholic Welfare Society for care arrangements. A few years later, the Local Council of Women criticized the appointment of a male lawyer to replace Magistrate Patterson, suggesting that women lawyers, including Parsons, were available. There was no comment from the Attorney General or from Parsons.[85]

Parsons was a member of the Local Council of Women and an accomplished musician who supported musical events. She was a member of the WLAO and attended a dance in April 1928 as well as the tea held in the home of Thompson McLay (1922) in Hamilton in 1938. She also responded to the toast to the bar at the WLAO annual dinner meeting in 1933, but she never served on the WLAO executive. Perhaps her focus on criminal law made her, or other WLAO members, uncomfortable. At a prestigious luncheon in Montreal celebrating the *Persons Case* decision of the Privy Council in 1929, Parsons was an invited speaker, along with Senator Dandurand, Joseph Mercier, MP, and William Tremblay, MLA. Parsons also represented the Child Welfare Council at a commission of inquiry about the York County Children's Aid Society, and she remained an executive member of the

85 *Toronto Star* (8 March 1930); and *Toronto Star* (22 November 1934) 10.

Ontario Farm Service Force when it absorbed the Ontario Women's Land Army in 1941.[86]

Parsons was counsel in a number of high-profile criminal law cases. One of her early clients was Allan Baldwin, who had been convicted of robbery and retained Parsons to appeal his conviction. While imprisoned in the hospital at the Don Jail, Baldwin and another man escaped from the jail, but one of the guards died during their escape, and Baldwin was charged with murder.[87] At the time, Parsons had yet to defend a client charged with murder, so she attempted to refer his defence to a more experienced lawyer, but no one would touch the case for fear that public opinion against the accused would tarnish their legal reputations. Since Parsons was convinced that Baldwin, "although a criminal, was not guilty of murder," she agreed to defend him, becoming the first woman lawyer in Ontario to defend an accused on a murder charge.[88] After a seven-day trial and eleven hours of

86 *Globe* (16 April 1928) 18; *Globe* (18 February 1929) 16; *Globe* (6 May 1932) 15; and *Globe and Mail* (6 August 1941). See also *Globe* (22 November 1929) 18, and (11 June 1934); WLAO, annual meeting program, 1933; and *Globe and Mail* (16 May 1938). Parsons was critical of alimony rules: "It is necessary to prove legal cruelty of an extreme nature—danger to life and limb, or the apprehension of such danger. In some cases, women have endured the greatest hardships, but have been unable to get alimony": *Toronto Star* (16 April 1934). She also commented on the case of Dorothy Blackwell in England, who had saved payments from her boarders between 1925 and 1941, but in 1943 the English Court of Appeal concluded that a wife's housekeeping money belonged to her husband. In critiquing this decision, Parsons quoted common law principles confirming a farmer's wife's entitlement to "butter and eggs money," and her classmate Grace Gordon (1924) announced in the press that the Local Council of Women would lobby for legislation: *Globe and Mail* (2 December 1943).

87 Rosenfeld, "The Lady ... and the Crooks," 46–47. In making his escape, Baldwin's rope broke, and he fell to the ground and fractured his arm. The police captured him, and he had surgery at the Toronto General Hospital, where Laura Down, later Legge (1948), was a nurse on duty. She recalled Baldwin's stay in hospital and the heavy police surveillance: Laura Legge, interview with M.J. Mossman (28 February 2008).

88 Rosenfeld, "The Lady ... and the Crooks," 17, 47. The first Canadian woman lawyer in a murder trial was probably S.M.G. Duff, associate defence counsel, in an Alberta case involving a charge of infanticide in the early 1920s: LSO Archives, WLAO fonds, SB, vol. 1, unidentified news report. In addition, Gertrude Bury, who practised in Olds, Calgary, and Red Deer, was cocounsel for the defence in a murder trial in Alberta in 1929 and "may have been the first woman in the British Commonwealth to address a jury at a murder trial": S. Petersson, "Women Lawyers and Law Students 1915–1935" (n.d.) 10:1 *Architypes* 4. Since both these women lawyers were cocounsel, Parsons was probably the first Canadian woman lawyer to defend an accused charged with murder on her own.

deliberation, the jury reported that it was unable to reach a verdict, and a second trial was ordered to be held four months later. Parsons used the months before the second trial doing extensive research about anatomy to discount the provincial pathologist's expert evidence. In the second trial, the jury accepted Parsons's arguments and returned a verdict of manslaughter rather than murder—thereby saving Baldwin from the gallows.[89]

In 1944, Parsons was appointed KC, the third woman in Ontario to receive the honour, and the press continued to report her success in criminal law defence cases.[90] Parsons defended a notorious criminal, Donald "Mickey" MacDonald, who had been charged in 1943 with armed robbery of a truck load of liquor valued at $35,000 and with kidnapping the truck driver. MacDonald was eventually sentenced to fifteen years in the penitentiary, but after Parsons appealed the trial decision, the Court of Appeal ordered a new trial. When the jury again convicted MacDonald in October 1945, Parsons appealed the verdict, both at the Court of Appeal and in the Supreme Court of Canada, but she failed to overturn either guilty verdict. "It was shortly after this final dismissal of the appeal that MacDonald made a sensational escape from Kingston Penitentiary [and he] has never officially been seen since."[91]

In 1944, Parsons explained her sense of legal (ungendered) professionalism:

> [H]er sex is neither a handicap nor an advantage in her court work. When she enters a trial court or appears before the Court of Appeal, she is just another black-robed advocate, and she asks no quarter from her legal adversaries. Her contacts with the seamy side of life haven't dulled a keen and sympathetic understanding of human nature … and there is a touch of the

89 Rosenfeld, "The Lady … and the Crooks," 47; *R v Baldwin* (1945) 84 CCC 159 (Ont CA); and *Globe and Mail* (12 October 1944) 4, (2 March 1945), (9 March 1945) 4, and (20 May 1945) 4.

90 In May 1945, the *Toronto Star*'s headline was "Portia Vera Winner Again: Woman Freed of Murder" after a jury deliberated for only four hours to reach a "not guilty" verdict in a knife slaying in January by Georgina Slemensky. As the news report explained, "It was the third time in nine weeks that Miss Vera Parsons had succeeded as defence counsel in a major criminal case": *Toronto Star* (16 May 1945) 3.

91 Rosenfeld, "The Lady … and the Crooks," 48; and *R v MacDonald* (1948) 84 CCC 177. Parsons also defended a father who, in a depressed state, administered medication overdoses to himself and his wife and three children. He alone survived and was found guilty of manslaughter: *R v Hillborn* (1946) 86 CCC 406 (Ont CA).

> reformer in her makeup. When her clients are young and not too far gone in criminality for redemption, Miss Parsons likes to tell them in man-to-man talk where they are heading unless they mend their ways.[92]

In another interview in 1944, Parsons suggested that there was "no good reason" why women could not be appointed Supreme Court judges in Canada, but added, "Of course, it lies with the ability of the individual woman and with the inclinations of the Minister of Justice."[93] She was later quoted about the need for reforms in the administration of criminal justice, including a larger probation staff and more extensive use of trade schools. She remained firmly focused on law, "quietly but firmly [resisting] attempts to become associated with women's social organizations."[94]

Parsons participated in discussions at the Canadian Bar Association and was among a minority of lawyers who voted not to abolish capital punishment, arguing her case vigorously. In 1963, she was identified as "one of the leading women lawyers," and in her final years she conducted a sole practice, concentrating on estates. She remained at work in her office until three weeks prior to her death in 1973 at the age of eighty-three.[95]

In January 1925, Edith Sheppard was called to the bar, perhaps encouraged by her father who believed that women should have a profession

92 *Globe and Mail* (20 October 1944) 13. Parsons also cautioned that legal work required long hours: "I don't think women should enter law without the thought of using it as an alternative for something else. Law is hard work and calls for long hours and plenty of study. I hardly think the study of law is a particularly good preliminary to marriage." In another report, Helen Tedman (1950) suggested that litigation was not suitable for most women lawyers but that her comments did not apply to "women of the calibre of Vera Parsons," Margaret Fraser (1928), Beatrice Lyons (1935), and Margaret Perney (1927): *Globe and Mail* (5 October 1954) 11.

93 *Globe and Mail* (28 October 1944) 11. Parsons did not challenge social conventions. She explained that she wore a hat in police court because "it is the correct thing to do" in a lower court, where barristers do not gown: *Globe and Mail* (23 January 1947) 12.

94 Hartt, "The Bench and the Bar," 23–24. Parsons also published an article about *R v Thomas* [1953] SCR 344, concerning evidence in a sexual assault case: *Obiter Dicta* (Winter 1953) 33–34.

95 *Toronto Star* (23 April 1954) 33; Rosenfeld, "The Lady ... and the Crooks," 48; and *Woman's Globe and Mail* (9 May 1963). By 1963, the firm was Graham, Parsons & Liscombe, and it remained so until 1972: *Canadian Law Lists*. See also obituary, *Toronto Star* (20 February 1973); LSO, "Diversifying the Bar," Vera I. Parsons; and J. Batten, *Learned Friends: A Tribute to 50 Remarkable Ontario Advocates, 1900–1950* (Toronto: Irwin Law, 2005) 10-11.

because "one never knows what circumstances may arise and they may have to support themselves." She graduated from the University of Toronto in 1921 and then attended Osgoode Hall. Her father owned the Georgian Bay Lumber Company and was a long-standing client of the McCarthy firm. It was probably this connection that resulted in her obtaining articles with Leighton McCarthy. After she was called to the bar in January 1925, Sheppard continued to be employed at the McCarthy firm, and the 1926 partnership agreement lists three partners and five associate lawyers, including Sheppard. She worked closely with William Beattie doing estates and real estate work.[96]

Sheppard thus became the first woman to be employed in a large corporate firm in downtown Toronto. Leighton McCarthy later described her as "the best student we ever had." Although her father encouraged Sheppard to set up her own practice, she demurred because she was uncertain about whether she could attract clients: "The poor people that do fall into my clutches have my sympathy—they are either very loath to entrust anything to me or are mildly amused by me as though I weren't to be taken seriously."[97] She joined the WLAO, and she attended at least one dinner meeting in April 1929, but later that year, she married a British soldier, Captain Revell, who was stationed with the Indian Army in Bombay. Sheppard ceased to practise law, and the couple moved to India, where Sheppard Revell's two children were born. Tragically, she died of peritonitis after an operation in the Bangalore Military Hospital in 1934, and her children, John and Elizabeth, were raised by their grandparents in Ontario after their father's death in 1945. Decades later, on 8 May 2003, the McCarthy firm held a celebration in honour of Sheppard, "the first woman lawyer to work in a downtown firm" in Toronto. The firm named a boardroom after her in 2004.[98]

96 C. Moore, *McCarthy Tétrault: Building Canada's Premier Law Firm* (Vancouver: Douglas and McIntyre, 2005) 57; and LSO Archives, OBBRP, "Edith Sheppard." See also McCarthy Tétrault file, "Edith Sheppard," (archived at the McCarthy Tétrault firm), which reported that Edith's sister became a chemical engineer.

97 McCarthy Tétrault file, "Edith Sheppard"; and C. Moore, "The First Woman to Practice in a Big Downtown Firm," *Law Times* (14 March 2005) 6.

98 LSO Archives, OBBRP, "Edith Sheppard"; LSO Archives, WLAO fonds, SB, vol. 1; Moore, *McCarthy Tétrault,* 57; and McCarthy Tétrault file, "Edith Sheppard." Sheppard was "highly regarded for her intellectual savvy and boundless energy": Media Room, McCarthy Tétrault, May 2003.

Irene Maw was also called to the Ontario bar in January 1925. Maw graduated from the University of Toronto in 1920 and then entered the law school. Her father, Henry Maw, was a lawyer in Toronto, and she may have articled at his firm, although Law Society records indicate that her principal was A. Macgregor in Toronto. Maw was involved, along with Helen Currie (1921) and Margaret Hyndman (1926), in organizing the WLAO's annual dinner meeting in March 1924 at the Madison Inn, and Maw was elected to the WLAO executive as corresponding secretary for the following year. After her call to the bar in 1925, she practised law in her father's firm, Maw & Macdonnell, for some years. However, she reported that she was needed at home and so she carried on a legal practice from her residence. She died in 1959, after practising law for thirty-five years. Maw was also an active member of the University Women's Club and a proud patron of Toronto music and theatre.[99]

Like Maw, Emily Lynch was a lawyer's daughter, and she was called to the bar in September 1925. Lynch practised law in Ford City and then in East Windsor, Essex County, but she established an office in Windsor in the early 1930s at 2545 Wyandotte Street East. She also served as an alderman in Windsor and was appointed QC in 1957. Lynch was among the small number of early women lawyers who were Catholic. She practised law until her retirement in the early 1960s. She died in 1962.[100]

In January 1926, two women were called to the bar. Ruby Wigle, the daughter of a Methodist minister, graduated from Mount Allison University. Initially, she worked as librarian at the Phillips Stewart Library, but in 1927 she purchased the law practice of Lida Pearson Sturdy (1921) in Preston. In the early 1930s, Wigle was probably the first woman to be appointed solicitor to a town council in Ontario, and she was also appointed solicitor for the Imperial Bank in Preston. In 1933, she married George Fish, an accountant at the bank and resold the Preston law practice to Pearson Sturdy. Wigle Fish moved with her spouse to various Ontario locations,

99 LSO Archives, OBBRP, "Irene Maw"; LSO Archives, WLAO fonds, SB, vol. 1; and LSO Archives, WLAO, annual report, 1923–24. Maw may have been "the first Ontario woman lawyer to practise law out of her home while acting as a primary caregiver": Bushby, "The Early Years," 4. See also obituary, *Globe and Mail* (18 December 1959).

100 LSO records suggest that Emily Lynch practised law with her father in Windsor: see LSO Archives, "Diversifying the Bar," Emily Lynch. In contrast, D.J. Lynch was practising law in Campbellford until the early 1940s: *Canadian Law Lists*. See also LSO Archives, WLAO fonds, SB, vol. 1.

including Sault Ste. Marie, Larder Lake, and Virginiatown, and the couple returned to Sault Ste. Marie in 1946. In 1954, they moved to Aurora, and Wigle Fish resigned her practice licence. She was active in many community organizations, including the Women's Institute, the University Women's Club, the Cancer Society, the Imperial Order Daughters of the Empire, and the United Church. She also published articles in *Saturday Night* and elsewhere.[101]

Wigle was called to the bar in the same ceremony as Margaret Hyndman and several male lawyers, where Justice Logie, the presiding judge, welcomed the young men to the profession. He also stated that it was "constitutionally impossible" for him to welcome young women to a profession "in which there was no room for them." Hyndman reported that she and Wigle "stood there smiling and said nothing," although Hyndman later learned that her father had been irate at the judge's remarks. Hyndman entered the law school as a matriculant, after growing up in Palmerston and graduating from high school in Listowel. She had also trained as a secretary to work in a law office "to find out how I could make myself necessary."[102]

Hyndman moved to Toronto and worked as a legal secretary at Bain Bicknell, but she also enrolled at the law school in 1921, at the age of nineteen. She first articled with Albert McMichael but then moved to the office of F.W. Wegenast. By contrast with her secretarial salary, her pay as an articling student was substantially lower. Since she was not assigned much legal work in Wegenast's office, Hyndman volunteered to help with research for his book on company law. As she explained, "company law [was] a bit of a rarity at this time," and Wegenast aspired to lay down the principles as well as explain decided cases, including British and American decisions. *The Law of Canadian Companies* was published in 1931, with Wegenast as its sole author—although it is now usually referred to as

101 G. Sinclair, "History Was Made by Aurora Lawyer," *Aurora Banner* (28 September 1961). See also LSO Archives, WLAO fonds, SB, vol. 1, news report about the call to the bar ceremony for Wigle and Margaret Hyndman (January 1926); Huckle, "List of Women Barristers and Solicitors"; *Canadian Law Lists*; and Wigle, "Sisters in Law."

102 OSCLH, oral history, "Margaret Paton Hyndman," 16–17, 24–32, 37–38, 40. To support herself while articling, Hyndman addressed envelopes for Wood Gundy and tutored three nights a week. She lived with her brother to whom she provided household help. Judge Logie had graciously welcomed Helen Kinnear (1920) when she appeared on a matter in his court: see Kinnear, in this chapter.

a co-authored book. Although Hyndman was called to the bar before the book's publication, she arrived at the office after her admission as a lawyer "and found my name on the door."[103]

Hyndman and her women classmates were the first women students to accept an invitation to attend the annual graduation dinner at Osgoode Hall: "[N]o group of women had ever gone to the annual dinner ... before us, and we made a few inquiries and found that they were always asked but they always said, 'thanks, they were busy that night.' Well, we decided that we weren't going to be busy that night except at the dinner. And whichever one of us was asked was to say she would pass the invitation on, and she was quite sure we would all be there." Hyndman recalled that this graduation dinner occurred during the constraints of Ontario's temperance legislation, and it was Ruby Wigle, daughter of a Methodist minister, who received the invitation. According to Hyndman, "Ruby [took] a long swallow, wondering what Father would think. But ... she was a bit of an actress," and she confirmed that all the women would attend—and that they would also contribute to a fund for liquor.[104]

While Hyndman was determined to ensure women's inclusion in student events at Osgoode Hall, her decision to create a Canadian chapter of Kappa Beta Pi, the American women lawyers' sorority, contributed to some exclusivity among Ontario women lawyers because its membership was restricted to women in active legal practice. After establishing the first Canadian chapter, Alpha Mu, in 1925–26, and later encouraging new

103 OSCLH, oral history, "Margaret Paton Hyndman," 41, 44–48, 47–52. Her obituary credited Hyndman with coauthorship of *The Law of Canadian Companies*: *Toronto Star* (21 January 1991) A11. See also *Globe and Mail* (25 January 1991) D8. The book was reprinted in 1979: *Toronto Star* (21 January 1991) A11; and C. Moore, "The Ontario Legal Alphabet: H is for Hyndman," *Law Times* (22 October 2001) 8. *The Law of Canadian Companies* (Toronto: Burroughs, 1931) initially sold for twenty to twenty-five dollars. Harold Kemp, who had joined the Wegenast firm, did not rejoin the firm after he returned from the Second World War because he was afraid Hyndman would "work him to death." Wegenast died in 1942, and Hyndman practised as a sole practitioner prior to joining Cassels Brock & Blackwell: L. Legge, "Tribute to M. Hyndman" (23 January 1991) in *Continuum* (Osgoode Hall Law School) (1991) 12 at 18.

104 OSCLH, oral history, "Margaret Paton Hyndman," 34. Hyndman also noted: "We had the Chief Justice there and when they offered him a drink, he was shocked. Of course, he had got himself well tanked at home where he had a pre-prohibition supply." She also noted it was not an issue of whether it was improper for women to drink; it was improper for anyone to drink in public at the time.

chapters in France and England, Hyndman was elected Grand Dean of the sorority in 1947, the first grand dean outside the United States. The sorority continued until 1983, when Hyndman concluded that it was no longer necessary because "the time has come when [women lawyers are] finally regarded as just 'persons.'" Although Hyndman was less active in the WLAO after the 1920s, she was awarded the WLAO President's Award in 1990.[105]

After her call to the bar, Hyndman's legal work at Wegenast, Hyndman & Kemp included estates, insurance, patents, securities, litigation, and company law, and in the late 1930s, she assisted Wegenast in a test case about the regulation of birth control. One of Wegenast's business clients, owner of the Kaufman Rubber Company and a man with advanced views about the treatment of employees, had opened several clinics in Ontario to offer birth control counselling and equipment to assist in limiting large families for his employees. In September 1936, Dorothea Palmer was arrested when she visited a home in Eastview (now Vanier), near Ottawa, to offer birth control information to a Kaufman employee and his spouse. Kaufman asked Wegenast to act for Palmer, and Wegenast successfully argued the "public good" defence in the *Criminal Code*'s prohibition of birth control in section 207. After a lengthy trial in Eastview, with "social workers, doctors, gynaecologists, psychiatrists" as experts, Palmer was acquitted, and the Ontario Court of Appeal dismissed the Crown's appeal in 1937.[106]

In 1939, as tensions increased in Europe, Hyndman organized a meeting at the King Edward Hotel to discuss the registration of women in the event of war. The Canadian Women's Voluntary Services (CWVS), modelled on a similar organization in the United Kingdom, created a databank of women volunteers for every constituency in Canada, including identifying homes prepared to receive British children in the event of their evacuation. In

105 LSO Archives, letter to Mary Atkinson (16 February 1972), citing *Golden Anniversary: History of Kappa Beta Pi, 1908–1958* at 20; and Kappa Beta Pi, *Quarterly* (December 1948) 276. See also OSCLH, oral history, "Margaret Paton Hyndman," 81, 85, 168–72; Hyndman recalled working with others to draft the first constitution for the WLAO.

106 *R v Palmer* [1937] 2 DLR 609 (Ont Mag Ct); [1937] OJ No 82; [1937] 3 DLR 493 (Ont CA); and OSCLH, oral history, "Margaret Paton Hyndman," 76–78. In the 1930s, Eastview's population was 71 per cent Catholic, and 17 per cent of families lived on social assistance: M. Dumont et al., *Québec Women: A History,* translated by R. Gannon and R. Gill (Toronto: Women's Press, 1987), 192–95. Dignitaries of the Catholic Church assisted the Crown, and Hyndman recalled that Kaufman paid the witnesses' expenses at the Chateau Laurier Hotel and sponsored a celebratory dinner there for the witnesses and the press after the verdict.

addition, at the winter meeting of the Canadian Bar Association–Ontario, in 1941, Hyndman proposed a system of free legal services for Armed Services members and their dependants. In one day, Ontario lawyers established voluntary services in most county towns for divorce or separation, estates, accident cases, and the guardianship of children, and this wartime legal aid service provided a precedent for publicly funded legal aid services in Ontario in the 1960s. During the war, Hyndman also assisted women in the Free French movement, arranging accommodation and speaking opportunities for them in Canada. At the end of the war, she was awarded the City of Paris Medal for these services.[107]

Hyndman was appointed KC in 1938. She was the second woman lawyer in Canada and the British Commonwealth, after Kinnear, to receive this honour. Her ongoing company law practice and her expert participation in a Senate Committee on Banking resulted in an invitation in 1945 to become the first Canadian woman to be appointed to a trust company board, the London and Western Trust Company. After the war, in the midst of concerns about the expense of butter, Hyndman also represented the new Canadian Association of Consumers as an intervenor in the reference to the Supreme Court of Canada with respect to the *Dairy Industry Act*'s prohibition of the manufacture, sale, or importation of margarine. When the decision was appealed to the Privy Council, Hyndman received notice to

107 Hyndman and Senator Iva Fallis, the second woman appointed to the Canadian Senate in 1935, met with the prime minister to discuss this registration of women volunteers. Hyndman also travelled by train to British Columbia, stopping in numerous cities and provincial capitals, where "there were halls crowded to beyond the doors" with volunteers. She also travelled to eastern Canada: OSCLH, oral history, "Margaret Paton Hyndman," 88–92, 102–5, 161–64.

appear on a motion, thus becoming the first Canadian woman lawyer to appear at the Privy Council.[108]

Hyndman's appearance at the Privy Council coincided with meetings of the Business and Professional Women's Clubs in London. Hyndman was very active in this organization, eventually becoming national president in Canada and then, in 1956, president of the International Federation. She met many women lawyers through this organization, including Helena Normanton, one of the first women to be called to the bar in England in 1922, following enactment of the *Sex Disqualification (Removal) Act 1919*. In 1947, on the twenty-fifth anniversary of Normanton's call to the bar, Hyndman contributed a cake to the celebration in London.

> The Lord Chief Justice was there and the ... Treasurer of each of the Inns of Court, and it was going to be a great big splash. But I knew that [because of post War rationing,] one thing that they wouldn't have much of would be cake, and I have a recipe for a wonderful light fruit cake and I ... made double the quantity and I sent it over to a very old firm of confectioners in London ... famous for ... icings on cakes. So, I wrote to them about it and they said ... that they couldn't possibly do their best, they needed so many pounds of icing sugar ... so many pounds of butter, and they couldn't possibly get that, and so many eggs to make the icing. So, I sent [all these ingredients] over by airmail. And the Lord Chief Justice was asked to cut the cake, with the Sword of Justice, and they found it didn't have any edge to it, it couldn't cut. And

108 *Globe and Mail* (24 December 1938) 1, 15; and OSCLH, oral history, "Margaret Paton Hyndman," 92–101, 108–14, 161–64. See also LSO Archives, WLAO fonds, SB, vol. 3. Before agreeing to the board appointment, Hyndman asked to see the financial statements, noting that she was not "stupid and silly enough to jump at the honour without investigating the company." See also *Reference re Dairy Industry Act (Canada) s 5* [1948] SCJ No 42; [1949] SCR 1; aff'd [1950] JCJ No 1; [1951] AC 179 (JCPC). Hyndman appeared on a motion, not the full hearing, and was not listed as counsel in the case report. She recalled borrowing an appropriate legal collar from her friend Sir Ernest MacMillan. At Christmas, Canada Packers presented Hyndman with a pound of yellow margarine, wrapped in gold paper. See also M. Strauss, "61 Years of Practicing Law," *Globe and Mail* (14 February 1987). A Canadian woman had appeared in the Privy Council (before Hyndman) as a self-represented litigant: C. Backhouse and N. Backhouse, *The Heiress versus the Establishment: Mrs. Campbell's Campaign for Legal Justice* (Vancouver: UBC Press/ Osgoode Society for Canadian Legal History, 2004).

they had to bring the chef in from the kitchen with his big knife to cut the cake. And that just brought the house down.[109]

Hyndman also promoted the creation of Women's College Hospital, and she joined its board in 1939. In addition, as a member of the Women's Emergency Committee for War Hospitals during the Second World War, she helped to lobby the federal government to complete construction of Sunnybrook Hospital to house wounded soldiers, many of whom were in "deplorable conditions" at the Christie Street Hospital. The Women's Emergency Committee had organized "yards and yards" of petitions, put together with cello tape, and Lady Eaton proudly led a placard-carrying procession down Yonge Street to meet the Minister of Defence. Hyndman also participated in the postwar lecture series organized by the Local Council of Women, in which she advocated for reform so women could sit on juries.[110]

In addition, as part of a committee of the Business and Professional Woman's Club, she lobbied Premier Frost's postwar government for equal-pay legislation. The club hired an economist to counter the government's concerns about negative impacts on the economy and organized women across Ontario to telephone their MPPs regularly to lobby for equal pay. In 1951, the *Female Employees Fair Remuneration Act* was enacted. Hyndman conceded that "it was a beginning," but she also believed that "the Bill didn't have any teeth in it." Two decades later, she represented Elizabeth Kennedy and Patricia Harris in their lengthy equal-pay case against Bell Canada pursuant to federal equal-pay legislation. Although a referee appointed to hear the complaint upheld the claims, Bell Canada's appeal to the Federal Court was successful. At the same time, publicity about the

109 OSCLH, oral history, "Margaret Paton Hyndman," 129, 133–37, 197–206; *Globe and Mail* (7 July 1953), (13 July 1956), (9 May 1966) 12, (8 January 1976), and (14 February 1987); LSO Archives, WLAO fonds, SB, vol. 6; and M. Porter, "The Legal Lady," *Maclean's Magazine*, (15 July 1949) 23. See also Bourne, *Helena Normanton*; and *Sex Disqualification (Removal) Act, 1919*, 9 & 10 Geo 5, c 71.

110 OSCLH, oral history, "Margaret Paton Hyndman," 173–78; *Globe* (25 May 1935); *Globe and Mail* (9 September 1944), (15 September 1944), and (3 October 1946) 13. See also S. Morrison, "The Self-Made Woman," *Board of Trade Journal* (May 1976) 46–47; and J. Bradbeer, "Sunnybrook Park Was Home to Elite Stables Before It Hosted a Hospital for Veterans," *Toronto Star* (28 August 2016) IN7. See also LSO Archives, WLAO fonds, SB, vol. 6, "Jury Work a Duty," *Globe and Mail* (16 February 1953).

case contributed to increasing acceptance of the concept of "equal pay for work of equal value" in Canada.[111]

Hyndman also contributed significantly to the work of the Royal Commission on the Status of Women, which reported in 1970, providing a template for reforms in women's interests. She was present in 1966 at the first meeting of representatives of women's organizations, arranged by Laura Sabia in the basement of the University Women's Club on St. George Street. After the meeting, Hyndman was part of a small group designated to contact government leaders. After news reports indicated that sixty women, representing thirty-two women's organizations, were heading to Ottawa to present a brief for a royal commission to Prime Minister Lester Pearson in November, the Commission was established, with Florence Bird (Anne Francis) as chair. Hyndman herself presented the brief of the Canadian Federation of Business and Professional Women's Clubs at the Royal York Hotel in Toronto in June 1968. Moreover, after the Commission's report was released in 1970, Hyndman actively promoted its 167

111 S. Tillotson, "Human Rights Law as Prism: Women's Organizations, Unions, and Ontario's Female Employees Fair Remuneration Act, 1951" (1991) 72:4 *Canadian Historical Review* 532 at 541. Tillotson identified Hyndman as the leader of the campaign of the Business and Professional Women's Club. See also M. Griffin Cohen, "Employment and Economic Issues: The Fair Employment Practices Committee" in B. Atcheson and L. Marsden, eds., *White Gloves Off: The Work of the Ontario Committee on the Status of Women* (Toronto: Second Story Press, 2018) 59 at 90–96; L. McDonald, "The Challenge Accepted: The Founding of the Ontario Committee on the Status of Women" in Atcheson and Marsden, eds., *White Gloves Off*, 33 at 47–51; OSCLH, oral history, "Margaret Paton Hyndman," 139–48; *Globe and Mail* (9 March 1951); and *Toronto Telegram* (9 March 1951); *The Female Employees Fair Remuneration Act*, SO 1951, c 26; and *Female Employees Equal Pay Act*, SC 1956, c 38. By 1961, all provinces except Québec and Newfoundland had enacted similar statutes: L. Bohnen, "Women Workers in Ontario: A Socio-legal History" (1973) 31 *University of Toronto Faculty of Law Review* 45 at 63; C. Kates, "'Identical or Substantially Identical': Bell Canada and the Struggle for Equal Pay, 1967–1976" (1990–91) 4 *Canadian Journal of Women and the Law* 133; and *Re Harris* [1976] 1 FC 84. See also OSCLH, oral history, "Margaret Paton Hyndman," 209–10, 248–53; E. Paris, "How Are the Nice Girls Doing in Places Like Banks, the Bell and Air Canada?," *Chatelaine* (September 1973) 48; Z. Bieler, "Sorry—But All the Lines to Equal Pay Are Busy," *Montreal Star* (22 November 1972) C-1; and M. Townson, "Bell Job-Plan Knocks Bias," *Financial Times of Canada* (10 March 1975) 19.

recommendations.[112] In the 1970s, Hyndman also participated pro bono as an intervenor in a challenge to the equality provision in the Bill of Rights in relation to "Indian" women's right to retain their status on marriage to non-Indigenous men. The challenge succeeded at the Federal Court of Appeal, but it was overturned in a five-four decision by the Supreme Court of Canada, a result that helped to galvanize women's participation in political action about the definition of "equality" in the *Canadian Charter of Rights and Freedoms* in the early 1980s.[113]

In the last two decades of her life, Hyndman received numerous honours, and many acknowledged her efforts on behalf of women's equality. She was appointed an Officer of the Order of Canada in 1973, and a dinner was held in Toronto in 1976 to celebrate the fiftieth anniversary of the Alpha Mu chapter of Kappa Beta Pi, with Lieutenant Governor Pauline McGibbon in attendance. Hyndman was one of four lawyers—and the only woman—to receive the first Law Society Medals, awarded in 1986, and she was one of five recipients of the Persons Award in 1988.[114] Yet, throughout her legal career, Hyndman steadfastly asserted that her gender was irrelevant: "Only the fact that I am a lawyer matters. That I am a woman is of no consequence." And she advised other women lawyers to "forget your sex and expect no quarter." As Justice M.M. Van Camp explained in 1990: "Margaret Hyndman never described herself as a 'woman lawyer'—though

---

112 *Globe and Mail* (29 June 1966) W2, and (3 November 1966) W6. See also *Globe and Mail* (4 June 1968) 13, (30 March 1971) 10; Royal Commission on the Status of Women, *Report of the Royal Commission on the Status of Women in Canada* (Ottawa: Information Canada, 1970); K. Macpherson, *When in Doubt, Do Both: The Times of My Life* (Toronto: University of Toronto Press, 1994) 150–51; F. Bird, *Anne Francis: An Autobiography* (Toronto: Clarke, Irwin, 1974); and B. Atcheson, "Equality Is a Woman's Place: The Royal Commission on the Status of Women" in Atcheson and Marsden, *White Gloves Off*, 23. In addition to equal pay, Hyndman advocated for women's access to post-secondary education and nondiscrimination in employment.

113 *Attorney General of Canada v Lavell* [1974] SCR 1349. Frances Smookler from the Business and Professional Women's Club assisted Hyndman: OSCLH, oral history, "Margaret Paton Hyndman," 149–60. Some Indigenous groups supported Lavell, while others supported the status quo. Hyndman may have become involved in this litigation because she had leased a Georgian Bay cottage situated on Indigenous lands and had good relationships with Indigenous women living there: OSCLH, oral history, "Margaret Paton Hyndman," 151–60.

114 *London Evening Free Press* (26 July 1973); *Toronto Sun* (9 January 1976), (13 January 1976); and *Globe and Mail* (28 February 1986) A17; (1986) 20:1 *Law Society of Upper Canada Gazette* n.p.; and *Toronto Star* (13 October 1988) M1 and M4.

she was a lawyer who took action on many of the issues which [affected] the lives of women."[115]

Indeed, Hyndman avoided looking for discrimination: "I haven't found any discrimination. I haven't looked for it. I think it's a very good rule to follow—not to look for discrimination, not to see it."[116] Nonetheless, during a press interview in the 1970s, Hyndman hinted at some ambivalence about discrimination in relation to her career. At the time, she was being interviewed in Ottawa about the implementation of the recommendations of the Royal Commission on the Status of Women.

> Asked if she is disappointed not to be a Supreme Court judge, she replied: "I have been at peace over unfulfilled ambitions for 20 years. Not appointing a woman judge has been discrimination. It was broken with the appointment of Mabel Van Camp. Again, as in most jobs, a woman has to be much better than a man. This applies to women judges."[117]

Hyndman might not have approved the heading for her obituary in 1991: "Lawyer Margaret Hyndman was a Woman's Rights Pioneer and a Leader in the Legal Profession." At the same time, the wording captured her exceptional work, not just as an outstanding member of the legal profession, but also as a lawyer who continually advocated for legal reforms concerning the rights of Canadian women.[118]

In May 1926, Elizabeth Davies joined the legal profession, but she may have practised only briefly, perhaps in Ottawa, and she had discontinued

---

115 Porter, "The Legal Lady," 23; LSO Archives, "Diversifying the Bar," Margaret Hyndman; and *Continuum* (Osgoode Hall Law School) (1991) 18.

116 *Globe and Mail* (14 February 1987) B1. After this comment, Hyndman continued: "That doesn't mean that there aren't judges who are prejudiced against women. I think there are. I think there are other male members of the profession who are prejudiced. But there are some who gargle their soup, there are some who spot their ties."

117 *Ottawa Journal* (16 March 1973). For Mabel Van Camp (1947), see Chapter Five.

118 *Toronto Star* (21 January 1991). In 1976, in honour of the fiftieth anniversary of her call to the Ontario bar, Hyndman's law firm, Blackwell Law, planted a beech tree on the north side of Campbell House. See also Batten, *Learned Friends*, 12–13.

her practice by 1931.[119] Four other women were called to the bar in November 1926, including Ethel Renwick, later Clark, who worked at Confederation Life in its Hamilton office for some years. After her marriage to Dr. E. Clark in 1936 in Caledonia, she ceased legal practice.[120] In contrast, Bertha Hawkins, who was also called to the bar in November 1926, continued to practise law for several decades. Hawkins articled with Hartley Dewart, KC, a former leader of the Ontario Liberal Party from 1919 to 1921.[121] After her call to the bar, she was employed continuously at Malone, Malone & Montgomery in Toronto, and she may also have been involved with the Toronto General Trusts Corporation, until her retirement. Her legal work focused on the Surrogate Court. Hawkins was appointed QC in 1958.[122]

Laura Lees, who entered the law school in 1921 as a matriculant, articled in Perth with John Hope at Hope & O'Donnell and later with Latchford & McKay. She practised for two years in Renfrew with T.M. Costello, who later became a judge of the County Court, and she was called to the bar in November 1926. In 1930, Lees began her lengthy employment at the Agricultural Development Board. When the Hepburn Liberals formed the new government in 1934 and initiated a program of austerity in the public service, both Lees and Margaret Perney (1927) were dismissed by the government because, in contrast to men, it was assumed that women

119 There is little information about Davies. Huckle, "List of Women Barristers and Solicitors," identified Davies as being located in Ottawa until her resignation from the Law Society in 1931, but WLAO records suggest she was in Toronto and not practising: LSO Archives, WLAO fonds, SB, vol. 1. Mitchell Thomas did not mention Davies as a woman lawyer in Ottawa: Mitchell Thomas, "The History of Women Lawyers in the County of Carleton Law Association," and there are no entries in the *Canadian Law Lists*, 1926–31.

120 LSO Archives, WLAO fonds, SB, vol. 1; and Huckle, "List of Women Barristers and Solicitors."

121 Dewart resigned in 1921 amid ongoing criticism and controversy in the Liberal Party. As the senior partner at Dewart, Maw & Hodgson, he was widely known for his courtroom skills, having successfully obtained a "not guilty" verdict in the celebrated case of Carrie Davies, who was charged with the murder of Bert Massey in 1915: C. Gray, *The Massey Murder: A Maid, Her Master, and the Trial that Shocked a Country* (Toronto: HarperCollins, 2013) 171–ff. In the early 1920s, Dewart was in his sixties, and his partner at the time of the Massey murder case was Henry Maw, the father of Irene Maw (1925). See also P. Oliver, *Public and Private Persons: The Ontario Political Culture, 1914–1934* (Toronto Vancouver: Clarke, Irwin, 1975).

122 LSO Archives, WLAO fonds, SB, vol. 1; Huckle, "List of Women Barristers and Solicitors"; and *Canadian Law Lists*. See also OSCLH, oral history, "Margaret Smith," 92–93.

did not need jobs to support their families. After organized resistance by WLAO members and women's organizations, both Lees and Perney were reinstated. Lees was often present at WLAO events, and she continued in government employment for the rest of her career. In 1960, both Lees and Lorna McWilliams (1922) were employed in the Department of Agriculture. Lees died in 1965.[123]

Grace Hunter graduated with an MA from the University of Toronto, and after attending Osgoode Hall she was called to the bar in November 1926. Her father and two brothers were also lawyers in Toronto, and she joined their firm, Hunter & Hunter, in the Temple Building, in the late 1920s. In addition, Hunter became president of University College Alumnae and a member of the Canadian Women's Press Club, publishing articles in *Saturday Night*. Her article about Helen Kinnear in 1934 suggested that "nobody looking at the new KC would suspect her of being a *bas bleu*." In 1936, Hunter reported on the visit of several WLAO members at the home of Mrs. Ward Wright (Geraldine Robinson, 1907) by Lord Thankerton, a member of the Privy Council in Britain.[124] Hunter travelled widely in Canada, the United States, and Europe, and she was active in political work: "She spent the summer of 1932 in Ottawa, preferring to attend the sittings of the Imperial Conference to a holiday in Muskoka." She was active in the WLAO and was elected president in 1930–31, and she was also involved with the Local Council of Women. In the early 1940s, Hunter worked as a librarian at the Phillips Stewart Library.[125]

In January 1927, there were thirteen women students at Osgoode Hall Law School, and two more women joined the bar that month: Elva Dunn and Gertrude Sinclair. Dunn articled with T.H. Crerar, KC, in Hamilton.

123 LSO Archives, OBBRP, "Laura Lees"; LSO Archives, WLAO fonds, SB, vol. 1; and *Canadian Law Lists*. See also OSCLH, oral history, "Margaret Smith," 95; J. Saywell, *"Just Call Me Mitch: The Life of Mitchell F. Hepburn* (Toronto: University of Toronto Press, 1991) 170–ff; and G.E. Reaman, *A History of Agriculture in Ontario* (Toronto: Saunders, 1970).

124 LSO Archives, WLAO fonds, SB, vol. 1, G. Hunter, "Our First Woman KC," *Saturday Night* (1934), a profile of Helen Kinnear KC; and G. Hunter, "Lady Lawyers and Lord Thankerton," *Saturday Night* (10 October 1936). Hunter's oldest brother, Gordon Hunter, became Chief Justice in British Columbia. For Robinson Wright, see Chapter Two.

125 LSO Archives, WLAO fonds, SB, vol. 1; and *Canadian Law Lists*. Huckle, "List of Women Barristers and Solicitors," identified Hunter as "practising" in Toronto, but the duration of her practice is unclear. As WLAO President, Hunter prepared the WLAO motion in 1931 about the need for women lecturers at Osgoode Hall: LSO Archives, WLAO fonds, SB, vol. 2, *Mail* (24 January 1931).

After her call to the bar, she worked with O'Reilly & O'Reilly but later became a solicitor in the Wills Department of the Toronto General Trusts Corporation. Dunn was active in the WLAO. She was elected to the executive in 1932–33 and became President in 1941–42.[126] Gertrude Sinclair, later Haines, was the daughter of Victor Sinclair, KC, Chair of the Workmen's Compensation Board. After being called to the bar, she worked briefly with her father as a claims officer, then practised with Holmstead & Sutton in Toronto until 1941. Sinclair had visited France with her sister in 1927, where they met with Suzanne Grinberg, a noted woman lawyer and a founding member of the Society of Women Jurists of France. Sinclair successfully encouraged this group to join Kappa Beta Pi, making France the second jurisdiction outside the United States to establish a chapter of the sorority.[127] Sinclair was involved with the WLAO, and she continued to practise law after her marriage to J.A. Haines, but she retired after the birth of her second daughter. She died in 1952.[128]

Two more women were called to the bar in the fall of 1927. Both Margaret Perney and Elizabeth Maclennan practised law for many years and neither married. Perney, the daughter of a director of education in Hamilton, completed one year at the University of Toronto in 1922 and then attended Osgoode as a matriculant while articling with Thomas Hobson, KC, at Lees, Hobson & Co. in Hamilton. She also worked briefly with the women's law firm of Daley and Thompson in Toronto. According to a news report at the time of her death, she chose to study law after her brother, Frank, was killed in the First World War: "It was her way of continuing a career he had started as a student in Osgoode Hall." After Perney's call to the bar, she opened an office in Hamilton, but after two years, she accepted an appointment as a solicitor with the Agricultural Development Board in Toronto, drawing up agreements and deeds. With Laura Lees, Perney was actively supported by the WLAO's lobbying when the Hepburn government

126 "Training for Portia Roles at Osgoode Hall," *Toronto Daily Star* (22 January 1927); LSO Archives, WLAO fonds, SB, vols. 1, 2: "Call 22 to the Bar, Two Feminine Ones"; and Bushby, "The Early Years."

127 LSO Archives, WLAO fonds, SB, vol. 2, unidentified news report, "Toronto Girl Forms Legal Sorority in France."

128 LSO Archives, WLAO fonds, SB, vols. 1, 6, "Funeral Wednesday for Mrs. J.A. Haines," *Toronto Star* (2 December 1952); Huckle, "List of Women Barristers and Solicitors"; and OSCLH, oral history, "Margaret Smith," 91. According to Smith, James Haines later practised law with Donald Lamont, the spouse of Mary Frawley Lamont (1937).

decided to terminate their employment in the early 1930s. Perney was active in the WLAO and served as President twice, in 1931–32 and again in 1939–40.[129]

In 1940, Perney opened her own law office in Toronto at 45 Richmond Street West, doing real estate and estates work, with an occasional civil court case. She was co-counsel with George Walsh in a major family law dispute, *Maynard v Maynard,* in the Supreme Court of Canada. Acting for the husband, Walsh and Perney successfully defended a court order for lump sum alimony and maintenance, an order that was based on the terms of a separation agreement signed by the spouses.[130] During her career, Perney was active in several community organizations: she was a board member of Women's College Hospital, an honorary member of the Business and Professional Women's Club, and a member of the Local Council of Women, the Law Association of Ontario, Kappa Beta Pi, the Progressive Conservative Eglinton Riding Association, and the Soroptomist Club, among others. She was appointed KC in 1950.[131] Beginning in 1954, Perney was elected continuously as a Toronto school trustee and was chair of the Toronto Metropolitan School Board when she died in 1960 at the age of fifty-eight. After her death, it was revealed that she had donated student scholarships anonymously: "Few people ever knew that Miss Margaret Perney, the constantly cheerful Toronto school trustee ... was a pioneer in city scholarships. It was typical of her that $500 scholarships donated to two Toronto honors Grade 13 graduates were kept secret—even from other

129 LSO Archives, OBBRP, "Margaret Perney"; LSO Archives, WLAO fonds, SB, vol. 1, obituary, *Globe and Mail* (10 September 1960); and *Telegram* (4 January 1950). See also Bushby, "The Early Years," 8.

130 Obituary, *Globe and Mail* (10 September 1960); *Telegram* (4 January 1950); LSO Archives, OBBRP, "Margaret Perney"; and *Canadian Law Lists.* See also *Maynard v Maynard* [1951] SCR 346, a case in which a wife, at a time when she was employed, agreed to a divorce and lump-sum maintenance and alimony in a separation agreement. When she subsequently had health issues and wanted to claim ongoing maintenance from her former spouse, the SCC decision confirmed that the agreement between the spouses (which had been included in the order of decree nisi) was valid and enforceable pursuant to the *Matrimonial Causes Act,* RSO 1937, c 208.

131 Obituary, *Globe and Mail* (10 September 1960); and LSO Archives, WLAO fonds, SB, vol. 6.

trustees. [Her appointment as KC] was an appropriate recognition of a woman who firmly believed in the public contribution of women."[132]

Like Perney, Elizabeth Maclennan entered the legal profession after the death of her brother R. Ward Maclennan, who had entered the law school in 1914, but joined the war effort and later died in an aviation accident. Elizabeth Maclennan graduated from the University of Toronto, and she was doing graduate work in history at the University of Oxford when her father asked her to take her brother's place in his firm, Mowat Maclennan. She began her law studies in 1924, articling with her father, and she was called to the bar in November 1927, at the age of twenty-eight. She was active in the WLAO for many years, becoming President in 1936–37. Maclennan was appointed a KC in 1948, and she was the second woman to be elected president of the York County Law Association in 1965. Maclennan died in 1973 in Aurora after a long career in the practice of law: "Elizabeth is remembered for her great kindness and generosity of spirit and her strong ethical and social conscience. Being earnestly concerned to help those who could little afford her services, she often worked for pennies and visited ill or aged clients who would have found the trip to her downtown office difficult or impossible."[133]

Three women were called to the bar in 1928. Edna Dawson, who was a graduate of the University of Toronto, obtained employment with the *Toronto Daily Star* after being called to the bar in June. There are few additional details about her and no mention of her in reports of WLAO activities.[134] Similarly, there is little information about Marjorie Reid, later Gunn, who was called to the bar in November 1928. Although she had a special interest in the work of the League of Nations, she did not engage in legal practice.[135]

132 LSO Archives, WLAO fonds, SB, vol. 6: J. Hutton, "Miss Perney Sponsored Scholarships," unidentified press report. Perney's law practice was taken over by Donna Haley (1955): LSO Archives, OBBRP, "Margaret Perney."

133 LSO Archives, OBBRP, "Elizabeth Maclennan"; *Continuum* (Osgoode Hall Law School) (Winter 2014) 32; Honsberger, *The County of York Law Association*, 105. By 1955, the firm was Mowat, Maclennan, Titus & Hilley: *Canadian Law Lists*.

134 LSO Archives, WLAO fonds, SB, vol. 1; Huckle, "List of Women Barristers and Solicitors"; and *Toronto Daily Star* (22 January 1927).

135 Reid married N.A. Gunn: LSO Archives, WLAO fonds, SB, vol. 1. See also Huckle, "List of Women Barristers and Solicitors," which described Reid as "non practising." The List included an additional surname for Reid: "Robertson."

By contrast with Dawson and Reid, Margaret Fraser entered legal practice in June 1928 and practised continuously until the late 1970s. The daughter of an Ottawa lawyer, Fraser graduated from the University of Toronto in 1925 and articled in Ottawa with Joseph Fisher. She joined the firm of Johnston, Grant, Dods & MacDonald, a firm of eight lawyers located in the Canada Permanent Building in Toronto.[136] Fraser did assistant counsel work. The firm's name changed as some lawyers left and others joined—by the mid-1960s, the firm was Adams, Fraser, Smith and Shaver, located at 200 University Avenue. Fraser was "a senior partner" in the firm. Her litigation practice involved appearances before the Ontario Court of Appeal and the Supreme Court of Canada. For example, she appeared successfully for the plaintiff in the Supreme Court of Canada in 1958 in *Gatz v Kiziw*, a case involving possessory title and the impact of Ontario's *Land Titles Act*.[137]

Fraser was appointed KC in 1948. She was an active member of the WLAO and was elected President in 1932–33, and she became vice-president of Kappa Beta Pi in 1939–40. In addition, Fraser's standing in the profession was recognized when she was elected President of the York County Law Association in 1953, the first woman to hold this post in the sixty-seven years of the association. Notwithstanding this accomplishment, the published history of the Association notes Fraser just once—for reviving dinner meetings after the Second World War. Fraser died in 1977.[138]

In 1929, seven women entered the profession. Janet Gibson, later VanEvery, was called to the bar in June, and practised with Gertrude Sinclair Haines (1927) at Holmstead & Sutton in the Royal Bank Building for about two years. She ceased practice prior to her marriage to her

136 LSO Archives, OBBRP, "Margaret Fraser;" and Huckle, "List of Women Barristers and Solicitors." Another record indicates that Fraser articled with her father, Angus Fraser, KC, of Perkins & Fraser in Ottawa: LSO Archives, WLAO fonds, SB, vol. 1.

137 Obituary, "Margaret Fraser, Senior Law Partner," *Toronto Star* (7 November 1977). Fraser became a partner at the firm in 1940; the *Canadian Law Lists* in 1941 identified Smiley, Shave, Adams, DeRoche and Fraser at 320 Bay Street. See also *Gatz v Kiziw* 1958 CanLII 12 (SCC), [1959] SCR 10, in which counsel for the defendant was W.B. Williston, QC. In addition to Fraser, Margaret Smith (1944) became a significant woman lawyer at this firm: see Chapter Five.

138 LSO Archives, OBBRP, "Margaret Fraser." See also A.O. Tate, "Took Lawyers 67 Years to Name Woman President," *Toronto Star* (23 January 1953); *Toronto Telegram* (26 January 1953); and Honsberger, *The County of York Law Association*, 49.

classmate Alan VanEvery in 1933.[139] Two women called to the bar in 1929 practised for many years in Hamilton. Frances Milne articled with Treleaven & Treleaven and practised at the firm in the Birks Building for her entire career. In the late 1930s, the firm's name included "Milne." She died in 1977.[140] Margaret Sullivan was admitted as a matriculant in 1924 and articled with her brother, Joseph D. Sullivan. She practised law with him as Sullivan & Sullivan at 28 James Street South for two decades. In 1950, she was still practising law as Sullivan & Sullivan, but on her own at 36 James Street South. She retired in 1970. Frances Milne and Margaret Sullivan were among the large number of women lawyers present at the WLAO tea, hosted by Mrs. W.S. McLay (Florence Thompson, 1922) in Hamilton in 1938.[141]

On 19 September 1929, Helen Grossman was called to the Ontario bar, making her the first Jewish woman lawyer in the province. Grossman was born in 1905 in Zitomar, Russia, the daughter of a merchant who immigrated to Toronto. She entered Osgoode as a matriculant in 1924 and articled with E.F. Singer, KC, a Jewish lawyer in Toronto. She continued to work at Singer's firm after her call to the bar. In 1930, she began a career with the Agricultural Development Board, but she returned to private practice around 1941, establishing a sole practice at 100 Adelaide Street.[142] Numerous press references to proceedings at Osgoode Hall suggest that

139 LSO Archives, WLAO fonds, SB, vol. 1; and *Bench and Bar* (May 1934) 8. VanEvery was then in practice with G.N. Cook on Bay Street: *Canadian Law Lists*. An undated news report later identified "Mrs. Alan VanEvery" as the newly elected Chair of the South Peel Board of Education: LSO Archives, WLAO fonds, SB, vol. 8.

140 LSO Archives, WLAO fonds, SB, vol. 1; Huckle, "List of Women Barristers and Solicitors"; and *Canadian Law Lists*.

141 LSO Archives, OBBRP, "Margaret Sullivan." This record identified Sullivan's father's occupation as "gentleman." See also *Canadian Law Lists*; Huckle, "List of Women Barristers and Solicitors"; and "Women Barristers at Hamilton Tea," *Globe and Mail* (16 May 1938).

142 LSO Archives, OBBRP, "Helen Grossman"; LSO Archives, "Diversifying the Bar," Helen Grossman; LSO Archives, communication from archivist Paul Leatherdale to M.J. Mossman (19 March 2018); and LSO Archives, WLAO fonds, SB, vol. 1. See also LSO Archives, "Diversifying the Bar," E.F. Singer, KC. Singer was called to the Ontario bar in 1912 and became the first Jewish member elected to the Ontario legislature in 1929, representing a Conservative riding in Toronto. Singer was active in promoting legislation to prohibit discrimination. Another Jewish lawyer, Fred Catzman, who won the silver medal at Osgoode Hall Law School in 1929, also experienced challenges in finding work: LSO Archives, OBBRP, "Frederick Catzman."

Grossman had an active legal practice, representing clients in a variety of legal matters, including divorce cases and estates.[143]

In 1955, Grossman received "floods of telephone calls, wires and personal visitations," all extending good wishes for success in the upcoming provincial election—although she was not a candidate! Eventually Grossman realized that radio listeners had confused her name with that of Allan Grossman because "Helen" and "Allan" sounded very similar on radio. She managed to reroute all these good wishes, but the publicity was undoubtedly useful to her practice. Her appointment as QC was announced on New Year's Day in 1956. She was the only woman QC in a group of seventy-five lawyers that year. She became a life member of the Law Society in 1979.[144]

Although there is evidence that some Jewish women lawyers experienced exclusionary practices by the WLAO, Grossman attended some WLAO events in the 1930s. For example, she proposed the toast to out-of-town members at the annual dinner meeting in 1932, to which Helen Kinnear responded. Grossman was also one of three women in her class, including Janet Gibson VanEvery and Annie Epstein Baker, who attended the event in the Great Hall at Osgoode Hall in 1979 on the fiftieth anniversary of their call to the bar. Grossman died in 1988.[145]

Three women were called to the Ontario bar in November 1929. Florence Sexton, later McMahon, articled and practised with Marquis, Pepler & Marquis in St. Catharines, the first woman to practise law in that city. The firm's name changed in 1936 to Marquis & Marquis, and in 1939, it changed again to Marquis, Marquis & Sexton. In the early 1940s, Sexton ceased

143 In 1950, Grossman was listed at 36a Prince Arthur Avenue, but her address was listed as Adelaide Street the following year: *Canadian Law Lists*. Examples of Grossman's litigation were reported regularly: see references in *Globe and Mail* (17 April 1940) 12, (20 May 1942) 19, (27 October 1944) 19, (16 June 1947) 21, (6 May 1958) 34, (9 January 1961) 32, (6 January 1967) 10, and (13 February 1979) 46.

144 *Globe and Mail* (16 June 1955) 16. Helen Grossman's law office was located in the same building as Alderman Allan Grossman's former office. Allan Grossman was elected MPP for the St. Andrew riding: P. Oliver, *Unlikely Tory: The Life and Politics of Allan Grossman* (Toronto: Lester and Orpen Dennys, 1985). See also *Globe and Mail* (2 January 1956) 5; and LSO Archives, OBBRP, "Helen Grossman."

145 *Toronto Star* (11 April 1932) 16; *Globe and Mail* (2 January 1956); and *Globe and Mail* (5 October 1979) 14. See also LSO Archives, OBBRP, "Helen Grossman."

practice in St. Catharines after she married and moved with her husband to New York City.[146]

Beatrice VanWart, who was also called to the bar in November 1929, married Captain Horace VanWart while they were both students at Osgoode. She practised with Davidson & Binkley in Toronto and was active in court work. Then, in the mid-1930s, she and her husband practised law as VanWart & VanWart at their firm at 350 Bay Street. By the 1940s, "Bea" VanWart, who was described as "most bright and most attractive," had obtained a divorce and moved to Ridgefield, Connecticut, where she married "wealthily." Her new husband was W.A.C. Miller. Although she was admitted to the bar of New York State, there is no evidence that VanWart Miller engaged in legal practice there.[147]

Annie Epstein, later Baker, the second Jewish woman lawyer in Ontario, was born in England and arrived in Toronto at age three with her mother and older brothers in 1911. They joined her father, who had immigrated earlier from eastern Europe to find work. Her parents were democratic socialists and involved in the Workmen's Circle, and although her grandfather was a rabbi, her family was not religious. Initially, they lived in a flat above a Chinese laundry but later moved to Kensington Market, "all Jewish" at that time. She attended Jarvis Collegiate and completed Grade 12 at age fifteen, but there was no money for her to attend university. Her mother arranged a visit to their landlord, William Clarke, who was a lawyer: "He was an old man ... [with] offices on King Street, above a tailor shop." After talking to Annie, Clarke said that she would be "a damn good lawyer," and he arranged her articles with Saul Isen (later Eisen) in an office above the bank at Bay and Queen. Epstein earned three dollars per week, mostly

146 LSO Archives, WLAO fonds, SB, vol. 1; *Canadian Law Lists*; and Huckle, "List of Women Barristers and Solicitors."

147 LSO Archives, WLAO fonds, SB, vols. 1, 3: *Star Weekly* (1938). This report identified Mrs. B.O. VanWart (1929) and Mrs. George Grover (Vida Harris, 1921) as women practising with their husbands in Toronto; and Mrs. H.L. Cartwright (Vera Robinson, 1920), practising with her husband in Kingston. See also *Canadian Law Lists*; Huckle, "List of Women Barristers and Solicitors"; and McWilliams, "Leaders among the Women Lawyers," 160–61. McWilliams described Captain VanWart as a "character." He served as a member of the Czech brigade in its counteroffensive in the Urals and its long retreat through Mongolia to China. According to McWilliams, Captain VanWart was a "shattered man" by 1922, but with the help of his wife and classmates, he completed law school. After the couple's divorce, he continued to practise law, and he was later appointed Czech consul.

running errands, but she went to motions and searched titles and learned by asking questions. She vividly recalled the quiet serenity in the Registry Office and the "gorgeous marble staircase going up to Land Titles."[148]

Epstein assisted Isen in a lawsuit against the "schwitz," a bathhouse on Centre Street in the Ward. The claim involved a watch and ring left by a patron with an attendant and not returned, and the "schwitz" was represented by David Goodman. After Isen won the case, Epstein recalled that "Mr Goodman decided to take away Mr Isen's good student," and he offered Epstein fifteen dollars per week. A bit later, she got a "very good job" with Leo Maldaver, also a friend of Goodman, and she remained in his office until her call to the bar. Epstein loved "the historical aspect of the law" in her real estate work, where she got to know who lived where and when.[149]

For her lectures at Osgoode Hall, Epstein always entered through the beautiful Benchers' entrance, but the two lecture halls were tiny, and although she enjoyed the lectures, she "hated the [academic] work," compared with her articling experience. She found law books a "bloody bore" and faced intellectual challenges in the Trusts course taught by Dr Cecil (Caesar) Wright. By contrast, Dean Falconbridge was "a joy; he was such a great guy." There were no student activities, and women students all sat in the front row for lectures, where the lecturers "didn't even notice them."

> You see, it was like an arena, banked up ... and we sat down here in the front row. So we never saw who was speaking. And the dais where the lecturer sat was quite high, there were two steps up, so he talked right over our heads. He never saw us. He was talking completely to the back row of this arena. [And the women didn't ask questions:] No. We didn't dare, we didn't open

148 OSCLH, oral history, "Annie Epstein Baker," 2–40, 45–48, 53–56. Epstein Baker related how Eisen had tried to avoid being tendered on a real estate deal by locking his office door. However, Sam Factor, the person attempting to tender, could see shadows of people through the frosted glass. He stood on two chairs and a desk to peep over the transom. "You can't hide from me," he said. At the Registry Office, Epstein also recalled leaving papers for duplicating in a basket on a pulley.

149 In 1929, when she graduated, Epstein was earning twenty-five dollars per week. She bought a gramophone. She believed that she was "a damn good [articling] student ... I was very creative, and I was very fast, and I was mentally agile." She said she was used to men and didn't flirt with them and thus earned their respect. During strikes in the bakeries, the bakers were clients of her principal, Moldaver: OSCLH, oral history, "Annie Epstein Baker," 58–66, 70.

our mouths. We just listened to the lecturer and then you took your books and you went away.[150]

Epstein was twenty-one when she was called to the bar on 21 November 1929, and "it was tough, because it was 1929 and I couldn't get a job ... because I was Jewish and I was a woman.... So, I went into practice by myself." Law offices were being partitioned as rental spaces, and she hired her cousin to work for her, setting up a telephone and a desk in her little office: "It was tough to make a living." Her father's connections with the Workmen's Circle created some work, and a client for whom she obtained a patent for an overhead garage door paid her five thousand dollars, a sum that she lived on for a year and a half. A few years later, she married her husband, a naval architect from New York, and they established a finance and loan business together, Baker Acceptance. After her three children were born, she worked only sporadically.[151]

In the 1980s, after the finance business ended, Epstein Baker began to practise law again, working in an office on Avenue Road with her son Donald, who had graduated from Osgoode Hall Law School in 1978. Epstein Baker did the typing and bookkeeping and answered the phone. She had remained a member of the Law Society and continued to read the law reports, and she was appointed QC in 1984. Although she lamented the newer trend for lawyers to be confrontational, she concluded that she would "stay right in the profession" if she were twenty years younger.[152]

At the same time, she recalled that it was difficult being a Jewish woman lawyer: "you never walked inside a non-Jewish place, you just didn't. It was

150 Epstein Baker described Janet Gibson, the daughter of Colonel Gibson, as "strictly Rosedale." Gibson kept Epstein in State Express cigarettes all through law school: OSCLH, oral history, "Annie Epstein Baker," 67, 72–73, 75–78.

151 Epstein was rejected for work in Jewish firms: some Jewish lawyers simply laughed and asked her whether she could work at night. Epstein Baker was identified incorrectly as the first Jewish woman lawyer in LSO Archives, "Diversifying the Bar," Annie Epstein Baker. Since Helen Grossman was called to the Ontario bar on 19 September 1929, two months before Annie Epstein Baker, Grossman is the first Jewish woman lawyer in Ontario: Huckle, "List of Women Barristers and Solicitors." After ceasing to practise law, Epstein Baker enjoyed life as "a lady about town" until she began to practise with her son a few decades later: OSCLH, oral history, "Annie Epstein Baker," 84, 86–92.

152 OSCLH, oral history, "Annie Epstein Baker," 100–1, 135; and LSO Archives, OBBRP, "Annie Epstein Baker." Her obituary identified the QC appointment as 1983: *Globe and Mail* (28 February 2005) S7.

as if there was a big sign outside...." And, although no one said that she could not be a lawyer because she was a woman, she acknowledged that some women experienced discrimination. Epstein Baker never joined the WLAO, describing it as women "huddled together ... [in] their own little world." At the same time, she recalled that early women lawyers were tough because they had to prove themselves by being tougher than men. She also expressed real enthusiasm for women in the legal profession in the 1980s and '90s.

> [Epstein Baker described] an incident about 10 years ago when she was waiting in a Supreme Court master's outer office before the hearing of motions. One after another, the chairs around his table became filled with women lawyers. "There were, I think, eight of us and not a man in the room. And the master walked in and he said, 'I don't believe what I'm seeing.' And I looked at him and I said, 'Believe it, master. It's going to get worse.'"[153]

Epstein Baker died in 2005, a few months before her ninety-seventh birthday.[154]

Between 1919 and 1929, fifty-five women joined the Ontario bar. Added to the eleven women who became lawyers between 1897 and 1918, a total of just sixty-six women lawyers were called to the Ontario bar in four decades after Clara Brett Martin. In contrast, only thirty-four women would join the legal profession between 1930 and 1939, the Depression years.

153 Osgoode Society, oral history, "Annie Epstein Baker," 59, 81–83, 137; and "She's Fought for 60 Years as a Lawyer," *Toronto Star* (10 April 1990).

154 LSO Archives, OBBRP, "Annie Epstein Baker."

## CHAPTER FOUR

# *"Unlimited Possibilities"? The Depression Years, 1930–39*

> *Misses Helen Kinnear and Janet Gibson, speaking to the toast to the future ... declared that the next few years would be, for women barristers, a time of great reward. Women were now recognized as an important entity of the professional world, and [they] would very shortly take their places among the leading counsel and most respected of the judiciary.... So far as the woman of the law was concerned, the best was yet to be—the future held for her unlimited possibilities.*[1]

This toast "to the future" for women lawyers was presented at the WLAO annual dinner in the spring of 1929. In October that year, there was also news that the Privy Council had overturned the decision of the Supreme Court of Canada and recognized women as "persons" in relation to eligibility for appointment to the Senate. The case was the culmination of a decade of litigation efforts by Emily Murphy and her four Alberta

1 Law Society of Ontario (LSO) Archives, Women's Law Association of Ontario (WLAO) fonds, SB, vol. 2, unidentified news report, 1929.

colleagues to obtain political rights for Canadian women.[2] At about the same time, the WLAO President, Marian James (1922), reported that more than sixty women had been called to the Ontario bar and that thirteen women were law students. James explained that women were "very excellent counsel," although they were not regularly involved in court work and generally worked in "advising, conveyancing, estate work and general solicitor work."[3]

By the autumn of 1929, the stock market crash and the beginning of the Great Depression were creating new challenges. As Eleanor Wachtel concluded, "Ironically, the victory in the Persons case coincided with the end of the first wave of feminism that revolved around the suffrage movement. For working women, the 1930s was a disaster. As unemployment skyrocketed, women were blamed for taking away jobs from men. Working conditions deteriorated, wages dropped and women's right to work was thrown into question."[4] In this context, the 1930s created new challenges for women lawyers, especially for those who were called to the bar during the Depression—for new women lawyers, opportunities were scarce or non-existent, especially for those without connections to the profession.

2 *Edwards v Attorney General for Canada* [1930] AC 128; and R. Sharpe and P. McMahon, *The Persons Case: The Origins and Legacy of the Fight for Legal Personhood* (Toronto: University of Toronto Press, 2007). Cairine Wilson, the first woman appointed to the Senate in February 1930, was a well-connected member of the Liberal establishment: V. Knowles, *First Person: A Biography of Cairine Wilson, Canada's First Woman Senator* (Toronto: Dundurn Press, 1988). The second woman appointed to the Senate, Iva Fallis, was appointed by the Conservative Prime Minister R.B. Bennett. Although women lawyers were not involved in the *Persons Case*, the lead lawyer for the "Famous Five" was Newton Rowell, a partner of Ward Wright whose wife was Geraldine Robinson Wright (1907). Since the Rowell Wright firm later became McMillan Binch, the firm marked the ninetieth anniversary of the case in 2019 (*Law Times*, 2019, n.p.) See also M. Prang, *N.W. Rowell, Ontario Nationalist* (Toronto: University of Toronto Press, 1975); and E. Harman, "Five Persons from Alberta" in M. Quayle Innis, *The Clear Spirit: Twenty Canadian Women and Their Times* (Toronto: University of Toronto Press/Canadian Federation of University Women, 1966) 158 at 173–78.

3 LSO Archives, WLAO fonds, SB, vol. 1, unidentified press report, ca. 1929–30. This press report also explained that a bill had (again) been introduced in the Québec legislature to permit women lawyers. An Ontario male lawyer was quoted as saying that Québec "need not fear either that there will be too many, or that the women who receive the gown will be unworthy."

4 E. Wachtel, "The Bumpy Road to Equality," *Canadian Living* (October 1989) 50 at 51.

Five women were called to the bar in October and November 1930. One was Lenore Colter, later Kayes, who responded to a toast to the graduating class at the WLAO annual dinner meeting in April 1930. Colter later practised law at her father's firm in Cayuga, and she was active in the Young Liberal Association. She may have ceased practice for a few years after her marriage to Walter Kayes, but in 1936 she was practising again at Colter and Colter in Cayuga. In 1939, she was listed as an employee at the Parliament Buildings in Toronto, but she later ceased to practise law.[5]

Belva Gordon, later Gibson/Hammell, was called to the bar with Colter. Born in the United States, she grew up in Hamilton, where her father was a doctor. As a matriculant, she articled with T.H. Crerar, KC, in Hamilton and with Elizabeth Newton at Jones & Leonard in Toronto while attending lectures at Osgoode Hall. In July 1930, Gordon was appointed to the Agricultural Development Board, but after her marriage in 1933 to another lawyer, J.A. Gibson, the couple moved to Galt to practise law as Gibson & Gibson. By 1942, Gordon Gibson had moved back to Toronto, where she joined Blake, Cassels & Graydon as the first female solicitor at the firm. Significantly, Gibson was advised that "the Firm had been reduced to ... hiring a female lawyer" because of the Second World War, and she was told not to expect the same remuneration or advancement opportunities accorded to her male counterparts. She was also warned that she would have to "fit into the scheme of things" when lawyers involved in the war returned to the firm. Although Gordon Gibson was initially expected to take on the mundane work of keeping the firm's dockets up to date, she also began to do more challenging legal work in the firm's conveyancing department—well

5 LSO Archives, WLAO fonds, SB, vols. 1, 3; E. Huckle, "List of Women Barristers and Solicitors in Ontario" (1897–1975) [unpublished, archived at Law Society of Ontario Archives]; *Toronto Star Weekly* (5 April 1930); and *Canadian Law Lists*. Huckle identified Colter's married name as "Keyes," but the LSO Archives records it as "Kayes": LSO Archives, communication from archivist Paul Leatherdale to M.J. Mossman (14 September 2020).

enough that she "easily broke the glass ceiling," becoming the first woman lawyer admitted to the partnership at Blakes in 1952.[6]

At some point, Gordon Gibson was widowed, and in 1957 she married John (Jack) Hammell, a wealthy Canadian mining magnate and widower. After his death in the United States, she returned to Toronto. As her obituary noted, Gordon Gibson was elected President of the WLAO in 1955–56 and appointed a QC in 1956. She died in July 1960.[7]

Three other women were called to the bar in November 1930. Sybil Bennett was the daughter of a Methodist minister who was an ardent Tory. Her grandparents were United Empire Loyalists and among the first families to settle in Halton County. Bennett graduated from Victoria College in 1926 and attended the law school while articling with W.J.G. Graydon in Toronto. After her call to the bar, she initially obtained employment at the Agricultural Development Board, but she moved to Georgetown in 1936 to enter into a law partnership with Leroy Dale. Bennett was appointed town solicitor for Georgetown, as well as acting solicitor for Brampton, and she continued to practise law. As a distant relative of the prime minister, R.B. Bennett, she proudly wore the KC gown he gifted her when she was

6 LSO Archives, Ontario Bar Biographical Research Project (OBBRP), "Alice Belva Gordon (Gibson/Hammell)"; LSO Archives, WLAO fonds, SB, vol. 1; T.D. Regehr, "Elite Relationships, Partnership Arrangements, and Nepotism at Blakes: a Toronto Law Firm, 1858–1942" in C. Wilton, ed., *Inside the Law: Canadian Law Firms in Historical Perspective* (Toronto: Osgoode Society for Canadian Legal History/University of Toronto Press, 1996) 207 at 213–4; obituary, *Toronto Telegram* (29 July 1960); A. Graydon, *Some Reminiscences of Blakes* (Paget, Bermuda: Beauregard, 1970) 55; and Osgoode Society for Canadian Legal History (OSCLH), oral history, "Margaret Smith," 97. Moore incorrectly reported "Alice Gordon" as being the first woman employed at a large downtown Toronto practice, the McCarthy firm, in 1942: C. Moore, *The Law Society of Upper Canada and Ontario's Lawyers, 1797–1997* (Toronto: University of Toronto Press, 1997), 221. He later identified Edith Sheppard (1925) as the first woman in such a practice: C. Moore, *McCarthy Tétrault: Building Canada's Premier Law Firm* (Vancouver: Douglas and McIntyre, 2005) 57.

7 *Globe and Mail* (16 October 1957); and obituary, "Jack Hammell," *Toronto Telegram* (9 May 1958). The Gordon-Hammell marriage "set the tongues wagging" because J.A. Hammell was also Gordon Gibson's client: P.K. McWilliams, "Leaders among the Women Lawyers—Revisited" (1987) 21:2 *Gazette* 157 at 160. See also obituary, "Alice Belva Hammell," *Toronto Telegram* (29 July 1960), and obituaries in the *Globe and Mail* and other papers in Stratford, Brantford, Montreal, and Hamilton.

appointed KC in September 1945, the fourth woman in the British Commonwealth to receive this honour.[8]

Sybil Bennett professed a lifelong commitment to the Progressive Conservative Party, and she engaged in political debates as a student at Osgoode Hall. In 1949, she became a Conservative candidate for the Halton riding in the federal election, losing by just 1,500 votes. By 1950, she was President of the National Women's Progressive Conservative Association and vice-president of the Ontario Association. As President of the Women's Progressive Conservative Association of Toronto in November 1950, Bennett attended a tea, along with Margaret Perney (1927), and she was an out-of-town delegate at the Ontario Association's annual meeting. In 1953, she was elected to Parliament for the Halton riding, "a riding as old as Confederation itself." Bennett was one of just three women members elected in 1953, and she was the first Ontario woman lawyer to achieve this political status. Press reports at the time often described Bennett's appearance, suggesting that she favoured "smartly-tailored suits and ultra-feminine hats," but these reports also confirmed that she was "one of the party's most effective speakers."[9]

Bennett sternly warned male politicians not to attend women's meetings to offer platitudes and patronizing speeches: "That may have been all right in grandma's day, but it doesn't go over now." In addition, she encouraged young women to become lawyers and to practise law outside larger cities:

> I wish that more young women would study law. I have found that women in my profession can succeed in a country practice. It is true that women lawyers are not adapted to some cases as well as men ... But in rural areas, a

8 LSO Archives, OBBRP, "Sybil Bennett"; *Globe and Mail* and *Toronto Daily Star* (13 November 1956); and LSO Archives, unidentified press report (11 September 1945). Some press reports incorrectly identified the year of Sybil Bennett's KC appointment as 1935: *Ottawa Evening Journal* (1 July 1953). Bennett may also have articled with Rowan, Parkinson & Co, and she became a "popular speaker on laws and citizenship for various organizations": LSO Archives, WLAO fonds, SB, vols. 1, 3. Bennett was one of three women appointed KC in 1945. Palen (1918) and Alford (1916) were appointed KC in November and December, respectively. In 1945 the Conservatives were again in power in Ontario under Premier George Drew. See also press photo of Sybil Bennett, Edra Sanders, and Lily Sherizen at their call to the bar in Ontario: *Victoria Daily Colonist* (25 November 1930).

9 *Toronto Daily Star* and *Globe and Mail* (13 November 1956); *Ottawa Evening Journal* (1 July 1953); and LSO Archives, unidentified press report (11 September 1945).

> woman seems to get in closer touch with the people. She understands more clearly the little problems of human nature. Besides that, she gets a wonderful training in public life and business.[10]

Bennett died in 1956 at the age of fifty-two after suffering ill health for two years.[11]

Edra Sanders, later Ferguson/Christopherson, was called to the bar with Bennett. Sanders attended the WLAO dinner in 1929 with its toast to the "unlimited possibilities" of the future, and she was elected to the WLAO executive as its student representative for 1929–30. Sanders's father practised law at Ingram & Sanders in the railway town of St. Thomas, and her family was well connected to the Conservative Party. Although as a young child, Sanders helped her father sort copies of the *Weekly Notes* in his office, he advised her that it would be a "complete waste of time" for her to study law.[12]

After graduating from grade thirteen, Sanders attended Alma College, a private girls' college in St. Thomas, where she studied drama and public speaking while also working in her father's law office. In 1925, she enrolled at the law school as a matriculant and articled with her father's law partner in St. Thomas. After she moved to Toronto to attend lectures at Osgoode Hall, Sanders's father "begrudgingly" telephoned McGregor Young at the office of the Official Guardian to arrange her articles in Toronto. Young disapproved of women lawyers, and although Sanders was involved in some litigation, she also had to fetch books and robes for Young during

10 *Globe and Mail* (13 November 1956); *Ottawa Evening Journal* (1 July 1953); and LSO Archives, unidentified news report (11 September 1945). Other reports affirmed that Bennett was "an energetic and faithful worker in the interests of her riding." See also *Toronto Daily Star* (13 November 1956): "It is believed that [Bennett] was one of the first women in Canada to enter private practice," a comment that may suggest a lack of visibility for other early women lawyers.

11 LSO Archives, unidentified news report (13 November 1956). Bennett's law partner, Leroy Dale, a Georgetown councillor, died in the same month as Bennett: *Conserv Tor* (15 November 1956). This press report described Bennett and Dale as "two distinguished lawyers and public servants."

12 LSO Archives, WLAO fonds, SB, vol. 2, unidentified news report; OSCLH, oral history, "Edra Sanders Ferguson," 12, 15–18, 27, 31–32, 35–37, 48. Sanders reported that her family employed live-in maids and domestic workers who were often Indigenous women. Her obituary identified her second husband, P.R. Christopherson, who had predeceased her: *Globe and Mail* (18 November 2011).

her articles. Unlike many Canadians in the early 1930s, Sanders was able to travel to Europe for several months after completing her legal education. Indeed, she later recalled that her family "had [no money problems] in the Depression ... [because] the money would come in from real estate transactions ... and we would loan a lot of money on mortgages and we would get paid a finder's fee."[13]

After being called to the bar, Sanders discovered that none of the male lawyers in St. Thomas would hire her. She joined her father's firm, becoming the first woman to practise law in St. Thomas. Her brothers also joined the family firm (Richard in 1935 and Frank in 1937), making it the first four-person family law firm, including a woman, in Ontario. To Sanders, working in a small town meant that she was not just "a cog. I was somebody who knew something."[14] She became active in the community and was elected President of the Business and Professional Women's Club in 1931. She also served on the board of the Children's Aid Societies in St. Thomas and Elgin County, and on the executive of the Liberal-Conservative Association, and vice-president of its branch in western Ontario. Her political aspirations were rewarded when she became the first woman alderman in 1936, heading the polls in St. Thomas, and she was elected by acclamation the following year. A contemporary report suggested that Sanders overcame "the handicap of lingering prejudice to achieve responsible office." She also gave speeches on women's rights,

13 During her articles, Sanders lived with two classmates, Belva Gordon and Lenore Colter, in a boarding house on St. George Street. Although Sanders believed the Depression did not affect her own family, she clearly recalled that "it affected my clients. It was terrible": OSCLH, oral history, "Edra Sanders Ferguson," 30–32, 35–37, 43, 47, 163; and *Globe and Mail* (21 June 2010).

14 Robinson Wright, also from St. Thomas, was called to the bar in 1907 but probably never practised law: see Chapter Two. Sanders' father articled for Robinson's father, and the latter warned Sanders to "never let [your daughter] be a lawyer" because his daughter had decided to marry and never practise law: "All that money I spent on Geraldine." Sanders decided that "things are going to be different [for her]," and she took on litigation at the firm. She became the first woman appointed a senator at the University of Western Ontario [now Western University]: OSCLH, oral history, "Edra Sanders Ferguson," 51–57, 66, 69, 77–84, 117–21, 132. See also "Edra Iles Sanders" (1937) 7:6 *Bench and Bar* 1; LSO Archives, OBBRP, "Edra Sanders Ferguson"; "The Way Things Were," *Continuum* (Osgoode Hall Law School) (Winter 2005); and *St. Thomas Times-Journal* (5 July 1966).

arguing that "woman has the same right and the same economic status as man, the right to take her place in the affairs of the world."[15]

In 1940, Sanders married Donald Ferguson, head of the history department at Guelph Collegiate Vocational Institute. She moved to Guelph, and the couple had two children. According to Sanders Ferguson, she combined motherhood with law practice by foregoing leisure, but she may have practised law only part-time for some years.[16] After her husband's death, Sanders moved to Toronto and was the first appointee to the newly expanded provincial Division Court (now Small Claims Court). Her courtroom was in a former munitions factory and was "overloaded and had no dignity." In addition, the summons list often had up to 360 names, even though the courtroom accommodated only 200 people, and Sanders Ferguson recalled the challenges of trying to assist unrepresented litigants.[17] As a Division Court judge, she also had some jurisdiction as a County Court justice, but she may not have been accepted by male judges. As she explained, "County Court judges would eat [lunch] in the Arcadian Court at Simpsons [and] Supreme Court judges would eat together in

15 (1937) 7:6 *Bench and Bar* 1; and LSO Archives, WLAO fonds, SB, vol. 8, unidentified press report (May 1936). Sanders was presented to the Governor General in Ottawa in 1934 by Anita Dateman Lawson, an Osgoode graduate (1918) who chose not to be called to the bar because her spouse was a member of Parliament: LSO Archives, WLAO fonds, vol. 2, unidentified news report (23 January 1934). For Dateman Lawson, see Chapter Two. See also LSO Archives, "Diversifying the Bar," Edra Ferguson.

16 *Toronto Star* (16 October 1962). Sanders Ferguson reported that she had hired a replacement at the St. Thomas firm but still attended at the office, especially during summer months: OSCLH, oral history, "Edra Sanders Ferguson," 157, 169–70.

17 This judicial appointment was the result of recommendations in *The Silk Report*, prepared by Eric H. Silk, assistant deputy Minister, Department of the Attorney General, and presented to Attorney General Kelso Roberts. The *Report*'s recommendations were intended to relieve heavy caseloads in the County Court. The creation of a dual jurisdiction for a judge of the Division Court and the Family and Juvenile Court was also designed to increase enforcement of child support orders: LSO Archives, WLAO fonds, SB, vol. 7, unidentified news report; and OSCLH, oral history, "Edra Sanders Ferguson," at 86–88, 190–206, 212–15. See also LSO Archives, OBBRP, "Edra Sanders Ferguson."

[Convocation Hall]." But she ate alone. In 1962, she was appointed to the Family and Juvenile Court of Ontario, serving until her retirement in 1975.[18]

As a judge, Sanders Ferguson expressed blunt views about women in law: "Women working with men should always make sex secondary ... forget any conspicuousness that arises from being female by becoming absorbed in the purpose of one's presence." And, although she conceded that a woman "has got to prove herself maybe twice as much as her brother," she also believed that it is not possible to discriminate against a person who didn't recognize they were being discriminated against. At a dinner meeting for women lawyers at the Third Empire and Commonwealth Law Conference in Sydney, Australia, in 1965, an Australian woman lawyer commented that "being as good as the next man isn't enough. Not if you're a woman. You've got to be a whole lot better to stand any sort of a show." As the press reported, "Judge Ferguson from Canada shot back: All right then, accept that and get on with it. The more women complain about sex prejudice, the more they draw attention to being women, rather than lawyers or doctors or what have you. Be confident. Be good at your job and you'll get there."[19]

Judge Ferguson received an honorary degree from the University of Western Ontario, and in 2011, at the age of 101, she became the oldest recipient of the Order of Canada for her contributions to law and women's rights. She was fondly remembered as "Ma Ferguson" by many lawyers and clients who appeared in her courts.[20]

---

18 Lunch arrangements that excluded women judges were common in earlier decades. In the United States, Nadine Gallagher ate sandwiches alone in her judicial chambers for ten years while her male colleagues lunched together elsewhere: R. Chester, *Unequal Access: Women Lawyers in a Changing America* (South Hadley, MA: Bergin & Garvey, 1985) 84.

19 OSCLH, oral history, "Edra Sanders Ferguson," 37–38; and LSO Archives, WLAO fonds, SB, vol. 8, *Australian Women's Weekly* (22 September 1966). See also *Toronto Daily Star* (16 October 1962); *Tribune* (3 September 1966); and *Sydney Morning Herald*, "Women's Section" (26 August 1965) for a report about the judges from Australia and the Commonwealth proceeding through Sydney streets, in robes and wigs, to the Town Hall, where they sat to hear the opening address of the conference by Lord Gardiner, Lord Chancellor of Great Britain. A photo of this occasion includes only two women: Judge Edra Ferguson, from Ontario, and Roma Mitchell, QC, then vice-president of the Law Council of Australia.

20 Obituary, *Globe and Mail* (18 November 2011).

Lily Sherizen, later Sharon, was the third woman called to the bar with Sanders and Bennett in November 1930, becoming the third Jewish woman lawyer in Ontario.[21] Sherizen was born in Mozir, Lithuania, the daughter of a wealthy man. In contrast, after the family immigrated to Canada, her father pressed clothes at Eaton's, and later opened a furniture store. Sherizen and her three brothers did not attend university because, as she explained, "I am a Cabbagetown kid." She applied for jobs in journalism without success, and then decided to try law as a way of assisting her father in his furniture business. To be admitted as a matriculant at Osgoode Hall, she had to complete three more high school courses, and she also struggled to find an articling position:

> If you are going into law, you had to article somewhere. And the doors were closed, and especially to little Jewish girls. Anne [Epstein] Baker got into a law office, and Helen Grossman got into a law office ahead of me. But they weren't very good examples apparently because I couldn't get in—people said, "no, they had enough," and they didn't want anymore little girls in their offices. [Then, after I told Mr. Goodman] that I was related to him and wanted to be a lawyer—and at $2 a week, what did he have to lose, he took me in![22]

As the only Jewish woman in her class at Osgoode Hall, Sherizen often felt isolated because her classmates did not include her in their social activities. Although one-third of all Jews in Canada were living in Toronto, the largest non-British ethnic group in the city, many were recent immigrants, especially from Poland, and they were concentrated in Wards Three, Four, and Five, where they dominated work in the needle trades. After Hitler rose to power in Germany in 1933, fascist organizations became prominent in the city, and swastikas frequently appeared at Jewish social occasions. The climax was the Christie Pits Riot in 1933, which

21 Sherizen later used her own surname as well as Sherizen-Sharon: see *Globe and Mail* (13 June 1956), (15 June 1957), and (4 June 1959). In contrast, Law Society records incorrectly identify her spouse as Leon Shanon: LSO Archives, OBBRP, "Lily Sherizen," while other records refer to Lily Sherizen Charon.

22 OSCLH, oral history, "Lily Sherizen Sharon," 1–9, 14; LSO Archives, OBBRP, "Lily Sherizen"; and LSO Archives, WLAO fonds, SB, vol. 1. David Goodman also provided positions to several able young Jewish lawyers when they were unable to secure positions elsewhere: LSO Archives, "Diversifying the Bar," David Goodman.

erupted when Nazi supporters in the stands at a baseball game taunted the Jewish team. Discrimination was compounded by increasingly restrictive immigration policies for Jews: only 5,000 Jewish immigrants entered Canada between 1933 and 1945.[23] Moreover, although the number of Jewish lawyers in Canada increased from 104 in 1921 to 351 ten years later, the number of Jewish women lawyers in Toronto remained at three: Grossman (1929), Epstein Baker (1929), and Sherizen (1930).[24]

After her call to the bar, Sherizen remained in the office of David Goodman, KC, until 1944. She was engaged in a variety of legal work, including defending an accused in a criminal case in Kitchener. She was also active in social organizations and president of the Iota Alpha Pi sorority, a literary society, when the artist Arthur Lismer was a guest speaker. In 1939, she participated in a Hadassah event to support refugees, and she organized a group of professional women to support the Zionist cause. Sherizen was one of a few women on the executive of the Zionist Organization of Canada.[25]

In 1944, when Sherizen was still receiving the same (articling) salary at Goodman's firm, she decided to set up her own sole practice, although it was challenging to rent space during the war. Dr. Gelber, who knew her through her volunteer activities at the Brunswick Street Schul, rented her a little office for fifteen dollars a week, and she "found a little old desk, and a reconditioned typewriter," and paid a secretary in a millinery office next door to answer the phone and type letters. As Sherizen recalled, she

23 M. Mandel, *The Jewish Hour: The Golden Age of a Toronto Yiddish Radio Show and Newspaper* (Toronto: Now and Then Books, 2016) 29–30, 60–63. As Mandel noted, Jews were first elected to the Ontario legislature in the 1930s: David Croll, representing Windsor Walkerville (1934–43); E.F. Singer, representing St. Andrew in Toronto, 1929–34), and J.J. Glass, representing St. Andrew (1934–43). See Legislative Assembly of Ontario, "Members," online: <http://ola.org/en/members/all>.

24 S. Sperdakos, "'A Forum for Discussion' and a Place of Respite: Jewish Lawyers and Toronto's Reading Law Club" (2012) 30 *Windsor Yearbook of Access to Justice* 163. Sperdakos identified four Jewish women lawyers in 1930 by including Edna [*sic*] Sanders Ferguson, although Sanders Ferguson was not Jewish. See also R. Dinovitzer, "Social Capital and Constraints on Legal Careers" (2006) 40:2 *Law and Society Review* 445.

25 OSCLH, oral history, "Lily Sherizen Sharon," 1–9, 12–21. Sherizen recalled that when a non-Jewish boy asked her out, he "ran away" when she told him that she was Jewish. Sherizen was also hired by the Council of Jewish Women to obtain pensions for elderly clients, and she did mother's allowance cases. See also *Globe* (12 December 1935); and reports in the *Globe and Mail* (22 April 1939), (24 October 1939), (12 June 1953), (13 June 1956), and (15 June 1957).

"stayed on, I plugged on, and got my own clients and then built [a practice] in a bigger office." Her general practice included family law, and Sherizen was actively involved in reforms to allow Supreme Court support orders to be enforced by family courts. Her brief on the need to reform arrangements for support enforcement was presented to both the Attorney General and Toronto City Council to explain why her many women clients could not afford enforcement motions in the Supreme Court with its "fancy counsel" and expensive fees.[26]

Fortuitously, her reform efforts succeeded. When Sherizen appeared in the Supreme Court in a divorce case before Judge Keiller MacKay, she requested him to record that the support order would be enforceable in the family court, "and he endorsed the record like that." MacKay had befriended Sherizen when she was a young lawyer at the Goodman firm, and MacKay's wife had invited Sherizen to speak at a meeting of the Welfare Committee in the MacKay home. In spite of Mrs. MacKay's welcome, Sherizen recalled that "I got the worst cold shoulder I have ever had in my life; I felt this coolness around me." In 1945, Sherizen assisted with the lectures organized by the Local Council of Women, serving as an usher at the family law lecture by Marjorie Brigden Henry (1921). She was also appointed counsel to the Women Electors Association, which "got everybody scared, even Joe Salzberg, who was then a Communist."[27]

Yet, as a Jewish woman, Sherizen continued to experience exclusion in the legal profession. On one occasion, when Earl Smith at the Law Society told her about an opening at McCarthy's, he also warned her that it was not likely they will take you "because you are a woman, and because you are Jewish." Sherizen tried not to take such decisions to heart: "There were a lot of people that didn't get positions, they were Jewish, there were a lot of people who never got Judgeships because they were Jewish. There are a lot of women who didn't get things because they were women. So, I

26 OSCLH, oral history, "Lily Sherizen Sharon," 22–24, 26, 30–31, 40–46.

27 OSCLH, oral history, "Lily Sherizen Sharon," 32–33, 36–37; and *Globe and Mail* (24 October 1945). In 1945, Judge MacKay gave judgment in *Re Drummond Wren* [1945] 4 DLR 674 (HC), which held that a covenant restricting the sale of land in Toronto to "Jews or persons of objectionable nationality" was invalid. Sherizen reported that she became the lawyer for the Women's Electoral Association after both Margaret Hyndman and Vera Parsons declined this appointment.

wasn't anything special."[28] Although Sherizen was not invited to join the WLAO or Kappa Beta Pi in the 1930s, apparently because she was Jewish,[29] some changes occurred in the early 1940s. Sherizen credited Margaret Fraser (1928) for inviting her to join the WLAO, although Sherizen advised the president, Elva Dunn, that she would join only if she could chair the Committee on Family Law and also take on a study of juvenile delinquency. As she explained to Dunn, "I will come but not for social reasons," thereby eliminating the need to be invited to members' social events, such as weddings and Christmas parties.[30]

Sherizen's WLAO committee submitted a brief with recommendations to Toronto's City Council in 1946, and the brief was resubmitted in 1949 with recommendations about juvenile delinquency and "domestic relations." A report was also submitted to the Royal Commission on Education in 1946, and Sherizen presented her report and resolutions to the midwinter meeting of the Ontario section of the Canadian Bar Association (CBA) in Niagara Falls in 1947. These reports identified the need for reforms in the context of postwar reconstruction and included recommendations relating to education, court processes, and alternative arrangements for delinquent children. Sherizen's law reform work received positive press reports: it was credited by the *Globe and Mail* with having "shown the way" in the

28 OSCLH, oral history, "Lily Sherizen Sharon," 42, 55. According to Sperdakos, Jewish lawyers established the Reading Club in 1947 because they were excluded from joining the Lawyers Club. Such exclusion "reflected prejudices that existed during this and subsequent years at all levels of the profession, including ... the hiring of articling students and associates, entry into law firm partnerships and appointments to the bench": Sperdakos, "A Forum for Discussion," 165. See also P. Berton, *Maclean's* (1 November 1948).

29 Sherizen Sharon recalled that her classmate Sybil Bennett had advised her that Jews were not welcome at the WLAO: OSCLH, oral history, "Lily Sherizen Sharon," 38–39. In addition, Sanders Ferguson recalled that it was Margaret Hyndman who wanted to exclude Jews and women students who were not good students from Kappa Beta Pi. According to Sanders Ferguson, women students were invited to join the sorority based on their marks in the first three months at Osgoode Hall, and she was the only woman student in her class to be invited to join the sorority: OSCLH, oral history, "Edra Sanders Ferguson," 41.

30 Sherizen noted that Fraser had promised that the WLAO would accommodate the food requirements of her religion. At the same time, Sherizen was aware that her four women classmates from Osgoode Hall often met for coffee or lunch, but she was never included until Belva Gordon Hammell invited her to a tea with classmates in the late 1950s (when Gordon Hammell was dying of cancer): OSCLH, oral history, "Lily Sherizen Sharon," 38–39, 44.

treatment of young offenders in that she advocated for reforms similar to the borstal system in England. Her report was also described as "an act of good citizenship" that could be followed by other women's groups.[31] In 1948, Sherizen joined the WLAO executive and she was elected President for two years (1951–53). With Elizabeth Newton (1921), she also convened a Hobby Show for lawyers, both male and female in 1951 and 1952, at which women lawyers revealed their talents for painting, ceramics, photography, and music. In 1951, she presided at a lunch for Canadian women lawyers attending the Canadian Bar Association meetings in Toronto, and she regularly attended meetings of the Ontario section of the CBA as the WLAO representative. Sherizen also presided at the WLAO Christmas dinner in 1952.[32]

Although few records about Sherizen's family law cases exist, her concern for women in poorer families is apparent in her comments about Ontario family law reforms in the 1970s and '80s.

> The Family Law Act had to change with the status of society and the amount of money people were making and the contributions that women were making ... I don't think the judge is saying it's ½ and ½ anymore, I think the Judge is deciding the worth of each family member ... But in my years, there was no question, nobody had anything, the men never had any money, we were just chasing them for support, and the only thing we had was the house [and a wife was protected by her dower right if the husband held title]. And I felt very badly when this family unit, the joint family ownership, now have a family home, and they are each entitled, no matter whose name the property

31 LSO Archives, WLAO fonds, *Report of the Committee on Public Welfare in Regard to Juvenile Delinquency and Domestic Relations Problems,* 1–3. Lily Sherizen, chair, and Margaret Chambers, secretary (1937), submitted it to Toronto City Council: *Toronto Star* (16 June 1946). The report was resubmitted for consideration by a committee headed by Dr. Goldring: *Report re Juvenile Delinquency and Domestic Relations Problems,* May 1949. See also agenda, midwinter meeting of the Ontario section of the CBA (25 January 1947); and A. Bushby, "From the Archives," *Without Prejudice* (WLAO) (Spring 1995) 4. Sherizen also addressed a dinner meeting of the University Women's Club in 1950: *Globe and Mail* (10 November 1950).

32 *Globe and Mail* (9 May 1951), (2 February 1952). See also (1951) 1:7 *Chitty's Law Journal* 176; and *Globe and Mail* (19 April 1948), (14, 15 September 1951), and (18 December 1952); LSO Archives, "Diversifying the Bar," Lily Sherizen; and LSO Archives, WLAO fonds, "Hobby Show Program," 1952. One item in the Hobby Show was "Literary Art," by Sherizen and Dorcas Kelly Landriau (1921).

> is in. Now, I don't think that is quite right, because in the smaller type of [case], where there [are] very poor people and they have a family home ... [the wife] is met with the theory that she has to sell the home, or she has to give her husband half, or he can control her; he can walk in there with a gun and scare the life out of her every day ... [When] the home is now worth a million dollars, [there are remedies], but what do you do with the poor little woman who has nothing?[33]

Sherizen was appointed QC in 1952 along with Theresa Cherrier (1918). They were the first two women to be appointed Queen's rather than King's counsel.[34] In the 1950s, Sherizen married Leon Sharon, but she continued in legal practice and as a member of the Toronto Zionist Council executive. In 1956–57, she was elected treasurer of the council, with responsibility for the council's support for Hebrew University. In 1960, Sherizen Sharon became a candidate for alderman in Ward 4. Her platform included promoting sound municipal government, low-cost housing, and the proper development of Ward 4, but her candidacy was unsuccessful. She continued a modest practice until she experienced back problems in the 1980s. She died in 1991 at the age of eighty-five.[35]

Only two women were called to the bar in the fall of 1931. Both had enrolled at the law school as matriculants in 1926, just before the admission requirements changed to require at least two years of university studies. Jean O'Rourke was the daughter of a hotel keeper in Caledonia

33 OSCLH, oral history, "Lily Sherizen Sharon," 30–31, 33–35.

34 Archives of Ontario, *Orders in Council re Her Majesty's Counsel Learned in the Law*, file 3058/52 (18 December 1952). There were sixty-nine QC appointments, including these two women lawyers, both of whom engaged in family law.

35 Leon Sharon shared an office with Sherizen, where he did commercial work: OSCLH, oral history, "Lily Sherizen Sharon," 24; and LSO Archives, OBBRP, "Lily Sherizen Sharon." See also *Globe and Mail* (12 June 1953), (13 June 1956), (15 June 1957), and (4 June 1959). In the 1960 election, Sherizen Sharon received 565 votes, but the winner was David Rotenberg with 1,440 votes: *Toronto* Star (22 November 1960); and *Globe and Mail* (30 November 1960), (6 December 1960). The *Toronto Daily Star* published an article about Sherizen on 22 November 1960, apologizing that her name had "inadvertently" been left off the list of candidates in Ward 4 a few days earlier. Ward 4 encompassed the area between Bathurst Street and University Avenue, and from just north of St. Clair Avenue to the waterfront, including the Toronto Islands. In 1962, Sherizen Sharon was an unsuccessful candidate for the Board of Education: *Globe and Mail* (20 November 1962). When she was profiled in (1989) 1:2 *Without Prejudice* (WLAO) 3, Sherizen stated she didn't get rich, but she "did things that she wanted to do."

and a Catholic. She had first articled with H. Arrell in Caledonia and then with Edward Murphy in Toronto, and she continued to practise in Murphy's office after being called to the bar in September 1931. She was actively involved in the WLAO, serving as President in 1938–39, and she was appointed KC in 1948. O'Rourke practised law until 1969. She died in 1974 and was buried in St. Patrick's Cemetery in Caledonia after a funeral mass there.[36]

The second woman, Lillian Sandler, later Gordon, was admitted to the bar in November 1931, the fourth Jewish woman lawyer in Toronto. Her parents were Polish immigrants who married after arriving in Toronto, and together they opened a tailor shop on Dupont Street. According to Sandler, her parents kept a kosher house, but they were not religious: "In the 1930s, most people [she knew] were socialists, you know, things were so tough that everybody who was young was looking to solve the problems that we were in." Because they were poor, Sandler recalled, "It was quite a deal when my family decided that I would go [to high school]"; they were "education mad." She enrolled at the law school as a matriculant and articled with Max Aiken in his general practice for two dollars per week. Her family provided a home and clothing, and Sandler was "busy ... and happy." She also loved law, including "reading cases ... I thought it was wonderful." Like other Jewish women law students, Sandler acknowledged that "anti-Semitism was really accepted," especially when it came to articling positions: "I really think a Jewish girl ... well, in the first place a girl, and in the second place a Jewish girl, just wouldn't try to get into a non-Jewish firm." For her call-to-the-bar ceremony, she rented a gown because "money we didn't have." Sandler was the first Polish-Canadian woman lawyer in Ontario.[37]

Sandler opened a sole practice at College and Yonge: "Now, that would be pretty daring, I was a female and a Jew ... a hell of a combination to have in one person." Although she had only a single office on the second floor and a secretary, Sandler connected with a real estate speculator in the

36 LSO Archives, OBBRP, "Jean O'Rourke," and obituary, unidentified press report. Murphy may have been a relative of O'Rourke. See also LSO Archives, WLAO fonds, SB, vol. 1; and "Diversifying the Bar," Jean O'Rourke. In 1960, O'Rourke was listed as a solicitor in the Provincial Secretaries Department: *Canadian Law Lists.* O'Rourke may also have been an executive member of the Legal and Literary Society in 1930–31: unconfirmed photo *Continuum* (Osgoode Hall Law School) (Winter 2015) 18.

37 LSO Archives, OBBRP, "Lillian Sandler"; OSCLH, oral history, "Lillian Sandler Gordon," 2–18.

West End and a business broker who bought and sold businesses, and they brought in clients.

> And that was the basis of my practice. In those days, there was not a really large real estate business; people didn't buy and sell houses; it wasn't until after the Second World War that people started to buy houses. In the late 1930s the basis of my clientele, [in addition to wills and women who needed divorces and would rather go to a woman, and didn't have any money to pay you] were businesses, very small, like rooming houses. They were mostly run by women too. [Sandler also described many of her clients as] "Off the street. Two-dollar clients."[38]

Sandler married Sam Gordon, probably in the 1950s. Gordon attended law school after he served in the Second World War and was called to the bar in 1956. The couple practised law together. According to Gordon, "By the time I met Lil she was doing very well for herself." She acted for developers buying lots and then placing mortgages on them, and she developed good relationships with National Trust and other banks. Gordon picked up divorce work and other matters at the firm. For Sandler Gordon, "It was a joy to be working" in her later years: "[I] had sat twiddling my thumbs for quite a number of years. I was a woman, remember, that was a big thing, and you weren't in a firm—you were the firm."[39]

Sandler Gordon acknowledged the challenges she faced as a Jewish woman lawyer. As a woman, "You were odd, you were very odd ... I came from a non-swearing family, and I decided ... to show how tough I am ... I learned to swear ... my expression was 'God damn it to hell' ... and I was known as a toughie." She also faced prejudice, including in relation to the WLAO: "There was prejudice, period. Wherever you went." She was also not invited to join the legal sorority. As Sandler recalled, Sarah Kaplan Goldstick (1943) later joined the sorority only "after a lot of yelling and screaming." And although Sandler and Gordon were aware that

38 OSCLH, oral history, "Lillian Sandler Gordon," 12–14, 26.

39 OSCLH, 5–6, 16–18. "Sam" Gordon's father was a baker, and Gordon worked in his father's shop from the age of sixteen. He was not Jewish and did not convert after he married Sandler, but this difference did not create problems for Sandler's family. The fifth Jewish woman, Sarah Kaplan, later Goldstick, was a classmate of Sandler who completed the courses at Osgoode Hall in 1931, but she married and was not called to the bar until 1943: see Chapter Five.

Charles Dubin, who was Jewish, worked for an elite, non-Jewish firm, they explained this discrepancy based on his being a "scholarship boy" and "a very brilliant man." Yet, despite the challenges, Sandler concluded: "I liked the [practice of law]. I had a personal relationship with all my clients. They all became friends ... I liked law for the fact that it wasn't a typewriter scene, it wasn't dull, you had a problem all the time. And you had to use your brains all the time, which was fine. All the time I practiced, I found it interesting." Sandler Gordon and her spouse retired in 1984, when both were in their seventies, and "gave" the practice, including a filing cabinet of wills, to another lawyer.[40]

Three women were called to the bar in 1932. Eleanor Richards graduated from the University of Toronto in 1928 and articled with Mulock, Millicken, Clarke & Redman. After her call to the bar in June, she continued to practise with the firm until the late 1930s, when she obtained a post in the legal department of National Trust.[41] A second woman, Tmima Littner, later Cohn, was inspired by her parents to study law. Her father was a Romanian Orthodox Jew who had marched in a suffragist parade in Toronto, and her mother was an early advocate of women's rights. Littner graduated from the University of Toronto in 1929 and, after graduating from Osgoode Hall, she was called to the bar in June 1932. She practised only briefly, in part because she found the profession unwelcoming to Jewish women. She married Martin Cohn and ceased practice after her children were born. The family moved to the United States, where she actively promoted environmental issues and the rights of women. She also volunteered her services at free legal clinics and spoke and wrote about women's legal rights. Littner Cohn died in 1989.[42]

A third woman, Marie Wilson, later McCullough/Sanders, was called to the bar in September 1932. She was the only child of parents who lived in Rosedale. Her father had established an insurance firm, AE Wilson & Co. Ltd, and her mother remained at home where the family had a live-in cook.

40 OSCLH, oral history, "Lillian Sandler Gordon," 23–24, 26–27, 28, 31–33, 40–43. Sandler and Gordon recalled that there were many Jewish male lawyers: "As a matter of fact, if you were a Jewish boy, that is where you headed."

41 LSO Archives, WLAO fonds, SB, vol. 1; Marie Wilson (1932) recalled Richards: OSCLH, oral history, "Marie Wilson," 49; and *Canadian Law Lists*.

42 LSO Archives, WLAO fonds, SB, vol. 1; LSO Archives, "Diversifying the Bar," Tmima Littner Cohn. Her classmate, Marie Wilson, recalled Littner Cohn: OSCLH, oral history, "Marie Wilson," 49.

Wilson attended Bishop Strachan School and completed a BA at University College in 1929. She later recalled that University College was a significant change since she "had never known any people except the kids in Rosedale and the ones in private school." At Osgoode Hall, most of the students in her class were university-educated, but even so, "there was quite a slaughter [that is, failures] after the first year."[43]

Women students were still assigned seats in the front row at Osgoode Hall, and Wilson found both the instructors and students to be friendly. Caesar Wright, who was "fresh from Harvard" and used a casebook, was excellent, although the Benchers were unhappy because so many students failed his course. For Wilson, Wright "could take you off on quite a speculation but you never got confused because he would always wind up saying, 'now, to come back to the bedrock,'" encouraging an inquiring mind without creating confusion between "which was the reality and which the speculation." Wilson articled with White, Bristol, a firm of about twenty lawyers that provided legal work for her father's insurance company. As a student, she was unpaid, a situation she believed to be the norm in "top offices" and not the result of the Depression. After being called to the bar, Wilson spent a year studying insurance law in the English syllabus in preparation for joining her father's insurance business in 1933.[44]

Once she joined, she continued to live at home and work with White, Bristol. She was the only in-house counsel at the firm, but she participated in litigating cases with different male counsel, including George Drew, who

43 OSCLH, oral history, "Marie Wilson," 1–17, 48–49. Although her parents did not drink alcohol, her father introduced her to Harvey's Bristol Cream so that she would know what to request if she was offered a drink.

44 Osgoode Hall did not yet offer an insurance course. The Depression made little impression on Wilson, even though she was the only employee who was paid below minimum wage, but she was living at home with practically everything paid for by her father. The White Bristol firm clearly distinguished between lawyers and clerical staff, and Wilson recalled how she was always treated as a "professional" even though she was female: OSCLH, oral history, "Marie Wilson," 46–77, 52.

relied on Wilson's detailed notes to argue in court.[45] Early in her career, Wilson appeared with senior counsel at the Supreme Court of Canada, where Chief Justice Duff suggested the court would like to "hear from the lady." Wilson recalled being accommodated by judges and lawyers in robing facilities: "Somebody else saw the problem, and I didn't have to really raise it myself ... some gentleman came forward with a solution." She described herself as a woman who never "had to fight my way." Although some lawyers in smaller centres were less friendly, Wilson concluded that she had been treated "awfully well—the worst I would say was that I puzzled them."[46]

In 1948, Wilson married Dr. R.J.P. McCullough. She described him as being concerned that she not "go domestic on him ... he wanted me to stay the way I was," and her father also wanted her to remain involved in the business: "He thought the value ... would go down greatly if I didn't." Thus, Wilson regularly went to the office for lunch with her father and then stayed for the afternoon, but her father was always "anxious that I would get home before my husband." In 1949, Wilson was appointed vice-president of the company, and after her father died in 1960, she became President. She recalled attending WLAO meetings, and she was involved in the insurance, negligence, and municipal sections of the CBA. Although she realized that women could not join the Lawyers Club, she had no concerns about this exclusion. Wilson was appointed KC in 1948, and in the mid-1970s she was appointed the first woman director of the Bank of Nova Scotia—and the bank installed a powder room on the directors' floor for the first time. In 1986, she was appointed to the Public Sector Pensions Advisory Board.[47] Wilson was widowed in 1954, and in 1977 she

45 The case with Drew was *Huycke v Town of Cobourg*, [1937] OR 682 (Ont CA). Apparently, Drew read her notes in making his argument. When the judge asked him whether "the lady [Wilson] has anything to add," Drew responded, "Well, the only reason that Miss Wilson has nothing to add, is because she has prepared my whole argument." Wilson remembered Drew as being not proud and self-centred and prepared to give her credit. Drew and Wilson represented the Town of Cobourg while J. Cartwright, KC, represented the plaintiff, who had fallen on an icy sidewalk. The plaintiff succeeded at trial, but the decision was overturned on appeal. Wilson also recalled Morden, McRae, and Robinette as good instructors at Osgoode Hall: OSCLH, oral history, "Marie Wilson," 53–64, 68–71, 73–76.

46 The judge in the Cobourg case permitted her to use his office as a robing room: OSCLH, oral history, "Marie Wilson," 26–32, 93–96.

47 OSCLH, oral history, "Marie Wilson," 97–110, 124–39.

married Richard Sanders, whom she had known as a student at Osgoode. Sanders died in 2001, and Wilson continued to live in her childhood home until her death at the age of ninety-eight in 2007.[48] In her view, she was "always ... a lawyer at heart [with] no regrets; I was right in the heart of it in the days when I was in court. I can't think of any other career I would have wanted."[49]

Four women were called to the bar in 1933, but three practised only briefly. Helen DeRoche, later Roberts, was the daughter of Judge G.E. DeRoche of the County Court in Belleville. She graduated from the University of Toronto in 1929 and, with her father's support, studied at Osgoode Hall, sharing an apartment with two other women downtown. DeRoche reported that the four "girls" in her class communicated only with one another. They sat together in the front row of the lecture hall and "did not look at, let alone talk with, their male classmates." She also recalled that the classes followed a strict lecture format, without questions from students.[50] De Roche also had trouble finding articles: "It was hard for anyone to find work because of the depression, but ... particularly for women [because] nobody wanted a girl." After her father "pressured" his contacts, she was hired at Briggs, Frost & Birks, but "not everybody at the firm was overly receptive to her," and her work mainly involved title searching and document deliveries. After her call to the bar in June, she was unemployed for a year, but her father's influence resulted in employment at Cameron & Cameron in Belleville. She was the only woman lawyer in the community.[51]

48 Richard Sanders was a brother of Edra Sanders Ferguson: OSCLH, oral history, "Marie Wilson," 120–23, 165, and OSCLH, oral history, "Edra Sanders Ferguson," 14. See also "Lives Lived: Marie Wilson McCullough Sanders," unidentified news report after her death, *Globe and Mail*; LSO Archives, OBBRP, "Marie Wilson"; "Home of the Week," *Globe and Mail* (1 February 2008) G13, which described a Rosedale property, the home of "maverick female lawyer Marie Wilson." Built in 1912, it had been acquired by Wilson's father in 1922. See also OSCLH, oral history, "Marie Wilson," 165.

49 OSCLH, oral history, "Marie Wilson," 109–11. See also *Orders in Council re Her Majesty's Counsel Learned in the Law* (16 December 1948). Wilson recalled being a member of the Rosedale Golf Club and the Granite Club, and she was appointed to the board of Standard Trust in the mid-1960s: OSCLH, oral history, "Marie Wilson," 124–57.

50 LSO Archives, "Nora's Interview with Torchy,'" unidentified interviewer of Helen ("Torchy") DeRoche. The interviewer noted that Torchy's granddaughter, Jana Cadsby, was then a law student and a childhood friend of the interviewer, but there is no other identifying information for "Nora." DeRoche's nickname resulted from her fiery red hair.

51 Gertrude Alford (1916) may have practised for a few years in Belleville, but by 1932 she was practising in Trenton: see Chapter Two.

DeRoche believed that although success came in later decades to women with academic ability, she had "needed somebody behind [her] with connections" in the 1930s. In addition, she noted that the firm's clerical staff tried to support her:

> The girls tried to shove people into my room. One time I was sitting in my room. A client walked into the office and wanted to see Mr Cameron. The girl said "I'm sorry, he's busy right now. Would you like to see Miss DeRoche?" The client said, "Mister who?" The girl said, "It's a lady lawyer with our firm." There was dead silence and after a moment, the client said, "No. I'll wait for Mr Cameron."[52]

DeRoche claimed she knew nothing about legal fees and did not take her legal work seriously because she expected to be taken care of financially by her father or husband. She practised for only three years and then married Greer Roberts and stopped work because, "in those days, your husband kept you." During the Second World War, the firm asked her to return to work to replace a lawyer who joined the military, but she declined because she had two young daughters. DeRoche Roberts resigned from the Law Society in 1966.[53]

One of DeRoche's classmates was Elsinore Wegenast, the daughter of F.W. Wegenast. After graduating from the University of Toronto, she articled in her father's firm in Brampton and was called to the bar in November. Wegenast married W.E.P. DeRoche, a brother of Helen DeRoche, in June 1933, and the couple moved to Ottawa. Wegenast DeRoche did not practise law.[54] Marion Niven, later Foran, who also graduated from the University of Toronto in 1930, was admitted to the bar in June 1933 and practised with Waldron, Bouke & Hetherington, but only briefly. She

52 LSO Archives, "Nora's Interview with Torchy," n.p.

53 LSO Archives, "Nora's Interview with Torchy," n.p.

54 LSO Archives, OBBRP, "Elsinore Wegenast"; and Huckle, "List of Women Barristers and Solicitors." Wegenast DeRoche resigned her Law Society membership voluntarily in 1965.

married Philip Foran and moved to Ottawa and ceased legal practice.[55] Thus, the only long-time woman practitioner in the class of 1933 was Ina Marion Bulloch, who was called to the bar in November. There is little information about her, although she responded to the toast to "the Barristers of 1933," proposed by Helen Palen (1918) at the WLAO annual dinner meeting in April 1933 at the Royal York Hotel. In 1956, she was practising law at 100 Adelaide Street, but by 1960 she was employed as a solicitor in the Department of Highways, employment that continued for some years. Bulloch was appointed QC.[56]

Three women were called to the bar in 1934. One was Mary Appleby from Islington, who acquired some prominence after she published an article in *Obiter Dicta* in January 1934, just a few months before her call to the bar in June. In the article, Appleby noted that it was "hard to imagine any prospective law student of the fair sex in 1934 suspecting that she might be refused admission to the Law Society simply because she was a woman," and she described the many challenges faced by Clara Brett Martin three decades earlier. She concluded: "Today, neither as a student at law nor as a practising lawyer, is a woman regarded as a curiosity by the other members of the profession." Thus, "it is only fair that a woman should not ask any special consideration because of her sex." At the same time, Appleby suggested that younger men showed more acceptance of their female colleagues, and she hoped that attitudes of older members would disappear as "women prove themselves to be successful in law."

Appleby also noted that women without legal connections often experienced problems in practice, and she recommended a basic knowledge of business for legal practitioners. Countering the assertion that there were no prominent women counsel, she argued that the lack of robing facilities at Osgoode Hall made such work challenging for women barristers. She

55 LSO Archives, WLAO fonds, SB, vol. 1; and Huckle, "List of Women Barristers and Solicitors." Marie Wilson identified Foran (1933) as a friend from Bishop Strachan School and the person who alerted the press about Wilson's brief appearance in the Supreme Court of Canada: OSCLH, oral history, "Marie Wilson," 29–32. Mitchell Thomas confirmed that Niven Foran was not employed in private practice or government in Ottawa: E. Mitchell Thomas, "The History of Women Lawyers in the Carleton County Law Association" in W. Johnson, ed., *The First Century: Essays on the History of the County of Carleton Law Association by Various Hands on the Occasion of the Association's Centenary, 1888–1988* (Ottawa: Bonanza Press, 1988) 107 at 113.

56 Huckle, "List of Women Barristers and Solicitors"; LSO Archives, OBBRP, "Ina Bulloch"; LSO Archives, WLAO fonds, SB, vol. 1; and *Canadian Law Lists*.

concluded by prophesying that “the time will come in the not-too-distant future when women will win equal distinction with men in every phase of the practice of law.” Appleby was listed as a lawyer in Islington for many years until the mid-1960s, and she may also have been employed in social service work.[57]

Constance Hunt, later McLean, was called to the bar with Mary Appleby in June 1934. Hunt’s father, John Hunt, KC, was one of the first Catholic lawyers in Hamilton, at a time when “religious affiliation shaped business and social life.” Her father’s practice flourished because of the large Italian (Catholic) population in Hamilton. Constance Hunt attended Central Collegiate and Loretto College, and she travelled with her parents to a conference of the CBA in England in 1924. She graduated with first-class honours from McGill, with a scholarship to study at the Sorbonne, but she decided to attend law school in Toronto since her mother was quite ill. Her parents gave her a car to travel back and forth from Hamilton, and she recalled few problems during the Depression. Since she had initially enrolled in the MA program in French at the University of Toronto, she lived in the University College residence for all three years of her studies at Osgoode Hall. Hunt articled with her father, who worked in his office on weekends. She learned how to value houses, did real estate work, and reviewed wills, but she avoided court work.[58]

Hunt described Osgoode Hall as “a gloomy old place,” but she was a good student, “fourth or fifth” in her graduating class. Her husband, who was a member of the same class, placed third. Hunt found Falconbridge “a darn poor lecturer” and Wright “one of the smartest lawyers I ever came across,” but she recalled that Wright lectured rather than using the case method. Her lectures were scheduled in the mornings until eleven or twelve o’clock, after which she worked in the office until about five. For some articling students, there was little work. One classmate in a big firm spent his time putting stamps on envelopes. Hunt described the women students’ washroom facilities as being “in the bowels of [Osgoode Hall]”

57 M. Appleby, “The Entry of Women into the Profession of Law and Their Hopes” *Obiter Dicta* (17 January 1934) n.p.; and Huckle, “List of Women Barristers and Solicitors.” According to Mary Hunt McLean, Appleby died around 2005: LSO Archives, “Memoir of Mary Constance Hunt McLean,” assisted by A. Kirk-Montgomery, 2007, at 33.

58 “Memoir of Mary Constance Hunt McLean,” 1–2, 18–26, 29–30, 49–55, 62. Hunt described herself as one of the poorest women students at McGill, but she also explained that she had “no recollection of [the] depression [because] I was away at McGill.”

and said it was hard to meet women students in other years of the law program because of their different class schedules. She joined the women's law sorority and attended a few meetings, and she remembered Margaret Hyndman as "the sort of person that you noticed."[59] In 1933, Hunt published an article in *Obiter Dicta* in which she described women students: "We aren't much trouble. We never take up ... time arguing with the lecturer. In class we offer no assistance in the interpretation of the intricate judgments, but then neither do we contribute our efforts to the occasional show of dissatisfaction marked by the stamping of feet."[60] Monty McLean, a male classmate, sat with the women students in the first row for the lectures because he was tall and needed room for his feet. Hunt and McLean fell in love while they were both students, and they became engaged, but they did not have money for marriage for three years.[61]

Although Hunt and McLean opened a small practice together on Ottawa Street in Hamilton, they both joined her father's firm at 34 Main Street in 1936. McLean was paid twenty-five dollars per week, but Hunt McLean was unpaid. As she explained, "I pretty well went along with whatever they wanted me to do." In subsequent years, only her husband practised with Hunt's father as Hunt & McLean, but during the Second World War, Monty McLean was on active service. Their family lived in Jamaica to guard the US coast and later in Ottawa, where McLean worked in the Judge Advocate General's Department. During this time, Hunt McLean was a homemaker with five children. After the war, her husband practised law with Walter Tuchtie, a Ukrainian-Canadian lawyer who practised mainly criminal law,

59 Hunt was fond of Robinette, who had a good sense of humour. She also remembered Clute, McRuer, Wishart Spence, Borden, and Morden. However, she recalled that Borden and Morden "stuck their nose up at girls in the class, while the older men were more respectful to women." Hunt also commented that "when I wrote exams, the minute I read the question, I could zero in on the point, and go right from there": "Memoir of Mary Constance Hunt McLean," 29, 35–41, and 46–48.

60 Memoir of Mary Constance Hunt McLean, 105–9, 112; and C. Hunt McLean, "Then the Camel Put Its Head in the Tent," *Obiter Dicta* (28 February 1933).

61 Monty McLean articled with Maurice Crabtree, a sole practitioner, from whom he claimed to have really learned law. He also returned to Woodstock in the summers to live with his widowed mother and worked in a law firm there. McLean's mother was concerned about her son marrying a Catholic, as the McLeans were Protestant. In due course, the five Hunt-McLean children received some Catholic training, but religion was not important in their home, "Memoir of Mary Constance Hunt McLean" 42–43, 49–51, 71–74.

and McLean was involved in collecting evidence in relation to the controversial *Dick* murder case in Hamilton.[62]

When her husband became unwell a few decades later, McLean Hunt returned to the practice at age sixty-five, eventually merging it with a new practice set up by two nephews. She retired at the age of eighty-five, when she no longer wanted to engage with the new technology required in legal practice.[63] Hunt McLean was celebrated as the earliest woman graduate to attend the Special Convocation in 1991 at York University, at which Osgoode Hall graduates from before 1960 received the LLB degree. When she crossed the platform to receive her degree, "the whole auditorium ... was standing up and clapping." Hunt McLean died in September 2010.[64]

Among the women graduates of 1934, Florence Forrest, later Evely/Wilson, practised law only briefly after she was called to the bar in October. Her office was located at 302 Bay Street until 1937, but she ceased to practise law after her marriage. Forrest created a stir as a law student when she rode a horse from her home in Port Hope to Osgoode Hall and arrived in Dean Wright's class in her riding habit. She was teased by the male students, and "Caesar Wright told her in no uncertain terms she was not to wear her riding habit again!"[65]

62 *R v Dick* [1947] OR 105 (ONCA); and LSO "Diversifying the Bar," Walter Tuchtie. Monty McLean developed Alzheimer's disease, and he died in 1989, "Memoir of Mary Constance Hunt McLean," 73–74, 125. See also obituary, "Mary Constance McLean," *Hamilton Spectator* (20 September 2010). She died one hundred days after her one hundredth birthday.

63 "Memoir of Mary Constance Hunt McLean," 96–98; and *Canadian Law Lists*. When Hunt McLean's son, Don, had an appeal to the Supreme Court of Canada, she attended and was invited to meet Chief Justice McLachlin. See also M. McKiernan, "Woman Lawyer, 100, Retains LSUC Membership," *Law Times* (28 June 2010) 3.

64 Hunt McLean's obituary noted her volunteer activity at St. Joseph's Hospital Auxiliary and the Birthright Pregnancy Service, where she was its volunteer director for fourteen years. However, "she wasn't a rabble rouser, she was a doer," obituary, *Hamilton Spectator* (20 September 2010). See also "Memoir of Mary Constance Hunt McLean," 37–ff.

65 Huckle, "List of Women Barristers and Solicitors." See also *Canadian Law Lists*; and "Memoir of Mary Constance Hunt McLean." According to Hunt McLean, "Caesar Wright didn't have a good sense of humour." Hunt McLean believed that Forrest was called to the Ontario bar in 1935. Another record in the *Canadian Law Lists* in the early 1960s identifies "Catherine I. Forrest, 35," as an employee at the Western Municipal News in Winnipeg in the early 1960s. This intriguing reference may, or may not, be related to Florence Catherine Forrest, called to the Ontario bar in 1934 or 1935. No information has been discovered about her marriages.

Five women were called to the bar in 1935. According to Hunt McLean, Emily Williamson was in the class of 1934, but Williamson was not admitted to the bar until June 1935. Williamson was a former legal secretary in her fifties when she entered Osgoode Hall. She may have had a sole practice in Burlington at 60 Water Street East until the mid-1950s.[66] Agnes Weir, later Randolph, practised law in Sarnia, probably the first woman lawyer in that community, at the firm of Weir & Weir. Charles Weir had been called to the bar in 1920. Agnes Weir was in practice at this firm until 1946, when she was listed as Mrs. A. Randolph, but a few years later, both the firm and Weir Randolph are absent from the *Canadian Law Lists*.[67]

Beatrice Lyons, later Mathews, was called to the bar in June 1935. She practised law in Newmarket in the firm of Mathews and Lyons, and the firm also had an office in Toronto at 171 Yonge Street. In 1939, the firm became Mathews, Lyons and Vale, and by 1955 it was a firm of nine lawyers, with offices in both Newmarket and Toronto. Lyons was active in the WLAO and served as President in 1948–49. In 1950, she was a special guest at a luncheon hosted by the Women's Division of the Canadian National Exhibition. A press report identified Lyons as the only woman among ninety members of the Council of the Canadian Bar Association and reported that the council was planning to meet with the American Association in Washington in September. At the meeting in Washington, Margaret Campbell (1937), President of the WLAO, and Judge Kinnear (1920) were elected to the CBA council, replacing Lyons, who had held the position for several years. Lyons had a general legal practice in Toronto, doing corporation work, as well as civil and criminal court work (including both prosecution

66 *Canadian Law Lists*; Huckle, "List of Women Barristers and Solicitors"; "Memoir of Mary Constance Hunt McLean," 33; and LSO Archives, WLAO fonds, box 98, death notice, ca. 1956–57.

67 *Canadian Law Lists*; and Huckle, "List of Women Barristers and Solicitors." Huckle indicated that Weir Randolph was "practising."

and defence). At some point, Lyons married Mathews, and both were appointed QC.[68]

Clara Halperin, later Muskat, was just nineteen years old when she began her legal studies at Osgoode Hall after becoming the only woman graduate in the honours law program at the University of Toronto in 1932. After she was called to the bar in June 1935, she had a job interview with a leading firm. During the interview, she was asked, "Halperin ... is that a Jewish name?" She responded affirmatively and heard nothing further from the firm. Early in her career, she worked closely with another Jewish lawyer, Onie Brown, and Halperin honoured him after he died by establishing a scholarship in his name for students in financial need at Osgoode Hall Law School. In 1937, she established a sole practice at 100 Adelaide Street West, but she later moved to 88 Richmond Street West. Halperin married C.M. Muskat, and she continued her solo practice in Toronto well into her eighties.[69]

A fifth woman lawyer, Helen Okuloski, was called to the bar in November 1935. She was the daughter of Polish immigrants who owned a chain of dry goods stores in Hamilton, and she became the first Polish Canadian woman lawyer in Hamilton. She attended the University of Toronto, but she enrolled at Osgoode Hall as a matriculant in 1930 and was called to the bar five years later. Although Okuloski paid fees to the Law Society for two years, there is no evidence of her in legal practice until 1938. Her sole practice began at 94 Barnsdale Avenue North in Hamilton, but she moved her office in the mid-1940s to Barton Street East. By 1950, she was sharing the practice with her brother Edward, who had been called to the bar in 1948.

68 Huckle, "List of Women Barristers and Solicitors"; A. Bushby, "The Early Years: Sources of an Enduring Tradition—The Women's Law Association of Ontario, 1919–1950" (80th Anniversary Celebration, 14 January 2000); and *Canadian Law Lists*. The CNE luncheon was in honour of "Canada's most representative grandmother," Mrs. George Ball from Edmonton: *Globe and Mail* (9 September 1950). This report also identified Lyons as a director of the Pilot Club, an international service organization. See also LSO Archives, WLAO fonds, SB, vol. 3, "The Washington Convention" (September 1950). A press report in 1944 noted that two women lawyers had appeared in court on opposite sides for the first time: Lyons was counsel for the Anglo-Canadian Leather Co. in Huntsville while Mary Lamont (1937) appeared for the Employees' Association: LSO Archives, WLAO fonds, SB, vol. 3, unidentified news report.

69 LSO Archives, "Diversifying the Bar," Clara Halperin Muskat; Huckle, "List of Women Barristers and Solicitors"; and *Canadian Law Lists*.

In the mid-1950s, the firm relocated to 928 King Street East, and in 1965 P.A. Marshall, who had been called to the bar in 1959, joined the firm.[70]

Hunt McLean recalled that Okuloski was a year behind her at Osgoode, and she remembered Helen's sole practice after her brother's death. Okuloski's sister explained that Helen provided legal services to "a large ethnic clientele because of her understanding of their needs and backgrounds" and that she was protective of her women clients' rights.[71] Significantly, Okuloski hired a Black lawyer who had received rejections at other firms. Edward Okuloski had encouraged Lincoln Alexander to apply to the Okuloski firm, and Alexander (later Lieutenant-Governor of Ontario) became a member of the firm for a brief period. As Alexander later explained, "some people have the guts to do the right thing."[72] Helen Okuloski later became a member of the American Trial Lawyers Association, and she was appointed QC in December 1954. She died in 1993.[73]

70 LSO Archives, "Diversifying the Bar," Helen Okuloski; Huckle, "List of Women Barristers and Solicitors"; and LSO Archives, Paul Leatherdale communication with M.J. Mossman (23 February 2018). Some records suggest that Okuloski completed the second year of the BA program at the University of Toronto but she was admitted as a matriculant in 1930 and was a student for five years at Osgoode Hall—even though the category of matriculant had been eliminated in 1926 and was not reintroduced until 1932. The decision to reintroduce the category was contentious, and the chair of the Legal Education Committee, M.H. Ludwig, KC, declared, "Here we have the banner province of this Dominion with the lowest standards of [law school] entrance": (2002) *Gazette* 40–41. Okuloski's sister recalled that Helen opened her practice in 1938, although Law Society records indicate that she paid her fees in both 1936 and 1937. The delayed start of her practice may have been a consequence of the Depression.

71 LSO Archives, "Diversifying the Bar," Helen Okuloski; and *Canadian Law Lists.* Based on Hunt McLean's recollection of Okuloski in the year behind Hunt McLean, Okuloski may have commenced her studies as a matriculant in 1933. According to Hunt McLean, Okuloski supported her brother, Edward, while he attended Osgoode Hall. She also suggested that John Sopinka articled with Helen Okuloski, but LSO records indicate that Sopinka articled with Walter Williston, QC, in Toronto: LSO Archives, "Memoir of Mary Constance Hunt McLean," 136; and LSO Archives, OBBRP, "John Sopinka."

72 LSO Archives, "Diversifying the Bar," Helen Okuloski. See also L. Alexander, *Go to School, You're a Little Black Boy: The Hon Lincoln M. Alexander—A Memoir* (Toronto: Dundurn Press, 2006) 66–67; and OSCLH, oral history, "Lincoln M. Alexander." Helen Okuloski also provided an articling position to Roxie Marshall (1952), who later practised law in Hamilton.

73 *Orders in Council re Her Majesty's Counsel Learned in the Law* (22 December 1954); LSO Archives, "Diversifying the Bar," Helen Okuloski; and *Canadian Law Lists.* Okuloski practised law for about fifty years.

In 1936, three women were called to the bar, but two married and did not practise law. Edythe Haughland, who was called to the bar in September, married H.R. Howden and moved to Detroit. Similarly, Isabell Hinds, later Wallbridge, who was admitted in October, moved to Welland. There are no records of her in legal practice.[74] In contrast, Bessie Adelman, later Wolfe, who was called to the bar in January, engaged in legal practice for some years in Toronto. She practised law at 248 Lippincott Street in the 1940s and then at 1034 Bathurst Street and 1713 Dufferin Street in the 1950s and early 1960s.[75] She was engaged in a sole practice during these years.

In 1937, eight women were called to the bar, but not all of them practised law. In January, Constance Nelson, the daughter of a printer in Hamilton, was called to the bar after articling with L.F. Stephens. She married and lived in Hamilton, but she did not practise law.[76] In contrast, Margaret Struthers, who was called to the bar in May 1937, practised with her lawyer husband, F.H. Chambers, who was called to the bar that same year. From 1942, Chambers & Chambers was located at several different locations in Toronto, but Margaret Chambers joined the Attorney General's Department in 1954, working as a solicitor for the Official Guardian's Office. In 1960, "Mrs. Margaret Chambers" was appointed a deputy judge of the Juvenile and Family Court for Metropolitan Toronto, "the first woman

74 Huckle, "List of Women Barristers and Solicitors."

75 Hunt McLean (1934) recalled Adelman as a classmate. The later date for Adelman's admission to the bar in 1937 might relate to a leave of absence because of the Depression, or the need to re-sit an examination: LSO Archives, "Memoir of Mary Constance Hunt McLean," 33; and *Canadian Law Lists*. Adelman Wolfe was the seventh Jewish woman to be called to the Ontario bar, following Grossman (1929), Epstein Baker (1929), Sherizen Sharon (1930), Sandler Gordon (1931), Littner Cohn (1932), and Halperin Muskat (1935). It is unclear whether these women interacted or provided mutual support.

76 LSO Archives, OBBRP, "Constance Nelson"; Huckle, "'List of Women Barristers and Solicitors"; and *Canadian Law Lists*. The name of her spouse was not identified, but Nelson was present in 1938, along with other women lawyers in Hamilton, at the tea hosted by Mrs. McLay (Florence Thompson, 1922): *Globe and Mail* (16 May 1938) 12. The LSO records indicate that Nelson resigned voluntarily at an undisclosed date.

judge in Toronto." According to the press, Judge Chambers's appointment disproved "the theory of prejudice against women in law."[77]

In June 1937, Margaret Fasken Baird, later Campbell, was called to the bar. Baird's father was a Scottish poet who also wrote for the *Manchester Guardian.* Baird Campbell described him as a "dreamer [and amateur inventor] who taught her about literature." Her mother was the second oldest of the large Fasken family, and the primary income earner in the Baird family: she designed homes, borrowed the money to build them, and then sold them to working men's families in Toronto on installment plans. Baird's mother may have had some financial help from her uncle, David Fasken, a highly successful lawyer in the Beatty Blackstock firm at the turn of the twentieth century. At the same time, Baird Campbell recalled that her family experienced poverty in the 1930s: she could not afford to go to the movies, and her family gave up their car in 1929. In addition, although she attended Bishop Strachan School, where the principal was a friend of her mother, her parents struggled to pay the required tuition. When she decided to go to university, Baird's parents told her that she would have to pay her way, and she then worked for several years in the Parks Department, both summers and winters.[78]

77 LSO Archives, OBBRP, "Margaret Chambers" (a record that identifies Chambers as male); and Huckle, "List of Women Barristers and Solicitors." In 1960, "M. Chambers" was still listed at the firm of Chambers & Chambers, suggesting that her appointment to the Official Guardian's office may have been part-time: *Canadian Law Lists.* See also *St. Catherines Standard* (22 November 1960), which suggested, probably incorrectly, that Struthers Chambers graduated from Osgoode Hall in 1935 but delayed her call to the bar to 1937. According to Hunt McLean (1934), Struthers was in her class at Osgoode, but she took a leave of absence to join the Oxford Movement: LSO Archives, "Memoir of Mary Constance Hunt McLean," 33. Chambers was identified as secretary, along with Lily Sherizen (1930), chair, of the WLAO committee's Report on Juvenile Delinquency and Domestic Relations in 1946. F.H. Chambers was appointed KC in 1950 and continued in practice as Chambers & Chambers. The first woman judge at the Family and Juvenile Court in Ontario was Bertha Thompson (1939); in 1962, the second woman—Edra Sanders Ferguson (1930)—was appointed to this court in Toronto: *Globe and Mail* (29 September 1962); and *Woman's Globe and Mail* (9 May 1963).

78 Huckle, "List of Women Barristers and Solicitors;" and OSCLH, oral history, "Margaret Baird Campbell," 1–38, 42–47. Baird described her mother as not a "radical" or a "feminist," but she was unhappy about not being able to vote until after the First World War since "any drunk lying in the gutter could vote." Baird also reported that her decision to study law had been supported early on by Uncle David (Fasken), although he died in 1929, before she entered Osgoode Hall.

Baird thrived at University College, she also discovered a passion for fairness: after learning that not everyone was eligible to join a sorority, she refused to become a member. She also participated in university rallies in support of Professor Frank Underhill, who had coauthored the CCF manifesto and been asked by the college administration to resign his political affiliation. After succeeding in her university studies, Baird entered Osgoode. Knowing that the Fasken firm disapproved of women lawyers, she arranged articles with a cousin, Arnold Ferguson, but his office closed before she completed her articles, and she transferred to Margaret Hyndman's office. Baird was not paid at Hyndman's firm, and she mainly did deliveries rather than court work, real estate, or corporate law. Although Baird had great respect for Hyndman as a lawyer, she also found her "rabidly anti-Roman Catholic," and Baird was annoyed when these views hurt her Catholic friend and classmate, Mary Frawley. Baird also concluded that there was great unfairness in the articling system because "the girls and the Blacks [and probably the Jews] were disadvantaged in trying to get articled ... something ... we had paid for ... and [so we] should have had the same training."[79]

Baird recalled seven women in her class of two hundred law students. She was pleased with her first meeting with Dean Wright, when he began by asking: "Well, sir, what can I do for you?" She and her classmate Aileen McGuire found one instructor "a lecherous old goat," and she described Robinette's embarrassment when teaching torts that involved "women in delicate conditions." She also recalled that when Colonel Foster, another instructor, announced that he could not tell a particular joke with women in the room, "they all got up and left." Baird liked Dean Wright's Socratic method of teaching, and she regarded him as a "challenging professor." In their graduation year, the women students decided, for the first time, to hold their own separate party rather than celebrating with their male classmates. They successfully claimed their share of funds from the Legal and Literary Society, but Baird lamented that the male graduates, "rather than fighting for justice," had held their celebration at a strip club.

79 Mary Frawley, later Lamont, was in Baird's class, although she was not called to the bar until September 1937, and Hyndman refused to admit Frawley to Kappa Beta Pi. Although Baird joined the sorority, she resigned when the US sorority rejected two Black women lawyers from Jamaica. Baird also disagreed with Hyndman's persistent efforts to allow women barristers to use the male barristers' robing room at Osgoode Hall: OSCLH, oral history, "Margaret Baird Campbell," 51–55, 65–72, 76–78.

Moreover, a decade after Hyndman's and Wigle's call to the bar ceremony in 1926, Baird recalled how Justice Kelly asked the gentlemen to rise in 1937, and, when Baird stood up, he commented, "I said gentlemen rise, I do not approve of women in the practice of law."[80] Baird worked with W.C. Davidson for ten dollars per week. Although she applied for legal work with the national railways, both corporations responded that they "couldn't have a woman living out of a suitcase." Then, after the war began, she had the opportunity to take over a Brantford law practice, Waterous & Wallace, whose partners went on active service. As the first woman lawyer in Brantford, she recalled being "the first one ever to break into that silent sea."[81]

In 1941, Baird married Sterling Campbell, originally from Woodstock and a former Hollywood technical adviser and assistant director, who had joined the war as a flight lieutenant. The couple had three children. In 1951, when her youngest child was three, Baird opened a sole practice in Toronto as "Margaret Baird" at 657 Yonge Street. Her first clients were her hairdressers, and she worked as a sole practitioner until 1967. Although Baird was interested in criminal law, she found the attitude toward women lawyers harsh in the criminal courts. At a later point, she did immigration work, assisting Christian Armenians, as well as real estate and family law. Her comments about the family court reveal its lowly status in mid-twentieth-century Ontario: "From the first time I went in before Judge Grudeff in that horrible little place in the cellar of the Registry Office next to the garbage department ... Right on through I had done a lot of

80 Baird Campbell referred to this experience when she was an elected member of the Ontario Legislature, stating that "I had been a gentleman around Osgoode Hall for three years" and that it did not offend her: Ontario, Legislative Assembly, *Official Report of Debates (Hansard)*, 31:2 Sess (10 March 1978) 596.

81 After another lawyer at the firm went to France with the military, Baird was left in charge of the office, and she also tutored his children. Although no records of her work in Brantford exist in the *Canadian Law Lists*, she recalled having to deal with a motion on her second day because the judge refused a request for an adjournment. She believed that he treated her poorly because she was an "outsider," but her gender may also have been a factor: OSCLH, oral history, "Margaret Baird Campbell," 61–66, 81, 88–90. However, when Baird Campbell was elected to the Board of Control in Toronto in 1966, the *Brantford Expositor* (6 December 1966) reported this achievement as "Brantford's First Female Lawyer Wins."

family law. I knew the law very well ... Some were [unpaying clients], but ... there were a lot who came to me because they knew that I knew that law."[82]

Baird Campbell became actively involved in community organizations, including the Canadian Bar Association and the WLAO, and she was elected WLAO president for two years (1949–51). After she presented a paper about taxation and family support payments at a CBA midwinter meeting in Niagara Falls, she was invited to speak to the CBA's taxation section at a dinner meeting at the (exclusively male) Lawyers Club. The invitation was immediately rescinded when it became known that M. Baird was a woman. Baird Campbell was appointed QC in 1960.[83]

As Margaret Baird Campbell, she was elected alderman in 1958, and she became a member of the Board of Control in 1966 and then budget chief in Toronto. She focused on the problems of waste disposal, poverty, housing, and battered wives and abused children, and she also tried to establish better links between family court orders for support and women's welfare payments—to avoid the many distress calls on Friday afternoons. She helped establish credit-counselling arrangements in North Regent Park, as well as supporting young lawyers who volunteered at a legal clinic there before the creation of the Legal Aid Plan in 1966.[84] In 1962, she promoted ideas about women in public office, suggesting that a woman had to "cease [looking on herself] as some sort of freak." Instead, a woman needed to:

> underplay the obvious differences between herself and her male colleagues and yet recognize that, for a time at least, she must have qualities beyond those of the norm of any given government in order to hold her own in the

82 *Toronto Daily Star* (22 April 1941); obituary, *National Post* (16 April 1999); and OSCLH, oral history, "Margaret Baird Campbell," 93–103, 147–49. Baird Campbell was the first non-Armenian to be granted honorary membership in the Armenian Revolutionary Federation, as recognition for her help in settling hundreds of Armenians in Canada: *Globe and Mail* (7 October 1957). Judge Grudeff, who was born in Bulgaria, was called to the Ontario bar in 1926 and appointed KC in 1945. He became a family court judge in 1949: LSO Archives, "Diversifying the Bar," John Grudeff.

83 Ontario, Legislative Assembly, *Official Report of Debates (Hansard)*, 31:2 Sess (10 March 1978) 597. Baird, like Lily Sherizen, was one of the first women lawyers to present a paper at a CBA meeting. See also *Business and Professional Woman* (June 1962), Edmonton Alberta. Baird Campbell lamented the profession's "narrow mindedness" that so often prevented women lawyers from making a greater mark as lawyers: D. Richardson, "Margaret Fasken Baird Campbell" (1989) 2:1 *Without Prejudice* (WLAO) 3.

84 OSCLH, oral history "Margaret Baird Campbell," 119–20.

> debate and voice of the council or legislature ... Second, she must cultivate a sense of humour—particularly an ability to laugh at herself. Nevertheless, there may be times when the very drive to prove herself may give the impression of petulance—this should be avoided at all cost. Above all, she must remember that she is ... a member of the governing body or directors of a large corporation and, accordingly, must devote much time to the understanding of business administration.[85]

In 1969, Baird Campbell ran for mayor of Toronto against William Dennison, the incumbent. For Campbell, Dennison was "a man of no imagination, no vision," and she campaigned to be a more energetic mayor because Toronto was becoming an important city in Canada and the world. She suggested creating a domed stadium on the Toronto waterfront for Toronto's hockey and football teams, and she also wanted Toronto to be "known throughout the world for its ethnic-type festivals, art, music, airports, clean air, sparkling water, [and] safe streets." David Rotenberg campaigned against her, telling constituents that "you don't want a woman to be Mayor, do you?" Baird Campbell confronted Rotenberg, suggesting that it would not be appropriate for her to campaign against a Jewish candidate for mayor. Rotenberg responded, "That is different."[86]

In spite of her efforts, Baird Campbell was defeated in the mayoralty campaign. She practised law briefly in a rented office in Karl Jaffary's firm, and in 1971 she was appointed a judge of the Provincial Court, Family Division.[87] As Judge Campbell, she lobbied for a better library for the family court, and she often tried to find practical solutions in the cases before her. For example, as a way of preventing a future problem for two boys accused of a minor offence, she "bawled the hell out of these kids" and threatened

85 LSO Archives, M. Baird Campbell, "For the Women in Public Life" (June 1962), unidentified news report. A press report identified her as "Meg the knife," providing details of her tough stance on numerous issues: *Globe and Mail* (27 November 1967). See also OSCLH, oral history, "Margaret Baird Campbell," 120–ff and 129–33.

86 LSO Archives, WLAO fonds, unidentified press report (21 October 1969); and OSCLH, oral history, "Margaret Baird Campbell," 133.

87 OSCLH, oral history, "Margaret Baird Campbell," 143–50; and M. Siggins, "Maggie Campbell: The Road Back?," *Telegram* (6 February 1970). See also *Globe and Mail* (13 May 1971), which identified Mrs. M.M. Chambers as the first woman appointed to the Family Division of the Provincial Court in Toronto in 1960 and stated that Kechin Wang, who was appointed along with Baird Campbell, was the first Chinese lawyer appointed to the Provincial Court, Family Division.

jail if they were returned to her court on another offence. She also lobbied for a registration desk on the main floor of the Jarvis Street courthouse for women clients. Because women were often present with children, and the children frequently needed to go to the bathrooms in the basement, the mothers sometimes missed their cases. "And her case would be dismissed because she wasn't there ... and I thought it was shocking."[88]

Although Baird Campbell was a "lifelong Tory," she became angry in the early 1970s with the William Davis government in Ontario because it "thinks people are less important than the bureaucracy that's supposed to be serving them." According to her, the government was failing to consult citizens. As a result, she accepted the Liberals' invitation to contest the by-election in the St. George riding in 1973 and thus "return to democratic government [by developing] a strong, experienced opposition." Because the Tory candidate was Roy McMurtry and the riding had been Conservative for thirty years, the press reported this contest as "Maggie vs. Blue Machine." Campbell was elected, becoming the Liberal Party's first woman MPP and the only Toronto Liberal in the legislature, and she continued to press issues forcefully.

> Being a small fish in a big pond of mostly male politicians did little to dampen her charge. Feisty and tough, she immediately began fighting for issues and ideas—some quite revolutionary for the times. Long before the gay community was even a community, she took on the cause of gay rights, fighting successfully to have sexual orientation included in the anti-discrimination law being passed. It was just one of the many causes she would take up for women and minority rights, believing it was her duty to provide a voice for those who had been denied one for so long.[89]

As Community and Social Justice critic and then Justice critic, Campbell voiced concerns about the Browndale schools. She also raised the issue of battered women, a hard battle that she "fought virtually alone in my time in the legislature. It didn't become popular until later." She conceded

88 OSCLH, oral history, "Margaret Baird Campbell," 116–18, 151–64. She also identified a general "lack of support [for] poor parents," which resulted in many children ending up in court.

89 Obituary, *National Post* (26 April 1999). See also "The Battle of St. George," *Toronto Sun* (6 March 1973); and *Toronto Sun* (16 February 1973). Baird Campbell resigned her judicial appointment to run in the by-election.

that she was not the most diplomatic of politicians, and although she enjoyed political life, she found it frustrating. She retired as MPP at the age of sixty-eight in 1981 to spend time with her husband, who was then eighty-four years old.[90] Campbell received the Order of Canada in 1983, and she was honoured the following year when the Liberal Party established the Margaret Campbell Fund to support women candidates in provincial elections. In 2014, there were renewed efforts to have her honoured by the City of Toronto.

> Over her career, Campbell championed women's rights and fought tirelessly on behalf of the homeless, especially street kids. She was one of the first politicians to focus on domestic violence and spoke of how hard it was in the 1960s to convince men that battered wives were found everywhere in Toronto, not just in poorer neighbourhoods such as Regent Park. Until just a few years before her death, she actively volunteered in the Out of the Cold program for the homeless. She also earned the respect of Toronto's gay community by speaking out in the 1970s in favour of allowing gay youth groups to meet at community centres.[91]

Margaret Baird Campbell died in 1999. Although she faced many challenges fearlessly, she also acknowledged some personal experiences of discrimination during a debate in the provincial legislature in 1978.

> When I look back over my career in the law, I have faced discrimination on a very personal basis, and I want every member of this House to know that when you do face discrimination it is a soul-searing thing. It makes you determined ... to spend the rest of your life fighting for the individual, for

90 OSCLH, oral history, "Margaret Baird Campbell," 166–72–ff. Baird Campbell reported that when she raised the issue of battered wives, "the Tories all snickered, the Liberals sat on their hands [as did the NDP]," leaving her to battle alone. Baird Campbell also argued that the rent-control legislation introduced by the Conservatives (Attorney General Roy McMurtry), with the support of the NDP (Jim Renwick), was beyond provincial jurisdiction. Although McMurtry and Renwick, like Campbell, were lawyers, it was Baird Campbell's legal advice that was upheld when the legislation was declared *ultra vires.*

91 *Toronto Star* (24 July 2014) A19: B. Hepburn, "Time for City to Honour Margaret Campbell," reporting that Joy Noguchi asked City Council to honour Campbell. See also "Lives Lived," *Globe and Mail* (6 May 1999).

> human rights, and for civil rights because ... anything less than that is totally unacceptable.

In spite of such experiences, Baird Campbell remained optimistic about women in law: "I think that women are finally able to be lawyers."[92]

In September 1937, three women were called to the bar. Aileen McGuire, later Worrall, joined the firm of McGuire, Boles & Co. at 67 Yonge Street, where the senior partner was W.H. McGuire, a senator who had been called to the bar in 1906. In 1942, the firm name was revised to McGuire, Boles & McGuire. After Aileen McGuire married James Worrall, who had been called to the bar in 1941, the name changed, in 1946, to McGuire, Boles and Worrall. Eventually, James Worrall took over the practice; Aileen McGuire did not practise law after the birth of their children.[93]

McGuire's friend at university as well as Osgoode Hall was Mary Frawley, later Lamont, the only child of the Catholic chief of obstetrics at St. Michael's Hospital. Frawley had completed an honours course in English and history at the University of Toronto in 1934, where she was also a friend of Margaret Baird. Although Dr. Frawley had been "wiped out" by investments in the stock market crash in 1929, and the family lost their home on Avenue Road, he arranged for his daughter to travel to Europe in the summer of 1934, an annual student trip organized by Major Ney. Frawley's trip proved rather perilous: "When you think back we were watching history unfolding, very ghastly history, and we were so dim witted that we didn't realize what was going on. We crossed the border between Italy and Austria ... ten days or two weeks after Dolphus was shot. And there were soldiers parading through the train with bayonets." The student group was also received by Mussolini in Rome.[94]

92 Ontario, Legislative Assembly, *Official Report of Debates (Hansard)* (10 March 1978) 596. On this occasion, Mrs. Campbell explained that she was "going to do something I really don't like to do in the House ... I'm going to talk ... about discrimination ... because that is the key to the position I take." Baird Campbell also reported that discrimination in her law practice made her work so difficult that she advised her two daughters not to become lawyers: LSO Archives, name file, "Margaret Fasken Baird Campbell (1912–1999)." See also OSCLH, oral history, "Margaret Baird Campbell," 176; and *National Post* (26 April 1999).

93 Huckle, "List of Women Barristers and Solicitors"; *Canadian Law Lists*; and OSCLH, oral history, "Margaret Smith," 101.

94 OSCLH, oral history, "Mary Frawley Lamont," 2, 7–9, 14–26.

When she began studies at Osgoode Hall, Frawley had doubts about whether she would get through the program, but she was "just so ornery that I decided to stick with it." All the same, after she had been called to the bar, Dean Wright remarked to her, "The greatest disservice I ever did the Ontario bar was to let you through," to which Frawley retorted, "Caesar, don't be rude, I have a certificate and you can't take it away from me." Her class of 150 students included a handful of women, all of whom still sat in the front row: "Nobody asked us if we liked it ... that is where we were." During her Osgoode studies, Frawley articled with McMaster, Montgomery, because her father and Montgomery were friends. Since she hated public speaking, Frawley did solicitor work and avoided court appearances. She was active in the WLAO and elected President for two years (1945–47), but she was excluded from the sorority.[95]

After her call to the bar, Frawley worked for Canada Life Insurance for three years in the "policy forms department," checking for mistakes. In 1941, she married Donald Lamont, an Osgoode Hall classmate, and ceased work at Canada Life. However, she worked as a court reporter for the Ontario Court of Appeal for two years (1942–44) and then joined her husband in practice as Lamont & Lamont. In 1944, the press reported a Labour Board case in which Beatrice Lyons (1935) appeared for the employer and Mary Lamont for the employees. After the birth of her children, Frawley Lamont ceased practice—although her husband sometimes telephoned her to consult about firm files.[96]

95 Frawley believed that the sorority was trying "to keep up the calibre of the membership," but it is unclear whether she was referring to her academic performance or her religion, as Margaret Hyndman's aversion to Catholics was widely known. Frawley believed that an important rationale for the WLAO was the Lawyers Club's exclusion of women, even though the WLAO had been created in 1919, three years before the Lawyers Club in 1922. Frawley also admired Lil Sherizen's work as WLAO President: "There was a lot of family law Lil was fussing with long before anybody else was": OSCLH, oral history, "Mary Frawley Lamont," 3, 33, 48–50.

96 LSO Archives, WLAO fonds, SB, vol. 3, unidentified news report; and see also Beatrice Lyons (1935). The court appearance related to an application for certification, filed by David Goldstick, the lawyer spouse of Sarah Kaplan Goldstick (1943). See also OSCLH, oral history, "Mary Frawley Lamont," 35–37, 61–63. Donald Lamont had set up practice with J.B. McLeod (McLeod & Lamont), but when McLeod died shortly thereafter, Frawley Lamont joined her husband, and the firm became Lamont & Lamont. The couple's son Don later practised with his father at the firm. See also D. Richardson, "Profile of Mary Lamont" (1989) 2:1 *Without Prejudice* (WLAO) 3.

In 1970, Frawley joined the Ontario Legal Aid Plan, working three days a week as an interviewing lawyer at the local Area Office. Her role was to determine the legal matter to be resolved, work that she found rewarding.

> The people ... who came to Legal Aid, many times were not only having legal difficulties ... but applicants had no one else to whom they could talk. And they had other problems that might not be related to their legal problems, and they had a great need to talk. I really did feel strongly that the people who were there ... and they may have waited an hour, two hours, whatever to speak to [someone]. The problems were very varied. A great many marital uproars as you can imagine. Great fuss and feathers over that. And people that had difficulties with estates, their rights under wills, and what not. And real estate. In ten years, I learned never to change my expression, no matter what anybody said to me.[97]

When she retired at Legal Aid in the 1980s, Frawley Lamont was sixty-seven. She credited a solid, comprehensive, and practical legal training, "Caesar Wright's opinion notwithstanding," for her success. She also recognized the benefits of both her father's connections and having a legal practice with her spouse: "I wasn't in a situation where you encountered [discrimination]."[98]

The third woman called to the bar in September 1937 was Marie (Marion) Darte, later Johnson. She also graduated from the University of Toronto in 1934 and then enrolled at Osgoode Hall. Probably because she was the daughter of an executive at Union Carbide, she obtained an articling position with Salter Hayden at the McCarthy firm, and she continued to be employed at the firm after her call to the bar until the late 1940s. Her work focused on real estate transactions. Darte was active in the WLAO and served as President in 1942–43. At some point, after she married J.T.

97 The process of applying for legal aid was complex, involving numerous forms as well as separate interviews with a lawyer and with the financial department to determine both legal and financial eligibility. A senior lawyer's opinion was required to issue a legal aid certificate. When Frawley Lamont asked the receptionist why she was receiving so many difficult applications, the receptionist responded: "Mrs. Lamont, you are the only one who will listen to them." She concluded that a background in social service would have been advantageous. Frawley Lamont recalled that she had worked with an "outstanding" Area Director, Bill Donkin: OSCLH, oral history, "Mary Frawley Lamont," 66–85.

98 OSCLH, oral history, "Mary Frawley Lamont," 28–32.

Johnson in 1947, she ceased to practise at the McCarthy firm, and she resigned from the Law Society in 1966.[99]

In November 1937, two more women were called to the bar. One was Lolo Boehmer, later Loucks, who practised law in St. Thomas. In 1939, she was at Leitch & McClurg, and a few years later, she worked at H.C. Cameron's firm while he was on active service. After the war ended, she may have been in a sole practice in 1946, using her married name, Loucks, but she ceased practice at some point and moved to Québec.[100] In contrast, Marie Copeland began to practise law in 1939 with G.B. Jackson, KC, as Jackson & Copeland in Cooksville. Copeland remained in this practice until 1946, when she and her spouse, Edgar Clement, who had been called to the bar in 1939, established a practice together. The couple continued this practice in Cooksville in the 1960s. Copeland died in 1993.[101]

For the first time since the end of the First World War, no women were among the lawyers called to the Ontario bar in 1938. Moreover, although two women graduated from the law school in 1939,[102] only one woman—Bertha Thompson, later Harrison—was admitted to the Ontario bar that year. The daughter of a printer, Thompson grew up in Thorold and graduated from McMaster University in 1936. After attending Osgoode Hall, she was called to the bar in September 1939, becoming the one hundredth

99 LSO Archives, OBBRP, "Marion Johnson [Marie Darte]"; Huckle, "List of Women Barristers and Solicitors"; and A. Bushby, "Presidents of the Women's Law Association of Ontario, 1919–2000," in Bushby, "The Early Years." The liberal attitude of Leighton McCarthy resulted in the firm having four women lawyers in the 1940s, including Darte: Moore, *McCarthy Tétrault*, 57. See also Chapter Four: June Ryan (1941); Jean Oldreive, later Carrie (1945); and Gretta Wong, later Grant (1946). And see OSCLH, oral history, "Margaret Smith," 104.

100 *Canadian Law Lists*; and Huckle, "List of Women Barristers and Solicitors." Sanders Ferguson reported that Boehmer was a woman lawyer in St. Thomas in the 1930s: OSCLH, oral history, "Edra Sanders Ferguson," 69. Québec enacted legislation permitting women to become lawyers in 1941, but no information exists about whether Boehmer Loucks engaged in practice there. See also Chapter One.

101 *Canadian Law Lists*; Huckle, "List of Women Barristers and Solicitors"; and LSO Archives, OBBRP, "Marie Copeland." Her engagement to Clement was announced in the *Globe and Mail* (26 January 1940).

102 Isabella Arthur became a student at Osgoode at the request of the Law Society of British Columbia. At some point, probably 1938, she was first vice-president of the Legal and Literary Society and was photographed at a Law Society lunch at the Royal York Hotel, along with Dean Falconbridge and R.S. Robertson, KC, Treasurer of the Law Society: LSO Archives, WLAO fonds, unidentified news report, ca. 1938.

woman lawyer to be admitted to the Ontario bar. Initially Thompson practised at the firm of Trapnell & Co. in St. Catharines, but she moved to Marquis & Co. in 1943, and in 1946 the firm's name changed to Marquis, Marquis & Thompson. Thompson remained at the firm until the early 1950s, then travelled and lived abroad for several years. In 1959, she returned to Ontario to accept an appointment as Deputy Juvenile and Family Court judge for Lincoln County, and she was appointed a Provincial Court judge in the family division in 1969. As a contemporary news report explained, the court was not well known, in part because its proceedings were closed to the public. Thompson became a life member of the Law Society in 1989 and died in the same year.[103]

In May 1939, King George VI and Queen Elizabeth had travelled to Canada for a royal tour, the first visit to Canada by reigning monarchs. During their nine-hour visit to Toronto, a city of 650,000, 2 million spectators swarmed the city, and veterans of the First World War especially welcomed them.[104] By the time Thompson was called to the bar on 21 September 1939, Britain and Canada had issued declarations of war against Germany, and just as in the Great War, many practising lawyers and law students volunteered for active service.[105] In addition, the absence of male students and lawyers during the war created some significant opportunities for women in law, although women lawyers continued to face gender challenges.

103 LSO Archives, OBBRP, "Bertha Thompson," which identified Thompson as "male." Thompson's employment at the firm of Marquis & Marquis occurred after Florence Sexton (1929) had already departed St. Catharines for the United States. See also *St. Catharines Standard* (23 May 1974); and *Canadian Law Lists.* According to Huckle, Thompson married Bernard Harrison, but she was appointed to the court in 1959 as "Bertha Thompson": Huckle, "List of Women Barristers and Solicitors."

104 "Royals Feel People's Love on Eve of War," *Toronto Star* (21 May 2017) A15. The royal visitors, who were scheduled to spend seven minutes in front of the Christie Street Military Hospital, were still shaking hands and offering comfort to veterans of the Great War forty-five minutes later. The ship on which the royal visitors travelled to Canada was accompanied by two warships carrying a secret cargo of gold worth $120 million in 1939, funds that would help pay for the looming war.

105 Britain and France declared war on Germany on 3 September, and Newfoundland, which was not yet a Canadian province, did so on 4 September. A declaration of war by the Canadian House of Commons and Senate received Royal Assent by Governor General Lord Tweedsmuir on 10 September 1939.

# *One Hundred Women Lawyers: "A Meagre, If Resourceful, Handful"*

*Although female doctors, police officers, accountants, veterinarians, ministers, psychologists, coroners, lawyers, engineers, forest rangers, film directors, university instructors, dentists, publishers, pilots, and undertakers were frequently mentioned in the periodical literature of the 1920s, and never entirely disappeared even in the 1930s, they were never more than a meagre, if resourceful, handful ... [D]uring a period that was very far from giving them an equal chance, but that also never entirely denied them the prospect of individual fulfilment, most women retained the courage to cope and the determination to make the most of whatever life offered.*[1]

Although one hundred women were admitted to the Ontario bar in the decades up to 1939, gender patterns often created discrepancies between women lawyers' aspirations and opportunities. New variations in women lawyers' experiences emerged in the interwar years with optimism about "a new day" for women after the First World War, and the achievement of female suffrage in the 1920s, but also significant challenges during the

1 V. Strong-Boag, *The New Day Recalled: Lives of Girls and Women in English Canada, 1919–1939* (Toronto: Copp Clark Pitman/Penguin, 1988) 5, 67.

Great Depression in the 1930s.[2] Fifty-five women gained admission to the Ontario bar between 1919 and 1929, but only thirty-four women became lawyers between 1930 and 1939.[3] In addition to the impact of the Depression, the exclusion of matriculants at Osgoode Hall after 1926 may have deterred women applicants, and the reversal of this policy in the early 1930s—in the midst of the Depression—did not result in many women applicants at Osgoode Hall. At the same time, some women matriculants in the interwar years enjoyed successful careers: Apha Hodgins (1919), Helen McTague (1924), Margaret Hyndman (1926), Margaret Perney (1927), Edra Sanders Ferguson (1930), Lily Sherizen (1930), Lillian Sandler (1931) Jean O'Rourke (1931), and Helen Okuloski (1935). In contrast, the number of women law students with university degrees, even in the 1930s, suggests a pattern of middle-class privilege.[4]

2 The 1941 census identified 8,621 lawyers in Canada, including 129 women: Law Society of Ontario (LSO) Archives, Women's Law Association of Ontario (WLAO) fonds, SB, vol. 3, unidentified news report. These numbers probably identified practising lawyers.

3 E. Huckle, "List of Women Barristers and Solicitors in Ontario" (1897–1975) [unpublished, archived at Law Society of Ontario Archives]. These eighty-nine women, called to the bar between 1919 and 1939, nonetheless suggest a significant expansion in the number of women lawyers in Ontario, following the admission of only eleven women to the legal profession between 1897 and 1918.

4 After September 1932, matriculants were once again entitled to enrol in the law program at Osgoode Hall, and it may be significant that five years later, in 1937, the largest number of women were called to the bar in the decade. Yet statistics suggest the number of students who entered as matriculants was small: nine students in first-year in 1937 and eight in 1939. This category of admission to the law school was finally eliminated in 1952–53: B. Bucknall, T. Baldwin, and J. Lakin, "Pedants, Practitioners and Prophets: Legal Education at Osgoode Hall to 1957" (1968) 6:2 *Osgoode Hall Law Journal* 139 at 196, 200, 224. Even in the 1920s, half of Ontario lawyers held a university degree, when only 3 per cent of Canadian youth had access to higher education: C. Moore, *The Law Society of Upper Canada and Ontario's Lawyers, 1797–1997* (Toronto: University of Toronto Press, 1997), 196, and Appendix 3. Between 1921 and 1925, 40 per cent of law students had university degrees; in contrast, between 1926 and 1930, 70 per cent had university degrees. Indeed, even after 1932, 72 per cent of law students held university degrees. Nonetheless, the success of matriculants in legal practice may have encouraged a new category of law school admission in later decades: "mature students," persons without university backgrounds but with experience in the workforce: Law Society of Upper Canada, *Report of the Special Committee on Legal Education* (Toronto: Law Society of Upper Canada, 1972). One goal of this new admission category was increased diversity in the profession: see Part Four.

In addition, all women law students and lawyers in the 1920s and '30s were white, and many had family connections to the legal profession, other professions, the business community, or public service, connections that were useful in obtaining articling positions and legal employment—that is, women lawyers in the 1920s and '30s were "professional gentlemen"—except for their gender.[5] In contrast, women lawyers who were "Outsiders" beyond gender—including Jewish and Catholic women and women from immigrant families—often struggled to gain footholds in the profession. Moreover, both the WLAO and the legal sorority engaged in exclusionary practices in these decades.[6] Yet, since these prejudices were also rampant in male clubs and elite Toronto law firms, it is difficult to untangle discrimination based on religion, class, family connections, and marital status from exclusion based on gender.

Significantly, the first cohort of Jewish women lawyers—Helen Grossman (1929), Annie Epstein Baker (1929), Lily Sherizen Sharon (1930), and Lillian Sandler Gordon (1931)—enrolled as law students prior to the new requirement for some university studies, adopted in 1926. The daughters of immigrants, these women contributed to the rising number of Jewish lawyers in Canada in the 1920s. By 1931, Jewish lawyers represented almost 9.5 per cent of Toronto lawyers, although there was not yet a Jewish judge or

5 Moore, *The Law Society of Upper Canada*, 197–99. At the same time, the "social class" of some women lawyers may have contributed to strong societal pressures to cease legal practice if they married.

6 For example, the legal sorority did not open its membership to Jewish women lawyers until the Second World War. Lily Sherizen (1930) recalled that Sarah Kaplan Goldstick (1943) successfully battled for entry to this organization. The situation is less clear with respect to the WLAO. While there are records of Helen Grossman attending some WLAO events, Lily Sherizen Sharon was advised that she was not welcome as a member of the WLAO. When she received an invitation in the late 1940s, she told them she would join the organization but on her own terms: Osgoode Society for Canadian Legal History (OSCLH), oral history, "Lily Sherizen Sharon," 38–44.

magistrate in the city.[7] Yet, while Jewish women experienced discriminatory behaviour at Osgoode Hall, it was access to articling positions that presented the greatest obstacle: as Moore suggested, "Immigration of poor and distinctly 'foreign' Jews from Eastern Europe had given new impetus to Canadian anti-Semitism, and many lawyers and their clients were determined to keep the sons (and even more the daughters) of rag merchants and scrap-metal dealers out of the legal profession altogether."[8]

In contrast, two Jewish women lawyers—Tmima Littner Cohn (1932) and Clara Halperin Muskat (1935)—graduated from the University of Toronto in the 1930s and were called to the bar. Yet Halperin's outstanding academic qualifications did not prevent her from experiencing discrimination in her job search, and Littner abandoned formal legal practice altogether because of its exclusionary practices. Nonetheless, four Jewish women who were called to the bar before 1939—Helen Grossman (1929), Annie Epstein Baker (1929), Lily Sherizen Sharon (1930), and Clara Halperin Muskat (1935)—were appointed QCs in later decades, confirming their success in spite of virulent anti-Semitism in the 1930s. Catholic women lawyers were also a minority in these early decades of the

7 See L. Rosenberg, *Canada's Jewry: A Social and Economic Study of Jews in Canada* (Montreal/Kingston: McGill-Queens University Press, 1993) 191–96. As Rosenberg noted, there were already Jewish judges in Britain and Australia in this period. According to his data, of 351 Jewish lawyers in Canada, only two were women, suggesting that the four Jewish women lawyers, called to the Ontario bar in 1929 and 1930, were not well-known. See also G. Tulchinsky, *Canada's Jews: A People's Journey* (Toronto: University of Toronto Press, 2018). The first Jewish magistrate in Ontario was Abraham Lieff, appointed by Premier Hepburn in the 1930s. Lieff became the first Jewish judge of the Superior Court of Ontario in 1963: LSO, "Diversifying the Bar," Abraham Lieff. Lieff was married to Sadie Lazarovitz, an early graduate of McGill's Faculty of Law, who was probably barred from legal practice in Québec.

8 Moore, *The Law Society of Upper Canada*, 200. Moore argued that most Jewish lawyers during the interwar years "came from families that had overcome poverty" and that virtually all had attended university, citing Bora Laskin as an example. This comment does not reflect the situation of many Jewish women lawyers in Ontario in the interwar years, several of whom were matriculants. Like Laskin, moreover, a number of Jewish male lawyers attained success: Norman Borins became the first Jewish Crown Attorney in Ontario, Jacob Finkelman was the first full-time Jewish professor at the University of Toronto's law school, and Lionel Davis, from an old Toronto Jewish family, joined the Beatty Blackstock firm in 1910: LSO, "Diversifying the Bar," Norman Borins, Jacob Finkelman, and Lionel Davis. Most Jewish women lawyers, including Rosalie Silberman Abella (1972), did not achieve similar success until later in the century: see Part Four.

twentieth century in the province's overwhelming majority of Protestants, especially in Toronto, but several practised law successfully for decades: Theresa Cherrier (1918) in Hamilton; Emily Lynch (1925) in Windsor; Jean O'Rourke and Mary Frawley Lamont (1931) in Toronto, and perhaps others.

At the same time, gender remained a defining feature of women lawyers' experiences in the 1920s and '30s. Women were still seated together in the front row at Osgoode Hall lectures—identifying them from the beginning as "Outsiders," and rendering them invisible to lecturers. Social events at Osgoode, including dances and the annual graduation celebrations, were primarily designed for the often-sexist amusement of male students: as *Obiter Dicta* reported in 1928, the third-year class was "entertained most interestingly by two girl-dancers from one of the local bureaus." In addition, the election of a "Ladies' Representative" on the Legal and Literary Society was treated quite superficially in *Obiter Dicta*: in the 1932 election, female candidates were described as "militant and enthusiastic females [who] had plenty of (executive) experience and would look well receiving at the At Home formal event." Male students were invited to choose "from this bevy of brains and beauty," who needed no other description of their achievements.[9]

Women were also excluded from school activities. They were invited to contribute articles for publication in *Obiter Dicta*, but they were absent from its editorial staff. They were also unwelcome in the formal moot court program at Osgoode Hall, prompting women students to form a "Ladies' Moot Court Club" in the 1930s to develop courtroom skills. Only a few women had friendships with male students, and by the late 1930s, women held a separate graduation dinner celebration. Moreover, there was one egregious occurrence when "Helen Grossman (1929) missed lectures for several weeks in 1927 after being hit in the head by a boot, apparently

9 M. Brunet, *Becoming Lawyers: Gender, Legal Education and Professional Identity Formation in Canada, 1920–1980* (PhD diss., University of Toronto, 2005) [unpublished] 222, 229, citing *Obiter Dicta* (3 April 1928) 4 and (15 April 1932) n.p. The position of ladies' representative was renamed in the 1930s as "first vice-president." Isabella Arthur, a student from British Columbia, was first vice-president of the Legal and Literary Society, ca. 1937–38.

thrown by a male student." She received special credit for a failed exam as a result.[10]

Among the one hundred women called to the Ontario bar between 1897 and 1939, several were located in Toronto in 1939, although they were often employed in trust companies, insurance firms, and the provincial government. A few were engaged in private practice in smaller firms or in practice with their spouses, but only Marion Darte (1937) was working in a major firm, McCarthy's, in 1939. Like Edith Sheppard Revel (1925), Darte was confined to a real estate practice, and she remained an employed lawyer in the firm, a pattern that was common for women in other large Toronto firms in later decades. Similarly, when Belva Gordon Gibson/Hammell (1930) was hired at Blakes "for the duration of the war," her work focused on real estate. In spite of this initial focus, she eventually succeeded in becoming a partner in the firm in the 1950s, the first woman to achieve this status at an elite Toronto firm. In addition to women lawyers in Toronto, there was at least one woman lawyer in practice in 1939 in many communities near Toronto: Brampton/Georgetown (Sybil Bennett, 1930), Burlington (Emily Williamson, 1935), Cooksville (Marie Copeland, 1937), Newmarket (Beatrice Lyons, 1935), and Bowmanville (Apha Hodgins, 1919).

Beyond Toronto, several women lawyers—Frances Milne (1929), Margaret Sullivan (1929), and Helen Okuloski (1935)—had joined Jean Cairns Morris (1913) and Theresa Cherrier (1918) in Hamilton. Constance Hunt Mclean (1934), who was also located in Hamilton, was married with children and may have been practising part-time. Ethel Renwick Clark (1926) had married and ceased her employment at an insurance agency by 1939, and Eileen Harron (1921) was not in practice. In Windsor, there were three women lawyers in practice in 1939: Lovedy Campeau Scott (1919), Helen McTague (1925), and Emily Lynch (1926). In other Ontario communities, including St. Catharines (Bertha Thompson, 1939, and Florence Sexton, 1929), Preston (Lida Pearson Sturdy, 1919), London (Evelyn Harrison, 1921), St. Thomas (Edra Sanders, 1930, and Lolo Boehmer, 1937), Sarnia (Agnes Weir Randolph, 1935), Port Colborne (Helen Kinnear, 1920), and

10 There are conflicting accounts of the establishment of *Obiter Dicta* in either 1927 or 1928: see Brunet, *Becoming Lawyers*, 194, 222; and Moore, *The Law Society of Upper Canada*, 214. Moore suggested that the incident involving Grossman reflected the school spirit defined by "the hearties," but since she was the first Jewish woman lawyer, it is difficult to know whether gender or religion, or perhaps both, provoked this incident.

Cayuga (Lenore Colter, 1930), women were practising law, although sometimes only for a few years. In contrast, only two women lawyers were in private practice in eastern Ontario in 1939: one in Trenton (Gertrude Alford, 1916), and one in Kingston (Vera Robinson Cartwright, 1920). And no woman was in private practice in Ottawa. By 1939, it is possible that Ruby Wigle Fish (1926) was still practising law in Sault Ste. Marie, but it is unclear whether Edyth Dyke (1921) was then practising in Fort William, although she returned to practice in the 1940s. Clearly, most women lawyers outside Toronto were "lone voyagers," usually the only woman lawyer in their communities in the interwar years.[11]

There are some patterns of professional success for women who were called to the bar in the 1920s and '30s. Two women lawyers, Helen Kinnear (1920) and Margaret Hyndman (1934) were appointed KC in the 1930s, and a number of others received KC or QC appointments in later decades.[12] Most women practitioners who received these appointments were in active legal practice, and they often remained unmarried. In the 1920s and '30s, some women lawyers, including Helen Kinnear (1920), Vera Parsons (1924), Margaret Hyndman (1926), Margaret Perney (1927), Margaret Fraser (1928), and Beatrice Lyons (1935) were appearing as litigators, and

11 The term was created by G.J. Clifford, *Lone Voyagers: Academic Women in Co-educational Universities, 1870–1937* (New York: Feminist Press, 1989).

12 The WLAO kept records of these appointments for several years after the initial KC appointments of Kinnear (1920) in 1934, Hyndman (1926) in 1938, and Parsons (1924) in 1944: see LSO Archives, WLAO fonds, SB, vol. 3; and Huckle, "List of Women Barristers and Solicitors." The WLAO list includes the three women appointed KC in 1945: Sybil Bennett (1930), Helen Palen (1918), and Gertrude Alford (1916). Elizabeth Newton (1921) was appointed KC in 1947. Four women were appointed KC in 1948: Margaret Fraser (1928), Jean O'Rourke (1931), Marie Wilson McCulloch Sanders (1932), and Elizabeth Maclennan (1927). Two women were appointed in 1949: Evelyn Harrison (1921) and Margaret Perney (1927). Two more women were appointed KC in 1950: Helen McTague (1924) and Lovedy Campeau Scott (1919). In 1953, QC appointments were awarded to two women: Lily Sherizen Sharon (1930) and Theresa Cherrier (1918). Some additional QC appointees included Helen Okuloski (1935), in 1954; and two in 1956, Emily Lynch (1925) and Belva Gordon Gibson Hammell (1930): Archives of Ontario, *Orders in Council re His/Her Majesty's Counsel Learned in the Law*, files 3329/54, 3241/56. Although these records do not include the names of QC appointees after 1956, Huckle, "List of Women Barristers and Solicitors," identified other women lawyers who were appointed QC but dates of their appointment are missing: Marian James Lamey (1922), Grace Gordon (1924), Mary Waddell (1924), Bertha Hawkins (1926), Helen Grossman (1929), Ina Bulloch (1933), and Margaret Baird Campbell (1937).

some argued cases in the Supreme Court of Canada. In 1943, Helen Kinnear (1920) became the first woman judge in the British Commonwealth, while Bertha Thompson (1939), Margaret Struthers Chambers (1937), Edra Sanders Ferguson (1930), and Margaret Baird Campbell (1937) were later appointed judges in Juvenile and Family courts in Ontario, and Edra Sanders Ferguson was also appointed to the Division Court.

Three women lawyers succeeded in politics. Sybil Bennett (1930) was one of the earliest women and the first woman lawyer elected to Parliament in the early 1950s; Margaret Baird Campbell (1937) was elected to both Toronto City Council and the Ontario Legislature in the 1960s and '70s; and Emily Lynch (1925) was elected an alderman in Windsor. In addition, like Clara Brett Martin (1897), Margaret Perney (1927), Evelyn Harrison (1921), and Lida Pearson Sturdy (1921) were elected school trustees in Toronto, London, and Preston, and both Ruby Wigle (1926) and Lida Pearson Sturdy (1921) became solicitors to the Preston Town Council. Margaret Fraser (1928) and Elizabeth Maclennan (1927) were both elected president of the York County Law Association in later decades. Among women lawyers in active practice, only Lida Pearson Sturdy, Edra Sanders Ferguson, and Margaret Baird Campbell were married with children.

These patterns reveal that most "successful" women lawyers remained unmarried: marriage was not attractive for some women because it meant giving up "income and economic independence."[13] However, among women called to the bar between 1919 and 1939, there were some exceptions: Constance Hunt McLean (1934), Vera Robinson Cartwright (1920), Belva Gordon Gibson Hammell(1930), and Mary Frawley Lamont (1937) practised law, at least for some years, in firms with their spouses, although those who were also mothers may have worked only part-time for some periods. Lida Pearson Sturdy (1921) continued to practise law in her own firm after marriage, perhaps a necessity during the Depression, but continued her practice in later decades. It appears that Ruby Wigle Fish (1926), Edra Sanders Ferguson (1930), Marie Wilson McCulloch Sanders (1932), and others also combined marriage and legal practice, at least to some extent. In addition, some women lawyers—Lovedy Campeau Scott (1919), Lily Sherizen Sharon (1930), and Lillian Sandler Gordon (1931)—married later in life, after establishing their legal practices. Others, including Annie Epstein Baker (1929) and Mary Frawley Lamont (1937), married and ceased

13 LSO Archives, "Diversifying the Bar," Helen Kinnear.

legal practice but returned to legal employment in later decades. These patterns suggest that only a few married women lawyers with children continued to practise law, while women lawyers who practised full-time generally remained unmarried. Moreover, several women who were called to the bar in the 1920s and '30s practised briefly, or not at all, before marrying and resigning as members of the Law Society, confirming that societal norms about women and marriage, especially for middle-class women, continued to limit opportunities for women lawyers in the 1920s and '30s.

Yet, even women who engaged in legal practice often faced both blatant and more subtle discrimination—including the negative judicial comments made to Margaret Hyndman and Ruby Wigle Fish, and later to Margaret Baird Campbell, at their call-to-the-bar ceremonies. Women and Jews were excluded from the Lawyers Club, although the club later voted to permit Jews to become members—several years before women became eligible.[14] In addition, Margaret Baird Campbell (1937) reported that women could become members of the Ontario Bar Association and pay fees in the 1930s, but they were not permitted to vote. And in Toronto, exclusive male clubs continued to create problems for women lawyers who were invited to "business lunches" well into the 1990s, an issue

14 In spite of its more progressive views about legal education, the Lawyers Club adopted rules in 1929 requiring that no applications for membership be considered unless the applicant was "under forty years of age, male, white and of the Christian religion." Because of this exclusion, Jewish lawyers later established their own club, the Reading Club: S. Sperdakos, "'A Forum for Discussion' and Place of Respite: Jewish Lawyers and Toronto's Reading Law Club" (2012) 30 *Windsor Yearbook of Access to Justice* 163 at 165. In 1958, the Lawyers Club removed its ban on non-Christian members and gradually absorbed the members of the Reading Club, but women and Blacks continued to be excluded until later decades: Moore, *The Law Society of Upper Canada*, 267–68.

that prompted a WLAO newsletter to explain how women could avoid "unexpected and sometimes embarrassing situations."[15]

In addition, women law students and lawyers experienced challenges because of the washrooms at Osgoode Hall and the robing facilities in Ontario courts. In the early 1930s, the Law Society began to alter arrangements for women students by designating the third-floor washroom as a women's washroom, a welcome change from the women's washroom in the basement.[16] In the late 1930s, the Law Society undertook renovations at Osgoode Hall to create a Lady Lawyers' Robing Room, although its effort suggested that women lawyers were still perceived as marginal. According to the committee's report: "As this room will be very little used, I suggest it be kept locked and the ladies furnished keys. It is proposed to put 10 lockers from the present locker room in here and the writing desk from the Benchers' room. The washroom is to be completely furnished with all the necessary accessories."[17] As noted, Margaret Hyndman (1926) believed that women lawyers should share the men's robing rooms, probably to ensure women's access to participation in legal negotiations. According to

15 Women were permitted at the Toronto Club for lunch or dinner only if accompanied by a male member, but they were required to enter by the ladies' entrance through the lobby of an adjoining building. The University Club accepted women members, and they could use the main restaurant for lunch or dinner, but they were not permitted to use the lounge and Grill Bar because these facilities could only be entered through the men's locker room. The York Club restricted women's membership to spouses or widows of members, and all women were required to use the Port Cochère entrance. The National Club did not permit women members at all, although women guests were allowed to eat in the ladies' dining room in the basement. Ironically, the 1991 WLAO newsletter, explaining these arrangements at male clubs, also reported on the first meeting of the WLAO in 1990–91, at which the Minister of Justice, the Honourable Kim Campbell, spoke, urging them to pursue the goal of being "catalyst[s] for change": (1991) 5:1 *Without Prejudice* (WLAO) 3. Campbell was the first federal female Minister of Justice, and later the first (and only) woman Prime Minister in Canada.

16 LSO Archives, report of A. MacMurchy, chair (19 February 1931). The new women's washroom required considerable repairs, as it had "cracked plaster, peeling paint, and leaking plumbing."

17 See LSO Archives, "Report on renovations" and "Letter re furnishings from the Robert Simpson Company Ltd" to A. Heeney (30 September 1938). As Moore noted, the use of funds for a major construction project, at a time when many lawyers were still experiencing the challenges of the Depression, was overlooked by the Benchers. Indeed, the Society had cash reserves of more than a half million dollars in the mid-1930s, even though many lawyers' Society fees were in arrears: Moore, *The Law Society of Upper Canada*, 211.

Margaret Baird Campbell (1937), "We had our own robing room. And she wouldn't go into it."[18]

Although male lawyers and judges often displayed exclusionary practices in relation to women and other Outsiders in the legal profession, most women lawyers in these decades expressed little concern about gender discrimination. Some, like Mary Frawley Lamont (1937), recognized that her father's connections and her law practice with her husband meant she did not face discrimination. In contrast, Lily Sherizen Sharon (1930) both witnessed and experienced discrimination but philosophically concluded that it was widespread and that she "wasn't anything special." Even Dean Wright contributed distinctly sexist views in a speech in 1931, in which he lamented that "husbands have lost the right to chastise their wives and seem to have little left except liability to pay the shot."[19] Thus, from the perspective of later decades, women lawyers' experiences in the 1920s and '30s reveal both blatant as well as more subtle forms of discrimination. In a twentieth-century interview with Helen DeRoche Roberts (1933), the interviewer was obviously puzzled by the clear contradictions between women lawyers' exclusionary experiences and their failure to acknowledge them.

> [She] was almost hostile to any suggestion that she had been discriminated against. Almost the first thing she told me was that she had always like[d] men and had always related to them well. But almost immediately upon the tails of saying she had never experienced any discrimination, she would give an instance of it. I don't know what to make of this. I think it would be kind of patronizing to say that she was oppressed but just didn't realize it. [Although she confirmed the significance of her father's support, DeRoche stated,] "You were far better off if you got along with people."[20]

18 OSCLH, oral history, "Margaret Baird Campbell," 78–79. Issues about robing facilities created controversy for decades: see Chapter Five.

19 OSCLH, oral histories, "Mary Frawley Lamont," 28, and "Lily Sherizen Sharon," 42; and A. Bushby, "Creating Culture: The Early Years of Ontario Women in the Legal Profession" (Presentation to the International Women's Day Celebration, Law Society of Ontario, Toronto, 2000). 10. See also LSO Archives, WLAO fonds, C. Wright, "Downtrodden Males Seek Women's Rights: Women Pampered Favourites of the Law," unidentified press report, ca. 1931. According to Bushby, it was Wright's speech that prompted the WLAO motion in 1931 to appoint a woman lecturer at Osgoode Hall: LSO Archives, WLAO fonds, SB, vol. 2.

20 LSO Archives, "Nora's Interview with Torchy," 3. See also the Epilogue.

In spite of women lawyers' denial about exclusionary practices in the legal profession, the WLAO challenged an incident of discrimination in the 1930s. When Premier Hepburn's new Liberal government in Ontario embarked on cost-cutting measures in the mid-1930s, Laura Lees (1926) and Margaret Perney (1927) were dismissed from their employment as solicitors in the Department of Agricultural Loans. In response, Marion Darte (1937), corresponding secretary of the WLAO, wrote to Premier Hepburn on 5 January 1940, requesting a meeting to discuss the women's dismissal, and when no action occurred, she requested help from the Ontario Women's Liberal Association. Mrs. Verna Stratton, corresponding secretary for the association, wrote to the Premier on 31 January, characterizing these dismissals as "a very backward step as far as women are concerned; and as long as these professions are open to us, there should be no distinction made." On 1 March, a letter from the secretary of the Ontario Liberal Association to the WLAO representative confirmed the success of this intervention: Margaret Perney and Laura Lees were "being continued in the service."[21]

Overall, patterns for women who were called to the bar between 1919 and 1939 suggest that some women lawyers enjoyed opportunities for legal work, in contrast to several women lawyers admitted to the bar up to 1918. In the 1920s, a robust economy created increased work for lawyers, and some women lawyers, particularly those with family connections to the profession, obtained employment in Toronto and other communities in Ontario. In the 1930s, some women lawyers succeeded in solo and small-firm practices, but those without middle-class connections often experienced major challenges. Most women lawyers who married did not practise law for long, although a few engaged in legal practice with their lawyer spouses. In addition, the profession continued to discriminate against other Outsiders on the basis of race, religion, and class, and women lawyers continued to face exclusionary gender practices. It was still a gentleman's profession.

21 LSO Archives, York County Law Association fonds, Miscellaneous Activities. This activity reveals the importance of relationships between the WLAO and other women's organizations. See also Bushby, "Creating Culture," 11. Women's salaries were often needed to support parents and other dependants, including elderly parents and family members who were veterans of the First World War. In spite of the revised decision, Perney resigned her government position and established a sole practice.

# PART THREE

## *Gendered Legal Contexts: War and Post-War Reforms, 1940–57*

## *Women Lawyers in War and Peace: Progress and Stasis*

*Both the assumption of great gains made by women during World War II and the bewilderment over the postwar reversals rest on an inadequate examination of the context of women's wartime employment and an inaccurate assessment of the degree to which attitudes towards women's proper role in society changed during the war. Canada's war effort, rather than any consideration of women's right to work, determined the recruitment of women into the labour force ... [At the end of the war, the] slight yet disquieting reconstruction of womanhood in the direction of equality with men was scrapped for a full-skirted and re-domesticated post-war model, and for more than a decade feminism was once again sacrificed to femininity.*[1]

During the Second World War, women worked in factories, offices, and farms, replacing men who joined the war, and the Canadian government also began recruiting women for the Armed Forces in 1941. By the end of the war, nearly fifty thousand women were in uniform: the Royal Canadian Air Force created a "woman's division," the army created the Canadian

1 R. Pierson, "Women's Emancipation and the Recruitment of Women into the Labour Force in World War II" in S. Mann Trofimenkoff and A. Prentice, eds., *The Neglected Majority: Essays in Canadian Women's History* (Toronto: McClelland and Stewart, 1977) 125, 220. See also H. Armstrong and P. Armstrong, "The Segregated Participation of Women in the Canadian Labour Force, 1941–1971" (1975) 12:4 *Canadian Review of Sociology and Anthropology* 370.

Women's Army Corps (CWAC), and the Women's Royal Canadian Navy Service (WRCNS) was established in 1942. Some women in these units were posted overseas, but women in the Armed Forces were generally paid less than men: "The attitudes toward these women reflected the division of labour that pre-existed the war and the pay differentials similar to civilian practices."[2] Nonetheless, women's participation rate in paid work rose from 24.4 per cent in 1939 to a high of 33.5 per cent in 1944, but it fell steadily thereafter to a low of 23.6 per cent in 1954. Although the rates of marriage increased in the postwar period and some married women continued in paid work, they often faced the pattern of a "double day of labour," both outside and within their homes.[3]

Women law students also joined the Armed Forces, sometimes postponing or interrupting their law studies, and some women lawyers replaced male lawyers who joined the war effort in law firms—significantly, many of these opportunities disappeared at war's end. As during the Great War, many male lawyers and law students joined Canada's military effort as well as wartime bureaucracies and war industries. Indeed, "men who attended Osgoode in these years recall how 'great chunks' of the student body would be found missing some mornings," and Dean Falconbridge and Dr. Wright took over the classes of two faculty members who had joined up. Student numbers dropped to the lowest in the school's history: from a total of 325 students in 1939–40 to 109 students in 1943–44, and 116 in 1944–45. The Law Society distributed an "Armed Forces Letter" to those in military service, which included information about cases as well as legal news and gossip, and Osgoode Hall sponsored an informal Commonwealth law school in enemy prison camps, where some students even wrote exams. In 1943, two Osgoode alumni at Oflag VII-B, a German prison camp, constituted themselves the teaching staff of the prison law school. By the end of the war,

2 L. Marsden, *Canadian Women and the Struggle for Equality* (Don Mills, ON: Oxford University Press, 2012) 76–77. In 1943, 255,000 women were working in war industries, and several thousand had volunteered for the Women's Divisions of the Armed Forces: Pierson, "Women's Emancipation," 128.

3 R. Roach Pierson, *"They're Still Women after All": The Second World War and Canadian Womanhood* (Toronto: McClelland and Stewart, 1986) 215–16. See also Marsden, *Canadian Women and the Struggle for Equality*, 78–79.

734 Ontario lawyers and 177 students had participated in active service.[4] Although the Law Society provided refresher courses for returned soldiers, the policy adopted after the First World War, which had permitted veterans to skip some courses and exams, was not replicated in 1945.

As E. Mitchell Thomas (1942) recalled, the status of women law students and lawyers changed during the war. "Instead of being the last to be considered for a job ... we became 'sought after' ... [because it was unlikely that women would] run off to the War."[5] As noted, Margaret Baird Campbell (1937) took over a law practice in Brantford for male lawyers who had joined the war effort, and Mary Frawley Lamont (1937) managed her husband's practice while he was involved in war service.[6] Indeed, the demand for "woman power" in war-related industries and in the Armed Forces meant that one in three adult women in Canada was engaged in paid work by 1944: women acquired both new skills and new confidence, and some received wages that corresponded to the rates of pay of male workers whom they were replacing. At least to some extent, women's experiences during the war contributed to the postwar campaign for Canada's first

4 B. Bucknall, T. Baldwin, and J.D. Lakin, "Pedants, Practitioners and Prophets: Legal Education at Osgoode Hall to 1957" (1968) 6:2 *Osgoode Hall Law Journal* 139 at 202–3. Morden and Edge, two part-time lecturers, were the instructors who went on active duty. Guards were posted at Osgoode Hall, and the law school established its own branch of the Canadian Officer Training Corps: C. Moore, *The Law Society of Upper Canada and Ontario's Lawyers, 1797–1997* (Toronto: University of Toronto Press, 1997), 223–24. See also Law Society of Ontario (LSO) Archives, Women's Law Association of Ontario (WLAO) fonds, SB, vol. 3, *Toronto Star* (20 June 1946). The article included a photo of three former prisoners of war being called to the bar: J.R. Turnbull, W.W. Cameron, and R.W. Davies. It noted that Turnbull passed some law exams in a prison camp. See also "Osgoode Hall Armed Forces Letter (No 18)" (21 November 1944), reproduced in Law Society of Upper Canada, "Professionalism: A Century of Perspectives" (2002) *Gazette* 42–43, announcing arrangements for "Post-War Refresher Courses" in fall 1945. Some law students remained at their desks, prompting criticism in *Obiter Dicta* for their failure to "heed their country's call to the task." In addition, as the war progressed, the federal government's efforts to boost enlistment included requiring universities to report students who failed exams or were placed in the lower half of their small classes: M. Brunet, *Becoming Lawyers: Gender, Legal Education and Professional Identity Formation in Canada, 1920–1980* (PhD diss., University of Toronto, 2005) [unpublished] 190.

5 LSO, WLAO fonds, SB, vol. 7, E. Mitchell Thomas, letter to the WLAO (18 January 1965), noting that she also served as WLAO President in 1943–45.

6 C. Morgan, "An Embarrassingly and Severe Masculine Atmosphere': Women, Gender and the Legal Profession at Osgoode Hall, 1920s to 1960s" (1996) 11:2 *Canadian Journal of Law and Society* 19 at 49. See also Chapter Three.

equal-pay statute, in Ontario in 1951.[7] Moreover, as early as 1943, women began to focus on their postwar roles. At a meeting of the Local Council of Women in Toronto, one speaker asserted that "the position of women after the war is most certainly going to be such as was never before dreamed of by her, or, what is more to the point, by man." Another speaker suggested a need for the world to be "adjusted" to accommodate women workers.[8] At war's end, the women's section of the Department of Veterans Affairs tried to ensure continued "fair play" in terms of equal treatment for women in the workforce, although these efforts were not entirely successful.[9]

The war and these postwar arrangements were relevant to aspiring women lawyers in two different ways. First, a number of women postponed admission to the law school or took leaves from their existing studies, in order to participate in the war effort. These women often benefitted, as did male students, from veterans' entitlement to educational support at war's

7 In 1943, the pay rate for women in the Armed Forces was raised to four-fifths that of men, from a previous rate of two-thirds: *Toronto Star* (24 July 1943); and D. Forestall, "The Necessity of Sacrifice" in J.M. Bumstead and L. Kuffert, eds., *Interpreting Canada's Past*, 3rd ed. (Don Mills: Oxford University Press, 2005) 367–69. See also L. Bohnen, "Women Workers in Ontario: A Socio-legal History" (1973) 31 *University of Toronto Faculty of Law Review* 45 at 58; and *Female Employees Fair Remuneration Act*, SO 1951, c 26. Ontario's statute was the first in Canada, but the federal government enacted the *Female Employees Equal Pay Act* in 1956, and by 1961 every province except Québec and Newfoundland had similar legislation. See also Ontario Women's Bureau, *Equal Pay Legislation: An Historical Review* (n.d.) [unpublished, archived at Ontario Women's Bureau, Toronto] 1, citing the recommendations of the Advisory Committee on Reconstruction, which included equal pay for women as well as equal terms of employment and equal opportunities for advancement.

8 *Globe and Mail* (17 November 1943) 9. Speakers represented the Federation of Canadian Business and Professional Women's Clubs and the Federation of Medical Women of Canada. Eileen Mitchell (1942), President of the WLAO, identified issues about equal pay for women, and several speakers emphasized the need to ensure women's opportunities for postwar work.

9 P. Neary and S. Brown, "The Veterans Charter and Canadian Women Veterans of the Second World War" (1994) 9:2 *British Journal of Canadian Studies* 249. The authors quoted Olive Ruth Russell, who supervised women's demobilization at the Department of Veterans Affairs: "Women had skills that should and must be used in the national interest, including supports for homemaking responsibilities." Nonetheless, restrictions on hiring married women in the federal public service, lifted during the war, were reinstated in 1947 and not revoked until 1955: Bohnen, "Women Workers in Ontario," 61, citing K. Archibald, *Sex and the Public Service* (Ottawa: Queen's Printer, 1970). See also J.E. Hodgetts et al., *The Biography of an Institution: The Civil Service of Canada, 1908–1967* (Montreal/Kingston: McGill-Queens University Press, 1972).

end, and women who acquired skills and worked alongside men during the war were perhaps more confident in the gentleman's profession. Yet societal views in the postwar decades generally characterized women's war work as exceptional, creating strong support for women, and especially married women, to return to full-time homemaking and children. In addition, governmental support for homemakers in the postwar years, such as the *Family Allowances Act* in 1944, reinforced ideas about differential sex roles.

> Because the allowances were intended as supplements to the male wage, they did not interfere with a husband's responsibility to maintain his family ... [The allowances represented] a general, conservative cultural consensus that transcended both class and gender boundaries and cohered around the cultural ideal of family independence and the liberty of individual men to pursue their goals untrammelled in the marketplace—ideals predicated on the maintenance of discrete gendered spheres between the home and workplace.[10]

10 N. Christie, "Conclusion: The Endangered Family" in N. Christie, *Engendering the State: Family, Work and Welfare in Canada* (Toronto: University of Toronto Press, 2000) 310 at 319. See also SC 1944–45, c 40; and Pierson, "Women's Emancipation," 136–44. The Liberals (under Mackenzie King and St. Laurent) were in power federally during the war and until 1957, when the Progressive Conservatives (under Diefenbaker) won the election. In Ontario, the Liberals (under Hepburn) were in power from 1934 to 1943, when they were defeated by the Conservatives (under Drew). Drew resigned in 1948 to lead the federal Conservatives, and he was replaced by Frost in Ontario: see D. Creighton, *The Forked Road: Canada, 1939–1957* (Toronto: McClelland and Stewart, 1976); J. Saywell, *"Just Call Me Mitch": The Life of Mitchell F. Hepburn* (Toronto: University of Toronto Press, 1991); and M. Stevenson, "George Drew: The Law of the Sea, and the Diefenbaker Government, 1957–1963" (2020) 31:2 *Diplomacy and Statecraft* 326.

In this context, women who became lawyers in the 1940s and '50s, just as in earlier decades, often relinquished the practice of law if they married.[11]

Thus, in spite of women's efforts to contribute to the war effort, the social climate after the Second World War tended to discourage women, and especially married women, from engaging in paid work, and women who practised law in the late 1940s and '50s often experienced gender discrimination. Although the United Nations General Assembly adopted the Universal Declaration of Human Rights in 1948, which included protection for "equality before the law,"[12] sex discrimination legislation did not yet exist in Canada.[13] Even after Ontario became the first Canadian province to enact human rights legislation, in 1962, it was not until 1971–72 that "sex" was added as a prohibited ground of discrimination in the *Ontario Human Rights Code*, and not until 1985 that sex equality was legally protected in the *Canadian Charter of Rights and Freedoms*, enacted in 1982.[14]

11 "Well girls, it looks as though the old game of employment by sex, rather than merit, is on the books again": K. Kent, unidentified quote in *Maclean's*, quoted in Neary and Brown, "The Veterans Charter," 378. In addition, federal funding for the extensive wartime program of day nurseries for mothers engaged in war work ceased in 1946. Although some provincial and municipal funding was provided for child care, a consensus emerged that the widespread employment of women was not appropriate after the war ended, and thus child care was no longer essential: A.M. Timpson, *Driven Apart: Women's Employment Equality and Child Care in Canadian Public Policy* (Vancouver: UBC Press, 2001); L. Madsen, "Citizen, Worker, Mother: Canadian Women's Claims to Parental Leave and Childcare" (2002) 19 *Canadian Journal of Family Law* 11; and D. McKenzie, "A Long History of Failure: Feeling the Effects of Canada's Childhood Policy" (2014) 29 *Canadian Journal of Law and Society* 397. The postwar cancellation of the tax concession available to employed married women was also in keeping with these official attitudes toward working women during the war: Pierson, "Women's Emancipation," 136–45.

12 M.A. Glendon, "John P. Humphrey and the Drafting of the Universal Declaration of Human Rights" (2000) 2 *Journal of the History of International Law* 250. Several women were involved in background discussions about the sex-equality provisions, including American Eleanor Roosevelt and Hansa Mehta, an Indian woman.

13 Ontario had enacted the *Racial Discrimination Act* and the *Fair Employment Practices Act*, but even though the latter prohibited employment discrimination on the basis of race or religion, it did not preclude sex discrimination.

14 K. Schucher, *Coercing Justice? Exploring the "Aspirations and Practice" of Law as a Tool in Struggles against Social Inequalities* (PhD diss., Osgoode Hall Law School, 2014) [unpublished]. See also *Women's Equal Opportunity Act, 1970*, SO 1970, c 33; *Ontario Human Rights Code Act Amendment Act, 1972*, SO 1972, c 119; and *Canadian Charter of Rights and Freedoms*, Part I of the *Constitution Act, 1982*, being Schedule B to the *Canada Act 1982* (UK), 1982, c 11.

Women who were called to the Ontario bar after the war had little choice but to cope with and, at times, confront "the gendered hierarchies and relations of power" in the legal profession.[15] Many women lawyers embraced a "quiet" professional identity as lawyers, ungendered.

After the many sacrifices of Canadians during the war, the postwar decades became "Canada's Golden Age," characterized by the rise of the welfare state, the emergence of an enlarged civil service, and an unprecedented economic expansion that continued after the war for nearly a quarter century. As Christopher Moore suggested, "lawyers benefited at every step."

> New layers of state regulation and public administration created new business for lawyers. Industrial development on a massive scale transformed corporate law practices and invented modern labour relations. As millions of Ontarians used their new prosperity to build homes, buy cars, marry, raise families, and accumulate property and services, they made work for lawyers at every stage. As Ontario surged forward, the legal profession rode the crest of the wave.[16]

In practice, however, it was more often male lawyers who "rode the crest of this [economic] wave" after the war.

In October 1945, Grace Gordon (1924) organized a series of lectures by women lawyers on law and legislation under the auspices of the Law Committee of the Local Council of Women. Judge Helen Kinnear (1920) initiated the series, giving a lecture "The Machinery of Justice." Her lecture was followed by five additional lectures: "Women and Investments," presented by Margaret Hyndman, (1926); "Labor Legislation," by Beatrice Lyons (1935); "Divorce," by Marjorie Henry (1921); "Making Wills," by Mary Frawley Lamont (1937); and "Succession Duties," by June Ryan (1941). The lectures, which were held at 88 Prince Arthur Avenue and at the YWCA auditorium, were a resounding success, attracting capacity audiences of up to five hundred people. Near the end of the series, Gordon noted that other communities were also interested in having such lectures and that a second series of lectures was being organized for fall 1946 in

15 Morgan, "An Embarrassingly and Severely Masculine Atmosphere," 61.
16 Moore, *The Law Society of Upper Canada*, 238.

Toronto.[17] In addition, the WLAO continued its activities, including a lunch in September 1951 at Winston's Theatre Grill on King Street, in conjunction with the annual meeting of the Canadian Bar Association.[18]

At Osgoode Hall, the retirement of Dr. MacRae led to the appointment of Bora Laskin in 1945. Because he was a former faculty member at Dean Kennedy's law program at the University of Toronto, Laskin's appointment at Osgoode renewed hopes for a more cooperative relationship between the two schools. Indeed, Premier Drew organized a meeting in 1947 between representatives of the university and the Law Society for this purpose, but no *rapprochement* occurred.[19] And, although Dean Falconbridge's efforts to establish a full-time academic program of legal education at Osgoode remained unsuccessful, the number of lectures increased to 1,044 in 1945, and new subjects were added to the curriculum: Administrative Law and Taxation Law in 1944, and Labour Law in 1945.[20]

After 1945, physical space at Osgoode Hall became not just inadequate, but often chaotic. There were 445 students enrolled in 1945–46 and 700 and 800 in the next two academic years: "The classrooms and Convocation Hall were busy six days a week," and in 1946, classes for second-year students were held in the hall of Metropolitan United Church. A press report in 1946 included photos of veterans at the law school, cramming for exams, noting that "out of 453 students, 345 are returned men." It also reported that "lucky" articling students might earn a salary of five dollars per week

17 LSO Archives, WLAO fonds, SB, vol. 3, *Globe and Mail* (4 October 1945) and *Toronto Evening Telegram* (1 November 1945). The second series of lectures took place in Willard Hall: the first lecture was presented by Helen Rodgers from Buffalo, the first woman to argue a case in the New York Court of Appeals. Five additional lectures were presented by Marie Wilson (1932), on insurance law; Jean O'Rourke (1931), "Criminals Are People"; Margaret Perney (1927), "The Home and Homeless: Landlord and Tenant"; Mary Gallagher (1940), on real estate; and Marjorie Henry (1921), "So This Is Marriage." Both lecture series attracted considerable press coverage for women lawyers after the war.

18 LSO Archives, WLAO fonds, SB, vol. 3, autograph signatures of women lawyers who were present.

19 Dean Wright was not impressed with Kennedy's Law School, describing it as "nothing more nor less than a department of the Faculty of Arts": C.I. Kyer and J.E. Bickenbach, *The Fiercest Debate: Cecil A. Wright, the Benchers and Legal Education in Ontario, 1923–1957* (Toronto: Osgoode Society for Canadian Legal History, 1987) 150.

20 Bucknall, Baldwin, and Lakin, "Pedants, Practitioners and Prophets," 204: Dean Falconbridge successfully requested more hours for lectures in his report to the Legal Education Committee, and lecture hours returned in 1945 to the arrangements established in 1934.

but that most were unsalaried.[21] Although the Law Society conceded that veterans could begin courses in mid-semester, there was no leniency with respect to examinations, and some students failed, especially in courses taught by Wright and Laskin. Moreover, some veterans were irate about Osgoode Hall instructors who had not experienced the hardships they had endured, but their ally, Hamilton Cassels, a Great War veteran who chaired the Legal Education Committee, approved virtually all grade appeals submitted by veterans.[22]

As during the Great War, there were increased numbers of women students at Osgoode Hall during the Second World War, perhaps because the Law Society welcomed women students—and their fees—in the absence of male students. Thus, eight women in a class of about fifty students were called to the bar in 1944, and for the first time since 1921, nine women joined the legal profession in one year, in 1948. Women students also became more visible after they established the Osgoode Women's Legal Society (OWLS) with its dinners and other social events. Moreover, women students picketed the law school twice, first to demand an end to their exclusion from moot court juries (women weren't eligible for jury duty until Ontario's 1951 *Jurors Amendment Act*).[23] Women picketed a second time to support women's eligibility for the position of president of the Legal and Literary Society, even though no women students were interested in the position: "It was a matter of principle." There were few law school activities during the war years: the Legal and Literary Society was generally inactive, and *Obiter Dicta* was published only monthly. In addition, as in the

21 Moore, *The Law Society of Upper Canada*, 227; and LSO Archives, WLAO fonds, *Globe and Mail* (26 April 1946). This press report also noted that earlier cohorts of articling students had paid law firms to accept them as articling students. The minor discrepancy in student numbers in 1946 probably reflects fluctuation during the academic year as some students dropped out.

22 Bucknall, Baldwin, and Lakin, "Pedants, Practitioners and Prophets," 205; and Moore, *The Law Society of Upper Canada*, 228.

23 *Jurors Amendment Act*, SO 1951, c 41. Gretta Wong Grant (1946) described the OWLS and these picketing activities prior to 1951: OSCLH, oral history, "Gretta Wong Grant," 43. The first woman to be called for jury duty was Mabel F. Smith, in 1953, at the Essex County courthouse, but the case was adjourned at the request of the Crown because the Crown's main witness had just given birth. Although the statute did not take effect until 1953, a court in Sault Ste. Marie summoned women for a jury panel in 1952: *Windsor Star* (6 January 1953).

universities, "male students set the 'patriotic standard' and women's contributions were circumscribed and considered voluntary."[24]

In the immediate postwar years, moreover, both students and faculty struggled: students were disadvantaged by a hopelessly inadequate library, and faculty members faced enormous piles of examinations to grade. Articling positions were scarce, and although some firms tried to support the veterans, there was initially too little "real" legal work. Moreover, with male veterans receiving preference, women experienced even greater challenges in finding articles and legal employment after 1945. As many students began to realize that they might become sole practitioners, they requested more office training. After a group of young Toronto barristers volunteered to lead discussion groups of twenty-five students each Monday evening, "practice groups" became compulsory at Osgoode Hall in 1947. A few years later, practice groups replaced office work for first-year students.[25]

Yet, in spite of such challenges, many law students graduated to "bright prospects" after the war: "Even as thousands of new lawyers entered the profession, old fields of legal practice expanded and subdivided and new fields emerged, creating business to support the lawyers at a previously unimagined standard ... It might be said that never in the history of Ontario had so many lawyers made so much money with such relative ease for so long," an assessment that probably overstates the success of women lawyers—and Outsiders—especially if they had few connections to the profession. Although the Law Society's preparations for peace were modest, intended "to preserve or to restore pre-war conditions," there were some new initiatives. These included refresher courses for returning veterans, which evolved as the Society's continuing legal education programs; and free legal advice for returning soldiers (and as wartime marriages became wartime divorces), for soldiers' spouses, a program that shaped ideas about legal aid services in the 1960s. The Law Society's introduction of a client compensation fund and an insurance company also offered new

24 OSCLH, oral history, "Gretta Wong Grant," 43; and Morgan, "An Embarrassingly and Severe Masculine Atmosphere," 48–49.

25 Moore, *The Law Society of Upper Canada*, 227; and Bucknall, Baldwin, and Lakin, "Pedants, Practitioners and Prophets," 204–5. The practice groups provided teaching opportunities for some women who became lawyers in the 1940s, including Mitchell Thomas (1942), Van Camp (1947), and Teagle MacDonald (1948).

opportunities for legal employment.[26] Yet, employment in elite private practice firms in Toronto remained relatively uncommon for women—they continued to find work in government and in trust and insurance companies, and some women lawyers opted to work as sole practitioners, especially in communities outside Toronto.

Notably, there were few reforms in legal education after 1945, a problem that erupted in public in 1949 as "the fiercest debate." Although legal education debates had occurred continuously at Osgoode Hall for decades, a consensus was emerging in Canada after the war that "university was the only place for higher education."[27] Thus, when Dean Falconbridge, the "gentle and contemplative scholar," announced his resignation as dean in January 1948, and the Benchers appointed Dean Wright to take his place, they faced "a man more impatient for reform." Wright had regularly identified deficiencies in Ontario's system of legal education, and he continued to promote reform proposals in public. In contrast, the Benchers, who had been trained under the existing system, were "neither familiar with, nor appreciative of, academic legal studies," and they pointedly asked Wright to cease public criticism of legal education at Osgoode Hall.[28]

The controversy escalated in January 1949 when the Law Society's Special Committee on Legal Education issued a new report. Established two years earlier and prior to Wright's appointment as dean, the committee issued a report with majority recommendations that were "contrary to everything Caesar Wright had publicly fought for," and confirmed the Benchers' continuing control over legal education—including the existing

26 Moore, *The Law Society of Upper Canada*, 226, 238–39, 249–50: A Law Society committee report at the end of the war proved to be "spectacularly wrong" in its suggestion that lawyers would face only weak prospects at the end of the war. The establishment of a compensation fund at the law society resulted in the need to promulgate rules about standards of practice, as well as more staff to examine members' accounts, and lawyers eventually faced more onerous reporting requirements.

27 Kyer and Bickenbach, *The Fiercest Debate*; and Moore, *The Law Society of Upper Canada*, 250.

28 Bucknall, Baldwin, and Lakin, "Pedants, Practitioners and Prophets," 207–10. See also C. Wright, "Law and the Law Schools" (1938) 16 *Canadian Bar Review* 579, recommending a full-time academic law program and a separate period of articling; and B. Laskin, "Cecil A. Wright: A Tribute" (1967) 45 *Canadian Bar Review* 213. In contrast, Mike Chitty, editor of the *Fortnightly Law Journal* and a Bencher, was firmly convinced that legal education must be controlled by lawyers: Kyer and Bickenback, *The Fiercest Debate*, 181.

system of full-time articles and part-time lectures. The report included a vague recommendation for further review by the committee, in collaboration with the dean, to ensure a balance between academic and practical courses. Dean Wright, who had not been consulted by the committee, first read the committee's recommendations in the morning newspapers.[29] Two days later, he and several other members of the full-time faculty resigned to join the law program at the University of Toronto.

This may have been "the most famous event in Osgoode's history."[30] Even though graduates of the program at the University of Toronto could not be called to the bar without completing all the requirements at Osgoode Hall, this event arguably resulted in a modest change in legal education at Osgoode Hall in 1950, and then recognition of academic legal education in Ontario universities in 1957.[31] Moreover, Osgoode Hall was facing severe overcrowding: between 1948 and 1952, more than 600 students crowded into facilities built to accommodate 300 students, and there were forecasts of about 1,500 students seeking admission to Osgoode Hall annually in the next ten years. As a private institution, funded by the Law Society and student fees, Osgoode Hall was also facing financial challenges, and the Benchers were pushed by the fiscal realities of modern mass

---

29 Bucknall, Baldwin, and Lakin, "Pedants, Practitioners and Prophets," 214–15, citing *Toronto Star* (21 January 1949) and Recommendation 2. The committee's report arguably ignored or rejected every progressive trend developed in the field of legal education in the preceding fifty years.

30 Kyer and Bickenbach, *The Fiercest Debate,* 210; Bucknall, Baldwin, and Lakin, "Pedants, Practitioners and Prophets," 215–16; and Wright's letter of resignation *Globe and Mail* (22 January 1949). Bora Laskin and John Willis resigned with Dean Wright. Stan Edwards, another full-time member of the Osgoode faculty who resigned, joined the firm of Fraser & Beatty.

31 Kyer and Bickenbach, *The Fiercest Debate,* 211. The protagonists attempted to achieve a smooth transition: the faculty at Osgoode Hall agreed to complete the current term, and Dean Wright spoke to students about the situation, emphasizing that the problem was a fundamental disagreement between the Benchers and the faculty at Osgoode Hall about how best to educate lawyers. There was some support for reform of legal education in Ontario: both *Obiter Dicta* and the Legal and Literary Society publicly supported Dean Wright, and some practitioners also sided with him. In contrast, other lawyers regarded Wright's persistent public criticism of the Benchers' decisions as inappropriate in a "gentleman's profession." A motion was passed at the midwinter meeting of the CBA Ontario branch, asking the Benchers to reconsider their decision to limit lecture hours, but attendees refrained from further comment because "it was not politic" to do so: Bucknall, Baldwin, and Lakin, "Pedants, Practitioners and Prophets," 222–23.

education to consider university legal education.[32] Queen's, Western, and Ottawa all wished to establish academic law programs.[33]

In January 1957, a significant negotiation occurred over a weekend at the Royal York Hotel with three representatives: Park Jamieson and John Arnup representing the Law Society and Alex Corry, vice-principal at Queen's, representing the universities.[34] The negotiation resulted in uniform requirements for admission to legal education in Ontario and an agreement that legal education would include three years of full-time academic studies at an approved law school, followed by fifteen months of articles and a six-month bar admission course at Osgoode Hall. Osgoode

32 Kyer and Bickenback, *The Fiercest Debate,* 248–49. The large numbers of prospective students probably reflected Osgoode's admission requirement of "any" university degree: the degree, rather than any specified level of standing, entitled a student to admission to Osgoode Hall: OSCLH, oral history, "Hilda Margaret McKinlay," 32–38. McKinlay attended Victoria College in 1947–51 while working full-time, so she attended only a few classes (although she recalled attending "all the parties.") As she reported, "all you needed to gain admission [to Osgoode] was a degree."

33 After 1949, Osgoode Hall revised its legal education arrangements to include four years: two years of full-time lectures, one year of articles, and a fourth year combining lectures and articles. In this context, the three-year academic law program at the University of Toronto was recognized as equivalent to *two years* of full-time lectures at Osgoode Hall, and this arrangement remained in place until 1957.

34 Kyer and Bickenbach, *The Fiercest Debate,* 259–61. Park Jamieson had authored the dissenting report of the Special Committee on Legal Education in 1949. Vice-Principal Alex Corry studied law at the University of Saskatchewan and was a Rhodes Scholar at Oxford before joining the Faculty of Political Science at Queen's University, where Principal Mackintosh wanted to establish a faculty of law to augment its strength in economics, commerce, politics, and industrial relations. Corry asked Bora Laskin at the University of Toronto's faculty of law to participate in this meeting, but Laskin declined. Corry's previous acquaintance with Jamieson and Arnup probably contributed to the positive outcome: J.A. Corry, *My Life and Work: A Happy Partnership* (Kingston: J.A. Corry/Queen's University, 1981) 151–56.

Hall retained its law school, offering a full-time program of academic legal education over three years.[35]

Thus, in the years between 1940 and 1957, most law students, including women, attended Osgoode Hall's three-year program prior to 1950 and its four-year program thereafter. Graduates of the University of Toronto's three-year law program were required to attend Osgoode Hall for three additional years up to 1950, and two additional years thereafter. After 1957, prospective law students had more options for studying law, including at universities located in different part of Ontario, and for full-time articling in students' home communities. The number of women lawyers accelerated after 1957, becoming "nothing short of revolutionary in the decades between the 1960s and '80s.[36] Just as the establishment of the law school in 1889 may have prompted Clara Brett Martin's application for admission in the 1890s, the 1957 agreement may have been one factor in increasing women's access to legal education. At the same time, there is no evidence that the agreement, in which representatives of the Law Society and the universities were all male, was designed to make the study

35 The Law Society required the universities to accept prescribed courses, and Corry happily assented to the Society's proposals: Corry, *My Life and Work*, 154. See also J. Arnup, "The 1957 Breakthrough" (1984) 18 *Law Society Gazette* 180. Although rising student numbers and financial pressures contributed to this outcome, long-standing developments in other provinces may have been significant: W.W. Pue, "Common Law Legal Education in Canada's Age of Light, Soap and Water" (1996) 23 *Manitoba Law Journal* 654. Debates continued in the 1950s: I. Rand, "Legal Education in Canada" (1954) 32 *Canadian Bar Review* 387; and M. Cohen, "The Condition of Legal Education in Canada" (1950) 28 *Canadian Bar Review* 267. See also LSO Archives, J.B. Dunlop, "Law Teaching Materials in Canada" (Graduate student paper submitted to Harvard Seminar on Legal Education, Boston, 1957).

36 In 1951, the population of Ontario was about 4.5 million. By that date, 159 women had been called to the Ontario bar, although only eighty were in active practice: D. Coyle, "Women in the Legal Profession in Canada" (1951–52) 38 *Women Lawyers' Journal* 14. Coyle reported that twenty-two women engaged in legal practice in British Columbia, five in Alberta, ten in Manitoba, thirty-eight in Québec, three in Nova Scotia, ten in New Brunswick, two in Newfoundland, and none in PEI. See also P. Axford, "Portias of the Province," *Saturday Night* (28 February 1948); and L. Millar, "Careers: The Modern Portia Has Won Professional Recognition," *Saturday Night* (25 August 1945). Although the number of male law students doubled between 1962–63 and 1980–81 in Canada, the number of female law students increased twenty-four times in this period: R. Abel, "United States: The Contradictions of Professionalism" in R. Abel and P. Lewis, eds., *Lawyers in Society: The Common Law World*, vol. 1 (Berkeley: University of California Press, 1988) 186 at 202.

of law more accessible for women and other Outsiders.[37] For women law students in Ontario between 1940 and 1957, the need to confront gender challenges remained.

37 Women lawyers' oral history recollections very seldom mention the 1949 "crisis," suggesting that the divisions among the Benchers was relatively unknown among (at least women) law students. See also Part Four. After the war, the press had also identified challenges facing foreign-trained lawyers, who were often required to complete both university and law courses: LSO Archives, WLAO fonds, SB, vol. 6: S. Gray, "Extra 6-Year Study for Lawyer," unidentified article about lawyers from Hungary, Czechoslovakia, and Italy.

CHAPTER FIVE

# "*Gendered Hierarchies and Relations of Power*," 1940–49

> *Women have broken down age-old prejudices and are demonstrating daily that they are as well equipped to practise law as their brothers at the bar. They have been accepted by the profession itself. Women now serve on the executives of both national and local bar associations and there are women chairman* [sic] *of their special committees. On a number of women has been conferred the honorary degree of King's Counsel* (KC) ... *A number of town solicitors are women and women lawyers are members of city and town councils.*[1]

These optimistic comments about positive prospects for women lawyers in 1945 reflect how some were attaining professional recognition. A few women lawyers were employed in Toronto law firms and in smaller Ontario communities, while others continued to be employed in government departments, insurance agencies, and trust companies. Some women who were called to the bar in the 1940s later achieved judicial and other appointments, but some practised law only briefly or not at all, especially if they

1 L. Millar, "Careers: The Modern Portia Has Won Professional Recognition," *Saturday Night* (25 August 1945).

married. These variations reflect the ongoing gendered hierarchies and relations of power among Ontario women lawyers in the postwar decade.[2]

Three women students completed their studies and were called to the bar in 1940. Beth Rowlin married her classmate F.E. Underhill, and they established a practice in London as Underhill & Underhill. Beth Underhill was the second woman lawyer in London, after Evelyn Harrision (1921), who had practised law there for two decades as the "only woman lawyer" in the city. In addition to her practice, Beth Underhill became a spokesperson for university women and women's rights. She was also part of a delegation of the National Council of Women when they presented resolutions to Prime Minister St. Laurent in 1950, recommending voting rights and more voice for "Indians" with respect to their education. Beth Underhill eventually joined the Canadian Bar Association in 1955. In the 1960s, with Gretta Wong Grant (1946), she established the Middlesex Women's Law Association, initially an informal organization that became more active as other women joined the London bar. In 1962, the MWLA hosted a successful one-day meeting in London for members of the WLAO.[3]

Mary Gallagher, later Gauthier, whose father was a land surveyor in northern Ontario, was called to the bar with Underhill in September 1940. She obtained a BA from the University of Toronto in 1937, and she articled in Toronto for Daniel Lang while attending Osgoode Hall. After her call to the bar, she worked at the Parliament buildings in 1941, and in the Office of the Public Trustee in Toronto from 1942 to 1946. By 1948, she had returned to Timmins and married Harold Gauthier, the son of a lawyer. Gauthier entered Osgoode Hall Law School in 1939, served in the Second World War,

2 C. Morgan, "'An Embarrassingly and Severely Masculine Atmosphere': Women, Gender and the Legal Profession at Osgoode Hall, 1920s to 1960s" (1996) 11:2 *Canadian Journal of Law and Society* 19 at 61.

3 F. Carter, *The Middlesex Bench and Bar* (London: Middlesex Law Association, 1969) 94, 120; and *Toronto Telegram* (1 November 1950). According to Gretta Wong Grant, Betty Underhill thought Wong Grant should have a QC, and Underhill organized the successful application: C. Backhouse, "Gretta Wong Grant: Canada's First Chinese-Canadian Female Lawyer" (1996) 15 *Windsor Yearbook of Access to Justice* 3 at 42–43, 45. Fred Underhill had joined the Middlesex Law Association in 1940, and Beth Underhill did so in 1960. Fred Underhill was later elected an alderman in London and appointed a QC. In the 1970s, *Canadian Law Lists* identified Beth Underhill as "Mrs. B.L. Underhill" at the firm of Underhill & Underhill, 478 Waterloo Street.

and was called to the bar in 1947.[4] The couple practised law as "Gauthier & Gauthier." Mary Gauthier was appointed QC in 1959, "the only woman QC in northern Ontario," and her spouse became QC in the same year. The Gauthiers were probably the first married lawyers to receive this honour together.

As the first woman lawyer in Timmins, Gauthier followed pioneer women lawyers in northern Ontario, including Eva Powley (1902) in Port Arthur and Edyth Dyke (1921) in Fort William. In 1962, when she became a candidate for the federal Progressive Conservative PC nomination in Timmins, the press identified Gauthier's many contributions to organizations in Timmins and Porcupine, as well as her membership in the WLAO. In 1971, H.W. Gauthier was appointed a judge in the Provincial Court (Criminal Division) in Cochrane. He died in 2002, and Mary Gauthier died in 2004.[5]

The third graduate of 1940, Marjorie Horenblas, later Jacobs, was called to the bar in November 1940. Between 1941 and 1946, she was listed at three locations in Toronto and may have been a sole practitioner, but she later married D.S. Jacobs and moved to Baltimore, Maryland.[6]

Only two women were called to the bar in 1941. One was Margaret (Marni) Griggs, later Abbott, who joined the Ontario legal profession in June. She moved to Québec and married her Osgoode classmate W.R. Abbott, and there is no record of her practising law in Ontario.[7] In September 1941, June Ryan was called to the bar. Her father was a farmer, and she graduated from the University of Toronto in 1938 and articled with H.B. Gardner. In 1942, she was employed at the Parliament buildings, but she

4 Law Society of Ontario (LSO) Archives, Ontario Bar Biographical Research Project (OBBRP), "Harold Wood Gauthier." He articled in Toronto with Everett Bristol.

5 E. Huckle, "List of Women Barristers and Solicitors in Ontario, 1897–1975" [unpublished, archived at Law Society of Ontario Archives]. In 1948, the law firm in Timmins was identified as "H.W. Gauthier," with Mary Gauthier's name in parentheses, but subsequent listings included both names. See also *Timmins Press* (18 April 1962); LSO Archives, OBBRP, "Harold Wood Gauthier" and "Mary Gauthier"; and *Canadian Law Lists*. After her spouse was appointed to the court, Mary Gauthier was listed at 158 Hemlock Street in Timmins, and she may have ceased to practise law. Mitchell Thomas, who was also from northern Ontario, was a classmate of Mary Gauthier, but Mitchell Thomas delayed her call to the bar until 1942: Osgoode Society for Canadian Legal History (OSCLH), oral history, "Eileen Mitchell Thomas," 39–40.

6 Huckle, "List of Women Barristers and Solicitors." Horenblas's address was listed on Beverley Street in 1941, on Bay Street from 1942, and on Richmond Street East in 1946: *Canadian Law Lists*.

7 Huckle, "List of Women Barristers and Solicitors"; and *Canadian Law Lists*.

then joined Marie Darte (1937) at McCarthy & McCarthy, "partly due to the liberal attitude of Leighton McCarthy," and both women worked as solicitors doing real estate transactions. In 1948, Ryan moved to the firm of C.M. Ricketts on Richmond Street West, and she remained at this firm, which became Ricketts, Farley and Cory, for a few years. Ryan was often involved in WLAO activities, and she may have become a sole practitioner at several locations in Toronto, but she suffered a serious illness and voluntarily resigned her Law Society membership in 1971.[8]

The third woman who graduated from Osgoode Hall in 1941—Angela Kerr, later Porter—was never called to the bar. Kerr Porter was a farmer's daughter from Elgin County who had trained as a teacher, but as a Catholic she had experienced discrimination in finding employment. At a community picnic attended by Premier Mitch Hepburn, her father, a loyal Liberal and a friend of Hepburn, asked whether his daughter could work for government, and Hepburn responded, "Yes, send her down." Kerr began working in the Corporations Tax department in Toronto, and she decided to enrol for lectures at Osgoode Hall, supporting herself with her government salary. Women students were no longer sitting in the front row in these wartime classes, and Kerr described how "Marni" Griggs sat with her boyfriend, later her husband, along with June Ryan. Kerr also recalled some of the instructors:

> They didn't ask us [women] very many questions. They didn't want to embarrass us. But this guy, Falconbridge ... I used to nearly die if I thought he was going to ask me a question, but he did ask me a question and I knew it, one day ... only one question in three years. [But] it wasn't a question-and-answer thing. They mostly lectured ... [Wright] was wonderful. He was very hard to get marks from, but he was such an interesting teacher ... He taught torts, and he also taught wills and trusts, and those were I think the three hardest courses.[9]

8 LSO Archives, OBBRP, "June Ryan"; C. Moore, *McCarthy Tétrault: Building Canada's Premier Law Firm* (Vancouver: Douglas and McIntyre, 2005) 67; and *Canadian Law Lists*. Gretta Wong Grant recalled Ryan as "a beautiful blonde ... she used to wear frills and things": Backhouse, "Gretta Wong Grant," 28. Ryan may have left McCarthy's because she found the practice "too much": OSCLH, oral history, "Margaret Smith," 103. Ryan may have suffered from schizophrenia, and the medical treatment may have impaired her ability to practise law: Laura Legge, interview with M.J. Mossman (28 February 2008).

9 OSCLH, oral history, "Angela Kerr Porter," 24–25, 28–29, 37–38.

By 1941, when she graduated, Kerr had been reassigned to the government's Succession Duty Department, and she decided to work and save money to be called to the bar in 1942. After she met and married her spouse, she abandoned a call to the bar because her husband did not believe in women working. Nearly thirty years later, in 1968, Kerr Porter's daughter, Mary Louise Porter, later Graham, graduated from Osgoode Hall Law School and was called to the bar in 1970—along with her spouse.[10]

Three women were called to the bar in 1942, including Eileen Mitchell, later Thomas, a graduate in 1940 who postponed her call to the bar. Her father, George Mitchell, had established a successful law practice in Cobalt during the mining boom in the early decades of the twentieth century. Mitchell, an only child, completed a BA in philosophy at Queen's in 1937. She worked in her father's practice during the summers, which, as she recalled, became more difficult during the Depression. After a faculty member at the University of Toronto discouraged her from pursuing graduate work, she enrolled at Osgoode in 1937, one of three women from northern Ontario in a class of one hundred students.[11]

Mitchell recalled turbulent times at the law school after 1939, when students left to join the war. Although records indicate that she articled with her father in Cobalt, she recalled doing negligence work at Lester & Russell and obtaining court experience with Frank Regan. After graduating in 1940, Mitchell attended the School of Social Work at the University of Toronto and later worked as an office manager for a company that manufactured radars. After saving enough money, she was called to the Ontario bar in May 1942 and worked briefly for the Judge Advocate General in Ottawa and

10 OSCLH, oral history, "Angela Kerr Porter," 19–25, 28–30, 37–38, 45, 49–50; and marriage announcement for Kerr and Captain Fredric Porter, *Toronto Star* (9 January 1943). See also Huckle, "List of Women Barristers and Solicitors": Mary Lou Porter married T.D. Graham. In contrast to Kerr Porter's experience in the 1940s, she noted that female students in the 1960s, including her daughter, engaged more with male students in social activities.

11 Huckle, "List of Women Barristers and Solicitors"; and OSCLH, oral history, "Eileen Mitchell Thomas," 1–40, 53–54, 76–78. Mitchell Thomas recalled that she was one of three women from northern Ontario in her first year in 1937, including Mary Gallagher (1940), later Gauthier, from Timmins, and Kathleen Morrison (1946), later Callahan, from Sault Ste. Marie. Mitchell Thomas also identified her father among the Osgoode male students in 1906 who alerted Grace Hewson (1908) to their prank: see Chapter Two.

later at Fennell Porter in Toronto, where she accompanied Dana Porter, later Attorney General, in his court appearances.[12]

Mitchell joined the WLAO and was President for two years in 1943–44. She recalled reserving a table for lunch with three other women lawyers at the Royal York hotel and how the server refused to seat her guests because the table was reserved for "a bunch of women lawyers." When Mitchell explained that she and her guests were the women lawyers, the staff member responded, "Oh, you can't be, you all look so nice." Mitchell also became the first woman lawyer in Canada to be elected to the National Council of the Canadian Bar Association, in 1942–43, although her participation was compromised at the council's dinner meeting in Montreal: it was scheduled for the male-only Montreal Club. Her offer to enter through the kitchen was refused, so after expressing her disgust to the president, she enjoyed a very nice dinner on her own. Mitchell regarded her work at Fennell Porter as highly successful, with a salary of $250 per month during the war. Nonetheless, her position was terminated in 1946—after she familiarized the firm's incoming students with arrangements for title searching.[13]

Significantly, Mitchell became the first woman lawyer to be appointed a practice-group instructor at Osgoode Hall in 1947—although the position was not a formal faculty appointment. Mitchell and her students were initially unhappy when all the women students were assigned to her group, but they "had such fun that we decided at the end that perhaps it would be a

12 OSCLH, oral history, "Eileen Mitchell Thomas," 41–48, 54–60. Mitchell Thomas described her minor role, along with Arthur Martin, in the trial of Mickey Macdonald when he was charged with murder: see also Vera Parsons, Chapter Three. Mitchell Thomas did not enlist in the war because she wanted to avoid being sent to "some remote location to wash dishes." See also LSO Archives, OBBRP, "Eileen Mitchell Thomas."

13 OSCLH, oral history, "Eileen Mitchell Thomas," 54–61, 70, 80–85. Mitchell Thomas was President of the WLAO for two years in 1943–45: A. Bushby, "The Early Years: Sources of an Enduring Tradition: The Women's Law Association of Ontario, 1919–1950" (80th Anniversary Celebration, 14 January 2000). Her work for the Judge Advocate General was similar to court martial work, and she "didn't like it a bit." While most women used a first initial, Mitchell Thomas' entry in the *Canadian Law Lists* at the Fennell Porter firm in 1943 and 1946 was "Eileen Mitchell." She regarded the WLAO as a way to provide women lawyers with strength in numbers, but she had no interest in a sorority, including Kappa Beta Pi.

better idea if we did stay together."[14] In 1946, Mitchell travelled to England for six months, where she worked to encourage British interest in Canada, and while there she observed the Youth Court and arrangements for young offenders—experiences that became useful later in her career. The British authorities also sent Mitchell to Nuremberg to observe the war trials.[15]

On her return to Canada, Mitchell married a former classmate from Queen's, Homer Thomas, an officer in the Royal Canadian Dragoons. The couple moved frequently for several years to postings in London, Kingston, and Ottawa. In London, Mitchell Thomas described having a modest sole practice and receiving helpful advice from Evelyn Harrison (1921). She also did appeals for her father's clients, and she received a secret apology from an appeal court judge after negative treatment from Justice Laidlaw, who wondered out loud, "what the hell is a woman doing in this court anyway?" In the early 1950s, she had two daughters. As she later commented, she might have pursued a different path without children because, by the 1950s, "Women were coming along a little better then ... and I might have been the head of my own firm or something."[16]

While her children were young, Mitchell Thomas did legal work from her home in Manor Park, Ottawa, including real estate transactions for Armed Forces employees who were moved frequently. She also acted in a dispute over the rate for sewer and water services after Manor Park was annexed by Ottawa. She recalled that Mayor Charlotte Whitton, who had opposed the Manor Park claim, was "mad as a wet hen" when the claim succeeded. In 1956, the family moved to a new posting in Toronto for two years, and Mitchell Thomas was employed part-time at Lang Mitchener doing real estate work.

14 OSCLH, oral history, "Eileen Mitchell Thomas," 62–63; and LSO Archives, Minutes of Convocation (1947), vol. 23, at 510–12. Judy LaMarsh (1950) was among fourteen women in first-year at Osgoode, and Mitchell gave her a very good evaluation: LSO Archives, S. Lewthwaite, "memo to file" (15 March 2001).

15 OSCLH, oral history, "Eileen Mitchell Thomas," 65–67; and C. Everett, "Woman's Place Not Only in the Home Says Ottawa's First Woman QC," *Ottawa Journal* (5 January 1960). Mitchell had visited Youth Courts in England where she met Mr. Watson, author of several books on young offenders. Juvenile delinquency and youth courts were becoming major social and legal issues in the 1950s: see United Nations Department of Social Affairs, *Comparative Survey on Juvenile Delinquency* (New York: United Nations Department of Social Affairs, 1952–53); and Lily Sherizen (1930), Chapter Four.

16 OSCLH, oral history, "Eileen Mitchell Thomas," 67–72.

When the family returned to Ottawa, she joined McNulty McClenaghan, where John McNulty, the brother of Mary McNulty Fix (1918), was the senior partner. Although Helen Currie (1921) worked for the federal Department of Revenue in the 1950s, Mitchell Thomas was the only woman in private practice in Ottawa. She was involved in applications for road widening and mechanics' liens in relation to construction and some trial work. In 1961, she was appointed legal counsel to the National Capital Commission, when it was empowered to expropriate seventeen thousand acres of land to form the Green Belt around the city.[17] Mitchell Thomas also accepted an appointment as a part-time municipal judge (two mornings each week) at Ottawa's Juvenile and Family Court, hearing cases about adoption, family disputes, wife assault, and youth theft. She eventually resigned, suggesting that these municipal courts were underfunded. They became part of the Ministry of the Attorney General a few years later. From 1962 to 1979, Mitchell Thomas was one of about forty lawyers employed at the federal Department of Justice, where she reported that the deputy minister was more interested in the quality of legal work than the sex of departmental lawyers.[18]

Like women lawyers in other Ontario communities, Mitchell Thomas described the dire situation of the robing rooms in the Ottawa courthouse. Although a small room had been designated for women barristers' use in the Daly Avenue addition in 1960, it was also used as the "holding room" for accused in custody, awaiting court appearances. Thus, women

17 E. Mitchell Thomas, "The History of Women Lawyers in the County of Carleton Law Association" in W. Johnson, ed., *The First Century: Essays on the History of the County of Carleton Law Association by Various Hands on the Occasion of the Association's Centenary, 1888–1988* (Ottawa: Bonanza Press, 1988) 107 at 108–9; and OSCLH, oral history, "Eileen Mitchell Thomas." No records of Mitchell Thomas in practice in London, Ottawa, or Toronto appear in *Canadian Law Lists* 1951 to 1956. She identified two cases in which she appeared in relation to expropriations: NCC *v Sheahan* [1971] SCR 406; and *Publiese v* NCC (1977) 17 OR (2d) 129; appeal dismissed [1979] 2 SCR 104.

18 OSCLH, oral history, "Eileen Mitchell Thomas," 62–72. McNulty required that she pay him three-quarters of her salary at the court. She also recorded that "a lot of hunger and poverty drove kids to steal." Mitchell Thomas worked at McNulty McClenaghan from 1959 to 1964, as a part-time Juvenile Court judge from 1961 to 1964, and at the Department of Justice from 1964 until she retired: LSO Archives, Eileen Mitchell Thomas file. In her Bencher biography in 1979, when she was an unsuccessful candidate, Mitchell Thomas identified her positions at the Department of Justice as "senior advisory counsel, director of legal services, and National Capital Commission": LSO Archives, "Candidates for Bencher 1979."

barristers were allocated an old holding room in the basement, where they left their coats in a former shower stall. There was "one chair, one small table and one telephone." Not surprisingly, women lawyers in Ottawa welcomed better facilities at the new Elgin Street courthouse.[19]

In 1959, Mitchell Thomas became the first Ottawa woman lawyer to be appointed QC by Ontario, and in 1971 she was appointed a federal QC as well. In January 1960, a press report quoted her view that women can successfully combine a career of homemaking with that of business; as she explained, "I'd be lost without my law practice."[20] Mitchell Thomas died at the age of ninety-one in 2007, a victim of Alzheimer's disease during the last years of her life. As an Ottawa woman lawyer commented, she was a "brave, determined woman [and] utterly unique in terms of being a female practising in [all] those years."[21]

In September 1942, Elsie Mills, later Nesbitt, was called to the bar, but she did not practise law for long. In 1943, she was listed in parentheses as "Mrs. E.D. Nesbitt" at the firm of W.P. Gregory in Stratford, and Gregory was identified as being "on active service." There are no listings for Mills Nesbitt after 1943, and by 1950 Gregory had joined McPherson & Co. in Stratford.[22]

Elsie Teasdale, the daughter of a merchant, was called to the bar in October 1942. Her brother had been killed in the First World War, and Teasdale worked for the provincial government for some years while supporting her elderly mother. When her employment was terminated as part of Premier Hepburn's austerity program, she worked for the Fire Marshall's office, and she enrolled at the University of Toronto to obtain a BA while working as a secretary between classes. Teasdale was thirty-nine

19 Mitchell Thomas, "The History of Women Lawyers," 111–12.

20 OSCLH, oral history, "Eileen Mitchell Thomas," 80–84. See also Everett, "Woman's Place Not Only in the Home." For many years, there were no other women in private practice in Ottawa: Mitchell Thomas, "The History of Women Lawyers," 113–14. Mitchell Thomas's federal QC was not the first, as Marguerite Ritchie, a federal civil servant, had been appointed a federal QC in 1963: obituary, Marguerite Ritchie, *Globe and Mail* (27 May 2016).

21 Obituaries, *Ottawa Citizen* and *Globe and Mail* (6 April 2007). Her son-in-law later published a comment about Mitchell Thomas: B. Cameron, "Lives Lived," *Globe and Mail* (26 April 2000). Mitchell Thomas regularly submitted letters to the editor. For example, she requested the names of more women in the list of executive appointments in the *Globe and Mail* (26 January 1987); and she published a comment on "custom and convention" in Canada's constitutional arrangements in the same paper (17 October 1981) 7.

22 Huckle, "List of Women Barristers and Solicitors"; and *Canadian Law Lists*.

years old when she entered Osgoode Hall Law School in February 1939, and she attended lectures in the early mornings and late afternoons while working as a secretary at Lang Mitchener. After her call to the bar, she joined Macfarlane & Co. around 1946, and in 1964 she became a partner in a new firm, Martin, Trites, Teasdale & Corston, which included several lawyers from the Macfarlane firm. Her name was not included in the firm listing after 1964 because of her death that year.[23]

In 1943, three women were called to the bar. Iva Sarah Kaplan, later Goldstick, was born in Yaraslov (Russia) in 1904 and immigrated to Canada with her parents. She graduated from the University of Toronto in 1928 and entered Osgoode Hall in October that year. Kaplan completed her studies at Osgoode and graduated in 1931, but she was not called to the bar. Two years earlier, in May 1929, she had married David Goldstick, who had been called to the bar in 1924 after obtaining a BSC at the University of Toronto, and the couple had two sons. David Goldstick was actively involved in the labour movement and a member of the Civil Liberties Association in Toronto. He also ran for alderman in Ward 4 in 1941, and he was involved in defending at least one communist in court.[24]

In 1943, David Goldstick's office was located at 414 Bay Street, but he died in March 1944 at Mount Sinai Hospital at the age of about forty-eight following a short illness. His obituary described him as "well-known in Jewish labor circles" and that he was survived by his widow, Sarah Iva

23 Huckle, "List of Women Barristers and Solicitors"; LSO Archives, OBBRP, "Elsie Teasdale"; and *Canadian Law Lists*. Law Society records indicate that she articled with C.R. Magone and D.R. Michener, and it is possible that her position at the Lang Mitchener firm may have included both secretarial and articling work. In any event, the Law Society "let it through," that is, recognized that Teasdale had met the articling requirement: OSCLH, oral history, "Margaret Smith," 105–6.

24 LSO Archives, OBBRP, "Sarah Kaplan Goldstick" and "David Goldstick. The couple's first son, Thomas, was born in the early 1930s; Daniel in 1940: Ontario Jewish Archives, Betty Goldstick Lindgren fonds; and LSO Archives, "Diversifying the Bar," David Goldstick and Sarah Kaplan Goldstick. In 1941, David Goldstick served on the Committee on Ukrainian Property, set up by the Civil Liberties Association, to address the government's confiscation of property (including 108 halls owned by the Ukrainian Labour Farmer Temple Association), an anticommunist measure. Other lawyer members of this committee included Andrew Brewin, J.L. Cohen, and John Osler, along with (among others) Morley Callaghan, E.B. Joliffe, Agnes Macphail, Rev. J.R. Mutchmor, and Drummond Wren: see L. Sefton MacDowell, *Renegade Lawyer: The Life of J.L. Cohen* (Toronto: Osgoode Society for Canadian Legal History/University of Toronto Press, 2001), 189–92, 339 n159.

"Caplan"; two sons, Tommy and Daniel; and his sister, Dorothy Dworkin.[25] Sarah Kaplan Goldstick informed the Law Society in January 1943 that she intended to practise law, after having worked from time to time as a law clerk in her husband's law office. She also explained that she had been interrupted by home duties and raising a family but that she had resumed her duties as a clerk in July 1942. By 1946, she was practising law at her late spouse's office location on Bay Street, in partnership with Jacob Kaplan. By 1958, she was a sole practitioner at this location, focusing on criminal, family, and real estate law. She practised briefly at 57 Queen Street West in the 1960s and then retired. Kaplan Goldstick was fondly remembered by Margaret Smith (1944), who explained that they both regularly joined Jean O'Rourke (1931) for lunch at the Arcadian Court. Although Smith was Anglican, O'Rourke Catholic and Goldstick atheist, Smith declared that they "never had an argument."[26]

In 1954, Kaplan Goldstick was among a group of women lawyers polled by the *Globe and Mail* about the death penalty in Canada. While Lorna Ireland McWilliams, president of the WLAO, suggested that it provided a useful deterrent to criminal behaviour, both Celia Corcoran (1948) and Margaret Campbell (1937) were "thoroughly opposed" to the death penalty. Grace Gordon (1924) explained that many persons convicted of murder suffered from mental illness and often had no money to pay for skilled legal counsel. In addition, Kaplan Goldstick offered her view:

25 Unidentified press report (6 March 1944); and *Canadian Law Lists*. Dorothy Dworkin was the wife, and later widow, of Harry Dworkin, and she became one of the first Jewish nurses in Toronto. She was active in the creation of Mount Sinai Hospital and in socialist politics: M. Mandel, *The Jewish Hour: The Golden Age of a Toronto Yiddish Radio Show and Newspaper* (Toronto: Now and Then Books, 2016) 27–28. Dworkin's brother, David Goldstick, was a socialist, but others referred to him as a communist. Margaret Smith identified Kaplan Goldstick as an "active communist": OSCLH, oral history, "Margaret Smith." See also C. Moore, *The Law Society of Upper Canada and Ontario's Lawyers, 1797–1997* (Toronto: University of Toronto Press, 1997), 267–68; and V. Hauch, "When Communists Were Elected to Office," *Toronto Star* (26 February 2017) A15.

26 Law Society Archives, archivist Paul Leatherdale communication to M.J. Mossman (19 March 2018). The records do not identify a relationship, if any, between Sarah Kaplan Goldstick and Jacob Kaplan. As of 1953, J. Kaplan was listed at 4 Albert Street. Margaret Smith (1944) recalled regular lunch meetings with Kaplan Goldstick and O'Rourke (1931), during which they tried (perhaps unsuccessfully) to persuade Goldstick to provide information about the Jewish faith to her younger son when he was becoming interested in Judaism.

> [The death penalty] punishes the innocent more than the guilty ... Capital punishment brutalizes the community [with extensive publicity about trials that provide] a terrible spectacle ... Countries without capital punishment have no greater incidence of crime that those with it ... I believe in re-education of these persons, and I really think they could be a help to society even behind bars. I don't believe in vengeance—"an eye for an eye"—and long-term prisoners might prove of value for research by doctors and social workers ... Life imprisonment is a greater punishment than death, if we are trying to punish ... And all lawbreakers should be deprived of too much publicity.[27]

Formal legislation abolishing the death penalty in Canada was enacted in 1976, ten years before Kaplan Goldstick's death in 1986.[28]

Two other women were called to the bar in September 1943. Sarah (Sadie) MacLean was a teacher prior to entering law school at the age of thirty-five., and she joined the legal sorority. After her call to the bar, during the last years of the war, she was employed at White, Ruel, Bristol in Toronto when six male members of the firm were on active service. Her position at the firm was terminated in 1946, and she worked briefly with H.J. Donley in Kenora and then at Dignan & Co. in Toronto in 1950. She may have been a sole practitioner for a few years in the mid-1950s at 46 Avenue Road, but in 1957 she joined the Ontario Department of Highways and relocated to the department's office in North Bay in 1960, the first woman lawyer in that community. In 1965, she was posted back to the department's office in Downsview and later worked at its office in London.[29]

Sadie MacLean was active in the Local Council of Women in Toronto in the early 1950s, and as convenor for town planning and housing, she presented a report about the housing shortage in a meeting at the Royal York Hotel. When she was among a group of women lawyers attending the annual meeting of the Canadian Bar Association in 1966, she explained, "We women ... have learned to keep our mouths shut until we have

27 "Abolition of Death Penalty Favored," *Globe and Mail* (10 April 1954) 15. There is no indication as to how women lawyers were selected for this poll, but the involvement of "Mrs. Goldstick" suggests her connection to the WLAO.

28 LSO Archives, OBBRP, "Sarah Kaplan Goldstick"; and amendments to the *Criminal Code*, July 1976.

29 LSO Archives, OBBRP, "Sarah MacLean"; Huckle, "List of Women Barristers and Solicitors"; *Canadian Law Lists*; and OSCLH, oral history, "Margaret Smith," 106.

something succinct to say." As WLAO president in 1989, MacLean was present at the ceremonial opening of the Clara Brett Martin Building, the new location of the Ministry of the Attorney General for Ontario. She participated in unveiling the plaque and cutting the ribbon to open the new building, which was renamed in the 1990s. MacLean died in 1996.[30]

Vivien Weekes, later Scott, was also called to the bar in September 1943. Like Edra Sanders (1930), who joined her father and brothers in their law firm in St. Thomas, Weekes initially joined her father, G.N. Weekes, and her two brothers, John and Rolfe, in their practice at 396 Rideout Street in London. Weekes became the third woman lawyer to practise in London after Evelyn Harrison (1921) and Beth Underhill (1940), but she soon joined the Canadian Red Cross Corps and went overseas during the Second World War. On her return, she rejoined the family firm, having graduated with a second law degree from the University of St. Andrews, Scotland. Weekes joined the Middlesex Law Association in 1946. After her marriage, she practised at the same London firm as "Mrs. V.N. Scott" from 1947 to 1954, but she later ceased to practise law, and she may have relocated to Islington. She died in 2010.[31]

In 1944, eight women were called to the bar, representing sixteen per cent of the diminished wartime class of forty-eight students. Among the four women called to the bar in June was Margaret Smith, daughter of a civil engineer at Canadian National Railway. After her father's death from Bright's disease when she was five years old, Smith and her mother lived

30 LSO Archives, OBBRP, "Sarah MacLean." MacLean's report concluded that efforts by all three governments had proved insufficient and that "the price of new homes is also prohibitive, and demand far exceeds supply": "All Levels of Government Must Tackle Housing Problem, Local Council Feels," *Toronto Telegram* (31 January 1951). See also L. Gibbons, "Women Lawyers and Judges Stay Mum during Bar Meet," *Tribune* (3 September 1966). The article also quoted Judge Edra Ferguson (1930), and it noted the presence of Fern Levis (1944) from Toronto and women lawyers from other provinces. At the opening of the Clara Brett Martin Building in Toronto in 1989, all three women judges of the Supreme Court of Canada (B. Wilson, C. L'Heureux-Dubé, and B. McLachlin) were present, along with other dignitaries: (1990) 3:1 *Without Prejudice* (WLAO) 2. After the discovery in the 1990s of antisemitic comments in the letter written by Martin (1897), her name was quietly removed from the building, and renamed the McMurtry-Scott Building.

31 LSO Archives, OBBRP, "Vivien Weekes"; *Canadian Law Lists*; LSO Archives, Women's Law Association of Ontario (WLAO) fonds, unidentified news report; Carter, *The Middlesex Bench and Bar*, 121; and Huckle, "List of Women Barristers and Solicitors."

with her aunt in Parkdale in the 1920s and '30s. Smith's aunt was a trained pianist who also worked for a brokerage firm, and she fostered Smith's expectations about working women: "I never questioned [what women could do.] It was something I accepted." With financial assistance from Smith's grandmother and two uncles, who were lawyers in Halifax, Smith graduated from Havergal, a private girls' school in Toronto, in 1938, and she obtained a BA from Trinity College in 1941. During the summers, she did volunteer war work in Halifax and vividly recalled all the ships in the harbour and the submarine nets at its entrance. Smith also attended a garden party in Halifax, hosted by her uncle's law firm during the annual meeting of the Canadian Bar Association. A woman law student at Dalhousie promoted Smith's interest in the profession, and she recognized that "you could make law very much what you wanted to make it."[32]

For Smith, "being a law student was a different world [from Trinity], going out as a law student and into the offices where some of the civil servants weren't very civil and would yell at you." In her first year, the women students sat in the front row, but not thereafter. In fact, as she was often late, she sat near the door and became friends with Charlie Dubin, Jack Kimber, and George McPhedran. Like other women law students, Smith experienced challenges in obtaining articles, and although she had worked for Gordon Balfour in the summer of 1941, she had no articles when classes started in September. Smith had earlier interviewed with Margaret Fraser (1928) at the Smily, Shaver firm, but the firm's policy of hiring only students whose families were known to firm members created a barrier. Then, after discovering an appropriate family connection, she obtained articles at the firm at three dollars per week. Smith worked in real estate, helping Fraser with title searches and deals, and she recalled a rude deputy clerk when she was searching for a quit claim. In another transaction, she was required to prepare an affidavit for an Italian client declaring "I am not an

32 OSCLH, oral history, "Margaret Smith," 2, 35–47, 52–53, 62–66. Smith also noted that her two uncles were admiralty lawyers and had appeared before the Privy Council and the Supreme Court of Canada. In addition, she described how, at dinner with her uncles, "the salts and peppers were usually ships crashing and collisions." Smith also experienced the loss of a cousin who was killed in the war. Women law graduates from Dalhousie in these years include Margaret Drummie (Saint John, NB) and Annie Hirsh (Sydney, NS) in 1939 and Maureen Allen (Halifax, NS) in 1940, and it was perhaps one of these women law students who inspired Smith: C. Wiktor, ed., *Dalhousie Law School Register, 1883–1983* (Halifax: Dalhousie Law School, 1983), student lists, 1939–40.

enemy alien." After being called to the bar, Smith accepted an offer at the Smily firm for thirty dollars per week with a promise of corporate work, her preferred area of specialization. Because she had graduated before tax was part of the Osgoode Hall curriculum, she studied on her own to acquire expertise in the taxation of companies.[33]

Smith worked closely with George Shaver, KC, in the firm's corporate law practice. When he died in 1948 and some clients left the firm, Smith concluded that their departures occurred because of her young age (twenty-seven), not her gender. She took over the remaining files and expanded the practice, working with Shaver's son, Grant, after his call to the bar in 1949, and she also helped to reorganize the firm's billing system. Smith was appointed QC in 1959. In the 1970s, her work for engineering and construction companies resulted in the presentation of briefs before committees of the House of Commons.[34]

Smith served on the executive of the WLAO for several years and attended meetings regularly. She recalled that she usually invited a number of women to drop in for a drink before the annual dinner meeting, and that Jean O'Rourke (1931) always did the same thing before the Christmas dinner. Smith also joined Kappa Beta Pi, and she was invited to a reception for women lawyers when the American Bar Association met in Toronto in 1988 because she knew many of them through her sorority contacts. Although Smith acknowledged some rivalry between the WLAO and the sorority, she was grateful for the sorority's support for women in active legal practice. She acknowledged "some kind of unwritten law against Jews in the Toronto chapter," but she explained that she was among a group of women students who planned to confront this exclusion in support of their classmate Fay Feldman. Yet, even before the students arrived at the meeting, the sorority had removed this exclusionary practice; thereafter, "there was never any Jewish bias." In addition, Smith recalled debates at the sorority's international meetings about the exclusion of Black women lawyers. Although the constitution was changed before Myrtle Blackwood,

33 Smith applied to about twenty other firms without success, but when she was offered other positions the following year, the Smily firm increased her pay to eight dollars per week. This increase allowed her to ride the "Hill bus," used by professionals, and to buy lunches and books, but her family continued to pay for tuition, food, and clothing. Smith noted that she "came from polite society" and that it was necessary to wear the right length of gloves: OSCLH, oral history, "Margaret Smith," 73–77.

34 OSCLH, oral history, "Margaret Smith," 76–77.

later Smith, was admitted to the Ontario bar in 1960, Blackwood did not respond to the sorority's invitation to become a member.[35]

According to Smith, sorority members decided that the organization was no longer needed in the 1980s because women lawyers had succeeded in the profession. At the same time, she described a sorority dinner in 1965 in the United States at which women lawyers who worked for corporations or government complained about challenges—to which Smith responded: "If you can't use the executive washroom, go and use it and show them. I used to go and use [the changing rooms] in the County Courts. I never made a petition to anyone, I did what I wanted to do. And I didn't talk about it. I think there is far too much talk." In March 1988, Smith's firm merged with Lang Mitchener, a decision intended to provide more opportunities and support for the firm's younger lawyers since both Smith and

35 OSCLH, oral history, "Margaret Smith," 98–99, 112, 117–24; and Huckle, "List of Women Barristers and Solicitors." With the declining health of her mother and her aunt, she missed some WLAO meetings, and she was also increasingly busy with the Business and Professional Women's Club. Thus, her attendance waned at the WLAO, although she asserted that "it wasn't that I had anything against the Women's Law, you just have to sort out your priorities": OSCLH, oral history, "Margaret Smith," 98–99, 117–24; and Huckle, "List of Women Barristers and Solicitors." Feldman later practised briefly in a firm in Ottawa and from her residence: see *Canadian Law Lists*; and Mitchell Thomas, "The History of Women Lawyers," 110, 113. Smith also recalled having lunch regularly for many years at the Arcadian Court with Sarah Goldstick (1943) and Jean O'Rourke (1931). She described Goldstick as "a very nice, kind person." Smith did not name Blackwood, but she did recall sending five letters to her, inviting her to join the sorority. She recalled being perplexed that she never received a response, a comment that may suggest Smith's lack of awareness about the impact of race (and racism) in the legal profession. Smith also identified chapters of the sorority in other countries and that Gertrude Sinclair Haines (1927) had established the chapter during her visit to Paris in 1927. She noted that chapters of the sorority existed briefly in London, West Germany, and China. She suggested that the main purpose of the sorority was networking and that it was less political than the WLAO and did not engage in lobbying the government: "Women's Law took itself more seriously than the sorority."

Grant Shaver planned to retire. Smith retired at the age of sixty-eight in 1989.[36]

In June 1944, three women were called to the bar with Smith. Helen McGregor Binkley, later Muehlman, was a teacher and single mother. There is no record of her practising law, perhaps because she could earn more money teaching than in a law practice. Similarly, Sydney Waugh, also from Toronto, appeared to be employed briefly at Osler, Hoskin in 1947. Over the next four years, she was at other locations in Toronto, where she may have worked as a sole practitioner until 1951. Waugh, who was afflicted with multiple sclerosis, died at a young age.[37]

Fern Levis, who was also called to the bar in June 1944, grew up in Etobicoke and graduated from the University of Toronto in 1941. She completed her articles with W.C. Davis and J.C. McRuer and then spent much of her legal career at the Ministry of the Attorney General and in the Office of the Public Trustee. Levis was highly regarded for her legal work and was appointed QC in 1969. She was a long-time supporter of the WLAO and she was elected President for 1966–68. She also attended many WLAO events, and the organization proudly announced her election to the executive of the Ontario branch of the Canadian Bar Association. Although women had been appointed as unofficial members of the executive for some years, Levis was the first woman lawyer to be elected to this position. She died in 2003.[38]

In September 1944, four women were called to the bar. Helen Tripp, whose father was a real estate broker, graduated from the University of Toronto. She articled with Fred Hetherington in St. Catharines and was employed briefly after her call to the bar at Mackenzie & Saunderson in Toronto. Tripp later joined the Toronto firm of Sinclair, Goodenough, Higginbottom & McDonnell in 1950. Tragically, she died in December

36 OSCLH, oral history, "Margaret Smith,"123–29, 131–36. Since the sorority was accredited only to Osgoode Hall, women at the university law schools after 1957 could not join until they were in the Bar Admission course. Smith also described the dinner in 1983 in honour of Laura Legge (1948) becoming the first woman Bencher and Lorraine Gotlib (1959) becoming the first woman President of the Canadian Bar Association—Ontario Section (later OBA). At this dinner, Margaret Hyndman (1926) presented the sorority's charter to Laura Legge, and the sorority disbanded. The charter is now in the LSO Archives. Smith also described some American women members, including Judge Florence Allen, and a meeting at the home of Bea Miller (Beatrice VanWart, 1929) in Chicago, "at her two-floor apartment overlooking Lake Michigan."

37 *Canadian Law Lists*; and Huckle, "List of Women Barristers and Solicitors."

38 LSO Archives, OBBRP, "Fern Levis"; *Canadian Law Lists*; and LSO Archives, WLAO fonds.

1955 after "accidentally [taking] an overdose of sleeping pills and was found dead in the University Women's Club on St George Street." She had obtained the sleeping pills from a physician who had been treating her for three years. At the time of her death, she was on the staff of the Law Society of Upper Canada.[39]

Johanna (Janie) Jansen, who was also called to the bar in September 1944, joined the Crown Life Insurance Co. in 1946 and worked there for about three years. Thereafter, records identify her at different locations in Toronto, where she may have worked as a sole practitioner until the mid-1950s. She participated in the WLAO Hobby Show, displaying her fine leatherwork. Although sources suggest that she moved to Nanaimo, British Columbia, there is no record of her practising law there. From 1959 to the late 1960s, she may have again established a sole practice at 35 Hayden Street in Toronto.[40]

Frances (Fay) Feldman, later Rossman/English, was the daughter of a merchant and she graduated from the University of Toronto in 1941. She articled with Herman Moscoe in Schumacher and with Wilfred Jenner in Toronto. Her surname changed to Rossman when she married in 1944, and then to English when she married again in 1962. Feldman remembered being asked at a hiring interview why she wanted to work: "Isn't your husband making enough to keep you?" Although the records are sparse, Feldman may have moved to Timmins to practise law initially. Later, Mitchell Thomas identified Feldman as being at the firm of Snipper & Cohen in Ottawa in 1958, and she also recalled that Feldman practised law from her home, doing conveyancing "with great success." From 1966, she was listed as "Mrs. Frances English" at 1883 Barnhart Place. Although she may have practised law only part-time, Feldman English was just the third woman lawyer in private practice in Ottawa, after Mary McNulty (1918)

39 Huckle, "List of Women Barristers and Solicitors"; OSCLH, oral history, "Margaret Smith," 68–69; *Canadian Law Lists*; and LSO Archives, OBBRP, "Helen Florence Tripp." See also LSO Archives, obituary, identifying Tripp's parents in St. Catharines; and unidentified news report, "Woman, 34, Killed by Sleeping Pills." The latter report included a coroner's explanation about how overdoses can occur: sleeping pills are taken and then a person wakes up and fails to remember taking them and takes another pill—which can be fatal.

40 Huckle, "List of Women Barristers and Solicitors," identified Jansen as a practitioner in Richmond Hill. See also *Canadian Law Lists*; and *Toronto Telegram* (7 February 1953).

and Mitchell Thomas (1942). She remained active in the local bar association after retiring from practice.[41]

Olga Chumak, later Chepesiuk, the first Ukrainian Canadian woman lawyer in Ontario, was also called to the bar in September 1944.[42] Her parents immigrated to Toronto from Galicia before the First World War, and she grew up in the Kensington Market area. Her father became head chef at the Albany Club around 1917–19, and he and his wife eventually owned two restaurants, the Parkway Tea Room on Bay Street and the Willow Tea Room on Queen Street.[43] Chumak, who graduated from the University of Toronto in 1941, joined a number of Ukrainian Canadian lawyers, including John Yaremko, who was also called to the bar in 1944. Chumak articled with

41 OSCLH, oral history, "Margaret Smith," 70–71; Mitchell Thomas, "The History of Women Lawyers," 110; and LSO Archives, OBBRP, "Frances Feldman Rossman English." There are no records for Feldman/Rossman/English in the *Canadian Law Lists*, 1944–70. Mitchell Thomas suggested that the interviewer's comment to Feldman was not unusual and that "we lawyers in the 1940's and '50's learned to accept the existence of such views." Mitchell Thomas identified the early Ontario women lawyers in Ottawa: Feldman and Mitchell Thomas in private practice; Mary McNultry Fix (1918), who practised only briefly; Helen Currie (1921), who was employed in the Department of Revenue; and Marion Niven, later Foran (1933), who did not practise law.

42 The first Ukrainian Canadian woman lawyer in Canada was probably Mary Wawryko in Manitoba, who was called to the bar in 1936. Wawryko was born in Saskatchewan, the daughter of Ukrainian immigrant farmers and supported herself through high school and university. She started to practise law from her home, but she retired after she married and had children. After she was widowed, when the children were still small, she returned to work. Wawryko was appointed a QC in 1965 and then a judge of the Winnipeg Juvenile and Family Court in 1968. She died in 1977 at the age of sixty-five: M. Kinnear, *In Subordination: Professional Women, 1870–1970* (Montreal/Kingston: McGill-Queen's University Press, 1995) 82, 207.

43 A. Kovalev, "Early Ukrainian-Canadian Lawyers in Toronto, 1923–1960" (2014) [unpublished, archived at Osgoode Hall Law School]. Kovalev examined the experiences of early Ukrainians called to the Ontario bar: Theodore Humeniuk (1923), Walter Tuchtie (1932), John Yatchew (1933), William Stasiv (1939), John Yaremko (1944), and Olga Chumak (1944). The earliest members of the immigrant Ukrainian community in Toronto arrived in 1903, and by 1914 there were four thousand Ukrainian immigrants concentrated around St. John's Ward and the Junction. The community doubled in size in the next ten years: Kovalev, "Early Ukrainian-Canadian Lawyers," 9, citing L.Y. Luciuk and I.L. Wynnyckyj, *Ukrainians in Ontario* (Toronto: Multicultural History Society of Ontario, 1988) 48, 53; and O.T. Martynowych, *Ukrainians in Canada: The Formative Period, 1891–1924* (Edmonton: Canadian Institute of Ukrainian Studies Press, 1991) 137. See also LSO, "Diversifying the Bar": Theodore Humeniuk, QC, the first Ukrainian lawyer to practise in Toronto and a leader in the Ukrainian community.

John Grudeff, who had immigrated to Toronto from Bulgaria and put himself through law school. After her call to the bar, Chumak joined Grudeff's firm as a partner, working in the Richmond Street office for a decade.[44] In 1954, after her marriage to Dr. Chepesiuk and the birth of their first child, she opened a solo practice with her brother, a notary public, at her home in Toronto: "For almost 20 years she worked out of the family home at 92 Roncesvalles Avenue. The main floor of the house was divided into 2 working areas: Olga's law practice at the back of the building and her husband's medical office at the front. The upstairs featured residential quarters big enough for the couple and their 3 children."[45]

Chumak Chepesiuk had a general practice, focused on wills and estates and real estate, and many of her clients were from the Ukrainian and other immigrant communities. In addition, she worked pro bono for the Ukrainian Museum of Canada. Although she was "primarily confined to the intra communal provision of relatively unsophisticated services, her passion and determination helped to break the barriers, both social and economic, [to enter] the previously unattainable ranks" of the legal profession. By bringing the law into the community, such legal services were essential for the functioning of the growing diaspora, and her strong community connections may have helped her to overcome gender barriers.[46]

Only two women were called to the bar in 1945. In June 1945, Jean Oldreive, later Carrie, was admitted to the bar, the first woman in the law school's history to win the gold medal. At the ceremony, she was presented to Chief Justice Robertson by Peter White, KC. Oldreive graduated from St. Thomas Collegiate and Alma College, and then completed a degree at the

44 Yaremko was the child of Ukrainian immigrants in Welland, Ontario, who graduated from university and from Osgoode Hall, where he was the gold medallist in 1944. In 1951, he was elected to the provincial legislature and served as a cabinet minister in the governments of Leslie Frost, John Robarts, and Bill Davis. Yaremko's niece, Hélène Yaremko Jarvis was President of the WLAO from 1989 to 1991: LSO Archives, "Diversifying the Bar," John Yaremko; *Toronto Star* (9 August 2010): and Bushby, "The Early Years." Grudeff was called to the bar in 1926 and appointed KC in 1945. He became a judge of the Juvenile and Family Court in Toronto in 1949: LSO Archives, "Diversifying the Bar," John Grudeff.

45 Kovalev, "Early Ukrainian-Canadian Lawyers," 17–18. Kovalev reported that the house was still in the family in 2014, when he interviewed Dr. William Chepesiuk, one of Chumak Chepesiuk's sons. Both sons became doctors, and they used the property for their offices. See also LSO Archives, "Diversifying the Bar," Olga Chumak and John Grudeff.

46 Kovalev, "Early Ukrainian-Canadian Lawyers," 18; and *Canadian Law Lists*.

University of Toronto. She articled at McCarthy & McCarthy with W.W. Davidson and W.R. West, and one of her references was Richard Sanders, a practitioner in St. Thomas and a brother of Edra Sanders (1930). At Osgoode Hall, Oldreive placed second in the examinations in the first two years, after J.S. Midanik. However, in third-year, she received the gold medal and the Chancellor Van Koughnett scholarship, while Midanik was awarded the silver medal and two prizes. Following her call to the bar, Oldreive was employed at the McCarthy firm until she married Alan Carrie in 1950, and she then worked as a sole practitioner until 1953. Although she ceased legal practice, Oldreive maintained her membership in the Law Society, eventually receiving a life membership. She died in 2022.[47]

In September 1945, Dorothy Jean Howard, later Reilly, was called to the bar. Howard and Oldreive were the only two women in their graduating class of twenty-six students, and Howard placed fourth in her final year. She was an only child, born in Gananoque, where her father was a telegrapher and station manager for the Canadian Pacific Railway. His seniority helped them manage financially during the Depression years, but family finances were only sufficient for Howard to pursue a pass course at the University of Toronto. Howard also worked as a waitress in Gananoque during high school, and she continued to work part-time during her studies at the university and at Osgoode Hall. With support from the railway's solicitor, she articled at Coatsworth & Richardson, doing a good deal of real estate and some corporate work, but she recalled that her articling salary was small.[48]

Howard attended Osgoode in the first year the tax course, taught by John Willis, was added to the curriculum.

> The way he taught it was more in a theory situation. How tax law evolved, why, what they were after. What they were trying to do. When he came in and

47 *Globe and Mail* (22 June 1945); Huckle, "List of Women Barristers and Solicitors;" *Canadian Law Lists*; and LSO Archives, Jean Carol Oldreive Carrie fonds. Although the number of students at Osgoode Hall in 1945 was small, the competition between Midanik and Oldreive suggests that Oldreive's gold medal was significant. Laura Legge described Oldreive Carrie as "brilliant," but also an "example of a woman who married and then ceased to practise law": Laura Legge, interview with M.J. Mossman (28 February 2008). See also obituary, *Globe and Mail* (3 September 2022).

48 OSCLH, oral history, "Dorothy Jean Howard Reilly," 20–32. In contrast, Reilly reported that Oldreive did only real estate work during her articles at the McCarthy firm.

> started his lecture, he said, "if you want to know how to, you buy Laneels & Smith's book, you are going to get none of that in this course." He was a real pet of a lecturer. He was a bit witty.

Howard recalled no problems with male students "other than trying to make us blush," and she and Oldreive sat in the first row. She attracted Dr. Wright's wrath by knitting in class; as he declared, "If I ever catch you knitting in here again, you are not going to pass Wills." Howard worked in the Great Library at night, probably becoming the first female night staff member, and she fondly remembered an old Jewish gentleman, a semi-retired lawyer, who studied every night and walked her to Bay Street to ensure her safety.[49]

After her call to the bar, Howard continued to practise at the Coatsworth firm for a few years. In 1949, Howard married T. Edgar Reilly, who had been called to the bar in 1942 and then served in the War. He started to practise law in 1946 in an office at 1596 Danforth Avenue, focusing on real estate and estates work ("buying and dying"), and he later employed a Czech lawyer, Stan Lander, as a paralegal. Her spouse also ran unsuccessfully for the Liberals in two federal elections. The couple had six children, including two who became lawyers. Howard Reilly did not practise law again until 1965, after her husband's death. She enrolled in refresher courses, and was later joined by her two lawyer children, who took on criminal and litigation work in the firm, "the office of T.E. Reilly" at 701 Coxwell Avenue. She had no regrets about being part of a small firm because "you could practise law the way you feel it should be practised. To the best of your abilities ... The big drawback is you have nobody to talk to. Talk things over with when you are trying to mull a problem." Jean Howard Reilly continued to practise law until her late eighties, and she maintained her licence until her death in May 2017.[50]

In March 1946, Ethel Fagan joined the Ontario bar by transfer. Born in 1886, Fagan worked as a stenographer and bookkeeper at the firm of Biggar

49 OSCLH, oral history, "Dorothy Jean Howard Reilly," 34, 36, 38–40; and obituary, *Toronto Star* (3 May 2017). Reilly recalled that the area around Osgoode Hall was rather unsafe at night.

50 OSCLH, oral history, "Dorothy Jean Howard Reilly," 43–63. Reilly was probably the first Ontario woman lawyer to have two children join the legal profession: Reilly's son, Tim, graduated from Osgoode Hall Law School, and her daughter, Mary Patricia, graduated in law at the University of Windsor. See also obituary, *Toronto Star* (3 May 2017).

& Burton in Toronto in 1914. In 1919, she began to serve articles with Burton, but after two years she learned that her articles had not been formally registered with the Law Society and that she would have to complete senior matriculation, repeat these two years, and attend Osgoode Hall lectures and article for three additional years. Faced with these hurdles in Ontario, Fagan relocated to Edmonton, where she was admitted to the LLB program at the University of Alberta in 1922 and graduated in 1925. With other students, Fagan received twenty-one hours of weekly lectures and was assigned readings in law reports and texts, as well as courses in history, legal psychology, and economics. After completing articling requirements during the summers at the Office of the City Solicitor in Edmonton and in the Department of the Attorney General, Fagan was called to the bar in Alberta in 1927.[51]

It is possible that Oliver Mowat Biggar assisted Fagan. He had been a member of the Biggar & Burton firm in Toronto and was a grandson of Sir Oliver Mowat, who had assisted Clara Brett Martin in her admission to the bar in Ontario in the 1890s. Biggar relocated to Edmonton in 1903, and later became a Bencher of the Law Society of Alberta. Like his grandfather, he supported aspiring women lawyers.[52] In a letter to the Law Society of Upper Canada in January 1946, Fagan explained that she had discovered that she could be admitted to the University of Alberta's law program and complete admission requirements more quickly than in Ontario.[53]

No records have survived concerning Fagan's practice in Alberta and elsewhere after 1927, but she was possibly employed in government. After

51 LSO Archives, letter to William Smith, Secretary of the Law Society of Upper Canada, from Ethel Fagan (12 January 1946), with details of her background. Although parts of her letter are redacted, it confirms her LLB degree in 1925 and her call to the bar of Alberta in 1927. See also Huckle, "List of Women Barristers and Solicitors." Harvey incorrectly identified Fagan as the first woman to earn the LLB degree in Alberta in 1921: C. Harvey, "Women in Law in Canada" (1970–71) 4 *Manitoba Law Journal* 9 at 17. Fagan's LLB degree in 1925 is not included in Petersson's study of women law graduates up to 1924: S. Petersson, "Ruby Clements and Early Women of the Alberta Bar" (1997) 9 *Canadian Journal of Women and the Law* 365 at 376.

52 Peterssen, "Ruby Clements," 379. For Ruby Clements, see Chapter One.

53 LSO Archives, letter from Fagan to William Smith (January 1946), a few months prior to her admission to the Ontario bar in March 1946, by transfer from Alberta; and confirmation from archivist Paul Leatherdale, LSO Archives. Huckle's "List of Women Barristers and Solicitors" may list admission to the Ontario bar incorrectly as March 1945, and by transfer from Saskatchewan.

being admitted to the Ontario bar in 1946, she became a sole practitioner, at 42 James Street North from 1955 until the early 1960s, and at RR 3 Mount Albion Road in the mid-1960s. Fagan was also involved in politics. An election poster for "Ethel B. Fagan, UEL, LLB as Alderman Ward One" in Hamilton in 1950 stated that Fagan believed "in genuine democracy with supreme authority in the voters." It also reported her efforts to secure railway service in the eastern and southeastern sections of the ward and a promise to work for an East End mountain approach, playgrounds, boy scout and girl guide camps, and improved railway crossings. Fagan was not elected on this occasion, and she was also an unsuccessful candidate for the Social Credit Party in Hamilton East in the federal elections of 1953 and 1957. Fagan died in 1967.[54]

In 1946, Osgoode Hall was overcrowded with returning veterans who comprised nearly three-quarters of students in all three years. Five women were among those called to the bar that year, all of whom practised law for lengthy periods. Margaret Grimshaw, the daughter of a physician, graduated from the University of Toronto in 1943. After being called to the bar in June 1946, she worked at Kingsmill & Co. at 86 Richmond Street West for two years, although she was never listed on the firm's card in *Canadian Law Lists*. In 1948, she accepted a position doing real estate work at Blake, Anglin, Osler & Cassels, which became Blake, Cassels & Graydon in 1953. As Allan Graydon recalled, lawyers at Blakes worked Saturday mornings in the 1920s and '30s, but many worked all day on Saturdays during the war, until the five-day week gradually returned in the late 1940s. Grimshaw was the second woman lawyer at Blakes, following Belva Gordon Gibson (1930), who had been hired in 1942. Grimshaw's work focused on real estate, and like Gordon Gibson, Grimshaw became a partner. She was appointed QC in 1959 and she may have been the oldest partner when she retired. Grimshaw died in 1990.[55]

54 Bushby, "The Early Years," citing LSO Archives, WLAO fonds, SB, vol. 4.

55 A. Graydon, *Some Reminiscences of Blakes* (Paget, Bermuda: Beauregard, 1970) 45, 55; LSO Archives, OBBRP, "Margaret Grimshaw"; *Canadian Law Lists*; and *Toronto Star* (20 June 1946): photo of Grimshaw and Kathleen Morrison, along with two male graduates, William Adams and Robert Sedgewick. See also OSCLII, oral history, "Dorothy Jean Howard Reilly," 41. According to Howard Reilly, Gibson tried to offer her a position at Blakes, and when Howard Reilly declined, Grimshaw joined the firm. For Gordon Gibson, see Chapter Three.

Kathleen Morrison, later Callahan, was born in Edmonton and graduated from Queen's University in 1937 at the age of twenty-three. Although she was admitted to Osgoode Hall in 1937, she was not called to the bar until June 1946, perhaps after participation in the war effort. A press photo of 1946 Osgoode graduates includes Morrison and Grimshaw as well as two male graduates. Morrison moved to Fort Frances, where she practised in the firm of T.H. Callahan, who had been called to the bar in 1945. Morrison became the first woman to practise law in Fort Frances. At some point, she married Callahan, and for a few years she paid bar fees only, suggesting a more limited law practice. After Callahan's death in 1952, she was listed as "Kathleen Morrison" in practice on Portage Avenue in Fort Frances, and she may later have practised at 348 Scott Street and in Thunder Bay. Morrison was appointed QC in 1961. In the 1970s, she was employed by the Department of Highways in Downsview and then by the Ministry of Transportation and Communication in Toronto.[56]

Two women were called to the bar in September 1946. Mary Margaret Bennett worked at the firm of Bennett & Bennett in the Sun Life Building in Hamilton until the late 1960s in a partnership with R.C. Bennett, who had been called to the bar in 1920. By 1970, the firm's address was 42 James Street South. She continued to be listed in practice as "Miss M.M. Bennett" and she probably had a general practice. Bennett's classmate Gretta Wong, later Grant, described her as a "very quiet, pleasant person."[57]

Helen Carefoot, the daughter of a country doctor in Markdale, was called to the bar in September 1946 with Bennett. Her parents had met at the St. Catharines General Hospital during the First World War, where her mother was a nurse, and the couple had several children. Carefoot

56 LSO Archives, OBBRP, "Kathleen Morrison"; and Huckle, "List of Women Barristers and Solicitors," which reported that Morrison practised law in Thunder Bay. See also *Canadian Law Lists*; and *Toronto Star* (20 June 1946). Gretta Wong Grant (1946) did not mention Morrison as one of her classmates, so it is possible that Morrison graduated from Osgoode Hall in 1945 but delayed her call to the bar: Backhouse, "Gretta Wong Grant," 30. Mitchell Thomas identified Morrison as a classmate in first-year in 1937 and, perhaps incorrectly, as being from Sault Ste. Marie: OSCLH, oral history, "Eileen Mitchell Thomas," 39–40.

57 LSO Archives, OBBRP, "Mary Margaret Bennett"; *Canadian Law Lists*; Huckle, "List of Women Barristers and Solicitors"; and Backhouse, "Gretta Wong Grant," 30. Wong Grant described other women classmates, including Ann Brown, who had dropped out in first-year, and Margaret Dufresne (1948), a matriculant who had to article for two additional years.

remembered that her parents treated girls and boys the same. Along with her two sisters, she played on a girls' hockey team in St. Catharines and Niagara Falls and later at Victoria College. Her father was a "buddy" of Agnes Macphail, and while still a student, Carefoot, was an unsuccessful candidate for the CCF in 1943. These connections probably contributed to her articling position with Brewin, Cameron and McRuer.[58]

Carefoot did not experience difficulties as a woman law student. She was a member of the mooting team and president of the debating society in her third year, the year when "all the men came flooding back from the War." She noted that some lecturers were uncomfortable discussing rape cases in the presence of women students, and she was outraged and spoke out against a case in which a woman was dying in childbirth, and the doctor asked the woman's husband to decide whether to save the mother or the child. She also expressed annoyance when Dean Wright declared in a speech that "women had no place in the practice of law," but she tried not to waste energy being angry: men, she stated, just liked their "old boys club," but few were "red hot anti-feminists." While she disagreed with the Chief Justice's comment that women were unsuited for court work because they were unable to project their voices, she understood that women lawyers were disadvantaged because they "weren't able to hobnob in the corridors, and the corridor gossip was not available to them ... I always found that a tremendous handicap."[59]

According to Carefoot, the WLAO was not active among women students during her three years at Osgoode Hall, and although she was invited to join the sorority, she declined because her friend Margaret Dufresne (1948) did not receive an invitation. Carefoot decided to practise law in Windsor after a major Toronto snowstorm created havoc during her final examinations. She, like other women lawyers, coped with inadequate women's robing rooms in the courts. At first, she changed in a washroom, and although she later obtained a locker in the barristers' lounge, everyone had to leave while she changed into her robes. When she travelled to the courthouse in Barrie, a male lawyer kindly gave her the key to his locker and

58 OSCLH, oral history, "Helen Carefoot," 1–8. Carefoot confirmed that Macphail was "very well thought of among farmers" and represented South-East Grey County in Parliament as a member of the United Farmers of Ontario and later the CCF (1921–40). She was involved in enacting the *Female Employees Fair Remuneration Act* in 1951, although critical of its deficiencies. Macphail died in 1954. See also Chapter Three.

59 OSCLH, oral history, "Helen Carefoot," 14–15.

departed: "I just nicely got my dress hanging in the locker, when the door burst open and a whole bunch of the lawyers came in, laughing at the top of their voices ... playing a joke on me ... [But] it didn't bother me, because I had a really nice slip."[60]

Carefoot joined a small firm in Windsor where legal work was assigned, and although she hoped to do criminal law, her firm believed that such work was not ladylike. Nonetheless, she appeared in some criminal cases, including serious ones such as robbery with violence, but her assignments were more often focused on mortgages and contracts. Although Lovedy Campeau Scott (1919), Helen McTague (1924), and Emily Lynch (1925) were all in practice in Windsor, Carefoot reported that she didn't find a women lawyers' network in the city. At the same time, she viewed women as "naturals for the practice of law," because "women possess ... a broad concern for human welfare, which qualifies them well for the challenge of law."[61]

In November, Gretta Wong, later Grant, became the fifth woman to be called to the bar in 1946, and she was probably the first Chinese Canadian woman lawyer in Canada. Her father, and later her mother, had each emigrated from China to London, Ontario, where they had eight children and were the only Chinese family. Her father established an elegant restaurant in London, where the children helped out during the Depression. Money was scarce, but all the children—both boys and girls—were encouraged to attend university with fees paid in installments. Gretta Wong, the second youngest child, attended the University of Western Ontario for a BA in political science and economics, and she entered Osgoode Hall in 1943. Finding articles was a challenge: "If you weren't WASP, Toronto was a pretty closed shop." Fortuitously, her brothers, who were chefs employed at the summer home of Leighton McCarthy, explained their sister's interest in law, and McCarthy didn't hesitate: "She has a place in my firm." At that time, Marion Darte (1937) and June Ryan (1941) were associate lawyers at McCarthy's, and Jean Oldreive (1945) was an articling student at

60 OSCLH, oral history, "Helen Carefoot," 16–17. According to her classmate Gretta Wong Grant, Carefoot was "the feminist" in their class, and the woman colleagues always supported her: OSCLH, oral history, "Gretta Wong Grant," 44.

61 OSCLH, oral history, "Helen Carefoot," 23–30. Carefoot was involved with the Business and Professional Women's Club, and she had some connections to Margaret Hyndman (1926) through her work and the club. See also S. VanKuren, "Law a Natural for the Fair Sex?," *Windsor Star* (4 December 1971). For Lovedy Campeau Scott (1919), Helen McTague (1924), and Emily Lynch (1925), see Chapter Three.

the firm. When all four women became involved in the WLAO, they were referred to as "McCarthy's Harem."[62]

Wong's articles focused on real estate and legal memos, and only male articling students attended at court. At some point, Wong was the only student available when Senator Hayden departed for the court and requested a student to deliver his bags there. In spite of her concerns that he would not wish to see a woman at the court, she "took the bag and started running ... and when we got to the robing room ... he took one look at me and grabbed the bag." In spite of some male chauvinism at the firm, Wong described it as a "very pleasant place to work." She also remembered friendly male students at Osgoode Hall, although they wanted women students to be feminine: they "tolerated us ... I think that some of them felt that we would never become Judges and the great advocates." Although her Chinese heritage did not create controversy, she witnessed Jewish students experiencing discrimination, and she recalled her colleagues' astonishment at McCarthy's when she accepted a date with a Jewish student. Wong participated in the Osgoode Women Law Students' (OWLS) protest in support of "matters of principle."[63]

Wong's admission to the bar ceremony was brief, with two other lawyers being admitted by transfer. Although Kew Dock Yip had received extensive press coverage as the first Asian Canadian lawyer after his admission to the Ontario bar a year earlier, in 1945, no one recognized Wong as the first

62 Backhouse, "Gretta Wong Grant," 3. According to Backhouse, it is difficult to prove this claim (as the first Chinese woman lawyer in Canada) authoritatively. OSCLH, oral history, "Gretta Grant," 1–29, 39–40; and Backhouse "Gretta Wong Grant," 3–13, 19–24, 26–29. Wong Grant also noted that she did not receive a warm welcome from the Chinese community in Toronto because she didn't speak Chinese well. Wong felt the support of Leighton McCarthy prevented her from encountering anti-Chinese discrimination at the McCarthy firm. While Wong articled at the firm, McCarthy was Canadian Ambassador to the United States, but he also conducted a monthly interview with Wong. Although she was formally articled to R. West, she had little interaction with him: OSCLH, oral history, "Gretta Grant," 39–40.

63 Backhouse, "Gretta Wong Grant," 28–31, 33; and OSCLH, oral history, "Gretta Grant," 39–44. Wong recalled that Leighton McCarthy and Senator Hayden had offices with their own receptionist, separate from the rest of the firm.

Chinese Canadian woman lawyer: "Not even Gretta."[64] McCarthy's did not offer her a position, and she declined Jean Oldreive's invitation to practise together because she wanted to study psychology related to juvenile delinquency. To finance her studies, Wong Grant worked for legal publishers for a year and then entered graduate studies in clinical psychology at the University of Toronto. Even before completing the degree, she was appointed a staff psychologist at the Andrew Mercer Reformatory for Women and later worked at the Cobourg Training School for Girls. In both locations, she recalled truly appalling conditions, including corporal punishment, and she faced major challenges in her efforts to provide rehabilitative counselling.[65]

A few years later, Wong married Alan Grant, an Osgoode graduate of 1947, and they moved to London, where he established a practice with a former university classmate. After the arrival of the first of four children, Wong Grant remained at home for some years, but she also paid Law Society fees, read the *Ontario Reports*, and occasionally assisted at her husband's office. In the late 1950s, she was appointed assistant city solicitor in London, one of the small number of women lawyers in the city, including Evelyn Harrison (1921), Beth Rowlin Underhill (1940), and Vivien Weekes Scott (1943) who had rejoined the Weekes family firm in 1947. After enactment of the *Legal Aid Act* in 1966, Gretta Grant was appointed the part-time Area Director of the London office, the beginning of her long association with legal aid administration in London, Stratford, and Woodstock. After Wong Grant's

64 Kew Dock Yip was one of twenty-three children of a Vancouver merchant born in China. Yip attended Columbia University, the University of Michigan, and the University of British Columbia, but because "Orientals" were excluded from admission to the bar in British Columbia, he moved to Ontario and entered Osgoode Hall in 1942 at the age of thirty-six. He spoke several Chinese languages and practised law in Toronto for forty-seven years. He was awarded the Law Society Medal in 1998 and died in 2001: LSO Archives, "Diversifying the Bar," Kew Dock Yip. See also Backhouse, "Gretta Wong Grant," 35–36; and B. Ryder, "Racism and the Constitution: The Constitutional Fate of British Columbia Anti-Asian Immigration Legislation, 1884–1909" (1991) 29 *Osgoode Hall Law Journal* 619.

65 Backhouse, "Gretta Wong Grant," 37–39. See also A. Glasbeek, *Feminized Justice: The Toronto Women's Court, 1913–34* (Vancouver: UBC Press, 2009).

husband died in 1967, she sold the practice in 1969 and worked full-time for the Ontario Legal Aid Plan until her retirement in 1988.[66]

Wong Grant became the first female trustee of the Middlesex Law Association and, in 1981, the first woman President of the association. Although there was a party (a "drunken brawl") at the male-only London Club in her first term as a trustee of the association, this arrangement was discontinued. Wong Grant recalled having a hard time being accepted at county and district law Presidents' meetings, where she often felt "elbowed out" by others: "I guess I could have stood up and done a little more screaming and yelling to be heard, but it became very difficult because the men always stepped forward, and they would be recognized probably before me."[67] Wong Grant was appointed QC in 1969, and she was awarded the Law Society Medal in 2000. As she later recalled, she had experienced "a really interesting life."[68]

In September 1947, three women were called to the bar. Esther Macdonald, later Marshall, grew up in Brantford, and then graduated from the University of Toronto in 1944. Her father, W.R. Macdonald, KC, was a Brantford lawyer, and she articled with his firm. When she was called to the bar, the press announced that "Girl Called to the Bar will Work with Dad." She became part of the firm of Macdonald, Macdonald, Brown & Binkley in Brantford, and she also worked in Ancaster and Hamilton. In 1948,

66 OSCLH, oral history, "Gretta Grant," 79–85, 87–104, 110–20; and Backhouse, "Gretta Wong Grant," 39–44. Wong Grant described her administrative innovations, including relocating the office for financial-eligibility assessments to the legal aid office, and her efforts to provide representation for children in child welfare proceedings, to speed up appeals, and to provide better legal services for Indigenous accused. She also promoted legal aid contacts within the community.

67 OSCLH, oral history, "Gretta Wong Grant," 107–9. Despite these difficulties, she was a highly respected Legal Aid Area Director and was often consulted by the plan's administrators in Toronto. In 1989, Wong Grant was appointed to the City of London's Race Relations Advisory Committee. See also K. Walter, "Gretta's Goal: A Greater London" *London Free Press* (28 March 1999); and "In Quest of Ontario's Legal Profession" *Ontario Lawyers Gazette* (Fall/Winter 2006) 34–35.

68 Backhouse, "Gretta Wong Grant," 45. Apparently, Wong Grant was nominated for the QC appointment by a woman's group, with the help of Betty (Beth) Underhill (1940). See also OSCLH, oral history, "Gretta Grant," 120; and LSO Archives, "Diversifying the Bar," Gretta Grant. In a group photo of postwar members of the Middlesex Law Association taken after the war, Wong Grant is seated front row centre. In the companion photo of "the Seniors" in 1969, Evelyn Harrison (1921) is seated front row centre: Carter, *The Middlesex Bench and Bar*, 114–ff.

Macdonald married J.S. Marshall, who had been called to the bar in 1948 and practised at the firm of Mewburn & Marshall in Hamilton. Macdonald Marshall relinquished legal practice around 1950, but she may have later engaged in some legal work in her spouse's firm.[69]

Harriet Clark, a graduate of the University of Toronto, was also called to the bar in September 1947, where she won the Wallace Nesbitt Essay Competition. She preserved memories of her experiences at Osgoode Hall, including timetables for classes, the names of instructors, and her own lecture notes. Beginning in 1945, for example, classes were scheduled at nine and ten o'clock in the morning and then a third hour of classes on Wednesdays at eleven. Wright taught Torts (first-year) and Wills (third-year), and Falconbridge taught Agency (second-year) and Conflict of Laws (third-year). In second-year, Clark had lectures on Mortgages at nine three mornings a week and Companies for two mornings. At ten, she had lectures in Agency one morning and on Equity and Property II for two mornings. In the additional hour on Wednesday mornings, at eleven, there was another lecture on Agency. Clark's notes include model examination questions and answers, as well as files she had created on topics such as the Statute of Frauds and specific performance.[70]

Clark's notes confirm that Osgoode Hall lectures focused on contemporary legal principles, and that there were few broader discussions of legal theory or social context. Clark was also present at the meeting of the Ontario section of the Canadian Bar Association in Niagara Falls in 1949, at which some lawyers expressed criticism of the report of the Special Committee on Legal Education and its recommendations, particularly the emphasis on office work rather than full-time legal studies. Clark contributed to the discussion, explaining that most of her office time during articles was "wasted": "When I went to Osgoode, I paid my own fees. I could not do it with the money I received from working in the law office.

69 Huckle, "List of Women Barristers and Solicitors"; LSO Archives, OBBRP, "Esther Macdonald Marshall"; and *Canadian Law Lists*. Huckle reported that Macdonald was not practising law, but at the time of her class reunion in 1967, twenty years after the call to the bar, she was identified as practising in Hamilton, perhaps in her husband's firm, Mewburn, Marshall & Reesor: LSO Archives, Harriet Clark fonds.

70 *Globe and Mail* (17 September 1947); LSO Archives, Harriet Clark fonds; and obituary, *Globe and Mail* (11 May 1992). The Clark fonds include her notes for Administrative Law, Companies, Conflict of Laws, Constitutional Law, Contracts, Criminal Law, Equity, and Evidence.

I got permission and took a part-time job, which left me only two or three hours a day in the law office. Nearly all that time was wasted, however, and I found myself just sitting around."[71]

Clark was the daughter of Herbert Clark, KC. Along with her parents, she attended the Commonwealth and Empire Law Conference in London, England, in 1955, and the conference in Ottawa in 1960, which included papers on federalism, criminal law, human rights, administrative tribunals, and matrimonial property.[72] She participated in the WLAO as well, and she contributed her needlework at its Hobby Show in February 1952. Clark also attended the CBA–Ontario Section meeting in Windsor in 1953, where she was photographed with Helen McTague, QC (1924), and Lovedy Campeau, QC (1919).[73]

After her call to the bar, Clark worked in association with Mulock, Milliken & Co, but she relocated to the Dominion Bank Building in the early 1950s and then to 68 Yonge Street in 1959. Her sole practice focused on wills and minor estates, and she also acted as a "buffer between old ladies and the Taxation Data Centre." Clark was a member of the Ontario Council of Women and became an honorary life member, and she was involved in the Canadian Historical Society, the University Women's Club, and Calvin Presbyterian Church in Toronto. She identified her greatest achievement

71 *Toronto Star* (5 February 1949). Several lawyers in attendance critiqued the Law Society's arrangements for legal education, including Arthur Kelly who suggested that the Benchers' report had "wrecked our system of education" and that it would be hard to attract teachers of any quality to Ontario. The reason for Clark's lack of useful work during her articles may be related to a lack of firm work, or perhaps a lack of work for women articling students.

72 LSO Archives, Harriet Clark fonds. Copies of some papers presented at this conference by several Ontario lawyers are in the Clark fonds: B.J. MacKinnon and E. McWhinney, "Problems of Federalism in the Commonwealth"; H.R.S. Ryan (Queen's University), "Necessity of Proof of Wrongful Intent in Criminal Cases"; R. Reid, "Administrative Tribunals and their Function in a Legal System"; B. Laskin (University of Toronto), "Human Rights and Civil Liberties"; and I. Baxter (Osgoode Hall Law School) and V. Parsons, "Matrimonial Property Laws within the Commonwealth."

73 *Windsor Daily Star* (2 February 1953). Lorna Brigden (1923), Joan Morris (1949), and Judy LaMarsh (1950) also showed needlework.

as helping to save Old Fort York from demolition at the time of the construction of the Gardiner Expressway. She died in 1992.[74]

The third woman called to the bar in September 1947 was M.M. (Mabel) Van Camp. She grew up in Blackstock, a village near Port Parry, where her father owned a garage. The eldest of four girls, she graduated from high school at the age of sixteen and obtained a BA from Victoria College in 1941. Although her family managed during the Depression by growing their own food, Van Camp needed financial support to attend university. In addition to a bursary, she obtained a position in the Toronto home of Joseph Sedgwick to provide live-in assistance to the family's children, after being recommended by a Blackstock neighbour. She lived with the family during her studies for the BA and again while she attended Osgoode Hall Law School.[75]

In 1942, Van Camp enrolled at the Ontario College of Education, intending to teach to obtain funding for law school. After only six weeks, she was asked to replace a teacher in South Mountain, a small community between Ottawa and Prescott, to teach Latin and home economics. She subsequently moved to Norwood, where she taught Latin and English. In 1943, she arranged a meeting with Dean Falconbridge to seek advice about studying law, but as she later recalled, "he persuaded me in the gentlest of terms that law was no profession for a lady, and I would be much happier if I did not take it." Although Sedgwick didn't overtly discourage her, Van

74 Obituary, *Globe and Mail* (11 May 1992); and LSO Archives, Harriet Clark fonds. The fonds include reports of other reunions of the class of 1947: the thirtieth, in November 1977 at the National Club; the thirty-fifth, in December 1982; and the fortieth, in 1987 in the library of the Royal York Hotel. John Robarts, Premier of Ontario, was a member of the class of 1947, along with two male politicians—Vern Singer (Liberal) and Jim Renwick (NDP). Several classmates later became judges, including Mabel VanCamp, the first woman to be appointed to the Supreme Court of Ontario: OSCLH, oral history, "Mabel Van Camp," 51.

75 OSCLH, oral history, "Mabel Van Camp," 1–30. Van Camp was the first person from her township to attend university, but Chancellor Bowles lived next door to the Van Camps in Blackstock, and he encouraged her to attend Victoria College, where Northrop Frye was one of her professors. According to Van Camp, Sedgwick usually played golf or poker with friends in the evenings, and she often read to the children at bedtime.

Camp knew he did not approve—in his view, "women were to be decorative and helpful."[76]

Van Camp persisted and entered Osgoode Hall in 1944 in a class of forty "very serious" students. She recalled that most instructors used straight lectures: "They appeared, they gave their lecture and they disappeared," but Dr. Wright used the Socratic method, and John Willis "stormed up and down the classroom ... all of a sudden asking a question of anybody whom he happened to be passing at that moment." Questions were not encouraged in class, and although instructors provided lists of cases for students to read at night, there was no instruction about researching cases or using the library. The courses focused on "what the decisions had been and how the changes had occurred. There was not much talk about changes that should be made ... It was mainly a history of the past."[77]

Sedgwick assisted Van Camp to find an articling position by introducing her to Jim McLennan at Macdonald & Macintosh, and McLennan agreed to accept her as an articling student. Van Camp described the firm as "one of the last of the old firms." Located on the fifth floor at 357 Bay Street, its entrance was a desk and a group of secretaries, and behind them was a long row of offices with a library and a room for prospectors in relation to the firm's mining clients. "Old Mr J.A. Macintosh," then in his late eighties, would open the letter book, which contained onionskin copies of all the letters sent out the day before. Each person in the office was called to account for letters that they had sent: "If there was one comma wrong in your letter, that was your responsibility," and it reflected on the reputation of the firm. Van Camp did research for McLennan, a litigator, and she often had to read microfiche copies of the *Globe and Mail*, a client of the firm, in relation to libel cases.[78]

---

76 OSCLH, oral history, "Mabel Van Camp," 38–40. She enjoyed teaching Latin, but she required some assistance with home economics from the woman in charge of the local inn where she boarded. Van Camp's students in South Mountain, a Catholic community, were good at Latin, and several students intended to become priests.

77 OSCLH, oral history, "Mabel Van Camp," 39, 48–50, 53–60. Van Camp noted that some male students wore their uniforms because they had no other clothes, and she recalled that they were often supporting wives and small babies in the cramped quarters of a third-floor flat, a challenging contrast to their recent lives as senior officers. Like Helen Carefoot (1946), Van Camp recalled the snowstorm in Toronto in 1944, when she skied across the Danforth Bridge and down Parliament Street to Osgoode Hall to write an exam.

78 OSCLH, oral history, "Mabel Van Camp," 62.

Van Camp found deliveries a chore, but "it was a way of meeting ... a relatively small group of people, the practicing bar. Bay Street was like my village, because when you went out the door on Bay Street, you spoke to almost every person you met because he would be a lawyer or a trust company person." She was the first student who did not have to pay for articles at the firm, but there was minimal instruction. After a one-day orientation to City Hall, the Surrogate Court office, the County Court office, and Osgoode Hall, students were on their own. Her call to the bar ceremony honoured Prime Minister Mackenzie King—a trying experience for Van Camp's father, an ardent Conservative. She also described the chancellor, Sir William Mulock, as very frail at the ceremony: when kneeling in front of him, students were half supporting him, "hoping that he wasn't going to collapse on top of you."[79]

After being called to the bar, Van Camp faced the challenge of finding employment.

> It was still not a time when women lawyers were accepted. You could work in a trust company, or you could work in government, but not in a law office. I went for interviews with firms who were advertising for lawyers ... and the interviews were courteous ... but you knew that there wasn't a chance of getting a job. It was very much like a men's club. They would just be uncomfortable with you around. The lawyers never would have considered having a woman as a member of the firm. And you really didn't expect it. Nobody got too upset about it, because it was just the pattern.[80]

79 OSCLH, oral history, "Mabel Van Camp," 62–69, 73–75. McLennan "kept you constantly at his elbow and as he was working, he would be tossing things to you."

80 OSCLH, oral history, "Mabel Van Camp," 85–94, 121. She found the WLAO and the sorority unable to help because so few of their members were in private practice; as she explained, the practitioners included Margaret Hyndman (1926), Vera Parsons (1924), Margaret Grimshaw (1946), and Elizabeth Maclennan (1927) as well as a few women in the Danforth area doing real estate and estate work from their homes. Van Camp also explained that a male lawyer would hesitate to hire a woman, "because he would know that his wife wouldn't be comfortable." Van Camp identified two women lawyers called to the bar shortly after her who started "the first women's law firm," probably a reference to June Bernhard and Janet Scott, called to the bar in 1951. The Bernhard and Scott firm was not the first women's law firm: see Chapter Three concerning two early women lawyers' firms in the 1920s: Robinson & Currie and Daley & Thompson.

Although it was disheartening, Van Camp persisted in her job search because she could not afford to start her own firm, and it was Sedgwick who eventually located a position for her. When the courts were closed for Armistice Day in 1947, he took a bottle and visited his friend Gerry Beaudoin at his office, and when Beaudoin complained of overwork, Sedgwick responded, "I know just the person for you." After interviewing Van Camp, Beaudown agreed to a "trial project," but he warned her that if his five secretaries (law clerks) were not happy, *she* would have to leave. Beaudoin, who started legal practice in the late 1920s and established his own office in the mid-1930s, mainly served French Canadian clients from Penetanguishene, the Maritimes, and Québec who worked in Toronto, many translating catalogues for Simpson's and Eaton's into French—but the firms' files were in English. Van Camp brought a significant asset to the firm because she could do divorces for Catholic clients, while Beaudoin, a devout Catholic, was prohibited by the Church from doing so.[81]

Van Camp's experience of family law in these decades, prior to the federal *Divorce Act* in 1968, was comprehensive, including separation, distribution of assets, and custody and access, and the firm was primarily involved in counsel work, with referrals from within and outside Toronto. Although Van Camp remained skeptical about clients' decisions to separate or divorce, because she believed that it was not "the answer to anything," she worked to achieve their wishes. Moreover, since divorce work was often accompanied by the purchase and sale of homes and the need to draft new wills, some divorce clients retained the firm for these additional legal matters, and Beaudoin's firm also did Senate divorces from Québec. At the time, there were just a few statutes and common law precedents about family law, and Van Camp recalled that family lawyers faced challenges in cases alleging cruelty because of the absence of women's shelters. There was also the difficulty of proof in claims of adultery involving paid co-respondents, and claims alleging a husband's homosexuality were especially challenging.

> When you were acting for a man, almost always the final paragraph of the statement of claim [by the other party] was an allegation that he was a

81 OSCLH, oral history, "Mabel Van Camp," 88–92. Although Van Camp seemed to be well accepted in Beaudoin's office, published records show her name in parentheses at the firm for several years after 1947: *Canadian Law Lists*.

> homosexual. And there was no way ... [he] could prove [otherwise]. And you couldn't have a trial ... if [he was] a man of any standing whatsoever, because all the papers [would report the homosexuality], none of the weakness of the evidence, none of the findings, not even the adultery. All that would come out is the headline ... And so, you just had to settle.[82]

Consistent with the firm's view that divorce was not always helpful, its policy was to send clients away for three months after the first interview—a strategy to encourage clients to seek counselling.[83]

For her first three years of practice, Van Camp lived at Fudger House on Sherbourne Street, a home built by the president of Simpson's for out-of-town employees but available to other women residents: there was Sunday afternoon tea, and the doors were locked every night promptly at eleven. During this time, she became an instructor in the practice groups at Osgoode Hall, offering practical skills: "How do you interview a client ... how do you issue a writ ... Most [students] knew the rules but hadn't a clue as to how one did it." From September to June, the practice groups were held once a week, there was no grading, and the focus was very practical: "Next year, [a student] would be in a small town, on his own, with no one to ask, and how was he going to start when the first client came in." Beaudoin's fees were low, and Van Camp earned very little, but she agreed to stay at the firm after Beaudoin's death in 1962, when Elliott Pepper, a former Queen's proctor at the Ministry of the Attorney General who oversaw the validity of evidence in adultery cases, bought the practice—on

82 OSCLH, oral history, "Mabel Van Camp," 99–110, 118–20. The firm also did annulments, but they were expensive and time-consuming.

83 OSCLH, oral history, "Mabel Van Camp," 107, 110, 117. Divorce was often regarded socially as a failure prior to the 1968 legislation, but Van Camp suggested that even where there was not a lot of money, "almost always you got the house for the woman and the children." Three-quarters of cases settled with separation agreements, but because there was no pretrial, a case that went to trial did so directly: "A Gallery of Women: M.M. VanCamp," *Globe and Mail* (23 April 1959). See also B. Atcheson et al., "Family Issues: Family Law, Childcare, Reproductive Issues" in B. Atcheson and L. Marsden, eds., *White Gloves Off: The Work of the Ontario Committee on the Status of Women* (Toronto: Second Story Press, 2018) 103; and L. Silver Dranoff, *Fairly Equal: Lawyering the Feminist Revolution* (Toronto: Second Story Press, 2017) 143.

condition that Van Camp remain in the firm. Pepper and Van Camp raised the fees and did not lose any clients. She was appointed QC in 1966.[84]

The firm also acted as solicitors for Catholic organizations, including the group that created the first French public school and high school in Toronto. Although Van Camp was not Catholic, some clients preferred to retain a woman, and she was increasingly involved in counsel work and in negotiating separation agreements. She recalled that she had sometimes lowered her fees rather than get involved in the reporting burdens of legal aid certificates. After the enactment of the *Divorce Act* in 1968, the focus of family law shifted—from ensuring evidence for divorce decrees to obtaining proof of assets and income for distribution. Van Camp enjoyed working in a small firm where "you knew your clients, you could give them the time they needed, you felt you really were performing a service ... that was helpful."[85]

By the late 1960s, pressure was mounting for the appointment of women judges in Canada, and in 1969, Réjane Laberge-Colas of Québec became the first woman judge of a Superior Court in Canada.[86] Van Camp, who had declined an appointment to the Family Court, believed that her

84 OSCLH, oral history, "Mabel Van Camp," 119–142, 147–51, 185–87; LSO Archives, OBBRP, "Mabel VanCamp"; and W. Stewart, "No Place for a Lady," *Vic Report* (Victoria College) (Winter 1993–94) 4. Van Camp believed that most instructors focused on what they thought had been missing in their own legal education, and instructors did exchange ideas from time to time. She also held a class on office management, focused on "the problems of running an office." The Queen's Proctor generally came [to the divorce court] as a friend of the court, having done the required investigation. Van Camp explained that family lawyers used private investigators to obtain evidence of adultery, but "you never put a private investigator on the stand. Or almost never. They had no credibility whatsoever." Moreover, one-night stands were seldom sufficient as evidence. According to Van Camp, evidence of adultery was often obtained at conventions, where other men were in and out of a husband's room and could provide evidence of his relationship with a woman. Annulments were difficult unless a husband was impotent, and good medical evidence was required. Her firm also did a few religious divorces, which were very time-consuming.

85 OSCLH, oral history, "Mabel Van Camp," 191–206, 214–16, 223–29; 236–29, and 570. See also R. Corelli, "First Woman High Court Judge Says Divorce 'Shouldn't Occur,'" *Toronto Star* (12 November 1971), a press report of an interview prior to her being sworn in as Justice Van Camp.

86 A graduate of the Université de Montréal in 1952, Laberge-Colas served as a judge for more than twenty-five years. She died in 2009: obituary, *Globe and Mail* (24 August 2009) S13.

lack of political connection precluded a judicial appointment, but the YWCA, an organization in which she had been active for many years, submitted Van Camp's name. As she recalled:

> There was pressure. There had been pressure, I think, of maybe two years. I have forgotten what was happening in the feminist movement at that time. But many groups were not so much [concerned] to have a woman on the Court, as to have women in public life in some way or other. And [Prime Minister] Trudeau was very receptive to it. Chief Justice Gale would have liked it to commence somewhere else. And in some other court. But they were going to add five [judges in Ontario's Superior Court] and it was difficult to add five and not have one of them a woman at that time.[87]

After Van Camp accepted this judicial appointment, effective December 1971, she and Chief Justice Gale conferred about the appropriate title for a woman judge. They rejected the English protocol of "Mrs. Justice Van Camp" in favour of "Madam Justice," without the "e."[88]

Van Camp served as a Superior Court judge until her retirement in 1995 at the age of seventy-five. She rejected the idea of a "woman judge's point of view," asserting that female judges' judgments differed from one another as much as those of male judges. Yet her judicial experiences were sometimes challenging. On one occasion when she travelled on circuit to northern Ontario, the sheriff did not recognize her when she stepped from the train, so she hired her own taxi to the courthouse. On arrival, she found the court in an uproar. The clerk explained, "We've lost the damn judge!" Van Camp quickly responded, "*I* am the damn judge."[89]

---

87 OSCLH, oral history "Mabel Van Camp," 240–45.

88 OSCLH, oral history, "Mabel Van Camp," 240–53; *Toronto Star* (18 December 1971); and *Globe and Mail* (13 May 1995). Van Camp's judicial salary was forty-four thousand dollars, more than she had earned in practice: *Toronto Star* (11 November 1971). The other appointments were Thomas Callon (Thunder Bay), David Cromarty (Welland), J.G. O'Driscoll (Toronto), and Mayer Lerner (London).

89 LSO Archives, OBBRP, "Mabel Van Camp"; and (1995) 10:1 *Without Prejudice* (WLAO) 4. Van Camp also reported that she had spent much of her life "walking into rooms full of strange men." Justice Van Camp decided an early case about marital property pursuant to the 1986 *Family Law Act*, which was overturned on appeal: *Caratun v Caratun* (1987) 9 RFL (3d) 337 (Ont HC); (1992) 42 RFL (3d) 113 (Ont CA). See also Stewart, "No Place for a Lady," 6.

Van Camp was active in the WLAO, serving as president from 1957 to 1962. The association was "a way of keeping in touch with what was happening in different offices ... You attended the WLAO activities to find out what [others] were doing ... because you were excluded from so many other groups." Indeed, Van Camp herself had experienced exclusion as an articling student when her principal invited all the firm's students to attend a Lawyers' Club meeting. Then, after discovering the club's male-only restriction, he arranged to take VanCamp for dinner—while all the other students attended the meeting. Van Camp was also a member (and former dean) of Kappa Beta Pi, the Canadian Institute of International Affairs, the Fudger House Chapter of the IODE (she was a regent), and the YWCA.[90]

Van Camp was described as "a curious blend of ultra-conservatism and reformist liberalism." During a visit to Osgoode Hall Law School at York University in 1975—to officially open the new office of the Women's Caucus—she cautioned women students not to isolate themselves from their male colleagues. In 1994, she also professed admiration for the quiet aspect of revolutionary change: "It is not enough to have women in the profession ... but after the change has been brought into effect, it is absolutely essential that there be women who will show that the change has been successful. The battle has not ended when you bring about change; the battle ends when you make that change a success.... [The WLAO] has tended to reflect what I call the quiet aspect of revolutionary change." Justice Van Camp was appointed to the Order of Ontario in 2003, and she died in 2012.[91]

In 1948, nine women were called to the Ontario bar, the largest number of new women lawyers in any year since 1921. In both these years, the admission of nine women lawyers occurred in the immediate aftermath of the two world wars, a pattern that may reflect women's greater opportunities for legal education when male students were absent on war service. Five of these new women lawyers were admitted to the legal profession in June, and they were photographed together in their barristers' gowns

90 Bushby, "The Early Years"; OSCLH, oral history, "Mabel Van Camp," 76–78, 82–83; and *Globe and Mail* (23 April 1959). She became the first female member of the Royal Canadian Military Institute.

91 J. Tintor, "Association for Women Lawyers Needed, but Must Not Divide Profession, Van Camp Says," *Law Times* (December 1994). See also LSO Archives, "Diversifying the Bar," Mabel Van Camp; and obituary *Globe and Mail* (9 August 2012).

outside Osgoode Hall.[92] Among them was Marion Smith, who graduated from Queen's University in 1943 with a BA. She served in the Women's Royal Naval Service during the war, as a visual signaller in Halifax and Prince Rupert, BC. After her call to the bar in Ontario, she worked for a year as a law clerk in Montreal. In September 1949, Smith married J.W. McKinnon, and the couple lived for a few years in Prince Edward Island before settling in Ottawa. Although Smith McKinnon was active in charitable work and in several organizations in Ottawa, she did not practise law. She suffered from dementia after 2012 and died a few days after her one hundredth birthday in November 2020.[93]

The remaining four women graduates engaged in legal practice in Toronto. Celia Corcoran, who completed a BA at the University of Toronto in 1938, joined the air force during the Second World War and entered Osgoode Hall in 1945. Corcoran practised law with her father, J.E. Corcoran, who had been called to the bar in 1917, at the firm of Godfrey and Corcoran at 10 Adelaide Street East. Corcoran's artistic abilities were evident in her unique contribution to the WLAO Hobby Show in 1952: "a lamp-stand and candle-holder made out of odd-shaped knotty pieces of wood [that had been] sanded and polished ... [They] were of such interesting shapes [that] they resembled wood-sculpture." After her father's death, Corcoran continued the firm's practice at 2 Toronto Street, and in 1963 M.M. Katzman, who had been called to the bar the previous year, joined her practice at 12 Richmond Street East. By 1970, Corcoran was in a sole practice at this location. Corcoran also served a term as President of the board of Women's College Hospital. She died in 2012.[94]

Kathleen (Kay) Killoran, the daughter of a physician, graduated from the University of Toronto in 1938 and joined the war effort. She worked in a laboratory for the Polymor Rubber Company, testing synthetic rubber,

92 Huckle, "List of Women Barristers and Solicitors"; LSO Archives, WLAO fonds, "Five Girls among 107," *Toronto Star* (26 June 1948).

93 Mitchell Thomas, "The History of Women Lawyers," 113; and *Canadian Law Lists*. Smith's war service was identified in OSCLH, oral history, "Betty Jean Teagle MacDonald" (1948) and "Laura Legge" (1948). See also obituary, *Globe and Mail* (14 November 2020) B22, which reported that a photo of Smith demonstrating semaphore is displayed at the Juno Beach Centre in France.

94 Huckle, "List of Women Barristers and Solicitors"; LSO Archives, OBBRP, "Celia Corcoran"; *Canadian Law Lists*; and LSO Archives, WLAO fonds, SB, vol. 6, "Show Hobbies of Lawyers at Dinner." See also OSCLH, oral history, "Mabel Van Camp," 153.

and was featured in a press photo with Bernice Galletly at the laboratory in 1943. Killoran entered Osgoode Hall in 1945 and was elected to the executive of the Legal and Literary Society in her final year. After her call to the bar, she was employed for two years at the Housing Corporation Ltd at 880 Bay Street, but then practised law with J.D. Bell, who had been called to the bar in 1941, at 171 Yonge Street. When the firm expanded, as Bell, Keith, Ganong & Griffiths, Killoran continued to practise at the firm's new location at 25 Adelaide Street West, but by 1965, she was working in the office of Guaranty Trust at 366 Bay Street. It appears that Killoran ceased practice about 1970. She died in 1979.[95]

Another woman graduate in June 1948 was Betty Jean Teagle, later MacDonald. Teagle was born in 1920, the daughter of a French officer who met her mother in England, and the couple immigrated to Canada after the First World War. Her family travelled to France every few years, except during the Depression, and her French grandfather showed Teagle the law courts, where she noted the large number of women lawyers: "It was just taken for granted." Teagle graduated from the University of Toronto and joined the Air Force. She was posted to Halifax and later to Newfoundland as a radar contact plotter. When the war ended, she entered Osgoode Hall, one of about ten women in a class of four hundred students, who attended lectures at the "overflow" location, the Metropolitan United Church Hall. Although she believed that women students were treated "very very fairly," she also noted that they usually spent time between classes in a small women's washroom.[96] Teagle described her first examination.

> I wrote all my exams up in Convocation Hall, facing the wall at the front so I could not see anyone ... The first exam was in real property and the course was Bora Laskin's, a wonderful man, I just loved him, when I got to know him, not during those days. Sometime later. He lectured to us in real property. And it was his first year, so, of course, there were no precedents to go by ... And I remember looking at the paper and thinking, "I am in the wrong

95 Huckle, "List of Women Barristers and Solicitors"; LSO Archives, OBBRP, "Kathleen Killoran"; and "The Executive Reports," *Obiter Dicta* (April 1948) 34: See also OSCLH, oral histories, "Mabel Van Camp" (1947) and "Laura Legge" (1948); and *Canadian Law Lists.*

96 OSCLH, oral history, "Betty Jane Teagle MacDonald," 1–50. Women were entitled to practise law in France when legislation was enacted there in 1900. By contrast, it was not until 1941 that Québec women became eligible to join the legal profession: see Chapter One.

> room. This is not the course we took" ... That was the most agonizing three and a half hours I have ever spent.[97]

Although the influx of students after 1945 made it difficult to obtain articling positions, Teagle articled at Henderson & Murray, working mostly on title searches and insurance. Although the firm also did divorce cases, the senior lawyers believed that Teagle should not be exposed to the details of such cases. When one of the firm's lawyers introduced her to Margaret Hyndman (1926), Teagle found her very impressive. After two years, Teagle transferred her articles to Bogart & McMaster, where the legal work was more varied, including litigation, although her former principals continued to be concerned that exposure to criminal law might have a "corrupting influence" on her.[98]

After her call to the bar, Teagle applied to work at External Affairs, but her application was not accepted. She held a succession of jobs, including a short time with the Ministry of Labour in Ottawa. After six months, she returned to Toronto, and Belva Gordon Gibson (1930) found her a position doing real estate transactions at Senior & Senior, where she was very busy in the midst of the postwar housing boom, since the firm acted for the Prudential Mortgage Company. In 1951, Teagle married Duncan MacDonald, who had been in the Air Force during the war and returned to complete university and Osgoode Hall. He was called to the bar in 1950 after articling at Senior & Senior. In addition to her work at the law firm, the Law Society invited Teagle MacDonald to lead one of the practice groups at Osgoode

97 OSCLH, oral history, "Betty Jane Teagle MacDonald," 48–50.

98 OSCLH, oral history, "Betty Jane Teagle MacDonald, 53–60. Lawyers at the former firm were particularly concerned because the Bogart & McMaster firm "even did murders."

Hall, mainly lecturing on real estate, as well as marking examinations and conducting oral exams.[99]

After the birth of her first child in 1954, Teagle MacDonald worked two days a week, doing title searches for her husband's law practice. Eight months after the birth of her second child, she hired full-time help at home and started work at White & Bristol with Janet Lang Boland (1950). Both women worked "by the hour," an arrangement that accommodated their need for flexibility with young children. Their work focused on real estate transactions, using dictation equipment to work at times when a secretary was unavailable, and Teagle MacDonald was paid $7.50 per hour. Few certified cheques were used in real estate transactions in these years, especially outside Toronto: "Back then, you knew who you could trust and who you couldn't." She experienced no difficulties, although sometimes surprise, as a woman in legal practice. She particularly recalled receiving support when a client used "bad words" to her on the phone, and the firm's partner immediately returned the client's file.[100]

After the White & Bristol firm amalgamated with another Toronto firm, Teagle MacDonald worked with Kenneth Kidd for eight years at 371 Bay Street, and she then joined her husband in practice, an arrangement that

99 Teagle briefly returned to real estate work at Bogart, McMaster & Fram in the Continental Life Building, and she later joined the provincial government office where Laura Lees (1926) was involved with the Junior Farmers' mortgage program: OSCLH, oral history, "Betty Jane Teagle MacDonald," 65–94. She continued to use her birth surname at the firm because the firm had five years of letterhead on hand, and her name was "up in gold on the door." After the birth of her daughter in 1954, when "Miss Teagle" was no longer appropriate, she used her married name. Teagle MacDonald identified Mabel Van Camp (1947) as the first woman to teach in the Osgoode Hall practice groups, unaware that Eileen Mitchell Thomas (1942) had done so earlier. She believed that it was important for women lawyers to be involved in teaching law, and she recalled using notes prepared for postwar "refresher courses" in her practice course; she also reported that she found marking examinations "devastating."

100 D.J. MacDonald initially established a firm with A.C. Heakes, who was also called to the bar in 1950, and their firm was located at 29 Main Street North in Weston. In 1965, the firm employed a woman lawyer, Alicia Forgie (1963): Huckle, "List of Women Barristers and Solicitors"; and *Canadian Law Lists*. See also OSCLH, oral history, "Betty Jane Teagle MacDonald," 101–17. Teagle MacDonald noted that there were almost no title searchers, and that the Registrar of Deeds, Mr. Dodds, did all the books by hand: "He had the most beautiful handwriting." She also described having to rush from the County Registry Office to the City Office and then to Land Titles; "you had to be really quite spry." In one of her cases, funds were tendered in cash, and it became an unreported leading case.

lasted from 1972 to the late 1980s. She was also involved with the WLAO, serving as President from 1968 to 1970. Although Teagle MacDonald was offered a QC, she declined because she never did court work, concluding that this honour had been offered "simply because she was a woman." She also recalled being inspired in her law work by Lang Boland, who encouraged her by saying, "Betty Jane, let's be the best."[101]

The call to the bar in June 1948 also included Laura Down, later Legge, one of seven children whose parents farmed in Delhi, near Tillsonburg, in southwest Ontario. Her parents were active in the Conservative Party, and her father was Reeve for many years, including during the Depression. Her parents encouraged education, and she learned to read before she started school at age seven. She attended high school in Tillsonburg, seven miles from the farm, and graduated in 1940 with scholarships to attend the University of Western Ontario. Although Down was interested in medicine, her parents were persuaded by university administrators to enroll her in the nursing program, and Down completed this program, winning prizes. She also completed extra courses for the university's BA during her practical nursing training at the Toronto General Hospital. Down then decided to change professions, entering Osgoode Hall in 1945: "On my own, I figured out that law was where I should be, because it was a profession where ... there is no end of studying and work and using your brain. Nothing becomes a matter of rote ... in law."[102]

Down entered Osgoode Hall in a class with three hundred returning veterans. She remembered Falconbridge teaching Contracts, illustrating his points with references to *Alice in Wonderland*: "A contract without consideration was the smile without the cat." He used a textbook, while Laskin and Wright used the casebook method, and she concluded that Laskin "was keen on the American judges" and that he might have been happier at Harvard. His Real Property exam was difficult, and Down failed to answer several questions, but when she passed the exam, she concluded that Laskin might have been "so sick of reading garbage" that he rewarded her

101 OSCLH, oral history, "Betty Jane Teagle MacDonald," 119–24. When her husband became ill with lupus erythematosus in 1972, she helped in his practice. Between 1985 and 1988, she was involved in closing the office, "the worst years I have ever spent." In relation to the QC, Teagle MacDonald believed that "it would have made a farce out of [this appointment]."

102 LSO Archives, Treasurers' transcripts, "Laura Legge," 1–27; and OSCLH, oral history, "Laura Legge," 46–49.

for writing nothing—"because I wasn't guessing." She found John Willis a "wonderful lecturer, who always made his wife the payee" in his course on Bills and Notes. In contrast, Wright always made "Susie Gluts" the woman who was gifted a hidden trust by a husband involved in adultery.[103] About 50 per cent of her class failed the examinations, including many wounded veterans who received no mercy from the Benchers: "They just chopped them, and this was how they controlled numbers ... it was exceedingly unkind." Down also recalled "a certain bond with the class of '48 because it was the first class after the war," a class of mature people, including men who had been through life and death experiences. There was no differential treatment for women students: "No, no. Never entered our minds. No. We were all law students."[104]

Down's first articling position was with William Laird, and she later articled with John Burden. Although "it was terribly difficult for anybody to take a girl's articles [because] girls who went into law in those years were oddities," she believed that her articling experience provided an excellent introduction to the practice of law: "In those years if you articled with a sole practitioner, you learned to do everything. You learned to keep books, you learned to do accounting, you learned to do real estate, estates. It was a marvellous general practice ... And it was a great experience, and he was

103 OSCLH, oral history, "Laura Legge," 51–65. Among her lecturers, those who used casebooks first explained the legal principle and then examined the cases illustrating the principle. Decades later, she described "the confusion of the way they are taught today, they are given a case and they try to find the legal principle involved, it is such garbage." She also found Laskin a "boring lecturer [who] pontificated [in a] deep, growling voice and one learned from him that all the judges were morons, the practicing bar really didn't know anything ... It is the same attitude that you have in the law schools today ... you would listen and listen to [Laskin], trying to get the point of what he had to say."

104 OSCLH, oral history, "Laura Legge," 64–66: Down Legge believed the high failure rate was because the Benchers "didn't want this number of lawyers," a concern that surfaced in Ontario again in the 1980s and '90s. See also LSO Archives, Treasurers' transcripts, "Laura Legge," 43–47, 50. Legge described the lectures at Metropolitan United Church in her second year and the overcrowding in Convocation Hall. There were three hours of lectures each morning and then afternoons at work in offices, as well as Saturday mornings.

a very good teacher. And he gave me free [rein]. He let me learn things and do things."[105]

After her call to the bar, Down worked as a junior at the Department of Health: "It was a natural fit having been a nurse and a lawyer to be with the Department of Health." Her work involved redrafting regulations under the *Public Health Act* and the *Hospital Acts,* and she researched a case about the procedure for closing a cemetery under the *Cemeteries Act.* Down was fortunate to have a government position because "there was very little work for lawyers in those years ... Toronto was a pretty dead city." Indeed, after her future husband, Bruce Legge, returned from the war and graduated in 1949, he did not find work until February 1950. The couple married in July 1950, and Legge gave birth to three children in 1952, 1954, and 1955, taking unpaid leaves for each child. Although she was adamant about not giving up law practice for marriage, she left the government in 1956 to have more flexibility in relation to her family, and she established a sole practice, initially practising from home.[106]

Legge soon established an office at Yonge and St. Clair, not far from her home, and she worked half days until the children were in school—with a housekeeper's help, she went home for lunch. She soon had an articling student and two other lawyers at the firm, and in 1973 her husband, who had been employed in the Department of Veterans Affairs and at the Workmen's Compensation Board, joined her in the practice as Legge & Legge. She did real estate and estate work and commercial work for local businesses, but she usually sent litigation to another firm so that she could be present in the office. Legge believed that "clients were completely unconcerned by your gender. All they cared about was the kind of work you did for them."

105 OSCLH, oral history, "Laura Legge," 53–58; and LSO Archives, Treasurers' transcripts, "Laura Legge," 39–51. According to Down Legge, she articled with Laird at Urquhart & Urquhart in the Confederation Life Building on Queen Street, and the firm shared offices with John Burden, a sole practitioner. Although it is unclear which of these two lawyers she was crediting with her excellent articling experience, it was probably Burden, the sole practitioner.

106 Huckle, "List of Women Barristers and Solicitors," identified the date of call as June 1948, but LSO Archives, OBBRP, "Laura Legge," shows the date of call as 1 January 1948. See also LSO Archives, Treasurers' transcripts, "Laura Legge," 41, 51–66; and OSCLH, oral history, "Laura Legge," 79–95.

> You see, I never thought of myself as a woman lawyer. I always thought of myself as a lawyer. And my generation did. We were, we were just lawyers. And if you married and had children, it was something that you accommodated, if you were working. But remember, very few women who married and had children worked ... It was not normal for women of my generation to marry, have children and practice. They just didn't. However, before I was ever married to Bruce Legge, I told him I was going to practice law if I married. I had no intention of having the degree ... and having worked as hard as I did to get it, not to use it.[107]

Legge joined the WLAO as a student and later served on the executive, including as President in 1964–66, and she was involved, along with Noreen Charlebois Stevens (1955), in pressing for women's robing rooms in Ontario courthouses. At the time, the women's robing room at Old City Hall consisted of a curtain which had been put up at the end of a hall. Moreover, "had the [WLAO] not intervened, they would have completed the courthouse on University Avenue with no robing rooms for women lawyers!" Legge joined Kappa Beta Pi, and she also attended executive meetings of the CBAO Council when she was WLAO president, but she believed women were not particularly welcome at the association: "You know they tolerated us and that was about it." Legge was appointed QC in 1966.[108]

107 LSO Archives, Treasurers' transcripts, "Laura Legge," 54, 56–62, and OSCLH, oral history, "Laura Legge," 155–66. In response to a comment by Joan Morris Hodgson (1949) that her husband did not want her to practise law, Legge sternly reported that Bruce Legge could not stop her. Legge also acknowledged receiving help from Celia Corcoran's father, who was delighted to see women lawyers, and she sometimes had lunch with two (unidentified) Jewish male lawyers from a nearby office. She did some Magistrate's Court work and frequently provided help to clients for "no fee, or very reduced fees" before the advent of legal aid. According to Legge, her husband joined the firm in 1973, after Premier Davis "fired" him from his position at the Workers Compensation Board: OSCLH, oral history, "Laura Legge," 118–24.

108 LSO Archives, Treasurers' transcripts, "Laura Legge," 127. Legge used to gown and then put her coat on, "and just put my outside gown on there." For details of her membership in a large number of other numerous organizations, see OSCLH, oral history, "Laura Legge," 133–34, 142–43; LSO Archives, "Diversifying the Bar," Laura Legge; and Treasurers' transcripts, "Laura Legge," 129–48. See also letter from A. Heeney, Architect, to K. Jarvis, Secretary of the Law Society (20 May 1970), LSO Archives, WLAO fonds, in which Heeney noted that he pointed out that "no accommodation is being provided for a robing room for Lady Barristers," and suggested that space should be provided for ten women.

In 1974, the Law Society appointed the first four "lay Benchers," including two women: Reginae Tait of Toronto and Roseanne Sutherland of Sudbury, the first time since the Society's incorporation in 1822 that women were Benchers. In 1975, Legge became the first woman to be elected a Bencher of the Law Society, a major accomplishment since women candidates in earlier Bencher elections had never succeeded. Indeed, Legge recalled that Margaret Hyndman had almost made it when she obtained sixteenth place at a time when there were only fifteen Benchers. Thus, when one of these Benchers was appointed to [the judiciary], Hyndman should have moved in, but [in the 1960s] there was no requirement that a Bencher with the next number of votes be moved in, "so they skipped her and appointed a man."[109] For the 1975 election, the WLAO decided to hold a run-off vote among its members to identify one woman to run for Bencher with full association support. Legge instead asked ten male lawyers to nominate her, including the managing partner at McCarthy's, and she received about five hundred letters from lawyers, all men, saying "we are thrilled that you are running, and you have our support and everybody in our firm." Legge believed she had been elected by men, stating, "I know for a fact that very few women voted for me." To Legge's chagrin, the WLAO announcement for the annual meeting in May stated: "We have finally done it. The Women's Law Association has finally managed to get a woman elected as a Bencher." It invited members to celebrate Legge's election.[110]

As a Bencher, Legge claimed that she experienced no discrimination whatsoever: the Benchers "never thought of me as a woman Bencher, they thought of me as a Bencher." When she decided to run for Treasurer, Roger Yachetti nominated her, Jack Ground seconded the nomination, and she was elected in June 1983 with thirty-one votes out of fifty-one. Legge's

109 "2 Women among Newest Benchers," *Globe and Mail* (13 December 1974) 13. See also OSCLH, oral history, "Laura Legge," 149–54. According to Legge, Hyndman "never once complained about it ... that is the kind of lady she is." The rules later changed.

110 OSCLH, oral history, "Laura Legge," 149–52. The managing partner at McCarthy's was John Clarry, spouse of Joy Kennedy Clarry (1951). Legge was persuaded to attend this event after warm support from Apha Hodgins (1919), Marian Lamey (1922), Margaret Smith (1944), and June Bushell (1953), although Legge claimed (perhaps an overstatement) that "I have always found that women are a pain in the neck, and they carry on about women supporting women and they do not support women." Legge was appointed to several Bencher committees, including replacing the chair of Admissions who became ill.

term as Treasurer was busy and sometimes controversial. For example, she promoted an internal appeal process in discipline cases, prior to access to the courts, and she was involved in issues about lawyers' advertising and access to the press. In spite of criticism, she also presided when Margaret Thatcher received an honorary degree from the Law Society, an invitation that had been extended by Legge's predecessor as Treasurer. She was also an outspoken critic of Ontario's new Family Law legislation in 1986 because it failed to provide protection for "women who choose to stay at home and raise their children."[111]

In the end, Legge believed that she had opened the way for women lawyers in her roles as Bencher and then Treasurer:

> I guess it made the men realize that just because you were female, you weren't a monster, and you weren't going to make a lot of waves. I never thought of myself ... as a woman lawyer. I always thought of myself as a lawyer. And when I became a Bencher, I thought of myself as a Bencher, and I was there to do a job as a Bencher. And I think that my male colleagues realized that I wasn't there with any hidden agenda, but to do my part ... it was acceptable.[112]

Legge was adamantly not a feminist, declaring in 1983, "I don't know what a feminist is ... Women have had equality for all my life. It's a question of them getting on with the job. I think the fact that I'm now Treasurer proves it." Her obituary declared that as the first woman to head Ontario's Law Society, she was "a tough but quiet barrier breaker." She herself declared in 1985, "I try to behave like a lady, as mother taught me I should. But don't

111 OSCLH, oral history, "Laura Legge," 159, 183–88, 189, 313–80; LSO, Treasurers' transcripts, "Laura Legge," 83–85, 90–100. Legge suggested that she had defeated Pierre Genest, the other candidate, because he had been a Bencher for only two years: in the view of many, "far too short a time to become Treasurer." See also *London Free Press* (21 March 1986).

112 LSO Archives, Treasurers' transcripts, "Laura Legge," 101.

kid yourself: no one ever pushes me around."[113] In 1987, the Law Society unveiled a bronze bust of Legge, and she was awarded an honorary LLD in 1988, the Award of Excellence by the Osgoode Hall Law School Alumni Association in 1997, and the Order of Ontario in 2003. The Law Society also created a special medal in her name, presented annually to honour a female lawyer for exemplary leadership. Legge died in 2010.[114]

In September 1948, four more women were called to the bar. Mhora MacInnis, later Hollingsworth, was the daughter of a lawyer in Sault Ste. Marie, John MacInnis, and she had graduated from Queen's University with a BA degree in 1945. She articled for her father and for T.E. Carmichael in Sault Ste. Marie. After her call to the bar, she returned to Sault Ste. Marie to work at the firm of Hamilton & Carmichael, solicitors for Algoma Steel and other mining companies. MacInnis was probably the first woman lawyer in Sault Ste. Marie, but after her marriage in July 1950 to F.S. Hollingsworth, there are no records of her practising law. She died in 2018.[115]

A second woman called to the bar with MacInnis was Margaret Dufresne. Dufresne was the wife of a lawyer, Paul Dufresne, who had been called to the bar in 1938. He served with the Canadian army during the war and then returned to his practice in Galt in 1946. Margaret Dufresne graduated from the Galt Collegiate Institute and married prior to entering Osgoode Hall in 1943 as a matriculant. She articled in Toronto with Hamilton Stuart, but then returned to her husband's office in 1946 to complete a final two years of articles in Galt. Dufresne was probably the first married woman to article with her spouse. Helen Carefoot (1946) recalled that she and Dufresne became friends as well as moot partners in second- and

113 *Toronto Star* (11 July 1983) B3. At a Benchers' meeting in 1990, Legge opposed a motion to grant full committee status to a Law Society subcommittee on Women in the Legal Profession: as she declared, a committee devoted to addressing women's concerns indicated that the Law Society viewed "women as weak and incompetent," a patronizing attitude: *Law Times* (30 September 1990). She made similar comments on being elected a Bencher (*Globe and Mail,* 25 April 1975) and on being elected Treasurer (*Toronto Star,* 11 July 1983, B3). See also obituary, *Globe and Mail* (30 October 2012); and E. Cameron, "Law's Happy Reactionary: Laura Legge," *Chatelaine* (February 1985) 106.

114 LSO Archives, "Diversifying the Bar," Laura Legge; "OBA Trailblazers," *York University Gazette* (16 April 1997); *Briefly Speaking* (March 2007); and obituaries, *Globe and Mail* (6 and 30 October 2010).

115 Huckle, "List of Women Barristers and Solicitors"; *Canadian Law Lists*; OSCLH, oral histories: "Helen Carefoot" (1946) and "Laura Legge" (1948); and Laura Legge, interview with M.J. Mossman (28 February 2008).

third-year, and that Carefoot declined an invitation to join Kappa Beta Pi because Dufresne had not received an invitation.[116]

Dufresne was called to the bar in 1948 with her brother, John, who entered Osgoode Hall in 1945 after serving in the war as a wing commander in the Royal Canadian Air Force. John Head and Margaret Dufresne were the first brother and sister to be called to the bar together: John was the father of a seven-year-old son, and Margaret the mother of a little boy, aged six months. Margaret Dufresne and her spouse practised law together, and a few years later the firm expanded as Dufresne, Gould & Dufresne, located at 24 Water Street North in Galt, a general practice focused on litigation, real estate, and estates. Margaret Dufresne worked at the firm three days a week, and she asserted that marriage and a career can work together if "the boss" in both home and office is the husband. She practised law until about 1960 and died in 1967.[117]

Marjorie Laird, later Palmer, also joined the legal profession in September 1948. She grew up in Manitoba, where her father was a Presbyterian minister, but after he became the chaplain at Camp Borden during the Second World War, Laird attended the University of Toronto for a BA and then graduated from Osgoode Hall in 1948. She initially joined the Farm Loans Branch of the Department of Agriculture and later worked in the Treasury Department. In 1952, she joined the Attorney General's Department, becoming an expert in constitutional law; and in 1957, she became the first woman appointed Senior Solicitor in the government of a Canadian province. An interview with Laird in 1959 focused on women's legal

116 OSCLH, oral history, "Helen Carefoot," 17; and LSO Archives, OBBRP, "Margaret Dufresne."

117 LSO Archives, OBBRP, "Margaret Dufresne"; *Canadian Law Lists*; and LSO Archives, WLAO fonds, "Brother, Sister Called to Bar: Her Husband Is Lawyer Too," *Evening Telegram*, unidentified news report. This report identified Margaret's father as a former alderman and insurance salesman in Galt, although LSO records incorrectly identify her father as John Head, a barrister, probably confusing her brother with her father. Dufresne was thirty-one years old when she entered Osgoode Hall, and her son was very young when she was called to the bar, while Backhouse, quoting Gretta Grant, reported that Dufresne was a married woman with grown children when she entered Osgoode Hall and that she practised law in Toronto: Backhouse, "Gretta Wong Grant," 30. Huckle, in "List of Women Barristers and Solicitors," identified Dufresne as "not practising," but there is a press report identifying the firm as Dufresne, Gould & Dufresne, after Ray Gould joined the Dufresnes in 1951: *LEX* (February 1951). After Margaret died of cancer, Paul Dufresne practised alone at 65a Ainslie Street North in Galt: *Canadian Law Lists*; and OSCLH, oral history, "Helen Carefoot."

rights, including the history of women's status in law, as well as issues about child support and family allowances. Noting Laird's expertise in constitutional law, the article also explained that "unlike most constitutional lawyers, she is a trim 123 pounds, has soft grey eyes and rich brown hair." It included her photo along with Attorney General Kelso Roberts. In December 1959, Laird resigned her government position "for personal reasons," stating that she intended to enter private practice and to edit a text on company law.[118]

In 1961, Laird joined Fraser, Beatty, Tucker, McIntosh & Stewart (later Fraser & Beatty), where several other women were in practice, including Noreen Charlebois, later Stevens (1955), and Patricia Bagwell Catalano (1958). Willa Carroll, later Corse (1958), also joined the firm in 1961, along with Laird. After Laird married William Palmer in 1962, she continued in private practice at Fraser & Beatty until 1968, and she was appointed QC in 1963. In the early 1970s, Laird Palmer was employed at JMPM Enterprises, perhaps reflecting her interest in being involved more directly in company law. No trace of a published text on company law has been found. Laird Palmer was adamant that "the time has come for women to stop campaigning for rights which they already have and prove by their ability that they can accept and hold them." She died in 1997.[119]

The fourth woman called to the bar in September 1948 was Joan Heath, a friend of Teagle MacDonald (1948), with whom she had worked during the war. Heath, a doctor's daughter, grew up in Hamilton and Toronto and graduated from the University of Toronto. After joining the Air Force, she spent two and a half years in Halifax at Eastern Air Command in

118 M.A.R. Laird, as told to J. Pollick, "Women Do Have Rights" (1959) 9:50 *Weekend Magazine* 2, 4. Laird was inspired to become a lawyer by Winnifred Yuill, daughter of a local lawyer in Melita, Manitoba. Laird reported that she went to school in St. Thomas, where her father was a minister for fourteen years: *St. Thomas Times-Journal* (31 December 1959). See also LSO Archives, name file, which identified her as "Marjorie Alice Palmer Ransier Laird (1923–97)," although Laird was Marjorie Alice Ransier Laird, and her surname changed to "Palmer" after her marriage in 1962: LSO Archives, OBBRP, "Marjorie Alice Ransier Palmer."

119 LSO Archives, OBBRP, "Marjorie Alice Ransier Palmer"; LSO Archives, "Diversifying the Bar," Marjorie Laird Palmer; *Canadian Law Lists*; Laird, as told to Pollick, "Women Do Have Rights," 2–4; and *St. Thomas Times Journal* (31 December 1959). See also S.T. Edwards, *Fraser & Beatty: The First 150 Years* (Toronto: Desktop Publishing Division, Fraser & Beatty, 1989) 31, 125; obituary, Pat Catalano, *Toronto Star* (12 June 2021); and "In Memoriam," Willa Corse, *Continuum* (Osgoode Hall Law School) (Winter 2014).

radar-tracking services, explaining that "the war was so awful, we wanted to do our part." Heath remembered thirteen women students in her Osgoode Hall class, but three women completed only first-year, and another died.[120] She also recalled that women students were generally accepted.

> The only time we ever really had a problem was ... [when] the first set of exam results ... came out and a lot of the men had been away from studying for five years and the first year they didn't all do so well ... For some reason the women did better. And they [the men] weren't very happy about that ... They were all doing much better after they had been there a couple of years ... It was for the most part a veterans' class, and many of them ... were not all that amenable to discipline ... they used to wander in and out when they felt like it. The professors would get mad and leave ... and eventually in our final year the whole law staff resigned and went to the University of Toronto law school ... The professors were not inclined to take [veterans'] circumstances into account, and the Benchers were. There was a continual battle, because the Benchers felt they should be given consideration, considering the years they had been away, and what they had been through.[121]

Heath recalled that there were no seat assignments for her class and that they fought with Bora Laskin because he had high standards—although they all became friends at reunions in later years. She also found it difficult to obtain an articling position because "they didn't want women, generally speaking." Eventually, after an intervention from friends, she obtained a position with MacBeth & MacBeth in Toronto, "even though the firm didn't have enough really for me to do." Initially, she was not paid a

120 OSCLH, oral history, "Joan Heath," 1–18, 21. Heath recalled that there was no opportunity for advancement during her war service, and the living conditions were challenging. Since there were no female barracks, she and another woman (perhaps Teagle) sublet from an RCMP couple and had hot plates. Heath recalled the three women who completed only first-year: Franny Allan, who married Roger Conant, a County Court judge; Marie Ballard, who married Mr. Allingham; and Mary Christilaw, who married Fritz Wigle. The woman who died was not identified.

121 OSCLH, oral history, "Joan Heath," 23–25. Heath's comment about the departure of Wright and his faculty is notable as this event was not often mentioned in oral histories of other women lawyers. The event occurred in January 1949, several months after Heath's graduation and call to the bar in 1948. Interestingly, Heath attributed Wright's departure to student behaviour, rather than to his disagreement with the Benchers about legal education.

salary, and she worked for a Mr. Davidson in second-year doing "personal stuff" and then at the Succession Duty office in third-year. Although she was paid five dollars a week in second-year and fifteen a week in third-year, she survived on her government pension of sixty dollars per month, and by living at home. She did some real estate and estate work during her articles but never any litigation. After her call to the bar, jobs were still hard to find; she worked initially with Kathleen Killoran at the Second Mortgage Housing Corporation, approving titles for mortgages. When the corporation disbanded and Killoran moved to a private firm, Heath worked at the Prudential Insurance Company, and then at the Ontario Treasury Department. She was later employed at the Agricultural Development Board with Laura Lees (1926), creating title abstracts and documentation about mortgages. Heath believed that the board was looking for women and Lees "was pretty well running the Department."[122]

In 1957, Heath's father died, and her mother decided to move to Guelph where she had family. Through her mother's connection to a childhood friend whose husband had practised law in Guelph before being appointed a judge, Heath obtained a position with Kenneth Blair and Alec Moon. At the time, the legal community in Guelph was entirely male, and Heath became the "only [woman] who actually practiced [in Guelph] for years and years and years." In 1958, Blair, Moon & Heath was located at 16 Douglas Street in Guelph. Heath focused primarily on real estate, as well as estates, and she sometimes appeared in chambers in mental incompetency cases or to pass accounts for estates: "You have to be a jack of all trades in a small ... town, because there just isn't the work to specialize only in one field." As Guelph's first woman lawyer, Heath generally felt well accepted by male lawyers, who were all gentlemanly, but she sometimes had problems with clients.

> I find it is very much harder for a woman to build up a clientele ... And the sad thing is, I often found that women were less eager to go to a woman than the men were. If a man liked the way you did his work, he was inclined to come

122 OSCLH, oral history, "Joan Heath," 24–29, 34.

> back without any problem. But women are a little inclined ... [to want] a man to discuss their worries with, rather than another woman.[123]

Heath was grateful for support from the WLAO; the women who had been called to the bar earlier "were awfully good to the younger group of women; they [wanted] to do their best for them."[124]

Heath recalled that her practice included oral commitments without a need for certified cheques in real estate transactions: "Nobody ever cheated anyone else. If they said something, they lived by it." She was a member and then chair of the Area Committee for Legal Aid, and she was the Area Director for thirteen years—she was paid an annual fee for her work, which went into her firm. She also expressed some frustration with legal aid arrangements, particularly in relation to applications for multiple divorces. In her view, legal aid should pay for only one divorce, and people should get counselling to avoid marrying "the same type of person who beat them up regularly." She also developed more expertise in criminal and family law in order to know "when you are being given the gears by someone who wants a certificate." Heath served as President of the Wellington County Law Association for a couple terms, and she promoted the *Family Law Reform Act* of 1978. She was also a member of the board of the Children's Aid Society, the Ontario Heritage Board, and other community agencies. Although she admitted that "some things ... haven't been easy," she did not regret becoming a lawyer, and she was pleased to have other women lawyers in Guelph, even though it was still hard.

> I don't know how I would feel about advising someone at this stage to go into it, if it was a female. In many respects, I think it is just as hard as it used to be for women, even though there are more of them in the profession, and more accepted than they used to be. But I think women have a double job there, they are getting married, and they are having children and they are having to

123 OSCLH, oral history, "Joan Heath," 39–52. Heath was aware that Edra Sanders Ferguson (1930) had lived in Guelph and that she "maybe did a bit [of law practice] from her house." She also knew that Mary MacDonald (1921) had worked as a librarian at the university. For Heath, the legal profession in Guelph was a very close group in the late 1950s, but it became less "old fashioned" as it grew. By the 1990s, moreover, other women lawyers had started to practise law in Guelph.

124 OSCLH, oral history, "Joan Heath," 36–37.

> try to run the house and run the children and run their profession, and it is pretty hard to do if you have a lot of night work.[125]

Five women were called to the bar in 1949, and four joined the legal profession in June. Joan Morris, later Hodgson, was born in Winnipeg, but her family moved to London, Ontario, when she started school, where she was placed in a gifted class. Her father worked for the Hobbes Glass Company in London, but he lost his job during the Depression, and the family moved to Oshawa, where he obtained work at another glass company. Morris attended the Ontario Ladies College in Whitby, graduating at age sixteen. She recalled feeling that, in the midst of the war, "the world turned over." Although her parents did not have postsecondary education, they encouraged her to attend university, and her women teachers, most of whom were unmarried, also encouraged their students to seek personal independence. After advice from her lawyer uncle, Morris enrolled in the four-year honours program in law at the University of Toronto in 1942.[126]

Her university class of twenty-five students was one-third WASP, one-third Jewish, and one-third Black, and she was the only woman. Many of the Black students were from the Caribbean, and since they were prevented from travelling to England for law studies during the war, the Inns of Court accepted the University of Toronto program as part of their bar admission process. It was Morris's first encounter with Black people, and she recalled being treated well by both Black and Jewish students—WASP students were less friendly. Thelma Kerr, later Thomson (1949), eventually joined the law course, and after completing the university program, the two women attended Osgoode Hall together. In addition, Eugenia Charles from Dominica joined their class. The daughter of the Dominican prime

125 OSCLH, oral history, "Joan Heath," 52–77. Laura Legge (1948) commented that Heath was "successful and very good": OSCLH, oral history, "Laura Legge," 67.

126 OSCLH, oral history, "Joan Morris Hodgson," 1–29. Morris's only sibling, Barbara, died of multiple sclerosis in 1937. During high school, Morris had a friend who owned a horse, which Morris was permitted to ride. At the time, most of the work to create the 401 was completed, but there was no concrete available for pavement because of the war, and Morris explained that she was "one of the few people who has ridden horseback on the 401."

minister, Charles hoped to establish a juvenile court there, which she did on her return. She also entered politics and later became Prime Minister.[127]

Morris described Dean Kennedy as "an absolutely mad Irishman," but he was very welcoming to female students. He taught Constitutional Law in all four years, spending a full year on each of the constitutions of Canada, the United States, and England, followed by a final year focused on world relations. Jacob Finkelman taught Labour and Administrative Law, and there were courses in economics, psychology, philosophy, and political science. As Morris explained: "Osgoode, of course, wouldn't have touched [such courses] with a ten-foot pole. And this was Kennedy's whole principle, that lawyers were not being educated, they were just being taught law. And that all the things that supported it in our modern learning system, which would contribute to the richness and the understanding of law, they were missing out on completely."[128]

In the fall of 1946, Morris entered Osgoode Hall as one of about thirty women in the first year, but many dropped out by Christmas, and only five women in her class completed three years successfully. There were lectures on the usual subjects—but "nothing but legal subjects." She was not a fan of Dr. Wright, describing him as a "woman hater" who believed that women should be in their place—and that place was certainly not in his course: "He would be talking, describing a tort case [involving some accident where] of course there was the usual miscarriage," and he would glare down the aisle at the women. One of her male colleagues told her that although he was awarded first place in Wright's Torts exam, she had

127 OSCLH, oral history, "Joan Morris Hodgson," 30–39. When the Black students went to England in 1946 to be admitted to the bar, they invited Morris to join them, but she declined because she did not feel sufficiently adventurous. Morris recalled that she naively arranged a date for a friend with a Jewish classmate, and that she was very surprised that it created difficulty.

128 OSCLH, oral history, "Joan Morris Hodgson," 41–45, 55, 63–64, 120. Although Morris described going to the Don Jail and the women's prison, there was no practical training; it was all academic, and all courses were compulsory. Kennedy also provided one lecture on relationships between men and women and "how you should treat them." Morris described becoming engaged to a soldier, but the engagement eventually ended. She wrote the Equity exam on VE Day. In 1946, she and her friends went to the parade when the 48th Highlanders returned home, and unbeknownst to her, her future husband, John Hodgson, was part of the parade. She recalled only one experience of exclusion at the university: when it was her turn to sit as a judge for a moot court, and the male student who was sitting as Chief Justice refused to have a woman member.

stood first. When Wright realized a woman stood first, he moved a man to the top.[129]

Morris also recalled a legal recruitment talk by a federal government representative at which her Osgoode classmate Sidney Dymond asked whether these jobs would be available to women. The recruiter paused and then suggested the possibility of good jobs in the secretarial ranks. The women in the class stood up and left. Morris became friends with Bora Laskin and his wife while living in a boarding house near the university campus, and she was grateful for the support offered by the "old guard" at the WLAO: Margaret Hyndman (1926), who always wore a hat in the office; Mabel Van Camp (1947); Vera Parsons (1924); Margaret Grimshaw (1946); and Mary Lamont (1937): "They just couldn't be kind enough, they were wonderful." And, although Morris initially joined the sorority, she resigned when she discovered the exclusion of Black members in the American Club.[130]

Morris obtained articles at Borden & Elliot because her father's employer was a client at the firm. At first, she was ignored, but after standing first in the Christmas examinations, Morris was assigned to prepare litigation briefs, but she obtained no other legal experience, including real estate (the area of law practised by most women in private practice firms). At Osgoode, there were lectures for half the day, articling for the other half, and studying at night. In the fall of third-year, Morris was thrilled when she was invited to join the firm after her call to the bar. Yet, after a senior partner objected to a woman lawyer at the firm, the offer was withdrawn. Morris was furious: "I have an Irish temper. And I was just wild with rage. But I didn't do anything, what could you do? This is 1949. All the veterans had returned, and I am complaining?" Morris interviewed at another firm, where the interviewer explained that the firm did not hire women because an earlier woman hire had made a mistake: "This was like a bomb blast. I

129 OSCLH, oral history, "Joan Morris Hodgson," 90–91, 96–99. Morris concluded that Laskin had given this information to the male student to pass to Morris, without identifying Laskin, because it was a decision that "Bora couldn't tolerate." Dean Kennedy and his family were very friendly toward Morris and invited her to dinner, often with Laskin, and she savoured being "exposed to those minds over the dinner table." Morris recalled the resignations of Dr. Wright and others at Osgoode Hall, but she identified the exodus as occurring in 1950.

130 Morris later realized that she was probably the only woman in Canada to be kissed at the Dominion Store meat counter by the Chief Justice of Canada (Laskin): "Women Alumni Memories," University of Toronto law, "Joan Hodgson." See also OSCLH, oral history, "Joan Morris Hodgson," 91, 93–94, 124.

stood up. I can remember this so vividly, and looked at him, and I said, 'I am delighted to hear that no man ever has.' And I walked out of his office and slammed the door." Morris described being discouraged, but she acknowledged that large numbers of lawyers were being "unloaded" on the market in 1949, and she also recognized her difficulty as a woman lawyer as well as her lack of real estate experience. In the end, her father's employer spoke to Henry Borden and told him to "get her a job, or else." Thus, Morris was hired as junior counsel at Brazilian Traction, a client of Borden and Elliot, where she did corporate legal work.[131]

In 1952, Morris married John Hodgson, an Osgoode classmate, although they did not meet at law school. Hodgson was well along in second-year at the University of Toronto when he was called up for war service in Italy. On his return, the university awarded him a BA without further study, so he entered Osgoode Hall in 1946. He articled at Blakes and then joined the firm, doing wills and estates and tax as well as legal work relating to charities. Morris continued to work for Brazilian Traction for a year until she became pregnant and resigned because "you didn't work when you were pregnant." Although her husband was initially supportive of her continuing to work after their children were born, society was less understanding, and Morris Hodgson opted to stay home with her children.[132]

Her spouse insisted that they continue to pay her Law Society fees, so Morris Hodgson did bylaws for charities and worked with Janet Lang Boland doing real estate searches. In 1970, during a trip with her husband, when he was President of the Ontario branch of the Canadian Bar Association, Joseph Cornish, Area Director for legal aid, asked whether she was working. When she said no, he responded, "This is ridiculous. I want you in my office [at the Ontario Legal Aid Plan] at ten o'clock on Monday morning. I need help." Morris Hodgson worked there three days a week

131 OSCLH, oral history, "Joan Morris Hodgson," 78–87, 100–101. When the board travelled from Brazil for the annual meeting, she was responsible for keeping all the wives entertained between formal occasions: "I had to keep them happy." She was well treated by the company, although the secretaries were often perplexed because they "couldn't get me into a slot."

132 OSCLH, oral history, "Joan Morris Hodgson," 70–71, 95, 103–4, 108–10, 127–28. According to Morris Hodgson, she had a "lovely time" as a mother, although she also recalled how she and two of her children had chicken pox at the same time. See also Graydon, *Some Reminiscences of Blakes,* 44–45, identifying John Hodgson's father, Gregory, who had worked at Blakes after being called to the bar in 1924.

for more than twenty years, conducting interviews for criminal and civil legal aid certificates. On one occasion, while helping a man with the application form, she asked whether he had a criminal record, and "he pulled himself up and looked at me and said, 'Ma'am, I am a professional criminal.'" Morris Hodgson recalled the plan in these early years as generous and caring: "To go back to that kind of thing after being away from law was great, because it combined being attached to the legal profession, but also keeping the feeling that you were doing good things." After the Law Society turned over legal aid to the government, it became more restrictive, and Morris Hodgson found that she was often being told what to do, or not, and it stopped being fun. She was happy to retire, although she continued to serve on a number of boards, and she was appointed QC.[133]

Morris Hodgson remained especially proud of her honours law graduation from the University of Toronto, having completed the additional courses and examinations for the LLB degree in 1948 during her time at Osgoode Hall. In contrast, she disparaged the LLB degrees conferred on lawyers who had graduated from Osgoode Hall up to 1960, at the special ceremony at York University in 1991. She died in October 2022. At her funeral, lawyer and god-daughter Caroline King explained how "to the last, she relished the law; its foibles, its possibilities and its power; and her mentorship and friendship were great gifts to all the young lawyers and people she encouraged and challenged."[134]

Morris Hodgson remembered her classmate, Elizabeth (Betsy) Robson, who was also called to the bar in June 1949. Robson graduated from McMaster University and then Osgoode Hall, and she articled in Hamilton with John O'Reilly. Robson practised for ten years in Hamilton, initially with J.A. Sweet, KC, where her name was listed in parentheses, and then at White, Paikin & Robson at 20½ King Street East. She was also employed as a trust officer for the Eastern and Chartered Trust Co. in Toronto for eight years, administering estates. In 1967, Robson was appointed Town Solicitor

133 OSCLH, oral history, "Joan Morris Hodgson," 117–27, 139–44, 146–50. Her spouse, John Hodgson, continued to work as a partner emeritus at Blakes until December 2010. He died in January 2011 after fifty-eight years of marriage: obituary, *Globe and Mail* (28 January 2011).

134 OSCLH, oral history, "Joan Morris Hodgson," 130–31, 102–3, Addendum. See also Osgoode Hall Law School of York University, "Special Convocation" (15 June 1991); and Caroline King, "Joan Weir Morris Hodgson, QC: Lawyer, Leader, Pioneer" (archived remarks forwarded by C. King to M.J. Mossman).

in Burlington, where her work required her to appear in court. As the press reported: "Quietly, almost gently, she questions her witness. Confident, efficient and to the point, a down-to-earth lawyer who conducts the case with the ease and self-assurance that can only come after years of training and hard work."[135]

Some regarded Robson's self-assurance in the courtroom as especially remarkable because she had been handicapped since childhood with deformed hands and feet. Others felt the challenge of overcoming such a disability made "Elizabeth Robson the person she is." In 1976, Robson was appointed a judge of the Waterloo Judicial District Court in Kitchener, and in 1981 she transferred to the Grey County Court in Owen Sound. Judge Robson sentenced a farmer to six months in jail after he lied to the bank about the size of his cattle herd, probably one of the first of the "farm gate defence" protests. Robson died of cancer in 1985 at the age of sixty. Ken Rae, Grey County's Crown Attorney, described Robson as a "very gallant lady" and among the earliest women lawyers appointed a County Court judge in Ontario.[136]

Barbara Duncan, also in the class of 1949, was called to the bar in June. She graduated from the University of Toronto with a BA before entering Osgoode Hall. As Morris Hodgson recalled, Duncan "was gorgeous looking and the men would be falling all over her." She articled with a real estate firm and then practised at Gregory, Armstrong, Kemp & Young at 372 Young Street. After several years, Duncan requested a leave from the firm to study in Geneva, but the request was denied, and Duncan "got fed up with [the firm and said] To hell with you." She resigned and went to Geneva to study international law, where she became friends with American students. She later settled in Boston, but because she had no wish to become an American citizen, she could not practise law. Thus, Duncan

135 LSO Archives, OBBRP, "Elizabeth Ann Robson"; *Canadian Law Lists*; OSCLH, oral history, "Joan Morris Hodgson," 76; and obituary, "Elizabeth Robson," *Toronto Star* (5 November 1985). See also "Female Lawyer: Adversity a Challenge," *Burlington Gazette* (15 September 1971). In her spare time, Robson translated books into Braille for the Canadian National Institute for the Blind.

136 Obituary, *Globe and Mail* (5 November 1985). In these farm gate defence protests, farmers regularly banded together physically to defend their farms from receivers.

worked in a trust company doing legal work with another lawyer signing her work.[137]

The fourth woman called to the bar in June 1949 was Sidney Dymond, the daughter of an investment broker in Toronto. Dymond's paternal grandfather was a lawyer who had worked as legislative counsel for the Parliament Buildings from 1891 until his death in 1932, and Dymond's mother was a Denton and a cousin of Laura Denton Duff (1920). After Dymond's parents separated, she and her brother lived with their mother in Unionville in the mid-1930s. At the age of twelve, Dymond started high school at St. Clements in Toronto, travelling to school from Unionville with a neighbour who was a lawyer on the Danforth. She recalled that he turned off the gas and coasted down hills to save money during the Depression. Dymond studied languages, math, and history at high school, but only one course in science was offered to students at that time. She was especially impressed by the principal of St. Clements, who instilled a sense of duty to the country, and to the world, in Dymond and her classmates. Although her family didn't suffer badly during the Depression, they learned to live economically and, like many others who lived through these years, she never got over the experience.[138]

Dymond enrolled at Trinity College in 1941, but after her brother went overseas in November, she began to have a guilty conscience because she was "progressing in school ... enjoying [herself], and he is overseas and that just didn't feel right at all." She knew that women were working in factories and picking fruit during the summer to support the war effort. At the end of her second year at Trinity, Dymond joined the women's division of the navy in July 1943. After training near Montreal and then Ottawa, she was posted to Moncton as a wireless operator. She was discharged in 1945 and completed her third year at Trinity in 1946—the university also granted her a fourth-year honours degree, based on her war service.[139]

137 OSCLH, oral history, "Joan Morris Hodgson," 105–6. According to Morris Hodgson, Duncan's parents had made a summer home in Kennebunkport, which Duncan inherited but eventually sold, and then had her new home built there.

138 OSCLH, oral history, "Madam Justice Sidney Dymond," 2, 6, 9–14, 24–29; and Huckle, "List of Women Barristers and Solicitors."

139 OSCLH, oral history, "Madam Justice Sidney Dymond," 33, 37–46, 70; and LSO Archives, OBBRP, "Sidney Dymond." The Department of Veterans Affairs paid for her third year of university, as well as tuition fees at Osgoode and a monthly allowance.

Dymond entered Osgoode Hall in the fall of 1946, and she articled with Harry Parkinson at Parkinson, Gardiner & Willis in Toronto, the firm where Sybil Bennett (1930) had articled. The Department of Veterans Affairs paid her tuition, and she earned five dollars per week at her articling position in the first year, rising to ten dollars per week in the third year. Dymond recalled that the instructors at Osgoode, including Wright and Laskin, lectured about cases and that students were expected to go to the library at lunch or in the evening to read them. She also explained that her large class, which began with 360 students, had lectures in Convocation Hall, and that she sat beside Thelma Kerr (1949). Dymond stood fifth in the graduating class of 248 graduates, but a large number of students failed because admission to Osgoode required only "the lowest of the pass BA's," and veterans were regularly admitted without any university education. Dymond also attended some WLAO meetings, which she recalled were held at members' homes, "a social group, meeting for cookies and coffee." She attended Kappa Beta Pi, known as "can you bake a pie?," but she ceased her involvement when she discovered that Black women were excluded.[140]

Dymond had trouble finding employment after being called to the bar in 1949 because "nobody would accept women." In addition, although she had spent six months articling at the Ontario Labour Relations Board, she found that both unions and companies did not want women in labour law. After her call to the bar, she worked briefly at the office of the Public Trustee, and then worked at the firm of Ryan, McAlpine & Ryan at 1865 Danforth Avenue; her name was added to the firm in 1951. Significantly, this firm expected its clients to accept a woman lawyer, explaining to them: "If you don't want her, then we don't want you." She had a general practice: real estate, estates, and company law, but she also did minor criminal litigation. In 1951, she acted for an accused charged with offences under the *Liquor Control Act*, and she succeeded in having the charges dismissed because her client had been charged pursuant to the wrong section of the Act. In addition, she embarrassed the police by noting that the seals on

140 OSCLH, oral history, "Madam Justice Sidney Dymond," 46, 60–69. Dymond recalled a consensus at Osgoode Hall that women law students were not able to succeed academically. She also described Convocation Hall as having little desks, with kitchen chairs, all in rows. The professor was in the middle with his back to the coloured windows and a little table in front of him. The microphone didn't always work. The room was packed, and there were students in the balcony. "It wasn't what you called conducive to good teaching for anybody." Dymond was unaware of students who were Jewish.

two bottles of liquor, which had been intact when they were introduced into evidence initially, had been broken—the bottles had been placed in a locker for which only three detectives had keys.[141]

In 1965, Dymond was invited to join the University of Toronto at its new Office of Research Administration, initially as executive secretary to the Vice-President, Research Administration. She was later appointed director of the office, and then Vice-Provost, Research Administration. She used her legal training in relation to research about patents, inventions, and copyright, and she was appointed QC in 1970.[142] A few years later, in 1973, Dymond was appointed Judge at Large for the County and District courts and was assigned to Brampton. At the time, she believed that she was the second woman appointed to the County Court after Janet Lang Boland (1950), who had been appointed in 1972. Dymond also explained that she did not apply for a judicial appointment: "I thought I would like to be a County Court Judge. And I mentioned this to a friend, who then put the wheels in motion and I just sat back and eventually had a call from Otto Lang [then Minister of Justice]. I didn't have to do anything, other than that one mention. Because there was no applying the way you do today.[143]

Dymond lamented the absence of formal judicial education, but she learned by watching other judges and seeking guidance from them. In 1975, she moved to the York Judicial District Court and became a County Court judge in 1983, and from 1990 to 1992, she was a justice of the Ontario Court of Justice (General Division). Although she kept a stern courtroom, Dymond also had a strong sense of compassion for victims. Nonetheless, when she presided over a rape case, in which for the first time the accused consented to being labelled a dangerous offender and requested a sentence of life imprisonment, Judge Dymond handed down an indefinite jail term: "I cannot ever say there is no hope for anyone." Dymond was a past board

141 OSCLH, oral history, "Madame Justice Sidney Dymond," 56, 70–77, 81; and OSCLH, oral history, "Joan Morris Hodgson," 75. See also "Who Broke Seals on Liquor, Portia Asks Police, Client Freed," *Telegram* (29 September 1951). The charge was dismissed by County Magistrate Martin. See also LSO Archives, OBBRP, "Sidney Dymond"; and Huckle, "List of Women Barristers and Solicitors."

142 OSCLH, oral history, "Madam Justice Sidney Dymond," 97–104. In her work at the University's Research Administration, Dymond regretted her lack of science in high school.

143 OSCLH, oral history, "Madame Justice Sidney Dymond," 105. Dymond was unaware that she was the third woman judge in the County Court, after Lang Boland and also Helen Kinnear (1920), who had been appointed decades earlier in 1943. Dymond described the Brampton courthouse as "a mess" and badly designed.

member of the Toronto General Hospital and the Ontario College of Art. Joan Morris Hodgson regarded her as a "very, very dear friend, a wonderful woman, and a brilliant judge." Moreover, Dymond had "a lot of drive because of who she was, and not her gender," an "outspoken lawyer [who] made her way in a man's world."[144]

In September 1949, Thelma Kerr, later Thomson, was called to the bar, the only woman in a group of sixty students. Her father was a chartered accountant, and she had attended Branksome Hall, a private girls' school in Toronto. With Joan Morris, Kerr attended the law program at the University of Toronto before enrolling at Osgoode Hall. At the university, Kerr recalled helping to create an International House for foreign students, including some refugees from Germany. Like other women in these years, Kerr experienced difficulty finding articles: "There was a feeling that a woman shouldn't be taking a place a veteran could." After her father's intervention, she obtained articles at McMillan Binch, the first female student at this firm. Although the firm had an office for law students, Kerr was relegated to the library "so they could watch me and make sure I wasn't demoralizing the male students." During articles, she was sent to arrest a ship in the harbour by pinning a warrant to the mast; she said she "imagined all the sailors peeping up my skirt."[145]

At the University of Toronto, Kerr helped another student, David Thomson, who had returned from war service to complete his degree, and they became friends. Thomson also attended Osgoode Hall and was called to the bar in 1948. Prior to his call to the bar, Thomson articled at the British American Oil Company, and when one of the clients at McMillan Binch sued the company, her firm asked Kerr to cease her relationship with Thomson. She responded by announcing their engagement, while also

144 LSO Archives, OBBRP, "Sidney Dymond"; Huckle, "List of Women Barristers and Solicitors"; and OSCLH, oral history, "Joan Morris Hodgson," 75, 106. See also obituary, *Toronto Star* (23 March 2000) B5. Dymond acknowledged that she might be softer in sentencing but that she was tougher on evidence, and she confirmed that she found criminal cases fascinating: OSCLH, oral history, "Madam Justice Sidney Dymond," 114, 122.

145 M.M. Cushnie-Mansour, *A 20th Century Portia: Biography of Thelma Bernice Kerr-Thomson* (Brantford, ON: Cavern of Dreams Publishing, 2011). See also Cushnie-Monsour, "Seniors: A 20th Century Portia," *Expositor* (28 July 2008); OSCLH, oral histories, "Joan Morris Hodgson," 32; and "Thelma Thomson, 48," *Nexus* (University of Toronto Faculty of Law) (Fall/Winter 2005). Kerr-Thomson suggested that she had married a poor preacher's son against her father's wishes and that, at the beginning of their practice together, they "worked over the same old tea bags for days."

explaining that they never discussed legal work. Kerr married Thomson in 1949; with a gift of one thousand dollars from her father, they set up a practice in Lindsay. Their office was located over a Chinese laundry and a café, and they lived in two rooms beside the office. Kerr Thomson was the first woman lawyer in Lindsay, and she frequently spoke at women's organizations, encouraging women to make wills and to serve on juries. At a celebration of the first anniversary of the establishment of a branch of the Business and Professional Women's Club in Lindsay in 1950, Kerr Thomson introduced Margaret Hyndman (1926), the guest speaker. The press report described Kerr Thomson as "Lindsay's Lady Lawyer, Mrs David Thomson." She was also elected secretary-treasurer of the Federation of Law Societies, District No. 6, at its annual meeting in Cobourg in 1950, and she was a featured speaker at a meeting of the Local Council of Women in 1953.[146]

Two sons were born in 1955 and 1957, and Kerr Thomson practised part-time at the office for a few years and then returned to full-time practice. On one occasion, she recalled having to obtain a client's signature—in the middle of a cow pasture, wearing heels, hose, hat and gloves, and "batting the cows aside with my briefcase." She also successfully defended a client charged with careless driving in police court by calling an expert witness (a mechanic), who gave evidence about a failure in the car's steering mechanism. In 1967, the Thomsons established a new office in Lindsay with additional lawyers, and Kerr Thomson opened a branch office in Fenelon Falls. She was a member of the board of the Ross Memorial Hospital in Lindsay as well as solicitor for the hospital, and she participated in the IODE, the Lindsay Art Guild, and the University Women's Club. The Thomsons were both active in the Liberal Party, and Kerr Thomson was elected to the constitution committee of the Ontario Women's Liberal Association and then appointed to the constitution committee of the Liberal Party of Ontario.[147]

With a specialty in wills and estates, Kerr Thomson was active in the Wills and Trusts section of the Canadian Bar Association. In 1973, she was one of four lawyers involved in a one-hour program on wills and estates,

146 *Watchman-Warder* (22 November 1950): "Mrs. Thomson" was an active member of the Business and Professional Women's Club." See also *Toronto LEX* (December 1950), which misspelled her name as "Thompson"; LSO Archives, OBBRP, "Thelma Kerr Thomson"; and OSCLH, oral history, "Joan Morris Hodgson," 32, 106. Morris Hodgson and Kerr Thomson stayed in contact after 1949.

147 Cushnie-Mansour, *A 20th Century Portia.*

part of thirteen recordings about legal subjects for cable television organized by a committee of the CBA–Ontario, chaired by Lorraine Gotlib (1959). In 1974, David Thomson was appointed a judge of the County Court in Windsor, although he later resigned for health reasons. In 1979, Kerr Thomson attended the thirtieth anniversary of her class at Osgoode Hall, and she recorded her views as a woman in law in a letter to Justice Bora Laskin, the guest speaker at the event.

> One of the things we [women graduates in 1949] had in common, apart from the general prejudice against females being privileged to partake of so much of the cup of knowledge, was the additional stress of competing against distinguished war veterans for whom the country was rolling out the red carpet and extending all favours from financial to obtaining articles of clerkship [creating a very real special problem for women in law at that time]."

Despite these challenges, Kerr Thomson concluded that she had enjoyed an interesting life. She died in Brantford in 2012.[148]

These stories of women who were called to the bar in 1940s reveal new wartime opportunities but also many postwar challenges. As Kerr Thomson (1949) noted, societal views about different—gendered—roles continued to create significant barriers for women in law in the 1950s

148 *Globe and Mail* (31 October 1973); Cushnie-Mansour, *A 20th Century Portia*; LSO Archives, OBBRP, "Thelma Kerr Thomson," and Thelma Kerr Thomson name file, letter to Justice Bora Laskin (26 May 1979).

CHAPTER SIX

# *Transitions in Law and Legal Education, 1950–57*

> *By displaying middle-class femininity and choosing less confrontational (and less prestigious) branches of law, women lawyers deviated from the ideal image of the lawyer but [they] also represented somewhat less of a threat in terms of gender expectations because they were not entirely acting like men either. This approach helped some women negotiate their way through sexism, although as late as 1956, Dean Smalley-Baker referred to the female students as "members of the contrary sex."*[1]

Societal views about women's primary role as homemakers, which began to regain strong currency after the war, created difficult challenges for women called to the Ontario bar in the 1950s. Male lawyers continued to be skeptical about women's professional aspirations, while the legal profession prioritized the needs of returning veterans for articling positions and employment. Thus, the number of women students at Osgoode Hall did not increase substantially in the 1950s, and some women graduates practised law only briefly. Between 1950 and 1957, only forty-two women joined

1 Brunet, M., *Becoming Lawyers: Gender, Legal Education and Professional Identity Formation in Canada, 1920–1980* (PhD diss., University of Toronto, 2005) [unpublished] 208, 235. See also "From Your Dean," *Obiter Dicta* (Fall 1956) 66.

the Ontario legal profession. In contrast, more than three hundred women became Ontario lawyers between 1958 and 1975.[2]

From 1950, the Osgoode Hall law program lasted four years, rather than only three, and graduates of the law program at the University of Toronto were required to complete only the final two years at Osgoode Hall to be called to the bar. But in 1950 seven women were called to the bar after completing the three-year program. Three women were admitted in June, when 34 of the 153 new lawyers were sons or daughters of lawyers. A news photo included Patricia Cooper and Janet Lang Boland, both of Toronto, and Judy LaMarsh of Niagara Falls.[3] Although Huckle reported that Patricia Cooper married F. Dullege and moved to Florida, there is some evidence that Cooper returned to Ontario in the 1950s, practising law as Patricia Cooper.[4]

Janet Lang, later Boland/Statten, grew up in Kitchener, one of three daughters. Her father, who encouraged her to enter law, was a vice-president of the Lang Tanning Company, the largest tanning company in the British Empire. Lang's family was Catholic, and she attended a Catholic high school in the United States and then Waterloo College. Although she did not recall financial challenges during the Depression, she remembered that her mother often provided sandwiches and blueberry pie to tramps on their back verandah. Lang recalled that her first-year class at Osgoode Hall in 1946 had about five hundred students, many of them men in uniform. Her favourite course was Torts with Dr. Wright, but she said Falconbridge was the best professor: "A pin didn't drop in his class." She

2 E. Huckle, "List of Women Barristers and Solicitors in Ontario, 1897–1975" [unpublished, archived at Law Society of Ontario Archives].

3 Law Society of Ontario (LSO) Archives (LSO), Women's Law Association of Ontario (WLAO) fonds, unidentified photo (June 1950). In 1950, the first women students were admitted to Harvard Law School: "Some Facts and a Few Figures," *Harvard Law School Record* (4 October 1950). In Ontario, the WLAO continued to offer support and collegial activities for women lawyers in the 1950s, and there were forty-one active members in 1951: LSO Archives, WLAO fonds, Scrapbook (SB), vol. 3, list of WLAO members, 1951.

4 Huckle, "List of Women Barristers and Solicitors"; and *Canadian Law Lists*. "Patricia Claire Cooper" was listed at Goodenough & Co, and at Higginbottom, McDonnell & Colville in the 1950s and '60s: *Canadian Law Lists*. She may have been suspended administratively: Law Society of Ontario, "Ontario Lawyer and Paralegal Directory," online database.

also recalled her classmate, Judy LaMarsh, and saw early signs that Judy would go into politics.[5]

Lang articled initially at Blake Cassels, working in real estate and doing title searches, estate work, and litigation. Department heads gave lectures once a month, followed by dinner and discussions about legal practice, and she especially enjoyed Arthur Patillo's sessions when he presented facts and then requested students' opinions. In 1947, after concluding that Blakes was too big, Lang transferred her articles to Beaton, Bell & Leek. She recalled that Beaton, a member of the Law Society's Legal Education Committee, shared the report that "fired" Dean Wright and Bora Laskin in 1949, a decision that she thought surprised many people. After the faculty departed, there were no longer courses in Evidence and Labour Law. Practitioners, including Arthur Martin, Charles Dubin, and John Robinette, were involved in teaching; and Colonel Foster continued to teach the Practice course.[6]

In her final year, Lang married John Boland, who attended law school after serving in the navy. He joined the Aetna Insurance Company, later becoming real estate manager of Crown Trust. After her call to the bar, Lang Boland practised from home. Although she had two little sons, she believed that lawyers in her graduating class often practised alone, at least initially: it was "very hard to get a job in those days [because the] market was glutted." Lang did real estate and wills, searched titles and interviewed witnesses for law firms, and reported for the *Ontario Weekly Notes* and in the Court of Appeal. Her husband's secretary worked for her at night, and she had a telephone-answering service. Lang recalled that her clients were diverse and that she served "hordes and hordes" of Chinese clients after

5 Osgoode Society for Canadian Legal History (OSCLH), oral history, "Janet Lang Boland," 1–38. Joan Morris Hodgson recalled that Janet Lang had been among several hundred students, including many returning veterans, in her first-year class in 1946 and that Lang was among the large number of students who failed first-year. Morris Hodgson recalled that Janet was a determined woman and that she re-entered the three-year program at Osgoode Hall in 1947: OSCLH, oral history, "Joan Morris Hodgson," 76–77; and LSO Archives, Ontario Bar Biographical Research Project (OBBRP), "Janet Lang Boland."

6 OSCLH, oral history, "Janet Lang Boland," 26–41, 122–23. It is possible that Lang could not continue articles at Blakes after failing first-year. LSO records indicate that Lang articled in Kitchener with James Sims, and there is no mention of articles at either of the Toronto firms identified by Lang Boland: LSO Archives, OPPRP, "Janet Lang Boland." Lang recalled enjoying her usual summer employment at the Taylor Statten camps in Algonquin Park after the first year at Osgoode Hall.

providing good service to a Chinese client who purchased a store with her help. She also obtained clients because she was a woman.

> In those days there were not very many women lawyers and [at a party, guests] would be interested in me because I am a woman, and particularly if it was a woman, although ... more of my clients were men ... and most people don't know lawyers and they don't know how to find them. And you couldn't advertise. And ... the next thing I would ... have a phone call, "will you draw me a will?" Or, "could you advise on this," or, "I need to buy a store," or "I want to adopt a baby," or any of these sorts of things.[7]

Lang Boland worked at home until her sons were aged six and four. She had been hired earlier at the White, Bristol firm to conduct title searches of the Bronfman properties, but she also acquired expertise in drafting shopping centre leases when she accompanied her husband to seminars on leases in the United States. Thus, when she joined White, Bristol, she became one of the first Toronto lawyers with expertise in this new area of practice. Eventually, Lang Boland took charge of real estate at the firm and remained there for eight years. She was appointed QC in 1966, and a few years later she followed a commercial lawyer colleague to the Lang Michener firm, where she was offered a partnership. At this firm, there were fifteen partners, including five senior partners; Governor General Roland Michener had practised there, and Senator Daniel Lang was also connected to the firm. Lang Boland had her own clients and did commercial and real estate work.[8]

Lang Boland recalled working with a senior partner whose client was a mortgagee for Rochdale College. She was required to attend at Rochdale each week to do minutes and arrange payments.

---

7 OSCLH, oral history, "Janet Lang Boland," 31–45, 49–51. A news report suggested that Lang Boland "plainly winked at Law Society Treasurer, Cyril Carson" as she was called to the bar: D. Howarth, "Woman Grad [Judy LaMarsh] Honored for Coffee Shop Help," *Telegram* (30 June 1950). Lang Boland described how Mr. Harvey asked her to write a case report for an important Court of Appeal decision, a task she undertook while in hospital after giving birth to her second child.

8 OSCLH, oral history, "Janet Lang Boland," 46–48, 54–60. Lang Boland noted that some of her shopping centre leases had spelling mistakes, which were also evident in leases drafted by other lawyers who used her templates. She regarded Peter White at White, Bristol as an outstanding lawyer.

> It was a horror story ... We would have a meeting of the Board of Directors and one of the Directors would be a white pussy cat, and so it really was like going into Alice in Wonderland, it was a wild place, and there would be people lying all over the place ... They had iron doors that would come down when the police were coming. It was a beautiful situation, there were all sorts of places to have lectures and lovely dining halls in residences that were just ruined by being painted and people were always jumping out of the windows on LSD ... It was scary.[9]

In 1972, after four years at Lang Michener, Lang Boland was appointed a junior judge of the York County Court (later District Court). She was the second woman appointed to the County Court in Ontario (after Helen Kinnear in Cayuga, in 1943) and the first in the County of York. The *Toronto Star* reported that she was appointed to the court because of "her brains and ability." Lang Boland never practised litigation, but she taught in the Bar Admission program, reported for the Court of Appeal, had a good grounding in commercial law, and read the law reports. She recalled receiving support from her new judicial colleagues, and how she heard jurors whispering when she entered the court for a jury trial because they had never seen a woman judge. She also had to learn criminal law. Her first case involved a charge relating to forty pounds of Chinese heroin. She found the accused guilty and sentenced him to life imprisonment: "I think it was the

9 OSCLH, oral history, "Janet Lang Boland," 61–64. Senator Dan Lang was still involved at the Lang Michener firm when Lang Boland (no relation) was there. Although Senator Lang was a Liberal, and others in the firm were active politically, Lang Boland was not active in politics.

first time anyone in the County Court in Toronto had given anyone a life sentence. So, I never looked back after that one."[10]

In 1976, Lang Boland was appointed to the Supreme Court of Ontario, becoming the second woman judge at the court after Mabel Van Camp (1947), who had been appointed in 1971. When John Boland died about six months after her appointment, and her third and youngest son was only fourteen, Chief Justice Estey suggested she take on family law to allow her to sit in Toronto. After a two-week course at the Judicial College in Nevada, she presided in the new Family Law Division for two years, hearing cases pursuant to the *Family Law Reform Act* of 1978, where she introduced the principle of joint custody in *Baker v Baker*. As Lang Boland recalled, the Family Law Division was a heavy load, with up to thirty-five motions each day: "You had to move and perhaps you didn't give lawyers as much time as they would like, and certainly as I would have liked to give them. But you had to keep moving." After two years of family law cases, Lang Boland returned to the assizes.[11]

In 1979, Justice Boland received an honorary doctorate from her alma mater, which had become Wilfrid Laurier University. She attributed her successful career to her helpful husband, her wonderful housekeeper, and

10 H. Worthington, "First Woman named Judge in York County," *Toronto Star* (4 February 1972); and "Metro Woman Named County Court Judge on Turner's Last Day," *Toronto Star* (2 January 1972). See also *Brantford Expositor* (22 February 1972); and obituary, *Globe and Mail* (16 March 2019) B21. Lang Boland's appointment occurred a few months after Mabel Van Camp had been appointed to the Supreme Court of Ontario, and John Turner, who appointed Boland, then relinquished his position as Minister of Justice to become Minister of Finance. Although Lang Boland recalled that a woman had been appointed to the County Court some years before her appointment, she did not recall her name: see Helen Kinnear (1920), who was appointed in 1943, and Chapter Three. Lang Boland described an early case in Small Claims Court in which she began to render judgment after hearing only the plaintiff, and she recalled how the clerk looked at her and said, "You know, the defendants have come from a long way away, don't you want to hear what they are going to say?": OSCLH, oral history, "Janet Lang Boland," 65–73.

11 OSCLH, oral history, "Janet Lang Boland," 80–121; LSO Archives, "Diversifying the Bar," Janet Lang Boland; and obituary, *Globe and Mail* (16 March 2019) B21. Lang Boland eventually presided over seventy-eight murder trials. Her family law decision in *Baker v Baker*, (1978) 3 RFL (2d) 193, was appealed to the Ontario Court of Appeal, where the court stated that since neither party had requested joint custody, there was no basis in evidence and no justification in law to award it in this case: see (1979) 23 OR (2d) 391 (Ont CA). A majority of the appeal court reached a similar conclusion in *Kruger v Kruger* (1979) 25 OR (2d) 673 (Ont CA), with a dissent by Wilson JA.

her sons' good health. Some colleagues suggested that she was an excellent judicial appointment because of her ability to understand people and to communicate effectively. Lang Boland herself suggested that "there's a great advantage in being a woman in law. The men take extra care of me." She never applied to become a judge, and she believed that she never encountered the glass ceiling: "It was just happening to be on the right corner at the right time, and I think John Turner was looking for a woman ... I didn't know John Turner, but he must have known a lot about my firm ... and that might have helped. I was very lucky to be in the right place at the right time."[12]

Lang Boland's classmate, who had shared her call-to-the-bar ceremony in 1950, was Julia (Judy) LaMarsh. She grew up in Chatham and Niagara Falls, where her father practised law, including criminal and municipal law. Her parents were Liberal supporters, and LaMarsh recalled the tears of joy in her home when "Mitch Hepburn's legions first took Ontario" in 1934. After high school, LaMarsh tried to join the Women's Division of the Air Force, but she was rejected because of poor eyesight. She attended the Normal School in Hamilton for a year to obtain a primary teaching certificate, intending to earn money as a teacher to pay for legal education. Instead, LaMarsh joined the Canadian Women's Army Corps, received training in drafting, and was posted to Halifax. Very soon, her ability to learn new languages resulted in an opportunity to study Japanese in Vancouver, a period that she described as "the hardest work of my life." Her proficiency in Japanese resulted in a secondment with two other Canadians to join a combined British, American, and Canadian operation in the United States engaged in translating thousands of pieces of paper picked up in the jungles of the Pacific. At war's end, using her veteran's entitlement, LaMarsh attended Victoria College at the University of Toronto and

12 *Toronto Star* (4 February 1972). See also OSCLH, oral history, "Janet Lang Boland," 66–68, 123–24; LSO Archives, "Diversifying the Bar," Janet Lang Boland; and *Globe and Mail* (23 November 1979). In 2000, Lang Boland married Dr. Taylor Statten: obituary, *Globe and Mail* (16 March 2019) B21.

completed all the courses for a degree in thirteen months. She enrolled at Osgoode Hall in the fall of 1947.[13]

LaMarsh said she experienced no discrimination at Victoria College or at Osgoode Hall, but she recalled a discouraging seminar about legal careers at the university, presented by John Arnup, who studiously ignored her presence. When she inquired "point blank" about conditions for women in the legal profession, LaMarsh recalled that: "He told me that women would not stick to their jobs, and that most law firms, forced to hire women during the war as law students, would refuse, now that the men were returning, to give women training because they would soon be leaving for marriage and motherhood."[14]

LaMarsh was called to the bar in June 1950 at the age of twenty-six, and, as President of the law school's Legal and Literary Society, she received a Gold Key honour award, based on her untiring efforts to establish a coffee shop and a Coke machine for students at Osgoode Hall. A steady but not brilliant student, she was one of the leading figures in the law school: "Everywhere you looked, there was Judy, organizing something." LaMarsh returned to Niagara Falls to practise law with her father for ten years, She was as noisy and effective in court as in school. Notably, in her first year in practice in 1951, she addressed a meeting of the Canadian Bar Association in Ottawa, proposing a motion to encourage the provincial government

13 A. Burke, "The Exuberant Miss LaMarsh" (1964) 3:2 *Weekend Magazine* 23; and J. LaMarsh, *Memoirs of a Bird in a Gilded Cage* (Toronto: McClelland & Stewart, 1968) 1–2. Credits for her one-year course at Normal School and her veteran's status may have helped to meet the requirements for the BA in record time. See also H. Robertson, "The Honourable Judy" in M. Kostash, et al., *Her Own Woman: Profiles of Ten Canadian Women* (Toronto: Macmillan, 1975) 1 at 10, reporting that LaMarsh was discharged from the army in 1945. In contrast, a report focused on her mark of 80 per cent in Japanese-language training, indicated that LaMarsh was discharged in 1946: K. Kritzwiser, "The MP Who Shuns Back Seats," *Globe Magazine* (7 January 1961) 7 at 20.

14 LaMarsh, *Memoirs of a Bird in a Gilded Cage*, 279. LaMarsh later reported that women students at Osgoode Hall found the best firms closed to them, and those that did take women gave only a minimum of experience and training and consistently paid them less than male students. Moreover, in 1968, when LaMarsh had retired from politics and was seeking work at a Toronto law firm, the firm's leader refused to associate with a woman in the practice of law. Law Society records indicate that LaMarsh articled with her father, W.C. LaMarsh, whose location was identified as "Toronto": LSO Archives, OBBRP, "Julia LaMarsh"; and *Canadian Law Lists*. Her date of admission as a student was 1942, perhaps confirming that she attended Normal School (1942–43) to work as a teacher to fund going to Osgoode Hall.

to keep closer checks on the ability and conduct of local magistrates, and she argued that magistrates should be lawyers. Her motion was seconded by her classmate Lillian Irwin; one report suggested that the two women tossed "a bombshell into the deliberations."[15] LaMarsh acted in a dozen rape cases and four murder cases, and she also defended an accused who had been charged with armed robbery, using a stolen car. It turned out to be *her* car! She also appeared in child custody cases, and her courtroom technique included both hard work and a bludgeoning tongue. When her father died in 1957, she took over the firm and succeeded him as solicitor for Stamford Township.[16]

During the 1950s, LaMarsh belonged to every civic and charitable organization in Niagara Falls and held offices in the Young Liberals, the Liberal Women, and the Liberal Party of Canada.[17] She was named the Liberal candidate for a federal by-election in 1960. Her ability to switch from being just "one of the boys" at industrial plants to a lady of perfect decorum at coffee parties won her respect—and votes. She entered Parliament at the age of thirty-five. Although she was the only woman in the Liberal opposition, she quickly established a reputation as a speaker who could use the weapons of ridicule and sarcasm—with lethal effect. Her first speech

15 Huckle, "List of Women Barristers and Solicitors"; *Telegram* (30 June 1950); and *Globe and Mail* (20 June 1950). See also D. MacDonald, "Ability of Magistrates Requires Closer Check Woman Lawyer Argues," *Globe and Mail* (31 March 1951). The meeting also discussed issues about courtroom facilities and legal aid services. See also "Lillian Irwin," in this chapter.

16 LSO Archives, WLAO fonds, "Her Car Used in Holdup, Lawyer Defends Accused," unidentified news report about an armed robbery; and W. Stewart, "The Fighting Lady of Parliament Hill" (ca. 1963) *Canadian Weekly* 2 at 3–4. An Osgoode Hall classmate described LaMarsh as a "loner and too noisy to have a boyfriend." LaMarsh herself compared her litigation style to that of John Diefenbaker. See also *Toronto Daily Star* (3 April 1957); and *Telegram* (4 April 1957). Ruby Wigle Fish (1926) and Lida Pearson Sturdy (1921) had been appointed earlier as town solicitors in Galt, and Elizabeth Robson (1949) was appointed town solicitor in Burlington: see Chapters Three and Five.

17 Robertson, "The Honourable Lady," 5. See also LaMarsh, *Memoirs of a Bird in a Gilded Cage*; *Welland-Pt. Colbourne Tribune* (22 April 1963); and K. Kelly, "I'm All I'm Ever Going to Be," *Winnipeg Free Press* (3 June 1963). In 1952, LaMarsh addressed the Ontario Women's Liberal Association, arguing that wives were second-class citizens, citing the new jury legislation that rightly exempted firemen but also their wives: "Wives Only Second-Class Speaker Tells Association," *Globe and Mail* (24 November 1952). LaMarsh was the only woman delegate to the NATO conference for young political leaders in Paris in 1958: Kritzwiser, "The MP Who Shuns Back Seats," 20.

occurred in a debate on national productivity: "Judy went straight to attack position, charging that one of the more immediate effects of emphasis on higher productivity would be accelerated automation, resulting in fewer jobs, not more." When she later engaged in a verbal battle with Labour Minister Michael Starr, CCF leader Hazen Argue interjected and asked the minister not to be mean to the lady. Starr responded: "Then let the lady be lady-like." When Pauline Jewett was elected for the Liberals in 1963, she was referred to as "a sort of female Judy LaMarsh."[18]

The Liberals formed government in 1963, and LaMarsh became the first Liberal woman Cabinet member after Prime Minister Pearson appointed her Minister of Health and Welfare. Nancy Morrison, a new lawyer who had arranged to work with LaMarsh in her Niagara Falls office, found herself in a sole practice. LaMarsh told her, "I've just been made Minister of Health and Welfare. Here are the keys to my house and here are the keys to my office. And here are the papers for a trial that's coming up in two weeks. Good luck."[19] LaMarsh played a major role in the creation of the (portable) Canada Pension Plan, which she argued was especially necessary for working people.

18 W. Stewart, "The Fighting Lady of Parliament Hill," 4. LaMarsh won the by-election with a plurality of five thousand votes and then doubled her margin in the general elections of 1962 and 1963 when the Progressive Conservatives under Diefenbaker were defeated: LaMarsh, *Memoirs of a Bird in a Gilded Cage*, 6–10, 45–46. See also *Northern Daily News* (Kirkland Lake) (27 April 1961), reporting her criticism of the salaries and expense packages for MPs. Ellen Fairclough, Margaret Aitken, and Jean Casselman were MPs in the Conservative government, but "the red carpet lay between them [and LaMarsh]": Kritzwiser, "The MP Who Shuns Back Seats," 7, 20. W.H. Herridge (CCF Kootenay West) commended LaMarsh for thorough preparation, a thoughtful assessment of the situation, and a deep concern for her constituents who were unemployed. A press analysis of LaMarsh and Jewett was published before the election in 1963: P. Gzowski, "The New Women in Politics," *Maclean's* (21 April 1962).

19 "Woman Judge was Employed in Office of Judy LaMarsh," *St. Thomas Times-Journal* (5 February 1973). Morrison worked in LaMarsh's law office for nearly four years, then returned to her home province, Saskatchewan, and then Vancouver, where she was appointed a Provincial Court judge in 1973 and, eight years later, a judge of the British Columbia Supreme Court: N. Morrison, *Benched: A Passion for Law Reform* (Calgary, AB: Durvile Pubs, 2018); and J. Batten, "Moving Testimony of a Pioneering Woman Lawyer," *Toronto Star* (22 December 2018) E12. In 1977, Morrison visited Osgoode Hall Law School at York University at the invitation of Patricia Hennessy, chair of the John White Society and later a member of the Superior Court of Justice in Ontario.

> We are just beginning to realize the importance of getting people ready to retire. We all know that early retirement is a death sentence. You know the ads, retire to Florida? That's fine but for many, retired early, the alternative is a job as a night watchman. Registering the night's guests at a motel. It's different for the top-level man. He has skills. He's snapped up ... Industry throws its men out too soon. Not nearly enough attention is being paid to this great area and to the waste of labor involved ... We must educate labour and industry not to throw people out at an arbitrary age ... I believe it's most important to be needed. This is true of our men and women.[20]

Although her combative style created problems in the final stages of the Bill's progress in Parliament—and LaMarsh always lamented how special arrangements were negotiated with Québec, her colleagues gave her credit for her back-breaking work. As Stanley Knowles commented, "I happen to know it wasn't easy." In 1965, LaMarsh was appointed Secretary of State with responsibility for Canada's centennial celebrations in 1967. As "virtual queen of the Centennial, she inspired 50,000 people to turn out for birthday cake and patriotism at a grand July 1 bash on Parliament Hill."[21] LaMarsh was instrumental in the appointment of Janet Scott (1951) as chair of the new Immigration Appeals Board in 1967, and she provided support in Cabinet for the Royal Commission on the Status of Women, also

20 *Ottawa Citizen* (23 April 1963). Ellen Fairclough, the first woman member of a federal Cabinet, was initially appointed Secretary of State, and later Minister of Immigration and Postmaster General by Prime Minister Diefenbaker, but she was defeated in the election in 1963. The only Conservative woman elected was Jean Casselman in Grenville-Dundas. For the Liberals, Pauline Jewett was elected for Northumberland and Margaret Konantz for Winnipeg South: *Niagara Falls Review* (23 April 1963). As Minister of Health and Welfare, LaMarsh gave up smoking: Burke, "The Exuberant Miss LaMarsh," 23; and Kritzwiser, "The MP Who Shuns Back Seats," 20–ff. LaMarsh also recommended public housing rather than nursing homes for the aged, and she commented on euthanasia and on beer sales in grocery stores.

21 *Ottawa Journal* (11 April 1968). In addition to her centennial year success, LaMarsh was responsible for the new *Broadcasting Act,* and she was credited with laying the groundwork for the Medical Care Insurance Bill completed by her successor Allan MacEachern: obituary, *Globe and Mail* (28 October 1980); and LaMarsh, *Memoirs of a Bird in a Gilded Cage*, Chapters 5 and 8. See also W. Michener, "The Trouble with Judy," *Chatelaine* (February 1968); and LaMarsh, *Memoirs of a Bird in a Gilded Cage*, 228, which suggested that during the centennial year, Canadians "cast off the bonds of ... conformity. The year 1967 changed us all profoundly."

in 1967.[22] When LaMarsh decided to retire in 1968, she was unsuccessful in gaining the Prime Minister's support for an appointment to the Ontario Court of Appeal—at a time when no woman had yet been appointed to a superior court in any Canadian province.[23]

Even without a judicial appointment, LaMarsh was ready to leave Ottawa because "she felt like a piece of tumbleweed" there, without real roots in a community. Before leaving, she supported Paul Hellyer in his failed leadership race against Pierre Trudeau that year. The press lamented her decision to leave politics: "A basically shy lady lawyer from Niagara Falls [had] transformed herself into a national figure, in part because she was colourful: she cussed openly, she wore miniskirts and fishnet stockings and smashing blonde wigs." Four years later, LaMarsh was practising law in St. Catharines: "The 47-year-old former health and welfare minister ... has settled into a comparatively prosaic career as a small-city lawyer—handling the usual variety of criminal and civil cases, lunching and talking shop with colleagues in a restaurant across from the courthouse and enjoying a seemingly uncharacteristic anonymity." Nonetheless, she publicly criticized the Trudeau government's handling of the October Crisis and asserted that the imposition of the *War Measures Act* was a disastrous mistake—a sorry record.[24] In 1972, she moved to Vancouver to host a hotline program on CKWX, where she quickly topped the king, Jack Webster, in the

22 LaMarsh, *Memoirs of a Bird in a Gilded Cage*, 293–95, 301–2. LaMarsh also tried unsuccessfully to appoint a woman to the superior court in Saskatchewan, but she reported that local interests raised voices to prevent this appointment.

23 Minister of Justice, John Turner, appointed Réjane Laberge-Colas to the Québec Superior Court in 1969 and Mabel Van Camp to the Ontario Supreme Court in 1971: obituary, Réjane Laberge-Colas, *Globe and Mail* (24 August 2009); and obituary, Mabel Van Camp, *Globe and Mail* (9 August 2012). The first woman appointed to the Ontario Court of Appeal was Bertha Wilson in 1975: E. Anderson, *Judging Bertha Wilson: Law as Large as Life* (Toronto: University of Toronto Press/Osgoode Society for Canadian Legal History, 2001) 83–85. LaMarsh also tried to promote Pauline Jewett's career after her election defeat in 1965: *Memoirs of a Bird in a Gilded Cage*, 308.

24 *St. Catharines Standard* (11 April 1968); and *Ottawa Journal* (11 April 1968). LaMarsh and Trudeau openly clashed in Cabinet about judicial appointments in Ontario, and she later acknowledged that she had objected in one case based on knowledge about unethical behaviour by a proposed appointee. Thus, when she counselled Hellyer to defer to Winters in the leadership contest so that "we can ... stop ... the bastard [Trudeau]," a comment picked up by microphones, she claimed it was a private comment: LaMarsh, *Memoirs of a Bird in a Gilded Cage*, 332, 347; and *Toronto Star* (11 April 1968).

ratings. LaMarsh was quoted frequently in the press and rumours circulated about her returning to politics.[25]

In 1973, LaMarsh received a senior appointment as a visiting professor at Osgoode Hall Law School at York University. Dean Harry Arthurs explained that she was the first woman to be appointed to a senior position in the faculty: "We hope that the law school and other legal institutions will be able to make many more such appointments in the years to come." LaMarsh was scheduled to teach two courses: Family Law, and Municipal and Planning Law, and she also agreed to write a weekly column for the *Toronto Star*.[26] She continued to speak out on issues of public concern, including at a conference on women and the law in Ottawa in 1974, where she criticized the Minister of Justice, Otto Lang, on the government's response to the abortion issue. She also advised women to be wary of

25 LaMarsh explained that she discovered that practising law was a young person's game. In addition, her Parliamentary pension of $174 per month often required her to take on several jobs at once: G. Russell, "Small-Town Judy with Big-City Punch," *Weekend Magazine* (17 January 1976) 5. LaMarsh publicly criticized the death penalty and the LeDain Commission on Non-Medical Use of Drugs, *Windsor Star* (14 March 1972); H. Robertson, "The Prime of Ms Judy LaMarsh," *Maclean's* (March 1975) 73; and LSO Archives, LaMarsh fonds, Bencher election file, 1979, when LaMarsh was a candidate. LaMarsh claimed that she buried the hatchet with Prime Minister Trudeau in 1973 and hoped to run in the next election. She also claimed that Trudeau refused to appoint her to Cabinet prior to the election because it was constitutionally improper. Thus, LaMarsh decided not to re-enter politics, claiming that she was supposed to spend ten days "getting myself elected, and the rest of the time running all over the bloody country trying to get *other* people elected," action she refused as a private member of the party: E. Rockett, "So, Judy LaMarsh, What Are You Up to Now?," *Chatelaine* (October 1973) 99.

26 *Toronto Star* (7 September 1973); and *Globe and Mail* (7 September 1973). Arthurs's comment failed to recognize that other law schools appointed women in tenure-track positions in the early 1970s: Baines, "Early Women in the Canadian Legal Academy" in A. Lund and V. Torrie, eds., *Early Women in the Canadian Legal Academy* (Vancouver, UBC Press, forthcoming 2024). In addition to her visitorship, LaMarsh was appointed a Unity Bank director, she conducted a weekly phone-in television show, and she appeared frequently as a political commentator for the CBC. She also attended meetings about the reform of family law and divorce: Robertson, "The Prime of Ms Judy LaMarsh," 73.

legislation based on the Ontario Law Reform Commission's recommendations on family law.[27]

Although LaMarsh's appointment to the faculty at Osgoode Hall Law School appeared to signal its interest in women faculty members, her appointment was not permanent—and it ended after two years, in 1975. At the time, she noted that she had felt like the figurehead for having women on staff, and she did a lot of public speaking for the law school, speaking that normally formed part of her income.[28] In February 1975, at a panel discussion about women and law, LaMarsh spoke about gender discrimination in the legal profession, and another panellist, Barbara Betcherman (1974), then an articling student, listed personal questions she had experienced in interviews: whether she was a virgin, whether she intended to marry, and what type of birth control she practised. LaMarsh confirmed that women continued to experience problems after passing the bar.

> The attitude toward women law students does not change when they are called to the bar, but becomes worse. Women are not given the same opportunities to advance and are often treated as glorified secretaries by their male counterparts ... Judges either want to pat you on the bottom or cop a feel if they can ... It's an attitude about what role 51 per cent of the population is expected to fulfill.[29]

27 *Ottawa Journal* (29 April 1974). The conference passed a resolution protesting the decision of the Québec Court of Appeal, which had overturned the acquittal of Dr. Henry Morgentaler on abortion charges. Described as a former MP and now an Osgoode Hall law professor, LaMarsh explained that "the Supreme Court decision which had denied Irene Murdoch an interest in the Alberta ranch she worked with her husband for 25 years had 'threatened' Canadian women into action": *Murdoch v Murdoch* [1975] 1 SCR 423.

28 *Weekend Magazine* (17 January 1976). As Dean Arthurs responded, "Judy is an original, independent, tough-minded person, whom I like very much. I'm sorry that a teaching career was not sufficient for a woman of her energy."

29 *Ottawa Journal* (7 February 1975). See also LSO Archives, LaMarsh fonds, unidentified news report (5 February 1975), presentation at McGill University in International Women's Year. LaMarsh criticized the Ontario government for its 1975 Women's Year program: K. Rex, "LaMarsh Waiting with Questions as Province Unveils $470,000 Women's Year Program," *Globe and Mail* (17 January 1975). LaMarsh was critical of the government's decision to lower the staff-child ratio in daycare centres, and she presented the keynote address at the conference of the National Association of Women and the Law in 1979: *Windsor Star* (26 February 1979); and *Globe and Mail* (28 February 1979).

In April 1975, Ontario premier Bill Davis appointed LaMarsh to chair the Royal Commission on Violence in Television. Noting that the influence of television on human behaviour had resulted in advertising regulations, the premier concluded that little was being done to diminish or restrict portrayals of violence, of casual brutality and killing, which might equally influence viewers, especially children. The work of the commission was controversial, particularly because LaMarsh was hosting a CBC radio program at the same time. She resigned from the radio program in 1976. In the end, the commission spent two years and $2.2 million and reported in 1977. Critics attacked many of its sixty-eight recommendations, suggesting that "the cure could be more serious than the disease."[30] By 1977, LaMarsh was writing two novels, thinly disguised studies about "who's who" in the seamy underside of Parliamentary politics. The novels were intended to finance a family law practice in Toronto, which opened in 1979, but in early 1980 LaMarsh became ill. She died of pancreatic cancer in October 1980 at the age of fifty-five.[31]

Tributes poured in at the news of her death. Prime Minister Trudeau lauded her many achievements in public life, both inside and outside politics. He added: "No tribute from me would be complete without reference to Judy's characterization of me at the 1968 leadership convention. Even when it was at my expense, I could not help admiring her colourful and frank style, which was always accompanied by an ongoing sense of dignity and a measure of good humor." Governor General Schreyer presented LaMarsh with the Order of Canada in a ceremony in Sunnybrook Hospital in July 1980, and York University established the LaMarsh Centre,

30 *Windsor Star* (15 April 1975); *Globe and Mail* (15 April 1975); and *Toronto Star* (14 February 1976), quoting Alan Borovoy of the Canadian Civil Liberties Association. See also *Report of the Royal Commission on Violence in the Communications Industry: Approaches, Conclusions, Recommendations* (Toronto: The Commission 1977). An *Interim Report* was published in 1976, after provincial consultations: see "Seek Involvement Here on Inquiry into Violence," *Pembroke Observer* (3 January 1976); and obituary, *Toronto Star* (28 October 1980) A14.

31 Judy LaMarsh, *A Very Political Lady: A Novel* (Toronto: McClelland & Stewart, 1979); LaMarsh, *A Right Honourable Lady: A Novel* (Toronto: McClelland & Stewart, 1980); and J. Timson, "Working on the Sequel," *Maclean's* (3 March 1980) 8–9. See also LSO Archives, LaMarsh fonds, re Bencher election, 1979; and obituaries, *Globe and Mail* (28 October 1980) 4, and *Toronto Star* (28 October 1980) A14. LaMarsh was appointed QC in 1963.

Ontario's first research unit to study violence.[32] Her obituary lauded her accomplishments.

> Judy LaMarsh was not the first woman Cabinet Minister in Canada. She was certainly the first to grab and hold public attention. And sometimes she was right—in the most undiplomatic language and at the top of her lungs ("Miss LaMarsh only opens her mouth to change feet," said ... T.C. Douglas). But the Canada Pension Plan would be healthier now if the late Prime Minister Lester Pearson had taken her advice ... The thing about Judy LaMarsh ... was that she was *interesting*. She is the only politician in our memory who said of a government grant at a public meeting, "Don't let anyone kid you. This isn't a gift from the government. It's your money." She kicked up the dust. Not a bad epitaph.[33]

Although LaMarsh became famous as a federal politician, she had practised law successfully, at the beginning and more sporadically at the end of her life. She did not initially identify with women's issues, regarding herself as an "incidental" woman: "Being the lone woman in the Cabinet and one of the few women MPs doesn't bother her. 'I never notice it. I never even noticed it when practising law. Either I'm dull-witted on this subject or else there hasn't been any discrimination. I've never looked for it and I never find it.'" In the 1970s, LaMarsh was more outspoken, perhaps as a result of her Parliamentary experiences. She was described as the "No 1 Spinster in Canada," as "an odd bod, a drill sergeant in jack boots, a dreadnought-sized Charlotte Whitton," and as a woman of nimble wit, unusual frankness, and unquestioned charm. Indeed, like other women lawyers working in 1960s and '70s, she was a transitional figure in the context of changing societal

32 Obituary, *Globe and Mail* (28 October 1980) 4; and LaMarsh Centre for Child and Youth Research, York University.

33 Obituary, *Globe and Mail* (28 October 1980) 4. LaMarsh's funeral in Niagara Falls was attended by large numbers of politicians, including Stanley Knowles, Flora MacDonald, John Munro, Herb Gray, Monique Bégin, William David, Roy McMurtry, and Keith Davey. Lieutenant-Governor Pauline McGibbon's eulogy described LaMarsh as "a gentle, generous, energetic, selfless, spunky woman—a fiercely strong Canadian." Six women were pallbearers: Edith Duggan and Florence Rosberg of Niagara Falls, Barbara Frum (daughter of Florence Rosberg), Pamela Walker, Doris Anderson, and Nancy Morrison: *Toronto Star* (30 October 1980).

views of women. Yet, as a "lone woman," she may have experienced more complex challenges than others.

> [LaMarsh went] through that kind of fire, alone, unshielded by convention, testing [herself], pushing ... to the limits of ... endurance and then beyond, harassed by critics, hounded by gossip and rumour ... faced constantly by a mirror which shows an exaggerated and distorted image—yet exhilarated at the same time by power, by the ability to alter the destiny of a nation, challenging the limits of ... intelligence, knowing the anxiety of responsibility and the joy of creativity.[34]

In September 1950, four women were called to the bar. Lillian Irwin, later Jackson, was born in Wawanosh, and her father was a police officer. She was admitted to Osgoode Hall as a matriculant in 1945, and she articled with Robert Hays in Goderich, becoming the first woman from Goderich to be called to the Ontario bar. Irwin practised law at the firm of Robertson, Lane, Perrett & Frankish in the Temple Building in Toronto for about three years, and it was Irwin who seconded LaMarsh's motion about magistrates at the CBA meeting in 1951. In 1954, Irwin married Raymond Jackson and moved to Montreal. The couple had four children and moved to Hartsdale, New York, in 1963. Irwin did not practise law after her marriage and resigned voluntarily from the Law Society in 1965.[35]

All three women who were called to the bar with Irwin Jackson practised law in Toronto. Mary West, whose father was a director, was born in Thorold and graduated from the University of Toronto in 1947. She articled with John Bench and then Joseph Keogh in St. Catharines. She was twenty-five years old when she was called to the bar, and she was featured in a news photo buying stamps for her diploma from Rolly Jones, the law-stamp

34 Kelly, "I'm All I'm Ever Going to Be;" and Robertson, "The Honourable Judy," 7 (quoting Angela Burke and Douglas Fisher) and 14. See also Stewart, "The Fighting Lady of Parliament Hill," 3; *Winnipeg Free Press* (3 June 1963); and Burke, "The Exuberant Miss LaMarsh," 3: LaMarsh regarded her political career as just "a period of my life," suggesting that women may see politics as an opportunity for public service rather than a life-long career.

35 Huckle, "List of Women Barristers and Solicitors"; *Canadian Law Lists*; and LSO Archives, OBBRP, "Lillian Walker Irwin Jackson." See also *Goderich Signal Star* (5 October 1950), announcing Irwin's call to the bar with three men from Goderich: Richard Donnelly, William Prest, and Joseph Priddle. Irwin Jackson moved first to Ville St. Laurent, Québec, and then to Westfield, New Jersey: Huckle, "List of Women Barristers and Solicitors."

distributor. In 1952, she obtained employment at the Hydro-Electric Commission Power Commission of Ontario, where she continued to work into the 1970s. She never married, and she died in 1986.[36]

Ena (Ina) Greenblatt, later Paul, was born in Poland and immigrated to Canada with her parents and two older siblings when she was three years old. Her father was a lumber merchant, and the family may have been Jewish. She attended the law program at the University of Toronto and while still a student married William Paul, a PhD student in pharmacology, in 1945. She graduated in 1947, entered Osgoode Hall, and articled with W.E. Brandon and with Norman Chisholm in Toronto. She and her husband lived apart for a year when he won a postdoctoral scholarship to Cambridge University in 1948, while she continued her studies at Osgoode Hall. When she was called to the bar, she was twenty-seven years old and was photographed with Helen Tedman, another graduate in September 1950.

Ena Paul's husband became a professor of clinical biochemistry at the University of Toronto, and Ena began to practise law with Elmer Brandon at 414 Bay Street. Her name was listed in parentheses as "Ena M. Paul." After Brandon's death, Paul practised on her own for some years, but she eventually relinquished full-time practice to care for her aging parents and the couple's four children, all of whom lived together in one house, where she regularly arranged family dinners on Friday nights. She "remained an advocate, helping people in need and demonstrating her commitment to just cause" after she ceased to practise law. She suffered a stroke in 2002 and was hospitalized for several months, and although she returned home, she died in 2003 from Parkinson's disease at the age of seventy-nine. Her obituary stated: "Her commitment to both intellectual and domestic life could never have been easy ... She was a working mother at a time when it was not fashionable."[37]

Helen McKee Tedman, who entered Osgoode Hall at the age of thirty-six, was also called to the bar in September 1950. She had completed a BA at the University of Toronto in 1933 and an MA in classics at the University of Michigan., and she then worked as a manager at Simpson's. She left this

36 LSO Archives, OBBRP, "Mary Margaret West"; *Globe and Mail* (29 September 1950); Huckle, "List of Women Barristers and Solicitors"; and *Canadian Law Lists*.

37 LSO Archives, OBBRP, "Ena M. Paul"; Huckle, "List of Women Barristers and Solicitors"; *Toronto Telegram* (29 September 1950); obituary, *Globe and Mail* (6 January 2004); and *Canadian Law Lists*. In the 1960s, the *Canadian Law Lists* identified Paul's location at 191 Parkside Drive, Toronto.

position when she married, and a few years later, with a young son at home, she arranged for her son to attend nursery school and entered the law program at Osgoode Hall in 1947. Tedman articled with R.A. Cranston at Lang, Michener, Day & Cranston. In the first-year exams, she placed sixteenth out of 325 students, and when she graduated with honours, she topped the 33 graduates. As a mature student who was nearly forty years old, she recalled being fully accepted, and she regarded her decision to study law as one of the happiest decisions in her life.[38]

Tedman was initially employed at Lang, Michener, Day & Cranston, but in October 1952 Tedman and Harold Day, who had been called to the bar in 1935, opened a law office as Day and Tedman. The firm was initially located at 38 King Street West, but it relocated in 1955 to 67 Yonge Street. By 1960, there was a new partnership, Day & Ault, and although Helen Tedman was listed at 67 Farnham Avenue, it is unclear whether she continued to practise law. In 1954, she had been featured in a press report in which she expressed her views about the practice of law, saying that it was necessary to enjoy solving problems: "If you fall into the muddle-brained category, better think twice ... because, if you can't think straight, the law is not for you." Tedman preferred corporate law, which did not often require attendance at court, and she suggested that male lawyers were more suited to court work, although this view did not apply to women like Vera Parsons (1924), Margaret Fraser (1928), Beatrice Lyons (1935), and Margaret Perney (1927), all of whom were excellent litigators. Tedman died in 1972 at the age of sixty-one.[39]

Eight women were called to the bar in June 1951, and three—Georgina "Jo" Davis, June Tarshis Bernhard, and Janet Scott—were photographed as the "Portias in a New Crop of Lawyers." A fourth woman, Katharine Hanlon, was also called to the bar at this June ceremony, at which Premier

38 LSO Archives, WLAO fonds, SB, vol. 3; and OBBRP, "Helen Beauchamp McKee Tedman." See also *Globe and Mail* (29 September 1950); and *Telegram* (29 September 1950), including a photo of Mrs. Tedman with her son, aged four and a half.

39 "Law Is Not Profession for the Muddle-Minded," *Globe and Mail* (10 May 1954). Tedman suggested that voice training and debating would be useful skills to acquire in relation to the practice of law. See also *Canadian Law Lists*; LSO Archives, WLAO fonds, SB, vol. 6; and OBBRP, "Helen Beauchamp McKee Tedman." Irene Domagalski, originally from Timmins and a graduate of the University of Toronto, articled with Tedman & Day and was called to the bar in 1958: LSO Archives. Tedman was listed at 92 Lawton Boulevard in 1970.

Frost was the guest speaker.[40] Georgina Davis graduated from the University of Toronto in 1947, was admitted to Osgoode Hall in July, and she articled in Toronto with Frederick Gardiner. After her call to the bar, she worked briefly at the Ontario Hydro-Electric Power Commission, but after her marriage to D.K. Frid and relocating to Dundas, there is no record of her in legal practice. Davis resigned voluntarily in 1972 and died in 2000.[41]

After her call to the bar, Katharine Hanlon worked at the Parliament Buildings in Toronto. A few years later, she married J.P. Meechan, but she continued her employment as Mrs. K.T.C. Meechan in the Provincial Secretary's Department. By 1960, she was listed as "Mrs. K Hanlon Meechan" at 14 Ixworth Road in Rexdale and later at 261 Ingelwood Drive. It is unclear whether she practised law at these locations.[42]

The other two women who were called to the bar in June 1951 practised law for many years, including as partners in their own firm for more than a decade. Initially, June Tarshis Bernhard worked at the office of the Public Trustee while Janet Scott was employed at the Parliament Buildings. Then, in 1952, they established their partnership, having become friends at law school. Both women believed that there was no room for high-strung women in the legal profession, but rather that law required "quick-mindedness, to know how to turn off her thinking on one subject and on to another, like a tap, without so much as the flicker of an eyelash."[43]

June Tarshis, the daughter of a machinery merchant in Toronto, had graduated from the University of Toronto in honours law in 1948. She married Hans-Dieter Bernhard when they were both law students. Her husband, the son of a German lawyer, had left Germany in 1938 at the age of fifteen and came to Canada from England in 1941 with other, mainly Jewish, evacuees, while his parents had emigrated to Chile. After being interned in New Brunswick and then released, Hans-Dieter Bernhard attended Harbord Collegiate, became a British subject in 1946, and graduated from the University of Toronto in law and entered Osgoode Hall in 1947. He articled with David Goodman, and after his call to the bar in 1950, he formed a

40 LSO Archives, WLAO fonds, SB, vol. 3, *Telegram*, unidentified photo.

41 Huckle, "List of Women Barristers and Solicitors"; LSO Archives, OBBRP, "Georgina Davis Frid"; WLAO fonds, SB, vol. 3; and *Canadian Law Lists*.

42 Huckle, "List of Women Barristers" and Solicitors; and *Canadian Law Lists*.

43 *Globe and Mail* (5 May 1960). See also Huckle, "List of Women Barristers and Solicitors"; and LSO Archives, WLAO fonds, SB, vol. 3, *Telegram*, unidentified photo of Bernhard and Scott at their call to the bar in 1951.

law partnership with his classmate at Osgoode, Murray Gruson, at 73 Adelaide Street West.[44]

In 1952, June Bernhard and Janet Scott opened their law partnership at the same address as Bernhard & Gruson, but the women lawyers later moved their office to 62 Richmond Street West. Bernhard & Scott was a general practice, including business contracts, tax, commercial law, and divorce. In an interview a decade later, they recalled working initially until nine three nights a week as well as Saturday mornings. By 1960, they were both looking forward to a holiday. The women believed that there were still difficulties for women in the legal profession—for example, women were generally unable to attend informal get-togethers after a case. At the same time, their sex might be an advantage, because "clients are intrigued, and it gets their attention." In addition, it could sometimes "throw the opposite side a bit off balance, to suddenly discover counsel has a cute smile and a fresh hairdo."[45]

Bernhard and Scott practised in partnership for eleven years. By the mid-1950s, Bernhard's husband was a sole practitioner, located at 330 Bay Street, Suite 1209, and the firm of Bernhard and Scott relocated to this same office address around 1960. Their partnership ended in 1962 when June Bernhard began to practise law with her husband. As "Mrs. J.T. Bernhard," she practised civil litigation while H.D. Bernhard did commercial law. The couple had three daughters. H.D. Bernhard was appointed QC in 1967, and J.T. Bernhard received a QC in 1968. In 1960, J.T. Bernhard described her views about the practice of law: "Law is for the individual who likes variety ... It is for the person who doesn't mind working long hours, taking what sometimes may be a tremendous amount of responsibility, [and] who is interested in people and their problems, and has a sympathetic ear when necessary."[46]

44 LSO Archives, OBBRP, "Hans Dieter Bernhard"; *Canadian Law Lists*; *Telegram* (30 June 1950); *Globe and Mail* (24 June 1950); and press reports in the *St. Catharines Standard* and Belleville *Ontario Intelligencer*. See also press reports re June Tarshis Bernard: *Toronto Star*, *Toronto Sun*, *Hamilton Spectator*, *London Evening Press*, and others (17 and 18 April 1979).

45 *Globe and Mail* (5 May 1960). Another report in 1952 about controversy over rooming houses in Rosedale identified Scott as representing rooming-house operators: *Globe and Mail* (29 October 1952).

46 *Canadian Law Lists*; and LSO Archives, OBBRP, "June Tarshis Bernhard" and "Hans-Dieter Bernhard." See also LSO Archives, June Tarshis Bernhard fonds, K. Rex, "More about Careers," *Globe and Mail* (2 February 1960), her speech to high school students on behalf of the Business and Professional Women's Club.

In 1979, Bernhard was appointed a judge of the Provincial Court (Criminal Division), the first woman judge in the court after its creation in 1971. Her judicial appointment was widely reported; she was described as a legal adviser and board member of the Elizabeth Fry Society and a member of the Advocates Society and the Family Law Section of the Canadian Bar Association. She had also completed the LLM degree at York University in 1977. Bernhard's spouse speculated that women judges had been absent in the criminal courts prior to the late 1970s because "the criminal courts are always in the public eye and it is quite possible the public itself wasn't ready for it."[47] Tarshis Bernhard described her experience as a woman lawyer as a struggle, and how she was often regarded as an "oddity," but she also noted that the situation for women in law had changed as their numbers increased.[48] After the couple's daughter Ella was called to the bar in 1982, she joined her father in the practice of law until his death in 1985. June Tarshis Bernhard died in 2013.[49]

J.T. Bernhard's original law partner, Janet Scott, was the daughter of a civil servant. She enrolled at Osgoode Hall in 1948, after graduating from the University of Toronto. Law Society records indicate she articled for three different principals in Toronto: Hamilton Stuart, J.D. McNish, and C.A. Thompson. When the partnership with J.T. Bernhard ended in 1962, Scott worked briefly at McDonald Davies Ward in the Prudential Building, and she then joined the Carswell Company, Canada's largest publisher, as

47 LSO Archives, June Tarshis Bernhard fonds, *Toronto Star* (17 April 1979); and *Hamilton Spectator* and *Toronto Sun* (18 April 1979). The *Toronto Sun* identified other family members in the legal profession and the judiciary, including her daughter, then a student in second-year at Osgoode Hall Law School, and her brother-in-law Judge H. Waisberg.

48 LSO Archives, June Tarshis Bernard fonds, unidentified news report (18 April 1979).

49 LAO Archives, OBBRP, "June Tarshis Bernhard" and "Hans-Dieter Bernhard." J.T. Bernhard may have remarried: see death notice, "June T. Bernhard-Teeter," *Continuum* (Osgoode Hall Law School) (Winter 2014) 31; and Osgoode Hall Law School, *Report on Giving, 2000–2001*(Osgoode Hall Law School, 2001) The couple's daughter, Ella Bernhard, established a practice focused on family law. In the late 1980s, she was the subject of a Law Society disciplinary hearing relating to her father's death by suicide, in which she maintained that her father's death and his private financial arrangements were not relevant to the law firm: *Globe and Mail* (August 1987). The outcome of this process is unknown, but a recent Law Society report identified Ella Bernhard as a member in good standing: LSO, "Lawyer and Paralegal Directory," online database, searched 2022.

Editor in Chief.[50] Four years later, she was appointed chair of the federal Immigration Appeals Board, which had become independent, rather than merely advisory, to the federal Department of Manpower and Immigration. At the time of her appointment, Scott stated bluntly: "It's a job that anyone with the proper ability and legal training could do. I hope the fact that I am a woman didn't enter into this. I like to think that I was selected on merit." Scott believed women had achieved full equality in the legal profession, and she opposed the investigations of the Royal Commission on the Status of Women in 1967, stating "It might be justified in certain areas, but for professional women it's completely unnecessary." According to Scott, professional women had achieved equality: "A woman is just another member of her profession. If she wants to get ahead, she has to be as good as or better than her competitors, but so do men."[51]

Scott was appointed QC in 1968, and in 1982 she was appointed a judge of the Waterloo Judicial District Court. She served as a justice of the Ontario Court of Justice (General Division) in Waterloo from 1990 to 1994. She died in 2000.[52] Although the Bernhard & Scott partnership was not the first women lawyers' partnership in Ontario, it endured longer than earlier women lawyers' partnerships, and it was the first partnership in which both women lawyers were later appointed to the judiciary.

In September 1951, four more women were admitted to the bar and featured in a news photo together. The records for Mary Roadhouse Malloney are sparse. It is unclear whether she practised law in the 1950s, although she appeared in a list of firm members at White, Bristol, Beck & Phipps in 1960 for one year. By the mid-1960s, she was listed at 178 Old Forest Hill Road, Toronto, but it is not clear whether she was practising law. She was active in the WLAO and was elected WLAO president in 1978–80. She recalled that her practice group at Osgoode Hall included a woman

50 LSO Archives, OBBRP, "Janet Scott," indicating her degree as BA, University of Toronto, but she may have graduated from the university's law program: *Fredericton Gleaner* (22 September 1967). See also *Globe and Mail* (29 October 1952), report and photo of Scott in discussion about rooming houses in Rosedale.

51 LSO Archives, WLAO fonds, *Fredericton Gleaner* (22 September 1967); *Globe and Mail* (3 August 1967); and *Canadian Law Lists*. See also C. Harvey, "Women in Law in Canada" (1970–71) 4 *Manitoba Law Journal* 9 at 23.

52 LSO Archives, OBBRP, "Janet Scott."

instructor and all women law students. According to Malloney, "We definitely felt segregated."[53]

Elizabeth Joy Kennedy was also called to the bar in September 1951, the fourth generation in her family to join the legal profession. Her grandfather was Frank Denton, KC, the lawyer who provided articling opportunities to early women lawyers, including Edith Paterson (1915). Kennedy served in the RCAF Women's Division, and she may have attended university as a veteran, since she was twenty-nine years old when she was called to the bar. For a few years, she practised at the firm of Frame & Rodger at 2 College Street, Toronto, and then worked in the City Solicitor's office until 1958. At some point, Kennedy married John Clarry, who became managing partner at the McCarthy firm, and she may have ceased practice after her marriage.[54] Kennedy Clarry was also a niece of Laura Denton Duff (1920), the law student who arranged the founding meeting of the WLAO in her father's office in 1919, and Kennedy Clary was active in the WLAO, serving as president in 1956–57. On one occasion, she made a presentation to the WLAO about her "Aunt Laura." Kennedy Clarry died in 1996.[55]

Mary Munro Weaver, a graduate of the University of Toronto, completed her studies at Osgoode Hall in 1950, but she was not called to the bar until

53 Huckle, "List of Women Barristers and Solicitors," reported that Roadhouse Malloney was practising law. See also *Canadian Law Lists*; and *Toronto Telegram* (14 September 1951). Since she was identified in the photo as Mary Roadhouse Malloney, she probably married before being called to the bar. See also J. Fielding, "Sisters in Law," *Weekend Magazine* (26 August 1978) 6a. Although Malloney disliked that women students were "segregated" in one practice group, she also explained that "no fuss was made."

54 Huckle, "List of Women Barristers and Solicitors": LSO Archives, OBBRP, "Joy Clarry," and WLAO fonds, SB, vol. 3, unidentified news report (September 1951); *Canadian Law Lists*; and photo of the four women graduates, *Toronto Telegram* (14 September 1951). For Edith Paterson, see Chapter Two. Laura Legge, who reported that her candidacy for Bencher was supported by the managing partner at McCarthy's, was probably referring to John Clarry, since both Legge and Kennedy Clarry were active in the WLAO.

55 LSO Archives, OBBRP, "Joy Clarry"; and *Canadian Law Lists*. See also WLAO fonds, SB, vol. 8, unidentified press report, and photo of Kennedy and other delegates to a convention of the Canadian Bar Association. This news report identified her as "Mrs. E.J. Kennedy, a barrister and solicitor," but it is amended in the WLAO file to show her as "Miss E.J. Kennedy." The other women in the photo were Mrs. L.S. Eckardt of Powell River, Mrs. W.H. Heffernan of Vancouver, and Mrs. Howard Emery of Edmonton.

September 1951.[56] She practised law at 2201 Kingston Road in the Township of Scarborough in the early 1950s. After relocating to Sudbury several years later, she worked with H.A. Doig in 1962 then joined the firm of Shea, Mossop & Stoner, which became Shea, Mossop, Stoner & Weaver in 1969, and later Weaver & Simmons. In 1983, Weaver was one of the first two women to be elected Benchers of the Law Society from outside Toronto. She was re-elected in 1987 as one of three women from outside Toronto and in 1991 as one of five women from outside Toronto.[57]

Weaver was appointed QC in 1979, and she served as a Bencher until 1995, when she retired. She was a member of the national council of the Canadian Bar Association and of the executive committee of the Ontario section, and she served as a board member of Laurentian University and as a trustee of the Algoma Hospital and the Ontario Mental Health Foundation. As a licensed pilot, Weaver often flew to locations outside Sudbury to meet her clients. In 2012, Weaver was honoured with the Laura Legge Award, presented annually to a woman lawyer who exemplifies leadership in the profession. According to her citation, Weaver "served as a significant

56 LSO Archives, WLAO fonds, SB, vol. 3, photo of three women called to the bar, including Kennedy, Malloney, and Weaver, *Toronto Star* (September 1951); and photo of four women graduates, including "Mrs. Mary Weaver," *Toronto Telegram* (14 September 1951). Another report, "Woman Lawyer," *Sudbury Star* (8 September 1971), indicated that Weaver "gave up her law practice for several years to raise a family." It also explained that two women, Charlotte Bell and Elizabeth Gray, were among 17 women in a group of 486 lawyers called to the bar in 1971 and that Bell and Gray then joined Weaver in the practice of law in Sudbury. Bell believed she was the first woman from northern Ontario to be called to the bar, in 1971, although there were several women who preceded her: Eva Powley (1902), Edyth Dyke (1921), Mary Gallagher Gauthier (1941), Eileen Mitchell Thomas (1942), Sarah MacLean (1943), Kathleen Morrison Callahan (1946), Mhora MacInnis Hollingsworth (1948), and Stella Panarites (1953). Some of these women were still in practice in northern Ontario in 1971: C. Ward, "The Changing Tide" (2009) *Continnum* (Osgoode Hall Law School) 14 at 16.

57 LSO Archives, Bencher fonds. In 1983, Judith Bell Oyen, who had graduated in law at Dalhousie in 1962 and was admitted to the Ontario bar 1964, was also elected a Bencher from outside Toronto. Bell Oyen practised law in Ottawa. By 1991, five women were elected from Toronto as well as five from outside Toronto, but a total of ten women Benchers was not achieved again until the 2003 election.

mentor and role model to new lawyers—particularly women lawyers—who went on to contribute to the provision of legal services in the north."[58]

The other woman admitted to the bar in September 1951 was Anne Levine, later Dubin. She graduated from the University of Toronto in 1948 and was the bronze medallist in her class at Osgoode Hall. Her future husband, Charles Dubin, had received the gold medal in 1944.[59] After she was called to the bar, Anne Dubin was appointed supervisor of practice groups at Osgoode Hall Law School, with responsibility for organizing lectures and marking examinations. When she resigned this position to enter private practice with her husband, she was honoured by the Benchers at lunch at Osgoode Hall, only the second woman to receive an invitation for such an occasion.[60] At Kimber & Dubin, Dubin's practice focused on com-

58 LSO, news release (14 March 2012) 4; LSO Archives, OBBRP, "Mary Weaver"; and Bencher fonds. Weaver was probably the first woman partner in a large law firm in northern Ontario, although Mary Gauthier (1940) practised in a partnership with her husband in Timmins, Edith Dyke (1921) practised in a small firm in Fort William, and Eva Powley (1902) worked in the Keefer firm in Port Arthur. See Chapters Two, Three, and Five; and LSO Archives, OBBRP, "Mary Weaver," which reported (incorrectly) that her QC was awarded in 1951.

59 LSO Archives, WLAO fonds, unidentified press report, photo of Lord Evershed, Master of the Rolls, congratulating Anne Levine, the bronze medal winner (September 1951). Although some Law Society records indicate that Dubin and Levine married in 1945, a year after Charles Dubin was called to the bar, others correctly identify their marriage as being in December 1951, after Levine had been called to the bar in September that year. In addition, the caption for the photo of women called to the bar in September 1951 identified her as "Anne Levine": *Toronto Telegram* (14 September 1951). See also LSO Archives, "Diversifying the Bar," Charles Dubin; LSO Archives, OBBRP, "Anne Dubin"; obituary, Anne Dubin, *Globe and Mail* (2 August 2007). Charles Dubin was appointed KC in 1962, the youngest man to receive the appointment in the British Empire, and he became the first Jewish Chief Justice of Ontario and was named to the Order of Canada. He died in 2008. See also Justice R. Armstrong, "Eulogy," Court of Appeal (29 October 2008). Anne Dubin was appointed QC in 1962. Charles and Anne Dubin established a memorial entrance award at Osgoode Hall Law School of York University: LSO Archives, "Diversifying the Bar," Charles Dubin; M. Aitken, "Between You and Me," *Telegram* (21 October 1955), focused on Anne Dubin; S. Martin, "Charles Dubin: Judge who Probed Use of Drugs in Sport Was a 'Complete Man of the Law'," *Globe and Mail* (21 October 2008); and "Osgoode Entrance Award Honours Memory of Charles and Anne Dubin," *Yfile*, York University (23 July 2009).

60 LSO Archives, Anne Dubin fonds, L. Dempsey, "Person to Person," *Globe and Mail* (10 October 1955). The other woman so honoured was Elizabeth Newton (1921), who had painted portraits of Dean Falconbridge and three Treasurers of the Law Society, D.L. McCarthy, G.W. Mason, and Shirley Denison.

mercial law while her husband practised almost exclusively in the courts. When Tory, Tory, DesLauriers & Binnington established a litigation department, the firm recruited Kimber and Dubin in July 1972. After Charles Dubin was appointed to the Ontario Court of Appeal in January 1973, Anne Dubin remained at the Tory firm and later became a partner. She was also appointed a director of Petro Canada Limited, Telemedia Communications, and the Morgan Trust Co. of Canada. She was the first woman to be appointed governor of the Toronto Stock Exchange. She was appointed QC in 1962, along with Lida Pearson Sturdy (1921).[61]

Early in her career, Anne Dubin became involved in penal reform, including the Elizabeth Fry Society in 1951 and chair of the Penal Reform for Women Joint Committee, which lobbied for reforms for women prisoners. In 1968, she appeared on a panel with Ian Baxter to discuss the Ontario Law Reform Commission's report about reforms to family property, and she was active in the Allied Arts Society (involving the Ballet Guild, the Opera Committee, and the Drama League). In addition, she was a member of the Ontario Law Reform Commission Advisory Board and the Attorney General's Advisory Committee on the Juvenile and Family Court of Metropolitan Toronto, vice-chair of the York County Legal Aid Plan, vice-chair of the Board of Governors of York University, trustee of the Toronto Hospital Foundation, honorary counsel of the Canadian Red Cross Society and the Museum Children's Theatre, director of the Clarke Institute, and trustee of the Ontario Mental Health Foundation. In 2007, her obituary noted that Anne Dubin would be remembered "for her intelligence, independence, indomitable spirit, and her dedication and loyalty."[62]

The number of women called to the bar after 1951 declined, perhaps reflecting the impact of the new four-year course at Osgoode Hall. In June 1952, only one woman was admitted to the bar: Roxie Marshall. Born in 1903, she graduated from McMaster University in 1948 and then attended Osgoode Hall. Marshall articled with Helen Okuloski (1935) in Hamilton, and she practised law in Hamilton after her call to the bar, initially at the

61 Obituary, *Globe and Mail* (3 August 2007); obituary, *Yfile*, York University (7 August 2007); *Toronto Star* (27 May 1976) C8; *Telegram* (3 January 1962); and Robertson, "Eulogy" (29 October 2008). For Pearson Sturdy, see Chapter Three.

62 Obituary, *Globe and Mail* (3 August 2007). Anne Dubin had served on the Board of Governors of York University, including as vice-chair, for twenty years (1973–93), and she was appointed an honorary governor in 1995: obituary, *Yfile*, York University (7 August 2007).

corner of James and Jackson Streets, but after 1955 at 288 Stanley Avenue. She continued to practise law until her death in 1970.[63]

In September 1952, a second woman was called to the bar: Bertha Haffa, later McCarney. She was born in Niagara Falls, New York where her father was an architect, and she graduated from the University of Toronto in 1948. While attending lectures at Osgoode Hall, she articled for three different principals: Arthur Kenny, Howard Alles, and Sylvester Ryan, all in Toronto. She was granted Canadian citizenship in May 1952. After her call to the bar, Haffa worked briefly for the Succession Duties Department, but there is no record of her practising law after her marriage and relocation to Oakville. Bertha Haffa's admission is of interest because her sister, Mary Agnes Haffa, later Bennett, was called to the bar three years later in June 1955, the first pair of sisters to become lawyers in Ontario.[64]

Two women were called to the bar in 1953, but June Bushell was the only woman at the ceremony in June, along with 146 men. The press photographed Bushell with two male graduates: Roderick Smith, a wartime ace who shot down thirteen enemy aircraft, and John (Jack) Dunlap, a Big Four football star with the Toronto Argonauts, Ottawa Roughriders, and Hamilton Tiger-Cats. Bushell studied law at the University of Toronto, where she found Dean Kennedy a great character and wonderful lecturer, although she also recalled that he told women students "you're lucky to be here." She also experienced anxiety about her exam results, which at that time were regularly published in the newspaper as lists of students who had

63 Huckle, "List of Women Barristers and Solicitors"; LSO Archives, OBBRP, "Roxie Isabelle Marshall"; and *Canadian Law Lists*. Marshall was forty-nine years old when she was called to the bar. Marshall may have served in the war and pursued further education with the veterans' support program.

64 Huckle, "List of Women Barristers and Solicitors"; LSO Archives, OBBRP, "Bertha Marie Haffa." The LSO record indicates that Haffa changed her name to "Mrs. Bertha H. McCarney" after her marriage, although the same record incorrectly identifies "McCarney" as her premarriage name. See also Harvey, "Women in Law in Canada," 28, who noted other pairs of sisters: Moira Mungovan, later Caswell (1962), and Deirdre Mungovan, later Harvey (1966); and Joan Robinette, later Sadlier (1957), and Dale Robinette, later Best (1971). He also identified three sisters at the Québec bar: Therese LeMay-Lavoie, Jeanne LeMay Warren, and Edith LeMay.

passed and failed.[65] Bushell graduated from the University of Toronto in law in 1951, and then completed the final two years of the law program at Osgoode Hall.

Bushell's greatest challenge was finding an articling position, an experience she described as "simply dreadful [because] no one wanted to hire a woman," and she recalled the advice of a professor that she should "go to parties and get married." Bushell persevered, and after her call to the bar, she found employment with the Department of Public Welfare in Toronto for two years and then in the commercial department at the Crown Trust Company. In the early 1960s, she joined Chappell, Walsh & Davidson, a small litigation firm, at 350 Bay Street. She recalled that the firm held a partnership meeting to discuss whether to hire her and that the partners also consulted with clients about whether it was acceptable to hire a woman. Eventually, Bushell established a strong practice in corporate, commercial, and real estate law. She was appointed QC in 1969. By the mid-1970s, the firm was Chappell, Bushell & Stewart, and it later relocated to the Eaton Centre. Bushell was also active in WLAO activities and served as president in 1962–63. She retired in 1989 after thirty-six years of legal practice. Bushell died in October 2023 at the age of 96, and she was remembered for her dedication to the profession and her mentoring, including the June Bushell Award at the WLAO for a woman who has "overcome adversity to excel in her career as a lawyer."[66]

In September 1953, Stella Panarites was called to the bar, an occasion much celebrated in her hometown of Cobalt. She was the first woman lawyer of Greek heritage in Ontario. Just two years earlier, the first Greek lawyer—Frederick Floras, who immigrated to Canada with his parents

65 Huckle, "List of Women Barristers and Solicitors"; and LSO Archives, WLAO fonds, SB, vol. 6, unidentified press report (June 1953). See also A. Bushby, "The Early Years: Sources of an Enduring Tradition—The Women's Law Association of Ontario, 1919–1950" (80th Anniversary Celebration, 14 January 2000); and "June Bushell '51," *Nexus* (University of Toronto Faculty of Law) (Spring/Summer 2006) 10.

66 "June Bushell," *Nexus*, 10: and *Canadian Law Lists*. In February 1989, the WLAO gave its President's Award to all past presidents of the association. Bushell responded to this honour, stating, "It was fun for us and a memory that I will treasure": (1989) 2:1 *Without Prejudice* (WLAO) 2. See also obituary, *Toronto Star* (2 November 2023).

after the First World War—had been called to the Ontario bar.[67] Panarites's father had arrived in Canada as an immigrant even earlier, in 1906 and had worked in a mine while running a candy business and establishing the Minerva Restaurant. Stella Panarites suffered two serious accidents as a child, including a bad fall and a hockey accident, which required long periods of hospitalization away from school, but she persevered. She graduated with a BA from Queen's in 1949, and then entered the new four-year program at Osgoode Hall, and she articled with four different principals in Toronto: Thomas Slater, Edmund Brown, William Inch, and Garth Moore. She was called to the bar at the age of twenty-nine.[68]

Panarites was celebrated when she triumphantly returned to Cobalt as a lawyer. Although she might have practised elsewhere in the province, she believed that Cobalt, a ghost town during the Depression, would boom again with increasing demand for metal. Her new law office was located on Silver Street, and the mayor and a host of citizens, ranging from miners to merchants, dropped by with congratulations on her first day of business. Panarites practised law in Cobalt until 1957, when she joined Evans & Evans, and practised in Cochrane and Timmins until 1962. She subsequently practised in North Bay at Wallace, Trussler & Carr, and then in Orillia with Marshall & Russell. In 1968, she was listed in parentheses at E.B. Kendall in Midland, and in the 1970s Panarites again worked at Wallace & Carr. She died in North Bay in 1986.[69]

Six women were called to the bar in June 1954. Gladys Roy, the only graduate of 1954 who did not marry, worked as a sole practitioner in Toronto. She was initially located at 62 Richmond Street West but she relocated a few years later to 106 Adelaide Street West. By 1963, she was

67 Born in Greece in 1924, Floras came to Canada with his parents. He joined the Royal Canadian Air Force during the Second World War and then attended the University of Toronto and Osgoode Hall with assistance from the Veterans Rehabilitation Act. He practised law in Toronto for forty-five years, doing real estate, corporate, and commercial law, especially for generations of Greek and Macedonian families, and he was awarded a QC: obituary, *Toronto Star* (13 June 2016).

68 Huckle, "List of Women Barristers and Solicitors"; LSO Archives, OBBRP, "Stella Avura Panarites"; and WLAO fonds, SB, vol. 6, "Stella Returns to Cobalt as Full-Fledged Lawyer," unidentified press report. While a student at Osgoode, Panarites was elected the WLAO student representative in 1952: *Globe and Mail* (1 May 1952).

69 LSO Archives, WLAO fonds, SB, vol. 6, unidentified press report. Huckle, "List of Women Barristers and Solicitors," indicated that Panarites practised in Cochrane. See also *Canadian Law Lists*; and LSO Archives, "Diversifying the Bar," Stella Panarites.

employed at the provincial government in the Department of Lands and Forests. In the 1970s she established a sole practice in Bowmanville at 9½ King Street West, becoming the second woman lawyer in Bowmanville, following Apha Hodgins (1919).[70]

The other women called to the bar in June 1954 married and continued to practise law. Georgia Riddell, who was born in Palmerston, Ontario, graduated from the University of Toronto with a BA in 1950 and was called to the bar in 1954. Initially, Riddell was employed at Graydon & Cook at 330 Bay Street, but in 1958 she joined Fasken, Robertson, Aitchison, Pickup & Calvin, later Faskens. After she married R.D.C. Bentley, she continued to practise at Faskens, using her own surname, but when she became pregnant, she was embarrassed to be called "Miss Riddell" and became "Mrs. Bentley." Like other women lawyers in larger Toronto firms at this time, her employment arrangement was marginal.

> From the beginning, "Mrs Bentley" was treated differently. She was on a salary and was assigned to [two elderly members of the firm] as a conveyancing lawyer. She also assisted [another male lawyer] in wills and estates. It would be many years before a woman in the firm did anything other than these family-related types of legal work. Although she practised with the firm for almost thirty years, developing a deep expertise in real estate, she was never seriously considered for partnership.[71]

70 Huckle, "List of Women Barristers and Solicitors"; and *Canadian Law Lists*. For Apha Hodgins, see Chapter Three.

71 C.I. Kyer, *Lawyers, Families, and Businesses: The Shaping of a Bay Street Law Firm, Faskens, 1863–1963* (Toronto: Osgoode Society for Canadian Legal History/Irwin Law, 2013) 224. Hilda McKinlay (1971) also did estates and trusts work but she left Faskens for Fraser & Beatty, where she became a partner within six months. McKinlay was appointed to the High Court (Supreme Court of Ontario) in 1983 and to the Court of Appeal of Ontario (1987–99): obituary, *Globe and Mail* (6 January 2024) B17. The first woman to join the partnership at Faskens was Eleanor Cronk, in 1983: Kyer, *Lawyers, Families and Businesses*, 248; and OSCLH, oral history, "Hilda Margaret McKinlay," 109–27.

A woman lawyer who later joined the Fasken firm described Riddell Bentley as "a very nice lady who had been with the firm for a long, long time" and worked in the real estate department. Riddell Bentley died in 2001.[72]

Anna Bacon, later Stevenson/Ker, was also called to the bar in June 1954. She graduated from the three-year academic law program at the University of Toronto in 1952 and then completed the two years required at Osgoode Hall. Bacon initially entered the Classics program at the university, but when she learned it was possible to do the university law program in three years and be called to the Ontario bar after two, she "hightailed" it out of Classics. Although Dean Wright initially declined her request to enter the law program, she responded by showing him her excellent grades, and she was admitted to the law school, becoming the only woman in her class during the three years she was there.[73]

Bacon had been the only woman in Classics, so she was not concerned about being the only woman in the law school, and she became "just one of the guys." She recalled an exceedingly polite and respectful environment, and the dean and other law professors—perhaps through the unsung force of the Faculty Wives Club—created a warm social circle and invited her to their homes for dinner. As she suggested, "They probably thought it was worse for me than I did." Like other women, Bacon experienced great difficulty finding an articling position, even though she stood second in her

72 OSCLH, oral history, "Hilda Margaret McKinlay," 108–9, 126; and LSO Archives, OBBRP, "Georgia Bentley." Bentley's LSO record is sparse and does not identify her parents' names, her university record, or her articling principal(s). In addition, no personal records about Riddell Bentley have been identified, and there is also no evidence of her relationship, if any, to Justice Riddell: see Chapter Two. Hilda McKinlay (1971) suggested that since Riddell Bentley did not work full-time, she did not become a partner. Although there were no women partners at Faskens while McKinlay was at the firm, there were several women lawyers at Fraser & Beatty: Willa Carroll, later Corse (1958), and Marjorie Laird, later Palmer (1948), who became a partner in 1964. In the 1950s, Noreen Charlebois, later Stevens (1955), and Patricia Bagwell, later Catalano (1958), were also employed at Fraser & Beatty: Edwards, *Fraser & Beatty: The First 150 Years* (Toronto: Desktop Publishing Division, Fraser & Beatty, 1989) 125. Corse died in 2013: *Continuum* (Osgoode Hall Law School) (Winter 2014) 31; and Catalano died in 2021: obituary, *Toronto Star* (12 June 2021) B14.

73 Huckle, "List of Women Barristers and Solicitors"; University of Toronto, Faculty of Law, Anna (Penina) Bacon Ker"; and *Nexus* (University of Toronto Faculty of Law) (Spring/Summer 2006) 77. Bacon entered the university law program at the age of nineteen on full scholarship, and her story suggests that the new two-year program at Osgoode Hall may have been attractive to law graduates at the University of Toronto.

university law class. With Dean Wright's help, she eventually secured a "hardly glamorous" position at Toronto General Trusts, drafting wills. After her call to the bar, she continued to work there for a few years, and after her first marriage, she worked there as "Anna Stevenson." However, she resigned when she recognized that "working and marrying ... it just wasn't done then. The times were not particularly comfortable for women."[74]

At a later point, Bacon married David Ker and had two children. She enjoyed a long and successful career in later years at the Federal Appeals Board, the provincial Electoral Commission, and the Refugee and Immigration Bureau. She was also appointed QC. Bacon Ker's sense of humour and her admiration for the academic law program at the University of Toronto comes through in an exchange in *Obiter Dicta* that occurred while she was a student at Osgoode Hall. Responding to a long poem "Advice to the Lawlorn," which suggested that students should not work too hard because those with marks above "B" would end up teaching at the University of Toronto, Bacon Ker published a riposte. Student with marks "below B" would suffer an even worse fate: "THEY would teach at Osgoode Hall." Bacon Ker died in 2006.[75]

Helen Burden, who was also called to the bar in June 1954, graduated with a BA from the University of Toronto in 1950. She articled in Toronto with her father, John Burden, as well as with two other lawyers, Frederick Cawthorne and I.C. Harries. Burden was employed at Armstrong, Kemp, Young & Burrows, along with Barbara Duncan (1949), at 372 Bay Street between 1957 and 1959, but by 1965 both women had resigned. Burden married Eric Murray in 1959 and did not practise law for some years, but her spouse, also called to the bar in 1954, joined with a classmate at the firm of Freedman, Cohl & Murray at 480 Lawrence Avenue West. The firm later became Cohl, Murray & Osak at 2788 Bathurst Street. Burden Murray had returned to law practice by 1970. After revising her name on the Law

74 University of Toronto, Faculty of Law. This history identified her as Anna (Penina) Bacon Ker. See also *Canadian Law Lists*.

75 "Anna Bacon Ker," *Nexus* (University of Toronto Faculty of Law) 77; and obituary, "Anna Bacon Ker QC," 89. The obituary identified her spouse and two children.

Society rolls to "Helen Murray," she was listed as a member of the firm. She retired in 1993 and died in 2008.[76]

Joan Bissett, later Neiman, was born in Manitoba, the daughter of a doctor, Edgar D.R. Bissett. He had been elected to Parliament as a Liberal/Labour member in 1926 but was defeated in the 1930 election. He served as a captain in the Canadian Army Medical Corps in World War II. Bissett's father grew up in Cape Breton and began his university studies at Mount Allison University, and Bissett decided to attend the same university. She graduated in 1941 with a BA and returned to Manitoba, where she completed a secretarial course and then applied to join the women's division of the Royal Canadian Naval Service during the war. Although Bissett was interested in being posted overseas, she spent most of the war in Ottawa, and retired in 1946 as a lieutenant-commander.[77]

In 1946, Bissett moved to Montreal to work as an assistant to a former naval officer who had been appointed a manager for the Montreal Shipping Company. After eighteen months, she left this position to join the National Research Council in Ottawa, and in 1950 she returned to Winnipeg, helping with the major flood conditions there for several weeks. When she was invited by another former naval office to work as an executive assistant in his family's law office in London, Ontario, Bissett decided that "if I am going to go down and work for a lawyer, I want to be a lawyer myself." Since the London office had a branch office in Toronto, Bissett arranged to article in the Toronto office while attending Osgoode Hall. During these

76 Huckle, "List of Women Barristers and Solicitors"; Huckle reported that Burden likely practised in Port Credit. See also LSO Archives, OBBRP, "Helen Murray"; and *Canadian Law Lists.* She was active in the Kappa Beta Pi sorority: a press report identified "Mrs. Helen Murray" as the chair of a celebratory meeting of Kappa Beta Pi at the Royal York Hotel in 1963: *Telegram* (22 June 1963). As noted earlier, Helen's father, John Burden, was an articling principal for Laura Down Legge (1948).

77 Senator Joan Neiman, interview with Tom Earle, 1985, Library and Archives Canada (LAC), R1026-73-5-E, vol/box no. 2564, item 3820145, 1–11. According to Neiman, she learned about her father's political affiliation from Prime Minister Diefenbaker during a visit to Parliament. Bissett's family lived in Pine Falls, and her father was the doctor for the Fort Alexander Reservation. She poignantly described how she became aware of the significant differences in the lives of residents on the reservation, in contrast with her own. She described her war work in Ottawa, as hard, especially as she became aware of every casualty list relating to the navy.

years, she was also actively involved in penal reform, including the Elizabeth Fry Society.[78]

Bissett entered the four-year program at Osgoode Hall in 1950 at the age of thirty. She felt like "a bit of a loner and being a woman a bit of a stranger, a strange animal out of [about] three hundred and twenty classmates." She was older than most students, and there were fewer veterans among the students than in earlier decades. Nonetheless, she served as the woman's representative on the Legal and Literary Society's executive in 1952. At the beginning of fourth-year, she married her classmate Clemens M. Neiman, and after they were called to the bar together in 1954, they established a practice at 38 King Street West with their classmate J.H. Seguin. The practice was Neiman, Bissett & Seguin, and Bissett practised as "Mrs. J.B. Neiman." In 1957, the practice relocated to 35 Hayden Street, and all three partners continued there until 1970. Clemens Neiman was the first Lithuanian lawyer in Toronto, and their firm acted for many Lithuanian immigrants, which helped to build their practice: "In our early days we just took anything and everything that came along. Eventually I concentrated as much as possible on wills, estates and family law ... [but] I always had to help in other areas, particularly real estate, if we were getting behind."[79]

Bissett Neiman and her spouse became active in the Liberal Party in their Etobicoke riding, where they supported Red Kelly when he was elected to Parliament in 1963, and Bissett Neiman was a candidate in Ontario provincial elections in both 1963 and 1967. Although she was defeated by Deputy Premier Rowntree, she gained more votes in the second election, and she remained active in Liberal organizations. In addition, she worked with organizations that promoted women's rights, although she acknowledged that women faced difficulty in becoming

78 LAC, interview with Senator Joan Neiman, 11–15. Bissett described visiting the Girls' Training School in Galt with Agnes MacPhail, and she served on the board of the Elizabeth Fry Society and was counsel to the organization for some years. Although she tried to volunteer with the John Howard Society, she was told that only men were involved in the organization, but she tried to establish a branch at Osgoode Hall. Bissett was also involved in lobbying efforts to abolish capital punishment. She described her work at the National Research Council as top secret: LAC, interview with Joan Neiman, 15–19.

79 LAC, interview with Joan Neiman, 14, 19. As Bissett Neiman noted, many of the Lithuanian immigrants were involved in construction, and their work helped to build the law practice. See also (1952) 26:2 *Obiter Dicta* 36; Huckle, "List of Women Barristers and Solicitors"; *Canadian Law Lists*; and Parliamentary biographies, "Joan Neiman" and "Edgar D.R. Bissett."

involved in public life, particularly becoming MPs in Ottawa in a large country like Canada.[80]

In 1970, Bissett Neiman's listing changed to 3828 Bloor Street West in Islington, and her spouse and Seguin formed a new partnership at 25 Adelaide Street West: Neiman, Seguin, Bloomenfeld & White. In 1972, Bissett Neiman was appointed to the Senate of Canada, the year when Muriel McQueen Fergusson, who had been admitted to the bar of New Brunswick in 1925, became the first woman speaker in the Senate. Bissett Neiman served as a senator for more than twenty years, and she chaired the Standing Committee on Legal and Constitutional Affairs for several years in the 1980s and was a member of the Special Science Policy Committee, among others. She also chaired the Special Senate Committee on Euthanasia and Assisted Suicide, and in 2006, Ontario premier Dalton McGuinty appointed Neiman to the Citizens Panel on Increasing Organ Donation. She also served as a member of Dalhousie Health Law Institute's End of Life Project, and represented Canada within the Inter-Parliamentary Union where she was appointed chair of Human Rights. Bissett Neiman, Ontario's first woman lawyer to be appointed to the Canadian Senate, retired at the age of seventy-five in 1995. She died in November 2022 at the age of 102.[81]

Rose Rabkin, who was also called to the bar in 1954, married Max Rosenfeld. She established a sole practice as "Mrs. Rose Rosenfeld" in Toronto, initially at 85 Richmond Street West and, from 1956, at 347 Bay Street. In the early 1960s, she moved to Israel and ceased to practise law.[82]

80 LAC, interview with Senator Joan Neiman, 20–31. As she explained, "It is difficult to combine family life and politics when you have young children and a husband who may be thousands of miles away." The Neimans had three children. They supported Robert Winters in the federal Liberal leadership campaign in 1968, but they eventually agreed to support Pierre Trudeau as their second choice.

81 Parliamentary biography, "Joan Neiman." In 1973, C.M. Neiman relocated to Fraser & McLauglin in Mississauga, while Seguin remained in practice at the Toronto firm: *Canadian Law Lists*. McQueen Fergusson had been a Senator since 1953: see Chapter One. Apparently, Clemens Neiman was also considered for a Senate appointment, but he was not interested in policy discussions, in contrast to election campaigns. As Bissett Neiman noted, several women's organizations were actively promoting women candidates for the Senate in the 1970s: LAC, interview with Senator Joan Neiman, 37–38, 40–41, 55–56. See also obituary, *Globe and Mail* (6 December 1922) B18.

82 Huckle, "List of Women Barristers and Solicitors"; and *Canadian Law Lists*.

Seven women were called to the bar in 1955, and a press photo identified the four women who joined the profession in June: Noreen Charlebois from Penetanguishene and Donna Haley, June Gross, and Daphne Byers, all from Toronto.[83] Noreen Charlebois was the first woman law student at Fraser & Beatty, and she became the first woman lawyer at the firm after her call to the bar. Her Osgoode Hall classmate Sinclair Stevens was also a student at the firm, and he remained there briefly after his call to the bar, but after Charlebois and Stevens married, Stevens established his own firm. Noreen Stevens, who was regarded as an excellent solicitor, practised at the firm in the real estate department until 1962 but ceased to practise law thereafter. She remained actively involved in the WLAO and served as President in 1963–64. Charlebois Stevens joined Laura Legge (1948) to lobby successfully, on behalf of the WLAO, for the creation of robing rooms for women lawyers when the new courthouse on University Avenue was under construction.[84]

Donna Haley, the daughter of a sales manager at Northern Electric in Walkerville, later part of Windsor, attended Trinity College in Toronto, graduating first in the Honours BA program in 1951, and then entered Osgoode Hall. Elizabeth Maclennan (1927), who was a cousin of one of Haley's college friends, introduced Haley to the firm of Mowat, Maclennan,

83 *Globe and Mail* (24 June 1955). According to Huckle, "List of Women Barristers and Solicitors," there were five women called to the bar in June, including Mary Agnes Haffa, later Bennett. See also LSO Archives, WLAO fonds, SB, vol. 6.

84 Edwards, *Fraser & Beatty*, 31. Charlebois's name was not listed in the firm's roster until 1957: *Canadian Law Lists*. The reason for Charlebois Stevens' departure is unknown, and there is no information about whether she had unrealized partnership expectations. She served as President of the WLAO in 1963–64, probably after her departure from the firm: Bushby, "The Early Years." Sinclair Stevens continued to practise in his own firm and was also engaged in business activities. In 1972, he was elected to Parliament and served as a Cabinet minister in the Progressive Conservative governments of Joe Clark and Brian Mulroney until 1986, when he was forced to resign as Minister of Regional Economic Development and Foreign Investment Review. In 1987, he was the subject of a public inquiry, headed by Justice William Parker, to investigate allegations that Stevens had violated conflict-of-interest guidelines by courting individuals doing business with his ministry for investments related to his private holdings. Although the inquiry concluded that Stevens violated the guidelines fourteen times, the Federal Court overturned the inquiry's results in 2004, eighteen years later: obituary, "William Parker," J. Coyle, "Judge Brought Down Federal Minister," *Toronto Star* (13 September 2016) GT3. See also LAC, Parliamentary biography, "Sinclair Stevens"; and OSCLH, oral history "Laura Legge," 132–33.

Titus & Hilley in Toronto. Haley articled in Toronto with E.B. Titus, KC, "Captain Titus," who had served in the First World War. As an articling student, Haley was scheduled to appear in Magistrate's Court in the basement of Old City Hall, but the police officer at the door would not permit her to enter, probably because she was young and female. She did eventually succeed in gaining admission to the court, but as she later explained, "things were different in those days for women."[85]

Haley recalled excellent lectures by practitioners: Arthur Martin in Criminal Law, William Howland in Mortgages, Walter Williston in Civil Procedure, and George Edmonds in Insurance Law, but she was less impressed with Dean Smalley-Baker and skipped some of his classes. There were only a few full-time members of faculty, including Alan Leal, Donald Spence, and David Smout, and all the instructors used a lecture format. Although Haley found the practice groups not particularly useful, she was active in many activities at Osgoode Hall. She was women's representative on the Legal and Literary Society executive in her second year, and cochair of the Luncheon Committee in her fourth. Haley was also active as a debater at Osgoode Hall, and she was awarded one of three Gold Keys when she graduated in 1955. She graduated within the top ten among two hundred students in her class, but at the call to the bar ceremony, she was admitted as "Dona Hally," an error that she never forgave.[86]

Haley was initially interested in litigation practice, but when she sought advice from Vera Parsons (1924), she was not encouraged. Haley briefly accepted a position at Horkins & Cory, but the firm determined that it could not afford her services—although Haley believed that it was once again "the woman problem." After seeking advice at the Law Society, she obtained a position with Frank Erichsen-Brown, who represented insurance companies and was seventy-five years old. Haley assisted in an insurance case involving a power plant in Windsor that was damaged in a riot, and although the insurers lost at trial and on appeal, they succeeded

85 OSCLH, oral history, "Madam Justice Donna Haley," 2, 8–10, 12–16, 20, 22; and LSO Archives, OBBRP, "Donna Haley." Haley recalled that her articling firm tried to have two students each year and that the firm also provided articles for two other women: Daphne Byers (1955) and Lorraine Gotlib (1959).

86 OSCLH, oral history, "Madam Justice Donna Haley," 14–15, 22. See also (1954) 28:3 *Obiter Dicta* 27; *Levana Journal*, Kingston, Ontario (6 February 1953); and "Gold Key Award Winners, 1954–55" (1955) 29:3 *Obiter Dicta* 25. The other two winners of the Gold Key in 1954–55 were Ian Outerbridge and Robert Stanbury.

in the Supreme Court of Canada, represented by B.J. McKinnon.[87] Haley's firm was also involved in several estate litigation cases, including *Hayward v Thompson*, a case that involved the testimony of an expert witness who had not interviewed the testatrix prior to her death. Instead, his expert opinion about the mental capacity of the testatrix was based on his attendance at the trial and his review of evidence presented there. The will left the testatrix's property to her sister, and Erichsen-Brown and Haley believed that the will had been signed under undue influence on the part of the sister, who had excluded the husband and daughter of the testatrix from access to her prior to her death. Although the challenge to the disputed will was unsuccessful at trial and in the appeal court, Erichsen-Brown and Haley appealed *in forma pauperis* to the Supreme Court of Canada. Haley recalled inquiring about a ladies' robing room at the court, and being directed to the ladies' washroom. The Supreme Court allowed the appeal with costs; the case report misidentified her as "Miss Dona J. Haley."[88]

Haley established an extensive estates practice, including drawing wills and probate, administration, and succession duties problems. When Margaret Perney (1927) died in 1962, she assigned her practice to Haley "through the good graces of Elizabeth Maclennan" (1927). At this time, Haley joined the Rohmer firm, eventually becoming a partner. In 1968, the firm was Rohmer, Cory & Haley at 480 University Avenue. Following a number of changes, Haley was in a sole practice by 1975, and she chaired the Royal Commission on the Status of Pensions in Ontario (1977–81), and served as chair of the Pension Commission of Ontario for 9 years. Haley was appointed QC in 1967, and in 1981 she was appointed a judge of the York Judicial District Court, "the tenth woman appointed a judge [in Canada] in the preceding twenty months by Justice Minister, Jean Chrétien." Haley worked extensively on pension reform and chaired the Canadian Association of Pension Supervisory Authorities, as well as assisting in the

87 OSCLH, oral history, "Donna Haley," 24–28. Bert McKinnon, QC, was later appointed to the Ontario Court of Appeal (1974–78) and became Associate Chief Justice of Ontario.

88 *Hayward v Thompson*, (1960) 25 DLR (2d) 545. See also OSCLH, oral history, "Donna Haley," 28–34. Because of the Supreme Court of Canada's decision, the testatrix's earlier will, in favour of her husband and daughter, was probated, but since the sister had moved to Ireland, there was a delay in obtaining the costs awarded, and the Irish pound was devalued in the interim. As Haley, concluded, "Mrs. Thompson [the sister] won in the end, in some fashion." Haley also noted that County Court Judge Frank McDonagh stipulated that women should not appear in his court.

preparation of a pensions report for the Royal Commission on the Status of Women, later presented by the Business and Professional Women's Club. In 1990, she became a justice of the Ontario Court of Justice (General Division) and, in 2002, of the Superior Court of Justice.[89]

During her years in practice and as a judge, Haley was involved in efforts to reform the law of succession, and she had ongoing concerns about inadequate protection for persons who lacked capacity. She also felt strongly about the use of simple language, eschewing Latin, and she preferred to apply "the intention of the testator, not for making it come out nicely for everybody in the end." And although Haley did not feel that her gender was of great significance, she apparently disagreed with Justice Dymond's determination to make gender irrelevant among members of the judiciary. Thus, after her judicial appointment, when Haley's office did not have an adjoining washroom, she strongly dissented from Dymond's advice to use the men's washroom along the corridor. Haley retired as a judge in 2002, and fulfilled a life-long dream to live beside the ocean in Sidney, British Columbia. She enjoyed legal practice very much, but also acknowledged that "being a judge, being on the other side of the fence, that was equally intriguing, and I enjoyed that too." Haley died in January 2023 a few days before her 94th birthday.[90]

June Gross, later Allan, who was also called to the bar in June 1955, was briefly employed in 1956 at Wray, Russell, Rogers & Beck, a firm of nine lawyers, including Gross. It appears that Gross married and moved to Rochester, New York, and she apparently ceased to practise law.[91]

Daphne Byers, later Rose, the daughter of an industrial engineer in Welland, also joined the legal profession in June 1955. She obtained a BA in philosophy at the University of Toronto prior to attending Osgoode Hall, and she articled with G.L. Howell and E.B. Titus in Toronto. After her call to the bar, she practised criminal law at the firm of H.R. Rose, QC, at 372 Bay

89 OSCLH, oral history, "Madam Justice Donna Haley," 40–46, and 86–87. See also "10th Woman Appointed to Bench," *Toronto Star* (31 October 1981). Haley confirmed that she did not apply for a judicial appointment. See also discussion of intention in a will in *Fox v Fox Estate* (1994) 5 ETR (2d) 179 (Gen Div); (1996) 28 OR (3d) 496 (CA); LSO Archives, OBBRP, "Donna Haley"; *Canadian Law Lists*; and obituary, *Globe and Mail* (28 January 2023) at B20.

90 OSCLH, oral history, "Madam Justice Donna Haley," 90, 100–101, 140, 147; and obituary, *Globe and Mail* (28 January 2023) at B20.

91 Huckle, "List of Women Barristers and Solicitors"; and *Canadian Law Lists*.

Street. In an interview not long after her call to the bar, Byers stated that criminal law in practice was quite different from legal theory:

> You see the other side of life ... When I first went to the courts, I believed everything a defendant said, every defendant. Since then, I have learned that not all are lily white ... So many people appear in court without counsel, and [then] plead guilty to charges or fail to defend themselves properly ... Perhaps one grows used to seeing the plight of some of the bewildered accused ... But I don't think I ever shall. Check back in five years.

Byers married Harry Rose, who had been called to the bar in 1929, and they practised together at the firm until Rose's death in 1964. In 1965, she was listed as "Daphne J.M. Rose" at the firm of Rose, Rose, Kerzner & Silver, with two lawyers who had been admitted to the bar in 1965. From 1966 to 1968, Byers Rose was listed as a sole practitioner at 347 Bay Street, and in 1970 she was listed at 70 Deslisle Avenue. Byers Rose died in 1975.[92]

A fifth woman called to the bar in June 1955 was Mary Agnes Haffa, later Bennett. Her sister, Bertha Haffa McCarney, had been called to the bar in 1952, making them the first pair of sisters to become lawyers in Ontario; a photo of them appeared in the press. Mary Agnes Haffa later married David T. Bennett and practised real estate law at the McCarthy firm from 1956. She was listed as "M.A. Bennett" after 1966. After her marriage, she may have practised part-time up to the 1970s. Haffa Bennett died in 2013.[93]

In September 1955, Eleanor Colleen Ball, later Purvis/Washington, was called to the bar. From 1957, she was employed as a solicitor in the Office of the Official Guardian. After her marriage to W.B. Purvis, around 1965, she continued to work for the office as Mrs. E. Purvis. She was active in the

92 LSO Archives, WLAO fonds, SB, vol. 6, G. Bryant, "Women Lawyers Learn Ropes of Court Work, Meet 'Rougher Element,'" unidentified press report. See also LSO Archives, OBBRP, "Daphne Rose"; and Huckle, "List of Women Barristers and Solicitors," where Byers's date of call to the bar is correct, although it is included in the list of women called to the bar in 1964. In her early years at the Rose firm, Byers's name was included in parentheses in the *Canadian Law Lists.*

93 LSO Archives, WLAO fonds, SB, vol. 6, photo of Haffa McCarney (1952) and Haffa, later Bennett (1955), *Globe and Mail* (24 June 1955); Huckle, "List of Women Barristers and Solicitors"; and *Canadian Law Lists.* Although M.A. Haffa was included in the McCarthy firm's listing after 1966, her name was not included in the firm's professional card after that date. See also *Continuum* (Osgoode Hall Law School) (Winter 2013) 31.

WLAO, and after a second marriage, she served as president in 1970–71 as "Colleen Purvis Washington."[94]

Shirley Tucker, later Parks, was also admitted to the Ontario bar, by transfer from Saskatchewan, in September 1955. The daughter of a lawyer, W.A. Tucker, she completed the BA and LLB degrees at the University of Saskatchewan, and she articled in Saskatoon with D.C. Disberry and in Ottawa with A.D. Wilson. She was called to the Saskatchewan bar in 1954. In Ontario, she was admitted to bar using her own surname, but she requested a revision in Law Society records after her marriage to Gordon Parks in 1958. Tucker Parks practised in Ottawa, where she was appointed Director of Legal Services for the federal Department of Health and Welfare. She was appointed QC in 1973.[95]

Four women were called to the bar in 1956, and two were admitted to the profession in June. One was Daisy McCullagh from Cobourg, who had served in several leadership positions in women's organizations there. After completing an honours degree at University College in 1952, she enrolled at Osgoode Hall at the age of thirty-eight, leaving her husband and two daughters, aged fifteen and seventeen, at home in Cobourg. As she explained, "The surprising thing is not that she is working towards a law career at her stage in life, but that she has a husband 'who will let me.'" McCullagh articled with John German in Cobourg and with Margaret Hyndman and Benjamin Grossberg in Toronto. McCullagh served with Donna Haley on the executive of the Legal and Literary Society at Osgoode Hall, where McCullagh was the women's representative; like Haley, McCullagh received a Gold Key award at her graduation.[96]

At the call to the bar ceremony in June 1956, McCullagh was one of two women in a graduating class of 159. She returned to Cobourg to practise law, the first woman lawyer in the community and "the only lady lawyer

94 Huckle, "List of Women Barristers and Solicitors"; and *Canadian Law Lists.*

95 Huckle, "List of Women Barristers and Solicitors"; and LSO Archives, OBBRP, "Shirley Tucker Parks," as revised in 1973. See also *Canadian Law Lists*; and E. Mitchell Thomas, "The History of Women Lawyers in the County of Carleton Law Association" in W. Johnson, ed., *The First Century: Essays on the History of the County of Carleton Law Association by Various Hands on the Occasion of the Association's Centenary, 1888–1988* (Ottawa: Bonanza Press, 1988) 107 at 113.

96 Huckle, "List of Women Barristers and Solicitors"; (1954) 26:3 *Obiter Dicta* 27; and LSO Archives, Daisy McCullagh fonds, D. Goudy, "Mother of 2 Studies Law, Plans Cobourg Practice," unidentified news report (10 February 1953). See also *Peterborough Examiner* (26 February 1953); and LSO Archives, OBBRP, "Daisy McCullagh."

in the United Counties." At first, she practised with John German, but she then established her own practice on Division Street and later purchased the McCullagh Building on King Street West, where she practised with Tom Hart. She was appointed QC in 1969, and after the practice and building were sold, her practice continued as McCullagh, Macklin, VanDuzer & Halls. McCullagh retired in the 1980s, after practising law for twenty-five years. She was honoured by the lawyers and judges of the Northumberland Bar Association at a special event, at which she received an honorary life membership. McCullagh was described as "a fine counsel, an honorable lawyer ... [and] a credit to the Law Society."[97]

The other woman who was called to the bar with McCullagh in June 1956 was Audrey Ross Rosenthal, and the two women appeared together in a press photograph. Ross Rosenthal's spouse, Harold Rosenthal, had been called to the bar in 1954 and was practising in Windsor at the firm of McTague and Co., where Helen McTague (1924) was still in practice. By 1958, however, it was Ross Rosenthal who was employed at the McTague firm while her spouse had established a sole practice in the Security Building in Windsor. In 1968, Ross Rosenthal was appointed Area Director for the Ontario Legal Aid Plan in Essex County, and in 1970 she became an assistant director of the plan. In 1973, she was appointed Legal Accounts Officer, a position she held as a member of the senior administration at the head office of the Ontario Legal Aid Plan in Toronto for the rest of her career.[98]

In September 1956, Moyra Seeger, later Nicholson, was admitted to the Ontario bar by transfer from Nova Scotia. She graduated from Dalhousie Law School, "the youngest student to graduate from a law school in Canada." She completed her law degree at the age of twenty. She articled with Syd Gillies and Richard Bell in Ottawa and married D.E. Nicholson. She practised law in Ottawa, initially at Greenberg, Wright and then with Hill, Hill and Hall. She later worked as part of the firm of Nicholson &

97 LSO Archives, WLAO fonds, SB, vol. 6, unidentified news report (June 1956); *Cobourg Sentinel Star* (3 May 1956); and "Prominent Lawyer Honoured on Her Retirement," *Cobourg Daily Star* (8 October 1981). See also LSO Archives, OBBRP, "Daisy McCullagh."

98 Huckle, "List of Women Barristers and Solicitors"; *Canadian Law Lists*; and LSO Archives, WLAO fonds, SB, vol. 6, unidentified news report. Ross Rosenthal replaced D.J. Thomas, QC, as Legal Accounts Officer when Thomas became an assistant director at the Ontario Legal Aid Plan. In the 1950s, Helen McTague (1924) was still heading the Windsor firm of McTague & Co.: see Chapter Three; and *Canadian Law Lists*.

Nicholson and in the federal government as Legal Advisor to the Department of Agriculture.[99]

In October 1956, Elaine Knight was called to the Ontario bar at the age of forty-one. She practised for two years at the firm of Lamont and Lamont (Mary Lamont, 1937) in the Temple Building in Toronto. In 1963, Knight was employed at Mathews, Dinsdale & Clark at 366 Bay Street, but by 1966, she had she relocated to Zimmerman, Haywood, Winters & Chambers at 111 Richmond Street West. From 1967 Knight was in a sole practice at 347 Bay Street. She died in 1978.[100]

In 1957, seven women were called to the bar. In April, Eileen MacLean Yates joined the Ontario legal profession by transfer from Nova Scotia and Alberta. MacLean was born in Port Hawkesbury, Nova Scotia, and she graduated with degrees in arts and law from Dalhousie University. She began her legal practice in Halifax, where she was secretary-treasurer of the Nova Scotia Barristers Society and registrar of the Nova Scotia Admiralty District. In addition, she worked as chief solicitor of the Workmen's Compensation Board of Nova Scotia. MacLean moved to Alberta, where she was appointed legislative counsel for the province and became a member of the Attorney General's Department. With her husband, George Yates, also a lawyer, she moved to Hamilton, where she articled with A.J. Polson, QC. After being called to the Ontario bar, she was hired to revise the municipal bylaws in Hamilton, and in 1959 she was appointed Acting City Solicitor.

The press reported that "Mrs. Yates was originally a Maritimer and has all the directness attributed to the people who hail from the eastern provinces. She does not permit any interference from council members in the legal proceedings being undertaken by the department." Another press report indicated that Yates was scheduled to represent Hamilton in a hearing in Ottawa about Bell Telephone's application for increased rates. When the Hamilton council subsequently appointed a new City Solicitor, Allen Stewart from Owen Sound, Eileen Yates joined her husband and they

99 Huckle, "List of Women Barristers and Solicitors"; and *Canadian Law Lists*. See also Mitchell Thomas, "The History of Women Lawyers," 110: Seeger's articles in Ottawa completed her barrister qualification in Nova Scotia as well as in Ontario.

100 Huckle, "List of Women Barristers and Solicitors"; LSO Archives, OBBRP, "Elaine Knight"; and *Canadian Law Lists*. Huckle indicated that Knight likely practised in Oshawa. Knight may have left the Lamont firm in 1960 after Irene Domagalski (1958) joined Lamont & Lamont that year.

practised law as Yates & Yates at 23 James Street South. MacLean Yates was appointed QC in 1968 and she died in 1979.[101]

In June 1957, three women were called to the bar. Records indicate that Nancy Curran, later Carnwath, graduated from the University of Toronto in 1952 and was employed in 1960 at Goodenough, Higginbottom, McDonell & Colville at 320 Bay Street. Her biography indicates that she worked for most of her career as a partner at McMillan Binch, where she specialized in commercial real estate until 1994. In that year, she was appointed counsel at Helsons, LLP, and she remained in this position until 2012, when she officially retired, although she continued to provide counsel at the firm on a part-time basis. Carnwath also lectured in real estate in the Bar Admission Course and contributed articles for continuing education about real estate and banking securities.[102]

Another woman called to the bar in June was Cezarina Wysocki. She graduated from the University of Toronto and studied at the Toronto Conservatory before entering Osgoode Hall. After her call to the bar, she was employed in 1958 in the Ministry of the Attorney General. In 1962, Wysocki was featured in a news report in Ottawa following her appointment as co-counsel for the Crown in a controversial criminal trial, in which the accused was Mrs. Adrienne Laroche, the former Eastview town treasurer. The Crown was also represented by special prosecutor R.P. Milligan from Cornwall; it was the first time a male-female team represented the Crown in a criminal case in Ottawa. A news report explained that "Miss Wysocki finds little discrimination against women lawyers," although she conceded that women might have to prove themselves a bit more than a man. Asked whether she planned to be a career woman or a housewife, Wysocki suggested that it was possible to have a legal career and a marriage, but not "when you become a mother." Wysocki continued to work in the provincial government, but she later transferred to the Ministry of Health.[103]

101 Huckle, "List of Women Barristers and Solicitors"; LSO Archives, WLAO fonds, SB, vol. 6 *Toronto Telegram* (8 November 1957); and *Canadian Law Lists*. See also LSO Archives, OBBRP, "Eileen MacLean Yates."

102 Huckle, "List of Women Barristers and Solicitors"; and *Canadian Law Lists*. See also Nancy Carnwath biography, Helsons, LLP, online: <http://helsons.ca/lawyers/nancy-carnwath>.

103 Huckle, "List of Women Barristers and Solicitors"; *Canadian Law Lists*; and J. Strachan, "A Charming Prosecutor," *Ottawa Citizen* (10 February 1962).

Margaret Archibald was also called to the bar in June 1957, at the age of thirty. Born in Kent County, she obtained a BA in 1948 from the University of Western Ontario. She worked as a secretary at Imperial Oil in Sarnia and later in Toronto, and she was admitted to the law school at Osgoode Hall in 1953. She articled with Ralph Steele in Chatham and with Joy Kennedy (1951) in Toronto. After being called to the bar, she was employed in the legal department of the California Standard Company in Calgary for three years, but in 1960 she returned to Ontario to practise law in Chatham and Dresden, the first woman lawyer in these communities. In 1966, she purchased the practice of Leigh Snider, QC, and continued to practise law in the 1970s and '80s. In 1974, Archibald spoke at the annual meeting of the YWCA in St. Thomas, and she was appointed to the new Ontario Status of Women Council, the only representative from southwestern Ontario. She was active in several civic and church committees and an ardent proponent of women's rights. In 1982, she was elected mayor of Chatham, serving until 1986. Archibald was probably the first Ontario woman lawyer to become mayor of an Ontario city. She and her husband, Frank Sysel, retired to Lake Huron, and she died in 2019 at the age of ninety-four.[104]

Three women were called to the bar in September 1957. Rainey Hunter, the daughter of an architect, completed a BA at the University of Toronto in 1952. While attending Osgoode Hall, she articled with Harold Steele. After her call to the bar, she found employment in the Provincial Secretary's Department in 1958 and later joined the staff of the York County Legal Aid office. Hunter was active in the WLAO, serving as President from 1973 to 1975. She died in 1991.[105]

Laura Gray was also called to the bar in September. Her father was the proprietor of Gray's Baggage Transport, and she graduated with a BA from the University of Western Ontario. Gray articled with George Mitchell in London, and after her call to the bar, she established a long-standing sole practice at 354 Waterloo Street in London. She was appointed QC in 1974.

104 Huckle, "List of Women Barristers and Solicitors"; *Canadian Law Lists*; and LSO Archives, OBBRP, "Margaret Archibald." The LSO record indicates that she discontinued her law practice in 1984, although her obituary suggested that she continued to practise law into the late 1980s: Forest Funeral Home, obituary, 2019. See also Dresden, "Chatham Lawyer to Practice Here," *North Kent Leader* (15 December 1966); and "To Address Annual Meeting of YWCA," *St. Thomas Times-Journal* (16 February 1974).

105 Huckle, "List of Women Barristers and Solicitors"; LSO Archives, OBBRP, "Esther Rainey Hunter"; and *Canadian Law Lists*.

Gray joined the Middlesex Bar Association in 1957, and she remained a member of the association, along with other women lawyers in London, including Evelyn Harrison (1921), Gretta Grant (1946), and Beth Underhill (1940). She died in London in 1983 at the age of fifty-five.[106]

Joan Robinette, later Sadleir, was also admitted to the bar in September. The daughter of J.J. Robinette, she was photographed with him in a press report, which noted that her grandfather was T.C. Robinette, "one of the greatest criminal lawyers to address a jury in Ontario." Joan Robinette clerked for J. McRuer, Chief Justice of the High Court of Ontario, and she worked briefly as a research assistant for the Law Society's Legal Education Committee, but she resigned in the fall of 1959. After her marriage to R.H. Sadleir, she did not practise law, but she was involved with her husband in the early days of Trent University and in numerous community groups in Peterborough and Toronto. Joan Robinette Sadleir died in August 2022.[107]

As a result of the "historic agreement" between the Benchers of the Law Society and the universities in 1957, arrangements for legal education in Ontario changed dramatically. In addition to academic programs at several Ontario universities, Osgoode Hall established its three-year full-time academic program at its downtown location and, after 1968, at York University. These new entry paths to the legal profession in Ontario probably contributed to the very significant increase in the number of women lawyers in subsequent decades.

106 Huckle, "List of Women Barristers and Solicitors"; *Canadian Law Lists*; and F. Carter, *The Middlesex Bench and Bar* (London: Middlesex Law Association, 1969). See also LSO Archives, OBBRP, "Laura Isabelle Gray," a record that identified Gray's mother as a "lady."

107 Huckle, "List of Women Barristers and Solicitors"; LSO Archives, WLAO fonds, SB, vol. 6; LSO, Minutes of Convocation (20 November 1959); and obituary, *Globe and Mail* (3 September 2022).

# *Achievements on the Margins of the Legal Profession*

> *Women, despite individual achievements ... remained on the margins of the profession. From the 1940s through the 1960s, a handful of women were called to the Ontario bar each year ... No women had yet been elected to convocation (or even come close), and the conviction that women were "okay for trust work" but inappropriate in most fields (and particularly in well-paid, prestigious, and influential ones) remained strong in the profession and among its principal clients.*[1]

Eighty-seven women entered the Ontario legal profession between 1940 and 1957, almost the same number who became lawyers between 1919 and 1939. Whereas Canada had 466 women doctors by 1957, only 187 women had become lawyers in Ontario, and not all of them practised law. The requirement of university studies and the four-year program in law at Osgoode Hall in 1950 might have created obstacles for some women who wanted to be lawyers, although recognition of the law program at the University of Toronto reduced attendance at Osgoode Hall for its graduates to two years. At the same time, the postwar preferential treatment of male veterans and the resurgence of traditional roles for women in the 1950s

1 C. Moore, *The Law Society of Upper Canada and Ontario's Lawyers, 1797–1997* (Toronto: University of Toronto Press, 1997) 268.

probably discouraged some women.[2] Yet, women continued to pursue admission to the Ontario bar, perhaps encouraged by Ellen Fairclough, the first woman member of the federal Cabinet, who had commented in 1951, "Anything the girls want badly enough they can get."[3]

The experiences of women lawyers between 1940 and 1957 continued to reflect gendered patterns, especially in relation to marriage. Among the nine women called to the bar in 1948, the largest cohort of new women lawyers up to 1957, three—Celia Corcoran, Joan Heath, and Kathleen Killoran—did not marry and they all practised law. Two—Marion Smith McKinnon and Mhora MacInnis Hollingsworth—married early and did not engage in legal work for long, although MacInnis Hollingsworth may have practised part-time after her marriage. Marjorie Laird Palmer, who married fifteen years after being called to the bar, continued to be employed, and three women—Bettie Jean Teagle MacDonald, Margaret Dufresne, and Laura Down Legge—practised law with their spouses.

Several other women, who married their classmates at Osgoode Hall, established legal practices with their spouses: Beth Rowlin Underhill (1940) in London, Mary Gallagher Gauthier (1940) in Timmins, and Thelma Kerr Thomson (1949) in Lindsay. In the 1950s, some women lawyers, including Anne Levine Dubin (1951) and Joan Bissett Neiman (1954), married and practised law with their spouses in small firms in Toronto. Similarly, June Tarshis Bernhard (1951) also eventually practised with her husband in Toronto. Two women lawyers, Dorothy Howard Reilly (1945) and Daphne Byers Rose (1955), practised law in their lawyer husbands' firms after their spouses died. Dorothy Howard Reilly also practised with two of her children. Sarah Kaplan Goldstick (1943) established her own practice in her husband's Toronto office after his death, and Kathleen Morrison Callahan (1946) did so in Fort Frances. Ina Greenblatt Paul (1950)

2 For graduates of the law program at the University of Toronto, including June Bushell and Anna Bacon Ker (1954), the new program at Osgoode Hall was attractive. But after the admission of matriculants to Osgoode Hall was abolished in the mid-1950s, university attendance became a permanent requirement for entry to Osgoode Hall.

3 Law Society of Ontario (LSO) Archives, Women's Law Association of Ontario (WLAO) fonds, "Career Field Wide for Modern Miss," *Toronto Telegram* (5 April 1951) 5: this report (perhaps inaccurately) identified only 113 women were lawyers in Canada. By 1951, 159 women had been called to the Ontario bar, although not all were practising: E. Huckle, "List of Women Barristers and Solicitors in Ontario, 1897–1975" [unpublished, archived at Law Society of Ontario Archives].

may have continued legal work from her home after her marriage and the birth of her children. A few women also practised law with other family members: Vivien Weekes Scott (1943), with her father and brothers in London; Celia Corcoran (1948), with her father in Toronto; and Judy LaMarsh (1950), with her father in Niagara Falls. Nonetheless, some women who married experienced exclusion: Anna Stevenson (1955) felt unwelcome as a lawyer in a trust company after her first marriage, and both Jean Oldreive Carrie (1945) and Joan Morris Hodgson (1949) practised for a few years and then married and abandoned practice, although Hodgson returned to work at the Legal Aid office in later years.

Many women lawyers in the 1940s and '50s continued to work in government, joining earlier women lawyers at the Parliament Buildings in Toronto: Fern Levis (1944) and Eleanor Ball Purvis Washington (1955) at the Office of the Official Guardian, Marjorie Laird Palmer (1948) and Cezarina Wysocki (1957) at the Ministry of the Attorney General, Katharine Hanlon Meechan (1951) in the Provincial Secretary's Department, and Laura Down Legge at the Ministry of Health. In Ottawa, Eileen Mitchell Thomas (1942), Shirley Tucker Parks (1955), and Moyra Seeger Nicholson (1956) were employed by the federal government. Women continued to be appointed City Solicitors, including Elizabeth Robson (1949) in Burlington, Joy Kennedy Clarry (1951) in Toronto, and Eileen MacLean Yates (1957) in Hamilton. With the advent of the Ontario Legal Aid Plan, moreover, women were appointed as Area Directors: Gretta Wong Grant (1946) in London, Joan Heath (1948) in Guelph, and Audrey Ross Rosenthal (1956) in Windsor; and Ross Rosenthal also became a senior administrator in the Head Office. In addition, Joan Morris Hodgson (1949) and Rainey Hunter (1957) were employed at the York County Legal Aid Office, along with Mary Lamont (1937).

Women who joined the legal profession in the 1940s and '50s generally obtained employment in small- to medium-sized firms, especially in communities outside Toronto: Helen Carefoot (1946) in Windsor, Joan Heath (1948) in Guelph, Judy LaMarsh (1950) in Niagara Falls, Mary Munro Weaver (1951) in Sudbury, Stella Panarites (1953) in Cobalt and other locations in northern Ontario, Daisy McCullagh (1956) in Cobourg, and Margaret Archibald (1957) in Chatham. In addition, several women lawyers obtained employment in small- to medium-sized firms in Toronto: Elsie Teasdale (1942), Olga Chumak Chepesiuk (1944), Margaret Smith (1944), Mabel Van Camp (1947), Sidney Dymond (1949), Joy Kennedy Clarry (1951), Helen Tedman (1950), June Bushell (1953), and Donna Haley (1955).

Some, including Harriet Clark (1947) and June Tarshis Bernhard and Janet Scott (1951) and others, established their own firms.

Yet women generally remained absent from large and prestigious Toronto law firms. Although Edith Sheppard Revel (1925) was employed briefly at the McCarthy firm in the 1920s, prior to her marriage and relocation to India, Belva Gordon Gibson Hammell (1930) was not hired at the Blakes firm until 1942, and initially only for the duration of the war. Both Gibson Hammell and Dorothy Grimshaw (1946) eventually became partners at Blakes, but most women who were hired in these large firms were contract employees, and their work focused almost exclusively on real estate transactions: Noreen Charlebois Stevens (1955) and other women lawyers at Fraser & Beatty, Mary Haffa Bennett (1955) at the McCarthy firm, and Georgia Riddell Bentley (1954) at Faskens. In this context, the recruitment of Janet Lang Boland (1950) as a partner at Lang, Michener in the late 1960s, and the recruitment of Anne Levine Dubin (1951) at Torys in the early 1970s were significant.

A few women in this cohort achieved political prominence in Parliament. Judy LaMarsh (1950) was the first woman lawyer in Canada to be appointed to Cabinet, in 1963, and Joan Bissett Neiman (1954) was the first Ontario woman lawyer to be appointed to the Senate, in 1972. In addition, Margaret Archibald (1957) was the first woman lawyer to be elected mayor of an Ontario city. Several women who were called to the bar in the 1940s and '50s were later appointed judges, arguably the result of societal pressures on "gatekeepers," the impact of the feminist movement, and the increasing number of women lawyers. The appointment of Mabel Van Camp (1947) in 1971 was followed by the appointment of Janet Lang Boland (1950) in 1972, Sidney Dymond (1949) in 1973, Elizabeth Robson (1949) in 1976, June Tarshis Bernhard (1951) in 1979, Janet Scott (1951) in 1982, and Donna Haley (1955) in 1981. Yet, as Mabel Van Camp announced at the time of her appointment, she had no intention of thinking of herself as a "woman judge": "I won't feel required to prove anything. I would imagine that from the moment I assume office I will be a judge ... I've been a lawyer for 24 years. I'm not a woman. I don't think like a woman while I am practising law."[4]

Many women who were called to the bar between 1940 and 1957 continued to come from the "professional class." Except for Gretta Wong Grant (1946), they were all white, and most came from middle-class families and had attended university. A few women who participated in the war effort succeeded in attending Osgoode Hall with their veterans' benefits, although others had to work part-time to attend law school. There was little diversity among these women lawyers. It is unclear whether Noreen Charlebois Stevens (1955) and Margaret Dufresne were members of the Franco-Ontarian community, and there were no women of colour or women with Indigenous heritage among those called to the bar up to 1957. As in earlier decades, there were a few women whose families had immigrated to Canada: Olga Chumak Chepesuik (1944) was the daughter of Ukrainian immigrants, Stella Panarites (1953) was the daughter of a Greek immigrant, and both parents of Gretta Wong Grant (1946) had emigrated from China. There was also little religious diversity. A large majority of the women were Protestant, although a few, including Janet Lang Boland (1950) and perhaps others, were Catholic. In addition, Elizabeth Robson (1949) may be the only woman lawyer in this cohort with a disability.

Moreover, only a handful of Jewish women were called to the bar in the 1940s and '50s: Sarah Kaplan Goldstick (1943), Frances Feldman English

4 In 1970, *The Report of the Royal Commission on the Status of Women* (Ottawa: Information Canada, 1970) 342 recommended the appointment of women judges, quoting the former Chief Justice of the Ontario Supreme Court J.C. McRuer, who suggested that women should be appointed not because of their sex but on the basis of merit: "There are many women who are practising at the Bar of Canada who would make better judges than some of the men that have been appointed" (Recommendation 33). See also LSO Archives, WLAO fonds, Scrapbook (SB), vol. 10, "First Woman High Court Judge Says Divorce 'Shouldn't Occur,'" *Toronto Star* (12 November 1971).

(1944), Anne Levine Dubin (1951), and Rose Rabkin Rosenfeld (1954).[5] Discrimination against Jewish women lawyers was muted. Both the WLAO and the sorority eventually abandoned their formal restrictions against the admission of Jewish women during and after the Second World War. Although Lily Sherizen Sharon (1930) was invited to join the WLAO and eventually became President, it is unclear whether others were fully welcomed, and the Reading Law Club, established in 1947 for Jewish lawyers, only welcomed male lawyers in the 1970s. There is some evidence that Sherizen Sharon (1930) argued for Jewish women's admission to the Reading Law Club, and the membership list for 1958 included (Sarah) Ida Goldstick (1943); Helen Grossman (1929), QC; Clara Muskat (1935); and Lily Sherizen (1930), QC, although they may not have attended club meetings.[6]

5 Others may have been Jewish, including Marjorie Horenblas Jacobs (1940), Ina Greenblatt Paul (1950), and June Tarshis Bernhard (1951). In the 1970s, Jewish lawyers in Toronto often established sole practices, and both Jewish and Catholic lawyers were overrepresented in small firms (two to five lawyers). In Toronto law firms with more than twenty-five lawyers, there were no Catholics and only a small percentage of Jews, and these larger Protestant law firms engaged in much of the corporate and commercial law work: H.W. Arthurs, J. Willms, and L. Taman, "The Toronto Legal Profession: An Exploratory Survey" (1971) 21 *University of Toronto Law Journal* 498 at 517. A later study of Toronto lawyers in the 1980s revealed greater diversity—as well as ongoing exclusionary practices: J. Hagan, M. Huxter, and P. Parker, "Class Structure and Legal Practice: Inequality and Mobility among Toronto Lawyers" (1988) 22 *Law and Society Review* 9. See also Part Four.

6 S. Sperdakos, "'A Forum for Discussion' and Place of Respite: Jewish Lawyers and Toronto's Reading Law Club" (2012) 30 *Windsor Yearbook of Access to Justice* 163. The Reading Law Club was named for an English barrister, Rufus Isaacs, elected to the House of Commons in Britain. He represented the town of Reading and became the first Jewish person to be appointed Lord Chief Justice. It is unclear whether women lawyers were welcome to attend meetings of the Reading Club or whether women called to the bar after 1939 expressed interest in membership. Jewish male lawyers continued to be excluded from the Lawyers Club after the Second World War. In 1948, Henry Rosenberg wrote to the President of the County of York Law Association to explain his decision not to attend the upcoming dinner because numerous members were also members of the Lawyers Club. Rosenberg was appalled that such "Hitlerian ideology" remained in the Lawyers Club's constitution after Canada's involvement in a war for freedom and democracy: LSO Archives, York County Law Association fonds, letter from H.S. Rosenberg to R.H. Sankey, President of the County of York Law Association (22 April 1948).

Moreover, discrimination against Jewish lawyers continued after the war and into the 1950s. When Dr. Wright addressed the WLAO in 1947 on the subject of legal education, he suggested that "students of different race or creed have an almost hopeless task in trying to obtain a place in better law offices," and it was not until 1955 that John Geller was admitted to the partnership at Campbell Godfrey, probably the first Jewish partner in a major Toronto firm.[7] Even after the Reading Law Club accepted an invitation to amalgamate with the Lawyers Club, members of the Reading Law Club failed to recognize that they would be joining a discriminatory organization—the Lawyers Club was still restricted to male members. As Sophia Sperdakos concluded, "This reflects the extent to which women's right to equal treatment within the profession lagged decades behind changes respecting other forms of discrimination, even among those groups who were themselves discriminated against."[8]

In the 1940s and '50s, the WLAO continued to provide support for women lawyers. There was a reception in honour of Helen Kinnear (1920) when she was appointed to the County Court in 1943 and for Helen Palen (1918) when she was appointed deputy registrar of the Supreme Court of Ontario in 1950. In addition, although several women achieved recognition when they were awarded KC or QC appointments, election as a Law Society Bencher was more elusive. It was not until 1975 that Laura Legge became the first woman elected a Bencher, even though Isadore Levinter

7 Moore, *The Law Society of Upper Canada*, 267, 179–80; and Sperdakos, "A Forum for Discussion." See also LSO Archives, WLAO fonds, "Race Discrimination Seen Hampering Law Students," unidentified news report (ca. 1947).

8 Sperdakos, "A Forum for Discussion," 186–87, quoting *Toronto Telegram* (26 March 1964). For the wives of lawyers, there was a Lady Reading Club, a social and charitable organization. According to Sperdakos, women lawyers were invited to join the Lady Reading Club, but none did so: Sperdakos, "A Forum for Discussion," 192–ff, n93. Like meetings of the WLAO, the Lady Reading Club met in members' homes. By contrast, the Reading Law Club and the Lawyers Club met at Osgoode Hall, and by the 1980s, the WLAO had also moved its meetings to Osgoode Hall: D.-L. Carlson, "WLAO Moves from Tea Parties to Policy Debates," *Law Times* (14 August 1994) 1, 6. As Carlson noted, the WLAO had traditionally "served largely as a social network offering support in the cold world of law," but by the 1980s it had "moved to being much more a support for women in their roles as full- or part-time practitioners," including assistance with developing law practices, career goals, and personal development.

had become the first Jewish Bencher when he was elected in 1956.[9] Women lawyers, including Elizabeth Newton (1921), Vera Parsons (1924), Margaret Hyndman (1926), and Marjorie Brigden Henry (1921), had been candidates for Bencher at least as early as 1946. In 1951, there were again four women candidates, with Helen Palen (1918) receiving the largest number of votes, although not nearly enough to be elected. Women lawyers were unsuccessful candidates again in the Bencher elections of 1956 and 1961. In 1966, Margaret Hyndman was the only woman candidate, and she came close to being elected.[10] Thus, Legge's success in 1975 was cause for celebration. Nonetheless, she was still the only woman elected a Bencher in both 1975 and 1979, and in 1983 she was still the only woman Bencher from Toronto.[11]

Overall, the stories of women lawyers called to the bar between 1940 and 1957 reveal increasing acceptance as well as frequent marginalization. Nonetheless, these women lawyers were laying the groundwork for the much larger cohorts of women who entered the profession in subsequent decades. Moreover, in the context of their small numbers, the WLAO remained an important source of support for women lawyers. The association's feisty commitment to the legal profession as women lawyers was

9 Sperdakos "A Forum for Discussion," 174 n41. See also Chapter Two, Chapter Three and Chapter Four.

10 LSO Archives, Bencher files. In the 1951 election, the other candidates were Elizabeth Newton, Vera Parsons, and Marjorie Brigden Henry. In 1956, only Henry was a candidate, and she received just 124 votes. Again in 1961, only Vera Parsons and Marjorie Brigden Henry were candidates, and both were unsuccessful. According to Legge, Hyndman was sixteenth in the election in 1966, at a time when there were still only fifteen Benchers. However, when one of the fifteen received a judicial appointment, the Benchers were entitled to exercise discretion, and they "skipped" Hyndman and appointed the man next on the list: OSCLH, "Laura Legge," 149–54. As Treasurer, John Arnup was responsible for the increase in the number of Benchers from fifteen to forty, with twenty being allocated to candidates outside Toronto: Moore, *The Law Society of Upper Canada*, 269. Although Arnup became Treasurer in 1963, the 1966 Bencher election involved fifteen lawyers from Toronto and fifteen from outside Toronto.

11 LSO Archives, Bencher files. In 1983, Judith Bell Oyen (1964) from Ottawa and Mary Weaver (1951) from Sudbury were elected Benchers from outside Toronto. See also Osgoode Society for Canadian Legal History (OSCLH), oral history, "Margaret Smith," 110–11, which described ongoing controversies among WLAO members with respect to Bencher candidates. The second woman elected from Toronto was Frances Kiteley (1976) in 1987. A news report in the mid-1990s suggested that some women Benchers were approaching issues differently from male Benchers: D.-L. Carlson, "Law Society a Study in Gender Politics in the '90s," *Law Times* (15 May 1994) 1, 3.

evident at its Christmas dinner in December 1947 in a song composed by Ruby Wigle (1926):

*We're Ontario's women lawyers*
*And a very happy band.*
*We know about first mortgages*
*And also sales of land.*
*We listen to the sages*
*And vamp Judges out of hand*
*Meanwhile we practise law.*

*Chorus:*
*Here's to Law—the best profession*
*We struggle on without concession*
*Title searching's our obsession*
*We love to practise law.*[12]

12 LSO Archives, WLAO fonds, SB, vol. 4. The first verse and chorus of the song, to be sung to the tune of "John Brown's Body," was attached to a letter from Wigle to "Vida" (Vida Harris Grover, 1921) on the letterhead of Osgoode Hall Law School.

PART FOUR

# *After 1957: Changing Gender Patterns*

# *Continuity or Transformation?*

> *More women are practising law, more women have been appointed to Boards, Commissions and Benches, more and more women are entering partnerships in large firms, more are going out on their own—these developments will only increase and take root over the next years ... We all chose this profession because it remains one of the most important and noble of professions. It is a profession richly enhanced by its women lawyers, at least as well as by its men, and the sooner both realize it, believe it, and practise it, the easier it will be for everyone.*[1]

Almost three decades after 1957, Justice Rosalie Abella's assessment identified important changes for women in law. In exploring some of these changes, this Part engages with Judith Bennett's argument that *changes* in women's work in different historical periods more often reflect *continuity*, rather than *transformation*, in women's status relative to men.[2] At least to some extent, the historical context in which women lawyers worked, and

1 Justice R. Abella, "Women in the Legal Profession" opening presentation (Toronto: Law Society of Upper Canada Continuing Legal Education program, 13 May 1986) 1 at 20–21.

2 J. Bennett, "Theoretical Issues: Confronting Continuity" (1997) 9:3 *Journal of Women's History* 73; and J. Bennett, *History Matters: Patriarchy and the Challenge of Feminism* (Philadelphia: University of Pennsylvania Press, 2006). See also the Prologue.

the gendered patterns that shaped their opportunities, provide connections to challenges faced by some contemporary women lawyers.

Clearly, increasing numbers of Ontario women lawyers after 1957 encouraged the appointment of women as judges, their election as Benchers of the Law Society, and leadership positions in law firms, corporations, government, and university law schools. Yet these changes did not always benefit all women lawyers, and some covert exclusionary practices may suggest patterns of continuity rather than transformation. In exploring these patterns, this Part briefly examines four developments that affected roles for women lawyers in Ontario after 1957:

- The expansion of women's opportunities to study law after the accreditation of university law programs;
- The "surge" in numbers of women lawyers after 1957 in the context of second-wave feminism;
- The dramatic expansion, diversification and globalization of legal work that created new challenges for legal practice and professional culture; and
- Increasing diversity among women lawyers, by contrast with the mostly white, Protestant and middle-class women who became lawyers in the decades up to 1957.

In spite of many changes, the stories of earlier generations of women lawyers arguably remain relevant because "knowledge of the past can fortify us in the present."[3] Thus, historical patterns of gendered experiences in the legal profession, and the strategies adopted by earlier cohorts of women lawyers to confront them, may have continuing relevance for contemporary women lawyers.

3 F. Wade, *Square Haunting: Five Writers in London Between the Wars* (London: Faber & Faber, 2020) 318-19, and review: R. Franklin, "Splinters and Mosaics: On Women's History and Biography," *Harper's Magazine* (June 2020) 76 at 80. Wade argued that historical patterns may reveal unexpected resonances of feeling and experience across time and place, creating a validating sense of solidarity.

### The Accreditation of University Law Schools

> *The critical event [in the creation of new university law schools was] the settlement of a long-standing controversy in Ontario between the Bar and the University of Toronto which led to the establishment of new law faculties at Ottawa, Queen's and Western.*[4]

The first women to graduate from university law schools were admitted to the Ontario bar in 1962. At least to some extent, women may have been encouraged to become lawyers after they could complete academic and articling programs in their home communities, as well as at the University of Toronto and Osgoode Hall. In addition, all university graduates (and those with two years of university studies, pursuant to the 1957 agreement) continued to be required to article and complete the Bar Admission Course at Osgoode Hall in Toronto.

In September 1957, women became members of the first law classes at Queen's University and the University of Ottawa, while others entered law faculties at the University of Western Ontario in 1959 and at the University of Windsor in 1968. Although Ontario universities were entitled to offer these academic law programs, the 1957 agreement allocated full control over course offerings to the Law Society, ensuring substantial uniformity in legal education in the province. At Queen's, second-year students took courses in Companies and Partnerships, Constitutional Law, Equity and Trusts, Jurisprudence, Evidence, Family Law, and Real Estate Transactions, and they were permitted to take one option, either Criminology or International Trade. It was not until 1969 that the Law Society's mandatory

4 M. Cohen, "Legal Education in Canada—Fifteen Years Later, 1949–1964" in Canadian Bar Association, Papers presented at the Annual Meeting, 1964, Montreal, Québec (Toronto: CCH Canadian Limited, 1965) 117 at 118–19. Although the Law Society traditionally permitted all students with basic qualifications to be admitted to Osgoode Hall Law School, failure rates were high. In 1949, the full-time faculty in eleven Canadian law schools numbered 41, but the number had grown to 155 in sixteen law schools by 1963–64. See also G. Killeen, "On Entering the World of Law" (1990) 24:4 *Gazette* 282.

courses were reduced to seven.[5] Moreover, the Law Society continued to monitor admission requirements and statistics: in 1964, most students with minimum admission requirements—two years of university with an average of 60 per cent—had obtained a place in one of five Ontario law schools.[6]

Queen's, like other Ontario universities, had a law school as early as 1853, but after the Law Society established its law school at Osgoode Hall in 1889, requiring all aspiring Ontario lawyers to graduate from its program, law programs at Queen's ceased.[7] Queen's vice-principal, Alex Corry, successfully participated, on behalf of the universities, in the 1957 negotiation with Law Society Benchers, and he recalled that "Park Jamieson promptly produced some fine Scotch to celebrate" its successful outcome. Corry also promised that a law school at Queen's would be ready to open

5 M. Walters, *"Let Right Be Done": A History of the Faculty of Law at Queen's University* (Kingston: Faculty of Law, Queen's University, 2007) 15, 19–20, a history published to celebrate the fiftieth anniversary of the law school; it was, also published in (2007) 32:2 *Queen's Law Journal*. The first-year courses were Civil Procedure, Constitutional Law, Contracts, Criminal Law and Procedure, Personal Property, Real Property, and Torts. See also W.R. Lederman, "Canadian Legal Education in the Second Half of the Twentieth Century" (1971) *University of Toronto Law Journal* 141. More recently, the Federation of Law Societies of Canada established a national requirement for law school programs as the basis for their accreditation, and this requirement included substantive and skills-based competencies and a course in ethics and professionalism, online: <https://flsc.ca> 1-5 (accessed 1 January 2018).

6 Law Society of Upper Canada, Minutes of Convocation (20 November 1964) x–xi. As Harry Arthurs later suggested, "thirty years ago, anyone could come to law school, and what they got there did not greatly tax their intellectual powers": H. Arthurs, "Law, Society and the Law Society" (1993) 27: 2 *Gazette* 85 at 86.

7 The Board of Trustees at Queen's voted to establish a law school as early as 1853, and the first program began in 1861. Five LLB degrees were conferred two years later, along with an honorary LLD to John A. Macdonald. The Faculty of Law then promptly folded, although it was revived briefly in the mid-1880s, and for several decades political science students were permitted to write exams set by local lawyers to obtain the Queen's LLB degree: Walters: *"Let Right Be Done,"* 5–8. See also D.D. Calvin, *Queen's University at Kingston: The First Century of a Scottish-Canadian Foundation, 1841–1941* (Kingston: Trustees of the University, 1941); and H. Neatby, *Queen's University*, vol. 1, *1841–1917: And Not to Yield* (Montreal/Kingston: McGill/Queen's University Press, 1978).

by September.[8] The new Faculty of Law commenced in September 1957 with great enthusiasm. Although its Law Library was initially located in the damp basement of a men's residence and required considerable effort to keep the plaster from falling, these arrangements did not dampen students' enthusiasm as they debated the legal issues of the day: adultery as the only ground for divorce, the need to recognize legal abortion, and the abolition of capital punishment.[9] Queen's appointed two faculty members in 1957, and they were joined the following year by the new dean, W.R. Lederman, a former faculty member at Dalhousie's law school and a distinguished constitutional scholar.[10]

Twenty-four male students enrolled at Queen's Law School in 1957, along with one woman, Mary Alice Murray, a former Latin teacher. In second-year, Murray was joined by Geraldine Tepper, who had completed first-year law at the University of Toronto. Both Murray and Tepper, along with sixteen male students, graduated in 1960 and, after articling in Kingston and completing Osgoode Hall's bar admission course, both women were called to the Ontario bar in April 1962. Tepper was married to a Kingston lawyer, Lou Tepper, and the local press included a photo of the couple at her Queen's law graduation under the caption "Wife with LLB." Geraldine and Lou Tepper practised law together for many years on Princess

8 There are diverging accounts of this meeting. Corry was uneasy about being the only university representative present at the meeting, and he invited Bora Laskin (University of Toronto) to join him, but Laskin declined because of the acrimonious relations between the Benchers and the university. See Part Three; and J.A. Corry, *My Life and Work: A Happy Partnership* (Kingston: J.A. Corry/Queen's University, 1981) 151–56. Stuart Ryan at Queen's provided the school's motto, *Soit Droit Fait,* a phrase used by medieval kings when assenting to Parliamentary bills, including the Petition of Right, and thus an expression of transcendent value: Walters, *"Let Right Be Done,"* 2–5. See also "1957–1960: A Small School with a Big Future," *Queen's Law Reports 2016* at 24.

9 Walters, "Let Right Be Done," 14; and "1957–1960: A Small School," 24–25. The small number of students and faculty meant that they "became a family."

10 The faculty of law at Dalhousie University was established in 1883, the first university law school in common law Canada, and it was highly influenced by new developments in legal education at Harvard: J. Willis, *A History of Dalhousie Law School* (Toronto: University of Toronto Press, 1979). W.R. Lederman was a prolific constitutional scholar with many published books and articles, including *Continuing Canadian Constitutional Dilemmas: Essays on the Constitutional History, Public Law and Federal System of Canada* (Toronto: Butterworths, 1981). The law professors in the first year at Queen's included Dan Soberman, Stuart Ryan, and Acting Dean Corry. See also "1957–1960: A Small School," 24.

Street in Kingston, and Geraldine continued in practice after her spouse's death in 1999. In addition to other awards, she received the Law Society's Bicentennial Award of Merit in 1997 for her many contributions to public service.[11]

After her call to the bar, Mary Alice Murray was appointed by Dean Lederman as secretary and registrar in the Faculty of Law at Queen's, positions she held until her death in 1981. She was beloved by generations of students for her individualized attention to their needs: as Geraldine Tepper explained, the first class had gifted its "class treasure" to the law school. Queen's granted Murray a Distinguished Service Award in 1980 in recognition that she had become the focus of the faculty's relationship with its alumni, the local bar and the bar at large. In addition, she was "a role model to support and encourage women both as students and as teachers of law."[12] At a special ceremony marking the law school's twenty-fifth anniversary in 1982, "Miss Murray" was awarded a posthumous QC by Ontario. It was accepted by Geraldine Tepper.[13]

The University of Ottawa had also established a Faculty of Law in the nineteenth century with a program for students wishing to practise law in both Québec and Ontario, but it languished after the Osgoode Hall program began in 1889. In September 1957, the new common law program commenced, occupying part of the fourth floor of the Arts Building alongside the civil law program. The first dean of both programs, Justice Gérald Fauteux of the Supreme Court of Canada, served until 1962. There was a strict attendance requirement for classes as well as a student code of conduct, which, for example, prohibited students from using the entrance to the building reserved for faculty. In addition to courses mandated by the Law Society, the university expressed interest in offering classes consistent

11 Walters, *"Let Right Be Done,"* 10, 15–16; and the Frontenac Law Association website. The association established the Lou Tepper Award in 1999, and Geraldine Tepper was the recipient in 2006. Geraldine Tepper was the first Jewish woman to graduate at Queen's in law.

12 Walters, *"Let Right Be Done,"* 17; "1957–1960: A Small School," 24; and Queen's University, obituary, unidentified news report. In 1982, the law school created the "Mary Alice Murray Memorial Fund": letter from Professor Stuart Ryan, Chair (archived with M.J. Mossman)

13 Walters, *"Let Right Be Done,"* 17. See also Faculty of Law, Queen's University, *Alumni Anecdotes* (Kingston: Faculty of Law, Queen's University, 1982) 1, 21, 27, 44, a book dedicated to M.A. Murray, whose posthumous QC was only the second awarded in Ontario. Murray was the first Catholic woman to graduate from Queen's in law.

with "a professional and liberal education tailored to the demands of public office and the business world."[14]

Rose Marie Perry was the only woman graduate in law at the University of Ottawa in 1960. She was called to the bar in June 1962 along with the Queen's law graduates, Tepper and Murray. The daughter of an insurance adjuster, Perry completed a science program at St. Patrick's College as the only woman in her class. Although she was advised at her law school admission interview that she would be "taking a man's place, [and] would marry and have children and never practise law," Perry enrolled in the common law program. Like other women students at the university, she faced challenges: "Many male students slurred not only ... women's intellectual capacities, but also their looks, manner of dress and grooming."[15] Perry's classmates also faced challenges in their examinations since, as the first law class, there were no practice questions for review. The "mortality rate" in first-year examinations remained relatively high in the 1960s: "It was

14 A. Turnbull, ed., *Réunion: Common Law History at the University of Ottawa: 30 ans en francais, 50 Years in English* (Ottawa: University of Ottawa Faculty of Law, 2007) 3–11, online: <https://www2.uottawa.ca/faculty-law/sites/g/files/bhrskd406/files/2022-02/reunion-uofo-common-law-eng-web.pdf>. The earlier common law program ceased in 1896. In 1962, when Fauteux returned to the Supreme Court of Canada, he appointed T. Feeney as Dean of the Common Law section and P. Azard as Dean of the Civil Law section.

15 E. Huckle, "List of Women Barristers and Solicitors in Ontario" 1897–1975 [unpublished, archived at Law Society of Ontario Archives]. Turnbull, *Réunion*, 11–12; and E. Mitchell Thomas, "The History of Woman Lawyers in the County of Carleton Law Association" in W. Johnson, ed., *The First Century: Essays on the History of the County of Carleton Law Association by Various Hands on the Occasion of the Association's Centenary 1888-1988* (Ottawa: Bonanza Press, 1988) 107 at 108–9. Mitchell Thomas identified Perry as the first native Ottawa woman lawyer, perhaps because Mary McNulty Fix (1918), also from Ottawa, had practised law only briefly after her call to the bar in 1918: see Chapter Two.

easier to get in, but harder to get out."[16] After her call to the bar in 1962, Perry joined Gowling & Henderson, where she practised intellectual property law. She became a member of the International Bar Association and was appointed QC. As she reported, "I was admitted. I took a man's place. I have worked my entire life in advancing my profession and I have thoroughly enjoyed it."[17]

While Perry was the only woman law student in her class, Elisabeth Slasor, the daughter of a chartered accountant who obtained a BA from Carleton University in 1958, was the only woman graduate in law in 1961. Slasor articled with H.P. Hill and was called to the bar in 1963. She was initially employed at the Hill firm in estates law but she later joined Gowling & Henderson. Slasor died in the mid-1980s.[18]

At the University of Western Ontario (now Western University), the London Law School had been established in 1885 by the Middlesex Law Association, but the school closed its doors after the Law Society established its compulsory law school in 1889 and refused to recognize

16 Turnbull, *Réunion,* 11–14, quoting Professor Soberman at Queen's law faculty that failure rates of 20 per cent, 30 per cent, and even 40 per cent were not unusual in first-year law in the mid-1960s: students gained admission more easily than in later decades, but they failed if they did not work hard enough. In 1960, University of Ottawa law students began to compete in the annual moot court competition, now the Gale Cup: Turnbull, *Réunion,* 15, 24–26. In addition to the University of Ottawa, the 1960 competition included Queen's, the University of Toronto, Western, and Osgoode Hall. A photo of the law school's internal competition in 1959 includes a diminutive Rose Perry in the middle of the second row. Ottawa law students Roydon Kealey and Lee Ferrier won the cup in 1961 and1962; and in 1971 Sheila Block and Joyce Harris—the only women participants in the Gale Cup that year—won the cup for the University of Ottawa. Block later recalled that the law school telephoned her after she applied for admission, inquiring whether, as a married woman, she really wished to attend law school.

17 Mitchell Thomas, "The History of Women Lawyers," 113; and Turnbull, *Réunion,* 11.

18 Law Society of Ontario (LSO) Archives, Ontario Bar Biographical Research Project (OBBRP), "Elisabeth Slasor"; Huckle, "List of Women Barristers and Solicitors"; Mitchell Thomas, "The History of Women Lawyers," 111; and Turnbull, *Réunion,* 12. Mitchell Thomas reported that Slasor died in 1986, although LSO records identify her death in 1983. There is also some discrepancy in the spelling of Slasor's first name; LSO Archives records it as "Elisabeth."

graduates of the London school.[19] After the 1957 agreement, a new Faculty of Law was established at Western in 1959, and retired Supreme Court of Canada justice Ivan Rand was its first Dean. The Faculty of Law was located for two years in the Engineering Sciences building and had a library of five thousand books in its first year. A new law school building was officially opened in a ceremony on 27 October 1961.[20]

The first class of thirty-five students created a "law society," later the Legal Society, during its first term and elected an executive: William Jarvis, president; Carol Torrens, later Creighton, secretary; and William Jenkins, treasurer.[21] Students were expected to dress and conduct themselves "in keeping with the standards of the profession they are preparing to enter": men were expected to wear coats and ties and women suits or dresses. The women's suits required skirts, not trousers. Western's Faculty of Law offered courses in the twenty-three subjects required by the Law Society as well as optional courses in labour law, community planning, and trade regulation. Dean Rand assumed a full teaching load in addition to his administrative work. In May 1962, seventeen students received the LLB degree.[22]

The only woman graduate in Western's first graduating class in law was Carol Torrens Creighton, the daughter of the head of the university's Romance Languages Department. In second-year, she married her classmate Jon Creighton. They graduated in 1962 and were called to the bar in 1964. When they were photographed by the local newspaper, Jon quipped that they planned to open a law firm, Creighton & Creighton and that no

19 In the decades between the 1880s and 1954, a Department of Law existed in the Faculty of Arts, and academic legal courses were offered in this and other departments until the late 1950s. In addition, the university awarded the LLB degree to students who met the requirements of the Department of Law and were later admitted to the bar: M. Banks, *Law at Western 1959–1984* (London, ON: Faculty of Law, University of Western Ontario, 1984) iii–iv.

20 Justice Rand, born in 1884 in New Brunswick, had a distinguished career as a lawyer, judge, and arbitrator in labour-management disputes. He was especially known for the Rand formula, created to end a deadlock in mediating the long and bitter Ford strike in Windsor in 1945. He retired, at age seventy-five, from the Supreme Court of Canada in 1959 and assumed responsibility as dean at the law school at Western. The new law building was named for a significant woman philanthropist at Western, Josephine Spencer Niblett: Banks, *Law at Western*, 1–5.

21 Banks, *Law at Western*, 2–3.

22 Banks, *Law at* Western, 4–7. Four additional students received the degree in September 1962. Creighton recalled that two other women students had enrolled in her class at Western, but both withdrew.

one would know who was the senior partner! In fact, Carol Creighton initially practised law at Giffen & Pensa in London and her husband practised at a different London firm until they both relocated to Toronto.[23]

In Toronto, Carol Creighton was appointed chief research assistant in the latter years of the Royal Commission Inquiry into Civil Rights, the McRuer Commission. According to McRuer's enthusiastic biographer, Patrick Boyer, commission researchers engaged in an immense task: "McRuer began a methodical study of hundreds of statutes and regulations and developed a detailed agenda of subjects to be considered ... All in all, thousands of letters and formal briefs were received, and hundreds of witnesses interviewed."[24] The five commissioners met monthly, but there were other smaller meetings in McRuer's office. In 1976, at a meeting about the commission's project on the law of evidence, for example, McRuer and the project's author, Allen Mewett, were present, along with commission counsel, Patricia Richardson, and staff lawyer, Carol Creighton.[25]

Creighton was subsequently employed as counsel in the Ministry of the Attorney General, and when the Constitutional Branch was established, she joined a group reporting to David Mundell. She later became deputy

23 Carol Torrens Creighton, email communication to M.J. Mossman (15 February 2016). She also recalled articling at Fraser and Beatty.

24 P. Boyer, *A Passion for Justice: The Legacy of James Chalmers McRuer* (Toronto: Osgoode Society for Canadian Legal History, 1994) 303–ff. When Premier Robarts asked McRuer to lead the Royal Commission inquiry in 1964, McRuer agreed but on condition that he also be named chair of a new commission on law reform. Although McRuer was then seventy-three years old, the Premier agreed to McRuer's request, and McRuer headed the Royal Commission inquiry from 1964 to 1971 as well as chairing the Ontario Law Reform Commission during its first year. After the first year, he relinquished the latter position to Alan Leal, but McRuer remained the Commission's vice-chair. The Royal Commission submitted three reports in five volumes in 1968, 1969, and 1971, reflecting McRuer's "distinctive vision of the law and of society." In the 1969 submission, McRuer again expressed "appreciation for the devoted services by Mrs. Carol M. Creighton, LLB, the Chief Research Assistant." However, not everyone approved McRuer's report: see J. Willis, "The McRuer Report: Lawyers' Values and Civil Servants' Values" (1968) 18:4 *University of Toronto Law Journal* 351.

25 Boyer, *A Passion for Justice*, 360–61. Meetings began promptly at 9:30 a.m., and they worked steadily, with absolutely no interruptions, no calls, no coffee, until noon. The group reassembled at 1:30 p.m. and continued to work until 4:30 p.m. According to Boyer, when "it was time to go ... McRuer would simply get up and leave." Creighton also worked as assistant counsel to Ron Atkey on the Courts project and with McRuer on the Evidence project: Torrens Creighton, email communication to M.J. Mossman (12 May 2020).

director and general counsel in the ministry, and she was appointed QC in 1984. When Creighton appeared as counsel in the Supreme Court of Canada, she gowned in the boiler room in the absence of a women's robing room. In addition, she experienced the "separate entrance" policy at a Toronto male club when she attended a lunch, as the only woman, with other members of the McRuer Commission.[26]

At the University of Windsor, the Board of Governors approved President Leddy's plan to establish a law school in 1966–67, but the plan did not receive support from the provincial government. Leddy finally told Premier Bill Davis, "All right if you won't give us a Law School, I will start campaigning for a Medical School," a much more expensive faculty. Premier Davis responded in mock horror, "I surrender." Mark McGuigan was recruited as the first Dean in 1967, but after he was elected to Parliament in June 1968, President Leddy appointed Walter Tarnopolsky as Dean, and he served from 1968 to 1972.[27] Significantly, the first faculty appointed at the Windsor law school in 1968 included a woman, Margaret Hughes, who later became the first woman Dean in a common law faculty in Canada in 1984 at the University of Calgary.[28]

As with other new university law schools, there was no law school building in Windsor. Ruth Deech, who arrived from the United Kingdom in 1968, found "a little building which had been used for driving tests, with a small sign, 'New Law School for Windsor.'"[29] In the first year, faculty had offices in a small house on Sunset Avenue, but all classes were held in one room

26 Banks, *Law at Western,* 2–3; and Torrens Creighton, email communications to M.J. Mossman (6 and 12 May 2020). In addition to McRuer, others present at this lunch included David Mundell, John Arnup, and Peter Cory. Creighton recalled no expressions of concern by these male lawyers when she was directed to a separate entrance.

27 Recollection of Dr. J.F. Leddy, recorded by Professor George McMahon in A. Demers, *A History of the University of Windsor Faculty of Law, 1968–2008* (Windsor: University of Windsor Faculty of Law, 2008) 12–13.

28 The appointment of Margaret Hughes, BA, LLB, LLM, MSW, was included in a news report announcing faculty appointments at the new law school: *Windsor Star* (16 February 1967). See also Demers, *A History of the University of Windsor Faculty of Law,* 130; and E. Sleeman, ed., *International Who's Who of Women* (2002) 259.

29 Demers, *A History of the University of Windsor Faculty of Law,* 19. Deech was briefly a sessional instructor at the law school, where she took over classes for McGuigan after he was elected to Parliament. She then returned to Oxford.

in Dillon Hall, where the faculty circulated in to teach. A new law school building was formally opened with great fanfare in September 1970.[30]

The first class included just one woman, Susan Sherk, who graduated in 1971 and was called to the bar in 1973. She practised law on Front Street in Thorold for over forty years before her retirement. At the law school's fiftieth anniversary in 2018, Sherk credited the faculty with providing a strong foundation for the core principles and values of law, and she fondly recalled her work on the student magazine, *The Oyez*. Sherk had authored a report in *The Oyez* about the opening ceremony for the new law school building on 24–25 September 1970.[31] In 1972, three more women—Faye Campbell, Donna Campbell, and Brenda Duncan—graduated at the law school in Windsor, and they were called to the bar in 1974; all three practised law for several years.[32]

The recognition of university law schools in 1957 was important for legal education in Ontario. Although the Law Society initially maintained control of the curriculum, university law schools established additional course options that reflected broader conceptions of legal education and lawyers'

30 In attendance were the Governor General, Roland Michener, Senator Paul Martin, Chief Justice Bora Laskin, and the Honourable J.C. McRuer: Demers, *A History of the University of Windsor Faculty of Law,* 16–18. Librarian/ Professor Roger Jacobs introduced the special guests and then presented a brief speech, explaining that the law was both an ancient heritage and a modern reality; his remarks also focused on *livery of seisin,* a medieval method of transferring a freehold estate. Dean Ron Ianni later reported that Windsor's legal education program aspired to prepare students for active and creative participation in the development of Canadian laws and institutions and that the law school offered a wide range of educational experiences, including contributions from other disciplines: Demers, *A History of the University of Windsor Faculty of Law,* 27; and Windsor Law calendar, 1978–79.

31 S. Sherk, "Livery of Seisin" (1970) 2:1 *The Oyez,* 3. See also University of Windsor Faculty of Law, *Bridging the Law: Fifty Years of Windsor Law* (Windsor: Biblioasis, 2018); and *Canadian Law Lists.*

32 Huckle, "List of Women Barristers and Solicitors"; and University of Windsor graduation class photos, 1971, 1972.

work and that were in line with offerings in other Canadian provinces.[33] The availability of university law programs in different parts of Ontario may have encouraged women to enrol as law students. Research suggests that "professions where entry is practitioner-controlled are least accessible to women" while gender equality is advanced where entry is controlled by universities or the state.[34] In addition, some women law students may have preferred to study law and complete their articling requirements in their home communities. In this context, it is significant that the first women law graduates at university law schools—Murray and Tepper in Kingston, Perry in Ottawa, and Creighton in London—were residents of cities where university law schools were created in 1957 and 1959. Sherk was resident in the Niagara area when she opted to study law at Windsor, and she established her practice in the Niagara Peninsula in Thorold.[35] Finally, the availability of university law programs in different Ontario communities may have encouraged Outsiders, both men and women, to pursue legal careers.

33 P. Girard, "The Making of the Canadian Legal Profession: A Hybrid Heritage" (2014) 21 *International Journal of the Legal Profession* 145. Academic perspectives also influenced the adoption in 1969 of a new approach to legal education in Ontario, when the Law Society reduced the number of required courses for the accreditation of academic law programs. In addition, many university law schools began to create graduate programs. Four decades later, the Law Society voted to accredit another Ontario law school: the Bora Laskin Faculty of Law at Lakehead University in Thunder Bay, intended to serve northern communities and to focus on Indigenous law. In 2020, the Lincoln Alexander Law School was also established at Toronto Metropolitan University (formerly Ryerson) with Donna Young, a graduate of Osgoode Hall Law School, as Dean. In contrast to other law schools, these two new university law schools were accredited with "practice-ready" programs, requiring students to engage in practical placements as well as academic courses during their three-year programs. Graduates of these law schools are not required to article, but they must pass the bar examinations: see websites of the Bora Laskin Faculty of Law and Lincoln Alexander School of Law.

34 M. Burrage, K. Jarausch, and H. Siegrist, "An Actor-Based Framework for the Study of the Professions" in M. Burrage and R. Torstendahl, eds., *Professions in Theory and History: Rethinking the Study of the Professions* (London: Sage, 1990) 203 at 223. The authors also suggested a need to assess the impact of "feminization" on the ideologies and strategies of the professions.

35 Most of these women established legal practices or legal work in their home communities, although Torrens Creighton moved from London to Toronto after initially practising in London.

### A Surge in Numbers and Second-Wave Feminism

> *A decade ago, fewer than five percent of Canadian lawyers were women. There has been an unprecedented influx of women into the profession, however, and within a generation, as many as a third of Canadian lawyers will be female. Will women change the law, or will the law change women?*[36]

The "surge" in women's admission to the bar after 1957 began gradually. Twenty-nine women were called to the Ontario bar between 1958 and 1961 and forty-five women between 1962 and 1967. The numbers increased more rapidly thereafter: 290 women became lawyers between 1968 and 1975. And, while only one hundred women had been called to the bar between 1897 and 1939, eighty-five women joined Ontario's legal profession in one year in 1975.[37] Law schools in Canada more than doubled their annual enrolments of both men and women between 1964 and 1970, arguably a response to increased demand for lawyers' services and their higher earnings.[38] Moreover, although women constituted about 3 per cent of

36 J. Fielding, "Sisters in Law," *Weekend Magazine* (26 August 1978) 6a.

37 Huckle, "List of Women Barristers and Solicitors." In 1968, women students constituted about 9 per cent of the first-year class at Osgoode Hall Law School, but they represented just over 36 per cent of students in first-year in 1979. Moreover, the percentage of women students who graduated was comparable to graduation rates for male students from 1969 to 1979: *Continuum* (Osgoode Hall Law School) (November 1980) 9.

38 D. Stager with H. Arthurs, *Lawyers in Canada* (Toronto: University of Toronto Press/Statistics Canada, 1990) 94.

enrolments in legal education in Canada at the end of the Second World War, they represented 47 per cent of Canadian law students by 1986.[39]

Increasing numbers of women students and lawyers resulted in new gender dynamics in law. Men's behaviour toward women colleagues deteriorated significantly: the "gentlemanly paternalism" and "boyish teasing" of a few women students, a feature of classes at Osgoode Hall in earlier decades, turned into "clear-cut misogyny" by the late 1960s. As the number of women law students and lawyers increased, male students began to resent their female classmates' excellent academic performance. In addition, as legal job markets declined during recessions in the 1970s and '80s, some male students and lawyers became resentful of the competition created by increasing numbers of women in law.

> It seemed the "invasion" previous generations had feared was finally happening. Men were concerned about how this would affect their own chances for success and, perhaps less consciously, how it would force them to rethink their professional identity as lawyers ... [In addition, for women to be accepted,] they would have to perform a tough balancing act: adopt a masculine attitude while remaining feminine ... In a profession controlled by

39 Stager with Arthurs, *Lawyers in* Canada, 94–98, Table 4.13, 149–50. The authors suggest a variety of explanations for this revolutionary increase in numbers, including increased governmental support for postsecondary education and new universities for the baby boom generation. For women, moreover, the declining demand for teachers, and law as a route to upward mobility, might also have been factors. The surge in the number of women lawyers in the 1970s and '80s resulted in many younger women lawyers: although female lawyers constituted only 21 per cent of the total number of Canadian lawyers in 1988, they represented 42 per cent of lawyers under the age of thirty. Stager and Arthurs suggested some reasons for increasing numbers of women lawyers: an increasing demand for family law legal services: more women with mothers who were employed, particularly in male-dominated work; views about legal work as suited to combining work and family; and the impact of lawsuits against large American law firms in the late 1970s. See also R. Abel, "United States: The Contradictions of Professionalism" in R. Abel and P. Lewis, eds., *Lawyers in Society: The Common Law World*, vol. 1 (Berkeley: University of California Press, 1988) 186; and C. Moore, *The Law Society of Upper Canada and Ontario's Lawyers, 1797-1997* (Toronto: University of Toronto Press, 1997) 205–8).

> white middle-class men, [women and Outsiders] were relegated to the rank of "others" and there were attempts to confine them to specific roles.[40]

Mélanie Brunet documented the rudeness and tiresome vulgarity at Osgoode's 1968 graduation banquet, and the extraordinary sexism of *Obiter Dicta*, the student newspaper. She also identified a palpable homophobic atmosphere at several university law schools in Canada, concluding that the unprecedented increase in the number of women law students created insecurity for some men—who responded by emphasizing a particularly aggressive hypersexualized masculinity.[41]

Women students were regularly asked to justify their place in law schools. As one woman explained in *Obiter Dicta*, "I do not come to catch a lawyer. Several thousand hours and dollars is a heck of an output just to trap a mate."[42] In addition, the increased number of women lawyers was accompanied by exclusionary employment practices: a 1971 survey of Toronto law firms revealed that 40 per cent openly admitted to a prejudiced attitude toward women applicants for articling positions, and a

40 M. Brunet, *Becoming Lawyers: Gender, Legal Education and Professional Identity Formation in Canada, 1920–1980* (PhD diss., University of Toronto, 2005) [unpublished] 265–66, 280–81. Brunet's dissertation focused on law schools at four universities: Dalhousie, Osgoode Hall at York, Laval, and the Université de Montréal. The 1997 Law Society exhibition in honour of the centennial of women's entry to the Ontario legal profession included a ceramic pig, presented at a reunion by the 1968 women law graduates of Osgoode Hall Law School to their male colleagues. The gift represented women students' response to *Obiter Dicta*, the student newspaper at Osgoode Hall Law School, with its sexist images of scantily dressed women in the 1960s and '70s: Brunet, 313–17.

41 Brunet, *Becoming* Lawyers, 293, 298, 301–4, 308–10. Brunet also noted that women students at Osgoode Hall did not agree about how to change these sexist attitudes. Some women students advocated constant "nit-picking," while others rejected being overly sensitive to minor issues because it would undermine credibility about more serious affronts.

42 M.V. MacLean, "Lady Lawyers and All That" (1966) 4:4 *Obiter Dicta* n.p. MacLean (1966) advised her male colleagues that she was not available "to take carbon copies for those who are suffering from hangovers, to watch the Leafs lose ... to type up your assignments or to make sandwiches."

1972 study identified a variety of discriminatory practices in Toronto.[43] In Kingston, a woman was dismissed from her articling position in 1974 because she refused to comply with the firm's prohibition against wearing a pantsuit to work, even on days when she was not appearing in court.[44] And in 1977, a lecturer in the Bar Admission Course was forced to apologize for blatantly sexist comments in the materials for the Law Firm Administration course.[45]

Earlier patterns of gendered segregation in legal work continued in the 1970s and '80s. In spite of the trail-blazing success of Vera Parsons (1924) in criminal law litigation, women lawyers were often regarded as unsuitable for criminal law practice. Maryka Omatsu (1977) recalled that a professor at Osgoode Hall bluntly stated that "no matter how good a woman is, she will never get more than a C in criminal law."[46] In addition, when Anne Barrett (1976) applied for summer employment at the office of the Crown Attorney for the County of York, her application was rejected by a senior Crown who suggested she would be a "disruptive" influence. After

43 R. Lowman, "Law Firms Accused of Discriminating in Hiring Students," *Toronto Daily Star* (3 September 1971); and L. Silver Dranoff, "Women as Lawyers in Toronto" (1972) 10 *Osgoode Hall Law Journal* 177 at 179–80. Dranoff was puzzled about women lawyers' responses to her survey, in which women lawyers often flatly denied the existence of gender discrimination in the profession; Dranoff suggested that these women might have been the "fortunate ones who knocked on open doors." Although some may have found open doors, it is clear that most early women lawyers denied gender discrimination as a necessary strategy for acceptance as lawyers: B. Dinerman, "Sex Discrimination in the Legal Profession" (1969) 55 *American Bar Association Journal* 951; E. Paris, "Which Professions Pay Off for Women, If Any?," *Chatelaine* (September 1974) 37; and Fielding, "Sisters in Law."

44 Huckle, "List of Women Barristers and Solicitors"; and K. Rex, "Law Student Lost Job for Wearing Pant Suit, Women's Council Is Told," *Globe and Mail* (18 January 1974). In response to this news report, Laura Sabia, chair of the Ontario Status of Women Council, planned to investigate, and an unidentified press report of 24 January 1974 confirmed that Cynthia Campling (1975) had obtained an articling position at Cunningham & Little in Kingston the following week.

45 M. Mironowicz, "Bar Admission Students Snap at Bra Remark, Sexist Text," *Globe and Mail* (15 November 1977). Students petitioned to have the offensive material removed from the text for the course, and Margaret Campbell (1937), MPP, raised the matter in the provincial legislature. The instructor, Albert Strauss, apologized to the class the next day: *Toronto Sun* and *Globe and Mail* (16 November 1977). See also Fielding, "Sisters in Law," 6a.

46 Brunet, *Becoming Lawyers*, 183. The professor was not identified. For Vera Parsons, see Chapter Three.

Barrett referred this decision to the Ontario Human Rights Commission, the director of Crown Attorneys for the province provided an assurance that this exclusionary practice would not be repeated.[47]

Barrett's legal response to her rejected application suggests the impact of second-wave feminism in the 1960s and '70s, when thousands of Canadian women were swept up in the women's movement: "Together we created a movement that uncovered, explored, critiqued, and attempted to transform the hierarchical relations between men and women in every aspect of social life."[48] In addition, some aspiring lawyers entered law schools because changing political and social thought in the 1960s characterized law as an instrument for social change. Recognition of sex discrimination as an issue of human rights, the creation of the Ontario Law Reform Commission, and the establishment of legal aid services in the 1960s also fuelled ideas about relationships between law and social change.[49] Moreover, following the 1970 report of the Royal Commission

47 J. Bankier, "Women and the Law School: Problems and Potential" (1974) 22:6 *Chitty's Law Journal* 171 at 173. Barrett's case occurred in the summer of 1973: D. O'Connor, telephone communication to M.J. Mossman. Barrett's response to her application was an example of the impact of the amendment to the *Ontario Human Rights Code,* which added "sex" discrimination to proscribed actions in 1971–72. At the same time, a survey about articling in 1971 reported that 35 per cent of law firms attached importance to the applicant's sex, 12 per cent to religion, and 27 per cent to race: F. Folk, "On Women and Law," 3, articling newsletter (1 September 1971); and *Toronto Daily Star* (3 September 1971). (Out of 800 inquiries, only 104 firms responded.) See also M. Irvine, "Women at Osgoode: Problems and Perceptions of the Growing Minority," *Long Range Academic Policy Committee of Osgoode Hall Law School,* Appendix A, 15 January 1974 [unpublished]. The first female assistant Crown Attorney was Barboura Ferns (1974): LSO, "Diversifying the Bar," Barboura Ferns; and Osgoode Society for Canadian Legal History (OSCLH), oral history, "Barboura Ferns," 26–27. See also D. Owram, *Born at the Right Time: A History of the Baby Boom Generation* (Toronto: University of Toronto Press, 1996).

48 R. Hamilton, *Gendering the Vertical Mosaic: Feminist Perspectives on Canadian Society* (Toronto: Copp Clark, 1996) 50. Hamilton also explored the strategies adopted by women's groups in their pursuit of gender equality: 54–ff. See also L. Marsden, *Canadian Women and the Struggle for Equality* (Don Mills, ON: Oxford University Press, 2012); and L. Silver Dranoff, *Fairly Equal: Lawyering the Feminist Revolution* (Toronto: Second Story Press, 2017).

49 Archives of the Law Society of Upper Canada, *Crossing the Bar: A Century of Women's Experience "Upon the Rough and Troubled Seas of Legal Practice in Ontario"* (Toronto: Archives of the Law Society of Upper Canada, 1993) 26. The *Ontario Human Rights Code* amendment came into force in 1972, the Ontario Law Reform Commission was established in 1967, and Ontario's first *Legal Aid Act* was enacted in 1966.

on the Status of Women, Canadian women's organizations became active in promoting its recommendations concerning laws and social norms that limited women's participation in Canadian society.[50] As the report noted, only 3 per cent of lawyers in Canada in 1960 were women, a statistic that may have contributed to a three-fold increase in the percentage of women lawyers in the 1970s: from 4.8 per cent in 1971 to 15.1 per cent in 1981.[51]

Moreover, feminist lawyers began using arguments about sex equality to achieve legal changes on behalf of women clients, as well as engaging in broader efforts to effect legal and social reform.[52] In 1974, women in law at the University of Windsor hosted a national conference to explore issues for women lawyers and law students, an event that resulted in

50 M. Wade Labarge, M.D. Johnston, and M.E. MacLellan, *Cultural Tradition and Political History of Women in Canada* (Ottawa: Information Canada, 1971) 21–23. See also Marsden, *Canadian Women and the Struggle for Equality* 150, 185–88; and Dranoff, *Fairly Equal*, 50–51.

51 S. Bashevkin, "Canada" (1984) 8 *Comparative Law Yearbook* 3 at 4–5; and Royal Commission on the Status of Women in Canada, *Report of the Royal Commission on the Status of Women in Canada* (Ottawa: Information Canada, 1970) 79, para 248. In contrast, 26 per cent of lawyers in France and 30 per cent in the USSR were women. The percentage of women lawyers in Canada was comparable to approximately 7 per cent of women physicians, 4 per cent of women dentists, and less than 1 per cent of women engineers. The report was critiqued for its failure to take account of how cultures reinforce biological gender with social conventions: N. Griffiths, *Penelope's Web: Some Perceptions of Women in European and Canadian Society* (Toronto: Oxford University Press, 1976) 217–21. See also M. Huxter, "Survey of Employment Opportunities for Articling Students and Graduates of the Bar Admission Course in Ontario" (1981) 15 *Law Society Gazette* 169; and J. Hagan and F. Kay, *Gender in Practice: A Study of Lawyers' Lives* (Oxford: Oxford University Press, 1995). In 1974, sixteen students signed a letter to the editor of *Obiter Dicta*, which critiqued another letter that had decried claims of discrimination against women lawyers. In response, these sixteen students (including four male students) argued that they were not prepared to countenance either overt discrimination against less fortunate women or stereotyped views of women in law: *Obiter Dicta* (28 February 1974) n.p.

52 Silver Dranoff, *Fairly Equal*. See also B. Symes, "From Litigator to Litigant and Back Again: Equality in Practice" in E. Sheehy and S. McIntyre, eds., *Calling for Change: Women, Law and the Legal Profession* (Ottawa: University of Ottawa Press, 2006) 267; and C. Menkel-Meadow, "Excluded Voices: New Voices in the Legal Profession Making New Voices in the Law" (1987) 42:1 *University of Miami Law Review* 29.

the creation of the National Association of Women and the Law.[53] Justice Claire L'Heureux-Dubé, then a member of the Superior Court of Québec, spoke at the conference, noting that, in 1974, only 4 of 293 judges of superior courts in Canada, and only 3 of 192 county court judges, were women. In this context, others argued that the appointment of women judges would depend on an active and successful women's movement, which could both encourage women lawyers' aspirations and create more pressure on gatekeepers to appoint women judges.[54] In Ontario, these views may have contributed to the appointment of Bertha Wilson (1959) to the Ontario Court of Appeal in 1976, and to become the first woman appointed to the Supreme Court of Canada in 1982. Although she had fewer years of appellate experience than some of her male colleagues, Justice Minister Jean Chrétien concluded that, so long as Wilson was qualified, it was more important "in the context of the times" to appoint her—rather than a male who might be "better" qualified in terms of appellate experience.[55]

In 1968, the first two women were appointed to faculties at Ontario law schools: Margaret Hughes at Windsor and Gladys Choquette in the common law program at Ottawa. Other women faculty members were

53 *Globe and Mail* (2 April 1974); Silver Dranoff, *Fairly Equal*, 67–68; and National Association of Women and the Law, "Work and Development," memo, 1976. At the 1974 conference, Law Society Treasurer Sidney Robins announced the inclusion of sex in the nondiscrimination provision of the Society's Professional Conduct Ruling. It applied to the employment of lawyers or articling students "or in other relations between him and his fellow members of the profession": Paris, "Which Profession Pays Off for Women?"

54 B. Cook, "Women Judges: A Preface to Their History" (1984) 14 *Golden Gate University Law Review* 573 at 575; Cook identified a need for two additional factors: increased numbers of women lawyers and an expansion of judicial positions. See also B. Cook, "Women as Supreme Court Candidates: From Florence Allen to Sandra O'Connor" (1982) 65:6 *Judicature* 315.

55 E. Goldenberg, *The Way It Works: Inside Ottawa* (Toronto: McClelland & Stewart, 2006) 89. The appointment of Sandra Day O'Connor to the US Supreme Court in 1981 created pressure on Justice Minister Chrétien to appoint a woman to the Supreme Court of Canada, especially in the context of new equality guarantees in the *Canadian Charter of Rights and Freedoms*. See also E. Anderson, *Judging Bertha Wilson: Law as Large as Life* (Toronto: University of Toronto Press/Osgoode Society for Canadian Legal History, 2001) 85–86.

appointed in most Ontario law schools in the late 1960s and early 1970s.[56] In addition, courses about women and the law began to appear in law schools across Canada.[57] Women lawyers also participated in efforts to achieve recognition for sex equality in sections 15 and 28 of the *Canadian Charter of Rights and Freedoms* in the early 1980s, and LEAF, the Women's Legal Education and Action Fund, was established in 1985 to support

56 Hilda McKinlay (1971), who had become a teaching fellow at Osgoode Hall for a year after completing the LLM degree at Columbia in 1968, was appointed to the Faculty of Law at the University of Toronto in 1969. Gail Brent was appointed at Queen's in 1972 and then at the University of Western Ontario, along with Winnifred Holland, in 1974. Although Judy LaMarsh was appointed a Visiting Professor at Osgoode Hall Law School in 1973 for two years, the first tenure-stream female faculty were Louise Arbour and Mary Jane Mossman in 1976–77. In other common law schools in Canada, Patricia Hyndman was a faculty member at the University of Manitoba in 1964 and at Dalhousie University in 1965. In Québec, Alice Desjardins was appointed to the Université de Montréal in 1961, and Gabrielle Chaussebourg was appointed to the Droit Civil program at the University of Ottawa in 1963: B. Baines, "Overview of Early Women in the Canadian Legal Academy," in A. Lund and V. Torrie, eds., *Early Women in the Canadian Legal Academy* (Vancouver: UBC Press, forthcoming 2024). Women were also appointed to contract and tutorial positions and several women lawyers were appointed law school librarians: see Chapter One.

57 Jane Banfield Haynes, a graduate of UBC in law and later a faculty member and adviser to the President on the Status of Women at York University, undertook a modest survey of course offerings in women and the law in Canadian law schools (common law and civil law) in the late 1970s. Her survey indicated that such courses were being offered in Ontario at the University of Ottawa (Judith Swan), Queen's University (Beverley Baines), the University of Toronto (Marie Huxter), the University of Western Ontario (Constance Backhouse), the University of Windsor (Kathy Lahey), and Osgoode Hall Law School (Mary Jane Mossman). There were some courses offered in law schools in other provinces, including at the University of New Brunswick (Anne McLellan), at the University of British Columbia (Barbara Findlay and Lynn Smith), and at the University of Manitoba (Janet Debicka and Linda Vincent). In some universities, instructors in these courses were male: J. Banfield Haynes, "Survey of Courses on Women and Law" (1977) [unpublished, archived at York University]. See also Baines, "Overview of Early Women in the Canadian Legal Academy."

litigation of women's equality issues.[58] And in 1986, the Law Society in Ontario sponsored its first continuing education program on Women and the Law.[59]

Although the surge of women lawyers in the 1960s and '70s coincided with second-wave feminism, not all women lawyers identified as feminists. Moreover, like women in earlier cohorts, some women lawyers continued to deny the impact of gender in the legal profession, and some traditions of the gentleman's profession continued.[60] For some women lawyers, a surge in numbers did not result in greater success; they remained at the margins of the profession. At the same time, Bertha Wilson's appointment to Canada's Supreme Court, as well as other societal changes, arguably

58 P. Kome, *The Taking of Twenty-Eight* (Toronto: Women's Press, 1983); C. Hosek, "Women and the Constitutional Process" in K. Banting and R. Simeon, *And No One Cheered: Federalism, Democracy and the Constitution Act* (Toronto: Methuen, 1983) 280. See also M. Eberts, "Women and Constitutional Renewal" and B. Baines, "Women, Human Rights and the Constitution," both in A. Doerr and M. Carrier, eds., *Women and the Constitution in Canada* (Ottawa: Advisory Council on the Status of Women, 1981) 9, 31. LEAF is a nonprofit advocacy organization that uses litigation to promote the *Charter*'s equality guarantees for women: Archives of the Law Society of Upper Canada, *Crossing the Bar*, 38; and website of the Women's Legal Education and Action Fund.

59 *Women in the Legal Profession* (Law Society of Upper Canada, Continuing Legal Education, Osgoode Hall, 13 May 1986) 20 [archived at Law Society of Ontario]. The program was controversial. A prominent woman lawyer in Toronto suggested there was no need for the program because women lawyers were simply "lawyers" and already equal. Nonetheless, Treasurer Arthur Scace asserted that issues about gender and professionalism were appropriate for a Law Society educational program: letter from A. Scace to M.J. Mossman, ca 1986).

60 See B. Luedetke, "'Ludicrous' to Call Lawyers Sexist," *Globe and Mail* (11 February 1975). In later decades, some women lawyers engaged in litigation about their treatment as lawyers. In 1998, Joy Casey sued her former employer, Blake Cassels & Graydon, for gender discrimination in relation to a denial of partnership and alleged misrepresentation about partnership prospects. The suit was settled, and Casey established her own firm. A decade later, Diane LaCalamita sued McCarthy Tétrault because of the firm's failure to promote her to partner, alleging that she had been promised this appointment when she joined the firm as an experienced intellectual property lawyer. A settlement was reached, but LaCalamita is no longer practising law in Ontario: K. Pullen, "The Problem with Women," *Toronto Life* (May 2010) 43; O. Bertin, "Report Analyzed Gender Balance at McCarthys" (2009) 29:17 *Lawyers Weekly* 1; K. Kidd, "Woman's Fight Opens Legal Titans' Secret Files" *Toronto Star* (3 September 2009) 1; and Law Society of Ontario, "Ontario Lawyer and Paralegal Directory," online database. See also J. Kaye, "Women Lawyers in Big Firms: A Study in Progress toward Gender Equality" (1988) 57 *Fordham Law Review* 111.

transformed the gender factor, at least for some women. That is, instead of a barrier, female gender sometimes became a beneficial, even necessary, attribute for professional legal advancement, and professional recognition became a reasonable ambition for some women lawyers because (female) gender was a necessary consideration for gatekeepers. As Hilda McKinlay (1971), the second woman to be appointed to the Ontario Court of Appeal, in 1987, suggested after her retirement, one reason for her decision to accept this appointment was because "the Court of Appeal needed a Dame. They really needed a woman on the court."[61] At the same time, the success of women lawyers was often inversely related to the extent of their expressed commitment to gender issues, especially to feminism, and these issues were regularly debated in the 1980s and '90s in Canada and elsewhere.[62] Yet, an assessment of the extent to which the surge created changes that reveal continuity—or transformation—in their work status requires an exploration of transformations in the legal profession after 1957.

61 OSCLH, oral history, "Hilda McKinlay," 227. In contrast to this post-retirement comment, McKinlay stated at the time of her appointment that she "couldn't say whether it was important that a woman be appointed at this time [to the Court of Appeal]" and that she believed that it was important that "qualified" persons be appointed: R. Hallechuk, "2nd Woman Named to Court of Appeal," unidentified news report, 1987. McKinlay was appointed to the High Court of Justice in 1983 and then to the Ontario Court of Appeal in 1987: LSO Archives, (OBBRP), "Hilda McKinlay"; and obituary, *Globe and Mail* (6 January 2024) B17.

62 For examples, see C. Menkel-Meadow, "The Comparative Sociology of Women Lawyers: The 'Feminization' of the Legal Profession" (1987) 24 *Osgoode Hall Law Journal* 897 at 899–900; B. Adam and K. Lahey, "Professional Opportunities: A Survey of the Ontario Legal Profession" (1981) 59 *Canadian Bar Review* 675; M. Harrington, *Women Lawyers: Rewriting the Rules* (New York: Plume Books, 1995); C. Fuchs Epstein, *Women in Law* (New York: Basic Books, 1981) and 2nd ed. (Chicago: University of Illinois Press, 1993); M. Thornton, *Dissonance and Distrust: Women in the Legal Profession* (Melbourne: Oxford University Press, 1996); G. Gatfield, *Without Prejudice: Women in the Legal Profession* (Melbourne: Oxford University Press, 1996); C. McGlynn, *The Woman Lawyer: Making a Difference* (London: Butterworths, 1998); and H. Sommerlad and P. Sanderson, *Gender, Choice and Commitment: Women Solicitors in England and Wales and the Struggle for Equal Status* (Dartmouth: Ashgate, 1998). See also J. Brockman, *Gender in the Legal Profession: Fitting or Breaking the Mould* (Vancouver: UBC Press, 2001); J. McKenzie Leiper, *Bar Codes: Women in the Legal Profession* (Vancouver: UBC Press, 2006); and three international studies: U. Schultz and G. Shaw, eds., *Women in the World's Legal Professions* Oxford: Hart Publishing, 2003); U. Schultz and G. Shaw, eds., *Gender and Judging* (Oxford: Hart Publishing, 2013); and U. Schultz et al., eds., *Gender and Careers in the Legal Academy* (Oxford: Hart Publishing, 2021).

### Transformations in Legal Practice and Professional Culture

> *Women have entered law during a period of dramatic change to a firmly established and intensely stratified profession. During the last 20 years, the Canadian bar has undergone impressive transformations in the forms of burgeoning numbers, rapidly expanding law firms with branch and international offices, mergers between large law firms, the decline of solo practice, rising numbers of lawyers working as employees in various settings, increasing specialisation and expanding bureaucratisation, together with declining prestige of the profession.*[63]

In contrast to modest changes in the focus and organization of private practice in earlier decades, legal practice and lawyers' roles were fundamentally changed in the last decades of the twentieth century. "Once primarily defenders and litigators, lawyers ... also become advisors and consultants to governments and businessmen," and they were increasingly engaged in preventing conflicts rather than settling matters in a courtroom. Lawyers were more often dealing with companies and governments rather than individual clients, with papers instead of people, and the rise of the welfare state led to more involvement in the lives of its citizens, creating new opportunities for legal work.[64]

The Canadian legal profession had been expanding since the mid-1960s, but the growth in the number of lawyers, coupled with a protracted

63 F. Kay and J. Hagan, "Social Mobility and Hierarchical Structure in Canadian Law Practice" in W. Felstiner, ed., *Reorganization and Resistance: Legal Professions Confront a Changing World* (Oxford: Hart Publishing, 2005) 281. The authors argued that these changes disadvantaged women in law in terms of access to elite specializations, senior management opportunities, and enhanced remuneration. They also noted that legal work had become "proletarianized," with technical expertise narrowly confined, routinization of activity more pervasive, and responsibilities less meaningful, especially for women lawyers (307). See also J. Wallace and F. Kay, "The Professionalism of Practising Law: A Comparison across Work Contexts" (2008) 29 *Journal of Organizational Behavior* 1021.

64 M. Brunet, *Becoming Lawyers*, 266, 268, 272–73. Brunet suggested that some law students became idealists who wished to use law to achieve progressive social change while others became realists who talked openly about Bay Street firms and five-figure incomes. Most students constituted a silent majority. Brunet did not identify members of these different groups according to gender.

economic recession, weakened the profession's control of the market for legal services and decreased individual and collective prospects for upward mobility. In addition, ongoing social stratification meant that new entrants were disproportionately persons from professional families and other privileged socioeconomic groups. In this context, law schools began to develop admission programs for mature students, Indigenous Peoples, and other qualified persons whose credentials were adversely affected by social or economic circumstances. Although the experiences of women in law were not often addressed, it was clear that elite firms in metropolitan areas, traditionally dominated by white Angle-Saxon Protestant males, were just beginning to hire a few high-qualified Jews, Catholics, women, and immigrants in the 1980s.[65]

Significantly, globalization also resulted in fundamental challenges in private practice in the last decades of the twentieth century: law firms expanded dramatically in size, and many established branch and international offices. Expansion required more associates relative to the number of firm partners and different roles for these groups: partners were expected to seek out and maintain major clients while associates provided administrative and research support for the firm's legal work. Thus, law firms were increasingly distinguished by a small group of partners, whose activities were supported by a much larger group of associates, and entry into the partnership became much more exclusive. One result was the emergence of two levels of partnership: equity (profit-sharing) partners and nonequity (salaried) partners. In addition, the globalization of law firms raised "new challenges for strategic decision-making and competitive expansion, networks of knowledge transfer and cohesive firm cultures, and professional autonomy in a managerial model of firm expansion." Many of these changes were accompanied by increased workloads and time pressures for both male and female lawyers. In this context, the absence of appropriate workplace policies to accommodate family responsibilities

65 H.W. Arthurs, R. Weisman and F.H. Zemans, "The Canadian Legal Profession" (1986) 3 *American Bar Foundation Research Journal* 447 at 450, 466–71. The authors described medium-sized firms, small firms, and sole practitioners in cities, as well as lawyers in small communities, business, government, and education. See also Consultative Group on Research and Education in Law, *Law and Learning* (Ottawa: Social Sciences and Humanities Research Council, 1983) 25; and Adam and Lahey, "Professional Opportunities."

often affected women lawyers negatively.[66] In contrast, workplace leaves for the purpose of working as in-house counsel, campaigning for election in politics, or serving in government—activities that more often reflect the careers of male lawyers—were viewed as more acceptable.[67] Indeed, some research concluded that women associates who wished to become partners were required "to embody standards that are an exaggerated form of a partnership ideal" and that such standards were uniquely imposed on women.[68] It was not until 1994 that the Law Society in Ontario decided to top up maternity benefits beyond a woman's entitlement to legislated employment insurance. In 2009, moreover, the Law Society launched its pilot program, the Parental Leave Assistance Program, recommended by the Society's Retention of Women in Private Practice Working Group. For some lawyers, the program created a sense of support while for others, it was a "life saver."[69]

66 F. Kay, S. Alarie, and J. Adjei, "Leaving Private Practice: How Organizational Context, Time Pressures and Structural Inflexibilities Shape Departures from Private Law Practice" (2013) 20 *Indiana Journal of Global Studies* 1223 at 1234–37. See also F. Kay and J. Hagan, "Cultivating Clients in the Competition for Partnership: Gender and the Organizational Restructuring of Law Firms in the 1990s" (1999) 33:3 *Law and Society Review* 517 at 548–59.

67 K. Hull and R. Nelson, "Assimilation, Choice, or Constraint? Testing Theories of Gender Differences in the Careers of Lawyers" (2000) 79:1 *Social Forces* 229. The authors concluded that many gender differences in lawyer careers were the result of gender inequality in legal employment. See also P. Tancred, "Outsiders/Insiders: Women and Professional Norms" (1999) 14:1 *Canadian Journal of Law and Society* 31.

68 F. Kay and J. Hagan, "Raising the Bar: The Gender Stratification of Law-Firm Capital" (1998) 63 *American Sociological Review* 728 at 728–31, 741. The authors engaged with Bourdieu's concept of cultural capital, suggesting that women must demonstrate extraordinary work commitment to obtain partnership status, by bringing in new clients, establishing a large network of corporate clients, returning from maternity leave, and continuing to docket high numbers of hours per week. Women also needed to express a commitment to firm culture. See also P. Bourdieu, *Distinction: A Social Critique of the Judgment of Taste* (Cambridge, MA: Harvard University Press, 1984).

69 *Globe and Mail* (10 May 1994); and "Parental Leave Assistance Program Gets Rave Reviews," *Ontario Lawyers Gazette* (Winter 2009) 32–33. The 2009 program was created as a three-year pilot.

Although the emergence of "mega firms" in the latter decades of the twentieth century may have created challenges for women lawyers, they also redefined the legal profession itself.[70]

> The rise of the large law firm and an accompanying loss of ground on the part of solo practitioners and small law firms have created two separate hemispheres, each with its own structures, identities, ideologies as well as ethics. The homogeneity of the legal profession has suffered serious erosion [and] the process of fracturing appears to be unstoppable. It is the inevitable outcome of law firms' exposure to market forces and lawyers having to respond to demands of powerful clients in industry, as the profession is undergoing a transformation from a liberal profession proud of its ethical stance to an entrepreneurial one working on purely commercial principles. In law firms this results in a process of hierarchization, with fewer positions at the top of the pyramid and a broadening of its base.[71]

In this context, commercialization tended to make the "gentleman's profession" a thing of the past, with women lawyers often becoming victims or passive bystanders. Statistics about gender and the legal profession in Ontario suggest that more women than men lawyers work in large private practice firms as associates or employees at the bottom of the pyramid, where they also earn less than their male colleagues.[72]

---

70 M. Galanter, "Mega-law and Mega-lawyering in the Contemporary United States" in R. Dingwall and P. Lewis, eds., *The Sociology of the Professions: Lawyers, Doctors and Others* (London: Macmillan, 1983) 152. See also M. Galanter and T. Palay, *Tournament of Lawyers: The Transformation of the Big Law Firm* (Chicago: University of Chicago Press, 1991).

71 Schultz, "Introduction" in Schultz and Shaw, eds., *Women in the World's Legal Professions*, liii–iv. Evidence suggests that male lawyers often occupy the top of the pyramid and that women lawyers are more often at its base: see also F. Kay and E. Gorman, "Women in the Legal Profession" (2008) 4 *Annual Review of Law and Social Science* 299; and M. Thornton, "Authority and Corporeality: The Conundrum for Women in Law" (1998) 6:2 *Feminist Legal Studies* 147.

72 Schultz, "Introduction" in Schultz and Shaw, eds., *Women in the World's Legal Professions* xli-xlvi; and M. Orenstein, *Racialization and Gender of Lawyers in Ontario: A Report for the Law Society of Upper Canada,* April 2010, 20–25, a report based on the 2006 census. See also the international report: M. Choroszewicz and F. Kay, "Understanding Gender Equality in the Legal Profession" in R. Abel et al., eds., *Lawyers in 21st-Century Societies*, vol. 2, *Comparisons and Theories* (Oxford: Hart Publishing, 2022) 127.

Thus, "the exposure of the profession to the full market is resulting in an every-increasing pressure on costs—in all sectors, and its colonisation by the forces of managerialism and entrepreneurialism." In addition, the dynamics of change in the profession are leading toward a universal calculus where "only those aspects of practice which can be measured, counted and priced have a place."[73]

In this context, many women lawyers remain on the margins of power and privilege, with discrimination occurring unwittingly or in the conviction that it can be rationally justified. For several decades after 1957, women lawyers remained primarily engaged in real estate, estates, and family law practices, and in spite of some notable exceptions, many male lawyers continued to believe that women lacked the aggressiveness necessary for civil or criminal litigation and were unsuited for corporate or labour law practices.[74]

As the nature of practice in large firms changed dramatically, women lawyers increasingly filled the need for routine paperwork at the bottom of the pyramid of firm hierarchies. Thus, when the WLAO celebrated its seventy-fifth anniversary in 1994, the invitation to its special reception was blunt: "'Look like a girl, think like a man, act like a lady, and work like a dog."[75] Moreover, as a woman lawyer who practised from the 1970s to the 2000s explained:

> We encountered awkward situations and we encountered outright discrimination. There were no policies or protocols to assist us in addressing these issues ... We developed strategies. Some were symbolic. Some colleagues always used their initials in correspondence, never their first names, so that at least at the beginning stages of litigation, opposing counsel would not be aware of their gender ... The most common strategy was to demonstrate our ability through very hard work—our motto: "Be over prepared."

73 H. Sommerlad, "Can Women Lawyer Differently? A Perspective from the UK" in Schultz and Shaw, eds., *Women in the World's Legal Professions*, 191 at 214–15.

74 Schultz, "Introduction" in Schultz and Shaw, *Women in the World's Legal Professions*, xli; and Brunet, *Becoming Lawyers*, 283. See also Part Three.

75 D.-L. Carlson, "WLA Moves from Tea Parties to Policy Debates," *Law Times* (14 August 1994) 1 at 6.

> There are still vexing problems for women, especially in the areas of advancement, compensation, and retention in the profession.[76]

To some extent, these challenges resulted in women lawyers increasingly seeking employment in government, academe, and corporations.

In the last decades of the twentieth century, professional organizations began to respond to these concerns. In 1991, Ontario's Law Society issued its *Transitions in the Ontario Legal Professions* report, which identified significant differences in the experiences of male and female lawyers who had been called to the bar between 1975 and 1990 and revealed that women lawyers continued to be marginalized in the practice of law.[77] An editorial in the press boldly concluded that the report's findings "suggest the blame can be laid squarely on the shoulders of the profession's Boy's Club attitudes, unrelenting career demands and discriminatory practices." It also cited the report's finding that 60.5 percent of unemployed lawyers who indicated they were not interested in working in the profession were women. In 1992, for the first time, the Canadian Bar Association–Ontario's Annual Institute of Continuing Legal Education presented a series of lectures focused on feminist analyses of law.[78]

76 J. Minor, "The Bumpy Road," *Nexus* (University of Toronto Faculty of Law) (Spring/Summer 2006) 108. Minor was in private practice for several years and then joined the Constitutional Law branch at the Ministry of the Attorney General; she later became an elected Bencher and Treasurer of the Law Society.

77 F. Kay, *Transitions in the Ontario Legal Profession: A Survey of Lawyers Called to the Bar between 1975 and 1990* (Toronto: Law Society of Upper Canada, 1991). The report identified how women lawyers were less likely to enter or remain in private practice and more likely to have career interruptions related to child care. In addition, it reported women's reasons for departure from legal work, including their dissatisfaction with law practice and child care responsibilities.

78 Editorial, *Law Times* (19 February 1990) 6. The report confirmed that within seven years of being called to the bar, only 6 per cent of women lawyers secured partnership, compared to 15 per cent of male lawyers. The study also reported that 28 per cent of lawyers working in education were women and that women represented 37 per cent of lawyers in government and 48 per cent in legal aid: P. Kulig, "Study Shows Firms Lack Women Partners," *Law Times* (19 February 1990) 1–2. See also Kay, *Transitions in the Legal Profession*; F. Kay, N. Dautovich, and C. Marlor, *Barriers and Opportunities within Law: Women in a Changing Legal Profession* (Toronto: Law Society of Upper Canada, 1996); and "Legal System Oppresses Women," *National* (Canadian Bar Association) (March 1992) 6. The CBA program resulted in the creation of the Feminist Legal Analysis Section of the Ontario Bar Association.

In the context of ongoing reports of exclusion and marginalization—as law students, in articling positions, and in legal practice—the Canadian Bar Association also established a task force to investigate gender issues in the legal profession chaired by retired Supreme Court of Canada Justice Bertha Wilson. The association held a national conference in 1992 in Toronto over three days, and 175 lawyers, the majority of whom were women, attended, including Justice Wilson; Paule Gauthier, the first woman president of the Canadian Bar Association; and the Honourable Kim Campbell, the first woman Minister of Justice of Canada.[79] Notwithstanding women's accomplishments, the task force's 1993 report, *Touchstones for Change,* documented barriers to gender equality in the profession and made 228 recommendations to overcome them, including lawyers' responsibilities in relation to standards of professionalism and the goals of equality, diversity, and accountability.[80] The report's introduction posed the fundamental question:

> Will the reforms the Task Force advocates be implemented as a free and dignified act of justice? Is the profession ready for equality of opportunity for all women—white women, Women of Colour, Aboriginal women, women with disabilities, lesbian women? Or will their male colleagues make them wait another fifty years until time will have robbed their

79 M. Polanyi, "CBA Breaks Glass Ceiling and an Old Girls' Club," *Canadian Lawyer* (August/September 1992); and K. Hudson, "Admit Inequality Exists in System, Law Conference Told," *Toronto Star* October 1992). At this conference, Justice Wilson explained her view that gender bias was "a man's problem and it's men who must solve it": M. Tenszen, "Gender Bias 'Akin to Racism' Former Justice Tells Lawyers," *Toronto Star* (October 1992).

80 Canadian Bar Association, *Touchstones for Change: Equality, Diversity and Accountability—The Report on Gender Equality in the Legal Profession* (Ottawa: Canadian Bar Association, 1993). After a recommendation from the conference in Toronto in 1992 for representation from Indigenous and Black women, Sharon McIvor and Judge Corinne Sparks joined the task force. The report's fourteen Appendices included reports of provincial and territorial working groups.

consent of its graciousness and tainted it with the meanness and cowardice of expediency?[81]

*Touchstones for Change* provided a comprehensive report about gender equality in the legal profession, including barriers to entry and equal treatment and statistical data about women's participation in the profession."[82] The report resulted in controversy, particularly in its recommendations that law firms accommodate family responsibilities and its evidence about the exclusionary practices experienced by women judges. In addition, the report recommended educational programs to provide "remedial human rights jurisprudence accessible to non-specialists" and that these programs should be repeated until they have created "a common understanding of our legal duties to our colleagues in the profession and beyond."[83] In spite of the report's failure to achieve complete acceptance of its recommendations, Justice Wilson confirmed that she was reasonably content with the pace of reform. Nonetheless, when she addressed women law students in the 1990s, she always advised them that they would have to prove

81 Canadian Bar Association, *Touchstones for Change*, 4–5. Justice Wilson's final question was based on the speech of Lord Buckmaster in the British Parliament in 1919, when the issue of women becoming barristers and solicitors was being debated. See also M.J. Mossman, Review of *Touchstones for Change* (1994) 7 *Canadian Journal of Women and the Law* 138. Wilson had earlier identified her experiences of injustice in law practice as the "messy contingencies of life," although she also remembered the male client who told her, "I don't want any bloody woman drafting my will": "Wilson to Lead Status of Women Probe," *London Free Press* (20 August 1991). A Dalhousie law graduate and a member of the Nova Scotia bar, Wilson articled at the Osler firm and was called to the Ontario bar in 1959. Like other women lawyers, she was excluded from travelling to a client meeting along with a male lawyer at the firm, without her spouse's permission, on the grounds of propriety, and she did not become a partner for nine years: Anderson, *Judging Bertha Wilson*. Janet Minor had a similar experience of exclusion from travel with a senior male lawyer for a case on which she had worked: Minor, "The Bumpy Road," 108.

82 Canadian Bar Association, *Touchstones for Change*, 267, and Chapters 1–15, which focus on women's experiences in private practice, government, corporate counsel, law faculties, administrative tribunals, and the judiciary as well as problems in family law practice and the role of Law Societies and the Canadian Bar Association. Its conclusion identified gender equality as "a momentous challenge for the profession."

83 Canadian Bar Association, *Touchstones* for *Change*, 271–72; and M.J. Mossman, "Engendering the Legal Profession: The Education Strategy" in U. Schultz and G. Shaw, eds., *Women in the World's Legal Professions*, 2003) 77. See also K. Keating, "*Touchstones for Change*: A Review" (1993) 51:6 *The Advocate* 843; M. Buckley, "*Touchstones for Change*: A Response" (1993) 51:6 *The Advocate* 853; and Mossman, Review of *Touchstones for Change*.

themselves *again and again* in their careers: "All your life as a woman you are proving yourself ... proving ... that you can do it. And you get tired of it."[84]

In the twenty-first century, studies have continued to identify exclusionary gender practices in the Ontario legal profession. In 2008, the Law Society introduced its Justicia project, designed to encourage the hiring and retention of women lawyers in major firms. Noting that women had been entering the legal profession in Ontario for decades but also "leaving in droves," the report argued that "the legal profession should not assume that change will occur without conscious efforts to create a shift in the legal culture."[85] As a male lawyer who was cochair of the working group suggested, "Clients today expect law firms not only to be committed to equality, but also to actively promote diversity in the workplace."[86]

A decade later, the Society's 2018 annual report revealed that while 12.4 per cent of lawyers in Ontario were male partners at law firms, only 4.3 per cent were female law partners.[87] Similarly, a study of salaries for in-house counsel in 2020 revealed continuing disparity based on gender, and in 2016, the Criminal Lawyers' Association identified continuing

84 Anderson, *Judging Bertha Wilson*, 200, 351, and Chapter 13. Notably, Wilson later joined the Royal Commission on Aboriginal Peoples (352–ff).

85 Law Society of Upper Canada, *Final Report: Retention of Women in Private Practice Working Group*, executive summary (22 May 2008), online, paras 1, 4. More than fifty firms joined the *Justicia* project: para 18. The project targeted firms with twenty-five lawyers or more in Toronto as well as the largest firms in other regions of Ontario, with plans to bring together firm representatives to share "best practices" and promote the retention and promotion of women in private practice. Participating firms agreed to track demographics on gender in their firms, to review policies about family leaves and flexible work arrangements, to share information about networking opportunities, and to develop mentoring and leadership skills.

86 "Fifty Law Firms Commit to Support Women in Private Practice," *Ontario Lawyers Gazette* (Winter 2008) 34–35. Regular updates were reported in the *Ontario Lawyers Gazette*: (Winter 2009) 32, (Spring 2009) 34; (Summer 2009) 32; and (Fall/Winter 2010) 33. In the same period, continuing problems were identified in K. Lunau, "My Brilliant, Brief Career," *Maclean's* (26 May 2008) 68–69.

87 Law Society of Ontario, annual report, 2018. See also A. Balakrishnan, "The Invisible Woman: Women in Law Summit Explores How to Help Women Lawyers and Partnership Numbers," *Canadian Lawyer* (2 April 2020); and Balakrishnan, "Women in Law: Tips for Success from Leading Female Lawyers in the Legal Industry," *Canadian Lawyer* (December 2021), online.

challenges for women who are criminal law practitioners.[88] Moreover, in spite of increasing diversity among law students and practitioners, studies continue to identify challenges and discriminatory practices in the experiences of some women and Outsiders.

> Even if women are inclined to bring change to the legal profession, they must operate within a series of constraints that sharply restrict their ability to do so, including cultural expectations for the lawyer role, the inherent emphasis in existing legal systems on establishing rights, lawyers' ethical duties to pursue their clients' interests at the expense of others, and the trend toward greater emphasis on commercialization and profit in legal practice.[89]

Such comments suggest that changes in opportunities for some women lawyers, even in the twenty-first century, may often reflect continuity rather than transformation in status relative to men. In addition, the legal profession has also confronted challenges relating to diversification.

### Diversifying the Bar

> *The legal profession in Ontario is changing dramatically. The number of lawyers who are women, Aboriginal and members of a visible minority continues to grow, transforming the face of a profession that until the early 1970s was primarily white and male. While women and racialized persons are transforming the face of the legal profession, they encounter barriers within the profession. The future will bring an increasingly diverse legal profession. Profound demographic changes will challenge the profession to achieve corresponding cultural change and equity within the profession.*[90]

---

88 C. Dobby, "Female In-House Lawyers Earn Less Than Men, Study Says," *Globe and Mail* (27 May 2020) B1, B4, identifying similar salary disparities for racialized and disabled lawyers; and N. Etienne, "Report Highlights Challenges of Criminal Law Practice for Women" *Canadian Lawyer* (April 2016) 9–10.

89 Kay and Gorman, "Women in the Legal Profession," 323. The authors suggested that although women might construct a different system if they could start from scratch, existing constraints may require them to behave as male lawyers to succeed. See also C. Menkel-Meadow, "Portia in a Different Voice: Speculations on a Woman's Lawyering Process" (1985) 1 *Berkeley Women's Law Journal* 39; and Choroszewicz and Kay, "Understanding Gender Equality in the Legal Profession," 127.

90 Orenstein, *Racialization and Gender of Lawyers in Ontario*, i–ii.

Most early women lawyers in Ontario were white, Protestant, and middle-class; only a few were Jewish, Catholic, or recent immigrants. Although some Black, Indigenous, and immigrant lawyers who were male were called to the Ontario bar in the nineteenth and early decades of the twentieth centuries,[91] similar diversity among women lawyers did not occur until the later decades of the twentieth century. These differences suggest that a combination of racial and gender discrimination created substantial obstacles for some women lawyers.

Myrtle Blackwood, later Smith, became a member of the first-year class at Osgoode Hall in 1954–55, and she briefly articled in the office of B.J. Spencer Pitt (1928) prior to Pitt's departure for medical treatment in New York. Blackwood became Ontario's first Black woman lawyer when she was called to the bar in 1960, although she was probably the second

91 For Robert Sutherland (1855) and Delos Rogest Davis (1884), see Chapter One. Davis' son, Frederick, was called to the Ontario bar in 1900: L.C. Talbot, "History of Blacks in the Law Society of Upper Canada" (1990) 24:1 *Law Society Gazette* 65 at 65–66; J. Isaac, "Delos Rogest Davis, KC" (1990) 24:4 *Law Society Gazette* 293; and Moore, *The Law Society of Upper Canada and Ontario's Lawyers*, 177–79. In the twentieth century, Black lawyer Lionel Cross (1924) employed several Black male articling students, including B.J. Spencer Pitt (1928). Pitt also employed Black male law students, including George Carter (1949), who became the second Black judge in Ontario. Pitt's nephew Romain Pitt, was appointed a Superior Court judge: obituary, *Toronto Star* (16 May 2020) A20. See also S. Lewthwaite, "Reconstructing the Lives and Careers of Lawyers: Ethelbert Lionel Cross, Toronto's First Black Lawyer" in C. Backhouse and W.W. Pue, eds., *The Promise and Perils of Law: Lawyers in Canadian History* (Vancouver: UBC Press, 2009) 193. Another Black male lawyer, Lincoln Alexander (1953), became part of a four-man firm in Hamilton in which the partners were Irish, Black, Japanese, and Indigenous. The firm "was a leader in addressing the issue of race and the practice of law [and] an inspiration to other visible minority lawyers": Law Society of Ontario (LSO), "Diversifying the Bar," Lincoln Alexander, Paul Tokiwa, and Peter Isaacs. Isaacs was appointed to the Ontario Court of Justice in 1995. Alexander became a QC (1965), the first Black federal member of Parliament (1968–85), the first Black federal Cabinet Minister, and the first Black Lieutenant-Governor (for Ontario) (1991). He was chancellor of the University of Guelph for fifteen years and a Companion of the Order of Canada. See also L. Alexander, *Go to School, You're a Little Black Boy: The Hon Lincoln M. Alexander—A Memoir* (Toronto: Dundurn Press, 2006); and P. Sworden, "'A Small United Nations': The Hamilton Firm of Millar, Alexander, Tokiwa and Isaacs, 1962–1993" in C. Wilton, ed., *Inside the Law: Canadian Firms in Historical Perspective* (Toronto: Osgoode Society for Canadian Legal History/University of Toronto Press, 1996) 469. See also LSO, "Diversifying the Bar," William Simcoe Kerr and Solomon White; and Chapter One.

Black woman lawyer in Canada.[92] Violet King, the daughter of a Calgary railway worker, had graduated from university with a combined arts and law degree in 1953 and was called to the Alberta bar in 1954, six years before Blackwood joined the legal profession in Ontario. Apparently, King's negative experiences as a Black lawyer in Canada resulted in her relocation to the United States, where she later worked as a senior administrator for the YMCA–YWCA.[93]

When she was called to the Ontario bar in 1960, Myrtle Blackwood explained that she was fulfilling a lifelong ambition, encouraged by her late father. Philip E. Band, a Bay Street lawyer, stated that Blackwood was an "exceptional young lady, neat, accurate and conscientious."[94] Although Blackwood's initial employment is unclear, she became a solicitor in the provincial Department of Economics and Development in 1964 and then moved, in 1966, to the Ontario Housing Corporation as a solicitor for several years. After she married Stephen Smith, she continued work at the

92 Talbot, "History of Blacks," 68; and LSO Archives, Osgoode Hall Law School, "List of Women Students, 1954–55." See also Chapter One.

93 King practised briefly in Calgary and later at the Citizenship Branch in Ottawa for about seven years. She then moved to Newark, New Jersey, to work with the YMCA–YWCA, concluding that "you don't come up against the colour barrier" in Newark as in Canada. King worked on urban social-planning programs for Blacks and later joined the Y administration in Chicago, where she was honoured for her outstanding record and became the first woman appointed to a management position with the Y's US national executive: LSO Archives, Violet King file, citing *Calgary Herald* (2 November 1996 and 2 December 1997). King died of cancer at age fifty-one in 1981. See also LSO Archives, letter from Brenda McCafferty, Legal Archives Society of Alberta, to Susan Lewthwaite, LSO Archives (11 October 2006). King articled in Alberta with Edward McCormick, and when he later spoke at a public meeting in Chicago, he was invited to a Black club for a drink. The only white person present, he felt a "chill in the air that you could almost pick icicles off the ceiling—until the host announced that McCormick was the Calgary lawyer who had trained Violet King. Then everyone wanted to shake his hand": LSO Archives, Violet King file, unidentified news report.

94 LSO Archives, WLAO fonds, "Law Grads Ceremony," unidentified news report (June 1960); and LSO Archives, "Philip Band, QC" (1914–2009), and obituary, *National Post* (nd). A list of women students at Osgoode Hall Law School in 1954–55 indicates that Blackwood began first-year with Irene Domagalski; Willa Carroll, later Corse; Violet Koson, later Bielski' and other women called to the bar in 1958: LSO Archives, "List of Women Students, Osgoode Hall Law School 1954–55: First Year"; and Huckle, "List of Women Barristers and Solicitors. Blackwood's call to the bar two years after these women may indicate that she was admitted as a matriculant just prior to the elimination of this admission category: see Chapter Six.

corporation as "Mrs. Myrtle I. Smith" until 1971. In 1971–72, Blackwood was located at 1073 Bloor Street West and in 1973–75 at 171 Yonge Street, where she may have conducted sole practices. At some point, Blackwood Smith moved to Montreal, although no record of her in legal practice in Québec exists. She later moved to Kitchener, where she worked at Callright Marketing for some years. One of her coworkers described her as a private person. Smith died of cancer in September 2020 at the age of ninety.[95]

A second Black woman was called to the Ontario bar eleven years after Blackwood. Marva Jemmott was the only Black woman among thirty-three women who joined Ontario's legal profession in 1971. At the age of twelve, Jemmott, who was born in Barbados, had immigrated with her parents to Toronto, where her father worked for the Canadian Pacific Railway. After high school at Jarvis and Harbord Collegiates, she attended the University of Toronto for her first degree. She was attracted to the University of Ottawa's law program because of its dual English–French and common law–civil law programs, but Jemmott was disappointed to discover that the two law school programs operated quite separately. She found Ottawa a less "meaningful" community than Toronto. She also experienced overt racism in the city, including an occasion when a complete stranger walked up to her and spat in her face, and several occasions when she was referred to with a common racial slur.[96]

Although 105 students enrolled in the LLB program with Jemmott in September 1966, only one-third remained after Christmas, and Jemmott was one of only three women in her graduating class in 1969. Jemmott returned to Toronto to article at Enfield, Kimberley & Henmerick, and she spent a few months in the Crown Attorney's office before attending the bar admission course. After being called to the bar in 1971, Jemmott established a sole practice near her home in the neighbourhood of Dufferin and

95 Huckle, "List of Women Barristers and Solicitors"; *Canadian Law Lists*; and Westmount Memorial Celebration Centre, "Obituary: Myrtle Smith," online: <www.dignitymemorial.com/en-ca/obituaries/kitchener-on/myrtle-smith-9347602>. Blackwood's spouse predeceased her, but her three children—Lyndon, Maxene and Renore—survived, and Smith was described as a long-time member of Highland Baptist Church in Kitchener. Blackwood's obituary did not identify her legal status, including her accomplishment in becoming Ontario's first Black woman lawyer. See also LSO, "Diversifying the Bar," Bertrand Joseph Pitt, which identified some of Pitt's Black articling students, including Blackwood.

96 Huckle, "List of Women Barristers and Solicitors"; and OSCLH, oral history, "Marva Jemmott," 5, 41, 57–58, 60–ff, 90, 93, 104, 113.

Eglinton. As she explained, most Black practitioners at the time established sole practices because they were seldom able to find employment in existing law firms.

> They didn't seem to go into groups, or law firms for some reason. I think you either had the ones that applied for government jobs because the government would hire you ... and there would be no problem there, or else they seemed to open up their own practice. I can just think of one fellow who was working for anybody ... and that was Charles Archibald, I think he was with Thomson, Rogers for a few years. [97]

In addition to working as a sole practitioner, Jemmott sometimes practised with other women lawyers, including Marlene Philip (1975), also a Black woman, who articled at Parkdale Community Legal Services and later practised immigration and family law. Philip recalled that she sometimes encountered subtle racism in her practice, including being mistaken in court for a client about to be deported.[98] Jemmott recalled that Black lawyers in these years supported one another: she often received client referrals from other Black lawyers, she provided articling positions for Black law students, and she tried to create a community among Black lawyers to "open doors" for them. Jemmott was appointed QC in 1984, and in 1994 she received the WLAO President's Award for her many accomplishments: she was a cofounder of the Delos Davis Law Guild, a participant in the Task Force on Policing, and coordinator of the legal section of the National Black Coalition of Canada.[99]

97 Huckle, "List of Women Barristers and Solicitors"; and OSCLH, oral history, "Marva Jemmott," 101, 122–24, 132–38, 141. Jemmott recalled that Janet Boland (1950) was an excellent bar admission instructor.

98 M. Ryval, "Women in Law: Ladies No Longer in Waiting" (December 1977) *Canadian Lawyer* n.p.: Marlene Philip, 17–ff. See also S. Thwaites, "1994 President's Award Recipients" (1994) 9:1 *Without Prejudice* (WLAO) 2. Jemmott suggested that she was only the third woman practising criminal law; it is unclear whether she was aware of the lengthy criminal law practice of Vera Parsons (1924). Jemmott also believed, incorrectly, that she may have established the first all-woman law partnership in Ontario, but there were several women partnerships in Ontario after the firm of Robinson & Currie was established in 1921: see Parts Two and Three. Nonetheless, Jemmott clearly established Ontario's first Black women's law partnership in Ontario.

99 OSCLH, oral history, "Marva Jemmott," 145; Thwaites, "1994 President's Award Recipients"; and Archives of the Law Society of Upper Canada, *Crossing the Bar* 33.

In 1977, Jemmott stated in a press report that she had experienced no real barriers, although her comment might have been an effort to "fit in" by denying experiences of racial exclusion. Fifteen years after this comment, when she was the keynote speaker in February 1992 at a reception at Osgoode Hall (which accompanied the inaugural Black Law Students' Association Canada's annual conference in Toronto), she was less guarded about describing the historical barriers faced by Blacks in the legal profession. In this speech, she saluted recent appointments of Black judges in Ontario—a crucial necessity at a time when relations between police and Blacks were at an all-time low. In 1992, all the Black judges in Ontario were male—the only Black woman judge in Canada was Corinne Sparks in Nova Scotia.[100]

In the 1990s, Jemmott experienced health problems that affected her law practice, and in 2008 a law society tribunal permitted her to surrender her licence to practice law.[101] Her very impressive accomplishments in the 1970s and '80s must be understood in the context of the "double discrimination" of gender and race experienced by many Black women

100 Ryval, "Women in Law": Marva Jemmott, 17–ff; and L.C. Talbot, "The Formation of the Black Law Students' Association (Canada)" (1992) 26 *Law Society Gazette* 187 at 191. See also C. Sparks, "Women of Colour in the Legal Profession: A Panoply of Multiple Discrimination" in Canadian Bar Association, *Touchstones for Change*, Appendix 10. Sparks was appointed to the family court in Halifax in 1987, the first Black woman to be appointed a judge in Canada and the first Black judge in Nova Scotia. In 1995, she acquitted a Black teenager who was accused of hitting a police officer with his bicycle when the officer was attempting to arrest another person. The Nova Scotia Court of Appeal overturned her decision, with a dissenting opinion, but in 1997 the Supreme Court of Canada reinstated a verdict of not guilty. The case attracted controversy because the Crown asserted a possible apprehension of bias on the basis of Judge Sparks's Black race: see *R v S(RD)* [1997] 3 SCR 484.

101 *Law Society of Upper Canada v Marva Maureen Jemmott* 2008 ONLSHP 0061. The three-person panel reviewed irregularities in Jemmott's accounts and records of her failure to respond to concerns but accepted the joint submission of counsel for Jemmott and for the Law Society that her health issues, age, and responsibility for a sole practice merited the decision to permit her to surrender her licence to practise. The three-person Hearing Panel included Joanne St. Lewis, the first Black woman Bencher. See also S. Scott, "The House Snatchers," *Chatelaine* 2007), an account of mortgage fraud, which named Jemmott as the lawyer acting for a fraudulent client.

lawyers: "Black women are never Black or women. They are always both."[102] Even in the late 1980s, barriers for Black women lawyers remained: the first Black woman lawyer was hired at a Bay Street firm in Toronto in 1988,[103] and it was not until 2003 that a Black woman lawyer was elected a Bencher. Joanne St. Lewis, a faculty member in the University of Ottawa's Common Law program, was elected from outside Toronto in 2003, and she served as a Bencher until 2009 and again in 2015–16. St. Lewis chaired the Law Society's Equity and Aboriginal Issues Committee, and she was faculty adviser to the Black Law Students' Association Canada for seventeen years.[104] In 2016, Tanya Walker (2006) became the first Black woman lawyer to be elected as a Bencher from Toronto.[105]

Racialized women lawyers were also appointed to academic positions and to the judiciary in the 1980s and '90s. Emily Carasco (1984), a South Asian woman who obtained her LLB degree in Uganda and then completed

102 J. Herbert, "'Otherness' and the Black Woman" (1989–90) 3 *Canadian Journal of Women and the Law* 269 at 274, quoting M.B. Lykes, "Discrimination and Coping in the Lives of Black Women: Analyses of Oral History Data" (1983) 39:3 *Journal of Social Issues* 79 at 82. Herbert's article critiqued M.J. Mossman, "'Otherness' and the Law School: A Comment on Teaching Gender Equality" (1985) 1:1 *Canadian Journal of Women and the Law* 213. See also E. Thornhill, "Focus on Black Women" (1985) 1:1 *Canadian Journal of Women and the Law* 168; S. Neallani, "Women of Colour in the Legal Profession: Facing the Familiar Barriers of Race and Sex" (1992) 5 *Canadian Journal of Women and the Law* 148; Black Law Students' Association and Attorney General of Ontario, *Black Access to the Legal Profession: The Timeroll Report* (Toronto: Attorney General of Ontario, 1996); J. St. Lewis and B. Trevino, *Racial Equality in the Canadian Legal Profession: The Challenge of Racial Equality: Putting Principles into Practice* (Ottawa: Canadian Bar Association, 1999); and J. St. Lewis and B. Trevino, *Virtual Justice: Systemic Racism and the Canadian Legal Profession* (Ottawa: Canadian Bar Association, 1999).

103 K. Makin, "Black Woman Lawyer on Bay Street Drawn to Career by Perry Mason," *Globe and Mail* (14 April 1988) A1. Some Black male lawyers also faced challenges: M. St. Patrick Baxter, "Black Bay Street Lawyers: Looking Back, Looking Ahead" (Keynote address, Third Annual Conference and Symposium of the Black Law Students' Association, Ottawa, 19 February 1994); and W. Ahmed, "How the Legal Profession Views My Brown Skin," *Toronto Star* (10 June 2020) A17.

104 University of Ottawa, Faculty of Law, Common Law Section, Faculty biography, Joanne St. Lewis, online; and LSO Archives, Bencher files. St. Lewis also served as a mid-term Bencher in 2001–3. The first Black male Bencher was Leonard Braithwaite (1958), in 1999: LSO, "Diversifying the Bar," Leonard Braithwaite. He was awarded the Order of Canada in 1997 and the Order of Ontario in 2005.

105 LSO Archives, Bencher files; and A. Robinson, "First Black Female Bencher Elected in Toronto," *Law Times* (11 July 2016) 1.

the LLM and SJD at Harvard, was appointed to the Faculty of Law at the University of Windsor in 1980, probably the first non-white woman to join a university law faculty in Ontario.[106] The University of Windsor law faculty was also the first in Canada to appoint an African Canadian woman dean. Juanita Westmoreland-Traoré (1997) became Dean in 1996 after working in the public service in Québec and Ontario, and in 1999, she was appointed a judge in Québec.[107] In 1992, Michelin Rawlins (1982), who practised as a Crown Attorney in Windsor, became the first Black woman lawyer appointed a judge of the Ontario Court of Justice.[108] In 2020, Charlene Theodore became the first Black lawyer and the tenth woman to be elected President of the Ontario Bar Association.[109]

Despite this recognition, some Black women lawyers continue to experience exclusionary practices in the legal profession, just as white women lawyers faced challenges as law students and lawyers. As a Black woman lawyer who tried to fit in on Bay Street explained in 2017: "As a person of colour, that's a roadblock that comes up again and again."[110] In 2010, a report for the Law Society in Ontario, based on the 2006 census, identified a "surge" in the number of visible-minority lawyers and revealed that the proportion of racialized women had increased relative to racialized men. It also confirmed differences in the experiences of members of the legal profession based on gender and race: while 40.8 per cent of women were associates or employees in law firms, only 26.9 per cent of men were in this

106 LSO Archives, "Diversifying the Bar," Emily Carasco. Both as an academic and in her work on Ontario government boards and commissions, Carasco advocated for equity, equality, and human rights, and she received an honorary LLD from the Law Society in 2006.

107 LSO Archives, "Diversifying the Bar," Juanita Westmoreland Traoré. In 2005, she received the Canadian Bar Association's Touchstone Award for promoting equality in the legal profession.

108 LSO Archives, "Diversifying the Bar," Michelin Rawlins. Rawlins graduated from the law school at the University of Windsor.

109 Theodore grew up in Brampton, graduated in law from Schulich Law School, Dalhousie University, and focused on legal work relating to international human rights, diversity, and inclusion: *Toronto Star* (2 September 2020) A11.

110 Hadiya Roderique, "Who Belongs on Bay Street?," *Globe and Mail* (4 November 2017) F1, F3, F5–6. In the 1980s, Thora Espinet (1984), an early Black woman lawyer, started her own law firm because she could not get a job; she later became a deputy judge of the Small Claims Court: LSO, "Diversifying the Bar," Thora Espinet. See also Black Law Students' Association and Attorney General of Ontario, *Black Access to the Legal Profession;* and St. Lewis and Trevino, *Racial Equality in the Canadian Legal Profession*; and St. Lewis and Trevino, *Virtual Justice.*

category; and although 44.6 per cent of racialized lawyers were associates or employees, only 30.5 per cent of white lawyers were in this category. The report concluded that "the systemic exclusion of racialized lawyers is the result of a complex filtering system beginning in law school and working through the many incremental steps in a lawyer's career."[111] For some Black women lawyers, these statistics reveal that both gender and race continue to define professional opportunities.

In 2011, the Law Society created a Working Group on Challenges Faced by Racialized Licensees, and its report was adopted by the Benchers in December 2016.[112] The report identified an increase in the percentage of racialized lawyers in Ontario—from 9 per cent in 2001 to 18 per cent in 2014—and it documented challenges experienced by Black and racialized lawyers. Its report was controversial, especially its recommendation that Ontario lawyers be required to agree to a "statement of principles" regarding lawyers' responsibility to promote equality, diversity, and inclusion. After continued opposition, this requirement was abolished by a vote of the Benchers in September 2019; it was replaced by an obligation for lawyers and paralegals to affirm a commitment to human rights in their annual reports to the Law Society.[113]

111 Orenstein, *Racialization and Gender of Lawyers in Ontario,* 20–25, 34–36: the data indicated that women lawyers were more often employees or associates than men, that women lawyers generally earned less than men, and that women lawyers were more often employed in government than in private practice. The report also noted that most young white men *and women* who were becoming lawyers had the same demographic and class backgrounds but that Indigenous and visible minority law students differed from white students in terms of their class backgrounds. See also F. Kay, "Social Capital, Relational Inequality Theory, and Earnings of Racial Minority Lawyers" (2019) 32 *Research in the Sociology of Work* 32; and C. Nelson, "The Conflicting and Contradictory Dance: The Essential Management of Identity for Women of Colour in the Legal Academy" in Sheehy and McIntyre, eds. *Calling for Change,* 117.

112 Law Society of Ontario, *Working Together for Change: Strategies to Address Issues of Systemic Racism in the Legal Professions* (LSO: Challenges Faced by Racialized Licensees Working Group, 2016). The report focused on "racialized" lawyers and law students, a term that includes more than Black lawyers. Although the report recognized that Indigenous lawyers also face barriers, it did not address this issue on the basis that it would be better addressed by the Law Society's Indigenous Advisory Group.

113 Convocation repealed Recommendation 3.1 regarding the Statement of Principles: Law Society of Ontario, Minutes of Convocation, September 2019. See also J. Gallant, "Diversity at Law Firms a Work in Progress, Analysis Finds," *Sunday Star* (29 September 2019).

Moreover, although Black male lawyers also experience exclusionary practices, these reports suggested that Black women lawyers often face more significant challenges. Thus, although increasing numbers of Black women lawyers may indicate change in the legal profession, these women lawyers may more often experience continuity rather than transformation in status in the gentleman's profession. At the same time, the combination of race and gender discrimination may suggest that Bennett's formulation does not fit well for Black women lawyers. For them, transformation must occur, not only relative to Black male lawyers but also in relation to white men and women in the legal profession.[114] Thus, for some Black women lawyers, a fundamental transformation in status remains elusive.[115]

Indigenous women lawyers have also faced challenges, even though two Indigenous men were admitted to the Ontario bar as early as the 1860s.[116] Norman Lickers (1938), who obtained a BA from the University of Western Ontario, was probably the first Indigenous person to become an Ontario lawyer in the twentieth century. In 1946, he was appointed counsel to the federal government's Standing Committee on Indian Affairs, which sponsored revisions to the *Indian Act* in 1951. Later, in 1969, he organized a protest against a policy that would have abolished special status for Indigenous Peoples.[117]

In contrast, Indigenous women lawyers did not appear in Canada until the late 1970s. The first Indigenous woman lawyer in Canada was Marion Ironquill, later Meadmore. She was a Cree-Ojibwe who grew up on a farm in Saskatchewan and attended a residential school in Manitoba. Ironquill

114 Bennett, "Theoretical Issues: Confronting Continuity"; and Bennett, *History Matters: Patriarchy and the Challenge of Feminism.*

115 In 1993, a Law Society report concluded that "the profession was in the past, and is still, overwhelmingly white, able-bodied, and middle class," even though activism in minority communities, changes in university admission policies, and efforts by the Law Society to address issues of under-representation may have had some impact in recent decades." See Law Society of Upper Canada, *Crossing the Bar*, 31.

116 For William Simcoe Kerr (1862) and Solomon White (1865), see Chapter One. White was elected a member of the provincial legislature, and he was appointed a KC: C. Moore, "Ontario's First Native Lawyer?," *Law Times* (26 October 1998) 8.

117 LSO Archives, "Diversifying the Bar," Norman Lickers. Lickers practised law in Brantford, and although he was later disbarred, he was a band councillor and active in establishing organizations to promote Indigenous culture. Lickers's granddaughter Kathleen Lickers is currently in private practice in Ohsweken, Ontario: LSO, "Ontario Lawyer and Paralegal Directory," online; and *Ontario Lawyers Gazette* (Fall/Winter 2006) 34.

married in 1954, and she raised three sons while participating actively in Indigenous organizations in Winnipeg. Among other activities, she established the first Indian and Métis Friendship Centre in Canada, she edited a newspaper focused on Indigenous issues, and she was involved in creating the National Indian Council, the Indigenous Bar Association, and the National Indigenous Council of Elders. In the 1970s, Ironquill Meadmore attended the new pre-law program for Indigenous students at the University of Saskatchewan and then entered the law faculty at the University of Manitoba. She graduated in 1977 with a law degree, and after completing one year of articles, she was called to the bar in Manitoba on 29 June 1978. Ironquill Meadmore practised law as the first Indigenous woman lawyer in Canada, and she remained active in Indigenous organizations for decades. She was awarded the Order of Canada in 1985.[118]

In the late 1970s, two Indigenous women graduated from Ontario law schools. In 1976, Roberta Jamieson, a member of the Six Nations of the Grand River, graduated in law at the University of Western Ontario (now Western University), becoming the first Indigenous woman law graduate in Canada and Ontario. She initially worked as executive assistant in the Indian Commission Office of Ontario, and she was called to the Ontario bar in 1981. In 1985, Jamieson was appointed Indian commissioner, and in 1989 she became the first woman Ombudsperson in Ontario, serving until 1999. In 2001, she became the first woman to be elected Chief of the Six Nations. Jamieson was appointed an *ex officio* member of a special House of Commons committee on "Indian" self-government, and she was involved in developing alternative dispute-resolution methods, particularly in relation to Indigenous land claims. In 1994, she became a member of the Order of Canada and she was promoted to officer in 2016. She was also named an Indigenous people's counsel, and she received more than twenty honorary

118 C. Goar, "Rediscovered Thread in National Fabric," *Toronto Star* (1 July 2013) A11. See also Law Society of Manitoba, records of Call to the Bar; and "Marion Ironquill Meadmore," *The Canadian Encyclopedia* online (accessed 25 October 2017). <https://www.thecanadianencyclopedia.ca>.

degrees at Canadian universities. In 2004, Jamieson became president and CEO of the National Aboriginal Achievement Foundation, now Indspire.[119]

The second Indigenous woman law graduate in Ontario was Delia Opekokew. She graduated from Osgoode Hall Law School in 1977, and in 1979 became the first Indigenous woman called to the Ontario bar. She was also the first Indigenous woman to be called to the bar of Saskatchewan, in 1983. Opekokew grew up in Saskatchewan, a member of the Canoe Lake Cree Nation, and she attended residential schools in the province. After high school, she took a secretarial course and then worked for the Saskatchewan government and the Federation of Saskatchewan Indians. In 1969, Opekokew moved to Toronto; a few years later, she and her spouse relocated to Winnipeg, where she became actively involved, along with Ironquill Meadmore, in the Indigenous community. Together, Opekokew and Meadmore decided to take a few undergraduate courses at the University of Manitoba, and after achieving success in these courses, they both attended the pre-law summer program for Indigenous persons at the University of Saskatchewan. While Meadmore enrolled at the law school at the University of Manitoba, Opekokew moved back to Toronto with her spouse and enrolled at Osgoode Hall Law School.[120]

Opekokew found her law school studies challenging, especially because she was one of only two Indigenous students—the other was Harry LaForme, later a member of the Ontario Court of Appeal.[121] In spite of many challenges, Opekokew made lasting friendships with other women

119 "Recent Appointments: Roberta Louise Jamieson" (1990) 3:1 *Without Prejudice* (WLAO) 3; and H. Ball, *Great Women Leaders* (Toronto: Second Story Press, 2004). Jamieson was a founding member of the Canadian Native Law Students' Association, and she received the National Aboriginal Achievement Award in 1998 for her work in law and justice. She was also a candidate for leadership of the Assembly of First Nations in 2003. See also "Roberta Louise Jamieson," *The Canadian Encyclopedia*, online.

120 Law Society Archives, "Diversifying the Bar," D. Opekokew; and LSO Archives, A. Kirk-Montgomery, interview with D. Opekokew (2011–12) 1–40.

121 Harry Laforme (1979) worked as a lawyer on behalf of Indigenous organizations, both in Canada and internationally. A member of the Mississaugas of the Credit First Nation, he was appointed to the Ontario Superior Court in 1994, and he became the first Indigenous appellate court judge in Canada when he joined the Ontario Court of Appeal in 2004: "Harry S. LaForme," *Indspire*, online: <https://indspire.ca/laureate/harry-s-laforme-2/>; and "Harry Laforme," Olthuis, Kleer, Townshend LLP, online, <https://www.oktlaw.com/team-members/harry-laforme/>. After retiring from the court in 2018, LaForme became senior counsel at this law firm, and for several years he taught the course on Rights of Indigenous Peoples at Osgoode Hall Law School.

students at Osgoode. After graduating in 1977, she articled and then, after her call to the bar, practised law with Norman Zlotkin in Toronto. In 1980, she returned to Saskatchewan as counsel to the Federation of Saskatchewan Indians. She worked for the Federation for five years and was involved in negotiations pertaining to Indigenous rights and the patriation of the Constitution. In 1985, Opekokew returned to Toronto as an associate at Blaney, McMurtry & Stapells, where she worked on Indigenous land claims in Ontario and in some western provinces.[122]

In 1990, Opekokew established a sole practice in Toronto and continued to work on behalf of Indigenous individuals and organizations. Among other cases, she was appointed one of three commissioners in an inquiry into the shooting death of Leo Lachance by a white supremacist. She was also counsel for the family after the death of "Dudley" George, killed by police at Ipperwash Provincial Park in 1995, which resulted in the creation of the Ministry of Aboriginal Affairs in Ontario. A year earlier, in 1994, Opekokew became the first woman to run for the position of Grand Chief of the Assembly of First Nations. She was also involved in a successful claim by Indigenous members of the Armed Forces to obtain their Veterans' Benefits, and in a land claim by the Canoe Lake Cree Nation regarding social and economic rights pursuant to Treaty 10 in lands occupied by the Primrose Lake Air Weapons Range. From 2008 to 2017, Opekokew acted as deputy chief adjudicator for the independent assessment process pursuant to the Indian Residential Schools Settlement Agreement. She was designated an Indigenous Peoples' Counsel in 2004, and she received the WLAO President's Award in 2012, the Law Society Medal in 2013, and an honorary doctorate from the Law Society of Ontario in 2019.[123]

Other Indigenous women followed Meadmore, Jamieson, and Opekokew into the Ontario legal profession. Terry Vyse (1980), a Mohawk,

122 LSO Archives, "Diversifying the Bar," D. Opekokew; Kirk-Montgomery, interview with Opekokew, 40–49; and C. Gerus and J. Widerman "This City," *Toronto Life* (August 1979). See also D. Opekokew, *The First Nations: Indian Government and the Canadian Confederation* (Saskatoon: Federation of Saskatchewan Indians, 1980); and D. Opekokew, *The First Nations: Indian Government in the Community of Man* (Saskatoon: Federation of Saskatchewan Indians, 1982).

123 LSO Archives, "Diversifying the Bar," Delia Opekokew; Kirk-Montgomery, interview with Opekokew, 50–87; "Delia Opekokew," *Indigenous Saskatchewan Encyclopedia*, online: <https://teaching.usask.ca/indigenoussk/import/opekokew_delia.php>; and "Law Society to Honour Trailblazing Advocate Delia Opekokew with Honorary Doctorate," *Law Society Gazette* (19 September 2019).

became the first Indigenous woman judge in the Ontario Court of Justice (Provincial Division) in 1991.[124] Rose Toodick Boyko (1982), a member of the McLeod Lake Indian Band, became the first Indigenous woman appointed to the Superior Court of Justice in Ontario in 1994.[125] Susan Hare (1995), a member of the M'Chigeeng First Nation on Manitoulin Island, became the first Indigenous woman to be elected a Law Society Bencher in 2007. In addition to her general practice in her community, Hare was appointed an adjudicator for the Grandview School for Girls settlement in Ontario and for the federal Indian Residential Schools claims process.[126] The first Métis woman lawyer in Ontario was probably Helen Pierce (1982), who practised law in Sault Ste. Marie until 2001, when she was appointed to the Superior Court of Justice in Thunder Bay. Pierce, probably the first Métis judge in Ontario, was appointed Regional Senior judge of the Northwest Region in 2009.[127]

But Indigenous women's experiences were not always positive after "the door was open." In 1988, Patricia Monture, later Monture-Angus (1994), a Mohawk woman and recent law graduate at Queen's University, filed an action against the Ontario Attorney General and the Law Society to challenge the requirement to pledge allegiance to the Queen for admission to the Ontario bar. For Monture, it was not appropriate to swear allegiance to a "foreign monarch." Instead, Monture wished to acknowledge her culture by carrying an eagle feather, symbolizing a commitment to tell the truth. In 1992, the Law Society voted to make the loyalty oath optional, and Monture was called to the bar. Nonetheless, as a legal academic, she remained highly critical of many aspects of Canadian law, including

124 "Recent Appointments: Terry Vyse" (1991) 5:2 *Without Prejudice* (WLAO) 2. Vyse was in private practice prior to her appointment, and she was also a director of the Niagara Regional Native Centre.

125 "Rose Toodick Boyko," *Wikipedia*. Boyko, an early Indigenous nurse, later graduated from Queen's in law, and she received an honorary degree from Queen's in 1999. See also "Rose Toodick Boyko," *Indspire*, online: <https://indspire.ca/laureate/rose-toodick-boyko-2/>.

126 LSO Archives, "Diversifying the Bar," Susan Hare. As a student at Osgoode Hall Law School, Hare worked with Professor Alan Grant to create the law school's special Intensive Program in Indigenous Lands, Resources and Governments. See also Evelyn Baxter (1993), an Oji-Cree from northern Ontario, who became the first member of the Nishnawbe Aski Nation (Treaty 9) to become a lawyer: LSO Archives, "Diversifying the Bar," Evelyn Baxter.

127 LSO Archives, "Diversifying the Bar," Helen Pierce.

gender-equality claims.[128] Although she acknowledged that litigation by white feminists had successfully established major precedents in the courts about gender equality pursuant to the *Charter*, she was concerned that the cases were based on white women as legal subjects, thus creating "a social construction of women that is already judicially determined, ill fitted, and potentially a new site of colonial imposition" for Indigenous women.[129] That is, neither the problems of discrimination nor appropriate legal solutions are always the same for white and Indigenous women.

In addition to challenges based on gender and race, other diversity issues may impede women lawyers' success. For example, women lawyers have sometimes confronted problems based on their sexuality, although there is evidence of more recent acceptance.[130] While some earlier Ontario women lawyers with disabilities, including Vera Parsons (1924) and Elizabeth Robson (1949), succeeded as members of the

128 P. Monture, "Now That the Door Is Open: First Nations and the Law School Experience" (1990) 15 *Queen's Law Journal* 179. See also T. Lindberg, "What Do You Call an Indian Woman with a Law Degree—Nine Aboriginal Women at the University of Saskatchewan College of Law Speak Out" (1997) 9 *Canadian Journal of Women and the Law* 301; E. Carasco, "A Case of Double Jeopardy: Race and Gender" (1993) 6:1 *Canadian Journal of Women and the Law* 142; and R. Csilag, "Aboriginal, Indigenous, Native? She Preferred Haudenosaunee," obituary, Patricia Monture, *Globe and Mail* (2 December 2010).

129 P. Monture, "The Right of Inclusion: Aboriginal Rights and/or Aboriginal Women?" in K. Wilkins, ed., *Advancing Aboriginal Claims* (Saskatoon: Purich, 2004) 39 at 46. See also E. Snyder, "Indigenous Feminist Legal Theory" (2014) 26 *Canadian Journal of Women and the Law* 365; J. Green, ed., *Making Space for Indigenous Feminism*, 2nd ed. (Halifax: Fernwood Publishing, 2017); and S. McIvor, "Aboriginal Women: Working in Coalition to Advance Sex Equality" in Sheehy and McInyre, eds., *Calling for Change*, 253.

130 Archives of the Law Society of Upper Canada, *Crossing the Bar*, 32. Susan Ursel (1986) was among the first openly Lesbian women lawyers. She practises labour, employment, and human rights law and advocates for the LGBTQ2S+ community in litigation matters, and she was awarded the Law Society Medal in 2019: LSO Archives, "Diversifying the Bar," Susan Ursel; and "Susan Ursel," UPFH, online: <https://www.upfhlaw.ca>.

Ontario legal profession, dis/ability often creates additional challenges.[131] Some women lawyers also faced discrimination as members of the Franco-Ontarian community, especially when they were precluded from gaining admission to the Ontario bar unless they could speak English, but recent developments have resulted in some francophone women lawyers achieving prominence.[132] Increasing numbers of women from immigrant

131 Disabled lawyers may experience practical challenges and prejudice and discrimination. For Parsons and Robson, see Chapters Three and Five. In recent decades, Mary Louise Dickson (1966), who practised law in a wheelchair, was appointed QC in 1983 and was elected a Bencher of the Law Society in 2007. She received the WLAO President's Award in 2005 and the Order of Ontario in 2009: Huckle, "List of Women Barristers and Solicitors"; "Mary Louise Dickson," Dickson Appell, online: <https://dicksonappell.com/who-we-are/mary-louise-dickson/>; and obituary, *Globe and Mail* (27 January 2024) B18. See also L. Hill et al., *Lawyers with Disabilities: Identifying Barriers to Equity, a Report of the Disability Research Working Group of the Equity and Diversity Subcommittee* (Vancouver: Law Society of British Columbia, 2000); and A. McChesney, R. Nolan, and M. Schmieg, *Advancing Professional Opportunities and Employment Accommodation for Lawyers and Other Law Graduates Who Have Disabilities* (Ottawa: REACH, 2001).

132 Archives of the Law Society of Upper Canada, *Crossing the Bar*, 31. Law school programs and trials in French have been introduced. Among francophone women lawyers, Monique Métivier (1979) was appointed a judge of the Superior Court of Justice in 1995 and became the first woman judge to become Regional Senior Justice for the eastern region of Ontario. Louise Charron (1977) was appointed a judge in 1988 for the District Court in Ottawa, and she was later appointed to the Ontario Court of Justice (General Division), the Ontario Court of Appeal, and the Supreme Court of Canada. Nathalie Boutet (1991), a francophone from Québec, succeeded in obtaining a commitment from the Law Society to amend the Rules of Professional Conduct to compel lawyers to advise bilingual clients of their right to use French or English in the courts: see LSO Archives, "Diversifying the Bar," Monique Métivier, Louise Charron, and Nathalie Boutet.

communities have also succeeded in becoming lawyers.[133] Some have been appointed to the judiciary in recent decades. Rosalie Abella (1972) became the first Jewish woman appointed to the Supreme Court of Canada, in 2004. Maryka Omatsu (1977), whose family experienced discriminatory treatment during the Second World War, became the first Japanese woman to be appointed to the Ontario Court of Justice, in 1993. Annemarie Bonkalo (1978), of Hungarian heritage, became the first female Chief Justice of the Ontario Court of Justice, in 2007. Sheila Ray (1981) became the first South Asian woman lawyer appointed to the Ontario Court of Justice.[134]

These examples of accomplished women lawyers reveal much greater diversity among women admitted to the Ontario bar in the decades after 1957, especially in the latter years of the twentieth century and in recent decades. At the same time, it is important to assess the legacy of the cohort of women who became lawyers in Ontario in earlier decades. To what extent does greater success for current women in law represent continuity or transformation in status for women lawyers in Ontario?

133 Alicia Natifidad (1983) became the first Filipino woman lawyer to practise law in Canada: LSO Archives: "Diversifying the Bar," Alicia Natifidad. Lucia Favret (1986) is recognized as the first Italian woman lawyer in Ontario; and Korean women lawyers Jenny Chu Steinberg (1886) and Kim Eunice (1987) have both engaged in specialized corporate law practices: LSO Archives, "Diversifying the Bar," Lucia Favret, Jenny Chu Steinberg, and Kim Eunice. In addition, Constance Sugiyama (1979), a third-generation woman of Japanese descent (*sansei*), an expert in corporate law, was one of the first Asian woman lawyers to become a partner in a major Canadian law firm: LSO Archives, "Diversifying the Bar," Constance Sugiyama. Two women lawyers of Chinese heritage were elected Benchers of the Law Society. Fatima Mohideen (1978) was elected from outside Toronto in 1991, and Avvy Yao Yao Go (1991), who was born in Hong Kong, became an in-term Bencher from Toronto in 2001: LSO Archives, "Diversifying the Bar," Fatima Mohideen and Avvy Yao Yao Go. Avvy Go also received the WLAO's President's Award in 2002. Iva Sareen (1979) was the first South Asian women to be called to the Ontario bar: LSO Archives, "Diversifying the Bar," Iva Sareen.

134 LSO Archives, "Diversifying the Bar," Rosalie Abella, Maryka Omatsu, Annemarie Bonkalo, and Sheila Ray. See also M. Omatsu, *Bittersweet Passage: Redress and the Japanese-Canadian Experience* (Toronto: Between the Lines, 1992).

### Women Lawyers: Still at the Margins?

> *At first glance, the dramatic rise in female participation in all key areas of law, including legal practice, creates the impression of a success story, as if the "woman question" had been resolved and women lawyers had made significant inroads into a previously inaccessible elitist profession. However, on closer inspection discrimination against women, however well concealed and refined and possibly subconscious, is still rife. Women lawyers tend to remain on the margins of power and privilege.*[135]

Women's experiences as lawyers are, of course, varied, both in the past and the present. Especially in recent decades, some women lawyers have gained recognition and attained success as members of the legal profession and the judiciary, in politics, legal education, and business, and in leadership positions in major law firms and the Law Society. These accomplishments deserve celebration. At the same time, exclusionary practices, which may be concealed or even subconscious, continue to create barriers for some women lawyers. In spite of increased access to legal education and an unprecedented increase in numbers, some women lawyers continue to be sidelined by new patterns of exclusion in professional culture and stratification in the context of globalization. As the "Women in Law Summit" in 2020 concluded, gender remains a significant barrier for some women lawyers.[136]

At least to some extent, recognition of gender issues in the legal profession coincided with a fundamental transformation of legal "professionalism," particularly with respect to corporate management demands. Moreover, policies about inclusion based on race, gender, and class—a paradigm shift from "exclusivity" to "representativeness"—has sometimes resulted in resistance to accommodation. Although some analysts suggest

135 U. Schultz, "Introduction" in Schultz and Shaw, eds., *Women in the World's Legal Professions*, xli. This 2003 report is similar to comments in the 1980s: see M. Huxter, "Survey of Employment Opportunities for Articling Students and Graduates of the Bar Admission Course in Ontario" (1981) 15 *Law Society Gazette* 169 at 212–13; and D. Lipovenko "Sexism in Court Tough to Admit, Tougher to Fight," *Globe and Mail* (11 April 1987) B4. See also L. Pope, "Women on the Walls," *Otherwords* (Osgoode Hall Law School) (27 February 1989), critiquing the all-male photos on law school walls.

136 A. Balakrishnan, "The Invisible Woman."

that professional statements about non-discrimination and equality of access may change attitudes and, over time, behaviour, these claims have yet to be proven.[137] Controversy about the law society's report on racialization in the legal profession, particularly its statement of principles, confirmed that issues for many racialized and minority lawyers in Ontario have not disappeared.[138]

In addition to women, many lawyers who are Outsiders continue to encounter barriers similar to those faced by women called to the Ontario bar up to 1957. Thus, although the exclusionary practices that created challenges for early women lawyers may have changed, the profession's ethical commitment to equality remains an ongoing challenge. As Charles Smith, equity adviser to the Canadian Bar Association, commented, "It is interesting and somewhat paradoxical that the very profession which has been the source of such insight and eloquence on equality requires a healthy dose of self-examination and positive action to address inequality and outright discrimination within its own ranks."[139]

137 Abel, *English Lawyers between Market and State: The Politics of Professionalism*, Chapter 4, especially 154–58. Focusing on entry to the profession, Abel noted the shift from ascribed criteria, such as family status, to achieved criteria, based on educational success. Yet, because family status may also contribute to educational criteria, he suggested that "greater inclusiveness simply moves unrepresentativeness downstream." At the same time, Abel suggested that achievements by "token" women lawyers may inspire other women in law. See also H. Sommerlad, "Managerialism and the Legal Profession: A New Professional Paradigm" (1995) 2: 2–3 *International Journal of the Legal Profession* 159; and F. Kay, "Professionalism and Exclusionary Practices: Shifting the Terrain of Privilege and Professional Monopoly" (2004) 11:1–2 *International Journal of the Legal Profession* 11.

138 C. Liao, "Power, Gender, and Race in the Legal Profession" (2022) 34:1 *Canadian Journal of Women and the Law* 174 at 182, referring to the "dumpster fire that is going on in the Law Society of Ontario regarding equity issues" a reference to the controversy among Benchers about recommendations concerning racism in the profession.

139 C. Smith, "Next Steps on the Road to Equality in the Canadian Legal Profession," *Touchstones Newsletter of the CBA's Standing Committee on Equality* (Ottawa: Canadian Bar Association, 2002). See also M. Buckley, "The Second Decade: The Role of the Canadian Bar Association in Implementing the *Touchstones* Report" in E. Sheehy and S. McIntyre, *Calling for Change* 325; and M.J. Mossman, "Engendering the Legal Profession: The Education Strategy" in Schultz and Shaw, eds., *Women in the World's Legal Professions* 77 at 83: In addition to education about equality, "a systematic analysis of the processes of change and of the barriers to change within the legal profession" is necessary to achieve equality goals.

Thus, while there is evidence that some contemporary women lawyers in Ontario have achieved greater success than women in earlier cohorts, success may continue to be influenced by race and class as well as religion, sexuality, dis/ability, and immigration status.

Moreover, even though male lawyers who are immigrants or racialized may also experience exclusion, gender remains a significant factor. Thus, while there is no denying that change has occurred since 1957 in terms of the gender composition of Ontario's legal profession, changes continue to result in continuity for many women lawyers. Moreover, even for those women lawyers who have enjoyed changes not available to women called to the bar before 1957, a transformation in status sometimes remains elusive. Gender equality and legal professionalism remain a work in progress for the contemporary legal profession in Ontario, a legacy of gendered patterns that all too often characterized the experiences of earlier cohorts of women in law.

# *A Legacy of Gendered Patterns*

## "Quiet Rebels"

*Their rebellion is a personal affair, not warfare waged on behalf of others. They pursue their own career interests with a minimal necessary antagonism of the sensibilities of society. They are individuals seeking individualised solutions to the problems they encounter ... While denying any ulterior political objective, the quiet rebel ... knows deep down that she is in the vanguard of social change [and that her efforts will make it easier for others to follow her ... But] her main concern is with her own personal development and success in a job that she chooses to do. Achieving this is difficult enough without worrying about changing the world at the same time.*[1]

The idea of "quiet rebels," women in pursuit of individual accomplishment in a man's world and without concerns about changing the world, is an apt description of many women lawyers who were called to the Ontario bar before 1957. As a tiny minority in the legal profession until the latter decades of the twentieth century, these women were "rebels at the bar" in

1 G.M. Breakwell, *The Quiet Rebel: Women at Work in a Man's World* (London: Century Publishing, 1985) xi–xii. See also D. Rhode, "Perspectives on Professional Women" (1988) 40 *Stanford Law Review* 1163 at 1202–ff.

the gentleman's profession.[2] Some women lawyers were also rebels in their determined challenges to societal norms about different gendered spaces for men and women (especially married women). A few were rebels in their determination to practise in areas of law that were regarded as unsuitable for women and in their rejection of a meek acceptance of women's "proper place" in the profession. But in contrast to some who rebelled, many of these early women lawyers rebelled quietly, if at all: they routinely remained silent (and often unseen) in classes at Osgoode Hall, they did not complain when they were denied articling opportunities, and they generally accepted their exclusion from clubs, legal organizations, the judiciary, the Law Society Benchers, and academe.

After Clara Brett Martin's persistent public efforts to challenge male exclusivity in the legal profession in the late nineteenth century, women lawyers in early decades of the twentieth century aspired to professionalism by performing their legal tasks with quiet competence—and frequently without complaint. As Mabel Van Camp (1947), the first woman appointed to Ontario's Supreme Court in 1971, explained in 1990, early women lawyers chose to remain quiet because "it was more important to fit in, to deny the differences."[3] In this context, many early women lawyers believed that their ability to practise law depended on silent acceptance of prevailing professional and social norms, including exclusionary gender practices. Moreover, it seems that many early women lawyers believed that their ability to practise law required them to completely deny the existence of gender discrimination as well as their status as "women" lawyers in the gentleman's profession.

In the early twentieth century, lawyers' work occurred in offices and courts and in male-only clubs and organizations, spaces that were gendered

2 J. Norgren, *Rebels at the Bar* (New York: New York University Press, 2013) 204. Norgren described the women who challenged male exclusivity in the legal profession in the United States as rebels who challenged patriarchy, law, arrogance, prejudice, and the fear of change, but she also cautioned that the entrance of women into the legal profession "is not served by hagiographic history."

3 "A Profile: Madam Justice Mabel M. Van Camp" (1990) 3:1 *Without Prejudice* (WLAO) 3. Van Camp believed that there were three phases in the struggle for women's equality. First, there were early women (including women lawyers) who were quietly competent. Second, there were the suffragettes in the UK, who chained themselves to railings and threw themselves under horses and were generally obnoxious. Third, there were women who succeeded by demonstrating their expertise: Osgoode Society for Canadian Legal History (OSCLH), oral history, "Mabel Van Camp," 82–83.

male, while middle-class women were discouraged from engaging in paid work outside their homes, spaces that were gendered female.[4] Thus, many law firms refused to consider women for articling positions well into the late twentieth century, and women often faced difficulties in finding employment after being called to the bar. At the same time, in becoming lawyers, early women were rebelling against the concept of separate and gendered spaces for men and women, at least to some extent, while also accepting ongoing discriminatory treatment as members of the legal profession. Moreover, most women lawyers who married faced societal pressures about their proper roles within gendered spaces, and they tended to practise law only briefly, or not at all—although women lawyers who married lawyer spouses sometimes succeeded in combining marriage and law practice.[5] But most women lawyers in these early decades who practised law full-time, often for many decades, remained unmarried.

The small number of women students at Osgoode Hall rendered them almost invisible to both lecturers and male classmates, and even as practitioners their numbers posed no threat to the status and livelihoods of male lawyers. Few early women lawyers were litigators, although the few who did court work experienced some success, and women who practised law in smaller Ontario communities generally focused on estates, real estate, and family law. Women lawyers who were employed in large- and medium-sized firms in Toronto in these early decades were generally assigned to real estate transactions, and their employment status generally excluded access to partnership. It is significant that Jewish women lawyers and some from immigrant families established solo practices, especially in the decades before the Second World War. They faced significant challenges, and although they may have enjoyed independence as sole practitioners, they probably had few other choices.

In the decades up to 1957, the small number of women lawyers meant that male lawyers and judges only rarely encountered women lawyers—perhaps sometimes in a courtroom or a registry office. Moreover, women

4 Women were becoming increasingly present in law firms in subservient roles as administrators and secretaries in these decades: E. Brunet, "The Law Office at the Turn of the Century," *Ontario Lawyers' Gazette* (May/June 1999) 32. See also L. Code, *Rhetorical Spaces: Essays on Gendered Locations* (New York: Routledge, 1995).

5 Many non-practising women lawyers were involved in social reforms relating to women's rights and suffrage, and they continued to be welcomed by the Women's Law Association of Ontario (WLAO).

lawyers' ongoing exclusion from male clubs and most legal organizations ensured the continuation of men's exclusive social and professional lives in these gendered spaces. In addition, with the exceptions of Helen Kinnear and a few women judges in the Family and Juvenile courts, both the judiciary and the Law Society's Benchers remained male preserves until the 1970s. Even robing rooms in courthouses regularly failed to accommodate women lawyers, a situation identified as late as 1983 by Chief Justice Howland: "The Ontario Government seems to have overlooked the fact that almost half the new law graduates are now women."[6]

Yet, in the context of exclusionary practices, many early women lawyers asserted that they were "lawyers," not "women lawyers," and they regularly denied the existence of any discrimination against women in law. In the context of systemic gender barriers that are now clearly evident, early women lawyers seemed to focus on "fitting rather than breaking the mould" of male dominance in the gentleman's profession.[7] Moreover, from the perspective of later generations of women lawyers, especially feminists, the stories of early women lawyers include "puzzles" and "silences," gaps and missing evidence, and even obvious self-censorship.[8] In assessing their stories, we need to understand how their individual contexts shaped their opportunities and their responses—and how their stories reveal strategic decision making about rebellions, both quiet and unquiet. By confronting male dominance in the gentleman's profession, early women lawyers created a legacy of individual and collective strategies in response to gendered patterns of discrimination.

As their stories, especially their oral histories, suggest, women explain their lives in different ways. Some women's stories are counternarratives, describing how they did not think, feel, or act according to prevailing societal norms about women's roles. Other women's stories suggest

6 Archives of the Law Society of Upper Canada, *Crossing the Bar: A Century of Women's Experience "Upon the Rough and Troubled Seas of Legal Practice in Ontario"* (Toronto: Archives of the Law Society of Upper Canada, 1993) 55: Chief Justice Howland, speech at an annual ceremony, "Opening of the Courts," Osgoode Hall, 1983.

7 Brockman, *Gender in the Legal Profession: Fitting or Breaking the Mould* (Vancouver: UBC Press, 2001).

8 Backscheider, *Reflections on Biography* (Oxford: Oxford University Press, 1999) 59; H. Lee, *Virginia Woolf's Nose: Essays on Biography* (Princeton, NJ: Princeton University Press, 2005) 5; and J. Ker Conway, *When Memory Speaks: Exploring the Art of Autobiography* (New York: Vintage Books, 1999) 15–16.

narratives of apparent acceptance of existing norms, but they demonstrate how these women devised subtle and inventive strategies to challenge societal norms to succeed in achieving their goals. Still others, who succeeded by accepting existing norms, may have contributed to the maintenance of "prevailing systems of gender domination."[9] Stories of women lawyers in Ontario up to 1957 reveal all three patterns, as well as variations within patterns, as early women lawyers adopted different strategies in differing contexts and in relation to different goals. For example, women lawyers who claimed they were simply "lawyers" were perhaps resisting exclusion by refusing to acknowledge gender discrimination at all. That is, they were acknowledging "the texture, the range and the limits of the possible" in their professional lives.[10] At the same time, it is possible that erasing women lawyers' gendered identities reinforced male dominance in the gentleman's profession at a time when there were very few women in law.

The many variations in early women lawyers' stories confirm Carol Sanger's advice that we need to avoid identifying them as role models: as she concluded, biographical subjects do not "live their lives in order to be role models for future women."[11] In addition, "whiggish claims" about early women lawyers, which rely on historical narratives such as the triumph of the individual over adversity, are not helpful, since such motifs completely fail to explain the "glacial pace of change in succeeding generations" of women lawyers.[12] In addition, while it is appropriate to acknowledge women lawyers' perseverance, as well as their quiet rebellions, it is not useful to characterize them as heroines. Especially because some women lawyers' stories reveal that their views, like those of many

9 Personal Narratives Group, *Interpreting Women's Lives: Feminist Theory and Personal Narratives* (Bloomington: Indiana University Press, 1989) 7.

10 P.M. Glazer and M. Slater, *Unequal Colleagues: The Entrance of Women into the Professions, 1891–1940* (New Brunswick, NJ: Rutgers University Press, 1987) 14.

11 C. Sanger, "Curriculum Vitae (Feminae)): Biography and Early American Women Lawyers" (1994) 46 *Stanford Law Review* 1245 at 1281.

12 C. Morgan, "An Embarrassingly and Severely Masculine Atmosphere': Women, Gender and the Legal Profession at Osgoode Hall, 1920s to 1960s" (1996) 11:2 *Canadian Journal of Law and Society* 19" at 21. See also C. Hemmings, "Telling Feminist Stories" (2005) 6:2 *Feminist Theory* 115; and N.G. Cott, *The Grounding of Modern Feminism* (New Haven, CT: Yale University Press, 1987) 233–34.

male lawyers in these early decades, do not accord with current principles of non-discrimination, heroism claims are blemished.[13]

Although insights from second-wave feminism in the late twentieth century informed this study of early women lawyers, it does not claim that these early women lawyers were feminists, even though some of them were quiet proponents of gender equality. As Linda Gordon suggested, contemporary ideas about feminism should be avoided in writing the history of women's lives because what counts as feminist now "is markedly different from what was considered so" in the past.[14] Similarly, Dea Birkett and Julie Wheelright emphasized the need to take account of both concrete historical contexts and "unpalatable facts" in women's lives: "To rewrite history to conform more exactly with current received notions of feminist thought serves to obscure rather than to clarify the past."[15] More pointedly, Gisela Bock argued that a true dialogue with women in the past means that we need to allow historical figures to "live within their own contexts" if we wish to understand their lives.[16] Such comments suggest a need to understand these early women lawyers within a radical social analysis that reveals the objective constraints under which individual woman achieved their goals as well as "how these women have been able to cope with, test, or challenge" such constraints.[17] Moreover, as the experiences of some current women lawyers confirm, contexts for women and Outsiders in the contemporary legal profession reveal a need to be particularly attentive to both "quiet" and "less quiet" rebellions.

13 See Chapter One, for discussion of Clara Brett Martin's anti-Semitism.

14 L. Gordon, "What's New in Women's History?" in T. De Lauretis, ed., *Feminist Studies/Critical Studies* (Bloomington: Indiana University Press, 1986) 20 at 29. See also L. Kealey, "Introduction" in L. Kealey, ed., *A Not Unreasonable Claim: Women and Reform in Canada 1880s-1920s* (Toronto: Women's Press, 1979) 1.

15 D. Birkett and J. Wheelright, "'How Could She?' Unpalatable Facts and Feminists' Heroines" (1990) 2:1 *Gender and History* 49 at 56. See also A. Diduck, "Women's Legal Histories" (1993) 8:2 *Canadian Journal of Law and Society* 181; and A. Shteir, "Bluestockings and Goddesses: Writing Feminist Cultural History" in M. Luxton and M.J. Mossman, eds., *Reconsidering Knowledge: Feminism and the Academy* (Halifax: Fernwood, 2013) 130 at 146–47.

16 G. Bock, "Women's History and Gender History: Aspects of an International Debate" (1989) 1:1 *Gender and History* 7 at 8–9.

17 B. Fisher, "The Models among Us: Social Authority and Political Activism" (1981) 7 *Feminist Studies* 100 at 101. See also C. Heilbrun, *Writing a Woman's Life* (New York: Ballantine Books, 1988); and C. Heilbrun, *Women's Lives: The View from the Threshold* (Toronto: University of Toronto Press, 1999).

The historical context for early women lawyers in Ontario was vastly different, in contrast to the experiences of many, but not all, women lawyers in more recent decades. In the six decades between 1897 and 1957, when only 187 women were called to the Ontario bar, women were greatly outnumbered by male law students and male practitioners: they were regarded as benign curiosities who posed no real challenge to the gentlemen's profession or to male lawyers. In addition, in contrast to contemporary women in law in Ontario, a majority of early women lawyers did not differ from male lawyers in terms of class, religion, and race. Yet their stories remain important, both for the complex history of the Ontario legal profession and for the variegated histories of these early women lawyers. Although their rebellions were often "quiet," their stories reveal that some early women lawyers adopted strategies of "unquiet" rebellions—often with the support of the WLAO. Although the "rebellion" against the government of Premier Hepburn was relatively public, most early women lawyers engaged with challenges and setbacks in private. Yet, stories of women lawyers reveal how some of them carefully selected occasions when "less quiet" views and actions were appropriate, and especially as their numbers increased, some women lawyers did not hesitate to rebel. As Jill Ker Conway suggested in relation to women's histories, "We should pay close attention to our stories, search for the ways we experience life differently from the inherited version and edit the plot accordingly."[18]

In more recent decades, some women lawyers have succeeded in becoming judges, including in provincial appellate courts and in the Supreme

18 Ker Conway, *When Memory Speaks*, 176–77. For discussion of the WLAO's rebellion against the Hepburn government, see Chapter Four. Interestingly, the WLAO recognized the contribution of many of these pioneer women lawyers at an awards dinner in September 1986, at which women who had been called to the bar in the early decades of the twentieth century were honoured: Law Society of Ontario (LSO) Archives, WLAO fonds, "Invitees to Awards Dinner, September 1986." The list (which may be incomplete) includes Marian James Lamey, QC (1922), Helen McTague, QC (1926), Margaret Hyndman, QC (1926), Bertha Hawkins, QC (1926), Helen Grossman, QC (1929), Lily Sherizan, QC (1930), Lillian Sandler (1931), Eleanor Richards (1932), Marie Wilson, QC (1932), Mary Appleby (1934), Helen Okuloski, QC (1935), Bessie Adelman (1936), and Edythe Haughland (1936). At the WLAO's ninetieth anniversary dinner, Chief Justice Beverley McLachlin was the featured speaker: Women's Law Association of Ontario, 90th Anniversary Gala, Toronto, 26 November 2009. In 2019, the WLAO celebrated its centenary with a gala event at which women Justices of the Supreme Court of Canada were honoured.

Court of Canada. Women have been elected Benchers and Treasurers at the Law Society, and they have established sole and small practices and been appointed managing partners in large Canadian law firms. Women lawyers are also now represented among faculty members and deans in university law schools, and they have succeeded in being elected to city councils, provincial legislatures, and the Parliament of Canada—and the Honourable Kim Campbell, a woman lawyer, became prime minister thirty years ago.

Although many exclusionary practices experienced by earlier generations of women lawyers have diminished, some women lawyers continue to feel subtle exclusion—they remain "invisible and unwelcome at the table."[19] In addition, when the Law Society of Ontario hosted the inaugural Treasurer's Roundtable on Women in Law in April 2021, participants identified "persistent challenges [that] face women in law, despite advances in the field." In response, the Law Society's report included detailed strategies to respond to the Roundtable's recommendations—including a resource hub to provide "practical tools that can be used to navigate professional challenges, workplace opportunities and career transitions."[20]

Thus, in the twenty-first century, Judith Bennett's question remains: Has a change in the number of women lawyers been accompanied by a *transformation in status*, or has there been change—but also continuity—at least for some women lawyers? Asking this question does not at all preclude a celebration of women lawyers who have found, or have created,

19 A. Balakrishnan, "The Invisible Woman," *Canadian Lawyer* (3 April 2020), quoting participants at the Women in Law Summit, Toronto, April 2020.

20 A. Maxwell-Alleyne, *Report from the Treasurer's Women in Law Advisory Group* (Toronto: Law Society of Ontario, 2022). The strategies also included data collection on women lawyers; creation of an enhanced resource hub; production of timely reports to assist the profession to address persistent gender inequities; support for mentorship and sponsorship programs; a commitment to becoming more vocal about harassment and discrimination and to reinforcing professional ethics; permission for licensees to make anonymous complaints to the Law Society; examination of best practices in organizations that address women's issues; provision of more dedicated resources to articling students and licensing candidates; and enhanced mental health resources.

open doors since 1957.[21] But the question of a more general transformation in status for women lawyers remains. At the same time, there is a need to ensure that women who wish to succeed in the legal profession can do so without adopting the gendered practices of the gentleman's profession. As Ursula Franklin noted in the context of women engineers some years ago, professional success all too often depends on women "quietly" eschewing feminism and becoming "gentlemen"; she also asserted that it is not women who have the primary responsibility for making changes in professions, even though "change there must be."[22] As the *Touchstones for Change* report argued in 1993, the responsibility for change lies with the legal profession: "The challenge is to ensure that the legal profession guarantees women equality of access and equality of opportunity for advancement."[23]

Thus, the stories of women lawyers who first confronted male exclusivity in the Ontario legal profession demonstrate how some succeeded in editing the plot, at least to some extent—and in spite of significant barriers to professional equality. Moreover, their assertions that they were not *women lawyers* but *lawyers* (ungendered), does not obscure the legacy of gendered patterns of exclusion. Their stories reveal different experiences in different historical contexts, and they demonstrate that while changes have occurred for women in law in the twenty-first century, some exclusionary patterns remain for some women lawyers—and Outsiders—despite substantially increased numbers.

21 J. Bennett, "Theoretical Issues: Confronting Continuity" 1997) 9:3 *Journal of Women's History* 73. In 1997, Susan Elliott, the second woman to be elected Treasurer of the Law Society of Upper Canada (LSUC), hosted a dinner to honour the anniversary of Clara Brett Martin's admission to the bar one hundred years earlier. Forty-three women lawyers—who were recognized as Presidents of local bar associations and legal organizations (including the WLAO), chairs of committees at the Law Society and other legal groups, and judges and deans of Ontario law schools—were invited to this event: Treasurer Susan Elliott, letter and invitation to Osgoode Hall, 2 April 1997; and LSUC Program, "Celebrating the Participation of Women in Law" (14 April 1999).

22 U. Franklin, "Will Women Change Technology or Will Technology Change Women?" in U. Franklin, *The Ursula Franklin Reader: Pacifism as a Map* (Toronto: Between the Lines, 2006) 243 at 250.

23 Canadian Bar Association, *Touchstones for Change: Equality, Diversity and Accountability—The Report on Gender Equality in the Legal Profession* (Ottawa: Canadian Bar Association, 1993) 1. See also M. Eberts, "Women in Law: Retreat and Renewal" in E. Sheehy and S. McIntyre, eds., *Calling for Change: Women, Law and the Legal Profession* (Ottawa; University of Ottawa Press, 2006) 83.

Moreover, there is some evidence that early women lawyers recognized their roles as quiet rebels for women lawyers of the future. The unusual toast at the WLAO celebratory dinner meeting in April 1927 suggested that they understood, and sometimes accepted, their roles as quiet rebels—while expressing determination that later generations of women lawyers would finally succeed in "editing the plot."

### The WLAO "Toast to the Future" 1927: Rewriting History?

> *[A] joke usually presupposes a social bond, joker and audience drawing freely on a stock of common knowledge involving a shared history, a familiar pattern of daily life, topical events, and popular assumptions and attitudes ... In social terms, there are times when people are free to make jokes, times when they need to make jokes, and times when joking is inhibited or disallowed.*[24]

What was the meaning of the "Toast to the Future" for women lawyers at the celebratory WLAO dinner meeting in 1927, when Aileen Silk Bicknell (1919) presented it "to the graduates of 1987, when only a few stray men would be called to the Bar and when all the judges would be women"? Was it more than a light-hearted moment for these early women lawyers at a time when their numbers were increasing, and they could look forward to greater opportunities for professional success in future years? Did these women lawyers feel free to make a joke?[25] Or was the dinner an occasion when women lawyers needed to make a joke? As suggested in the Prologue, the toast might have been just a moment of fun at the association's 1927 dinner meeting, looking ahead sixty years to 1987 and envisioning a complete gender transformation in Ontario's legal profession and the judiciary. But is it possible the toast had a more significant meaning?

Jokes can draw attention to significant social issues. Perhaps this toast was an oblique acknowledgement of the difficult challenges these women lawyers faced. Couched in humour, the toast may have been a disguised

24 W. Nash, "Humour" in T. McArthur, ed., *The Oxford Companion to the English Language* (Oxford: Oxford University Press, 1992) 486 at 486–87.

25 See A. Bushby, "De Facto" (1991) 5:2 *Without Prejudice* (WLAO) 4, a quiz about the history of the WLAO. The quiz included a question asking which response most accurately described the toast. Although the response identified as "correct" was "a funny comment," it is possible that the toast had more significance beyond its humour. See also the Prologue.

recognition of their common experiences of professional exclusion and disappointment—and perhaps it also served to cement bonds of mutual support among women who were confronting systemic gender barriers, both as students and as legal practitioners. Especially in a context where most early women lawyers asserted that they were simply lawyers, ungendered, this toast may have quietly signalled their hope for a different future for later cohorts of women in law. And since women lawyers were vastly outnumbered by men in the legal profession in 1927, and no women had yet been appointed as judges, the toast about such a complete gender transformation in the profession and the judiciary in 1987 may have identified a charming, yet very serious, aspiration for these early women lawyers.

Regardless of the toast's meaning, the women lawyers who attended this celebratory dinner would have been astonished at the changes that had occurred for women in law by 1987, and even later. By 1987, there were six university law schools in Ontario, including Osgoode Hall Law School at York University; women law students numbered close to half of Ontario law students; women lawyers were being appointed as judges and elected as Law Society Benchers; and some were forging successful careers in legal practice and as legal academics.[26] Ironically, it was in this context, in 1987, that Osgoode Hall Law School became the site of a new gender controversy when the President of York University appointed a man as the new law school dean, rather than the other candidate for the position, a woman.[27] More than one hundred women law academics, lawyers and, law students launched a formal complaint to the Ontario Human Rights Commission.

26 See Part Three, which explores how these changes, especially increasing numbers of women law students and lawyers, created new tensions for male students and lawyers.

27 I was the woman candidate for dean, so the discovery of this 1927 toast in the WLAO fonds at the LSO Archives seemed auspicious, particularly because of its reference to 1987. Although the complaint focused on systemic, not individual, discrimination, and I was not a signatory, I maintained regular communication with the complainants. I also remained a member of faculty at Osgoode Hall Law School until I retired in 2017. See also M.J. Mossman, "'Herculean Obstacles and Intrepid Complainants': The Sex Discrimination Complaint at Osgoode Hall Law School, 1987–1994" in U. Schultz et al., eds., *Gender and Careers in the Legal Academy* (Oxford: Hart Publishing, 2021) 425; and C. May, "Still a Boys' Club," *Canadian Lawyer* (November 1987) 15 at 17, 45.

The defendants were York University, its president, and Osgoode Hall Law School.[28]

The human rights complaint epitomized women's grievances about law schools and the legal profession in the 1980s.

> Something happens when a minority group evolves from being one or two token members of the graduating class to making up almost half the student body. [In the 1980s, women law students] began demanding certain things as a right that they'd only asked for as a favour before: more respect and less ogling from professors, more female staff and faculty, more courses on gender and the law. But many of their male fellow students, who in previous years had acted indulgently toward the interlopers sparsely scattered through their ranks, now began feeling quietly resentful. [With intense competition for jobs, they realized that] there were enough female students around to start threatening what they believed to be the natural balance. Who did these women think they were?[29]

The complaint demonstrated that gender issues remained significant for women in law sixty years after the WLAO's toast to the future. Although increasing numbers of women were becoming law students, male culture in most Canadian law schools in the 1980s remained dominant. As Mélanie Brunet argued, thinking like a lawyer was often equated with thinking like a man. In addition, Cecilia Morgan concluded that some male law students felt that their advantageous position—as law students who were white, middle-class men—was being severely threatened by large numbers

28 *Mary Lou Fassel et al v York University, President Harry Arthurs, and Osgoode Hall Law School,* "Complainants' Statement pursuant to the *Ontario Human Rights Code.*" The complaint alleged "continuing systemic discrimination against women at Osgoode Hall Law School ... and discrimination on the basis of sex": para 2. In a press interview a decade earlier in 1978, Harry Arthurs had explained that although women law students in the 1960s and '70s were "slightly older than the men, slightly brighter academically, and more likely to be social activists," he suggested that women students in the late 1970s were similar to men in their reasons for attending law school: they wanted "money, prestige and power": J. Fielding, "Sisters in Law," *Weekend Magazine* (26 August 1978) 6a. The complaint to the Human Rights Commission seems to confirm that some women lawyers and law students remained activists in 1987.

29 B. Drainie, "Trials and Errors: Women and Men at Osgoode Hall Law School: The Jury Is Still Out," *Toronto Life* (August 1991) 27–28.

of women law students.[30] Indeed, by 1987, women law students constituted 40.8 per cent of the graduating class at Osgoode Hall Law School, although, in contrast, only seven of Osgoode's nearly fifty faculty members were women. In 1987, there were only two women deans in Canadian law schools, at the University of Calgary and Laval.[31] There had never been a woman dean at Osgoode Hall Law School. Moreover, gender issues were becoming more widespread in the 1980s as the American Bar Association began to conduct its well-publicized hearings about gender and legal professionalism for its major report, released in 1988.[32]

The formal complaint focused on systemic, rather than individual, discrimination, building on a decision of the Supreme Court of Canada that recognized a need for legal redress in such cases.[33] Early on, the complainants notified the defendants of their upcoming strategy: they planned a letter campaign to Osgoode alumnae, requesting that women direct financial contributions to the complaint, rather than to the Law School's forthcoming fundraising campaign. In this context, the defendants agreed to participate in settlement discussions. The settlement process initially resulted in an agreement that the law school would undertake several important initiatives, including the appointment of an expert to assess gender issues at the law school, the inclusion of gender issues in courses, and the creation of an Institute for Feminist Legal Studies at Osgoode Hall Law School. As settlement discussions became more protracted over the following years, and the university's fundraising initiatives were less successful than expected, Osgoode's new dean announced that the promised

30 M. Brunet, *Becoming Lawyers: Gender, Legal Education and Professional Identity Formation in Canada, 1920–1980* (PhD diss., University of Toronto, 2005) [unpublished] 282; and Morgan, "An Embarrassingly and Severely Masculine Atmosphere."

31 Margaret Hughes was Dean at the University of Calgary, and Thérèse Rousseau-Houle was Dean at Laval. See also *Fassel v York*, paras 13–14, 20; and *Toronto Star* (5 June 1987) B1–B2. I became a decanal candidate after serving as both assistant dean and associate dean at the law school, and I was well known in the university and in legal communities and among feminist academics in Canada and elsewhere. In the context of considerable publicity about the fact that a woman was a decanal candidate at Osgoode for the first time, I had considered seriously whether I should withdraw to avoid negative publicity for the law school if a male were selected. Dean John McCamus assured me that there would be "no problem."

32 ABA Commission on Women in the Legal Profession, "Summary of Hearings," 1988 (chair, Hillary Rodham Clinton).

33 *Action Travail des Femmes v CNR* (1987) 76 NR 161.

financial contribution to the institute would be reduced to an amount far less than had been promised in the settlement agreement. The complainants then considered a lawsuit against the university to enforce the agreement, but in the context of concerns expressed by some women faculty at Osgoode, this strategy was abandoned.[34]

For many women involved, the outcome of the complaint was deeply disappointing:

> [The complaint] is very much the story of a legal system that responds slowly and inadequately to issues of discrimination ... It raises the very fundamental question of whether it is worth trying to challenge a male-dominated, male-defined institution [Osgoode Hall] through an institution that is equally and similarly male-dominated and male-defined [law and legal processes]. It is a reminder that every single step along the road to even the smallest change is a struggle and that even when you think that you have made a step, you often find that your step triggered the erection of a new barrier ... It is a story of the terrible personal costs exacted from those who try to challenge the discrimination and how attempts to circumvent those costs for the central person for whom the costs would be most staggering are, by and large, fruitless.[35]

In the end, the complaint was finally settled in 1993–94 by a new dean, Marilyn Pilkington, the first woman dean at Osgoode Hall Law School.[36]

The research for this book began before the 1987 controversy, but the experiences of women who became students at Osgoode Hall and were called to the Ontario bar in the first half of the twentieth century—and especially their unusual toast in 1927—are part of the same story. Just as women law students and lawyers in earlier decades faced invisible barriers

34 The complainants abandoned a possible lawsuit because it would have required women (and men) faculty members to be named as defendants, a requirement strongly opposed by some faculty.

35 D. Majury, "Collective Action on a Systemic Problem" in Social Science Federation of Canada, *Toward a New Equality* (Ottawa: Social Science Federation of Canada, 1991) 19. See also J. Besant, "'Smoking Guns': Reflections on Truth and Politics in the University" in M. Thornton, ed., *Through a Glass Darkly: The Social Sciences Look at the Neoliberal University* (Canberra: ANU Press, 2014) 229.

36 The final settlement included no additional gender commitments. A second woman dean, Mary Condon, was appointed at Osgoode Hall Law School in 2019.

in the practice of law, the complaint in 1987 revealed ongoing constraints for women seeking professional and academic success as lawyers.[37] As Rosabeth Moss Kanter concluded in 1988, most organizations exhibit invisible standards that promote social conformity: "The more closed the circle, the more difficult it is for Outsiders to break in." Similarly, as Margaret Thornton suggested, homosocial reproduction may result in "senior men [seeing] youthful images of themselves as the ideal candidates within the recruitment process ... It's like looking in a mirror."[38]

Thus, the experiences of early women lawyers and their legacy of gendered patterns in the legal profession still resonate for some members of the contemporary legal profession. Yet, as Part Four, any similar toast to future cohorts of women lawyers must also address the professional aspirations of Outsiders, who are not white, gentile, middle-class, Canadian-born, physically able, and/or heterosexual. In this way, understanding the historical challenges faced by earlier generations of women in law, and their strategies for overcoming or side-stepping exclusionary practices, may have ongoing relevance for current members of Ontario's legal profession, in addition to women. As Joan Wallach Scott argued, women's histories can expose "the often silent and hidden operations of gender that are ... present and defining forces in the organization of most societies." Her comment may also apply to silent and hidden societal norms that create barriers for Outsiders. In this way, stories about early women lawyers in Ontario contribute to a "rewriting of history."[39]

37 See also M.J. Mossman, "'Invisible' Constraints on Lawyering and Leadership: The Case of Women Lawyers" (1988) 20:3 *Ottawa Law Review* 567; and J. Kelly, "The Doubled Vision of Feminist Theory" in J. Kelly, *Women, History and Theory: The Essays of Joan Kelly* (Chicago: University of Chicago Press, 1984) 51.

38 R. Moss Kanter, *Men and Women of the Corporation* (New York: Basic Books, 1977) 68; and M. Thornton, "Hegemonic Masculinity and the Academy" (1989) 17 *International Journal of the Sociology of Law* 115 at 122. See also A. Simeone, *Academic Women Working towards Equality* (South Hadley, MA: Bergin and Garvey Publishers, 1987); and A. Theodore, *The Campus Troublemakers: Academic Women in Protest* (Houston, TX: Cap and Gown Press, 1986).

39 J. Wallach Scott, "Women's History" in J. Wallach Scott, *Gender and the Politics of History* (New York: Columbia University Press, 1999) 15 at 27.

APPENDIX

# *Statutes in Canada re the Admission of Women as Lawyers*

**Ontario: 1892, 1895, and 1927**

*An Act to Provide for the Admission of Women to the Study and Practice of Law*, SO 1892, c 32, permitting women to become solicitors "in the discretion of the Law Society."

*An Act to Amend the Act to Provide for the Admission of Women to the Study and Practice of Law*, SO 1895, c 27, permitting women to become barristers "in the Society's discretion."

The society's discretionary power was removed in 1927: RSO 1927, c 192, s 41(2).

**New Brunswick: 1906**

*An Act to Remove the Disability of Women so far as relates to the Study and Practice of Law*, SNB 1906, c 5.

**Newfoundland: 1910**

*An Act to Amend Chapter 54 of the Consolidated Statutes (second series), entitled "Of the Law Society, Barristers and Solicitors,"* SN 1910, c 16, s 1.

**British Columbia: 1912**

*An Act to Remove the Disability of Women so far as relates to the Study and Practice of the Law*, SBC 1912, c 18.

**Manitoba: 1912**

*An Act to Amend "An Act to Amend the Law Society Act,"* SM 1912, c 32.

**Saskatchewan: 1912–13**

*An Act to Amend the Statute Law*, SS 1912–13, c 46, s 27, amending the *Legal Profession Act*, RSS 1909, c 104.

**Nova Scotia: 1917**

*An Act to Amend Chapter 164, Revised Statutes of 1900, "The Barristers and Solicitors Act,"* SNS 1917, c 41, s 2.

**Prince Edward Island: 1918**

*An Act to Amend an Act to Incorporate a Law Society and Amending Acts*, SPEI 1918, c 14, s 6.

**Alberta: 1930**

*The Sex Disqualification (Removal) Act, 1930*, SA 1930, c 62, retroactive to 1 September 1905.

**Quebec: 1941**

*An Act Respecting the Bar*, SQ 1941, c 56, s 1.

# *Selected Bibliography*


**Archival Sources**

Archives of Ontario

Belleville Public Library, Belleville, ON

Bibliothèque Royale, Brussels Belgium
    Section des Manuscrits, Papiers Frank

Centre for Newfoundland Studies Archives, Memorial University of Newfoundland, St. John's, NL

City Archives, Kitchener, ON

Dalhousie University, Schulich Law School Archives, Halifax, NS

Lake of the Woods Museum, Kenora, ON

Law Society of British Columbia, Legal Archives of British Columbia
    E.L. Paterson fonds

Law Society of Ontario Archives
    Women's Law Association of Ontario (WLAO) fonds

Legislature of Ontario: Debates

Library and Archives Canada
W.L. Mackenzie King fonds

McCarthy Tétrault Archives

McGill University, Faculty of Law Archives, Montreal, PQ

Ontario Jewish Archives
Betty Goldstick Lindgren fonds

Osgoode Society for Canadian Legal History
Oral History Project, Transcripts of interviews

Province of New Brunswick Archives, Fredericton NB

Provincial Archives, Victoria, BC

Thunder Bay Museum, Thunder Bay, ON

University of Texas at Austin, Tarlton Law Library
Rare Books and Special Collections

Wilton Wilson Family, archival records

**Books**

Abel, R., *English Lawyers between Market and State: The Politics of Professionalism* (Oxford: Oxford University Press, 2003).

Abel, R., and Lewis, P., eds., *Lawyers in Society: The Common Law World*, vol. 1 (Berkeley: University of California Press, 1988).

Abbott, A., *The System of Professions: An Essay on the Division of Expert Labor* (Chicago: University of Chicago Press, 1988).

Alexander, L., *Go to School, You're a Little Black Boy: The Hon Lincoln M. Alexander—A Memoir* (Toronto: Dundurn Press, 2006).

Alpern, S., J. Antler, E. Israels Perry, and I. Winther Scobie, eds., *The Challenge of Feminist Biography: Writing the Lives of Modern American Women* (Urbana: University of Illinois Press, 1992).

Anderson, E., *Judging Bertha Wilson: Law as Large as Life* (Toronto: University of Toronto Press/Osgoode Society for Canadian Legal History, 2001).

Anderson, J.S., *Lawyers and the Making of English Land Law, 1832–1940* (Oxford: Clarendon Press, 1992).
Archibald, K., *Sex and the Public Service* (Ottawa: Queen's Printer, 1970).
Auerbach, J.S., *Unequal Justice: Lawyers and Social Change in Modern America* (New York: Oxford University Press, 1976).
Babcock, B., *Woman Lawyer: The Trials of Clara Foltz* (Stanford, CA: Stanford University Press, 2011).
Bacchi, C., *Liberation Deferred? The Ideas of the English-Canadian Suffragists, 1877–1918* (Toronto: University of Toronto Press, 1983).
Backhouse, C., *Claire L'Heureux-Dubé: A Life* (Vancouver: UBC Press/Osgoode Society for Canadian Legal History, 2017).
———, *Petticoats and Prejudice: Women and Law in Nineteenth-Century Canada* (Toronto: Osgoode Society for Canadian Legal History, 1991).
Backhouse, C., and N. Backhouse, *The Heiress versus the Establishment: Mrs. Campbell's Campaign for Legal Justice* (Vancouver: UBC Press/Osgoode Society for Canadian Legal History, 2004).
Backscheider, P., *Reflections on Biography* (Oxford: Oxford University Press, 1999).
Ball, H., *Great Women Leaders* (Toronto: Second Story Press, 2004).
Banks, M., *Law at Western, 1959–1984* (London, ON: Faculty of Law, University of Western Ontario, 1984).
Bannerman, J., *Leading Ladies* (Belleville: Mika, 1977).
———, *Leading Ladies: Canada, 1639–1967* (Galt, ON: Highland Press, 1967).
Bateson, M.C., *Composing a Life* (New York: Penguin, 1989).
Batten, J., *Learned Friends: A Tribute to 50 Remarkable Ontario Advocates, 1900–1950* (Toronto: Irwin Law, 2005).
Bell, D., *Legal Education in New Brunswick: A History* (Fredericton: University of New Brunswick, 1992).
Bell, S. Groag and M. Yalom, eds., *Revealing Lives: Autobiography, Biography and Gender* (New York: State University of New York Press, 1990).
Bennett, J., *History Matters: Patriarchy and the Challenge of Feminism* (Philadelphia: University of Pennsylvania Press, 2006).
Berton, P., *The Great Depression, 1929–1939* (Toronto: McClelland and Stewart, 1990).
———, *My Times* (Toronto: Random House - Seal Books, 1996).
Betcherman, L.R., *The Little Band: The Clashes between the Communists and the Canadian Establishment, 1928–1932* (Ottawa: Deneau Publishers, 1982).
Bird, F., *Anne Francis: An Autobiography* (Toronto: Clarke, Irwin, 1974).
Bledstein, B.J., *The Culture of Professionalism: The Middle Class and the Development of Higher Education in America* (New York: W.W. Norton, 1976).

Bolt, C., *The Women's Movements in the United States and Britain from the 1790s to the 1920s* (Amherst: University of Massachusetts Press, 1993).

Bourdieu, P., *Distinction: A Social Critique of the Judgment of Taste* (Cambridge, MA: Harvard University Press, 1984).

———, *Outline of a Theory of Practice,* translated by R. Nice (Cambridge: Cambridge University Press, 1977).

Bourne, J., *Helena Normanton and the Opening of the Bar to Women* (Hook, Hampshire: Waterside Press, 2016).

Boyer, P., *A Passion for Justice: The Legacy of James Chalmers McRuer* (Toronto: Osgoode Society for Canadian Legal History, 1994).

Brandt, G. Cuthbert, N. Black, P. Bourne, and M. Fahrni, *Canadian Women: A History,* 3rd ed. (Toronto: Nelson Education, 2011).

Breakwell, G.M., *The Quiet Rebel: Women at Work in a Man's World* (London: Century Publishing, 1985).

Brittain, V., *The Women at Oxford: A Fragment of History* (London: G. Harrap, 1960).

Brockman, J., *Gender in the Legal Profession: Fitting or Breaking the Mould* (Vancouver: UBC Press, 2001).

Burke, P., ed., *New Perspectives on Historical Writing,* 2nd ed. (Philadelphia: Pennsylvania University Press, 2001).

Burrage, M., and R. Torstendahl, eds., *Professions in Theory and History: Rethinking the Study of the Professions* (London: Sage Publications, 1990).

Buss, H., *Canadian Women's Autobiography in English: An Introductory Guide for Researchers and Teachers,* CRIAW papers, no. 24 (Ottawa: Canadian Research Institute for the Advancement of Women, 1991).

Calvin, D.D., *Queen's University at Kingston: The First Century of a Scottish-Canadian Foundation, 1841–1941* (Kingston: Trustees of the University, 1941).

Carter, F., *The Middlesex Bench and Bar* (London: Middlesex Law Association, 1969).

Cartwright, H., *The Ontario Statute Citator, 1935* (Toronto: Canadian Law List, 1937).

Cartwright, V. Robinson, *The Canada Statute Citator, 1935* (Toronto: Canadian Law List, 1937).

Charrier, E., *L'Évolution intellectuelle féminine* (Paris: Éditions Albert Mechelinck, 1931).

Chester, R., *Unequal Access: Women Lawyers in a Changing America* (South Hadley, MA: Bergin and Garvey, 1985).

Chunn, D., *From Punishment to Doing Good: Family Courts and Socialized Justice in Ontario, 1880–1940* (Toronto: University of Toronto Press, 1992).

Cleverdon, C., *The Woman Suffrage Movement in Canada* (Toronto: University of Toronto Press, 1950).

Clifford, G. Jonçich, *Lone Voyagers: Academic Women in Co-educational Universities, 1870–1937* (New York City: Feminist Press, 1989).

Code, L., *Rhetorical Spaces: Essays on Gendered Locations* (New York: Routledge, 1995).

Coney, S., *Standing in the Sunshine: A History of New Zealand Women since They Won the Vote* (Auckland: Viking, 1993).

Conway, J. Ker, *When Memory Speaks: Exploring the Art of Autobiography* (New York: Vintage Books, 1999).

Cook, R., and W. Mitchinson, eds., *The Proper Sphere: Woman's Place in Canadian Society* (Toronto: Oxford University Press, 1976).

Cook, T., *At the Sharp End: Canadians Fighting the Great War, 1914–1916* (Toronto: Viking, 2007).

———, *Shock Troops: Canadians Fighting the Great War, 1917–1918* (Toronto: Penguin Canada, 2009).

Corry, J.A., *My Life and Work: A Happy Partnership* (Kingston: J.A. Corry/Queen's University, 1981).

Cott, N.F., *The Grounding of Modern Feminism* (New Haven, CT: Yale University Press, 1987).

———, *Public Vows: A History of Marriage and the Nation* (Cambridge, MA: Harvard University Press, 2000).

Creighton, D., *Canada's First Century, 1867–1967* (Toronto: MacMillan, 1970).

———, *The Forked Road: Canada, 1939–1957* (Toronto: McClelland and Stewart, 1976).

Crowley, T., *Agnes Macphail and the Politics of Equality* (Toronto: Lorimer, 1990).

Cushnie-Mansour, M.M., *A 20th Century Portia: Biography of Thelma Bernice Kerr-Thomson* (Brantford, ON: Cavern of Dreams Publishing, 2011).

Demers, A., *A History of the University of Windsor Faculty of Law, 1968–2008* (Windsor: University of Windsor Faculty of Law, 2008).

Derry, L. Miller, *Digest of Women Lawyers and Judges.* (Louisville, KY: Dune Press, 1949).

Drachman, V.G., *Sisters in Law: Women Lawyers in Modern American History* (Cambridge, MA: Harvard University Press, 1998).

———, *Women Lawyers and the Origins of Professional Identity in America: The Letters of the Equity Club, 1887 to 1890* (Ann Arbor: University of Michigan Press, 1993).

Dranoff, L. Silver, *Fairly Equal: Lawyering the Feminist Revolution* (Toronto: Second Story Press, 2017).

———, *Women in Canadian Law* (Toronto: Fitzhenry and Whiteside, 1977).

Dumont, M., M. Jean, M. Lavigne, and J. Stoddart (Clio Collective), *Québec Women: A History*, translated by R. Gannon and R. Gill (Toronto: Women's Press, 1987).

Edwards, S.T., *Fraser & Beatty: The First 150 Years* (Toronto: Desktop Publishing Division, Fraser & Beatty, 1989).

Epstein, C. Fuchs, *Women in Law* (New York: Basic Books, 1981).

———, *Women in Law*, 2nd ed. (Chicago: University of Illinois Press, 1993).

Faculty of Law, Queen's University, *Alumni Anecdotes* (Kingston: Faculty of Law, Queen's University, 1982).

Figler, B., *Sam Jacobs, Member of Parliament* (Gardenville, Québec: Harpell, 1959).

Flexner, E., *Century of Struggle: The Woman's Rights Movement in the United States* (Cambridge, MA: Belknap Press/Harvard University Press, 1959).

Frank, L., *La Femme-avocat: Exposé historique et critique de la question* (Paris: V. Giard et E. Brière, 1898).

Friedman, J., *America's First Woman Lawyer: The Biography of Myra Bradwell* (Buffalo, NY: Prometheus Books, 1993).

Galanter, M., and T. Palay, *Tournament of Lawyers: The Transformation of the Big Law Firm* (Chicago: University of Chicago Press, 1991).

Gallichan, G., *Les Québécoises et le barreau: L'histoire d'une difficile conquête, 1914–1941* (Québec City: Septentrion, 1999).

Gatfield, G., *Without Prejudice: Women in the Law* (Wellington: Brooker's, 1996).

Geison, G.I., ed., *Professions and Professional Ideologies in America* (Chapel Hill: University of North Carolina Press, 1983).

Gibson, D., and Gibson L., *Substantial Justice: Law and Lawyers in Manitoba, 1670–1970* (Winnipeg: Peguis, 1972).

Gidney, R.D., and W.P.J. Millar, *Professional Gentlemen: The Professions in Nineteenth-Century Ontario* (Toronto: University of Toronto Press, 1994).

Gillett, M., *We Walked Very Warily: A History of Women at McGill* (Montreal: Eden Press Women's Publications, 1981).

Gilmore, W.C., *Newfoundland and Dominion Status: The External Affairs Competence and International Law Status of Newfoundland, 1855–1934* (Toronto: Carswell, 1988).

Glasbeek, A., *Feminized Justice: The Toronto Women's Court, 1913–34* (Vancouver: UBC Press, 2009).

Glazer, P.M., and M. Slater, *Unequal Colleagues: The Entrance of Women into the Professions, 1891–1940* (New Brunswick, NJ: Rutgers University Press, 1987).

Gluck, S. Berger, and Patai G., eds., *Women's Words: The Feminist Practice of Oral History* (New York: Routledge, Chapman and Hall, 1991).
Goldenberg, E., *The Way It Works: Inside Ottawa* (Toronto: McClelland and Stewart, 2006).
Gooptu, S:, *Cornelia Sorabji: India's Pioneer Woman Lawyer* (New Delhi: Oxford University Press, 2006).
Gray, C., *The Massey Murder: A Maid, Her Master, and the Trial that Shocked a Country* (Toronto: HarperCollins, 2013).
Graydon, A., *Some Reminiscences of Blakes* (Paget, Bermuda: Beauregard, 1970).
Green, J., *Making Space for Indigenous Feminism*, 2nd ed. (Halifax: Fernwood Publishing, 2017).
Griffiths, N., *Penelope's Web: Some Perceptions of Women in European and Canadian Society* (Toronto: Oxford University Press, 1976).
———, *The Splendid Vision: Centennial History of the National Council of Women of Canada, 1893–1993* (Ottawa: Carleton University Press, 1993).
Hacker, C., *The Indomitable Lady Doctors* (Toronto: Clarke, Irwin and Company, 1974).
Hagan, J., and F. Kay, *Gender in Practice: A Study of Lawyers' Lives* (Oxford: Oxford University Press, 1976).
Hallowell, G., *Prohibition in Ontario, 1919–1923* (Ottawa: Lowe, 1972).
Hamilton, R., *Gendering the Vertical Mosaic: Feminist Perspectives on Canadian Society* (Toronto: Copp Clark, 1996).
Harrington, M., *Women Lawyers: Rewriting the Rules* (New York: Plume Books, 1995).
Harris, A., *Broken Patterns: Professional Women and the Quest for a New Feminine Identity* (Detroit: Wayne State University Press, 1995).
Harris, B., *Beyond Her Sphere: Women and the Professions in American History* (Westport, CT: Greenwood Press, 1978).
Harvey, C., ed., *The Law Society of Manitoba, 1877–1977* (Winnipeg: Peguis, 1977).
Heilbron, H., *Rose Heilbron: The Story of England's First Woman Queen's Counsel and Judge* (Oxford: Hart Publishing, 2012).
Heilbrun, C., *Women's Lives: The View from the Threshold* (Toronto: University of Toronto Press, 1999).
———, *Writing a Woman's Life* (New York: Ballantine Books, 1988).
Heron, C., *Booze: A Distilled History* (Toronto: Between the Lines, 2003).
Hodgetts, J.E., W. McCloskey, R. Whitaker, and V.S. Wilson, *The Biography of an Institution: The Civil Service of Canada, 1908–1967* (Montreal/Kingston: McGill-Queen's University Press, 1972).

Hoff, J., *Law, Gender, and Injustice: A Legal History of US Women* (New York: New York University Press, 1991).

Honsberger, J., *The County of York Law Association: A History of the First Hundred Years, 1885–1985* (Toronto: County of York Law Association, 1989).

———, *Osgoode Hall: An Illustrated History* (Toronto: Osgoode Society for Canadian Legal History, 2004).

Horn, M., ed., *The Dirty Thirties: Canadians in the Great Depression* (Toronto: Copp Clark, 1972).

Iacovetta, F., and M. Valverde, eds., *Gender Conflicts: New Essays in Women's History* (Toronto: University of Toronto Press, 1992).

Kanter, R. Moss, *Men and Women of the Corporation* (New York: Basic Books, 1977).

Kay, F., N. Dautovich, and C. Marlor, *Barriers and Opportunities within Law: Women in a Changing Legal Profession* (Toronto: Law Society of Upper Canada, 1996).

Kealey, L., and J. Sangster, eds., *Beyond the Vote: Canadian Women and Politics* (Toronto: University of Toronto Press, 1989).

Kessler, D., *A Century on Spring Street: Wanda Lefurgey Wyatt of Summerside, Prince Edward Island, 1895–1998* (Charlottetown: Indigo Press, 1999).

Kimble, S., and M. Röwekamp, eds., *New Perspectives on European Women's Legal History* (New York: Routledge, 2017).

Kinnear, M., *In Subordination: Professional Women, 1870–1970* (Montreal/Kingston: McGill-Queen's University Press, 1995).

Kirk, H., *Portrait of a Profession: A History of the Solicitor's Profession: 1100 to the Present Day* (London: Oyez, 1976).

Kitz, J., *Shattered City: The Halifax Explosion and the Road to Recovery* (Halifax: Nimbus, 2004).

Knowles, V., *First Person: A Biography of Cairine Wilson, Canada's First Woman Senator* (Toronto: Dundurn Press, 1988).

Kome, P., *The Taking of Twenty-Eight* (Toronto: Women's Press, 1983).

Kramer, R., and T. Mitchell, *When the State Trembled: How A.J. Andrews and the Citizens' Committee Broke the Winnipeg General Strike* (Toronto: University of Toronto Press, 2010).

Kugler, I., *From Ladies to Women: The Organized Struggle for Women's Rights in the Reconstruction Era* (Westport, CT: Greenwood Press, 1987).

Kyer, C.I., *Lawyers, Families, and Businesses: The Shaping of a Bay Street Law Firm, Faskens, 1863–1963* (Toronto: Osgoode Society for Canadian Legal History/Irwin Law, 2013).

Kyer, C.I., and J.E. Bickenbach, *The Fiercest Debate: Cecil A. Wright, the Benchers and Legal Education in Ontario, 1923–1957* (Toronto: Osgoode Society for Canadian Legal History, 1987).

LaMarsh, J., *Memoirs of a Bird in a Gilded Cage* (Toronto: McClelland and Stewart, 1968).

———, *A Right Honourable Lady: A Novel* (Toronto: McClelland and Stewart, 1980).

———, *A Very Political Lady: A Novel* (Toronto: McClelland and Stewart, 1979).

Lang, E., *Handy Guide to the Laws of Ontario* (Toronto: Copp Clark, 1918, 1923, 1929).

Lang, E.M., *British Women in the Twentieth Century* (London: T. Werner Laurie, 1929).

Langstaff, A.M., *French-English, English-French Law Dictionary* (Montreal: Wilson and Lafleur, 1937).

Larson, M. Sarfatti, *The Rise of Professionalism: A Sociological Analysis* (Berkeley: University of California Press, 1979).

Lederman, W.R., *Continuing Canadian Constitutional Dilemmas: Essays on the Constitutional History, Public Law and Federal System of Canada* (Toronto: Butterworths, 1981).

Lee, H., *Virginia Woolf's Nose: Essays on Biography* (Princeton, NJ: Princeton University Press, 2005).

Leiper, J. McKenzie, *Bar Codes: Women in the Legal Profession* (Vancouver: UBC Press, 2006).

Lorinc, J., M. McClelland, E. Scheinberg, and T. Taylor, *The Ward: The Life and Loss of Toronto's First Immigrant Neighbourhood* (Toronto: Coach House, 2015).

Luciuk, L.Y., and I.L. Wynnyckyj, *Ukrainians in Ontario* (Toronto: Multicultural History Society of Ontario, 1988).

MacDonald, C., *Adelaide Hoodless: Domestic Crusader* (Toronto: Dundurn Press, 1986).

MacDowell, L. Sefton, *Renegade Lawyer: The Life of J.L. Cohen* (Toronto: Osgoode Society for Canadian Legal History/University of Toronto Press, 2001).

MacGill, E.G., *My Mother, the Judge* (Toronto: Ryerson Press, 1955).

Macpherson, K., *When in Doubt, Do Both: The Times of my Life* (Toronto: University of Toronto Press, 1994).

Magarey, S., and K. Round, *Roma the First: A Biography of Dame Roma Mitchell* (Adelaide: Wakefield Press, 2007).

Mandel, M., *The Jewish Hour: The Golden Age of a Toronto Yiddish Radio Show and Newspaper* (Toronto: Now and Then Books, 2016).

Marsden, L., *Canadian Women and the Struggle for Equality* (Don Mills, ON: Oxford University Press, 2012).

Martynowych, O.T., *Ukrainians in Canada: The Formative Period, 1891–1924* (Edmonton: Canadian Institute of Ukrainian Studies Press, 1991).

McClean, S., *A Woman of Influence: Evlyn Fenwick Farris* (Victoria: Sono Nis Press, 1997).

McGlynn, C., *The Woman Lawyer: Making a Difference* (London: Butterworths, 1998).
McLachlin, B.,*Truth Be Told: My Journey Through Life and the Law* (New York: Simon and Schuster, 2019).
Miller, I.H.M., *Our Glory and Our Grief: Torontonians and the Great War* (Toronto: University of Toronto Press, 2002).
Moore, C., *The Law Society of Upper Canada and Ontario's Lawyers, 1797–1997* (Toronto: University of Toronto Press, 1997).
———, *McCarthy Tétrault: Building Canada's Premier Law Firm* (Vancouver: Douglas and McIntyre, 2005).
Morello, K.B., *The Invisible Bar: The Woman Lawyer in America, 1638 to the Present* (New York: Random House, 1986).
Morgan, H.J., ed., *The Canadian Men and Women of the Time: A Handbook of Canadian Biography* (Toronto: W. Briggs, 1898).
Morrison, N., *Benched: Passion for Law Reform* (Calgary, AB: Durville Pubs, 2018).
Morton, D., *Canada and War: A Military and Political History* (Toronto: Butterworths, 1981).
Mossman, M.J., *The First Women Lawyers: A Comparative Study of Gender, Law and the Legal Professions* (Oxford: Hart Publishing, 2006).
Mullins, C., and A. Harvey, *Russell & DuMoulin: The First Century, 1889–1989* (Vancouver: Russell & Dumoulin, 1989).
Neatby, H., *Queen's University*, vol. 1, *1841–1917: And Not to Yield* (Montreal/ Kingston: McGill-Queen's University Press, 1978).
Neatby, H. Blair, and R. Dawson MacGregor, *William Lyon Mackenzie King: The Lonely Heights, 1924–1932* (Toronto: University of Toronto Press, 1963).
Norgren, J., *Rebels at the Bar* (New York : New York University Press, 2013).
———, *Stories from Trailblazing Women Lawyers: Lives in the Law* (New York: New York University Press, 2020).
November, J., *In the Footsteps of Ethel Benjamin* (Wellington: Victoria University Press, 2009).
Oliver, P., *G. Howard Ferguson: Ontario Tory* (Toronto: University of Toronto Press/ Ontario Historical Studies Series, 1977).
———, *Public and Private Persons: The Ontario Political Culture, 1914–1934* (Toronto Vancouver: Clarke, Irwin, 1975).
———, *Unlikely Tory: The Life and Politics of Allan Grossman* (Toronto: Lester and Orpen Dennys, 1985).
Omatsu, M., *Bittersweet Passage: Redress and the Japanese-Canadian Experience* (Toronto: Between the Lines, 1992).
Opekokew, D., *The First Nations: Indian Government and the Canadian Federation* (Saskatoon: Federation of Saskatchewan Indians, 1980).

———, *The First Nations: Indian Government in the Community of Man* (Saskatoon: Federation of Saskatchewan Indians, 1982).

Owram, D., *Born at the Right Time: A History of the Baby Boom Generation* (Toronto: University of Toronto Press, 1996).

Personal Narratives Group, *Interpreting Women's Lives: Feminist Theory and Personal Narratives* (Bloomington: Indiana University Press, 1989).

Pierson, R. Roach, *"They're Still Women after All": The Second World War and Canadian Womanhood* (Toronto: McClelland and Stewart, 1986).

Pilarczyk, I., *"A Noble Roster": One Hundred and Fifty Years of Law at McGill* (Montreal: McGill University Faculty of Law, 1999).

Prang, M., *N.W. Rowell: Ontario Nationalist* (Toronto: University of Toronto Press, 1975).

Prentice, A., P. Bourne, G. Cuthbert Brandt, B. Light., W. Mitchinson, and N. Black, *Canadian Women: A History*, 2nd ed. (Toronto: Harcourt Brace Canada, 1996).

Pue, W.W., *Law School: The Story of Legal Education in British Columbia* (Vancouver: University of British Columbia Faculty of Law, 1995).

Pue, W.W. and D. Sugarman, eds., *Lawyers and Vampires: Cultural Histories of the Legal Professions* (Oxford: Hart Publishing, 2003).

Purvis, J., *Emmeline Pankhurst: A Biography* (London: Routledge, 2002).

Reaman, G.E., *A History of Agriculture in Ontario* (Toronto: Saunders, 1970).

Rosenberg, L., *Canada's Jewry: A Social and Economic Study of Jews in Canada* (Montreal/Kingston: McGill-Queen's University Press, 1993).

Rowbotham, S., *Hidden from History* (New York: Pantheon, 1974).

Sachs, A., and J. Hoff Wilson, *Sexism and the Law: A Study of Male Beliefs and Legal Bias in Britain and the United States* (New York: Free Press, 1978).

Sangster, J., *Dreams of Equality: Women on the Canadian Left, 1920–1950* (Toronto: McClelland and Stewart, 1989).

———, *Through Feminist Eyes: Essays on Canadian Women's History* (Edmonton: Athabasca University Press, 2011).

Saywell, J., *"Just Call Me Mitch": The Life of Mitchell F. Hepburn* (Toronto: University of Toronto Press, 1991).

Schultz, U., and G. Shaw, eds., *Gender and Judging* (Oxford: Hart Publishing, 2013).

———, *Women in the World's Legal Professions* (Oxford: Hart Publishing, 2003).

Schultz, U., G. Shaw, M. Thornton, and R. Auchmuty, eds., *Gender and Careers in the Legal Academy* (Oxford: Hart Publishing, 2021).

Scutt, J., *Women and the Law: Commentary and Materials* (Sydney: The Law Book, 1990).

Sharpe, R., and P. McMahon, *The Persons Case: The Origins and Legacy of the Fight for Legal Personhood* (Toronto: University of Toronto Press, 2007).

Shaw, R., *Proud Heritage: A History of the National Council of Women* (Toronto: Ryerson Press, 1957).

Simeone, A., *Academic Women Working towards Equality* (South Hadley, MA: Bergin and Garvey Publishers, 1987).

Slater, J.G., *Minerva's Aviary: Philosophy at Toronto, 1843–2003* (Toronto: University of Toronto Press, 2005).

Smyth, E., S. Acker, P. Bourne, and A. Prentice, eds., *Challenging Professions: Historical and Contemporary Perspectives on Women's Professional Work* (Toronto: University of Toronto Press, 1999).

Sommerlad, H., and P. Sanderson, *Gender, Choice and Commitment: Women Solicitors in England and Wales and the Struggle for Equal Status* (Dartmouth: Ashgate, 1998).

Sorabji, R., *Opening Doors: The Untold Story of Cornelia Sorabji* (New Delhi: Penguin Books, 2010).

Stager, D., with H. Arthurs, *Lawyers in Canada* (Toronto: University of Toronto Press/Statistics Canada, 1990).

Steedman, C., *Landscape for a Good Woman: A Story of Two Lives* (London: Virago Press, 1986).

Stevens, R., *Law School: Legal Education in America from the 1850s to the 1980s* (Chapel Hill: University of North Carolina Press, 1983).

Strong-Boag, V., *The New Day Recalled: Lives of Girls and Women in English Canada, 1919–1939* (Toronto: Copp Clark Pitman/Penguin, 1988).

Struthers, J., *No Fault of Their Own: Unemployment and the Canadian Welfare State, 1914–1941* (Toronto: University of Toronto Press, 1983).

Taylor, G.V., and F.C. Snider, *Annotations to the Revised Statutes of Ontario, 1927* (Toronto: Carswell, 1927).

Theodore, A., *The Campus Troublemakers: Academic Women in Protest* (Houston, TX: Cap and Gown Press, 1986).

Thornton, M., *Dissonance and Distrust: Women in the Legal Profession* (Melbourne: Oxford University Press, 1996).

Timpson, A.M., *Driven Apart: Women's Employment Equality and Child Care in Canadian Public Policy* (Vancouver: UBC Press, 2001).

Tucker, E., *Administering Danger in the Workplace: The Law and Politics of Occupational Health and Safety Regulation in Ontario, 1850–1914* (Toronto: University of Toronto Press, 1990).

Tulchinsky, G., *Canada's Jews: A People's Journey* (Toronto: University of Toronto Press, 2018).

Turnbull, A., ed., *Réunion: Common Law History at the University of Ottawa: 30 ans en français, 50 Years in English* (Ottawa: University of Ottawa Faculty of Law, 2007).

University of Windsor Faculty of Law, *Bridging the Law: Fifty Years of Windsor Law* (Windsor: Biblioasis, 2018).

Wade, F., *Square Haunting: Five Writers in London between the Wars* (London: Faber and Faber, 2020).

Waite, P.B., *In Search of R.B. Bennett* (Montreal/Kingston: McGill-Queen's University Press, 2012).

Walsh, M.R., *"Doctors Wanted: No Woman Need Apply": Sexual Barriers in the Medical Profession, 1835–1975* (New Haven, CT: Yale University Press, 1977).

Walters, M., *"Let Right Be Done": A History of the Faculty of Law at Queen's University* (Kingston: Faculty of Law, Queen's University, 2007).

Wandersee, W., *Women's Work and Family Values, 1920–1940* (Cambridge, MA: Harvard University Press, 1981).

Watts, A., *History of the Legal Profession in British Columbia, 1869–1984* (Vancouver: Law Society of British Columbia, 1984).

Wegenast, F.W., [and M. Hyndman], *The Law of Canadian Companies* (Toronto: Burroughs, 1931).

Wiktor, C., ed., *Dalhousie Law School Register, 1883–1983* (Halifax: Dalhousie Law School, 1983).

Williams, G., *Learning the Law* (London: Stevens and Sons, 1969).

Willis, J., *A History of Dalhousie Law School* (Toronto: University of Toronto Press, 1979).

Wilton, C., *Inside the Law: Canadian Law Firms in Historical Perspective* (Toronto: Osgoode Society for Canadian Legal History/University of Toronto Press, 1996).

Witz, A., *Professions and Patriarchy* (London: Routledge, 1992).

Woolf, V., *Three Guineas* (London: Hogarth Press, 1977).

Wyatt, R., *Agnes MacPhail: Champion of the Underdog* (Montreal: XYZ Publishing, 2000).

## Book Chapters

Abel, R., "United States: The Contradictions of Professionalism" in R. Abel and P. Lewis, eds., *Lawyers in Society: The Common Law World*, vol. 1 (Berkeley: University of California Press, 1988) 186.

Alpern, S., J. Antler, E. Israels Perry, and I. Winther Scobie, "Introduction" in S. Alpern, J. Antler, E. Israels Perry, and I. Winther Scobie, eds., *The Challenge of Feminist Biography: Writing the Lives of Modern American Women* (Urbana: University of Illinois Press, 1992) 1.

Atcheson, B., "Equality Is a Woman's Place: The Royal Commission on the Status of Women" in B. Atcheson and L. Marsden, eds., *White Gloves Off: The Work of the*

*Ontario Committee on the Status of Women* (Toronto: Second Story Press, 2018) 23.

Atcheson, B., W. Lawrence, I. Melville, C. Morrison, and L. Marsden, "Family Law, Childcare, Reproductive Issues" in B. Atcheson and L. Marsden, eds., *White Gloves Off: The Work of the Ontario Committee on the Status of Women* (Toronto: Second Story Press, 2018) 103.

Baines, B., "Overview of Early Women in the Canadian Legal Academy" in A. Lund and V. Torrie, eds., (Vancouver: UBC Press, forthcoming 2024).

———, "Women and the Law," in S. Burt, L. Code, and L. Dorney, eds., *Changing Patterns: Women in Canada* (Toronto: McClelland and Stewart, 1988) 157.

———, "Women, Human Rights and the Constitution" in A. Doerr and M. Carrier, eds., *Women and the Constitution in Canada* (Ottawa: Advisory Council on the Status of Women, 1981) 31.

Baker, B., "Legal Education in Upper Canada, 1785–1889: The Law Society as Educator" in D. Flaherty, ed., *Essays in the History of Canadian Law*, vol. 2 (Toronto: Osgoode Society for Canadian Legal History/University of Toronto Press, 1983) 49.

Barber, M., "The Women Ontario Welcomed: Immigrant Domestics for Ontario Homes, 1870–1930" in A. Prentice and S. Mann Trofimenkoff, eds., *The Neglected Majority: Essays in Canadian Women's History, Volume Two* (Toronto: McClelland and Stewart, 1985) 102.

Bashevkin, S., "Independence versus Partisanship: Dilemmas in the Political History of Women in English Canada" in V. Strong-Boag and A. Claire Fellman, eds., *Rethinking Canada: The Promise of Women's History* (Toronto: Copp Clark Pitman, 1986) 246.

Besant, J., "Reflections on Truth and Politics in the University" in M. Thornton, ed., *Through a Glass Darkly: The Social Sciences Look at the Neoliberal University* (Canberra: ANU Press, 2014) 229.

Bittenbender, A.M., "Women in Law" in A.N. Meyer, ed., *Women's Work in America* (New York: H. Holt and Company, 1891) 222.

Bloomfield, E., "Lawyers as Members of Urban Business Elites in Southern Ontario, 1860 to 1920" in C. Wilton, ed., *Beyond the Law: Lawyers and Business in Canada 1830 to 1930* (Toronto: Osgoode Society for Canadian Legal History, 1990) 112.

Brockman, J., "Exclusionary Tactics: The History of Women and Minorities in the Legal Profession in British Columbia" in H. Foster and J. McLaren, eds., *Essays in the History of Canadian Law*, vol. 6, *British Columbia and Yukon* (Toronto: Osgoode Society for Canadian Legal History, 1995) 508.

Buckley, M., "The Second Decade: The Role of the Canadian Bar Association in Implementing the *Touchstones* Report" in E. Sheehy and S. McIntyre, eds., *Calling for Change: Women, Law, and the Legal Profession* (Ottawa: University of Ottawa Press, 2006) 325.

Burke, P., "Overture—The New History: Its Past and Future" in P. Burke, ed., *New Perspectives on Historical Writing*, 2nd ed. (Pennsylvania: Pennsylvania University Press, 2001) 1.

Burrage, M., K. Jarausch, and H. Siegrist, "An Actor-Based Framework for the Study of the Professions" in M. Burrage and R. Torstendahl, eds., *Professions in Theory and History: Rethinking the Study of the Professions* (London: Sage, 1990) 203.

Bushby, A., "Presidents of the Women's Law Association of Ontario, 1919–2000" in A. Bushby, "The Early Years: Sources of an Enduring Tradition: The Women's Law Association of Ontario, 1919–1950" (80th Anniversary Celebration, 14 January 2000).

Choroszewicz, M., and F. Kay, "Understanding Gender Equality in the Legal Profession" in R. Abel, H. Sommerlad, O. Hammerslev, and S. Schultz, eds., *Lawyers in 21st-Century Societies*, vol.2 *Comparisons and Theories* (Oxford: Hart Publishing, 2022) 127.

Christie, N., "Conclusion: The Endangered Family" in N. Christie, *Engendering the State: Family, Work, and Welfare in Canada* (Toronto: University of Toronto Press, 2000) 310.

Cohen, M., "The Condition of Legal Education in Canada—Fifteen Years Later, 1949–1964" in Canadian Bar Association, Papers presented at the Annual Meeting, 1964, Montreal, Québec (Toronto: CCH Canada Limited, 1965).

Cohen, M. Griffin, "Employment and Economic Issues: The Fair Employment Practices Committee" in B. Atcheson and L. Marsden, eds., *White Gloves Off: The Work of the Ontario Committee on the Status of Women* (Toronto: Second Story Press, 2018) 59.

Corbett, M., and D. Corbett, "Helen Kinnear (1894–1970)" in R.M. Salokar and M.L. Volcansek eds., *Women in Law: A Bio-biographical Sourcebook* (Westport, CT: Greenwood Press, 1996) 129.

Eberts, M., "Women and Constitutional Renewal" in A. Doerr and M. Carrier, eds., *Women and the Constitution in Canada* (Ottawa: Advisory Council on the Status of Women, 1981) 9.

———, "Women in Law: Retreat and Renewal" in E. Sheehy and S. McIntyre, eds., *Calling for Change: Women, Law and the Legal Profession* (Ottawa: University of Ottawa Press, 2006) 83.

Errington, J., "Pioneers and Suffragists" in S. Burt, L. Code, and L. Dorney, eds., *Changing Patterns: Women in Canada* (Toronto: McClelland and Stewart, 1988) 51.

Etter-Lewis, G., "Black Women's Life Stories: Reclaiming Self in Narrative Texts" in S. Gluck Berger and D. Patai, eds., *Women's Words: The Feminist Practice of Oral History* (New York: Routledge, 1991) 48.

Forestall, D., "The Necessity of Sacrifice" in J.M. Bumstead and L. Kuffert, eds., *Interpreting Canada's Past*, 3rd ed. (Don Mills, ON: Oxford University Press, 2005) 367.

Franklin, U., "Will Women Change Technology or Will Technology Change Women?" in U. Franklin, *The Ursula Franklin Reader: Pacifism as a Map* (Toronto: Between the Lines, 2006) 243.

French, D., "Agnes Macphail" in M.Q. Innis, ed., *The Clear Spirit: Twenty Canadian Women and Their Times* (Toronto: University of Toronto Press, 1966) 179.

French, M.P., "The Legal Parental Rights of Women in New Brunswick" in International Congress of Women, *Report of the International Congress of Women, June 24th–30th, 1909* (Toronto: Geo Parker and Sons, Printers, 1910) 203.

Galanter, M., "Mega-law and Mega-lawyering in the Contemporary United States" in R. Dingwall and P. Lewis, eds., *The Sociology of the Professions: Lawyers, Doctors and Others* (London: Macmillan, 1983) 152.

Gérin-Lajoie, H., "Legal Status of Women in the Province of Québec," in National Council of Women, *Women of Canada: Their Life and Work* (Paris: Paris International Exhibition, 1900) 41.

Giffen, P.J., "Social Control and Professional Self-Government: A Study of the Legal Profession in Canada" in S.D. Clark, *Urbanism and the Changing Canadian Society* (Toronto: University of Toronto Press, 1961) 127.

Glucksmann, M., "The Work of Knowledge and the Knowledge of Women's Work" in M. Maynard and J. Purvis, eds., *Researching Women's Lives from a Feminist Perspective* (London: Taylor and Francis, 1994) 149.

Gordon, L., "What's New in Women's History" in T. de Lauretis, ed., *Feminist Studies/Critical Studies* (Bloomington: Indiana University Press, 1986) 20.

Gorham, D., "Flora MacDonald Denison: Canadian Feminist" in L. Kealey, ed., *A Not Unreasonable Claim: Women and Reform in Canada, 1880s–1920s* (Toronto: Women's Press, 1979) 47.

Grossberg, M., "Institutionalizing Masculinity: The Law as a Masculine Profession" in M.C. Carnes and C. Griffen, eds., *Meanings for Manhood: Construction of Masculinity in Victorian America* (Chicago: University of Chicago Press, 1990) 133.

Hagan, J., and F. Kay, "Hierarchy in Practice: The Significance of Gender in Ontario Law Firms" in C. Wilton, ed., *Inside the Law: Canadian Law Firms in Historical Perspective* (Toronto: Osgoode Society for Canadian Legal History/University of Toronto Press, 1996) 530.

Harman, E., "Five Persons from Alberta" in M. Quale Innis, *The Clear Spirit: Twenty Canadian Women and Their Times* (Toronto: University of Toronto Press/ Canadian Federation of University Women, 1966) 158.

Heilbrun, C., "Women's Autobiographical Writings: New Forms" in M.W. Brownley and A.B. Kimmich, eds., *Women and Autobiography* (Wilmington, DE: Scholarly Resources, 1999) 15.

Hosek, C., "Women and the Constitutional Process" in K. Banting and R. Simeon, *And No One Cheered: Federalism, Democracy and the Constitution Act* (Toronto: Methuen, 1983) 280.

Kadar, M., "Afterword" in H.M. Buss and M. Kadar, eds., *Working in Women's Archives: Researching Women's Private Literature and Archival Documents* (Waterloo, ON: Wilfrid Laurier University Press, 2001) 115.

Kay, F., and J. Hagan, "Social Mobility and Hierarchical Structure in Canadian Law Practice" in W. Felstiner, ed., *Reorganization and Resistance: Legal Professions Confront a Changing World* (Oxford: Hart Publishing, 2005) 28.

Kealey, L., "Introduction" in L. Kealey, ed., *A Not Unreasonable Claim: Women and Reform in Canada 1880s–1920s* (Toronto: Women's Press, 1979) 1.

Kelly, J., "The Doubled Vision of Feminist Theory" in Kelly, *Women, History and Theory: The Essays of Joan Kelly* (Chicago: University of Chicago Press, 1984) 51.

Lewthwaite, S., "Reconstructing the Lives and Careers of Lawyers: Ethelbert Lionel Cross, Toronto's First Black Lawyer" in C. Backhouse and W.W. Pue, eds., *The Promise and Perils of Law: Lawyers in Canadian History* (Vancouver: UBC Press, 2009) 193.

Lowe, G., "Women, Work and the Office: The Feminization of Clerical Occupations in Canada, 1901–1931" in V. Strong-Boag and A. Clair Fellman, eds., *Rethinking Canada: The Promise of Women's History* (Toronto: Copp Clark Pitman, 1986) 107.

Majury, D., "Collective Action on a Systemic Problem" in Social Science Federation of Canada, *Toward a New Equality* (Ottawa: Social Science Federation of Canada, 1991) 19.

Martin, C.B., "Legal Status of Women in the Dominion of Canada (Except in the Province of Québec)" in National Council of Women, *Women of Canada: Their Life and Work* (Paris: Paris International Exhibition, 1900) 34.

Maynard, M., and J. Purvis, "Doing Feminist Research" in M. Maynard and J. Purvis, eds., *Researching Women's Lives from a Feminist Perspective* (London: Taylor and Francis, 1994) 1.

McDonald, L., "The Challenge Accepted: The Founding of the Ontario Committee on the Status of Women" in B. Atcheson and L. Marsden, eds., *White Gloves Off: The Work of the Ontario Committee on the Status of Women* (Toronto: Second Story Press, 2018) 33.

McIvor, S., "Aboriginal Women: Working in Coalition to Advance Sex Equality" in E. Sheehy and S. McIntyre, *Calling for Change: Women, Law and the Legal Profession* (Ottawa: University of Ottawa Press, 2006) 253.

Monture, P., "The Right of Inclusion: Aboriginal Rights and/or Aboriginal Women?" in K. Wilkins, ed., *Advancing Aboriginal Claims* (Saskatoon: Purich, 2004) 39.

Mossman, M.J., "Becoming the First Women Judges in Ontario: Women Lawyers, Gender and the Politics of Judicial Appointment" in U. Schultz and G. Shaw, eds., *Gender and Judging* (Oxford: Hart Publishing, 2013) 51.

———, "Engendering the Legal Profession: The Education Strategy" in U. Schultz and G. Shaw, eds., *Women in the World's Legal Professions* (Portland, OR: Hart Publishing, 2003) 77.

———, "'Herculean Obstacles and Intrepid Complainants': The Sex Discrimination Complaint at Osgoode Hall Law School" in U. Schultz, G. Shaw, M. Thornton, and R. Auchmuty, eds., *Gender and Careers in the Legal Academy* (Oxford: Hart Publishing, 2021) 425.

Nash, W. "Humour" in T. McArthur, ed., *The Oxford Companion to the English Language* (Oxford: Oxford University Press, 1992) 486.

Nelson, C., "The Conflicting and Contradictory Dance: The Essential Management of Identity for Women of Colour in the Legal Academy" in E. Sheehy and S. McIntyre, eds. *Calling for Change: Women, Law and the Legal Profession* (Ottawa: University of Ottawa Press, 2006) 117.

Olgiati, V., "Professional Body and Gender Difference in Court: The Case of the First (Failed) Woman Lawyer in Modern Italy" in U. Schultz and G. Shaw, eds., *Women in the World's Legal Professions* (Oxford: Hart Publishing, 2003) 419.

Pierson, R. Roach, "Women's Emancipation and the Recruitment of Women into the Labour Force in World War II" in S. Mann Trofimenkoff and A. Prentice, eds., *The Neglected Majority: Essays in Canadian Women's History* (Toronto: McClelland and Stewart, 1977) 125.

Pierson, R. Roach, "Experience, Difference, Dominance and Voice in the Writing of Canadian Women's History" in K. Offen, R. Roach Pierson, and J. Rendell, eds., *Writing Women's History: International Perspectives* (Bloomington: Indiana University Press, 1991) 79.

Popelin, M., "Laws of Marriage and Divorce in Belgium" in *Report of the International Congress of Women, June 24th–30th 1909* (Toronto: Geo Parker and Sons, 1910) 248.

Pue, W.W., "Canadian Legal Education, 1900–1930" in R. McQueen and W.W. Pue, eds., *Misplaced Traditions: British Lawyers, Colonial Peoples*, symposium issue (1998–1999) 16:1 *Law in Context* 80.

———, "Cultural Projects and Structural Transformation in the Canadian Legal Profession" in W.W. Pue and D. Sugarman, eds., *Lawyers and Vampires: Cultural Histories of the Legal Professions* (Oxford: Hart Publishing, 2003) 367.

Purvis, J., "Biography as Microscope or Kaleidoscope? The Case of 'Power' in Hannah Cullwick's Relationship with Arthur Munby" in L. Stanley, ed., *The Autobiographical I: The Theory and Practice of Feminist Auto-biography* (Manchester: Manchester University Press, 1992) 158.

Regehr, T.D., "Elite Relationships, Partnership Arrangements, and Nepotism at Blakes: a Toronto Law Firm, 1858–1942" in C. Wilton, ed., *Inside the Law: Canadian Law Firms in Historical Perspective* (Toronto: Osgoode Society for Canadian Legal History/University of Toronto Press, 1996) 207.

Risk, R., "The Nuisance of Litigation: The Origins of Workers' Compensation in Ontario" in D. Flaherty, ed., *Essays in the History of Canadian Law*, vol. 2 (Toronto: Osgoode Society for Canadian Legal History, 1983) 418.

Roberts, W., "'Rocking the Cradle for the World': The New Woman and Maternal Feminism, Toronto, 1877–1914" in L. Kealey, ed., *A Not Unreasonable Claim: Women and Reform in Canada, 1880s–1920s* (Toronto: Women's Press, 1979) 15.

Robertson, H., "The Honourable Judy" in M. Kostash, M. McCracken, V. Miner, E. Paris, and H. Robertson, eds., *Her Own Woman: Profiles of Ten Canadian Women* (Toronto: Macmillan, 1975) 1.

Sangster, J., "The 1907 Bell Telephone Strike: Organizing Women Workers" in V. Strong-Boag and A. Claire Fellman, eds., *Rethinking Canada: The Promise of Women's History* (Toronto: Copp Clark Pitman, 1986) 137.

———, "The Role of Women in the Early CCF" in L. Kealey and J. Sangster, *Beyond the Vote: Canadian Women and Politics* (Toronto: University of Toronto Press, 1989) 118.

Savage, J., "The Problems of Wealth and Virtue: The Paris Bar and the Generation of the *Fin-de-Siècle*" in W.W. Pue and D. Sugarman, eds., *Lawyers and Vampires: Cultural Histories of the Legal Professions* (Oxford and Portland OR: Hart Publishing, 2003) 171.

Schultz, U., "Introduction" in U. Schultz and G. Shaw, eds., *Women in the World's Legal Professions* (Oxford: Hart Publishing, 2003) liii.

Scott, J. Thomson, "Introduction" in J. Thomson Scott, *The Conditions of Female Labour in Ontario* (Toronto: Warwick and Sons, 1892).

Scott, J. Wallach, "American Women Historians, 1884–1984" in J. Wallach Scott, *Gender and the Politics of History* (New York: Columbia University Press, 1999) 178.

———, "Women's History" in J. Wallach Scott, *Gender and the Politics of History* (New York: Columbia University Press, 1999) 15.

Shteir, A., "Bluestockings and Goddesses: Writing Feminist Cultural History" in M. Luxton and M.J. Mossman, eds., *Reconsidering Knowledge: Feminism and the Academy* (Halifax: Fernwood, 2013).

Sommerlad, H., "Can Women Lawyer Differently? A Perspective from the UK" in U. Schultz and G. Shaw, eds., *Women in the World's Legal Professions* (Oxford: Hart Publishing, 2003) 191.

Strong-Boag, V., "Canada's Women Doctors: Feminism Constrained" in L. Kealey, ed., *A Not Unreasonable Claim: Women and Reform in Canada, 1880s–1920s* (Toronto: Women's Press, 1979) 109.

———, "'Setting the Stage': National Organization and the Women's Movement in the Late 19th Century" in S. Mann Trofimenkoff and A. Prentice, eds., *The Neglected Majority: Essays in Canadian Women's History*, (Toronto: McClelland and Stewart, 1977) 87.

Sugarman, D., and W.W. Pue, "Introduction: Towards a Cultural History of Lawyers" in W.W. Pue and D. Sugarman, eds., *Lawyers and Vampires: Cultural Histories of the Legal Professions* (Oxford: Hart Publishing, 2003).

Sworden, P., "'A Small United Nations': The Hamilton Firm of Millar, Alexander, Tokiwa and Isaacs, 1962–1993" in C. Wilton, ed., *Inside the Law: Canadian Firms in Historical Perspective* (Toronto: Osgoode Society for Canadian Legal History/ University of Toronto Press, 1996) 469.

Symes, B., "From Litigator to Litigant and Back Again: Equality in Practice" in E. Sheehy and S. McIntyre, eds., *Calling for Change: Women, Law and the Legal Profession* (Ottawa: University of Ottawa Press, 2006) 267.

Thomas, E. Mitchell, "The History of Women Lawyers in the County of Carleton Law Association" in W. Johnson, ed., *The First Century: Essays on the History of the County of Carleton Law Association by Various Hands on the Occasion of the Association's Centenary, 1888–1988* (Ottawa: Bonanza Press, 1988) 107.

Trofimenkoff, S. Mann, "Thérèse Casgrain and the CCF in Québec" in L. Kealey and J. Sangster, eds, *Beyond the Vote: Canadian Women and Politics* (Toronto: University of Toronto Press, 1989) 139.

Wilton, C., "Introduction" in C. Wilton, ed., *Inside the Law: Canadian Law Firms in Historical Perspective* (Toronto: Osgoode Society for Canadian Legal History/ University of Toronto Press, 1996) 13.

Woolf, J., "Silent Witness: Memory and Omission in Natalia Ginzburg's *Family Sayings*" in T.L. Broughton and L. Anderson, eds., *Women's Lives/Women's Times: New Essays on Autobiography* (New York: State University of New York Press, 1997) 203.

## Journal Articles

Abella, I., "The Making of a Chief Justice: Bora Laskin, the Early Years" (1991) 25:3 *Gazette* 422.

Acorn, A., "Snapshots Then and Now: Feminism and the Law in Alberta" (1996) 35:1 *Alberta Law Review* 140.

Adam, B., and K. Lahey, "Professional Opportunities: A Survey of the Ontario Legal Profession" (1981) 59 *Canadian Bar Review* 675.

Albisetti, J.C., "Portia Ante Portas: Women and the Legal Profession in Europe, ca. 1870–1925" (2000) 33 *Journal of Social History* 825.

Anderson, A., "The First Woman Lawyer in Canada: Clara Brett Martin" (1980) 2:4 *Canadian Women's Studies* 9.

Appleby, M., "The Entry of Women into the Profession of Law and Their Hopes" *Obiter Dicta* (17 January 1934).

Armstrong, H., and P. Armstrong, "The Segregated Participation of Women in the Canadian Labour Force, 1941–1971" (1975) 12:4 *Canadian Review of Sociology and Anthropology* 370.

Arthurs, H., "Law, Society and the Law Society" (1993) 27:2 *Gazette* 85.

Arthurs, H., R. Weisman, and F.H. Zemans, "The Canadian Legal Profession" (1986) 3 *American Bar Foundation Research Journal* 447.

Arthurs, H., J. Willms, and L. Taman, "The Toronto Legal Profession: An Exploratory Survey" (1971) 21 *University of Toronto Law Journal* 498.

Auchmuty, R., "Recovering Lost Lives: Researching Women in Legal History" (2015) 42:1 *Journal of Law and Society* 34.

———, "Whatever Happened to Miss Bebb? *Bebb v. The Law Society* and Women's Legal History" (2011) 31:2 *Legal Studies* 199.

Backhouse, C., "Gretta Wong Grant: Canada's First Chinese-Canadian Female Lawyer" (1996) 15 *Windsor Yearbook of Access to Justice* 3.

———, "'To Open the Way for Others of My Sex': Clara Brett Martin's Career as Canada's First Woman Lawyer" (1985) 1 *Canadian Journal of Women and the Law* 1.

Balakrishnan, A., "The Invisible Woman: Women in Law Summit Explores How to Help Women Lawyers and Partnership Numbers," *Canadian Lawyer* (3 April 2020).

Bankier, J., "Women and the Law School: Problems and Potential" (1974) 22:6 *Chitty's Law Journal* 171.

Bashevkin, S., "Canada" (1984) 8 *Comparative Law Yearbook* 3.

Bennett, J., "Theoretical Issues: Confronting Continuity" (1997) 9:3 *Journal of Women's History* 73.

Bertin, O., "Report Analyzed Gender Balance at McCarthy's" (2009) 29:17 *Lawyers Weekly* 1.

Betcherman, L.R., "Clara Brett Martin's Anti-semitism" (1992) 5:2 *Canadian Journal of Women and the Law* 280.

Bilson, B., "'Prudence Rather than Valor': Legal Education in Saskatchewan, 1908–23" (1998) 61 *Saskatchewan Law Review* 341.

Birkett, D., and J. Wheelright, "'How Could She?' Unpalatable Facts and Feminists' Heroines" (1990) 2:1 *Gender and History* 49.

Blackburn, R. Stewart Goodwin, "Heart and Home: A Memoir" (2008) 32 *Legal Studies Forum* 683.

Bock, G., "Women's History and Gender History: Aspects of an International Debate" (1989) 1:1 *Gender and History* 7.

Bohnen, L., "Women Workers in Ontario: A Socio-legal History" (1973) 31 *University of Toronto Faculty of Law Review* 45.

Boigeol, A., "French Women Lawyers (*Avocates*) and the 'Women's Cause' in the First Half of the Twentieth Century" (2003) 10:2 *International Journal of the Legal Profession* 193.

Bourne, J., "Great Expectations and Hard Times: The Advent of the Sex Disqualification (Removal) Act 1919 and Women's Entry to the Legal Profession (2023) 32:6 *Women's History Review* 793.

Brockman, J., and D. Chunn, "'A New Order of Things': Women's Entry into the Legal Profession in British Columbia" (2002) 60:3 *The Advocate* 185.

Brunet, E., "The Law Office at the Turn of the Century," *Ontario Lawyers' Gazette* (May/June 1999) 32.

Brunet, M., "'One of the Most Capable and Astute Barristers Practicing in Our Criminal Courts': Vera Parsons (1889–1973)" (2011) 32:4 *For the Defence* 31.

Buckley, M., "*Touchstones for Change*: A Response" (1993) 51:6 *The Advocate* 853.

Bucknall, B., T. Baldwin, and J. Lakin, "Pedants, Practitioners and Prophets: Legal Education at Osgoode Hall to 1957" (1968) 6:2 *Osgoode Hall Law Journal* 139.

Burnett, D., "The Society's Computer" (1977) 11 *Law Society Gazette* 70.

Burton, A., "The *Purdahnashin* in Her Setting: Colonial Modernity and the *Zenana* in Cornelia Sorabji's Memoirs" (2000) 65 *Feminist Review* 145.

Bushby, A., "De Facto" (1991) 5:2 *Without Prejudice* (WLAO) 4.

———, "From the Archives," *Without Prejudice* (WLAO) (Spring 1995) 4.

Cahill, B., "'Everybody Called Her Frank': The Odyssey of an Early Woman Lawyer in New Brunswick" (2001) 2 *Journal of New Brunswick Legal Studies* 55.

Cairns, J., "The Law Affecting Married Women's Property in Ontario" (1915) 5:3 *Women Lawyers' Journal* 19.

———, "Wills—Ontario" (1916) 5:7 *Women Lawyers' Journal* 52.

Campbell, R., "That Girl with the Terrible Name" (1975) 49 *Law Institute Journal* 502.

Carasco, E., "A Case of Double Jeopardy: Race and Gender" (1993) 6:1 *Canadian Journal of Women and the Law* 142.

Carlson, D. L., "Law Society a Study in Gender Politics in the '90s," *Law Times* (15 May 1994) 1.

———, "Portrait of the Judge as a Trail-Blazing Woman," *Law Times* (10–16 May 1993) 4.

———, "WLAO Moves from Tea Parties to Policy Debates," *Law Times* (14 August 1994) 1.

Cartright, V.A., "Friend to Forgotten Women: The Elizabeth Fry Society at Kingston," (1958) unidentified journal.

Chunn, D., and J. Brockman, "'She Never Did Anything by Halves': Mildred Elizabeth Louise Gordon" (2003) 61:5 *The Advocate* 725.

Cohen, M., "The Condition of Legal Education in Canada" (1950) 28 *Canadian Bar Review* 267.

Cole, C., "A Developmental Market: Growth Rates, Competition and Professional Standards in the Ontario Legal Profession, 1881–1936" (1984) 7 *Canada-United States Law Journal* 231.

Cook, B., "Women as Supreme Court Candidates: From Florence Allen to Sandra O'Connor" (1982) 65:6 *Judicature* 315.

———, "Women Judges: A Preface to Their History" (1984) 14 *Golden Gate University Law Review* 573.

Cook, T., "Canada's Warlord: Prime Minister Sir Robert Borden's Leadership during the Great War" (2011) 13:3 *Journal of Military and Strategic Studies* 1.

Coyle, D., "Women in the Legal Profession in Canada" (1951–52) 38 *Women Lawyers' Journal* 14.

Cronkite, F.C., "Legal Education—Which Trend" (1935) 13 *Canadian Bar Review* 359.

De Buerger-Van Lierde, F., "A l'Origine du Mouvement Féministe en Belgique: 'L'Affaire Popelin'" (1972) 50 *Revue Belge de Philologie et d'Histoire* 1128.

———, "Louis Frank, Pionnier du Mouvement Féministe Belge" (1973) 4:3–4 *Revue Belge d'Histoire Contemporaine* 377.

Denison, S., "Legal Education in Ontario" (1924) 2 *Canadian Bar Review* 85.

Diduck, A., "Women's Legal Histories" (1993) 8:2 *Canadian Journal of Law and Society* 181.

Dinerman, B., "Sex Discrimination in the Legal Profession" (1969) 55 *American Bar Association Journal* 951.

Dinovitzer, R., "Social Capital and Constraints on Legal Careers" (2006) 40:2 *Law and Society Review* 445.

Dranoff, L. Silver, "Women as Lawyers in Toronto" (1972) 10 *Osgoode Hall Law Journal* 177.

"Edra Iles Sanders" (1937) 7:6 *The Bench and Bar* 1.

Elgqvist-Saltzman, I., "Straight Roads and Winding Tracks: Swedish Educational Policy from a Gender Perspective" (1992) 4:1–2 *Gender and Education* 41.

Etienne, N., "Report Highlights Challenges of Criminal Law Practice for Women," *Canadian Lawyer* (April 2016) 9.

Ewan, E., "Scottish Portias: Women in the Courts of Mediaeval Scottish Towns" (1992) 3 *Journal of the Canadian Historical Association*, new series, 27.

Fisher, B., "The Models among Us: Social Authority and Political Activism" (1981) 7 *Feminist Studies* 100.

Greig, G. Flos, "The Law as a Profession for Women" (1909) 6 *Commonwealth Law Review* 145.

Foster, L., "Lida B Pearson Sturdy, 1895–1987" (1991) 79 *Waterloo Historical Society (Journal)* 40.

Gibson, S., "Fairly Determined" (2002) 29:3 *University of Toronto Magazine*, souvenir ed., 46.

Gilliam, N., "A Professional Pioneer: Myra Bradwell's Fight to Practice Law" (1987) 5 *Law and History Review* 105.

Gillis, E., "Legal Education in Ontario: An Historical Sketch" (1904) 4 *Canada Law Review* 197.

Girard, P., "The Making of the Canadian Legal Profession: A Hybrid Heritage" (2014) 21 *International Journal of the Legal Profession* 145.

Glendon, M.A., "John P. Humphrey and the Drafting of the Universal Declaration of Human Rights" (2000) 2 *Journal of the History of International Law* 250.


Greig, G. Flos, "The Law as a Profession for Women" (1909) 6 *Commonwealth Law Review* 145.

Hagan, J., "Transitions in the Legal Profession" (1993) 27:2 *Gazette* 91.

Hagan, J., M. Huxter, and P. Parker, "Class Structure and Legal Practice: Inequality and Mobility among Toronto Lawyers" (1988) 22 *Law and Society Review* 9.

Hartt, E.P., "The Bench and the Bar," *Obiter Dicta* (Spring 1952) 23.

Harvey, C., "Women in Law in Canada" (1970–71) 4 *Manitoba Law Journal* 9.

Hemmings, C., "Telling Feminist Stories" (2005) 6:2 *Feminist Theory* 115.

Herbert, J., "'Otherness' and the Black Woman" (1989–90) 3 *Canadian Journal of Women and the Law* 269.

Howsam, L., "'Sound-Minded Women': Eliza Orme and the Study and Practice of Law in Late-Victorian England" (1989) 15 *Atlantis* 44.

Hull, K., and R. Nelson, "Assimilation, Choice or Constraint? Testing Theories of Gender Differences in the Careers of Lawyers" (2000) 79:1 *Social Forces* 229.

Huxter, M., "Survey of Employment Opportunities for Articling Students and Graduates of the Bar Admission Course in Ontario" (1981) 15 *Law Society Gazette* 169.

Isaac, J., "Delos Rogest Davis KC" (1990) 24:4 *Law Society Gazette* 293.

Kates, C., "'Identical or Substantially Identical': Bell Canada and the Struggle for Equal Pay, 1967–1976" (1990–91) 4 *Canadian Journal of Women and the Law* 133.

Kay, F., "Professionalism and Exclusionary Practices: Shifting the Terrain of Privilege and Professional Monopoly" (2004) 11:1–2 *International Journal of the Legal Profession* 11.

———, "Social Capital, Relational Inequality Theory, and the Earnings of Racial Minority Lawyers" (2019) 32 *Research in the Sociology of Work* 32.

Kay, F., S. Alarie, and J. Adjei, "Leaving Private Practice: How Organizational Context, Time Pressures and Structural Inflexibilities Shape Departures from Private Law Practice" (2013) 20 *Indiana Journal of Global Studies* 1223.

Kay, F., and E. Gorman, "Women in the Legal Profession" (2008) 4 *Annual Review of Law and Social Science* 299.

Kay, F., and J. Hagan, "Cultivating Clients in the Competition for Partnership: Gender and Organizational Restructuring of Law Firms in the 1990s" (1999) 33:3 *Law and Society Review* 517.

———, "Raising the Bar: The Gender Stratification of Law-Firm Capital" (1998) 63 *American Sociological Review* 728.

Kaye, J., "Women Lawyers in Big Firms: A Study in Progress toward Gender Equality" (1988) 57 *Fordham Law Review* 111.

Keating, K., "*Touchstones for Change*: A Review" (1993) 51:6 *The Advocate* 843.

Kercher, B., "A Convict Conservative: George Crossley and the English Legal Tradition" (1999) 16:1 *Law in Context* 24.

Kernaghan, L., "The Madonna of the Law," *Hearsay* (Dalhousie University) (Fall 1991) 26.

Killeen, G., "On Entering the World of Law" (1990) 24:4 *Gazette* 282.

Kinnear, H., "The County Judge in Ontario" (1954) 32:1 *Canadian Bar Review* 21.

———, "The County Judge in Ontario" (1954) 32:2 *Canadian Bar Review* 127.

Kirk, L., "Portia's Place: Australia's First Women Lawyers" (1995) 1 *Australian Journal of Law and History* 75.

Kulig, P., "Study Shows Firms Lack Women Partners," *Law Times* (19 February 1990) 1.

Kyer, C.I., "Parading Their Ignorance of Financial Transactions: The Smith/Jarvis Fraud Trial of 1924" (2021) 36 *Banking and Finance Law Review* 339.

Laskin, B., "Cecil A. Wright: A Tribute" (1967) 45 *Canadian Bar Review* 213.

Law Society of Upper Canada, "Professionalism: A Century of Perspectives" (2002) *Gazette* 42.

Lederman, W.R., "Canadian Legal Education in the Second Half of the Twentieth Century" (1971) *University of Toronto Law Journal* 141.

Legge, L. "Tribute to M. Hyndman," *Continuum* (Osgoode Hall Law School) (23 January 1991) 12.

Liao, C., "Power, Gender, and Race in the Legal Profession" (2022) 34:1 *Canadian Journal of Women and the Law* 174.

Lindberg, T., "What Do You Call an Indian Woman with a Law Degree: Nine Aboriginal Women at the University of Saskatchewan Speak Out" (1997) 9 *Canadian Journal of Women and the Law* 301.

Lykes, M.B., "Discrimination and Coping in the Lives of Black Women: Analyses of Oral History Data" (1983) 39:3 *Journal of Social Issues* 79.

Lynch, M.L., "Women in the Law" (1950) 3 *University of New Brunswick Law Journal* 12.

MacLean, M.V., "Lady Lawyers and All That" (1966) 4:4 *Obiter Dicta* n.p.

Maclennan, R.J., "Legal Education in Canada" (1922) *Canadian Law Times* 319.

Madsen, L., "Citizen, Worker, Mother: Canadian Women's Claims to Parental Leave and Childcare" (2002) 19 *Canadian Journal of Family Law* 11.

Matsuda, M., "The West and the Legal Status of Women: Explanations of Frontier Feminism" (1985) 24 *Journal of the West* 47.

May, C., "Still a Boys' Club," *Canadian Lawyer* (November 1987) 15.

Mazer, B., "An Analysis of Gender in Admission to the Canadian Common Law Schools from 1985–86 to 1994–95" (1997) 20 *Dalhousie Law Journal* 135.

McKenzie, D., "A Long History of Failure: Feeling the Effects of Canada's Childhood Policy" (2014) 29 *Canadian Journal of Law and Society* 397.

McKiernan, M., "Woman Lawyer, 100, Retains LSUC Membership," *Law Times* (28 June 2010) 3.

McLean, C. Hunt, "Then the Camel Put Its Head in the Tent," *Obiter Dicta* (28 February 1933) 1.

McLeod, C., "The Morris Dynasty," *Canadian Lawyer* (August/September 1992) 52.

McPaul, B., "A Woman Pioneer" (1948) 22 *Australian Law Journal* 1.

McWilliams, P.K, "Leaders among the Women Lawyers of Ontario—Revisited" (1987) 21:2 *Gazette* 157.

Menkel-Meadow, C., "The Comparative Sociology of Women Lawyers: The 'Feminization' of the Legal Profession" (1987) 24 *Osgoode Hall Law Journal* 897.

———, "Excluded Voices: New Voices in the Legal Profession Making New Voices in the Law" (1987) 42:1 *University of Miami Law Review* 29.

———, "Portia in a Different Voice: Speculations on a Woman's Lawyering Process" (1985) 1 *Berkeley Women's Law Journal* 39.

Minor, J., "The Bumpy Road" *Nexus* (University of Toronto Faculty of Law) (Spring/Summer 2006) 108.

Monture, P., "Now That the Door Is Open: First Nations and the Law School Experience" (1990) 15 *Queen's Law Journal* 179.

Moore, C., "1902 Not So Different from 2002 for Lawyers," *Law Times* (14 January 2002) 8.

———, "Breaking Ground for Women Lawyers," *Law Times* (26 August 2002) 8.

———, "The First Woman to Practice in a Big Downtown Firm" *Law Times* (14 March 2005) 6.

———, "The Ontario Lawyers' Alphabet: R Is for Riddell" *Law Times* (25 November 2002) 7.

———, "The Ontario Legal Alphabet: H Is for Hyndman," *Law Times* (22 October 2001) 8.

———, "Ontario's First Native Lawyer?," *Law Times* (26 October 1998) 8.

Morgan, C., "'An Embarrassingly and Severely Masculine Atmosphere': Women, Gender and the Legal Profession at Osgoode Hall, 1920s to 1960s" (1996) 11:2 *Canadian Journal of Law and Society* 19.

Morrow, W.G., "An Historical Examination of Alberta's Legal System—The First Seventy-Five Years" (1981) 29 *Alberta Law Review* 148.

Mossman, M.J., "'Invisible' Constraints on Lawyering and Leadership: The Case of Women Lawyers" (1988) 20:3 *Ottawa Law Review* 567.

———, "'The Law as a Profession for Women': A Century of Progress?" (2009) 30 *Australian Feminist Law Journal* 131.

———, "'Otherness' and the Law School: A Comment on Teaching Gender Equality" (1985) 1:1 *Canadian Journal of Women and the Law* 213.
———, "Portia's Progress: Women as Lawyers—Reflections on Past and Future" (1988) 8 *Windsor Yearbook of Access to Justice* 252.
———, "Precedents, Patterns and Puzzles: Feminist Reflections on the First Women Lawyers" (2016) 5:4 LAWS at 39, MDPI online: <http:www.mdpi .comjournalslaws>.
———, Review of Canadian Bar Association report, *Touchstones for Change* (1994) 7 *Canadian Journal of Women and the Law* 138.
Mulcahy, L., and D. Sugarman, "Introduction: Legal Life Writing and Marginalized Subjects and Sources" (2015) 42:1 *Journal of Law and Society* 1.
Munro, K.B., "The Hon. Helen Kinnear, a Personal Memoir" *Canadian Lawyer* (June/July 1993) 15.
Neallani, S., "Women of Colour in the Legal Profession: Facing the Familiar Barriers of Race and Sex" (1992) 5 *Canadian Journal of Women and the Law* 148.
Neary, P., and S. Brown, "The Veterans Charter and Canadian Women Veterans of the Second World War" (1994) 9:2 *British Journal of Canadian Studies* 249.
Orme, E., "The Legal Status of Women in England" (1893) 25 *Chicago Legal News* 431.
Palen, H.B., "Drafting a Judgment or Order" (1950) 24:2 *Obiter Dicta* 15.
Parsons, V., "*R v Thomas*," (Winter 1953) *Obiter Dicta* 33.
Pazdro, R., "Of British Columbia Suffragists and Barristers" (1980) 2:4 *Canadian Women's Studies* 15.
Petersson, S., "Ruby Clements and Early Women of the Alberta Bar" (1997) 9 *Canadian Journal of Women and the Law* 365.
———, "Women Lawyers and Law Students 1915–1935" (n.d.) 10:1 *Architypes* 4.
Platt, P., "Vera Parsons: Some Pieces of a Life" (1975) 11:5 *The Advocate* (University of Toronto Faculty of Law) 11.
Polanyi, M., "CBA Breaks Glass Ceiling and an Old Girls' Club" (August/September 1992) *Canadian Lawyer* np.
Proudfoot, P., and G. Pun, "Edith L. Paterson" (2010) 68:1 *The Advocate* 84.
Pue, W.W., "Common Law Legal Education in Canada's Age of Light, Soap and Water" (1996) 23 *Manitoba Law Journal* 654.
Rand, I., "Legal Education in Canada" (1954) 32 *Canadian Bar Review* 387.
Resnik, J., "Ambivalence: The Resiliency of Legal Culture in the United States" (1993) 45 *Stanford Law Review* 1525.
Rhode, D., "Perspectives on Professional Women" (1988) 40 *Stanford Law Review* 1163.

Richardson, D., "Margaret Fasken Baird Campbell" (1989) 2:1 *Without Prejudice* (WLAO) 3.

———, "Profile of Mary Lamont" (Winter 1989) 2:1 *Without Prejudice* (WLAO) 3.

Riddell, W., "Women as Practitioners of Law" (1918) 18 *Journal of Comparative Legislation* 200.

Robinson, A., "First Black Female Bencher Elected in Toronto," *Law Times* (11 July 2016) 1.

Robinson, L., "Women Lawyers in the United States" (1890) 2 *Green Bag* 10.

Roth, T., "Clara Brett Martin—Canada's Pioneer Woman Lawyer" (1984) 18 *Law Society Gazette* 323.

Ryder, B., "Racism and the Constitution: The Constitutional Fate of British Columbia Anti-Asian Immigration Legislation, 1884–1909" (1991) 29 *Osgoode Hall Law Journal* 619.

Ryval, M., "Women in Law: Ladies No Longer in Waiting" (December 1977) *Canadian Lawyer* n.p.

Saks, M., "Removing the Blinkers? A Critique of Recent Contributions to the Sociology of Professions" (1983) 31 *Sociological Review* 1.

Sanger, C., "Curriculum Vitae (Feminae): Biography and Early American Women Lawyers" (1994) 46 *Stanford Law Review* 1245.

Sangster, J., "Telling Our Stories: Feminist Debates and the Use of Oral History" (1994) 3:1 *Women's History Review* 5.

Sedgwick, J., "Sir William Mulock, PC KCMG, A Recollection" (1991) 25 *Law Society of Upper Canada Gazette* 287.

Sherk, S., "Livery of Seisin" (1970) 2:1 *The Oyez*, 3.

Smith, C., "Next Steps on the Road to Equality in the Legal Profession" (2002) *Touchstones Newsletter of the CBA's Standing Committee on Equality* (Ottawa: Canadian Bar Association, 2002).

Snyder, E., "Indigenous Feminist Legal Theory" (2014) 26 *Canadian Journal of Women and the Law* 365.

Sommerlad, H., "Managerialism and the Legal Profession: A New Professional Paradigm" (1995) 2: 2–3 *International Journal of the Legal Profession* 159.

Sperdakos, S., "'A Forum for Discussion' and Place of Respite: Jewish Lawyers and Toronto's Reading Law Club" (2012) 30 *Windsor Yearbook of Access to Justice* 163.

Stanley, L., "Moments of Writing: Is There Feminist Autobiography?" (1990) 2:1 *Gender and History* 58.

Stevenson, M., "George Drew, the Law of the Sea, and the Diefenbaker Government, 1957–1963" (2020) 31:2 *Diplomacy and Statecraft* 326.

Sugarman, D., "From Legal Biography to Legal Life Writing: Broadening Conceptions of Legal History and Socio-legal Scholarship" (2015) 42:1 *Journal of Law and Society* 7.

Talbot, L.C., "The Formation of the Black Law Students' Association (Canada)" (1992) 26 *Law Society Gazette* 187.

———, "History of Blacks in the Law Society of Upper Canada" (1990) 24:1 *Law Society Gazette* 65.

Tancred, P., "Outsiders/Insiders: Women and Professional Norms" (1999) 14:1 *Canadian Journal of Law and Society* 31.

Thomas, E. Mitchell, "The History of Woman Lawyers in the County of Carleton Law Association" (1988) 22:4 *Law Society Gazette* 397.

———, "Sisters-in Law'" (1991) 25:3 *Gazette* 298.

Thwaites, S., "1994 President's Award Recipients" (1994) 9:1 *Without Prejudice* (WLAO) 2.

Thornhill, E., "Focus on Black Women" (1985) 1:1 *Canadian Journal of Women and the Law* 168.

Thornton, M., "Authority and Corporeality: The Conundrum for Women in Law" (1998) 6:2 *Feminist Legal Studies* 147.

———, "Hegemonic Masculinity and the Academy" (1989) 17 *International Journal of the Sociology of Law* 115.

Tillotson, S., "Human Rights Law as Prism: Women's Organizations, Unions, and Ontario's Female Employees Fair Remuneration Act, 1951" (1991) 72:4 *Canadian Historical Review* 532.

Tintor, J., "Association for Women Lawyers Needed, but Must Not Divide Profession, Van Camp Says," *Law Times*, (December 1994).

Walker, J.W., "Race and Recruitment in World War I: Enlistment of Visible Minorities in the Canadian Expeditionary Force" (1989) 70:1 *Canadian Historical Review* 1.

Wallace, J., and F. Kay, "The Professionalism of Practising Law: A Comparison across Work Contexts" (2008) 29 *Journal of Organizational Behavior* 1021.

Walters, M., "'Let Right Be Done': A History of the Faculty of Law at Queen's University" (2007) 32:2 *Queen's Law Journal* n.p.

Ward, C., "The Changing Tide" (2009) *Continuum* (Osgoode Hall Law School) 14.

Wigle, R., "Sisters in Law" (1927) 6 *Canadian Bar Review* 419.

Willis, J., "The McRuer Report: Lawyers' Values and Civil Servants' Values" (1968) 18:4 *University of Toronto Law Journal* 351.

Wilton, P., "Inappropriate for Women ..." *Law Now* (November 1992) 23.

Wright, C., "Law and the Law Schools" (1938) 16 *Canadian Bar Review* 579.

Yorke, L., "Mabel Penery French (1881–1955): A Life Re-created" (1993) 42 *University of New Brunswick Law Journal* 3.

## Theses and Dissertations

Brown, C., *Ethel Benjamin: New Zealand's First Woman Lawyer* (BA honour's thesis, University of Otago, 1985) [unpublished].

Brunet, M., *Becoming Lawyers: Gender, Legal Education and Professional Identity Formation in Canada, 1920–1980* (PhD diss., University of Toronto, 2005) [unpublished].

Cole, C., *"A Learned and Professional Body": The Professionalization of the Ontario Bar, 1867–1929* (PhD diss., University of Western Ontario, 1987) [unpublished].

Hoffman, J.D., *Farmer-Labour Government in Ontario* (Master's thesis, University of Toronto, 1959) [unpublished].

Kimble, S., *Justice Redressed: Women, Citizenship and the Social Uses of the Law in Modern France, 1890–1939* (PhD diss., University of Iowa, 2002) [unpublished].

MacLeod, J., *The United Farmer Movement in Ontario* (Master's thesis, Queen's University, 1958) [unpublished].

Neary, H. Bates., *William Renwick Riddell: A Bio-bibliographical Study* (Master's thesis: University of Western Ontario, 1977) [unpublished].

Schucher, K., *Coercing Justice? Exploring the "Aspirations and Practice" of Law as a Tool in Struggles against Social Inequalities* (PhD diss., Osgoode Hall Law School, 2014) [unpublished].

Sissons, C., *Elsie Gregory MacGill: Engineering the Future and Building Bridges for Canadian Women, 1918–1980* (PhD diss., University of Ottawa, 2008) [unpublished].

Takayanagi, M., *Parliament and Women, c 1900–1919* (PhD diss., King's College, London, 2012) [unpublished].

## Reports

ABA Commission on Women in the Legal Profession, "Summary of Hearings," 1988 (chair, Hilary Rodham Clinton).

Archives of the Law Society of Upper Canada, *Crossing the Bar: A Century of Women's Experience "Upon the Rough and Troubled Seas of Legal Practice in Ontario"* (Toronto: Archives of the Law Society of Upper Canada, 1993).

Black Law Students' Association and Attorney General of Ontario, *Black Access to the Legal Profession: The Timeroll Report* (Toronto: Attorney General of Ontario, 1996).

Bureau of Municipal Research, *What Is "The Ward" Going to Do with Toronto? A Report* (Toronto: The Bureau,1918).

Canada, J.C. McRuer, *Report of the Royal Commission on the Law of Insanity as a Defence in Criminal Cases* (Hull: Queen's Printer, 1956).

Canadian Bar Association, *Touchstones for Change: Equality, Diversity and Accountability—The Report on Gender Equality in the Legal Profession* (Ottawa: Canadian Bar Association, 1993).

———, Task Force on Gender Equality, Yukon Report, 1993.

Consultative Group on Research and Education in Law, *Law and Learning* (Ottawa: Social Sciences and Humanities Research Council, 1983).

Hill, L. and 1999/2000 Research Working Group (H. Bjarnason, H. Vlug and K. Kramer), *Lawyers with Disabilities: Identifying Barriers to Equity, a Report of the Disability Research Working Group of the Equity and Diversity Subcommittee* (Vancouver: Law Society of British Columbia, 2000).

International Congress of Women, *Report of the International Congress of Women, June 24th–30th, 1909* (Toronto: Geo Parker and Sons, Printers, 1910).

Irvine, M., "Women at Osgoode: Problems and Perceptions of the Growing Minority," Appendix A in *Long Range Academic Policy Committee of Osgoode Hall Law School*, 15 January 1974 [unpublished].

Kay, F., *Transitions in the Ontario Legal Profession: A Survey of Lawyers Called to the Bar between 1975 and 1990* (Toronto: Law Society of Upper Canada, 1991).

Labarge, M. Wade, M.D. Johnston, and M.E. MacLellan, *Cultural Tradition and Political History of Women in Canada* (Ottawa: Information Canada, 1971).

Law Society of Ontario, *Working Together for Change: Strategies to Address Issues of Systemic Racism in the Legal Professions* (LSO: Challenges Faced by Racialized Licensees Working Group, 2016).

Law Society of Upper Canada, *Final Report: Retention of Women in Private Practice Working Group*, 22 May 2008.

———, *Report of the Special Committee on Legal Education* (Toronto: Law Society of Upper Canada, 1972).

Maxwell-Alleyne, A., *Report from the Treasurer's Women in Law Advisory Group* (Toronto: Law Society of Ontario, 2022).

McChesney, A., R. Nolan, and M. Schmieg, *Advancing Professional Opportunities and Employment Accommodation for Lawyers and Other Law Graduates Who Have Disabilities* (Ottawa: REACH, 2001).

Ontario, *Public Accounts of the Province of Ontario, 1930–31* (Toronto: Herbert H. Ball, 1932).

Ontario, *Public Accounts of the Province of Ontario, 1934* (Toronto: Herbert H. Ball, 1934).

Orenstein, M., *Racialization and Gender of Lawyers in Ontario: A Report for the Law Society of Upper Canada*, April 2010.

Royal Commission on the Criminal Law, *Report of the Royal Commission on the Criminal Law Relating to the Criminal Sexual Psychopaths* (Ottawa: Queen's Printer1958).

Royal Commission on the Status of Women, *Report of the Royal Commission on the Status of Women in Canada* (Ottawa: Information Canada, 1970).

Royal Commission on Violence in the Communications Industry, *Report of the Royal Commission on Violence in the Communications Industry: Approaches, Conclusions, Recommendations* (Toronto: The Commission,1977).

Sparks, C., "Women of Colour in the Legal Profession: A Panoply of Multiple Discrimination" in Canadian Bar Association, *Touchstones for Change: Equality, Diversity and Accountability—The Report on Gender Equality in the Legal Profession* (Ottawa: Canadian Bar Association, 1993), Appendix 10.

St. Lewis, J., and B. Trevino, *Racial Equality in the Canadian Legal Profession: The Challenge of Racial Equality: Putting Principles into Practice* (Ottawa: Canadian Bar Association, 1999).

———, *Virtual Justice: Systemic Racism and the Canadian Legal Profession* (Ottawa: Canadian Bar Association, 1999).

United Nations Department of Social Affairs, *Comparative Survey on Juvenile Delinquency* (New York: United Nations Department of Social Affairs, 1952–53).

## Other Sources

Abella, R., "Women in the Legal Profession" (Presentation to Law Society of Upper Canada Continuing Legal Education program, Toronto, 13 May 1986).

Backhouse, C., "Gender and Race in the Construction of 'Legal Professionalism': Historical Perspectives" (Paper presented at Colloquium of the Chief Justice of Ontario's Advisory Committee on Professionalism, Toronto, 20 October 2003).

Baxter, M. St. Patrick, "Black Bay Street Lawyers: Looking Back, Looking Ahead" (Keynote address, Third Annual Conference and Symposium of the Black Law Students' Association, Ottawa, 19 February 1994).

Bushby, A., "Creating Culture: The Early Years of Ontario Women in the Legal Profession" (Presentation to the International Women's Day Celebration, Law Society of Ontario, Toronto, 2000).

Cole, C., "A History of Osgoode Hall Law School, 1889–1989" (1995) [unpublished, archived at Osgoode Hall Law School Library].

Dunlop, J.B., "Law Teaching Materials in Canada" [paper submitted to Harvard Seminar on Legal Education, Boston, 1957].

Haynes, J. Banfield, "Survey of Courses on Women and the Law" (1977) [unpublished, archived at York University].

Huckle, E., "List of Women Barristers and Solicitors in Ontario" (1897–1975) [unpublished, archived at Law Society of Ontario Archives].

Kovalev, A., "Early Ukrainian-Canadian Lawyers in Toronto, 1923–1960" (2014) [unpublished, archived at Osgoode Hall Law School].

Ontario Women's Bureau, *Equal Pay Legislation: An Historical Overview* (n.d.) [unpublished, archived at Ontario Women's Bureau, Toronto].

Ryan, S., "A Pilgrim's Progress: Clara Brett Martin's Campaign for Admission to the Bar of Ontario" (1999) [unpublished, on file, M.J. Mossman].

Servinis, J., "The Exclusiveness of the Legal Profession in Canada and How One Nova Scotian Woman Rose to the Challenge: M. Grace Wambolt" (1998) [unpublished paper, archived at Dalhousie Law School].

Sperdakos, S., "A Woman's Proper Place: The Entry of Women into the Legal Profession" (Presentation to Law Society of Upper Canada, Toronto, June 1997).

## *Index of Names of Women Lawyers*

Note: This Index includes the names of women who were called to the bar of Ontario and other jurisdictions (including women judges) who are discussed in this book. Names of a few women law graduates who were not called to the bar, but who are discussed in this book, are also noted.

# *Index of Subjects*